25th Ibero-American Conference on Software Engineering (CIbSE 2022)

Held online

Cordoba, Argentina
13-17 June 2022

ISBN: 978-1-7138-5558-3

Printed from e-media with permission by:

Curran Associates, Inc.
57 Morehouse Lane
Red Hook, NY 12571

proceedings.com

Some format issues inherent in the e-media version may also appear in this print version.

CIbSE - IberoAmerican Conference on Software Engineering
c/o Luca Cernuzzi
Universidad Católica "Nuestra Seóra de la Asunción",
Campus Universitario, Asunción
Barrio Santa Ana, C.C.1683, C.P. 1364
Asunción - Paraguay

Phone: +595 21 334650
Fax: +595 21 310587

lcernuzz@uca.edu.py

Additional copies of this publication are available from:

Curran Associates, Inc.
57 Morehouse Lane
Red Hook, NY 12571 USA
Phone: 845-758-0400
Fax: 845-758-2633
Email: curran@proceedings.com
Web: www.proceedings.com

Table of Contents

Main Conference

1 **A Literature Study to Characterize Continuous Experimentation in Software Engineering**
Vladimir Erthal (UFRJ), Bruno Souza (UFRJ), Paulo Sérgio Santos (UNIRIO) and Guilherme Travassos (UFRJ)

16 **A Metrics-based Approach for Assessing Architecture-Implementation Mappings**
J. Andres Diaz-Pace (UNICEN), Rodrigo Cian Berrios (UNICEN), Antonela Tommasel CONICET-UNCPBA and Hernan C. Vazquez (UNICEN)

31 **A Survey on the Differences of Using User Story and Tasks in the ASD Effort Estimation in Brazil**
Diego De Morais (USP), Fabio L. Siqueira (USP) and Jorge R. Almeida Jr. (USP)

46 **Advances in a DSL to Specify Smart Contracts for Application Integration Processes**
Eldair F. Dornelles (UNIJUI), Fernando Parahyba (UNIJUI), Rafael Z. Frantz (UNIJUI), Fabricia Roos-Frantz (UNIJUI), Antonia M. Reina Quintero (University of Seville), Carlos Molina-Jiménez (University of Cambridge), José Bocanegra (Universidad de los Andes) and Sandro Sawicki (UNIJUI)

61 **An experiment on how graduating students represent software designs**
Silvana Moreno (Universidad de la República), Diego Vallespir (Universidad de la República) and Martin Solari (Universidad ORT Uruguay)

76 **An Overview of Software Architecture Education**
Brauner Roberto do Nascimento Oliveira (USP), Lina Garcés (UNIFEI), Kamila Takayama Lyra (USP), Daniel Soares Santos (USP), Seiji Isotani (USP) and Elisa Yumi Nakagawa (USP)

91 **Automatic identification of web API change types in consumer applications**
Graciela Vidal (Universidad Nacional de la Patagonia Austral), Sandra Casas (Universidad Nacional de la Patagonia Austral) and Franco Herrera (Universidad Nacional de la Patagonia Austral)

105 **Autonomy and turnover in Distributed Software Development projects: a systematic literature review**
Amanda Maria Chaves (UFPE), Luís Amorim (UFRPE), Marcelo Marinho (UFRPE), Ivaldir Farias Junior (UPE) and Hermano Perrelli de Moura (UFPE)

120 **Centrarse en las personas para facilitar abordajes de Diseño Participativo**
Cynthia Lorena Corso (CIDS/UTN/FRC/UNLP) and Cecilia Challiol (LIFIA/UNLP/CONICET)

128 **Detección automática de problemas de accesibilidad a partir de eventos de interacción de usuario**
Maximiliano Toledo (Facultad de Informatica-UNLP), Alejandra Garrido (Facultad de Informatica-UNLP) and Julián Grigera (Facultad de Informatica-UNLP)

143 **Experimento para evaluar el uso de patrones de negocio para facilitar la comprensión del modelo conceptual de un sistema de gobierno electrónico**
Oscar Medina (Facultad Regional Córdoba), Marcela Genero (Universidad de Castilla-La Mancha), Marcelo Marciszack (Facultad Regional Córdoba), Alicia Bratti (Facultad Regional Córdoba) and Ana Strub (Facultad Regional Córdoba)

158 **Extending the Sustainability-Quality Model for supporting the design of Persuasive Software Systems**
Marcela Quispe-Cruz (Universidad Nacional de San Agustín de Arequipa) and Nelly Condori-Fernández (University of A Coruña)

173 **Investigating the Perception of Success in Software Projects Among Developers from a Brazilian Software Company**
Cláudio Nascimento (CEFET/RJ) and Rafael de Mello (UFRJ)

188 **MethApp4Mob: A Methodological Approach for Mobile Applications Development**
Iris Galeano (Universidad Católica Nuestra Señora de la Asunción), Mauricio Merín (Universidad Católica Nuestra Señora de la Asunción), Magali Gonzalez (Universidad Católica Nuestra Señora de la Asunción) and Luca Cernuzzi (Universidad Católica Nuestra Señora de la Asunción)

203 **On the Need to Use Smart Contracts in Enterprise Application Integration**
Fernando Parahyba (UNIJUI), Eldair F. Dornelles (UNIJUI), Fabricia Roos-Frant (UNIJUI)z, Rafael Z. Frantz (UNIJUI), Carlos Molina-Jiménez (University of Cambridge), Antonia M. Reina Quintero (University of Seville), José Bocanegra (Universidad de los Andes)and Sandro Sawicki (UNIJUI)

218 **Outsourcing with distributed teams in large-scale environments**
Rafael Camara (UFPE), Marcelo Marinho (UFRPE), Suzana Sampaio (UFRPE), Ivaldir Honório (UPE) and Hermano Moura (UFPE)

233 **Perceptions of knowledge management in Brazilian software development companies**
Juliana Oliveira dos Santos (UTFPR, Guilherme Martins (UTFPR), Érica Ferreira de Souza (UTFPR), Katia Romero Felizardo (UTFPR) and Giovani Volnei Meinerz (UTFPR)

248 **Pivoting in software startups. Motivations, process, and evaluation**
Karina Lanata (Universidad ORT Uruguay), Pablo Benítez (Universidad ORT Uruguay) and Gerardo Matturro (Universidad ORT Uruguay)

263 **Refactoring Assertion Roulette and Duplicate Assert test smells: a controlled experiment**
Railana Santana (UFBA), Luana Martins (UFBA), Tássio Virgínio (IFTO), Larissa Soares (UFBA), Heitor Costa (UFLA) and Ivan Machado (UFBA)

278 **Syntactic and Semantic Similarities and Discrepancies between Terms of Glossaries for Software Testing**
Guido Tebes (UNLPam), Philip Lew (XBOSoft) and Luis Olsina (UNLPam)

292 **Tool support to aligning requirements and testing through behaviour-driven requirements patterns**
Pollyana Ribeiro (UFG), Ernesto Veiga (UFG), Mariana Martins (UFG), Auri Vincenzi (UFSCAR), Taciana Kudo (UFG) and Renato Bulcão-Neto (UFG)

300 **Towards an ontology-based recommender system for agile practices adoption**
María Luciana Roldán (INGAR/CONICET/UTN), Verónica Bollati (UTN F. Reg. Resistencia) and Silvio Gonnet (INGAR/CONICET/UTN)

315 **Tratamento de Requisitos de Confiabilidade de Sistemas-de-Sistemas: Uma Revisão Sistemática da Literatura**
Sidny de Almeida Molina (UFMS), Debora Maria Barroso Paiva (UFMS) and Maria Istela Cagnin (UFMS)

330 **Understanding Refactoring Tasks over Time: A Study Using Refactoring Graphs**
Aline Brito (UFMG), Andre Hora (UFMG) and Marco Tulio Valente (UFMG)

Table of Contents

Doctoral Symposium

345 **Blockchain Governance using Reference Architectures**
Luis Esteban Florez (Universidad de los Andes)

352 **Definición de patrones a partir de Buenas Prácticas para el desarrollo de sistemas de Gobierno Electrónico**
Oscar Medina (Universidad Tecnológica Nacional)

360 **Diseño e implementación de un entorno de desarrollo integrado para robótica educativa soportado por una máquina virtual para plataformas de computación física**
Ricardo Moran (Universidad Abierta Interamericana)

368 **Evaluation and Improvement of Narrative Visualizations**
Andrea Lezcano Airaldi (National University of the Northeast)

376 **Framework socialmente consciente para criação de RPGs para contribuir com o processo de ensino e aprendizagem de Engenharia de Software**
Flávia Haddad (Universidade Federal do Paraná e Universidade Tecnológica Federal do Paraná)

384 **How to Identify Programming Skills from Source Code?**
Johnatan Oliveira (Federal University of Minas Gerais)

392 **Metodología Basada en Modelos en Tiempo de Ejecución para la Construcción y Operación de Sistemas Autoconscientes de Internet de las Cosas**
Lenin Erazo-Garzón (Universidad del Azuay)

400 **Modelo para Amparar o Desenvolvimento de Protótipos de Sistemas IoT**
Eduarda Almeida (Universidade Federal do Paraná e Universidade Tecnológica Federal do Paraná)

408 **On the Continuous Delivery in IoT Systems**
Igor Pereira (Federal University of Ouro Preto)

416 **Open-Source Software Projects Curating Model for Empirical Software Engineering Studies**
Juan Carruthers (National University of the Northeast)

CIbSE 2022

XXV Ibero-American Conference on Software Engineering

Córdoba, Argentine Republic - June 13 to June 17, 2022

PROGRAM COMMITTEE CHAIRS

Monalessa Barcellos (Federal University of Espírito Santo, Brazil)
Jose Luis de la Vara (University of Castilla-La Mancha, Spain)

DOCTORAL SYMPOSIUM CHAIRS

Kelly Garces (Universidad de los Andes, Colombia)
Carla Silva (Federal University of Pernambuco, Brazil)

JOURNAL FIRST CHAIRS

Xavier Franch (Universitat Politècnica de Catalunya, Spain)
Marcela Ruiz (Zurich University of Applied Sciences, Switzerland)

EIbAIS CHAIRS

Alejandra Garrido (Universidad Nacional de La Plata, Argentina)
Ivan Machado (Federal University of Bahia, Brazil)

INDUSTRY TALKS CHAIRS

Alvaro Ruiz de Menderozqueta (SimTLiX & UTN-FRC, Argentina)
Iris Gastañaga (Kinetic & UTN-FRC, Argentina)

GENERAL CHAIRS

Marcelo Martin Marciszack (Universidad Tecnológica Nacional (UTN-FRC), Argentina)
Roberto Muñoz (Universidad Tecnológica Nacional (UTN-FRC), Argentina)

PROCEEDINGS CHAIR

Davi Viana (Federal University of Maranhão, Brazil)

Preface

On behalf of the CIbSE 2022 Organizing Committee, we are proud to present the proceedings of the 25th Iberoamerican Conference on Software Engineering (CIbSE 2022). The conference was held virtually from Córdoba, Argentina. The hosting institution was the Universidad Tecnológica Nacional. Despite the social distancing, the conference joined the Software Engineering community together in a high-quality event.

CIbSE is the leading research forum on Software Engineering in Ibero-America. Its primary objective is to promote high-quality scientific research in Ibero-American countries and, thus, support the researchers in this community in publishing and discussing their work. In addition, the conference fosters collaboration and cross-fertilization among academics, students, and practitioners from industry. CIbSE has distinct characteristics as it welcomes contributions in three languages: Portuguese, Spanish or English.

In this edition of the conference, the three traditional tracks (Software Engineering, Requirements Engineering, and Empirical Software Engineering) were merged into a single main conference. Sixty-two papers were submitted. Each submission was reviewed by at least three members of the Program Committee, formed by leading experts. After a careful peer-review process, 24 papers were finally selected (38,7% acceptance rate). Five distinguished papers were be invited to submit an extended version to the Science of Computer Programming journal, and the best paper received an award certificate. In addition to the 24 original papers, six papers were accepted in the Journal First category, offering an opportunity for the authors to discuss their work with the community as well as to enrich the CIbSE technical program.

CIbSE 2022 hosted the Doctoral Symposium, which aims at bringing together doctoral students working on foundations, techniques, tools, and applications of Software Engineering and giving them the opportunity to present and discuss their research in a constructive and international atmosphere where a board of experts discuss with the students to suggest new perspectives and improvements to the PhD theses. Ten ongoing doctorate research projects were presented. Moreover, prof. Marcos Kalinowski (Pontifical Catholic University of Rio de Janeiro, Brazil) presented the keynote "Survey Research Methods in Software Engineering".

CIbSE 2022 also hosted the 5th edition of the Ibero-American School on Software Engineering (EIbAIS). EIbAIS aims at promoting a forum for discussions regarding Software Engineering, its related technologies and theoretical foundations, allowing the participation of practitioners, undergraduate and graduate students, and researchers.

This year, EIbAIS presented five tutorials, discussing general and specific topics of Software Engineering: Specification and Design of Vibrotactile Haptic Feedback (Andrés Rodriguez, Universidad Nacional de La Plata), Developing IoT Devices: Challenges for the Software Engineer (Federico Balaguer, Stream S.A.), A Look into Programmers' Heads: Measuring Program Comprehension with Neuro-Imaging and Eye Tracking (Janet Siegmund, Chemnitz University of Technology), The Use of Natural Language in Requirements Engineering (Leandro Antonelli, Universidad Nacional of La Plata), and Software Engineering in the DevOps Era (Nicolas Paez, Universidad de Buenos Aires).

CIbSE 2022 included the Industry Talks, which aims at providing the industry and practitioners means to discuss and work together in exploring how Software Engineer processes, methods, techniques, and tools can provide the industry with better solutions. Four experts from the industry shared their experience with the CIbSE audience.

The conference had two renowned keynote speakers. Coral Calero (University of Castilla La Mancha, Spain) discussed sustainability in software development and our responsibility for it. Tayana Conte (Federal University of Amazonas, Brazil) approached the importance of user experience and what software engineers can do to provide good user experience in the software they develop.

Finally, CIbSE 2022 counted with the CIbSE 25 years Panel to celebrate the 25th anniversary of the conference. Several researchers that have influenced CIbSE and have been influenced by it discussed the conference past, present and future. CIbSE has been of paramount importance for the research in Software Engineering in Ibero-America and there is a promising and fruitful road ahead.

CIbSE 2022 was possible only because many people collaborated. Hence, we would like to thank all who contributed to this event. The quality of the technical program is a result of the dedication of the members of the Program Committee together with the additional reviewers. We would also like to thank all members of the organizing committee, authors, keynotes, panelists, instructors, session chairs and all the participants for their collaboration in making CIbSE 2022 a success. We express our gratitude to the CIbSE Steering Committee for their great support, particularly to Marcela Genero and Renata Guizzardi. Finally, we are thankful for the opportunity of serving as chairs for this conference.

Monalessa Barcellos and Jose Luis de la Vara
CIbSE 2022 PC Chairs

Main Conference

PC Chairs

Monalessa Barcellos (Federal University of Espírito Santo, Brazil)
Jose Luis de la Vara (University of Castilla-La Mancha, Spain)

Program Committee

Fernanda Alencar (Federal University of Pernambuco, Brazil)
Leandro Antonelli (LIFIA, Facultad de Informática, UNLP, Argentina)
Joao Araujo (Universidade NOVA de Lisboa, Portugal)
Hernan Astudillo (Universidad Tecnica Federico Santa María, Chile)
Claudia Ayala (Universitat Politècnica de Catalunya, Spain)
Clara Ayora (Tree Technology S.A., Spain)
María-Cecilia Bastarrica (Universidad de Chile, Chile)
Pablo Becker (UNLPam, Argentina)
Veronica Andrea Bollati (Universidad Tecnológica Nacional, Argentina)
Regina Braga (Federal University of Rio de Janeiro, Brazil)
Antonio Brogi (Università di Pisa, Italy)
Carlos Cares (Universidad de La Frontera, Chile)
Bruno Cartaxo (Federal Institute of Pernambuco, Brazil)
Juan-Pablo Carvallo (Universidad del Azuay, Ecuador)
Jaelson Castro (Federal University of Pernambuco, Brazil)
Luca Cernuzzi (Universidad Católica Nuestra Señora de la Asunción, Paraguay)
Carlos Cetina (San Jorge University, Spain)
Nelly Condori-Fernández (Universidade da Coruña, Spain)
Tayana Conte (Federal University of Amazonas, Brazil)
Heitor Costa (Federal University of Lavras, Brazil)
Jose-Antonio Cruz-Lemus (University of Castilla-La Mancha, Spain)
Breno de França (UNICAMP, Brazil)
Juan de Lara (Universidad Autonoma de Madrid, Spain)
Rafael de Mello (Federal University of Rio de Janeiro, Brazil)
Andrea Delgado (Universidad de la República, Uruguay)
Edna Dias Canedo (University of Brasília, Brazil)
Oscar Dieste (Universidad Politécnica de Madrid, Spain)
Eduardo Figueiredo (Federal University of Minas Gerais, Brazil)
Efraín Fonseca (Universidad de las Fuerzas Armadas ESPE, Ecuador)
Awdren Fontão (Federal University of Mato Grosso do Sul, Brazil)
César França (Federal Rural University of Pernambuco, Brazil)
Kelly Garces Pernett (Universidad de los Andes, Colombia)
Vinícius Garcia (Federal University of Pernambuco, Brazil)

Alejandra Garrido (LIFIA-Facultad de Informatica-UNLP, Argentina)
Marcela Genero (University of Castilla-La Mancha, Spain)
Giovanni Giachetti (Universidad Andrés Bello, Chile)
Enyo Gonçalves (Federal University of Ceará, Brazil)
Miguel Goulão (Universidade Nova de Lisboa, Portugal)
Renata Guizzardi (Federal University of Espírito Santo, Brazil)
Graciela Hadad (Universidad Nacional del Oeste, Argentina)
Luis Iribarne (University of Almería, Spain)
Clemente Izurieta (Montana State University, USA)
Marcelo Jenkins (University of Costa Rica, Costa Rica)
Marcos Kalinowski (Pontifical Catholic University of Rio de Janeiro, Brazil)
Miguel Katrib (Universidad de la Habana, Cuba)
Uirá Kulesza (Federal University of Rio Grande do Norte, Brazil)
Maria Lencastre (Federal University of Pernambuco, Brazil)
Adriana Lopes (Federal University of Amazonas, Brazil)
Lidia Lopez (Barcelona Supercomputing Center, Spain)
Marcia Lucena (Federal University of Rio Grande do Norte, Brazil)
Ivan Machado (Federal University of Bahia, Brazil)
Beatriz Marín (Universidad Diego Portales, Chile)
Anna Beatriz Marques (Federal University of Ceará, Brazil)
Johnny Marques (Aeronautical Technological Institute, Brazil)
Silverio Martínez-Fernández (Universitat Politècnica de Catalunya, Spain)
Santiago Matalonga (University of the West of Scotlannd, Scotlannd)
Denisse Muñante (SAMOVAR, Télécom SudParis, Institut Polytechnique de Paris, France)
Elisa Yumi Nakagawa (University of São Paulo, Brazil)
Vânia Neves (Fluminense Federal University, Brazil)
Toacy Oliveira (Federal University of Rio de Janeiro, Brazil)
Luis Olsina (UNL La Pampa, Argentina)
Cristina Palomares (Universitat Politècnica de Catalunya, Spain)
José Ignacio Panach Navarrete (Universitat de València, Spain)
Oscar Pastor (Universidad Politécnica de Valencia, Spain)
Giani Petri (Federal University of Santa Maria, Brazil)
Ernesto Pimentel (University of Malaga, Spain)
João Pimentel (Federal Rural University of Pernambuco, Brazil)
Claudia Pons (Universidad Nacional de La Plata, Argentina)
Rafael Prikladnicki (Pontifícia Universidade Católica do Rio Grande do Sul, Brazil)
Carme Quer (Universitat Politècnica de Catalunya, Spain)
Christian Quesada-López (Universidad de Costa Rica, Costa Rica)
Sheila Reinehr (Pontifical Catholic University of Paraná, Brazil)
Marcela Ridao (INTIA UNICEN, Argentina)
Luis Jorge Enrique Rivero Cabrejos (Federal University of Maranhão, Brazil)
Gustavo Rossi (LIFIA, Faculdad de Informática, UNLP, Argentina)
Marcela Ruiz (Zurich University of Applied Sciences, Switzerland)
Daniela Cruzes (Norwegian University of Science and Technology, Norway)
Juan Sánchez (Universidad Politécnica de Valencia, Spain)

Victor Santander (Western Paraná State University, Brazil)
Gleison Santos (Federal University of the State of Rio de Janeiro, Brazil)
Rodrigo Santos (Federal University of the State of Rio de Janeiro, Brazil)
Carla Silva (Federal University of Pernambuco, Brazil)
Sergio Soares (Federal University of Pernambuco, Brazil)
Martin Solari (Universidad ORT Uruguay, Uruguay)
Isabel Sofia Sousa Brito (Instituto Politécnico de Beja, Portugal)
Simone Souza (ICMC/USP, Brazil)
Vítor Souza (Federal University of Espírito Santo, Brazil)
Guilherme Travassos (Federal University of Rio de Janeiro, Brazil)
Pedro Valderas (Universitat Politècnica de València, Spain)
Natasha Valentim (Federal University of Paraná, Brazil)
Diego Vallespir (Universidad de la República, Uruguay)
Davi Viana (Federal University of Maranhão, Brazil)
Jéssyka Vilela (Federal University of Pernambuco, Brazil)

Additional Reviewers

Aboua Ange Kevin N'Da
Adriano Gomes
Allan Mori
Ana Carolina Moises de Souza
Carolline Pena
Hector Oliveira
Marcelo Costa
Milene Rigolin
Rodrigo de Campos Soares
Sebastián Pizard
Vinicius Santos
Williby Ferreira

Doctoral Symposium

DS Chairs

Kelly Garces (Universidad de los Andes, Colombia)
Carla Silva (Federal University of Pernambuco, Brazil)

DS Committee

María Cecilia Bastarrica (Universidad de Chile, Chile)
Cristina Cachero (Universidad de Alicante, Spain)
Luca Cernuzzi (Universidad Católica Nuestra Señora de la Asunción, Paraguay)
Nelly Condori-Fernández (Universidade da Coruña, Spain)
Breno de França (UNICAMP, Brazil)
Marcela Genero (University of Castilla-La Mancha, Spain)
Renata Guizzardi (Federal University of Espírito Santo, Brazil)
Emanuel Irrazabal (FaCENA – UNNE, Argentina)
Marcos Kalinowski (Pontifical Catholic University of Rio de Janeiro, Brazil)
Marcelo Martin Marciszack (UTN FRC, Argentina)
Beatriz Marín (Universitat Politècnica de València, Spain)
Luis Olsina (UNLPam, Argentina)
Gleison Santos (Federal University of the State of Rio de Janeiro, Brazil)
Vitor Souza (Federal University of Espírito Santo, Brazil)
Diego Vallespir (Universidad de la República, Uruguay)

A Literature Study to Characterize Continuous Experimentation in Software Engineering

Vladimir M. Erthal[1], Bruno P. de Souza[1], Paulo Sérgio M. dos Santos[2], Guilherme H. Travassos[1]

[1]PESC/COPPE – Federal University of Rio de Janeiro (UFRJ)
Rio de Janeiro – RJ – Brazil

[2]Department of Applied Informatics – Federal University of the State of Rio de Janeiro
Rio de Janeiro – RJ – Brazil

[1]{vladimirerthal, bpsouza, ght}@cos.ufrj.br, [2]pasemes@uniriotec.br

Abstract. *Continuous Experimentation (CE) has become increasingly popular across industry and academic communities. Given its rapid evolution in software engineering (SE), the lack of a common understanding of CE can jeopardize new implementations and justify research efforts. Therefore, this literature study characterizes CE in SE based on its definitions, processes, and strategies for experimentation available in the technical literature. Seventy-six sources of information provided many different definitions, processes, and experimental procedures used to describe CE in SE. Despite the increasing use of CE in SE, it is impossible to observe a common terminology yet to support its characterization and use.*

1. Introduction

Continuous Experimentation (CE) has emerged as a new development practice for software systems. It aims to support software systems engineering through a systematic definition of *hypotheses*, continuous delivery to the end-users, and monitoring metrics to assess the acceptance or rejection of *hypotheses* based on evidence of actual use [Fagerholm et al. 2017]. It arose from the context of agile practices with a strong basis on the *Lean Startup* methodology of "build-measure-learn" [Fagerholm et al. 2014].

CE plays a fundamental role in supporting collaboration between the customer and the development team to discover new software requirements [Olsson and Bosch 2013a]. Also, using controlled experiments, CE guides software development organizations to evaluate and prioritize their development efforts, such as implementing a specific requirement/feature based on users' data [Olsson and Bosch 2014] and discovering the real needs of the users to create value and innovation in the product. It has been widely implemented by several big companies, mainly in web and mobile software systems. Large organizations such as Facebook, Google, Microsoft, LinkedIn, and Netflix have reported their experience using CE to evolve their software products [Auer et al. 2021].

Beyond CE, different expressions have been proposed to refer to this practice in the technical literature, such as Data-Driven Development (DDD) [Bosch and Olsson 2017], Innovation Experiment System (IES) [Bosch 2012], Online Controlled Experiments (OCE) [Kohavi et al. 2013], among others. As a result, the studies report countless processes and strategies from the vast array of expressions [Auer et al., 2021]. Therefore, it is not easy to observe a common understanding regarding continuous experimentation in software development. Moreover, these multiple understandings and perspectives make it difficult to synthesize the papers' contributions. Sometimes, it uses different expressions of the same concept or other words for different concepts. The lack of a common terminology motivated us to understand better and consolidate CE's definitions, processes, and experiment strategies. We believe it can contribute to the technical discussion regarding CE in software engineering (SE) by providing a common knowledge base. Therefore, we performed a literature study to identify and characterize its different definitions, processes, and experimental strategies to support the initial discussions towards organizing a common terminology of continuous experimentation in software engineering.

Besides this introduction, this paper offers the following parts. Section 2 describes the related work used as a seed for this investigation. Next, section 3 introduces the literature study protocol. Section 4 reports the main findings regarding CE's definitions, strategies, and processes. Next, section 5 discusses such findings and presents the implications of CE in SE. Section 6 shows the threats to validity. Finally, section 7 concludes by suggesting some future actions.

2. Related Works

Continuous experimentation has been an object of secondary studies since 2018, as it can be observed in six secondary studies dedicated to this topic. First, Auer and Felderer (2018) published an extensive systematic mapping of 82 primary studies. They addressed questions such as the amount of research activity, the intensity of collaboration between industry and academia, the kind of contributions provided, the most frequently investigated research topics, and the terms used for CE. In the same year, Ros and Runeson (2018) also published a mapping study with 62 primary sources regarding questions focused on the main topics researched within CE, the kind of organizations that use CE, and the characteristics of the experiments that have been used with CE. Also, in 2018, Mattos, Bosch, and Olsson (2018) published a literature review on 42 papers, but in this case, with a focus on CE adoption by embedded systems.

In 2020, Auer, Lee, and Felderer (2020) performed a secondary study with 14 papers focused on experiment characteristics. They proposed a taxonomy for creating experiments used in CE, seeking characteristics, guidelines, checklists, and review processes. Giaimo, Andrade, and Berger (2020) published a literature review with eight papers focused on applying CE in cyber-physical systems in the same year. Finally, in 2021, Auer, Ros, Kaltenbrunner, Runeson, and Felderer (2021) published a systematic literature review on 128 papers addressing three questions: the core constituents of a CE framework, the experiment strategies (that they call technical solutions) applied within CE and its challenges and benefits.

These secondary studies [Auer and Felderer 2018] [Ros and Runeson, 18] [Olsson, 18] [Auer et al., 20] [Giaimo et al., 20] [Auer et al., 21] define CE in different ways. It evidences the lack of a common definition of CE. These studies use CE as a general term, encompassing different perspectives, such as Data-Driven Development, Online Controlled Experiments, and Innovation Experiment Systems. As far as we could experience on our software projects, even though these different terms can share common practices, they do not represent the same concept. Therefore, they can blur the perspectives of practitioners and researchers when selecting CE practices that best apply to their specific software system projects.

3. Literature Study

3.1. Planning

Previous secondary studies (see Section 2) investigated CE, although with different goals from our study. They identified many primary sources of information. Therefore, we understood that a search strategy based on database searches was unnecessary. Thus, we first executed an *ad-hoc* search, including the secondary studies, to create the seed to perform our literature study using the Snowballing technique. Further, for the remaining phases of the review, we followed the practices of literature studies in software engineering as suggested in [Kuhrmann et al. 2017] for replicability and auditing of the results. It includes defining appropriate research questions, a search string, inclusion and exclusion criteria, data collection, dataset cleaning, and study selection.

Following the GQM (Goal/Question/Metric) paradigm [Basili et al. 1794], this study aims *to analyze* Continuous Experimentation practice *with the purpose of* characterizing its definitions, common expressions, processes, models, and experiment strategies *from the point of view of* SE researchers *in the context of* the SE technical literature provided by the Scopus database and snowballing. The Research Questions (RQs) detail the main aspects of the investigation [Table 1].

The term "models" is any graphical representation of any part of the experimentation approach, such as processes, frameworks, lifecycles, and architectures. This definition was used to compare the papers' organizational practices suggested or reported. Similarly, "experiment strategies" refer to obtaining and analyzing the user data needed to conduct the experiments in a CE process.

The initial *ad-hoc* search was performed using the Scopus database, a stable and large coverage search engine, basing the search on widespread expressions and limiting the search period for the last six years (2015 to 2021). The inclusion and exclusion criteria allowed us to get acquainted with the literature and create the seed for snowballing. Table 1 shows all these features. The snowballing technique searches for a research theme related to the initial articles by looking at those referenced by the initial set (backward) and those referred to (forward) [Wöhlin 2014]. The same inclusion and exclusion criteria supported the decision on the suitability of the sources of information.

Table 1. Summary of the literature study.

Research Questions	RQ1: Which are the expressions and definitions associated with the CE concept?
	RQ2: Which are the processes used for CE?
	RQ3: Which are the experiment strategies used for conducting CE?
Search String	("continuous experimentation" OR "continuous software experimentation" OR "experiment systems" OR "data-driven development" OR "A/B tests" OR "A/B testing" OR "online controlled experiments" OR "online controlled experimentation" OR "innovation experiment system" OR "Experiment-driven software development")
Inclusion Criteria	I1. The paper must be in the context of CE and Software Engineering.
	I2. The paper must report a primary or a secondary study.
	I3. The paper must provide data to answer at least one of the research questions.
	I4. The paper must be written in the English language.

Exclusion Criteria	E1. Duplicate publication/self-plagiarism.
	E2. Register of proceedings/posters.
	E3. Papers that are not peer-reviewed.
Technical Report	https://bit.ly/3DLj0uM

3.2. Execution

The search has been performed with Scopus by March 13th, 2021. It resulted in 1125 suggestions of articles, from which we selected 33 papers [S1][S2][S5][S14][S16][S17] [S18] [S20] [S22] [S25] [S26] [S28] [S29] [S31] [S42][S43][S46][S48][S49][S50][S51] [S53][S57][S59][S61][S62][S64][S68][S69][S70][S72][S76] because they provide models or experiment strategies of CE and deal with other contexts beyond the web context.

The papers were selected according to the defined inclusion and exclusion criteria. Then, two researchers analyzed the collection of selected sources to respond to each research question. The level of agreement was high among researchers, and the differences were resolved by analyzing the papers together. One last researcher reviewed the selection process—the snowballing identified 43 additional primary sources from 2007 until 2021. The final set of papers contains 76 selected papers. We consider this final set of articles relevant because of the different search strategies and objectives of our study and the appearance of [S6][S13][S15][S18][S24][S25][S28][S31][S42][S45][S46][S47][S48] [S49] [S50] [S51][S52][S53][S54][S55][S57][S58][S59][S65][S66] [S68] [S70] [S76], which are not present in the dataset of the last and large systematic literature review [Auer et al., 21].

4. Results

4.1. Continuous Experimentation Expressions and Definitions (RQ1)

In the selected papers, we identified 21 different expressions to describe the practice of applying experiments to guide a software system development process. Despite some similarities observed in their definition, some of these expressions have different definitions in various papers. Therefore, to facilitate the analysis, we decided to group the less cited expressions under the most cited ones. To do that, we first identified five terms that have citations in ten or more papers: Continuous Experimentation (30), Online Controlled Experiment (16), Data-Driven Development (12), Innovation Experiment System (10), and A/B Tests (10). However, analyzing the "Online Controlled Experiment" definitions, we realized that most of these matched this expression with A/B Tests. So, we decided to group the expression "A/B Tests" under "Online Controlled Experiment," reducing the categorization to four groups. The other terms were organized into these groups first by the similarity of their definitions in the papers: "Systematic Experimentation" and "Controlled Continuous Experimentation" into "Continuous Experimentation"; "Experiment-Driven Software Development," "Customer-Driven Development," and "Experiment-Driven Approach" into "Data-Driven Development"; and "Continuous Innovation," and "Innovation Process" into "Innovation Experiment System." Then, the remaining expressions were analyzed in its papers, and we identified that all of them were matched to A/B Tests. So, we organized them into "Online Controlled Experiment." All the researchers agreed with this categorization. Table 2 shows all the found expressions and their categorization. In this table, the 'Qty' column indicates the hits of each term in the papers. All the cited expressions were counted when a paper had citations to more than one expression. Still, only one hit was calculated for each term in each paper.

Table 2. Used expressions to describe the practice of applying experiments to guide the development process of a software system.

Group expression	Expressions	Qty
Continuous Experimentation	Continuous Experimentation [S1][S2][S3][S13][S19][S20][S22][S24][S25][S26][S27][S28][S29][S34][S35][S40][S44][S45][S46][S52][S53][S62][S63][S64][S65][S68][S70][S73][S75][S76]	30
	Systematic Experimentation [S40]	1
	Controlled Continuous Experimentation [S69]	1
Online Controlled Experiment	Online Controlled Experiment [S10][S11][S13][S15][S16][S17][S18][S31][S33][S37][S38][S39][S42][S43][S55][S59]	16
	A/B Tests [S10][S21][S30][S36][S37][S39][S43][S59][S72]	9
	Experimentation [S9][S15][S23][S32][S49][S50][S51][S74]	8
	Controlled Experiments [S30][S36][S72]	3
	Live Experimentation [S21][S67]	2
	Control/Treatment [S36]	1
	Parallel Flights [S36]	1
	Randomized Experiments [S36]	1
	Split Tests [S36]	1
	Test-and-learn [S55]	1
Data-Driven Development	Data-Driven Development [S5][S6][S14][S41][S43][S52][S55][S56][S58][S59][S61][S71]	12
	Experiment-Driven Software Development [S43][S48][S53][S76]	4
	Customer-Driven Development [S57]	1
	Experiment-Driven Approach [S41]	1
Innovation Experiment System	Innovation Experiment System [S4][S6][S12][S34][S44][S55][S60] [S62][S66][S7]	10
	Continuous Innovation [S22][S34][S60][S66]	4
	Innovation Process [S8]	1

4.2. Continuous Experimentation Processes (RQ2)

Twenty-four models are proposed in the analyzed papers to guide the CE development process, implant CE into an organization, or deal with specific CE aspects [Table 3]. We classified them into six dimensions. First, development processes establish ordered activities to develop a software system guided by experimentation. Second, maturity processes propose a path to transition a traditional development process into an experimentation-driven one. Third, architecture models illustrate the software experiment structures. Fourth, logical flows show an experiment's paths. Finally, lifecycle and management help structure these specific parts of the experiment.

Each model was analyzed in its activities and purposes by two researchers. As a result, we classified eleven items as development processes, six as maturity processes, three as architecture models, two as logical flows, one as lifecycle, and one as management.

Table 3. CE models proposed in the technical literature.

Dimension	Model Name	Characteristics
Development Processes	Facebook's deployment pipeline [S21]	Development and deployment with canary release
	Hypotheses Engineering [S48]	Creating and managing hypothesis
	Explanatory CTP model for customer touchpoints and feedback data collection [S66]	Model focused on the interactions with customers
	HYPEX model [S56]	Shows how to close the "open-loop problem" between requirements and user data
	Unnamed model [S4] [S12]	CE model for embedded systems
	The HURRIER Process [S46]	CE model for business-to-business (B2B) systems
	The Qualitative/quantitative Customer-driven Development (QCD) model [S57] [S58]	Focused on customer feedback techniques to generate hypotheses
	Bing's experimentation process [S35]	Focused on validating data to iterate, ship, or abandon the hypothesis
	Experimentation Process Framework [S43]	Detailed CE model with activities, artifacts, inputs/outputs, and stored data
	Fagerholm et al. process [S19]	Based on the Lean Startup methodology, lists activities and roles
	RIGHT process model for Continuous Experimentation [S20]	Based on the Lean Startup methodology, lists activities and roles (update of [S19])
Maturity Processes	Transitioning towards experiment-driven development [S41]	Areas that the company needs to evolve up to CE
	Experimentation Evolution Model [S14]	Areas that the company needs to evolve up to CE
	Experimentation Growth (EG) Model [S15]	Areas that the company needs to evolve up to CE (update of [S14])
	Data-Driven Development Adoption Process [S59]	Steps that a company needs to follow to achieve CE
	eXperimentation Progression (XPro) model [S50]	Steps that a company needs to follow to achieve CE
	The Stairway to Heaven (StH) model [S6] [S34] [S60]	Steps that a company needs to follow to achieve CE
Architecture Models	Bing's experiment system architecture [S38]	Architecture for experimentation
	Giaimo and Berger model [S25]	Architecture for experimentation in automotive systems
	Evidence-Based Engineering [S5]	Architecture for experimentation in smart systems
Logical Flow	High-level flow for A/B test [S37] [S10]	Architecture for A/B Test
	Logic flow for A/B test [S38]	Architecture for A/B Test
Lifecycle	The experiment lifecycle [S17] [S18]	Experiment lifecycle
Management	A model of hypotheses engineering in startups [S52]	Management of hypothesis

4.3. Experiments Strategies (RQ3)

We identified several experimental strategies to adopt when performing CE. We perceive that A/B testing is the most applied and known experimental strategy cited in the selected studies. Our findings identified 47 different empirical strategies, including A/B tests. The experimental strategy tests a hypothesis and determines how the software will be updated. They determine how the experiment will be conducted, who will participate in it, in which project phase it will occur, what type of user data will be extracted, and how it will be analyzed.

Analyzing the experimental strategies, we perceived qualitative and quantitative approaches. Also, the strategies have different goals. For example, one experiment can use different strategies to test a hypothesis. An A/B Test can be deployed as a canary release and utilize overall evaluation criteria (OEC) to analyze the results for a quantitative example. Thus, we identified three main goals in the quantitative strategies [Table 4].

We named **Controlled experiments** (six items) the strategies that deal with the form of the experiments, i.e., how the experiments will be conducted. These strategies normally involve the end-user after developing the product or feature. Similarly, we called **Metrics measurement** (13 items) the strategies that indicate what type of user data will be extracted, which will also determine how this data will be analyzed. Some of these strategies require code parametrization in the software, while others can be measured externally. Finally, we named **Deploy mode** (nine items) the strategies that determine who will be selected for the experiment, influencing how the analysis will be conducted. These strategies are always applied in the deployment phase.

For qualitative strategies [Table 4], we identified two main groups with different goals, which we named **Participatory requirements** (six items) and **Partial appraisal** (13 items). These groups are other than the quantitative strategies because the participatory requirements strategies need the client or user representative to participate in the requirements elicitation phase. So, it defines who will participate in the experiment and the project phase. The experiments' conduction and the data collected and analyzed shall be selected from the partial appraisal strategies. However, these strategies can also be utilized without a participatory requirement, determining other selection of participants and different project phases. It can even be used with quantitative strategies to extract data that metrics measurement could not obtain.

Table 4. Experiment strategies categorization.

Quantitative strategies	**Controlled experiments**	A/B test, A/B/n test (or multivariate tests - MVT), Quasi-controlled experiments, MVP/MVF, Cross-over experimental design, and multi-armed bandits.
	Metrics measurement	Landing pages, fake door tests, wizard of oz MVP, metaheuristic search, bug reports, support logs, Google analytics, advertising, BASES testing, labs website, internal metrics collection, cognitive mapping, and overall evaluation criteria.
	Deploy mode	Alpha and beta testing (or early-access), canary releases (or partial rollouts or canary flying), blue/green deployment, gradual rollout, dark launches (or passive launch), parallel execution, serial execution, downsampled execution, selected customers (or proxy/lead users or expert reviews).
Qualitative strategies	**Participatory requirements**	Participatory design (or cooperative design, or joint-application design), scenarios, user stories, use cases, joint requirements sessions, and solution/innovation jams.
	Partial appraisal	Case studies (or field experiments or user studies), focus groups, surveys, interviews, observation, mockups (or sketches), prototypes, walkthroughs, feature voting, open testing, customer unit workshop (or customer conference or trade show testing), product seminar, and ethnographic studies.

5. Discussion and Implications

5.1. Continuous Experimentation Expressions and Definitions

We noticed that the expressions "Continuous Experimentation," "Data-Driven Development," and "Innovation Experiment System" are the ones having more similarities to themes expressed in their definitions. The noticed themes were recurrence, a data-driven approach, and the use of user data to validate the experiments. It indicates that these expressions share the same intentions. However, the papers using the term "Innovation Experiment System" come mostly from the works of one research group [S4][S6][S7][S12][S34][S44][S55][S60][S66]. On the other hand, the expression "Online Controlled Experiment" diverges from the others because almost half the papers use this expression as synonymous with A/B Tests in the online domain. Besides, it has many citations to user data, but citations to data-driven approaches and recurrence are less common. A/B Tests can be used both in a data-driven and non-data-driven company. However, the three other expressions are applicable only in companies intending to be guided by the behavior of the end-users, transforming the possible requirements into hypotheses, and even creating theories through data obtained from the users.

This result expresses the current lack of consensus among researchers about which expressions should refer to the continuous experimentation approach in software development. The bigger quantity of CE usage indicates a trend to adopt this expression. However, the other terms are still very used. We believe that these expressions should be better distinguished to facilitate the research and express different approaches to software experimentation. Future works are needed to make clear this distinction.

Table 5. Phases of experimentation classify CE development processes. In each stage, "S" means "superficial," "D" means "detailed," and "NA" means "not addressed."

Process Name	Experimentation Phases				
	Ideation	Experiment Design	Implementation	Execution	Analysis
Facebook's deployment pipeline [Feitelson et al., 13]	NA	NA	S	D	NA
Hypotheses Engineering [Melegati et al., 19a]	D	S	NA	S	S
Explanatory CTP model for customer touchpoints and feedback data collection [Sauvola et al., 15]	D	D	NA	NA	D
HYPEX model [Olsson and Bosch, 14]	S	S	S	S	D
Unnamed model [Eklund and Bosch, 12] [Bosch and Eklund, 12]	S	NA	S	D	S
The HURRIER Process [Mattos et al., 20b]	D	NA	D	D	NA
The Qualitative/quantitative Customer-driven Development (QCD) model [Olsson and Bosch, 15a] [Olsson and Bosch, 15b]	D	D	NA	S	D
Bing's experimentation process [Kevic et al., 17]	S	S	S	S	D
Experimentation Process Framework [Mattos et al., 18a]	D	S	D	S	D
Fagerholm et al. process [Fagerholm et al., 14]	S	S	D	S	D
RIGHT process model for Continuous Experimentation [Fagerholm et al., 17]	S	S	D	S	D

5.2. Continuous Experimentation Processes

This study considered only the eleven development processes identified in [Table 3] because its objective is generally to analyze CE's conduction. Two of them were designed for specific software contexts [Eklund and Bosch 2012] [Bosch and Eklund 2012] [Mattos et al. 2020b], and the others are for general purposes. Table 5 shows these eleven processes classified according to the five phases of experimentation presented by [Auer et al. 2021], identifying whenever a phase is cited superficially, detailed, or not addressed in the model. We consider that a stage is detailed if more than one step in that phase or if the one-step has associated characteristics. This classification shows that none of the processes has all phases detailed. Six processes (54,5%) do not present all the stages. However, all the processes have at least one detailed phase. It indicates that all these processes aim to explore a specific part of the development process guided by experimentation. Since the processes have different clear stages, we understand that the processes have complementary parts. Therefore, the practitioners could benefit not from choosing just one of them but from utilizing some of them together.

5.3. Continuous Experimentation Strategies

The findings indicate a lack of consensus about which strategies to use for a CE process, even with many references about A/B Tests, mostly through collecting metrics. Therefore, more studies are needed to show which strategies should be used in CE processes. Furthermore, it is important to understand the qualitative strategies and their role in CE, particularly when quantitative data does not support answering questions or refuting hypotheses. For instance, it does not indicate which part of the software needs improvement. Qualitative strategies are required in this regard [Ros 2020].

Furthermore, there is a need to discuss whether participatory requirements should be used within the CE process, as stated in some analyzed papers, or should not, as in the processes in the matrix. For example, the works [Melegati et al. 2019a] [Melegati et al. 2019b], and [Melegati et al. 2020c] advocate that the requirement concept is inadequate in the CE context and that the *hypotheses engineering* should replace the requirements engineering in these cases. According to them, requirements engineering is an important component of "traditional requirements-driven development." However, in "experiment-driven software development," the *hypotheses* guide the elicitation of the users' needs, and they evolve together with the coding. So, as experiment-driven software development, CE would benefit from *hypotheses engineering* to better identify, prioritize, specify, analyze, and manage its hypotheses and reduce the waste of resources and time. In this way, the participatory requirements strategies should be adapted to this new concept to gain statistical relevance and be used as useful data-driven strategies in CE processes in software engineering.

6. Threats to Validity

As expected in any empirical study, threats to validity deserve attention. First, regarding reliability, we selected the works from technical literature following good search practices and considering an initial set of secondary studies (Section 2). Although they do not assure full replication, we described the elementary features that allow repeatability of results. Further, we have provided each article's inclusion and exclusion criteria [Table 1] and applied snowballing techniques to enlarge coverage and reduce this threat, including six secondary studies. Also, we have a larger list of selected primary sources than most previously identified secondary studies, including papers that do not appear.

To mitigate the bias of the selected papers and the interpretation bias of researchers, two researchers determined the articles, and two others reviewed the final set. The research protocol aims at promoting its data traceability. Additionally, an *ad-hoc* analysis supported this literature study. Thus, the interpretation and synthesis of the articles can be subjective. However, the researchers' experience with coding practices and data synthesis can naturally influence how such an analysis is conducted.

7. Conclusion

Continuous Experimentation has become widely known as a valuable development practice by practitioners and researchers. However, understanding the planning and implementation of CE in SE is still difficult because of the plurality of interpretations in the technical literature. In this context, based on the current body of knowledge examined utilizing a literature study, we characterize CE in its definitions, processes, and experimentation strategies.

We identified results regarding the definitions in which "continuous experimentation" shares the same intentions as "data-driven development" and "innovation experiment system," However, the distinct approaches are different from "online controlled experiment," which is an expression for A/B Test. The lack of a common terminology creates difficulties for researchers to discover and understand the different terms used in the available studies. To the best of our knowledge, no other research has discussed these expressions' differences.

We also identified 24 models regarding CE, eleven of which were development processes. We noticed that these development processes share common activities. Still, each has parts that deal with different experimentation aspects, making them complementary. This plurality of expressions and diverse highlights makes selecting the appropriate process for a specific context a challenge.

Finally, we identified 47 experimentation strategies, categorized them into two groups, subcategorized them into five subgroups, and created a correlation matrix of the processes and the strategies. We noticed that the A/B test is the most applied strategy known by both practitioners and researchers. However, the number of strategies found and the fact that most of them appear in few papers state that more studies are needed to determine the contributions of each strategy for CE.

We also identified that dealing with hypotheses is a little-explored challenge for CE. The relation between the conjectured software properties and requirements is unclear. Therefore, the recently raised concept of Hypotheses Engineering could help to align these approaches in the context of CE in SE. Continuous experimentation is not just collecting data, but it represents a systematic method having its concepts, processes, and strategies. It needs to be understood and aligned with the organization's strategic objectives to succeed in engineering software systems using CE. Therefore, despite its increasing use, it is impossible to observe a common terminology yet to support its characterization and use in SE. Further studies are necessary to organize such concepts and taxonomically represent them to make continuous experimentation less blurred in software systems projects.

Acknowledgments

This work is partially supported by the Coordenação de Aperfeiçoamento de Pessoal de Nível Superior - Brasil (CAPES) - Finance Code 001 and by CNPq. Prof. Travassos is a CNPq researcher (Grant 304234/2018-4) and CNE FAPERJ (Grant E-26/201.170/2021).

References

Basili, V. R., Caldiera, G., Rombach, H. D. (1994) "The goal question metric approach"; Encyclopedia of software engineering, 528-532.

Kuhrmann, M., Fernández, D. M., Daneva, M. (2017) "On the pragmatic design of literature studies in software engineering: an experience-based guideline"; ESE 22.6.

Wohlin, C. (2014) "Guidelines for snowballing in systematic literature studies and a replication in software engineering"; Proceedings of the 18th EASE.

Selected Publications

[S1] Auer, F. and Felderer, M. (2018) "Current state of research on continuous experimentation: a systematic mapping study"; 2018 44th Euromicro SEAA, IEEE.

[S2] Auer, F., Lee C. S., and Felderer, M. (2020) "Continuous experiment definition characteristics"; 2020 46th Euromicro SEAA, IEEE.

[S3] Auer, F. et al. (2021) "Controlled experimentation in continuous experimentation: Knowledge and challenges"; Information and Software Technology 134, 106551.

[S4] Bosch, J., Eklund, U. (2012) "Eternal embedded software: Towards innovation experiment systems"; ISoLA, Springer, Berlin, Heidelberg.

[S5] Bosch, J. and Olsson, H. H. (2016) "Data-driven continuous evolution of smart systems"; 2016 IEEE/ACM 11th SEAMS, IEEE.

[S6] Bosch, J., and Olsson, H. H. (2017) "Toward evidence-based organizations: lessons from embedded systems, online games, and the Internet of Things"; IEEE Software 34.5.

[S7] Bosch, J. (2012) "Building products as innovation experiment systems"; International Conference of Software Business, Springer, Berlin, Heidelberg.

[S8] Bosch-Sijtsema, P. and Bosch, J. (2015) "User involvement throughout the innovation process in high-tech industries"; JPIM 32.5, p. 793-807.

[S9] Buchert, T. et al. (2015) "A survey of general-purpose experiment management tools for distributed systems"; Future Generation Computer Systems 45, p. 1-12.

[S10] Crook, T., et al. (2009) "Seven pitfalls to avoid when running controlled experiments on the web"; 15th ACM SIGKDD.

[S11] Deng, A., and Shi, X. (2016) "Data-driven metric development for online controlled experiments: Seven lessons"; 22nd ACM SIGKDD.

[S12] Eklund, U. and Bosch, J. (2012) "Architecture for large-scale innovation experiment systems"; IEEE/IFIP Conference and European Conference, IEEE.

[S13] Esteller-Cucala, M., Fernandez, V., and Villuendas, D. (2020) "Towards data-driven culture in a Spanish automobile manufacturer: A case study"; JIEM 13.2.

[S14] Fabijan, A., et al. (2017) "The evolution of continuous experimentation in software product development: from data to a data-driven organization at scale"; IEEE/ACM 39th ICSE, IEEE.

[S15] Fabijan, A., et al. (2018a) "Experimentation growth: Evolving trustworthy A/B testing capabilities in online software companies"; J. Softw.: Evol. Process 30.12.

[S16] Fabijan, A. et al. (2018b) "Online controlled experimentation at scale: an empirical survey on the current state of A/B testing"; 44th Euromicro SEAA, IEEE.

[S17] Fabijan, A. et al. (2018c) "The online controlled experiment lifecycle"; IEEE Software 37.2, p. 60-67.

[S18] Fabijan, A., et al. (2019) "Three key checklists and remedies for trustworthy analysis of online controlled experiments at scale"; IEEE/ACM ICSE-SEIP, IEEE.

[S19] Fagerholm, F. et al. (2014) "Building blocks for continuous experimentation"; 1st international workshop on rapid continuous software engineering.

[S20] Fagerholm, F., et al. (2017) "The RIGHT model for continuous experimentation"; Journal of Systems and Software 123, p. 292-305.

[S21] Feitelson, D. G., Frachtenberg, E. and Beck, K. L. (2013) "Development and deployment at Facebook"; IEEE Internet Computing 17.4, p. 8-17.

[S22] Fitzgerald, B. and Stol, K.J. (2017) "Continuous software engineering: A roadmap and agenda"; Journal of Systems and Software 123, p. 176-189.

[S23] Gerostathopoulos, I., et al. (2018) "Cost-aware stage-based experimentation: challenges and emerging results"; 2018 IEEE ICSA-C, IEEE.

[S24] Giaimo, F. and Berger, C. (2017) "Design criteria to architect continuous experimentation for self-driving vehicles"; IEEE ICSA.

[S25] Giaimo, F. and Berger, C. (2020) "Continuous Experimentation for Automotive Software on the Example of a Heavy Commercial Vehicle in Daily Operation"; ECSA.

[S26] Giaimo, F., et al. (2016) "Continuous experimentation on cyber-physical systems: challenges and opportunities"; Proceedings of the scientific workshop XP2016.

[S27] Giaimo, F., Berger, C., and Kirchner, C. (2017) "Considerations about continuous experimentation for resource-constrained platforms in self-driving vehicles"; ECSA.

[S28] Giaimo, F., Andrade, H. and Berger, C. (2019) "The automotive take on continuous experimentation: a multiple case study"; 45th SEAA, IEEE.

[S29] Giaimo, F., Andrade, H. and Berger, C. (2020) "Continuous experimentation and the cyber-physical systems challenge: An overview of the literature and the industrial perspective"; Journal of Systems and Software 170, 110781.

[S30] Gomez-Uribe, C. A. and Hunt, N. (2015) "The Netflix recommender system: Algorithms, business value, and innovation"; ACM TMIS 6.4, p. 1-19.

[S31] Gupta, S. et al. (2019) "Top challenges from the first practical online controlled experiments summit"; ACM SIGKDD Explorations Newsletter 21.1, p. 20-35.

[S32] Gutbrod, M., Münch, J. and Tichy, M. (2019) "How do software startups approach experimentation? Empirical results from a qualitative interview study"; PROFES.

[S33] Jiang, S., Martin, J. and Wilson, C. (2019) "Who's the Guinea Pig? Investigating Online A/B/n Tests in-the-Wild"; Proceedings of the ACM FAccT.

[S34] Karvonen, T. et al. (2015) "Hitting the Target: Practices and Steps for Moving Towards Innovation Experiment Systems"; LNBIP.

[S35] Kevic, K. et al. (2017) "Characterizing experimentation in continuous deployment: a case study on bing"; 2017 IEEE/ACM 39th ICSE-SEIP, IEEE.

[S36] Kohavi, R., Henne, R. M. and Sommerfield, D. (2007) "Practical guide to controlled experiments on the web: listen to your customers, not to the hippo"; 13th ACM SIGKDD.

[S37] Kohavi, R., et al. (2012) "Trustworthy online controlled experiments: Five puzzling outcomes explained"; 18th ACM SIGKDD.

[S38] Kohavi, R., et al. (2013) "Online controlled experiments at large scale"; 19th ACM SIGKDD.

[S39] Kohavi, R., et al. (2014) "Seven rules of thumb for website experimenters"; 20th ACM SIGKDD.

[S40] Lindgren, E. and Münch, J. (2015) "Software development as an experiment system: A qualitative survey on the state of the practice"; ICASD.

[S41] Lindgren, E. and Münch, J. (2016) "Raising the odds of success: the current state of experimentation in product development"; IST 77, p. 80-91.

[S42] Liu, S. et al. (2019) "Enterprise-Level Controlled Experiments at Scale: Challenges and Solutions"; 45th Euromicro Conference on SEAA, IEEE.

[S43] Mattos, D. I., et al. (2018a) "An activity and metric model for online controlled experiments"; PROFES, Springer, Cham.

[S44] Mattos, D. I., Bosch, J., and Olsson, H. H. (2018b) "Challenges and strategies for undertaking continuous experimentation to embedded systems: Industry and research perspectives"; ICASD.

[S45] Mattos, D. I., et al. (2020a) "Automotive a/b testing: Challenges and lessons learned from practice"; 46th Euromicro Conference on SEAA, IEEE.

[S46] Mattos, D. I., et al. (2020b) "Experimentation for business-to-business mission-critical systems: a case study"; Proceedings of the ICSSP.

[S47] Melegati, J. and Wang, X. (2020) "Hypotheses Elicitation in Early-Stage Software Startups Based on Cognitive Mapping"; ICASD, Springer, Cham.

[S48] Melegati, J., Wang, X., and Abrahamsson, P. (2019a) "Hypotheses Engineering: first essential steps of experiment-driven software development"; 4th International Workshop on RCoSE/DDrEE, IEEE.

[S49] Melegati, J., et al. (2019b) "Enablers and inhibitors of experimentation in early-stage software startups"; PROFES, Springer, Cham.

[S50] Melegati, J., Edison, H., and Wang, X. (2020a) "XPro: a Model to Explain the Limited Adoption and Implementation of Experimentation in Software Startups"; IEEE TOSEM.

[S51] Melegati, J., et al. (2020b) "MVP and experimentation in software startups: a qualitative survey"; 46th Euromicro Conference on SEAA, IEEE.

[S52] Melegati, J., Guerra, E., and Wang, X. (2020c) "Understanding Hypotheses Engineering in Software Startups through a Gray Literature Review"; IST, 106465.

[S53] Melegati, J. (2019) "Improving requirements engineering practices to support experimentation in software startups"; 27th ACM Joint Meeting on ESEC/FSE.

[S54] Olsson, H. H. and Bosch, J. (2013a) "Post-deployment data collection in software-intensive embedded products"; ICSOB, Springer, Berlin, Heidelberg.

[S55] Olsson, H. H. and Bosch, J. (2013b) "Towards data-driven product development: A multiple case study on post-deployment data usage in software-intensive embedded systems"; LESS, Springer, Berlin, Heidelberg.

[S56] Olsson, H. H. and Bosch, J. (2014) "From opinions to data-driven software R&D: A multi-case study on how to close the 'open loop' problem"; 40th EUROMICRO SEAA.

[S57] Olsson, H. H. and Bosch, J. (2015a) "Towards continuous validation of customer value"; Scientific Workshop Proceedings of the XP2015.

[S58] Olsson, H. H. and Bosch, J. (2015b) "Towards continuous customer validation: A conceptual model for combining qualitative customer feedback with quantitative customer observation"; International Conference of Software Business. Springer, Cham.

[S59] Olsson, H. H. and Bosch, J. (2019) "Data-driven development: Challenges in online, embedded and on-premise software"; PROFES, Springer, Cham.

[S60] Olsson, H. H., Bosch, J. and Alahyari, H. (2013) "Towards R&D as innovation experiment systems: A framework for moving beyond agile software development"; IASTED ().

[S61] Olsson, H. H., Bosch, J. and Fabijan, A. (2017) "Experimentation that matters: a multi-case study on the challenges with A/B testing"; ICSOB, Springer, Cham.

[S62] Rissanen, O. and Münch, J. (2015) "Continuous experimentation in the B2B domain: a case study"; IEEE/ACM 2nd International Workshop on RCoSE, IEEE.

[S63] Ros, R. and Bjarnason, E. (2018) "Continuous experimentation scenarios: a case study in e-Commerce"; 44th Euromicro Conference on SEAA, IEEE.

[S64] Ros, R. and Runeson, P. (2018) "Continuous experimentation and a/b testing: A mapping study"; 2018 IEEE/ACM 4th International Workshop on (RCoSE), IEEE.

[S65] Ros, R. (2020) "Continuous Experimentation with Product-Led Business Models: A Comparative Case Study"; ICSOB, Springer, Cham.

[S66] Sauvola, T. et al. (2015) "Towards customer-centric software development: a multiple-case study"; 41st Euromicro Conference on SEAA, IEEE.

[S67] Schermann, G. et al. (2016) "Bifrost: Supporting continuous deployment with automated enactment of multi-phase live testing strategies"; 17th IMC.

[S68] Schermann, G., Cito, J., and Leitner, P. (2018a) "Continuous experimentation: challenges, implementation techniques, and current research"; Ieee Software 35.2, p. 26-31.

[S69] Schermann, G., et al. (2018b) "We're doing it live: A multi-method empirical study on continuous experimentation"; Information and Software Technology, v. 99.

[S70] Sveningson, R., Mattos, D. I. and Bosch, J. (2019) "Continuous experimentation for software organizations with low control of roadmap and a large distance to users: An exploratory case study"; PROFES, Springer, Cham.

[S71] Tang, D., et al. (2010) "Overlapping experiment infrastructure: More, better, faster experimentation"; 16th ACM SIGKDD International Conference on KDD.

[S72] Xu, Y. and Chen, N. (2016) "Evaluating mobile apps with A/B and quasi A/B tests"; 22nd ACM SIGKDD International Conference on KDD.

[S73] Yaman, S. G., et al. (2016) "Transitioning towards continuous experimentation in a large software product and service development organization–a case study"; PROFES.

[S74] Yaman, S. et al. (2017) "Notifying and involving users in experimentation: ethical perceptions of software practitioners"; ESEM.

[S75] Yaman, S., Mikkonen, T., and Suomela, R. (2018) "Continuous experimentation in mobile game development"; 2018 44th Euromicro Conference on SEAA, IEEE.

[S76] Yaman, S., et al. (2020) "Patterns of user involvement in experiment-driven software development"; Information and Software Technology, v. 120, p. 106244.

A Metrics-based Approach for Assessing Architecture-Implementation Mappings

J. Andres Diaz-Pace[1], Rodrigo Cian Berrios[2], Antonela Tommasel[1], Hernan C. Vazquez[2]

[1]ISISTAN Research Institute – UNCPBA University-CONICET
Campus Universitario Tandil – Tandil – Buenos Aires – Argentina

[2]Facultad de Ciencias Exactas – UNCPBA University
Campus Universitario Tandil – Tandil – Buenos Aires – Argentina

{andres.diazpace,antonela.tommasel}@isistan.unicen.edu.ar
cianrodrigo@gmail.com, hvazquez@exa.unicen.edu.ar

Abstract. *Several automated techniques for assisting engineers in creating mappings between source code (e.g., classes) and architecture elements (e.g., modules) have been proposed. They are generally assessed via precision and recall metrics. However, these metrics can only be evaluated post-mortem, i.e., once an expert created and validated all the mappings. In practice, given a set of mappings, engineers would like to assess their quality without (effortfully) validating the whole set. In this context, we explore a suite of quality metrics as an architectural fitness function for a ranking of mappings, which helps engineers select a useful list of those mappings. We empirically analyzed the evolution of our metrics in two projects using different mapping techniques.*

1. Introduction

The software architecture of a system is a blueprint that captures the main design decisions for satisfying the quality attributes (e.g., performance, modifiability, reliability, among others) posed by the system stakeholders [Bass et al. 2021]. These decisions are reflected in different architectural views (e.g., modules, components), which prescribe how the system should be implemented. Even when the architectural decisions are appropriately communicated to the development teams, there are usually *divergences* between the architecture "as designed" (e.g., the module view) and the architecture "as implemented" (i.e., the source code implementing those modules). When these divergences are not identified and properly controlled by the engineers, the benefits of architecture-centric development regarding the desired quality attributes tend to vanish, as the implementation no longer reflects the key design decisions. In this context, performing periodic conformance checks between the architecture and its implementation becomes necessary. A well-known approach for such checks is Reflexion Modeling (RM) [Murphy et al. 2001], which analyzes differences between the dependencies defined in the architecture blueprint and those found in the code. An RM prerequisite is the provision of mappings from source code elements to architecture elements.

Establishing the *architecture-implementation mappings* is often a tedious and error-prone task for engineers, as they must analyze many implementation details. Thus, several automated techniques (and tools) for assisting in creating and maintaining such mappings have been developed [Olsson et al. 2022]. These techniques take different information sources (e.g., the system dependency graph, source code, or descriptions of architectural components) and have recently incorporated Machine Learning (ML) developments. Since the output of these tools is often a ranking of proposed mappings, their performance can be evaluated in terms of ML metrics, such as precision and recall, which require knowing the valid mappings for a system in advance (ground truth). Unfortunately, this situation seldom happens in a project, either because the ground truth is unknown or an expert must validate all the mappings proposed by a tool, which entails a considerable effort. Nonetheless, engineers would still need to assess the mappings suggested by a tool and select promising ones, without waiting until the end of the process (when all mappings are established and validated).

In this paper, we propose a suite of metrics for assessing the architecture-implementation mappings for a system, assuming they can be somehow ordered in a ranking. These metrics are taken from the literature [Guimarães et al. 2018, Lange and Chaudron 2004] and are agnostic of the particular technique or tool being used for mapping generation. The metrics include aspects such as: level of abstraction, consistency, completeness and code coverage. Unlike existing approaches, we do not require a ground truth of mappings. In our proposal, the metrics work as an *architectural fitness function* [Ford et al. 2017], providing hints about the quality (or usefulness) of the mappings. For instance, if a metric indicates that the number of architectural divergences increases as more mappings (of a given ranking) are accepted, the engineer might be prefer to keep only the top-k mappings of the ranking. Here, a related question is how many mappings from a ranking should be accepted. We approach this decision as a *parameter optimization problem*, which considers the evolution of the metrics and seeks to identify a cut-off point in the mapping ranking that (mostly) satisfies the engineer's preferences over the metric values. We evaluated the proposed framework in two projects using six mapping techniques. In those projects, the optimization procedure showed that $\approx 35\%$ of the mappings (of the rankings) can lead to satisfactory results, in terms of both useful mappings and precision/recall for the process. Although in initial stages, this work contributes to the practical application of architecture conformance techniques in projects and tools.

The rest of the paper is organized into 5 sections as follows. Section 2 provides the main concepts of architecture conformance and defines the mapping problem. In Section 3, our approach based on mapping metrics and optimization is presented. Section 4 reports on an initial evaluation of the approach with case-studies. Section 5 covers related work. Finally, Section 6 gives the conclusions and outlines future work.

2. Background

It is common to structure and organize systems in terms of views. On the one hand, we assume that the system implementation will be described by a *code view* that captures the main implementation units and how they depend on each other. An implementation unit can be materialized by a class (or a package), while a dependency is any method invocation or any other usage relation between classes (or packages). For instance, Figure 1 (right side) shows a simplified code view with five classes. On the other hand, we assume that the software architecture will be described by a *module view* that identifies intended system-level units, called *modules*, which group cohesive functions. These modules have dependencies (or interactions) with each other, usually via provided/required interfaces. The example in Figure 1 (left side) shows a 3-tier architecture with three modules.

A standard approach for linking the architecture and code views is to structurally map them via the RM mechanisms. This approach requires engineers to establish one-to-many correspondences between code and architectural elements. In Figure 1, these mappings are exemplified by the dotted arrows from classes to modules. Based on the mappings, convergences and divergences between the relations prescribed by the architecture and those existing in the code can be discovered, as indicated by the green and red symbols, respectively. Divergences are also referred to as *architecture violations*.

We define below the main concepts for the architecture-implementation mapping problem, which serve as a conceptual framework for our proposal.

2.1. Formalization

Let $ArchView =< A, uses >$ be a graph (or tuple) that captures a static system view, in which $A = \{m_1, m_2, ..., m_N\}$ is a set of N modules and $uses$ is a binary relation between $m_i, m_j \in A$ denoting that the first module relies on services provided by the second module. Let $CodeView =< C, dependsOn >$ be a graph (or tuple) that represents a system implementation, in which $C = \{jc_1, jc_2, ..., jc_P\}$ is a set of P Java classes (with unique names) and $dependsOn$ is a relation between $jc_k, jc_l \in C$ indicating that the first class requires (or uses) methods defined in the second class. Dependencies between classes are often due to implementation needs.

The mapping can be seen as a matching between $ArchView$ and $CodeView$. More specifically, let $mappings = \{(jc, m) | jc \in C \wedge m \in A\}$ be a partial relation between elements at different levels of abstraction. This is a partial relation because some classes might have no correspondences with modules. A module, in turn, can relate to one or more classes. Along this line, the solution to the matching consists of finding (or approximating) $mappings$ as a function $f : C \rightarrow A$. Given the mappings, three possible types of differences between $ArchView$ and $CodeView$ arise: convergences, divergences, or absences. Divergences (violations) are of particular interest for architecture conformance because they imply that an intended module dependency is not followed in the code. Violations have quality-attribute effects concerning system modifiability, among other qualities [Brunet et al. 2012, Bass et al. 2021].

2.2. Mappings as similarity functions

RM does not prescribe how mappings should be established. For instance, engineers could rely on naming conventions of classes to link them to modules. Mapping generation is often done in a semi-automated way. In practice, either a tool suggests an initial set of mappings (or seeds) to the engineer, or the engineer provides an initial mapping that the tool then uses to infer additional mappings. From this perspective, the tool works as a *recommender system* [Robillard et al. 2014] that implements $f : C \rightarrow A$ and returns a *ranking of mappings*. We assume that each particular mapping has a goodness score in the range $[0..1]$, in which 1 refers to a perfect mapping (or similarity) between a pair of elements and 0 indicates a very unlikely mapping [Olsson et al. 2022].

A common strategy for generating likely mappings is to compute the similarity between all pairs (jc, m), being jc a class and m a module, respectively. In other words,

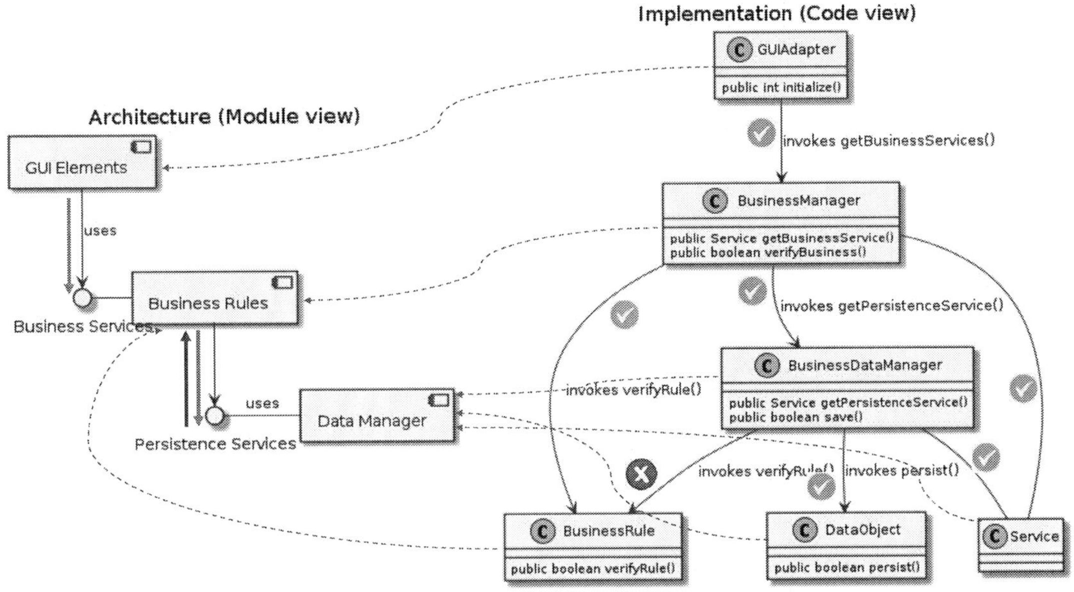

Figure 1. Example of mappings between architecture and implementation views.

we take the Cartesian product $C \times A$, under the constraint that any class can match only a single module. For a given class, the module with the highest similarity is chosen. Various similarity criteria between classes and modules can be applied. In this work, we focus on the following three similarity functions:

- **Linguistic similarity (L).** It compares the names of the class and module being mapped. To this end, the original names are split into tokens, and text similarity metrics are applied. In particular, we relied on a semantic metric provided by the SEMILAR toolkit [Rus et al. 2013].
- **Concern similarity (C).** A software concern is any aspect that impacts the design and implementation of a system, usually with cross-cutting effects on several artifacts [Robillard and Warr 2005]. For instance, a security concern might affect several classes and more than one module. Other examples of concerns include performance, persistence, or error handling. In terms of similarity, we say that a class matches a module if they "share" the same set of concerns.
- **Structural similarity (S).** It is based on the graph structure (or topology) of the module and code views. Similarity is treated as a graph matching problem. This function departs from an initial set of pairs of graph nodes (seeds) and then propagates the similarity to neighboring nodes, as proposed in [Melnik et al. 2002]. The seeds are either provided manually by the engineer or result from applying any of the previous functions.

As an example, Table 1 shows a matrix with the similarity scores computed by the three functions for the modules and classes of Figure 1. The best scores (for the mappings) are shown in bold. Note that the similarity functions might have different performance for the same pairs. This effect is caused by the heuristic nature of each function but it might also depend on class and module information. More details on the similarity functions above can be found in [Vázquez et al. 2015, Olsson et al. 2022].

	GUIAdapter			BusinessDataManager			BusinessRule		
	L	C	S	L	C	S	L	C	S
GUI Elements	**0.5**	**1.0**	**0.84**	0.25	0.0	0.52	0.28	0.0	0.0
Business Rules	0.0	0.0	0.0	**0.63**	**1.0**	**1.0**	**1.0**	**1.0**	**0.38**
Data Manager	0.0	0.0	0.0	0.71	0.0	0.0	0.28	0.0	0.37

Table 1. Examples of mapping scores using different similarity functions.

2.3. Performance evaluation

The traditional assessment of the mappings produced by a similarity function (as supported by a tool) is based on computing precision and recall metrics [Ricci et al. 2015], particularly when the ground truth (or reference mappings) is known or the mappings can be validated by an expert. The precision/recall formulas are given by Equations 1 and 2.

$$Precision = \frac{mappings \cap referenceMappings}{mappings} \quad (1)$$

$$Recall = \frac{mappings \cap referenceMappings}{referenceMappings} \quad (2)$$

In general, a tradeoff will exist between precision and recall, which is also affected by the goodness value of the mappings. High precision means that the suggested mappings are correct, while high recall implies that most of the real mappings were suggested. If high recall is accompanied by low precision, there will be some false positive mappings. In this regard, Figure 2 shows the evolution of these two metrics for a ranking of 120 class mappings (X axis) produced by a linguistic similarity function. Note also that the goodness value of the mappings (top-level chart) decreases, suggesting that the mappings beyond the 40th position (or with a goodness score < 0.5) should be considered spurious by the engineer. According to the charts, precision degrades significantly after that point ($k_{step} = 40 \approx 33\%$ of 120 mappings) at the cost of a slight improvement in recall. We refer to k_{step} as the *cut-off* point of the mapping ranking. Determining a good enough cut-off (for a given project) is important for the engineer to get the most of the performance of the mapping strategy (when the ground truth is not available), and it is the main driver of our approach.

3. Approach

Let us assume a scenario in which an engineer wants to map a code view to a module view using any automated strategy, and gets a ranking of suggested mappings. The engineer has to provide the architecture and code views as inputs for a mapping tool. Let us also assume that the tool is equipped with an arbitrary strategy for generating a ranking of mappings, as sketched in Figure 3. Since the real performance metrics (of the technique) will not be known in advance, the engineer can resort to "surrogates" for those metrics that we will refer to as a *fitness function* [Ford et al. 2017]. A fitness function is an instrument that provides an objective integrity assessment of some architectural characteristics. In our case, we are interested in conformance-related characteristics, and thus, we propose a *suite of metrics* for a ranking of mappings. Furthermore, these metrics can be computed at

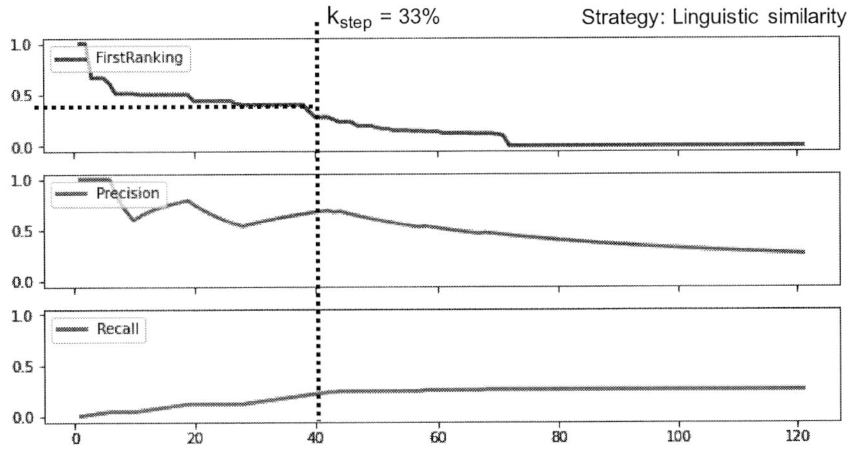

Figure 2. Evolution of goodness value of a ranking of mappings with respect to precision and recall.

different cut-off of the ranking to reflect how many mappings are accepted by the engineer and how much of the final metric values are retained. Note that the proposed metrics do not require having a ground truth, as it is the case of precision or recall.

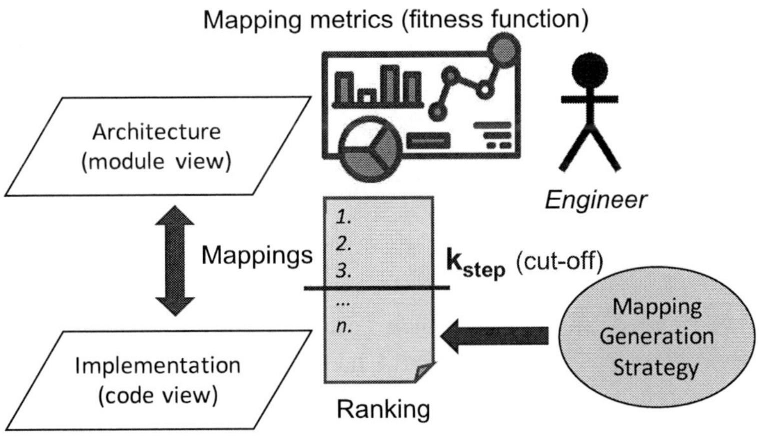

Figure 3. Main concepts of the proposed approach.

For instance, if we look at precision in Figure 4 for the case that the engineer would accept the full ranking (120 mappings), the global precision (of the technique) is 0.32 (*Precision*). Alternatively, we can assess the values of other metrics in the radar chart (e.g., *LevelAbstraction*, *Completeness*, *Consistency*, and *PackageCoverage*), as depicted by the blue area. A high value for *Consistency* suggests that the mappings introduced several violations, while a high value for *PackageCoverage* suggests that packages are evenly mapped to modules. If the engineer would instead take 17% of the mappings, then different metric values would be obtained, as depicted by the red area. Then, the engineer could either manually add the rest of the mappings, or re-run the tool with 17% of the mappings as seeds for getting more mapping suggestions. Specifically, when $k_{step} = 17\%$ we see that *Precision* goes up, *LevelAbstraction* stays the same, and *Completeness* and

Consistency go down. The mappings seem to have induced fewer violations while also lowering the package coverage. This means that considering a subset of the ranking can lead to better performance results. Although *Precision* is included for comparison purposes, its values will not be available, as the ground truth is unknown. In practice, the engineer should monitor the values of the four remaining metrics. Furthermore, an ideal k_{step} for the ranking should keep those metrics closer to their best reachable values.

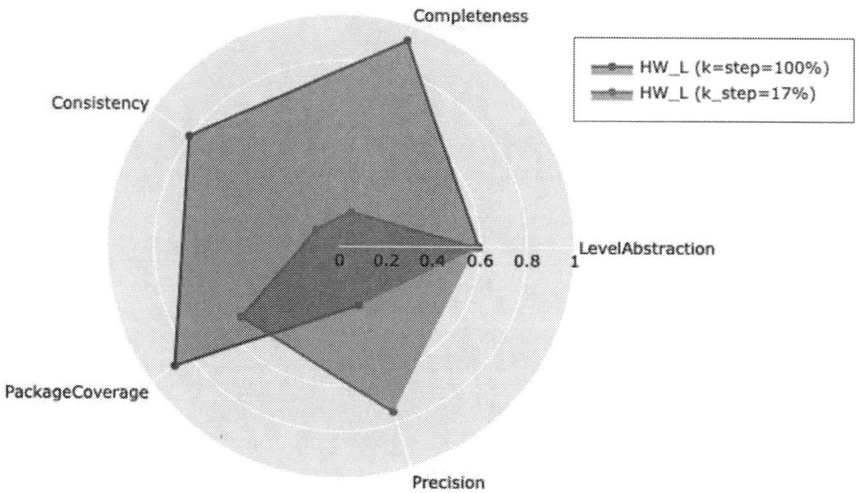

Figure 4. Comparison of metric values at two cut-off points of the ranking.

More formally, we define a fitness function $F = \{f_1, f_2, ..., f_m\}$ as a collection of metrics f_i, each one having the form $f_i\,(A, C, mappings_k) \rightarrow [0..1]$. The $mappings_k$ parameter results from applying a given mapping strategy S and then using k as the cut-off point for the corresponding ranking.

3.1. Suite of metrics

Our framework includes four metrics, in its current version, as described below. We chose these metrics inspired by [Lange and Chaudron 2004] and adapted code coverage ideas (from the testing field) to architecture conformance checking. All the metrics are monotonic with either increasing or decreasing trends.

- **Level of Abstraction**. This metric assesses the "distance" between the module and the code views, as computed by Equation 3. The smaller the value, the more detailed the abstraction level of the architecture, and vice versa. For instance, in the case of one single module mapped to most classes (which would not be very useful), $LevelAbstraction \approx 1$. In the opposite case, if there is a one-to-one mapping between each class and module, $LevelAbstraction = 0$. Ideally, an intermediate value for $LevelAbstraction$ is expected. This metric can be computed either for individual modules or the whole architecture. To this end, the code elements realizing each module ($\#classes(m_i)$) need to be identified.

$$LevelAbstraction(A) = \frac{1}{N}\sum_{i=1}^{N} LoA(m_i) = \frac{1}{N}\sum_{i=1}^{N}(1 - \frac{1}{\#classes(m_i)}) \quad (3)$$

- **Completeness**. A given architecture is said to be complete if, for each module, there is at least a (mapped) code element that implements the module. The metric is computed as the ratio between the number of modules that are not mapped to any class ($\#unmapped(A)$) and the total number of modules, as indicated in Equation 4. $Completeness = 1$ means that all modules are mapped to at least one class. An architecture can be incomplete in two cases: i) some modules are yet to be implemented, and a partial implementation is being considered, or ii) a subset of the mappings has been accepted, and there are modules still unmapped.

$$Completeness(A) = 1 - \frac{\#unmapped(A)}{N} \quad (4)$$

- **Inconsistency.** An architecture is entirely consistent when no differences result from the mappings between the module and code views. Three types of differences are accounted for in this metric: i) dependencies between modules that are not present in the mapped classes (*absences*), ii) dependencies between classes that are not prescribed in the corresponding modules (*divergences*), and iii) dependencies between modules that also occur between the mapped classes but in the opposite direction (*divergences*). $Inconsistency$ is computed as the number of detected differences (for any of the above types), as shown in Equation 5. High values imply that the implementation fails to conform to the architecture blueprint (based on the mappings). This metric is normalized to $[0..1]$.

$$Inconsistency(A) = \#divergences(A) + \#absences(A) \quad (5)$$

- **Code coverage** (**$PackageCoverage$**). This metric refers to the number of code elements effectively mapped to at least one module ($\#unmapped(C)$). A code element can be a class or a group of classes, such as a package. In this work, we consider Java packages as proxies for "modules" in the code. $PackageCoverage$ bears similarities with the notion of test coverage, revealing how much code is mapped by the architecture. The metric is analogous to $Completeness$, but considering the implementation point of view, as shown in Equation 6. $PackageCoverage = 1$ indicates a full architectural coverage of the code.

$$PackageCoverage(C) = 1 - \frac{\#unmapped(C)}{P} \quad (6)$$

The metrics above can be easily implemented by tool (e.g., a plug-in for an IDE), which should store the architecture blueprint (e.g., as a list of modules and their relations) and keep track of their mappings to the source code. We are currently implementing a prototype Eclipse plug-in based on the ideas of the $ConcernMapper$ tool [Armentano et al. 2015, Robillard and Warr 2005]. The normalization parameters for the metrics can be determined either from the rankings or from the list of packages/classes recognized by the tool.

3.2. Optimal selection of the cut-off point

The analysis of the metrics when considering the order of the mappings of a given ranking shows that values increase (or decrease) with different trends. Depending on the system, certain metrics tend to reach their peak values earlier (in the ranking) while others move more slowly. In this context, the engineer should choose a cut-off point k_{step} that maximizes the chances for most metrics to reach their peak values. This choice is not straightforward, as the gain obtained for one metric might be in detriment of another metric, as shown in Figure 4. Let q_{metric} be the percentage of the metric final value that the engineer would like to achieve when selecting a subset of the mappings. For instance, if $PackageCoverage$ had a maximum value of 0.87 (when considering all the mappings), the engineer could prefer to get at least a 75% of that value when the cut-off is set. In general, the same kind of preferences can be stated for the four metrics in our framework.

The problem can be cast as a multi-objective optimization that depends on parameters k_{step}, q_{metric} and a particular mapping strategy S, given views A and C along with the $mappings$ between them. Furthermore, we can define upper, lower and target values as desirable for each metric to favor values closer to the target and penalize values outside the predetermined limits. This situation is exemplified in Figure 5 for the $PackageCoverage$ metric. The target is set to 75% of the (final) metric value (top-level chart), and two cut-offs are proposed, one above the target and another one below it. The "utility" of these points is quantified by means of a so-called *desirability function* [Derringer and Suich 1980] for $PackageCoverage$. A desirability function seeks to find preferred response values for another function (i.e., our metric). In the figure, the desirability function (bottom-level chart) favors metric values being greater than 0.6 ($q_{metric} \geq 75\%$). Different stereotypes for desirability functions have been proposed[1], such as response-maximization, response-minimization, or response-target-is-best, among others. We apply these stereotypes to our four metrics as follows: *LevelAbstraction* is response-target-is-best, $Completeness$ is response-maximization, $Inconsistency$ is response-minimization, and $PackageCoverage$ is response-maximization.

Coming back to our fitness function $F = \{f_1, f_2, ..., f_m\}$, we translate each f_i to a desirability function counterpart d_i, and then combine them into a global function $D = \prod_i d_i$ to be maximized, as suggested in [Derringer and Suich 1980]. In this way, we formulate a single-objective optimization for D and perform a grid search of over different parameter configurations for k_{step} and q_{metric}. Since the rankings are dependent on the chosen mapping strategy S, it becomes a third parameter for the grid search.

4. Evaluation

To evaluate our proposed approach, we performed experiments with two Java systems, in which we executed different mapping strategies and also computed the suite of metrics described in Section 3.1 for the mappings resulting from those strategies. The main goal was to numerically determine k_{step} for each system while balancing the values of the metrics. We were also interested in analyzing q_{metric} and the role of the mapping strategy S with respect to the cut-off points.

[1] `shorturl.at/lmDG9`

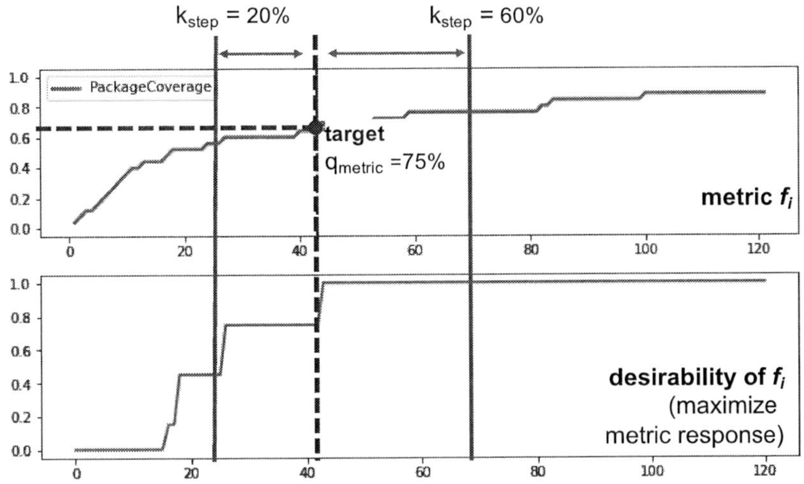

Figure 5. Quantifying preferred values for a metric using a desirability function.

The systems used as case-studies were Health Watcher (HW) and Mobile Media (MM) [Soares et al. 2002, Young 2005]. HW is a system for collecting and managing public health complaints and notifications, while MM is a software product line for mobile applications. The HW codebase has 120 classes (8697 LOC), and its architecture blueprint consists of 7 modules[2]. The MM codebase has 40 classes (3015 LOC), and its architecture blueprint consists of 15 modules[3]. Since the systems were relatively small (in size), we were able to compute different mapping strategies and understand the differences between one ranking or another. In both cases, reference mappings were available [Vázquez et al. 2015] in order to compute precision and recall metrics for comparison purposes. The reference mappings were determined by the original system developers, which is the standard practice in existing approaches to architecture conformance. We tested the strategies of Section 2.2, either in isolation or combined (e.g., applying linguistic and structural similarities in a sequence).

The optimization of the desirability functions was implemented in *Optuna*[4], a hyper-parameter optimization library for efficiently searching parameter configurations based on Bayesian techniques [Akiba et al. 2019]. Figure 6 depicts the values of the parameters explored by the optimization for both case-studies (darker points depict the progress of the Bayesian search). After 2000 trials, the best k_{step} was 35% and q_{metric} was 60% in both systems. This is the optimal cut-off for keeping 60% of all metric values, despite differences between HW and MM due to characteristics of their module and code views which might affect the performance of the similarity functions. It should be noticed that the mappings for the two systems revealed different levels of abstraction. We observed that a higher q_{metric} could be taken, at the risk of slightly decreasing the overall desirability function. This effect seems more noticeable in MM. Regarding the mapping strategy, a pure linguistic similarity (L) worked best in both systems. When comparing the strategies, Figure 6 shows that other linguistic variants combining structural and

[2]Notebook with experiments for HW: `shorturl.at/bdtG2`
[3]Notebook with experiments for MM: `shorturl.at/pDFI0`
[4]`https://optuna.org/`

hierarchical aspects (e.g., L_S_H) could work as well. This suggests that S can be an influential factor when selecting k_{step} in the rankings.

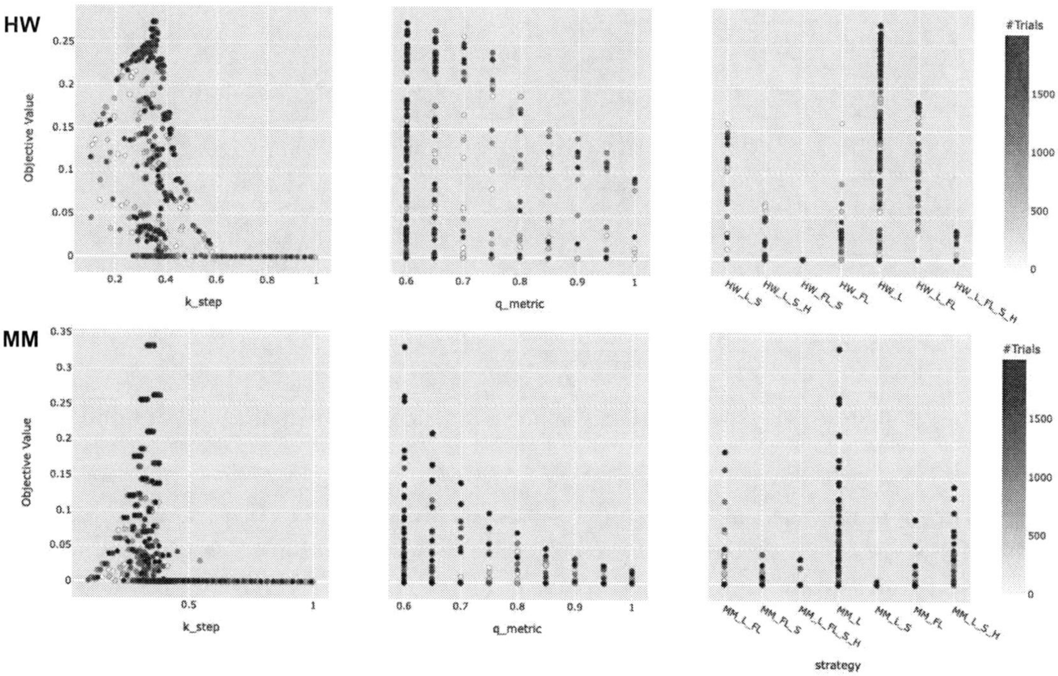

Figure 6. Slice plots with parameter values explored by *Optuna*.

In practice, our approach does not include precision and recall in its suite of metrics, and they were not part of the optimization process above. Nonetheless, we still used them in these experiments to have some kind of post-mortem performance indicators. Figure 7 shows the evolution of precision and recall for different mappings in the rankings. The X axis represents the ordered list of mappings (i.e., classes) considered in the rankings, which consequently affect the temporal evolution of the values. For instance, the top-left chart ($HW - precision$) shows that all mapping strategies degrade over time, but we can still distinguish two groups with different characteristics. The top-performing group starts with high precision values (when considering a few mappings) and goes down slowly around the 45th mapping position (which corresponds to 35% of the mappings). The strategies based on linguistic similarity (L) are included in this group. The other group reaches maximum precision values of 0.4 (which is deemed low) and degrades very quickly as more mappings are considered. These two groups were also detected for recall (top-right chart), although with the opposite effect, as recall increases steadily around the 45th position. Analogous trends can be observed for MM around the 15th position in the X axis.

In general, despite some variations between HW and MM, the plots show that most strategies yield a good precision for (approximately) the first half of the rankings, with some exceptions for a few low-performing strategies. We found correlations between the k_{step} determined by the optimization and the "natural" cut-offs exhibited by the plots of Figure 7. We should keep in mind that the computation of our fitness function is not based on precision nor recall. Thus, this result would indicate that the fitness function was a good surrogate for the traditional performance metrics for architecture-implementation mappings. Nonetheless, more experiments and case-studies should be analyzed in order to confirm these trends.

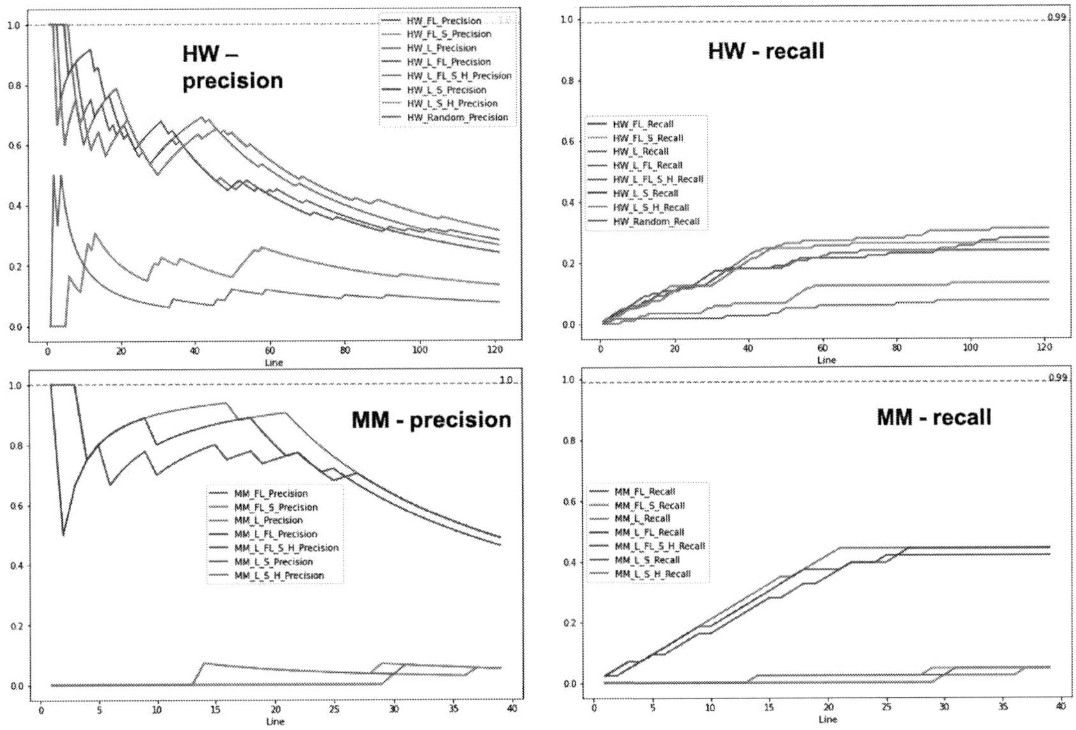

Figure 7. Precision/recall metrics of different mapping strategies for HW and MM.

5. Related work

Automated and semi-automated techniques for mapping code entities to modules have been proposed in the literature. These techniques traditionally rely on computing metrics and deriving a "similarity" or "module attraction" score for a code entity, and then assigning the entity to the module with the highest similarity. Other alternatives are based on training classification models. Various metrics have been introduced to this end. For example, [Christl et al. 2007] proposed to rely on the number of dependencies between entities and a modularity computation over the module dependency graph, while [Bittencourt et al. 2010] used latent semantic indexing (LSI). The main difference between existing metrics and strategies and our approach is that they rely on a mapping ground truth to assess performance. Existing strategies, however, are good candidates to extend our framework and the evaluation thereof. Furthermore, the notion of cut-off point for the mappings has not been explicitly addressed in the previous works.

Olson et al. [Olsson et al. 2022] extended both [Christl et al. 2007] and [Bittencourt et al. 2010] definitions to include module dependency information in their textual representation as part of an iterative mapping process. Although in [Olsson et al. 2022] the authors claim that considering the textual representation of modules allows to include semantic information in the orphan matching, the chosen LSI technique might not have been the best option, as it still requires a level of lexical matching between texts, and sufficient documents for the statistical computations to be significant. In this sense, recent advances in software engineering embeddings (such as [Feng et al. 2020] or [Efstathiou et al. 2018]) could help to improve the semantic perspective of the analysis.

All the reported works in the literature rely on the existence of a ground truth to train and evaluate the corresponding models. As mentioned, this could require a considerable manual efforts from engineers. Conversely, in our proposal, we do not depend on having a ground truth, as our suite of metrics focuses on evaluating the quality of mappings. Thus, our framework intends to be more general and flexible in this regard.

6. Conclusions

In this paper, we have presented a framework based on metrics for assessing the quality of a ranking of architecture-implementation mappings, as generated by an automated strategy via similarity functions. This work aims at assisting engineers in selecting a good-enough list of mappings from the ranking rather than to develop alternative mapping strategies. We proposed four metrics based on characteristics of both the module and code views of the system. These metrics work as surrogates for precision and recall, assuming that the latter are not always available in real-life projects. Regardless of the mapping strategy being used, this is a practical contribution of our approach when compared to existing techniques.

We have formulated a multi-objective optimization of the metric values using desirability functions to determine the cut-off point for a ranking. We performed an initial evaluation with two relatively small Java systems that showed encouraging results. In the parameter optimization, both systems converged to similar values (35% of the mapping rankings for 60% of the metric values), which would indicate some regularity in the evolution of the metrics. As for the mapping strategy, using a linguistic similarity produced the best outcomes. Nonetheless, we observed different characteristics in the analyzed systems (e.g., levels of abstraction, number of modules and classes, or usage of naming conventions, among others). Therefore, these findings should be interpreted as preliminary and still require further experimentation.

As future work, we plan to add additional metrics as well as more advanced mapping strategies, such as [Olsson et al. 2022, Feng et al. 2020, Efstathiou et al. 2018], to the framework. These extensions could strengthen the approach and help us gain insights into how promising mappings should be chosen. Regarding empirical studies, we would like to investigate the effects of using the selected mappings as seeds for additional executions of the mapping strategy. Finally, to foster practical adoption of these techniques, the framework and metrics should be integrated with an architecture conformance tool (e.g., SonarQube, ArchUnit, or Codiga, among others).

References

Akiba, T., Sano, S., Yanase, T., Ohta, T., and Koyama, M. (2019). Optuna: A next-generation hyperparameter optimization framework. In *Proceedings of the 25th ACM SIGKDD International Conference on Knowledge Discovery & Data Mining*, KDD '19, page 2623–2631, New York, NY, USA. Association for Computing Machinery.

Armentano, M., Soldavini, L., Díaz Pace, J. A., Vidal, S., and Marcos, C. A. (2015). Conformidad estructural de arquitecturas combinado con análisis de impacto de cambios. In *Simposio Argentino de Ingeniería de Software (ASSE 2015)-JAIIO 44 (Rosario, 2015)*.

Bass, L., Clements, P., and Kazman, R. (2021). *Software Architecture in Practice*. Addison-Wesley Professional, 4th edition.

Bittencourt, R. A., Santos, G. J. d., Guerrero, D. D. S., and Murphy, G. C. (2010). Improving automated mapping in reflexion models using information retrieval techniques. In *2010 17th Working Conference on Reverse Engineering*, pages 163–172.

Brunet, J., Bittencourt, R. A., Serey, D., and Figueiredo, J. (2012). On the evolutionary nature of architectural violations. In *2012 19th Working Conference on Reverse Engineering*, pages 257–266.

Christl, A., Koschke, R., and Storey, M.-A. (2007). Automated clustering to support the reflexion method. *Information and Software Technology*, 49(3):255–274. 12th Working Conference on Reverse Engineering.

Derringer, G. and Suich, R. (1980). Simultaneous optimization of several response variables. *Journal of Quality Technology*, 12(4):214–219.

Efstathiou, V., Chatzilenas, C., and Spinellis, D. (2018). Word embeddings for the software engineering domain. In *Proceedings of the 15th International Conference on Mining Software Repositories*, MSR '18, page 38–41, New York, NY, USA. Association for Computing Machinery.

Feng, Z., Guo, D., Tang, D., Duan, N., Feng, X., Gong, M., Shou, L., Qin, B., Liu, T., Jiang, D., et al. (2020). Codebert: A pre-trained model for programming and natural languages. *arXiv preprint arXiv:2002.08155*.

Ford, N., Parsons, R., and Kua, P. (2017). *Building Evolutionary Architectures: Support Constant Change*. O'Reilly Media, Inc., 1st edition.

Guimarães, E. T., Vidal, S. A., Garcia, A. F., Pace, J. A. D., and Marcos, C. A. (2018). Exploring architecture blueprints for prioritizing critical code anomalies: Experiences and tool support. *Software: Practice and Experience*, 48:1077 – 1106.

Lange, C. and Chaudron, M. R. V. (2004). An empirical assessment of completeness in uml designs. *IET Conference Proceedings*, pages 111–119(8).

Melnik, S., Garcia-Molina, H., and Rahm, E. (2002). Similarity flooding: a versatile graph matching algorithm and its application to schema matching. *Proceedings 18th International Conference on Data Engineering*, pages 117–128.

Murphy, G., Notkin, D., and Sullivan, K. (2001). Software reflexion models: bridging the gap between design and implementation. *IEEE Transactions on Software Engineering*, 27(4):364–380.

Olsson, T., Ericsson, M., and Wingkvist, A. (2022). To automatically map source code entities to architectural modules with naive bayes. *Journal of Systems and Software*, 183:111095.

Ricci, F., Rokach, L., and Shapira, B. (2015). Recommender systems: introduction and challenges. In *Recommender systems handbook*, pages 1–34. Springer.

Robillard, M. P., Maalej, W., Walker, R. J., and Zimmermann, T. (2014). *Recommendation Systems in Software Engineering*. Springer Publishing Company, Incorporated.

Robillard, M. P. and Warr, F. W. (2005). Concernmapper: simple view-based separation of scattered concerns. In Storey, M. D., Burke, M. G., Cheng, L., and van der Hoek, A., editors, *Proceedings of the 2005 OOPSLA workshop on Eclipse Technology eXchange, ETX 2005, San Diego, California, USA, October 16-17, 2005*, pages 65–69. ACM.

Rus, V., Lintean, M., Banjade, R., Niraula, N., and Stefanescu, D. (2013). SEMILAR: The semantic similarity toolkit. In *Proceedings of the 51st Annual Meeting of the Association for Computational Linguistics: System Demonstrations*, pages 163–168, Sofia, Bulgaria. Association for Computational Linguistics.

Soares, S., Laureano, E., and Borba, P. (2002). Implementing distribution and persistence aspects with aspectj. *ACM Sigplan Notices*, 37(11):174–190.

Vázquez, H. C., Díaz Pace, J. A., and Marcos, C. A. (2015). Uso de ontologías para mapear una arquitectura de software con su implementación. *Jornadas Argentinas de Informática e Investigación Operativa*, 44.

Young, T. J. (2005). Using aspectj to build a software product line for mobile devices. In *University of British Columbia, Department of Computer Science*.

A Survey on the Differences of Using User Story and Tasks in the ASD Effort Estimation in Brazil

Diego de Morais[1], Jorge Rady Almeida Jr.[1], Fabio Levy Siqueira[1]

[1]Departamento de Computação e Sistemas Digitais (PCS)
Universidade de São Paulo (USP) – São Paulo – SP – Brazil

{diego.morais, jorgerady, levy.siqueira}@usp.br

Abstract. *This paper investigates the state of the practice of ASD estimation based on User Stories. We conducted a survey with 85 Brazilian professionals experienced in ASD estimating. The survey analyzes what is used in the estimation (User Story, task, or both), its differences, how the estimate is made (especially if there is any segmentation), and the average precision of the effort estimates. The main findings are: 1) Planning Poker is the most used technique and points with a Fibonacci scale as a metric; 2) User Stories are broken down into tasks in the vast majority of teams; 3) Teams that estimate both: User Stories and tasks/subtasks showed greater accuracy compared to the others; 4) At least ¼ of the teams make estimates for the team segmenting by some criteria.*

1. Introduction

Effort estimation is the process by which effort is evaluated in terms of the number of resources needed to deliver an activity that meets the requirements, playing a critical role in any software development project [Trendowicz and Jeffery 2014]. In Agile Software Development (ASD), effort estimation is made during planning, which happens iteratively and at different levels. For example, in Scrum it is done in release planning, sprint planning, and current-day planning [Cohn 2006]. Depending on the agile approach and the project's particularities, it can be performed at different times, with different objects, estimating different activities and using different techniques [Cohn 2006; Trendowicz and Jeffery 2014]. There are several studies on ASD effort estimation investigating these variations [Dantas et al. 2018; Fernandez-Diego et al. 2020; Usman et al. 2014a, 2015]. However, they do not address some specific issues, such as what is used for estimating, the impact of estimating tasks to the detriment of User Stories, and whether estimates are made for the whole team or individually.

The challenges of estimating effort in ASD have been an even more critical theme given the mandatory remote work due to the pandemic (COVID-19), in which distractions, interruptions, and focus have very different characteristics from face-to-face work [Agren and Knoph 2021]. Therefore, this study aims to investigate the state of the practice of ASD estimation based on User Stories, analyzing what is used for estimating (user story, task, or both) and how the estimation is made. In particular, this work investigates the objects and metrics used to estimate, and the existence of segmentation in the teams' estimates and capabilities. Furthermore, following the related works, the average precision of the effort estimates was also evaluated, relating them to the object and metrics used.

The instrument used was a survey, based on a previous survey from Usman, Mendes, and Börstler (2015). The population was limited to Brazilian professionals with experience in estimating ASD and who have used User Stories to represent requirements in a recent project. Our main contribution is presenting the current state in Brazil of effort estimation practice in ASD using User Story. One of the findings is that a significant portion of the teams makes effort estimates for the team segmenting by some criteria. This result will be further investigated as part of our Master's Dissertation.

The remainder of this paper is organized as follows: Section 2 provides the theoretical background for requirements, metrics, estimation, and estimation objects in the context of ASD, while Section 3 summarizes related work. The research methodology is described in Section 4, with its distribution method at the end. The results are discussed in Section 5, along with threats to the validity of this study. Finally, Section 6 describes our findings and future work opportunities.

2. Background

This section provides a theoretical foundation for effort estimation in ASD, covering requirements, size metrics, accuracy metrics, and estimation techniques.

2.1. Requirements and Metrics

There are different representations of requirements that can be used in ASD. A systematic literature review in 2014 on effort estimation [Usman et al. 2014b] found that most works used User Story and Use Case as requirements representation. A survey in 2015 [Usman et al. 2015] found that only 10% of agile projects used Use Case as a requirements specification, with User Story being used in 61% of the projects. These values remained consistent in 2020, according to a systematic literature review [Fernandez-Diego et al. 2020]. Thus, this study is only focused on User Story as requirements representation.

According to Cohn (2004), a User Story describes the functionality valuable to a software user. For industrial professionals, User Story has a crucial aspect: it is the most granular representation of a requirement that developers use to build new features [Lucassen et al. 2016]. User Stories are generally measured in story points [Dantas et al. 2018; Fernandez-Diego et al. 2020], which is a size measurement unit. In most projects, only a predefined set of possible values is used [Cohn 2006]. By definition, story points are relative. Therefore, a User Story that receives two points is assumed to require twice as much effort as a User Story assigned a value of one point. The value can be assigned based on the effort involved, the complexity, and the risk inherent in developing a feature [Coelho and Basu 2012]. A story point usually, albeit not necessarily, corresponds to an ideal workday [Cohn 2006].

Estimating models cannot be evaluated without applying appropriate metrics to measure their accuracy. The most used accuracy metric is Magnitude of Relative Error (MRE) [Fernandez-Diego et al. 2020] – but it is out of our scope to investigate accuracy metrics.

2.2. Estimation Techniques and Objects

According to Usman et al. (2015), most agile teams use estimation techniques that rely on subjective expert evaluation to arrive at a forecast. The most prevalent techniques are Planning Poker, expert opinion, and analogy. It is observed that using these techniques in combination is directly associated to relatively more accurate estimates [Usman et al. 2015]. There is also a notable tendency to study data-intensive techniques using artificial intelligence [Fernandez-Diego et al. 2020].

Planning Poker, expert opinion, and analogy involve subjective evaluations to a greater or lesser extent. Considering studies of human judgment and decision-making by cognitive psychologists [Shepperd et al. 2018], it has been found that human beings generally use heuristics, that is, simple mental strategies that can lead to bad judgments, while sufficient in most circumstances.

In Scrum and Extreme Programming, the team members break down User Stories into individual tasks in the iteration planning [Alyahya et al. 2016]. In this scenario, estimation could be done on only User Stories (requirements), only tasks/subtasks (activities), or both: User Stories and tasks/subtasks. Due to the lack of a generic name for these items, we will use the term estimation object in this study. For example, functional specification, Use Case, User Story, task, and subtask would be estimation objects.

3. Related Works

Three systematic literature reviews (SLR) were conducted to synthesize the state of the art for effort estimation models and practices in agile software development. The first SLR was carried out in 2014 [Usman et al. 2014b], analyzing 25 primary studies from 2001 to 2013. Afterwards, two new SLR updates were performed, the first in 2018 [Dantas et al. 2018], analyzing 15 primary studies between 2014 and 2017, and the other in 2020 [Fernandez-Diego et al. 2020], analyzing 73 primary studies between 2014 and 2020. The results show that effort estimation methods were used in six agile methods (Scrum, XP, TDD, Agile Unified Process, Kanban, and Distributed Agile Software Development). It also shows that Planning Poker has become the most used estimation method. These results also show that the most frequently used size metrics (story points) is closely related to the requirements representation (User Story). Another result is that expert-based estimation methods continue to play an important role and that there is a prominent tendency to study data-intensive techniques. These works conclude that the accuracy of effort estimation models in ASD remains inconsistent and is still a challenge in most analyzed works, although some significant improvements have been identified, such as an increasing number of works reporting adequate ranges of accuracy values [Fernandez-Diego et al. 2020].

Another related work studied the state of practice in 2015 through an online questionnaire with 60 ASD practitioners from 16 countries [Usman et al. 2015]. The study concludes that most agile teams use estimation techniques that rely on subjective expert assessment (Planning Poker, analogy, and expert judgment) and use story points as size metrics. Another result is that the dominant tendency is to underestimate the effort. The main reasons perceived for inaccurate estimates are requirements and management issues.

These researches did not address a specific issue: breaking User Stories into tasks. This theme has already been identified as present in industry practice [Liskin et al. 2014]. Furthermore, the related works do not address the possibility of segmenting (splitting it based on some criteria) the team's estimate and capacity, either.

4. Research Method

This section presents the survey planning based on Kitchenham and Pfleeger (2002).

4.1. Research Questions

Our goal is to obtain the state of practice on how effort estimates are made using User Story in agile software development. The research goes deeper into the issue of breaking User Stories into tasks, the possible impacts of estimating tasks as opposed to User Stories, the average accuracy of estimates, and segmentation in team's effort and capacity estimates. The following research questions were formulated:

- **RQ1:** What objects are used for effort estimation in ASD?
  - **RQ1.1:** What effort estimation techniques are used for each object?
  - **RQ1.2:** What metrics of effort size and scale are used for each estimation object?
- **RQ2:** What is the average accuracy of effort estimation in ASD?
  - **RQ2.1:** How do estimation objects affect the effort estimation accuracy?
  - **RQ2.2:** How do estimation metrics affect the effort estimation accuracy?
- **RQ3:** Are the capacities and effort size estimates segmented during iteration planning in ASD?

RQ1 seeks to understand the objects used to estimate (RQ1.1 and RQ1.2). This study focuses on comparing the estimation of User Stories and tasks/subtasks.

RQ2 focuses on the accuracy of estimates in ASD and the impacts of estimation objects (RQ2.1) and estimation metrics (RQ2.2) used. The intention is to obtain this information from the respondent's perception, without assessing the accuracy metric used, in the same way as in a related survey [Usman et al. 2015].

Finally, RQ3 investigates whether the estimates are made for the whole team or segmented by any criteria, such as specialty (e.g., front-end, back-end, QA).

4.2. Target Audience

The target audience of this study is Brazilian professionals with practical experience in estimating effort in agile software development projects and who work in teams that use User Story to represent requirements. To select experienced professionals, we filtered respondents who participated in the effort estimation process for at least two iterations/sprints. User Stories were chosen as requirement representation because they are the most used according to the related works [Fernandez-Diego et al. 2020; Usman et al. 2015].

4.3. Survey and Planning

The survey was conducted using a self-administered questionnaire written in Portuguese[1]. One concern was to keep it as concise as possible.

Two pilot evaluations were executed with experienced professionals, the first being a business expert (product owner) and the second a senior developer. Based on their feedbacks, we simplified some questions and improved the text, question order, and answer options.

Table 1. Questions of the survey form, indicating its type (T). (C: Closed; O: Open; P: Partially open) and related research questions (goal)

#	Question	T	Goal
Q1	How long is your industry experience with estimating effort in ASD?	C	Filter
Q2	How are user needs and requirements represented?	P	Filter
Q3	What company do you work for?	O	RQ1
Q4	What is the approximate size of the company you work for?	P	RQ1
Q5	What is your main role within the team?	P	RQ1
Q6	Which agile methods does your team practice?	P	RQ1
Q7	How long have most of the team members worked together?	P	RQ1
Q8	What is the nature of the team's main demands?	P	RQ1
Q9	At what moments are effort estimates made?	P	RQ1
Q10	At what moment does the team commit to what will be done?	P	RQ1
Q11	What development activities are taken into consideration when estimating during iteration/sprint planning?	P	RQ1
Q12	What other activities are estimated during iteration/sprint planning?	P	RQ1
Q13	Are user needs and requirements broken down into tasks?	C	RQ1
Q14	What object are estimates made from?	P	RQ1,2,3
Q15	Which estimation technique is most frequently practiced by your team in iteration/sprint planning?	P	RQ1
Q16	In sprint/iteration planning, the capacities and estimates are made for the entire team or are they separated by any criteria?	C	RQ3
Q17	What is the effort size metric used to estimate?	C	RQ1,2
Q18	If the estimate is made in points, which scale is used?	P	RQ1
Q19	What is the average accuracy of the estimates compared to the efforts made by your team?	C	RQ2

The questions formulated are presented in Table 1. The questionnaire starts by filtering the target audience (Q1, Q2), followed by the professional, team, and company context questions (Q3 to Q8), questions about effort estimation (Q9 to Q18), and ends with a question on the accuracy of the estimates (Q19). In the question "Which object are

[1] The survey form in Portuguese is available at https://doi.org/10.6084/m9.figshare.17014184. This survey form file is in its original format, including tool control questions and other questions that will be covered in another paper. The question numbers do not correspond to the numbers in Table 1.

the estimates made from?" (Q14), when answering "both: User Stories and tasks/subtasks", an option was enabled to answer the following questions related to the object (Q15, Q16, Q17, and Q18) for both: User story and task/subtask. Four other questions were asked with complementary objectives to this study, which are subjects for future works.

4.4. Distribution of the Questionnaire

The questionnaire was available between April and May 2021. We recruited participants via: 1) Publications on the authors' profiles in LinkedIn (www.linkedin.com); 2) Emails and messages to the authors' contacts network; 3) Message to professionals working in agile software development teams in a working group of a non-profit independent private law foundation located in the city of São Paulo/Brazil; 4) Snowball effect.

The questionnaire was hosted in Google Forms. The text contained a brief introduction with basic information about the study' objective, justification for the choice, and the importance of the respondent's participation. Participants were also informed about the study privacy policies in a clear and detailed manner.

5. Results and Discussion

We obtained 139 responses[2]. Considering the target audience (Section 4.2), we excluded responses from people without experience in ASD estimation (Q1), who used a requirements representation different from User Story (Q2), or from professionals from teams that did not make estimations (Q14). Therefore, 54 responses (6, 47, and 1 respectively) were removed, resulting in 85 valid responses for this analysis.

In this sample, 5% of responses are from a single company (Q3). The authors infer that most companies are in Brazil due to convenience sampling and because the question form is in Portuguese.

The size of the companies the respondents work for (Q4) is mostly large – more than 100 employees (85%) – and most professionals perform the role (Q5) of developer (45%). Most of them use a combination of Scrum and Kanban (63%) as agile methods (Q6), followed by only Scrum (28%). Most of their team members have worked together (Q7) for 1 to 3 years (35%). The nature of their teams' main demands (Q8) is mainly new developments (90%) versus only 10% for support/maintenance.

The effort estimation can happen at several moments in the same team (Q9 – multiple selections), being the sprint planning ceremony the predominant one, as shown in Figure 1 – A. The sprint planning is also the most common ceremony in which the team commits to what will be done (i.e., the backlog items that the team commits to completing during the sprint - Q10). More specifically, this is typically done after estimating and after calculating the team's capacity, as shown in Figure 1 – B.

---

[2] The survey dataset (in Portuguese) is available in the following link: https://doi.org/10.6084/m9.figshare.17014214 - The answers for Q3 were removed to preserve anonymity.

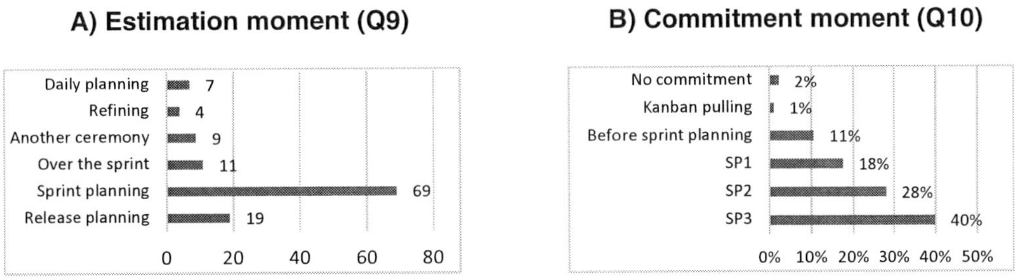

Caption:
SP1: During the sprint planning – before estimating
SP2: During the sprint planning – after estimating and after calculating the team's capacity
SP3: During the sprint planning – right after estimating

Figure 1. Estimation and commitment moments

Coding and testing are the most frequent development activities taken into account when estimating (Q11 – multiple selections), followed by deploy, as shown in Figure 2 – A. Other activities are also considered when estimating (Q12 – multiple choice), with meetings and support margin (i.e., time retention to troubleshoot production bugs or other maintenance activities) being the most frequently chosen, as presented in Figure 2 – B.

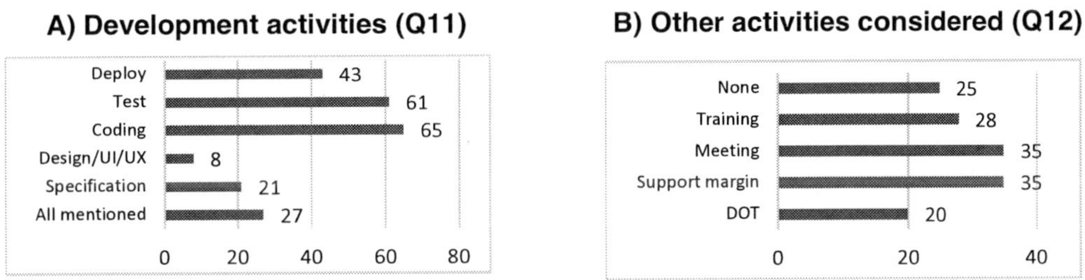

Caption:
DOT: Demands from other teams

Figure 2. Activities estimated

5.1. What Objects are Used for Effort Estimation in ASD? (RQ1)

User Stories are broken down into tasks (Q13) by the teams of 73% of respondents. For 21% it varies – some are broken, and some are not. The User Stories are not broken for only 6% of respondents, as seen in Figure 3 – A.

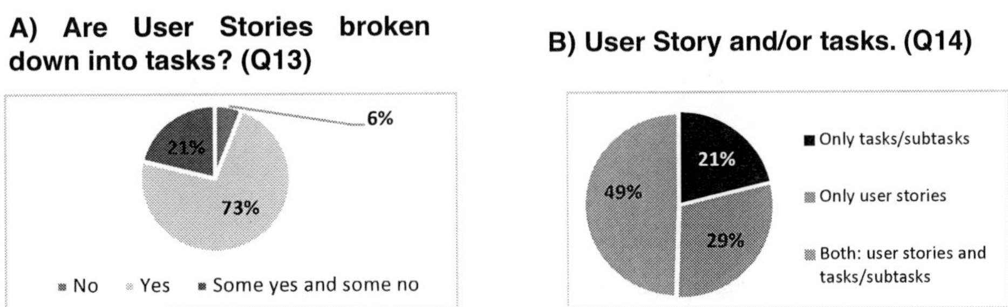

Figure 3. Estimation objects used

Almost half (49%) of teams estimate effort on “both: User Stories and tasks/subtasks” (Q14), although a little more than ¼ (29%) estimate “only User Stories” and the rest (21%) estimate “only tasks/subtasks”, as shown in Figure 3 – B.

RQ 1.1: What effort estimation techniques are used for each object?

In the question about the effort estimation technique (Q15), when the respondent selected that he estimated “both: User Story and task/subtask”, the option for answering an equal or different technique for each object was enabled. Therefore, each respondent of “both: User Story and task/subtask” has two responses counted, one in the object user story (identified as “User story - in both option”) and another in the object task/subtask (identified as “Task - in both option”). The other respondents have a single response in the corresponding object (“only User Story” or “only task/subtask”).

In this question, we included the answer option “By who will implement” even though this is not an estimation technique per se.

Planning Poker was the predominant technique for all estimation objects. When the object is “only User Story”, Planning Poker is even more prevalent with 72%, and the other techniques are less used. The same does not occur when the object is “User story - in both option” or “Task - in both option”, there is a more even distribution of the techniques, as shown in Figure 4.

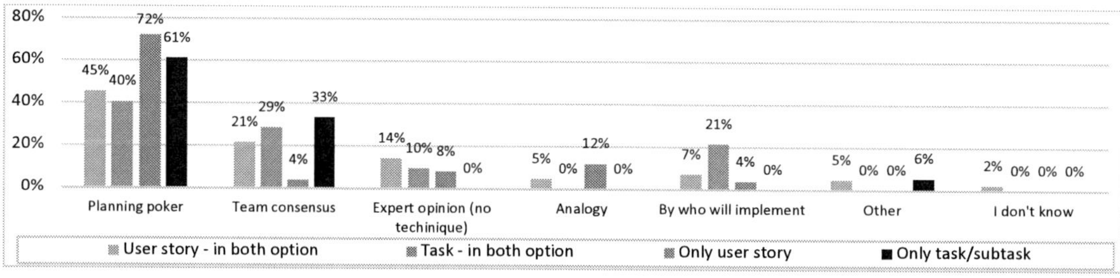

Figure 4. Estimation technique by the object used

The values indicate differences in the technique used concerning the estimation object, with a clear distinction of technique when the use of the object is exclusive (only an estimation object, i.e. “only User Story” or “only task/subtask”) or combined (“both: User Story and task/subtask”).

RQ 1.2: What metrics of effort size and scales are used for each estimation object?

The most commonly used effort size metrics (Q17) are Points for User Story, either when the object is exclusive (“Only User Story) or combined (“User story – in both option”), representing 80% and 69%, respectively. When the objects used are tasks/subtasks, the metrics were well distributed between points and hours, either when it is “only tasks/subtasks” (39% in hours and 61% in points) or the object is combined “Task – in both option” (48% in hours and 38% in points). Few teams use “days” as a metric. The results are shown in Figure 5 – A.

The scale used for the points was complemented with another question (Q18), whose results are shown in Figure 5 – B. When the estimation object was “both: User

Stories and tasks/subtasks", the scale was asked once. It was not asked for each object separately (which can be considered a problem in the survey protocol). The most used scale was Fibonacci, with dominant 95% for "only User Stories", 69% for "only tasks/subtasks", and 50% for "both: User Stories and tasks/subtasks". The object "only tasks/subtasks" obtained a relevant use of T-shirt size (33%).

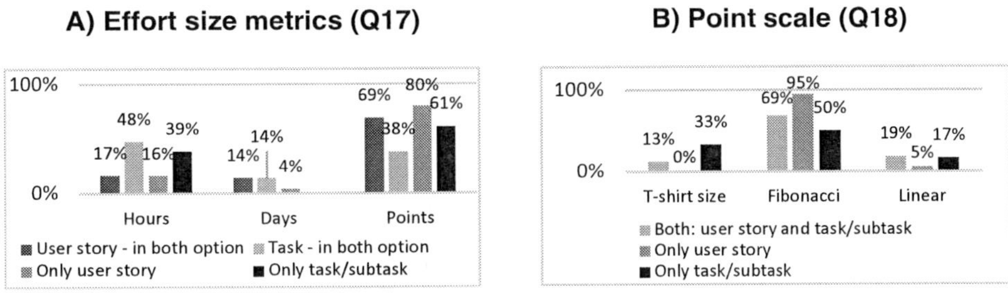

Figure 5. Effort size metrics by the object used

Considering the answers that use Planning Poker as the estimation technique (Q15) and User Story ("both: User story" and "only User Stories" from Q14), we analized the answers of size metrics (Q17). The answer "points" got the vast majority of responses (32 – 86%). In comparison, "hours" got 3 responses (8%) and "days" only 2 responses (5%). There is a clear relationship between the most used effort size metric (Points), the primary estimation technique (Planning Poker), and how requirements are specified in ASD (User Story). This relationship and result are consistent with related works [Fernandez-Diego et al. 2020].

5.2. What is the Average Accuracy of Effort Estimation in ASD? (RQ2)

Of the 85 valid respondents in this study, 13 (15%) responded that they did not know the mean accuracy of their team's estimates, 32 (38%) said they did not measure (Q19), and only 40 (47%) respondents evaluated the estimates. More than ⅓ of the responses do not measure the estimates accuracy. Similarly, the related RSLs [Fernandez-Diego et al. 2020; Usman et al. 2014a] also reported some primary studies not presenting the accuracy of the metric used, 26% and 33%, respectively.

It is not the focus of this study to analyze how accuracy is measured. Therefore, the answers only reflect the respondent's perception, similarly to Usman et al. (2015). We presented fixed value ranges as answer options, converted to the average for presentation in the graphs of Figures 6, 7, and 8.

The highest number of answers (11) was the best average accuracy ("between underestimated 5% and overestimated 5%"), followed by the following two ranges ("underestimated between 5% and 25%", and "overestimated between 5% and 25%") in the second place – both with 8 responses each, as shown in Figure 6. These results differ from those in Usman et al. (2015), whereby the range with most responses (35% of the total) was "underestimated between 25% and 50%", suggesting a greater tendency to underestimate than to overestimate.

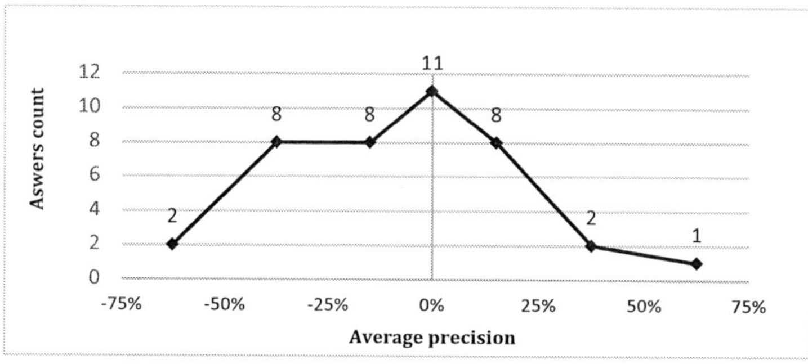

Figure 6. Average accuracy by answers count

RQ 2.1: How do estimation objects affect the effort estimation accuracy?

Of the 40 respondents who measure the estimate, 19 (47%) use "both: User Stories and tasks/subtasks", 12 (30%) use "only User Stories", and 9 (23%) "only tasks/subtasks".

The estimation object "both: User Stories and tasks/subtasks" was the only one to present a high number of responses in the best range (between underestimated 5% and overestimated 5%). In contrast, the others have a more uniform distribution between the ranges, as shown in the graph of Figure 7.

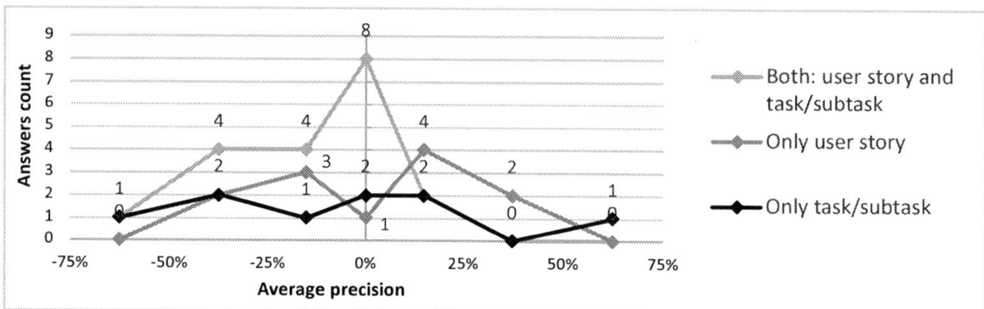

Figure 7. Average accuracy by the estimation object used

RQ 2.2: How do estimation metrics affect the effort estimation accuracy?

When the respondent answered "both: User Stories and tasks/subtasks" as the estimation object in Q14, the effort size metric was asked separately in Q17 – for User Stories and tasks/subtasks – but only one for accuracy was asked in Q19. To avoid inferring an answer and to make sure that the same answer was not counted twice, only answers that have the same effort size metric were considered when the person selected "both: User Stories and tasks/subtasks". Table 2 presents how we considered the data. With this process, 14 respondents were excluded from this analysis. Respondents who answered "only User Stories" and "only tasks/subtasks" were considered normally.

Table 2. Exclusion filter example for insufficient data (RQ 2.2)

	Estimate object (Q14)	Size metrics (Q17)		Result
		User Story	Tasks/subtasks	
Respondent A	Both: User Stories and tasks	Points	Points	considered
Respondent B	Both: User Stories and tasks	Points	Hours	not considered
Respondent C	Only tasks/subtasks	-	Hours	considered
Respondent D	Only User Stories	Days	-	considered

The metric "Points" was the only one to present the highest concentration of responses in the best ranges ("between underestimated 5% and overestimated 5%", "underestimated between 5% and 25%", and "overestimated between 5% and 25%"). In contrast, the others have a more uniform distribution between the intervals, as shown in Figure 8.

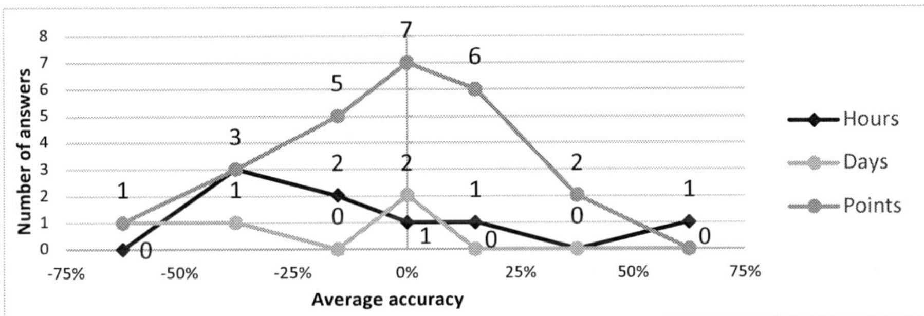

Figure 8. Average accuracy by effort size metric

5.3. Are the Capacities and Effort Size Estimates Segmented During Iteration Planning in ASD? (RQ3)

According to Stray et al. (2018), the first introduction of autonomous teams in software engineering was made by the agile manifesto [Beck et al. 2001], referring to the self-organization of teams as the origin of the best architectures, requirements, and designs. Stray et al. complements saying that perhaps the most straightforward definition of autonomous teams comes from a knowledge management perspective, as those exhibit three conditions: autonomy, cross-fertilization, and self-transcendence [Stray et al. 2018]. For the context of this study, the definition of cross-fertilization becomes particularly important: "refers to the team being formed from individuals with different specializations, behavior, and thinking so that regular interaction improves their understanding of each other's perspectives." [Lundene and Mohagheghi 2018 p. 2]

With teams having different technical specializations and, consequently, different skills in each specialization, we suspect that some teams have difficulties performing a single capacity estimation and planning for the whole team. This suspicion is based on the observation of Brazilian companies' ASD practice, in which specializations such as front-end, back-end, and quality assurance (QA) are specific to different professionals. The questionnaire shows that some teams segment the effort estimation (Q16) by different criteria, as presented in Figure 9. For example, a User Story or task may be estimated to be 2 points for the front-end, 2 points for the back-end, and 1 point for QA – instead of simply 5 points (this example was presented in the questionnaire to explain what segmentation is).

Most teams perform a single effort estimation for the whole team. User Stories have a higher rate for this response, either in exclusive form ("only user stories") or combined form ("User story – in both option"), representing 80% and 69%, respectively. Segmented by specialty (e.g., back-end, front-end, and QA) occupies second place. When the estimation object is tasks/subtasks, it is even more representative, 38% for the combined form ("Task – in both option", and 28% for the exclusive form ("Only tasks/subtasks").

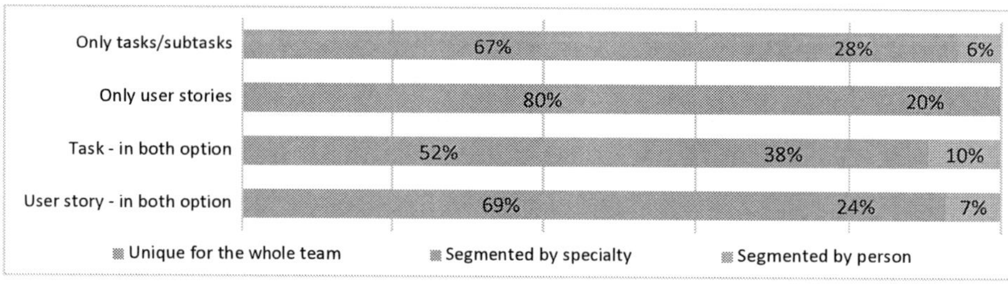

Figure 9. Segmentation of estimates by the object used

A similar distribution of responses among all objects indicates that the separation by estimation objects is not decisive for segmentation.

5.4. Threats to Validity

This section discusses threats to the validity of this work. We use the organization suggested by Wohlin et al. (2012).

The construct validity concerns the threats that may arise due to the improper construction of the research instrument. One threat is that the questions might not be adequate for what we want to measure. To mitigate this threat, we used questions from a related survey [Usman et al. 2015] (Q11, Q15, Q17 and Q19), as we believe they are already more mature and validated. Another threat is that the questionnaire might not address all the research questions. During the questionnaire construction process, each question was mapped to a research question to mitigate this.

Internal validity is concerned with issues such as relevant respondents, confounding factors, and bias in results. One threat is that the selected respondents were not part of the target audience. The answers to the first two questions in the questionnaire were used as exclusion criteria to ensure that the respondent belonged to the population. This procedure led to the exclusion of many responses (as discussed in Section 5). In addition, the respondent was asked about his role within the team (Q5) to identify biases and possible limitations in the answers for not participating in a team or not having visibility of the process. Another threat is respondents not being honest in responses that show problems in their organization. Respondents were assured of their anonymity to minimize this. Finally, another threat is the respondents' failure to understand the issues. A pilot test was conducted with experienced professionals (Section 4.3) to mitigate it.

Conclusion validity concerns whether the conclusions drawn are reasonable regarding the data collected, such as the relationship between factors or inappropriate statistical measures. This study used only frequencies and percentages to identify common patterns or practices to point out potential areas or relationships for future research efforts. Furthermore, only complete answers were considered in the result analysis.

External validity is related to generalizing the results. The main threat is that we used a convenience sample. To mitigate the risk of respondents not being representative, questions Q3 to Q8 identify the respondent's context. To obtain a broad population sample, actions such as announcing the survey in the authors' social network and a snowball approach were taken. Analyzing the data, we verified that responses from a single company did not exceed 5%. The authors believe that these steps contributed to obtaining a heterogeneous sample in terms of company, team, and role.

6. Conclusion and Future Work

This work presented a survey to investigate the state of the practice of ASD estimation on projects that use User Stories. We analyzed what is used for estimating (User Story, task, or both), its differences, and how the estimation is made (particularly if there is any segmentation). Following Usman et al. (2015), we also evaluated the average accuracy of the effort estimates. The survey was applied between April and May 2021, collecting 139 responses, with 85 considered valid, given our target audience.

The combination of Kanban and Scrum is the most used agile method among respondents. The most used estimation technique is Planning Poker, similar to the results of related works [Dantas et al. 2018; Fernandez-Diego et al. 2020]. Fibonacci scale points are the most effort size metric that respondent teams use. User Stories are broken down into tasks in most teams, and half of them estimate for both: User Stories and tasks. We investigated the relationship between estimation objects (Q14) and the characteristics of the company, project, and team (Q4-Q12). We did not find any correlation between the variables, considering a two-sample Z test [Zou et al. 2003] and $\alpha = 0.05$.

About ⅓ of the teams do not assess the accuracy of the effort estimate (RQ2). The teams that used both: User Story and task/subtask for estimating presented a better accuracy than the others in this study (RQ2.1). Future work may investigate the reasons for these results. Regarding the greater accuracy, we suspect that estimating both allows for refining requirements and understanding the team's problem and solution more accurately. However, a detailed analysis of each estimation moment needs to be researched, including evaluating this approach positive and negative impacts.

At least ¼ of the teams make effort estimates for the team segmenting by some criteria, with the segmentation by technical specialty (technical functionality) being the most answered. We did not find studies about effort estimation segmentation despite our perception of its existence in the Brazilian scenario. We observe the Brazilian industry considering technical specialization, such as back-end, front-end, and QA, as different competencies in the same team, with professionals working exclusively in one of them.

To summarize, this study contributes to presenting the current state of effort estimation practice in ASD using User Story (in Brazil):

- Confirm that Kanban and Scrum remain the most used agile methods with User Story, as well as the Planning Poker estimation technique;
- Evidence that many teams continue not to measure the accuracy of effort estimates.

Moreover, this study brings new relevant information to the academy (at least for this sample):

- Most teams break down User Stories into tasks, and half of them estimate for both;
- The teams that used both: User Story and task for estimating presented a better accuracy than the others;
- A significant portion of the teams makes effort estimates for the team segmenting by some criteria.

As future work, our Master's Dissertation study will continue investigating the topic of segmentation within the team to estimate effort and effort capacity through the Grounded Theory qualitative analysis method. We hope to understand the motivation, how it works, the difficulties and benefits of the teams that segment, in addition to the differences for the teams that do not segment. We also hope to understand better the relationship of segmentation to user stories and tasks.

References

Agren, P. and Knoph, E. (2021). *COVID-19's Impact on Agile Software Development*. Master thesis.

Alyahya, S., Alqahtani, M. and Maddeh, M. (2016). Evaluation and improvements for agile planning tools. *2016 IEEE/ACIS 14th International Conference on Software Engineering Research, Management and Applications, SERA 2016*, p. 217–224.

Beck, K., Grenning, J., Martin, R., et al. (2001). Manifesto for Agile Software Development. *The Agile Alliance*, p. 12–14.

Coelho, E. and Basu, A. (13 aug 2012). Effort Estimation in Agile Software Development using Story Points. *International Journal of Applied Information Systems*, v. 3, n. 7, p. 7–10.

Cohn, M. (2004). *User stories applied : for agile software development*. 13th. ed. Addison-Wesley.

Cohn, M. (2006). Agile estimating and planning. In *VTT Symposium (Valtion Teknillinen Tutkimuskeskus)*. . , [accessed on Oct 2].

Dantas, E., Perkusich, M., Dilorenzo, E., et al. (2018). Effort Estimation in Agile Software Development: An Updated Review. *International Journal of Software Engineering and Knowledge Engineering*, v. 28, n. 11–12, p. 1811–1831.

Fernandez-Diego, M., Mendez, E. R., Gonzalez-Ladron-De-Guevara, F., Abrahao, S. and Insfran, E. (2020). An Update on Effort Estimation in Agile Software Development: A Systematic Literature Review. *IEEE Access*, v. 8, p. 166768–166800.

Kitchenham, B. A. and Pfleeger, S. L. (2002). Principles of survey research part 2. *ACM SIGSOFT Software Engineering Notes*, v. 27, n. 1, p. 18–20.

Liskin, O., Pham, R., Kiesling, S. and Schneider, K. (2014). Why we need a granularity concept for user stories. *Lecture Notes in Business Information Processing*, v. 179 LNBIP, p. 110–125.

Lucassen, G., Dalpiaz, F., Van der Werf, J. M. E. M. and Brinkkemper, S. (2016). The use and effectiveness of user stories in practice. In *Lecture Notes in Computer Science*. . Springer, Cham.

Lundene, K. and Mohagheghi, P. (21 may 2018). How autonomy emerges as agile cross-functional teams mature. In *Proceedings of the 19th International Conference on Agile Software Development: Companion*. . ACM. https://dl.acm.org/doi/10.1145/3234152.3234184.

Shepperd, M., Mair, C. and Jørgensen, M. (9 apr 2018). An experimental evaluation of a de-biasing intervention for professional software developers. In *Proceedings of the ACM Symposium on Applied Computing*. . Association for Computing Machinery.

Stray, V., Moe, N. B. and Hoda, R. (2018). Autonomous agile teams: Challenges and future directions for research. *ACM International Conference Proceeding Series*, v. Part F1477, p. 1–5.

Trendowicz, A. and Jeffery, R. (2014). *Software Project Effort Estimation*. 1. ed. Cham: Springer International Publishing.

Usman, M., Mendes, E. and Börstler, J. (27 apr 2015). Effort estimation in Agile software development: A survey on the state of the practice. In *ACM International Conference Proceeding Series*. . Association for Computing Machinery.

Usman, M., Mendes, E., Weidt, F. and Britto, R. (17 sep 2014a). Effort estimation in Agile Software Development: A systematic literature review. In *ACM International Conference Proceeding Series*. . Association for Computing Machinery.

Usman, M., Mendes, E., Weidt, F. and Britto, R. (17 sep 2014b). Effort estimation in Agile Software Development: A systematic literature review. In *ACM International Conference Proceeding Series*. . Association for Computing Machinery.

Wohlin, C., Runeson, P., Höst, M., et al. (2012). *Experimentation in software engineering*. 1. ed. Berlin, Heidelberg: Springer Berlin Heidelberg. v. 9783642290

Zou, K. H., Fielding, J. R., Silverman, S. G. and Tempany, C. M. C. (2003). Hypothesis testing I: Proportions. *Radiology*, v. 226, n. 3, p. 609–613.

Advances in a DSL to Specify Smart Contracts for Application Integration Processes

Eldair F. Dornelles[1], **Fernando Parahyba**[1], **Rafael Z. Frantz**[1], **Fabricia Roos-Frantz**[1], **Antonia M. Reina Quintero**[2], **Carlos Molina-Jiménez**[3], **José Bocanegra**[4], **Sandro Sawicki**[1]

[1]Unijuí University, Brazil

[2]Department of Language and Systems, University of Seville, Spain

[3]Department of Computer Science and Technology, University of Cambridge, UK

[4]Department of Systems and Computing Engineering, Universidad de los Andes, Colombia

{eldair.dornelles, fernando.parahyba}@sou.unijui.edu.br,

{rzfrantz, frfrantz, sawicki}@unijui.edu.br,

reinaqu@us.es, carlos.molina@cl.cam.ac.uk,

j.bocanegra@uniandes.edu.co

Abstract. *Several languages have been developed for writing smart contracts for specific domains, such as health, finance, and business processes. However, none of them includes the constructors needed for writing smart contracts used in application integration processes which have their own particularities. Such smart contracts are responsible for monitoring the communication between the process and the applications to guarantee that the rights of the parties involved in the integration process are observed. To cover the gap, this paper discusses a domain-specific language for writing smart contracts in the application integration domain. It provides constructors to write smart contracts with a level of abstraction close to the natural language used in conventional contracts.*
Keywords: *Smart Contract, Integration Process, Integration Solution, Domain-specific Language, Enterprise Application Integration.*

1. Introduction

Companies of different segments and sizes rely on applications to support their business activities. Typically, a business environment uses a set of applications that exchange data and share functionalities. We use the term "application" to refer to any software artefact capable of processing data or providing functionality programmatically. To manage the communication between applications in this environment, companies usually use integration processes. An integration process is a software artefact developed using tools provided by the Enterprise Application Integration (EAI) community to orchestrate the integrated applications. Thus, an integration process acts as a middleware that communicates individually with each application, performing specific operations to read, write data, or request or respond to a given function or service.

Usually applications used to support business activities include external applications. Some applications do not belong to the owner of the integration process. Therefore, it is advisable to monitor the communication between the integration process and the external applications. Monitoring needs to be able to observe a set of constraints. This constrains can be related to service level (e.g., number of requests, hours and days in which access is allowed) or to business level which specify constraints related to the business rules (e.g., required data, type of services or products provided). Current integration platforms do not provide mechanisms for performing this type of monitoring. Therefore, if needed, the monitoring system has to be developed ad hoc as a separate system.

Communication constraints in an integration process can be specified as a smart contract. A smart contract is a self-execution contract that can be written using a general-purpose language (e.g., Java, Javascript, or Python), a Cross-domain language (e.g., Solidity, Michelson, or Plutus), or a domain-specific language (DSL) (e.g., Ergo, DSL4SC or ADICO-Solidity). General-purpose languages do not incorporate natural constructors to write smart contracts; i.e., they only provide generic constructors that make the task unnecessarily cumbersome. Cross-domain languages are languages for writing smart contracts that provide general constructors of contracts. However, they do not have the level of abstraction needed or constructors aimed at specific domains. So, writing smart contracts in these languages requires advanced programming skills. On the other hand, a domain-specific language is a language with a level of abstraction that is adequate for the domain. A DSL incorporates the vocabulary of a specific domain and provides constructors closer to natural language. Thus, writing smart contracts in a DSL is simpler and does not require advanced programming skills.

Recently, [Varela-Vaca and Reina-Quintero 2021] carried out a systematic mapping study of the languages used to write smart contracts. They found several domain-specific languages aimed at distinct domains, such as healthcare, finance, business processes, legal, and others. However, no language was found to support the EAI domain. We have noticed that existing DSLs do not incorporate the essential concepts of EAI, such as application, process, type of operations, and messages. Therefore, in this article, we argue that a DSL aimed at the EAI domain will be welcome by the EAI community. Such a DSL needs to incorporate typical contract constructors explicitly (e.g., contract, clause, type of clause, party, condition) and concepts that are intrinsic to the EAI domain —we highlight them in this paragraph.

In this paper, we present Jabuti, a domain-specific language to write smart contracts in the EAI domain. This DSL has a high-level abstraction, providing constructors close to the natural language used in conventional contracts. Jabuti includes contract concepts (i.e., contract, party, condition, and types of clause) and incorporates the EAI domain's vocabulary (i.e., application, process, type of operations, and messages). These features make Jabuti intuitive. It is easy to learn and produces easy-to-write and read smart contracts. We believe that it will be accessible to non–technical people who will be able to read and possibly write smart contracts. In addition, Jabuti was designed to be platform independent, i.e., a smart contract written using Jabuti can be translated into other languages, such as general-purpose languages: Java, Javascript, or Python; or cross-domain blockchain languages: Solidity, Michelson, or Plutus, to be deployed and activated.

The rest of this paper is organised as follows: Section 2 discusses related work. Section 3 presents the basic concepts of EAI. In Section 4, we present the metamodel of Jabuti. Section 5 presents a case study and a smart contract that has been written in

Jabuti. In addition, we present a snippet of Solidity code that reflects some parts of the code written with Jabuti. Section 6 concludes this paper.

2. Related Work

Since blockchain is receiving substantial mainstream attention from industry and academia, a plethora of smart contract languages have appeared. Thus, in [Varela-Vaca and Reina-Quintero 2021] 101 different smart contract languages were analysed. These languages range from high-level languages, such as Solidity [Ethereum Foundation 2021] to intermediary languages, such as Simplicity [O'Connor 2017], or low-level languages, such as Ethereum Virtual Machine bytecode [Wood 2014]. Furthermore, high-level languages can be general-purpose languages or domain-specific languages. We consider as related work the approaches that propose a high-level domain-specific language for smart contracts.

Existing domain-specific languages can be grouped according to their purpose. The group that is most related to our approach is that of languages designed to specify legal contracts or legal bindings. This group includes CML [Wöhrer and Zdun 2020], Ergo [Accord Project 2019], DSL4SC [Tateishi et al. 2019], Das Contract [Skotnica and Pergl 2019], ADICO-Solidity [Frantz and Nowostawski 2016], SPEC [He et al. 2018], SLCML [Dwivedi et al. 2021] and Symboleo [Sharifi et al. 2020]. In this group, the most related approaches to ours are DSLs that are designed having in mind Event-Condition-Action (ECA) rules, that is, they provide constructors for events, conditions, and actions. CML is the most related to our approach in the sense that is devised as a high-level language that is subsequently translated into Solidity. Ergo is a DSL proposed by the Accord project to specify smart legal contracts. DSL4SC is an intermediate language that is used as a formal model to generate statecharts. This approach uses templates to deal with high-level concepts that are managed in a contract and then transforms these templates into DSL4SC models. Das Contract is a visual DSL that combines concepts of the DEMO methodology [Skotnica et al. 2017] and BPMN [Object Management Group 2014] to model contracts. ADICO-Solidity aims to capture high-level institutional constructs to express rules, regulations, and laws. SPESC is a language whose goal is to collaboratively specify smart contracts in the sense that IT experts, domain practitioners, and business experts collaborate in the specification of the contract. SLCML is an XML-based language for specifying cross-organizational business smart contracts. Finally, Symboleo is a formal specification language for legal contracts whose concepts are based on an ontology that extends the UFO ontology [Griffo et al. 2020]. Although these languages share some concepts with Jabuti such as *Party*, *Obligation*, or *Event*, they are not devised to be applied in an EAI context, and, as a consequence, they can not naturally handle operations that are specific for EAI such as push, pull, and others.

Another group of DSLs includes languages that are devised to specify financial contracts. To this group belong SmartFin [Dean 2019], Egelund-Müller et al. [Egelund-Müller et al. 2017], Findel [Biryukov et al. 2017] and Marlowe [Seijas et al. 2020]. The concepts managed by this group of DSLs are more distant from the concepts managed in the EAI domain. SmaCoNat [Regnath and Steinhorst 2018] is a DSL for expressing smart contracts in natural language syntax. Finally, there are approaches to specifying smart contracts in other domains, such as supply chain [Bistarelli et al. 2021]. None of the previous DSLs can be used directly in the EAI domain.

3. Background

In this section, we introduce some basic concepts of the enterprise application integration and smart contracts, which are required to understand our proposal.

3.1. Enterprise Application Integration

Enterprise application integration is a field of software engineering concerned with developing methodologies, techniques, and tools for designing integration processes. An integration process is a software artefact that acts as a middleware orchestrating the communication between integrated applications. Integration platforms are used to design integration processes. An integration platform is a tool that provides the needed resources to design, implement, and execute integration processes. Figure 1(a) shows an integration process that is composed of two applications (App 1, App 2), a set of tasks (T1, T2, T3), slots (S1, S2, S3, S4, S5) and communication ports (P1, P2, P3). Tasks perform atomic actions on messages, such as split, filter, translate, and merge. Through these actions, tasks transform the message data, get the relevant content, and translate them into the format of the target application. Slots are buffers that connect a task to another task and to ports and help to desynchronize tasks. Ports are mechanisms that implement low-level protocols that enable the integration process to interact with their integrated applications. Ports can be unidirectional or bidirectional, as shown in Figure 1(b).

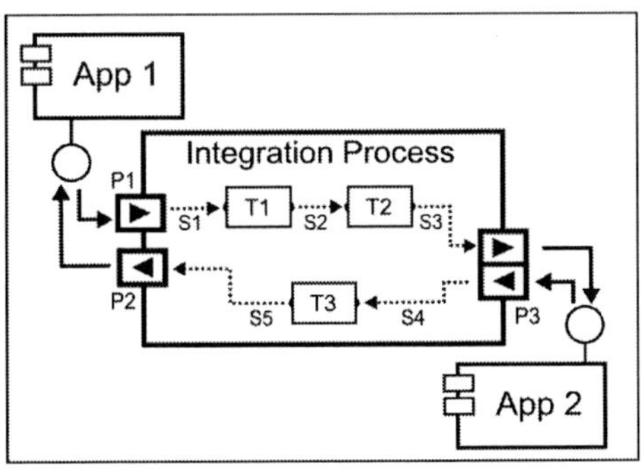

(a) Integration process structure.

	Port		Operation/Performer	
	Name	Notation	Process	Application
Unidirectional	Entry		Read	Push
Unidirectional	Exit		Write	Poll
Bidirectional	Solicitor		Request	Response
Bidirectional	Responder		Response	Request

(b) Types of ports and their operations.

Figure 1. Integration Process: Basic concepts.

There are two types of unidirectional ports, namely entry and exit ports. An entry port is used to input data into the integration process. Ports support read and push operations. Read is performed by the integration process to read data from its applications. Push is performed by an application to input data into its integration process. On the other hand, an exit port is used by an integration process to input data into an application. Exit ports, support write, and poll operations. Write is performed by the integration process to input data into an application. Poll is performed by an application to consume data that have been processed by the integration process. There are two types of bidirectional ports: solicitor and responder ports. A solicitor port is used by the integration process to perform a request against an application. Solicitor ports are used by the integration process to perform a request operation to request data or services against the application. The application performs a response operation to provide the data requested by the integration process. On the other hand, a responder port is used by the application to perform requests to the integration processes. The application uses a responder port to perform a request operation to request data from the integration process; next, the latter performs a response operation to provide the requested data.

3.2. Smart Contracts

Smart contracts are self-executing digital contracts that aim to ensure that agreements entered between two or more parties are fulfilled [Szabo 1997]. That is, smart contracts are computer programs that define the rules and consequences in the same way as a traditional contract, defining the obligations, rights, prohibitions, and the possible penalties to the involved parties. In addition, smart contracts make it possible to automate the execution of contracts and allow the parties to observe all execution, i.e., which clauses were executed and which of them it lake to execute yet.

A smart contract is made up of a set of attributes, which represent the general properties of the contract, such as the duration of the contract, the parties involved, the asset being traded, and a set of clauses. There are many ways to model smart contracts: financial, technical, and business, among others. One of the most used is the one with a focus on business, as the words attributed and used are closer to the knowledge of business people and therefore more friendly to use. The words attributed to this model are presented below:

- **Contract**: Represents an agreement between two or more parties. It is composed of a set of clauses which arbitrate whether or not a specific action can be performed.
- **Party**: A party represents a natural or legal person involved in the agreement signed in the contract.
- **Action**: An action represents an operation that can be performed by one of the parties. The execution of one action results in one event, which defines the next step in executing the contract.
- **Condition**: A condition is part of a clause; it defines a rule which must be met so that a specific action can or cannot be performed.
- **Clause**: A clause establishes a relationship between a part, a condition, an action, and possible penalties. Clauses can express a right, an obligation or a prohibition.
  - **Right**: A right clause sets out some conditions under which one of the parties can perform a certain action.
  - **Obligation**: An obligation clause determines the conditions under which one of the parties is obligated to perform a certain action.
  - **Prohibition**: A prohibition clause defines the conditions under which one of the parties cannot perform a certain action.
- **Event**: An event is a result generated by the execution of an action. That is, whenever an action is executed, an event is generated. This event can trigger another clause, a penalty or terminate the contract.

In the enterprise application integration domain, smart contracts can be used to define the clauses that express the conditions under which the operations described in the subsection 3.1 may or may not be performed. In our approach, we associate a smart contract with each port. The contract defines the clauses that govern the communication between the integration process and a given application.

4. The DSL Metamodel

In this Section, we present the metamodel of Jabuti and describe its elements. Figure 2 shows the metaclasses and the relationships between them in the metamodel, as well as the properties and operations on each metaclass. Jabuti provides constructors that allows us to model contract concepts, such as `Contract`, `Party`, and `Clause`, as well as concepts that are specific to the application integration domain, i.e. the parties involved in the contract (`Process` and `Application`) and the types of `Operations` that are carried out by ports (`PUSH`, `POLL`, `WRITE`, `READ`, `REQUEST`, `RESPONSE`).

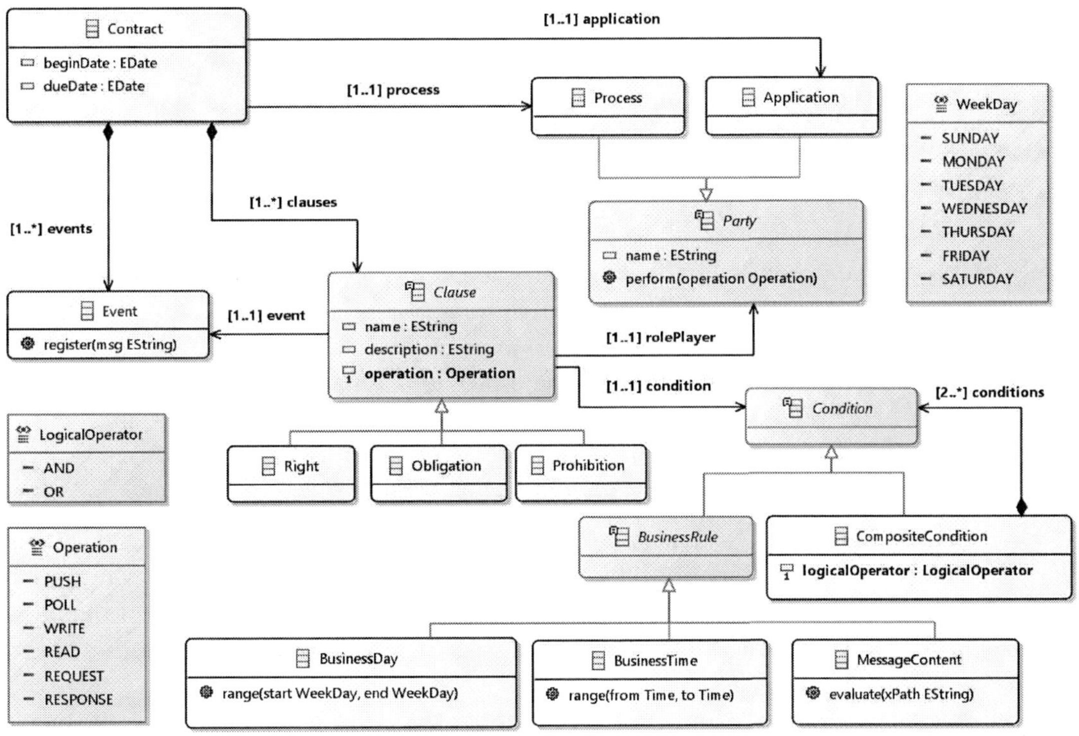

Figure 2. Jabuti metamodel.

The **Contract** metaclass defines the scope of the contract. A contract involves two parties, a `Process` and an `Application`, one or more `Clauses`, and one or more `Events` generated by the contract execution. In addition, the contract contains a start and expiration dates (`beginDate` and `dueDate`).

The **Party** metaclass is used to represent the parties involved in the contract. A party can be a `Process` that represents the integration process or an `Application` that represents the integrated application. The `perform` method defined in this metaclass represents the action performed by the parties during the execution of the integration process. The parties are associated with the clauses. Each clause declares an active party. This active party is defined by the property `rolePlayer` and indicates which party will trigger the clause.

The **Clause** metaclass is used to specify the condition under which the rolePlayer will be able or not to perform the operation associated with the clause. The operation property can assume the values: push, poll, write, read, request, or response, and represents the operations executed at the port during the execution of the integration process. Clauses can be of the following three types: `Right`, `Obligation` or `Prohibition`. A `Right` clause defines the right of the `rolePlayer` to perform an operation. An `Obligation` clause specifies that the `rolePlayer` must perform the operation specified in the clause. The `Prohibition` clause defines the condition under which the rolePlayer is not allowed to perform the operation specified in the clause.

The **Condition** metaclass is used to define the service-level and business-level rules. The service-level rules are modelled by the metaclasses `BusinessDay` and `BusinessTime`, which have the `range` method that is used to specify the period in which a given operation can be performed. The business-level rules are modelled by the `MessageContent` metaclass, which specifies the conditions related to the business domain. The `MessageContent` metaclass has an evaluation method, which receives an XPath expression (String), which is used to query the content of the received message (XML format) and check whether the business rule is satisfied or not.

The **Event** metaclass is used to model messages with details on the execution of a clause. When a clause calls an event, the event collects some data of this clause, such as name, clause type, rolePlayer, description, execution time, and execution status, to generate the message. In addition, the message generated by the event may contain custom text that the contract designer should provide. Finally, the **Event** metaclass logs the message in the repository using the `register` method.

5. Example of Application

Our study case is based on a real problem (simplified in this paper) involved in the docking process of ships in the port of Seville, Spain. Before docking at the port, the maritime agent (the ship) must request permission to dock from the port authority. This permission is requested by sending an e-mail to the port authority. This e-mail must specify the intended arrival and departure dates and time, the name of the ship, the tonnage of the ship, the Maritime Mobile Service Identity (MMSI) [1], the International Maritime Organization (IMO) [2], and the required port services. In this study case, we consider that the ships can not dock at the port on Sundays and from 10 p.m. to 8 a.m. on the other weekdays. Upon receiving the docking request, the port authority registers it and checks if a dock could be assigned to the ship during the requested dates. A confirmation or denying response is sent by e-mail back by the port authority to the maritime agent. If the e-mail sent is a confirmation, then it should include a proposal with the total cost. This proposal will be valid for 60 minutes. If there is no available berth for those dates, the response includes available dates. If the maritime agent accepts the port authority

[1] MMSI is an unique identifier of a ship station for telecommunication purposes

[2] The IMO number is a unique identifier for ships

proposal and budget, she sends within 60 minutes another e-mail requesting the booking, which includes the identification number of the received proposal. Once the reservation request is received, the port authority registers the reservation and sends a confirmation message by e-mail to the maritime agent.

5.1. The Integration Process

We have used Guaraná DSL [Frantz et al. 2011, Frantz et al. 2016, Frantz et al. 2020] to design a solution to support and automate the docking process of ships introduced in our study case. Figure 3 shows the integration process that we have used, which orchestrates the e-mail server of the port authority and its berthing application.

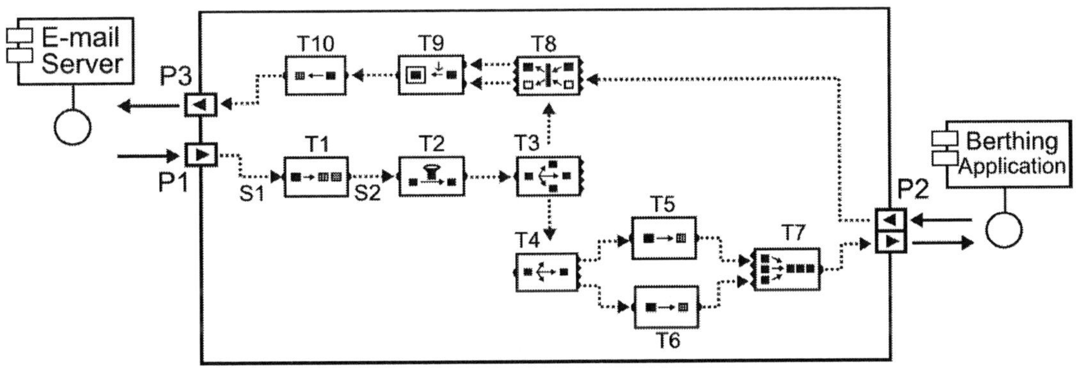

Figure 3. The berthing integration process.

Communication between the e-mail server and the integration process is carried out through the entry port P1 and exit port P3, which are responsible for reading and writing e-mails from and to the server, respectively. For every read operation performed by port P1 in an interval of 15 minutes, a new message is introduced in slot S1. Because messages at this point may contain data from more than one e-mail, the splitter task (T1) splits a message into two or more messages and writes them to slot S2, so that each message carries only the data of a single e-mail. The e-mails could be about several subjects. Due to this, the filter task (T2) filters these messages and keeps in the workflow only the messages related to the berthing requests or booking confirmations. The messages that remain in the workflow are replicated in the replicator task (T3) and forwarded to the dispatcher task (T4) and the correlator task (T8). Task T4 checks the content of the messages and identifies the subject. Messages related to the berthing requests are dispatched to the translator task (T5). The messages related to booking confirmation are dispatched to the translator task (T6). Task T5 creates a berth permission request message based on the received e-mail content from task T4. On the other hand, task T6 uses the content of the e-mail to build a request message to confirm the berth booking. The request messages created by the tasks T5 and T6 are forwarded to the merger task (T7), which gathers these messages and routes them to port P2.

Each message that arrives at port P2, produces a request to the Berthing Application. The application responds to the port either confirming or denying and providing a budget for docking the ship or confirming the booking to the maritime agent, according to the message request type received. Task T8 correlates this response with the original message containing the data of the e-mail received from the maritime agent. Task T9 enriches the original message with the response, and task T10 transforms the content of this message into text in natural language to be wrapped in an e-mail and sent using port P3 as a formal response to the maritime agent.

5.2. Clauses

Taking into account the description of the study case, we have defined five clauses to monitor the communication between the integration process and the Berthing Application, which occurs through the port P2. In this paper, we present only the smart contract associated with the port P2.

Clause 1: The integration process has the `right` to perform a berthing request operation against the Berthing Application. This request is performed under the following condition: the request must include the arrival and departure dates and times, the name of the ship, the tonnage of the ship, the MMSI, the IMO, and a list of the required services.

Clause 2: The Berthing Application has the `obligation` to perform a response operation against the integration process with a berthing proposal. This response is performed under the following conditions: the Berthing Application must respond within 60 minutes, and must include the berthing dates and budget.

Clause 3: If the maritime agent accepts the proposed berthing conditions, the integration process has the `right` to perform a request operation to book the berthing dates. This request is performed under the following conditions: the request must respond to the Berthing Application within 60 minutes, and must include the identification number of the proposal received.

Clause 4: The Berthing Application has the `obligation` to perform a response operation to the integration process with the booking confirmation. This response is performed under the following conditions: the Berthing Application must respond within 60 minutes, and must include the identification number of the berthing proposal.

5.3. Contract in the DSL

In this section, we introduce a smart contract developed using Jabuti to monitor the interaction between solicitor port P2 of the integration process designed in our study case and the integrated Berthing Application (cf. Figure 3).

The queries to dock the ship received by the integration process at port P1 give place to the execution of request operations at port P2 so that the Berthing Application has to analyse the request and respond to the port with a message denying or containing a proposal with the date, the time, and the cost to dock the ship at the port. Responses are delivered by e-mail to the maritime agent via port P3. Listing 1 presents the smart contract that we have implemented in our editor. This contract is composed of a set of attributes, the implementation of the four clauses introduced in our study case, and an event to register eventual failures in the execution of any clause.

The attributes (Atr) on lines 2 to 5 declare the basic and general information of the contract, such as the start and end dates and time of the contract, as well as the parties involved in this contract. The first clause, (C_1), declares a `right` of the integration

```
1  Contract BerthingAndServicesRequest{
2       beginDate = "2022-01-28 12:00:00"
3  Atr  dueDate =     "2023-01-27 11:59:59"
4       application = "Berthing Application"
5       process =     "Integration Process"
6
7       Right requestBerthing {
8           description = "Required data to be able to request berthing."
9           rolePlayer = process
10          rolePlayer.perform(Operation.REQUEST)
11          condition {
12 C1           MessageContent.evaluate('//arriveData != ""') AND
13              MessageContent.evaluate('//departureData != ""') AND
14           R  MessageContent.evaluate('//MMSI != ""') AND
15              MessageContent.evaluate('//IMO != ""')AND
16              MessageContent.evaluate('//portServices!=""')
17          }
18          onBreach(registerFailing, "Error sending berthing request.")
19      }
20
21      Obligation respondToBerthingRequest{
22          description = "Timeout for responding and required data."
23          rolePlayer = application
24          rolePlayer.perform(Operation.RESPONSE)
25          condition {
26 C2           Timeout(3600) AND
27              MessageContent.evaluate('//arriveData!=""') AND
28              MessageContent.evaluate('//departureData!=""') AND
29              MessageContent.evaluate('//portServices!=""') AND
30              MessageContent.evaluate('//budget!=""') AND
31              MessageContent.evaluate('//proposalID!=""')
32          }
33          onBreach(registerFailing, "Error responding to berthing request.")
34      }
35
36      Right requestTheBookingOfBerthingDates{
37          description = "Timeout to respond to the port proposal."
38          rolePlayer = process
39          rolePlayer.perform(Operation.REQUEST)
40 C3       condition {
41              Timeout(3600)AND
42              MessageContent.evaluate('//proposalID!=""')
43          }
44          onBreach(registerFailing, "Error requesting the booking dates.")
45      }
46
47      Obligation respondConfirmingTheBerthingBooking{
48          description = "Timeout to confirm the booking has been made."
49          rolePlayer = application
50          rolePlayer.perform(Operation.RESPONSE)
51 C4       condition {
52              Timeout(3600) AND
53              MessageContent.evaluate('//proposalID!=""')
54          }
55          onBreach(registerFailing, "Error confirming booking has been made.")
56      }
57
58      Event registerFailing(msg : String) {
59 Ev       register(msg)
60      }
61 }
```

Listing 1. Berthing smart contract in Jabuti.

process to execute a request against the integrated application when the conditions (R) of this clause are met. If this clause is breached, then the method `onBreach`, in line 18, is executed, and a message detailing the breach is forwarded to event Ev in line 58.

Clause C_2 declares the `obligation` of the application to perform a response operation by sending a berthing proposal to the integration process, and the condition that must be met to perform this operation. Clause C_3 declares the `right` of the integration process to perform a request operation to book the berthing dates when the conditions of this clause are met. Clause C_4 declares an `obligation` of the application to execute a response operation to the integration process to confirm the booking of the berthing dates. Event Ev at line 58 invokes the `register(msg)` method, which is responsible for registering the message log regarding the breach of the clause.

5.4. Contract in Solidity

Smart contracts gained more prominence with the emergence of blockchain technology which provides several services including indelible data, reliability, transparency and consensus without the involvement of central authorities. Currently, there are several blockchain platforms and smart-contract languages, Solidity is one of the best known. It is a cross-domain language that allows the specification of smart-contracts that can be run on Ethereum, one of the leading blockchain platforms. Solidity is supported by a development environment that help programmers to write, test, and deploy smart contracts. It has been used in a wide variety of domains. In this section, we map the Jabuti constructors into their equivalents in Solidity (Table 1). `Application` and `Process` constructors are mapped into addresses. `Clause` is mapped into Function. `BusinessRule` is mapped into require. `Operation` and `WeekDay` are mapped into enum, and `Event` is mapped into event.

Table 1. Mapping of Constructors from Jabuti into Solidity.

Jabuti	Solidity
Application, Process	address
Clause	function
Operation, WeekDay	enum
BusinessRule	require
Event	event

The equivalent Solidity code of part of the berthing smart contract written using Jabuti, (see Listing 1), was hand-coded and is shown in a snippet in Listing 2. The essential attributes of our contract are declared using the Solidity constructors in the snippet from line 8 to line 11 (Atr). Function C_1 in this snippet corresponds to clause C_1 in Listing 1. The conditions of clause C_1 in the contract are represented by the requirements (R) from line 27 to 31 in the snippet.

The algorithms shown in Listing 1 and 2 demonstrate the high level of abstraction provided by Jabuti in comparison to Solidity. Jabuti provides constructors that are frequently used in contract of the EAI domain, such as the `Application` or `Process` and `Clause`. These constructors are close to natural language as opposed to their corresponding constructors (`address` and `function`) in Solidity. Furthermore, the executable smart contract code in Solidity (or any other cross-domain language) can be automatically generated from Jabuti using model-driven engineering text-to-text transformations. This turns smart contracts written in Jabuti into blockchain platform independent code. Automatic transformation minimises coding errors, such as integer overflow and

```
// SPDX-License-Identifier: MIT
pragma solidity ^0.8.7;
pragma experimental ABIEncoderV2;

contract BerthingAndServicesRequest{
        uint beginDate;
        uint dueDate;
        address process;
        address application;

        RequestForm[] requestList;
        ResponseForm[] proposalList;
        uint[] approvedProposalId;
        uint requestCounter;
        uint proposalCounter;

        ...

        constructor(address _process, address _application, uint _beginDate, uint _dueDate){
            ...
        }

        function requestBerthing( uint _arvDate, uint _dptDate,
                        string memory  _mmsi,    string memory _imo) public {

            require(msg.sender == process, "Error sending berthing request.");
            require(_arvDate >= block.timestamp && _dptDate > _arvDate,
                                    "Error sending  berthing request.");
            require(!isEmpty(_mmsi), "Error sending berthing request." );
            require(!isEmpty(_imo), "Error sending berthing request." );

            requestList.push( RequestForm(
                                {   requestId: requestCounter++,
                                    arriveDate: _arvDate,
                                    departureDate: _dptDate,
                                    mmsi: _mmsi,
                                    imo: _imo,
                                    portServices: "",
                                    timestamp: block.timestamp,
                                    status: Status.WAITING
                                })
                            );
        }
        ...
}
```

Listing 2. Snippet of berthing contract in Solidity.

underflow or re–entrancy and dependency timestamp [ConsenSys Diligence 2020]. As a result, the coding effort is significantly reduced, and so is the number of errors compared to ad–hoc Solidity coding which is known to be error prone. In summary, the abstraction provided by Jabuti can increase code efficiency, clarity, flexibility and reduce the number of coding errors.

6. Conclusion

Companies use a set of applications to support their business management activities. These applications frequently involve external applications owned by third parties. The field of EAI provides methodologies, techniques, and tools for designing integration processes to allow the communication process among these applications. Usually, this communication process needs to comply with some business rules. Therefore, due to some applications belonging to third-party companies, it is essential to monitor this communication process and provide mechanisms to define the rights, obligations, and prohibitions of the involved parties. Smart contracts can be used for this purpose. However, there is no domain-specific language for writing smart contracts in the EAI domain.

In this paper, we present a domain-specific language called Jabuti to write smart contracts in the application integration domain. Jabuti delivers a high level of abstraction that properly incorporates contract concepts and includes the vocabulary managed in the enterprise application integration domain. Jabuti is user-friendly, enjoys a short learning curve, and produces easy-to-read smart contracts. These features help business experts even with no programming skills to develop their smart contracts. Smart contracts written in Jabuti can be translated into a general-purpose or a cross-domain language.

As a future work, we will implement the translators to automatically convert smart contracts written in Jabuti to Solidity and deploy them on a blockchain. In addition, we intend to develop a monitoring application that will provide the necessary resources to monitor the communication between an application (e.g., Berthing application) and the respective integration process. This monitoring application will capture the information related to the executed operations in the integration process and, on the basis of this information, will trigger the clauses of the corresponding smart contract.

Acknowledgements

This work was supported by the Research Support Foundation of the State of Rio Grande do Sul in Brazil (FAPERGS), under grant 19/2551-0001782-0; the Coordination for the Brazilian Improvement of Higher Education Personnel (CAPES); and, the Brazilian National Council for Scientific and Technological (CNPq) under grant 309315/2020-4. Antonia M. Reina has been funded by projects AETHER-US (PID2020-112540RB-C44/AEI/10.13039/501100011033), COPERNICA (P20_01224) and METAMORFOSIS (US-1381375). Carlos Molina has been partially funded by UKRI CAMB (G115169) project[3].

References

Accord Project (2019). Ergo language guide. `https://docs.accordproject.org/docs/logic-ergo.html`. Last accessed on 15 Dec 2021.

Biryukov, A., Khovratovich, D., and Tikhomirov, S. (2017). Findel: Secure derivative contracts for ethereum. In *Financial Cryptography Workshops*, pages 453–467. Springer.

Bistarelli, S., Faloci, F., and Mori, P. (2021). Towards a graphical DSL for tracing supply chains on blockchain. In *International Workshop on Future Perspective of Decentralized Applications*, pages 1–12. Springer.

ConsenSys Diligence (2020). Ethereum smart contract best practices. https://consensys.github.io/smart-contract-best-practices/attacks/. Last accessed on 01/04/2022.

Dean, D. (2019). Smartfin - implementing a financial domain-specific language for smart contracts. Technical report, Imperial College London.

Dwivedi, V. K., Norta, A., Wulf, A., Leiding, B., Saxena, S., and Udokwu, C. (2021). A formal specification smart-contract language for legally binding decentralized autonomous organizations. *IEEE Access*, 9(1):76069–76082.

Egelund-Müller, B., Elsman, M., Henglein, F., and Ross, O. (2017). Automated execution of financial contracts on blockchains. *Business & Information Systems Engineering*, 59(6):457–467.

Ethereum Foundation (2021). Solidity documentation. `https://solidity.readthedocs.io/en/latest/`. Last accessed on 5 Jan 2022.

Frantz, C. and Nowostawski, M. (2016). From institutions to code: Towards automated generation of smart contracts. In *2016 IEEE 1st International Workshops on Foundations and Applications of Self* Systems*, pages 210–215. IEEE.

Frantz, R. Z., Corchuelo, R., Basto-Fernandes, V., Rosa-Sequeira, F., Roos-Frantz, F., and Arjona, J. L. (2020). A cloud-based integration platform for enterprise application integration: A model-driven engineering approach. *Software - Practice and Experience*, 51(4):824–847.

Frantz, R. Z., Corchuelo, R., and Roos-Frantz, F. (2016). On the design of a maintainable software development kit to implement integration solutions. *Journal of Systems and Software*, 111(1):89–104.

Frantz, R. Z., Reina-Quintero, A. M., and Corchuelo, R. (2011). A domain-specific language to design application integration solutions. *International Journal of Cooperative Information Systems*, 20(2):143–176.

Griffo, C., ao Paulo A. Almeida, J., and Guizzardi, G. (2020). Towards a legal core ontology based on alexy's theory of fundamental rights. In *Multilingual Workshop on Artificial Intelligence and Law*, pages 1–12. CEUR-WS.org.

He, X., Qin, B., Zhu, Y., Chen, X., and Liu, Y. (2018). SPESC: A specification language for smart contracts. In *2018 IEEE 42nd Annual Computer Software and Applications Conference*, pages 132–137. IEEE Computer Society.

Object Management Group (2014). Business Process Model and Notation (BPMN), Version 2.0.2. Technical Report formal/2013-12-09, Object Management Group.

O'Connor, R. (2017). Simplicity: A new language for blockchains. In *Proceedings of the 2017 Workshop on Programming Languages and Analysis for Security*, pages 107–120. ACM.

Regnath, E. and Steinhorst, S. (2018). Smaconat: Smart contracts in natural language. In *2018 Forum on Specification Design Languages*, pages 5–16. IEEE.

Seijas, P. L., Nemish, A., Smith, D., and Thompson, S. J. (2020). Marlowe: Implementing and analysing financial contracts on blockchain. In *Financial Cryptography Workshops*, pages 496–511. Springer.

Sharifi, S., Parvizimosaed, A., Amyot, D., Logrippo, L., and Mylopoulos, J. (2020). Symboleo: Towards a specification language for legal contracts. In *2020 IEEE 28th International Requirements Engineering Conference*, pages 364–369. IEEE.

Skotnica, M. and Pergl, R. (2019). Das contract - A visual domain specific language for modeling blockchain smart contracts. In *Advances in Enterprise Engineering XIII*, pages 149–166. Springer.

Skotnica, M., van Kervel, S. J. H., and Pergl, R. (2017). A DEMO machine - A formal foundation for execution of DEMO models. In *Advances in Enterprise Engineering XI*, pages 18–32. Springer.

Szabo, N. (1997). Formalizing and securing relationships on public networks. *First Monday*, 2(9):1–15.

Tateishi, T., Yoshihama, S., Sato, N., and Saito, S. (2019). Automatic smart contract generation using controlled natural language and template. *IBM Journal of Research and Development*, 63(2/3):6:1–6:12.

Varela-Vaca, Á. J. and Reina-Quintero, A. M. (2021). Smart contract languages: A multivocal mapping study. *ACM Computing Surveys*, 54(1):1–38.

Wöhrer, M. and Zdun, U. (2020). Domain specific language for smart contract development. In *2020 IEEE International Conference on Blockchain and Cryptocurrency*, pages 1–9. IEEE.

Wood, G. (2014). Ethereum: A secure decentralised generalised transaction ledger. `https://gavwood.com/paper.pdf`. Last accessed on 20 Jan 2022.

An experiment on how graduating students represent software designs

Silvana Moreno[1], Diego Vallespir[1], Martin Solari[2]

[1]Universidad de la República, Uruguay

[2]Universidad ORT Uruguay

{smoreno, dvallesp}@fing.edu.uy, martin.solari@ort.edu.uy

Abstract. *As a practice, software design seeks to contribute to developing quality software. For graduating students, the design is difficult to understand, and building a good design seems to require a certain level of cognitive development. In this study, we report an experiment to know how students habitually represent detailed design (what artifacts and ways of design representation they use) and if there is an effect on software quality when they deliver the design representation. We found that students design on a basic level, they do not achieve complete designs that combine several artifacts to model dynamic and static aspects. Also, the delivery of design representation did not improve software quality.*

1. Introduction

Software design is one of the most important components to ensure the success of a software system [Hu 2013]. Software design has two main activities: architectural design and detailed design. During architectural design, high-level components are structured and identified. During detailed design, every component is specified in detail [Bourque and Fairley 2014]. Our work is explicitly focused on detailed design.

From a learning point of view, design is a complex discipline for undergraduate students to understand, and success (i.e., building a good design) seems to require a certain level of cognitive development that few students achieve [Carrington and K Kim 2003, Hu 2013, Linder et al. 2006]. In fact, several studies found that students do not manage to produce a good software design [Chen et al. 2005, Eckerdal et al. 2006a, Eckerdal et al. 2006b, Loftus et al. 2011, Tenenberg 2005].

This article presents an experiment to study how graduating students represent software designs. This experiment is a part of a family of experiments carried out in the context of the School of Engineering of Universidad de la República, in Uruguay. From 2012 to 2018, we conducted 7 experiments.

The **Baseline** experiments carried out in 2012, 2013, and 2014 were aimed at learning about the effort (measured in minutes) dedicated by students to detailed software design [Moreno and Vallespir 2018]. Results showed that students spend at least 3 times more time coding than designing. The **Template** experiments carried out in the years 2015, 2016, and 2017, were aimed at knowing about the effect on design effort and software quality when students represent the design using a specific set of design templates [Moreno et al. 2020, Moreno et al. 2021]. We found that the use of design templates did not improve code quality and that students who use templates dedicated more significant development effort to designing than to coding.

In this article, we present the last experiment of the family. We want to study how students habitually represent detailed design (what artifacts and ways of design representation they use) and know if there is an effect on software quality when they deliver the design representation to the teachers as part of a course.

We used the term graduating for our students because they are in the fourth year of the degree of the School of Engineering. The curriculum of the School of Engineering is a five-year degree, similar to the IEEE/ACM's proposal for the Computer Science undergraduate curriculum [Joint Task Force on Computing Curricula - ACM and IEEE Computer Society 2013]. Students have already passed courses where detailed software design is taught: design principles, artifacts and design diagrams, UML, design patterns.

The document is structured as follows: Section 2 presents the categorizing student software designs; Section 3 presents the related work; Section 4 presents the research methodology; Section 5 presents the results, and Section 6 is the discussion; threats to validity are mentioned in Section 7, and Section 8 presents the conclusions and future work.

2. Categorizing Student Software Designs

Some researchers have proposed frameworks to analyze and categorize design artifacts [Eckerdal et al. 2006a, Thomas et al. 2014]. Eckerdal's category categorizes the design artifacts students produce, and Thomas' category categorizes how students understand software design. In our experiment, we used these categories, and therefore we describe them below. Both categorizations use a scalar measurement approach, from basic descriptions to more sophisticated design representation

Eckerdal et al. developed a categorization of students design artifacts of six levels [Eckerdal et al. 2006b]:

- 0N - Nothing: little or no intelligible content.
- 1R - Restatement: merely restating requirements in some fashion from the task description.
- 2S - Skumtomte: a small amount restatement of the task with a small amount of information in text, or some unimportant implementation details with no description of its design.
- 3FS - First step: some significant work beyond the description. Either a partial overview of the system with the parts identified, but generally no identification of how they are related in the system; or the design of one of the system's components.
- 4PD - Partial design: providing an understandable description of each of the parts and an overview of the system that illustrates the relationships between the (may be incomplete) parts without completely described communications between the parts.
- 5C - Complete: showing a well-developed solution, including an understandable overview, part descriptions that include responsibilities, and explicit communication between the parts.

Thomas et al. investigated students' understanding by asking them for a task to "produce a design" [Thomas et al. 2014]. The authors analyzed the designs made by students and categorized them based on the following characteristics that express the different ways in which students understand the design phenomenon:

- 0ID - Informal design: does not include formal artifacts. Generally, text but may include detailed pictures without reference to software.
- 1A - Analysis: uses some formal notation for analysis (use case diagrams/not describe system structure or behavior).
- 2SS - Static structure: focus on design techniques of software engineering, expressing the components and their structural relationships using notations like class or architecture diagrams.
- 3DB - Dynamic behavior: focus on design techniques, expressing the components and some sequential behavior using notations like sequence diagrams or flowcharts.
- 4MRA - Multiple related artifacts: use multiple artifacts and relates components across different artifacts.
- 5EC - Expert category: the notations are relaxed, and only the essential artifacts are included.

3. Related Work

Software design involves identifying and abstractly describing the software system and its relationships. It is a creative activity, which can be done in different ways: implicitly, in the developer's mind before coding, on a sketch on paper, through diagrams, using both formal and informal languages or tools [Chemuturi 2018].

Research shows that students have (still) difficulties in designing. Building good designs requires a certain level of cognitive development that few students achieve [Carrington and K Kim 2003, Hu 2013, Linder et al. 2006]. This cognitive development is related to the ability to recognize design patterns, architectural design styles, and related data and actions that can be extracted into appropriate design abstractions [Hu 2013].

Students' ability to build a good design is related to the abstraction, understanding, reasoning, and data-processing ability [Kramer 2007, Leung and Bolloju 2005, Siau and Tan 2005]. In fact, it is more difficult for students learning to design than learning to code. Besides, there is no single method for designing software. Students may confuse the different methods and may not appreciate the similarities, differences, and their uses [Carrington 1998].

How students design software has been studied previously from different points of view [Eckerdal et al. 2006a, Eckerdal et al. 2006b, Thomas et al. 2014, Thomas et al. 2017, Loftus et al. 2011, Tenenberg 2005, Hu 2016].

A study reported by Tenenberg describes the skills that students have when designing software [Tenenberg 2005]. They used the designs elaborated by two types of students: first competency students and graduating students. Each participant is given the specification of a "super alarm clock" (system to get people to sleep) to produce a design. The results indicate that graduating students use less textual design notations and more graphical and standardized notations. In addition, a large number of students underestimated the importance of representing structural groupings and interactions between design parts.

Eckerdal et al. undertook a detailed examination of the design artifacts produced by graduating students also using the "super alarm clock" task [Eckerdal et al. 2006a, Eckerdal et al. 2006b]. The designs constructed by the students are grouped using Eckerdal's categorization. They found that 62% of the students cannot design a software system. The percentages associated with the proposed categories indicate that: 3% produce nothing, 18% restatement, 41% skumtomte, 29% first step, 7% partial design and, 2% complete.

The study published by Eckerdal et al. [Eckerdal et al. 2006a] was subsequently reviewed by Loftus et al. [Loftus et al. 2011]. This work aims to find out if students about to graduate (graduating) are able to design in groups and if they are able to recognize good and bad designs produced by others. The results confirm those reported by Eckerdal et al. In addition, they found that the main things missing from the students' designs were descriptions of system behavior and consistency between the use case diagrams and the implemented designs.

A study presented by Lynda Thomas et al. [Thomas et al. 2014] expanded on the research of Eckerdal et al.[Eckerdal et al. 2006a]. They used the task, "super alarm clock," and Eckerdal's categorization. The results obtained do not turn out to be as bad in the area of students' design skills as previously reported. Most of the designs were mapped in the first step and partial design. Furthermore, the authors built the list of fundamental characteristics that differentiate how students understand the design phenomenon presented in Section2 as Thomas' category.

Chenglie Hu continues this line of work by reporting an experiment in which graduating students perform the design to the same "super alarm clock" [Hu 2016]. The results show that 50% of the designs were categorized in the partial design category, 16.6% in the first step, and 33.3% in the complete category.

Years later, Thomas et al. studied software designs of students who were halfway through their 3-year undergraduate computing degree [Thomas et al. 2017]. Students were asked to "Produce a design" using a problem that appeared to require about the same design skill level as the "super alarm clock" problem. They used Eckerdal's categorization. Then, the authors compared the results with those obtained from a group of graduating students from the same university [Thomas et al. 2014].

The results show that most of the designs from both cohorts were in the first step category, followed by the skumtomte category. The graduating students produced a few more partial and complete designs but were relatively low cases.

In general, studies have shown that most graduating students are not competent in designing software [Eckerdal et al. 2006a, Eckerdal et al. 2006b, Loftus et al. 2011]. Students do not describe the behavior of the system [Loftus et al. 2011], do not seem to understand what kind of information they should include [Eckerdal et al. 2006a] and produce incomplete class diagrams, sequence diagrams with missing responsibilities, and objects at inconsistent abstraction levels [Sien 2011].

4. Research Method

We conducted the experiment in the context of an undergraduate course to study how graduating students habitually design software and if there is an effect on software quality when they deliver the design representation to course teachers.

4.1. Course context

The course lasts 9 weeks. In the first week (week 1), a base process (that students must follow) is taught, and the practical work dynamics are explained. Students participate in the course voluntarily.

The base process is a defined process that intends to help the software development tasks and collect product and process metrics. The process has different phases, scripts that guide the work in each phase, and logs that are used to collect data (see **Figure 1**).

The base process is divided into the following phases: plan, design, code, compile, unit test (UT), and postmortem. In each phase of the process, students must log the time dedicated to the phase and data on the defects they remove (injection phase, removal phase, and time spent to correct it). Students log the size (using a web tool) in lines of code of the program built in the postmortem phase.

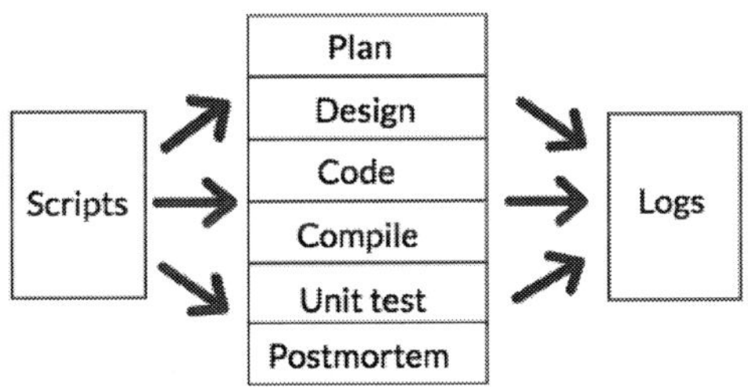

Figure 1. Base Process

The practical work consists of each student developing 8 small projects following the base process and recording the process data in the tool. Students carry out the projects individually, consecutively and at home. Project 2 does not begin until project 1 has been completed and so on. From week 2 to week 9, one project is assigned per week. At the beginning of each week, a teacher sends the student the project requirements. Each student's submission must contain the code that solves the problem, the test cases executed, and the export of the data registered in the tool.

Before starting the first exercise each student must choose the programming language to be used throughout the course. Our interest is to collect data on the execution of the development process using a programming language that the student masters. All the students have passed the courses Programming 3, Programming 4, Programming Workshop, and Software Engineering. During these courses, software design artifact and techniques, programming languages, algorithms and fundamental software engineering concepts are taught. We consider the group of students who participated to be homogeneous, since they are students at a similar stage of their career.

Projects are small in size and of low and similar complexity so design phase refers to detailed design (i.e. identifying classes, attributes, operations, program scenarios, status changes, and pseudo-code). Seven projects deal with numerical and statistical analysis problems, and one deals with a text-processing problem (project 2).

Previous studies using the same projects, showed that the nature of project 2 is different from the other projects, the process measures and product measures in project 2 are extremely different than in the rest of the projects (i.e., project 2 is an outlier), and it is usually discarded in statistical analysis [Grazioli et al. 2014]. Therefore, we excluded the data of this project from the analyzes presented in this article.

4.2. Goals and research questions

The goals of our experiment are, first, get to know if there is an effect on software quality when they deliver the design representation. We pose this goal to determine whether asking for the delivery of the habitual design representation changes student behavior and affects the software's quality. Second, get to know how students habitually represent software design (what artifacts and ways of design representation they use).

To get students to deliver the design representation they would habitually build, we do not request the use of templates or specific approaches to design representation (as we did in previous iterations of the family of the experiment).

We defined the following research questions and the corresponding research hypotheses:

RQ1: Is there any improvement in the quality of the products when students deliver the representation of their habitual design?

H1.0: Deliver the design in the habitual way does not modify defect density in the unit test phase.
H1.1: Deliver the design in the habitual way modifies defect density in the unit test phase.

We defined the defect density as the number of defects found in the unit test phase (UT) per every thousand lines of code. The consequence of high defect density in UT in software engineering is typically seen in the form of defect-fixing or rework effort incurred in projects, which results in poor quality products.

RQ2: How do students habitually represent the design?

To answer RQ2, we analyze using Eckerdal's categorization, Thomas' categorization and direct observations of the delivered designs handed by the students.

4.3. Experimental design

We carried out the experiment in 2018, and 15 students took part. Experimental design is of repeated measures of one factor (software design representation) with two alternatives: submitting the design representation or not.

To address the goals, students submit the habitual representation of their designs as part of the solution to each project. With the submission of the design representation, we seek to know the students' design practices. Even though it is an optional submission (i.e. the student can decide not to design in the design phase of the base process), we emphasize the importance of designing in the way they habitually do so, following their usual design representation. Besides, students are told that their designs will not influence the grading.

Students carry out the first four projects following the base process. Then, students are randomized divided into two groups: "habitual design delivery" (*HDD*), and "without

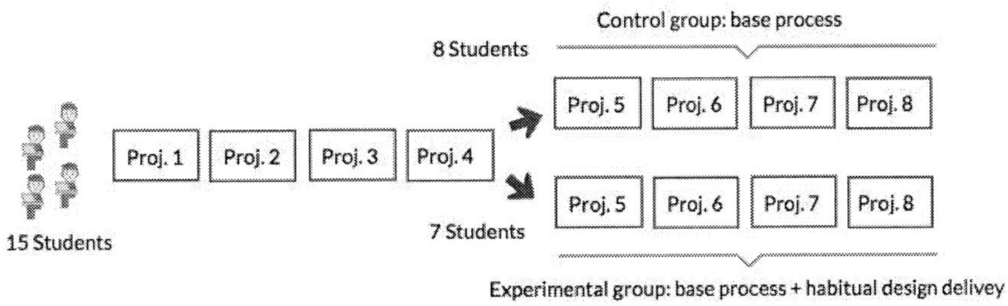

Figure 2. Experimental design

habitual design delivery" (*noHDD*). The control group (*noHDD*) carries out projects 5 to 8 following the base process. The *HDD* group continues applying the base process and also has to submit their design representations. The only difference between groups is the submission of the representation. However, it is important to remark that the students of both groups should produce a design for each of the programs as part of the design phase of the base process. In the *HDD* group, 7 students participated, and in the *noHDD* group, 8 students participated (see Figure 2).

The response variables considered in this experiment are external quality, measured as the defect density in the unit test phase of the base process, and the design quality. The design quality is measured using the design categorizations already mentioned.

5. Analysis and Results

5.1. Quality Improvement

To answer RQ1: "Is there any improvement in the quality of the products when students deliver the representation of their habitual design?" we analyzed the following hypothesis test:

H1.0: Delivering the habitual design does not change the defects density in unit test
H1.1: Delivering the habitual design does change the defects density in unit test

For each student, we calculated two average defect density in UT: for projects 1, 3 and 4, and projects 5 to 8. The calculation of each sample for projects 5 to 8 is as follows (the same applies for projects 1, 3, and 4):

$$1000 * \frac{\sum_{n=5}^{8} \#defectsUT_n}{\sum_{n=5}^{8} \#LOC_n} \quad (1)$$

Table 1 presents the average defect density (dd) in UT for the 8 students in the *noHDD* group and the 7 students in the *HDD* group projects 1, 3, and 4 and projects 5 to 8.

First, we studied if exists a difference in the quality of the products between the group's *HDD* and *noHDD* in projects 1, 3, and 4. During projects 1, 3, and 4, both groups apply the base process, so comparing the software quality of both groups during those projects allows to confirm that they are homogeneous groups. For this analysis, we defined the following hypothesis test:

Table 1. average defect density (number of defects in the unit test phase per every thousand lines of code) for the students in both groups

Group	St.	dd134	dd58	Group	St.	dd134	dd58
noHDD	1	30.51	28.05	*HDD*	1	27.78	58.82
noHDD	2	11.63	24.69	*HDD*	2	9.48	28.90
noHDD	3	8.47	21.18	*HDD*	3	85.71	120.00
noHDD	4	98.98	82.88	*HDD*	4	26.12	14.13
noHDD	5	15.56	19.17	*HDD*	5	31.25	15.47
noHDD	6	7.35	0.00	*HDD*	6	60.61	52.12
noHDD	7	62.50	21.19	*HDD*	7	19.48	70.51
noHDD	8	60.47	55.56				

H1.0: Median(Def. density in UT i) = Median(Def. density in UT j)
H1.1: Median(Def. density in UT i) <> Median(Def. density in UT j)
being i, j the students of HDD and noHDD groups in projects 1, 3 and 4.

The value of the median and the interquartile range of the defects density for the *noHDD* group are (23.0, 33.5) and for the *HDD* group are (27.8, 26.5) respectively. In this case, the samples correspond to defects density in UT of different students. So, we applied the Mann-Whitney-Wilcoxon test for independent samples.

Defects density in UT for students in the *HDD* group (Mdn = 27.8) did not differ significantly from students in the *noHDD* group (Mdn = 23.0) when considering projects 1, 3, and 4, W = 24 and p = 0.694. So, we can assume that both groups have similar or homogeneous behavior with respect to defect density.

To know if software quality changes when students deliver their habitual design representation, we analyzed the defect density between and intra groups. Between groups refers to knowing if exists a significant difference in the software quality between the groups. Intra groups refers to studying software quality in the *HDD* group before and after the delivery of the design representations.

Between groups

The hypothesis test is similar to the one described before but considering projects 5 to 8 instead of 1, 3, and 4. We applied the Mann-Whitney-Wilcoxon test again as the samples are independent. The values of the median and the interquartile range for the *HDD* group are (52.1, 37.2) and for the *noHDD* group are (25.7, 25.8).

Defects density in UT for students in the *HDD* group (Mdn = 52.1) did not differ significantly from students in the *noHDD* group (Mdn = 25.7) when considering projects 5 to 8, W = 20 and p-value = 0.397. Students who deliver their habitual designs did not differ significantly from those who do not deliver their habitual designs.

Intra groups

We also studied if there is any change within the group who delivered their habitual design (*HDD* group). We compared the defect density when they did not delivered their design (projects 1, 3 and 4) and when they delivered their design (projects 5 to 8). For this analysis, we defined the following hypothesis test:

H1.0: Median(Def. density in UT i) = Median(Def. density in UT j)
H1.1: Median(Def. density in UT i) <> Median(Def. density in UT j)
being i the students of HDD in project 1, 3 and 4, j the students of HDD in project 5 to 8.

The values of the median and the interquartile range for the *HDD* group in projects 1, 3 and 4 are (27.7, 26.5) and for the same group in projects 5 to 8 are (52.1, 37.2).

The samples are paired since the sampled pairs (Def. density in UT i, Def. density in UT j) correspond to the same student, so we applied Wilcoxon signed-rank test.

Defects density in UT for students in the *HDD* group in projects 1, 3 and 4 (Mdn = 27.7) did not differ significantly from students in the HDD group in projects 5 to 8 (Mdn = 52.1), V = 6, p-value = 0.219. That is, the delivery of the design representation did not differ significantly from the non-delivery of the design representation.

5.2. Habitually software design representation

To answer research question RQ2: "How do students habitually represent design?" we analyzed the 28 design representations submitted by the 7 students of *HDD* group from project 5 to project 8 using Eckerdal et al. categories, Thomas et al. categories, and direct observations. In this case, we do not have a control group because we do not have the design representation for students in the *noHDD* group. Therefore, it is not possible to answer this question using the framework of controlled experiments, but we do it in an exploratory and analytical way.

We mapped each design to Eckerdal's categorization and Thomas's categorization. The first author of the paper did the mapping, and the second author evaluated it both resolved discrepancies by discussion. Figure 3 illustrates the mapping associated with Eckerdal's and Thomas's categorizations for the 7 students for projects 5 to 8.

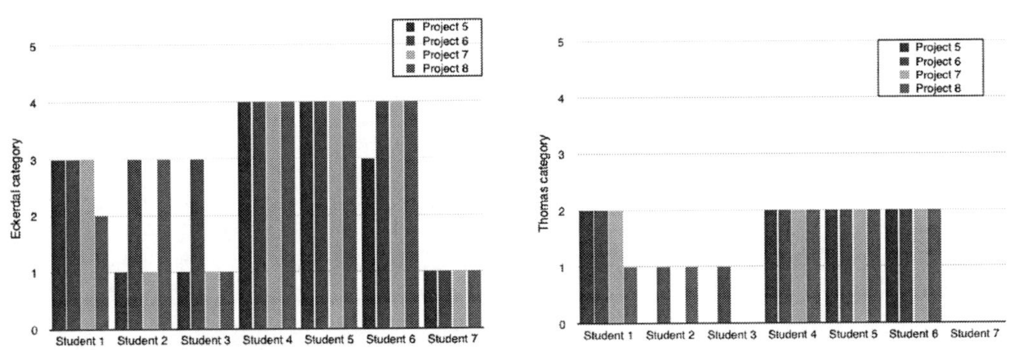

(a) Eckerdal (b) Thomas

Figure 3. Eckerdal and Thomas categories for the 7 students in projects 5 to 8

From Figure 3 arise that the ranking of some students' designs (students 1, 4, 5, 6 and 7) across the different projects does not change much. That is, their design is relatively consistent according to these categorizations.

Furthermore, it can be observed how some students (students 4, 5, and 6) managed to elaborate intermediately designs mapping to Eckerdal's categories 3-4. On the other hand, students 2, 3, and 7 elaborate more basic designs that categorize in the lowest Eckerdal and Thomas categorizations.

Some interesting aspects of the results associated with Eckerdal's categorization are observed. Students 4, 5 and 6 produced designs that provide an understandable description of each of the parts and an overview of the system that illustrates the relationships between the parts, without completely describing communications between the parts. Student 3 (in three of the four projects) and 7 handled designs that merely restated the requirements (i.e., it is not a software design). Student 1 generally manages to describe the system and its parts partially but fails to relate them. Finally, student 2's designs vary, ranging from only transcribing the requirements (half of the projects) to partially describing the system and its parts (the other half of the projects).

Using Thomas's categorization, it can be observed that the students manage basic designs. The delivery of students 2, student 3 and student 7 are in most of the projects (in 9 projects out of 12) text notations (category 0ID). In the remaining 3 projects students manage to identify some part of the system in an incompetent way (category 1A). Designs of students 4, 5, and 6 fall into category 2SS.; that is, their designs use static notation. Specifically, the designs elaborated by these students consist of incomplete class diagrams of the system. Student 1 elaborates incomplete class diagrams in the delivery of projects 5, 6, and 7 (category 2SS.), and identifies some incomplete part of the system for project 8 (category 1A)

Finally, no designs fall into categories 3DB, 4MRA and 5EC, which implies the ability to represent dynamic design with multiple related artifacts.

To add a complementary perspective to the students' design analysis, we analyzed project 8 in detail as a sample of the projects submitted. Table 2 presents for the 7 students a description of the main characteristics of the design submitted, the defect density in UT (dd), the Eckerdal's category and Thomas' category for project 8.

It can be observed that students 4 and 5 manage to represent designs using both class diagrams and pseudo-code. According to the categorizations of Eckerdal et al. and Thomas et al., these two students were the ones who categorized their designs better. It could be observed that these two students are the ones with less defect density in UT for project 8 (see Table 2). The rest of the students represent their design more informally, transcribing the requirements to natural language, doing a pseudo-code, or incomplete class diagrams. In these cases, the defect density in UT is higher.

In order to illustrate what kind of design the students deliver, some of the designs are presented as they were delivered in project 8 (the most complex project of the course). Figure 4 illustrates a part of the delivery of the design representation for students 5, 6 and 7. Student 5 makes a pseudo-code of a part of the project, student 6 develops an incomplete class diagram and student 7 transcribes the requirements into natural language. Figures correspond to the actual capture sent by the students of their design reflected on the sheet.

6. Discussion

In our experiment, we observed that the submission of the habitual design representation does not have an impact on the software quality produced by students. The results of the

Table 2. Main characteristics of the design submitted, the defect density in UT, the Eckerdal's category and Thomas' category for project 8

St.	Design description	dd	Eck.	Tho.
1	uses natural language to explain that he will extend a class by adding a method	33.78	2S	1A
2	performs a pseudo code of a part of the project	43.80	3FS	1A
3	transcribe the requirements to natural language, inputs and expected outputs of the project	66.67	1A	1R
4	performs a pseudo code of a part of the project, identifying classes, methods and attributes	14.71	4PD	2SS
5	performs a pseudo code of a part of the project, identifying classes, methods and attributes	8.40	4PD	2SS
6	makes a class diagram, identifying attributes and relationships between classes	43.48	4PD	2SS
7	transcribe the requirements to natural language	142.86	1R	0ID

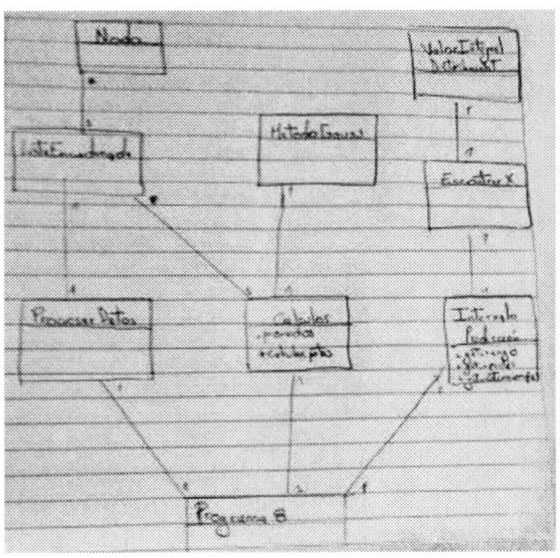

(a) Student 6

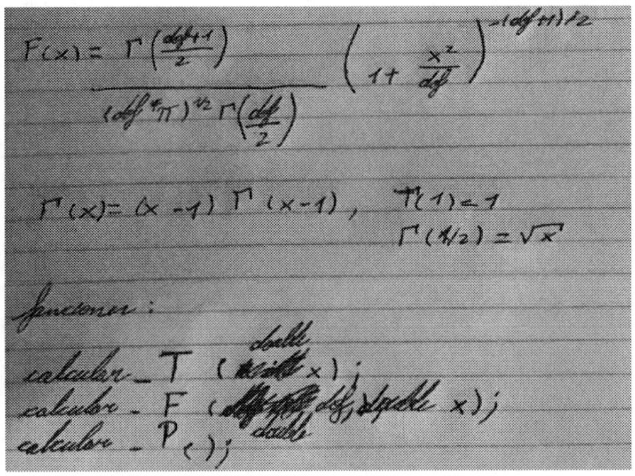

(b) Student 7

```
h := 0 /* Initialization of the pivot row */
k := 0 /* Initialization of the pivot column */
while h < m and k < n
        /* Find the k-th pivot: */
        max = abs(A[h,k])
        i_max = h
        for i = h+1, h < m i++
                if abs(A[i,k]) > max
                        i_max = i
                end
        end

        if A[i_max, k] = 0
                /* No pivot in this column, pass to next column */
                k := k+1
        else
                //swap rows(h, i_max)
                        aux = A[h]
                        A[h] = A[i_max]
                        A[i_max] = aux
                /* Do for all rows below pivot: */
                for i = h, h<m, i++:
```

(c) Student 5

Figure 4. Habitual design representation for students 5, 6 and 7 in project 8

statistical tests applied (intra and between groups) indicate that the quality of the group delivering the design representation does not vary significantly concerning the quality of the group that does not deliver it. However, the median value indicates that the submission of the usual design representation seems to negatively impact the software compared to the non-submission of the usual representation. This comes to our attention because we did not expect any difference between groups (considering that the experimental group was handling their habitual design). Furthermore, if there were differences in the medians (as is the case), we would expect the opposite results (i.e., students "caring" more about submitting their design and this having a positive impact on software quality). New questions arise from this: How does the design request affect the student's usual design-code process? Does the design request modify the student's habitual way of coding?

Using the categorizations by Ekerdal et al. and Thomas et al., we can affirm that students (in our Engineering School) design on a basic level. Even though they do not achieve complete designs that combine several artifacts to model dynamic and static aspects simultaneously, they manage to produce simple designs. We can observe that using natural language to transcribe requirements (restatement category) is a habitual practice of some students to represent their designs (student 2, student 3, and student 7). Two of these three students manage to describe the system and its parts in some exercise partially. Students 4, 5, and 6 provide an understandable description of the system's parts that illustrates the relationships between them (partial design category). Finally, student 1 manages to partially describe the system without relating its parts (first step category). No student used sequence, use case, collaboration, or dynamic diagrams. Furthermore, the delivered designs vary between text notations, the incomplete identification of the parts of the system, and the use of static notations to describe the system.

Some previously reported results are similar to ours [Eckerdal et al. 2006a, Eckerdal et al. 2006b, Thomas et al. 2014, Thomas et al. 2017]. Most of the designs categorized by Eckerdal et al. are associated with basic categories (18% restatement, 41% skumtomte, 29% first step) [Eckerdal et al. 2006a, Eckerdal et al. 2006b]. In the study reported by Thomas et al. [Thomas et al. 2014], the majority of designs categorized was in the first step and in partial design. Results from their following study [Thomas et al. 2017] shows most designs categorized were in the first step, followed by the skumtomte category. These authors agree that students do not know how to design, and our results show the same.

This experiment and the previous experiments in our family of experiments allowed us to know how graduating students are currently designing, their habitual practices, and the effects of design on software quality [Moreno and Vallespir 2018, Moreno et al. 2020, Moreno et al. 2021]. From the family results, we believe that a usual practice of the students when developing software is to follow the code-and-fix model. That is to say, they do not stop to think of a solution (design), but instead, they rush to code. Students dedicate at least three times less time to design than to coding. Also, using templates for the design representation did not help the students develop software products of a higher quality. These results in addition to those obtained in this experiment reveal that students do not have a great domain of design techniques and how to combine them. We believe, just as Loftus et al. [Loftus et al. 2011], that students have difficulties in designing software. Within the context of graduating students, those difficulties may be associated with several reasons: the lack of experience, the lack of awareness of the importance of design on quality, and the lack of education regarding design techniques among others.

7. Threats to validity

This section describes the threats to validity we have detected.

Internal validity - The fact that the context of the experiment is a course implies that the students do not develop naturally. We tried to minimize this threat with a non-graded course, that is, a course in which the student passes or fails. Besides, we remarked on the importance of monitoring and registering the process just as it was, and we emphasized that students' assessments would not be done according to results, defects found, efforts made, or delivered designs.

External validity - In our experiment, students voluntarily took part in a course, and they signed an informed consent that the data recorded and the designs delivered in the process could be used for research purposes, guaranteeing anonymity. Conversely, the results obtained in this experiment (academic context) cannot be generalized to the student's design practice in a professional context.

Construct validity - We measured software quality as the number of defects in UT and design quality using design categorizations (Eckerdal and Thomas). Although we used software quality and design quality scales from previous research, these are complex constructs to measure, and there could be a bias between theory and construction.

Conclusion validity - The number of students in the research constitutes a threat to the statistical conclusion (only 15). This causes the statistical analysis to be carried out using non-parametric tests with lower statistical power than the parametric tests. To measure this threat, we completed the non-parametric tests with descriptive statistics and in an observational way.

8. Concluding Remarks and Future Work

In this paper, we report the results from an experiment to know how students habitually represent detailed design (what artifacts and ways of design representation they use) and know if there is an effect on software quality when they deliver the design representation.

We analyzed the software quality (defect density) between and intra groups. The results of the statistical tests applied in both groups indicated that the quality of the group delivering the design representation does not vary significantly concerning the quality of the group which does not deliver it.

Also, we analyzed the design representations delivered by the students and categorized them using the categorizations by Eckerdal and Thomas.We found that the delivered designs vary between text notations, the incomplete identification of parts of the system, and the use of static notations to describe the system. Our results are similar to those reported in the literature [Eckerdal et al. 2006a, Eckerdal et al. 2006b, Thomas et al. 2014, Thomas et al. 2017], and we agree with them on the fact that students do not know how to deliver a design representation beyond using basic artifacts.

We propose a new experiment and conduct interviews with students as they carry out the projects as future work. Our interest is to know how they face design thinking during the design phase, if they carry out any design aspect during the code, why they choose the design artifacts they use, if they know others, why they are not used, etc.

References

Bourque, P. and Fairley, R. E. (2014). *Guide to the Software Engineering Body of Knowledge - SWEBOK v3.0.* IEEE Computer Society, 2014 version edition.

Carrington, D. (1998). Teaching software design and testing. In *FIE'98. 28th Annual Frontiers in Education Conference. Moving from'Teacher-Centered'to'Learner-Centered'Education. Conference Proceedings (Cat. No. 98CH36214)*, volume 2, pages 547–550. IEEE.

Carrington, D. and K Kim, S. (2003). Teaching software design with open source software. In *33rd Annual Frontiers in Education.*

Chemuturi, M. (2018). *Software Design: A Comprehensive Guide to Software Development Projects.* CRC Press/Taylor & Francis Group.

Chen, T.-Y., Cooper, S., McCartney, R., and Schwartzman, L. (2005). The (relative) importance of software design criteria. *SIGCSE Bull.*, 37(3):34–38.

Eckerdal, A., McCartney, R., Moström, J. E., Ratcliffe, M., and Zander, C. (2006a). Can graduating students design software systems? In *SIGCSE Bull.*, page 403–407. ACM, Association for Computing Machinery.

Eckerdal, A., McCartney, R., Moström, J. E., Ratcliffe, M., and Zander, C. (2006b). Categorizing student software designs: Methods, results, and implications. *Computer science education*, 16(3):197–209.

Grazioli, F., Vallespir, D., Pérez, L., and Moreno, S. (2014). The impact of the psp on software quality: Eliminating the learning effect threat through a controlled experiment. *Adv. Soft. Eng.*, 2014.

Hu, C. (2013). The nature of software design and its teaching: an exposition. *ACM Inroads*, 4(2).

Hu, C. (2016). Can students design software? the answer is more complex than you think. In *Proceedings of the 47th ACM Technical Symposium on Computing Science Education*, Computer Science Education 2016, page 199–204, New York, NY, USA. Association for Computing Machinery.

Joint Task Force on Computing Curricula - ACM and IEEE Computer Society (2013). *Computer Science Curricula 2013: Curriculum Guidelines for Undergraduate Degree Programs in Computer Science.* Association for Computing Machinery, New York, NY, USA.

Kramer, J. (2007). Is abstraction the key to computing? *Commun. ACM*, 50(4):36–42.

Leung, F. and Bolloju, N. (2005). Analyzing the quality of domain models developed by novice systems analysts. In *38th Hawaii International Conference on System Sciences.*

Linder, S. P., Abbott, D., and Fromberger, M. J. (2006). An instructional scaffolding approach to teaching software design. *Journal of Computing Sciences in Colleges*, 21.

Loftus, C., Thomas, L., and Zander, C. (2011). Can graduating students design: revisited. In *Proceedings of the 42nd ACM technical symposium on Computer science education*. ACM.

Moreno, S., Casella, V., Solari, M., and Vallespir, D. (2020). La representación del diseño detallado utilizando plantillas y sus efectos en la calidad del software. In *En Proceedings XXIII Ibero-American Conference on Software Engineering (CIBSE 2020)*.

Moreno, S. and Vallespir, D. (2018). ¿los estudiantes de pregrado son capaces de diseñar software? estudio de la relación entre el tiempo de codificación y el tiempo de diseño en el desarrollo de software. In *Conferencia Iberoamericana de Ingeniería de Software 2018*.

Moreno, S., Vallespir, D., Solari, M., and Casella, V. (2021). Representation of software design using templates: impact on software quality and development effort. *Journal of Software Engineering Research and Development*, 9(1):1 – 15.

Siau, K. and Tan, X. (2005). Improving the quality of conceptual modeling using cognitive mapping techniques. *Data & Knowledge Engineering*, 55(3). Quality in conceptual modeling.

Sien, V. Y. (2011). An investigation of difficulties experienced by students developing unified modelling language (uml) class and sequence diagrams. *Computer Science Education*, 21(4):317–342.

Tenenberg, J. (2005). Students designing software: a multi-national, multi-institutional study. *Informatics in Education*, 4.

Thomas, L., Eckerdal, A., McCartney, R., Moström, J. E., Sanders, K., and Zander, C. (2014). Graduating students' designs: Through a phenomenographic lens. In *Proceedings of the Tenth Annual Conference on International Computing Education Research*, page 91–98. Association for Computing Machinery.

Thomas, L., Zander, C., Loftus, C., and Eckerdal, A. (2017). Student software designs at the undergraduate midpoint. In *Proceedings of the 2017 ACM Conference on Innovation and Technology in Computer Science Education*, ITiCSE '17, page 34–39, New York, NY, USA. Association for Computing Machinery.

An Overview of Software Architecture Education

Brauner R. N. Oliveira[1], Lina Garcés[2], Kamila T. Lyra[1], Daniel S. Santos[1], Seiji Isotani[1], Elisa Y. Nakagawa[1]

[1] University of São Paulo (USP)
São Carlos – SP – Brazil

[2]Federal University of Itajubá (UNIFEI)
Itajubá – MG – Brazil

{brauner,kalyra_03,danielss}@usp.br, lina@unifei.edu.br

{sisotani,elisa}@icmc.usp.br

Abstract. *Software architecture comprises the most relevant structure of a software system and is a factor to enable systems to achieve qualities that are crucial to the system's goals. In this sense, teaching software architecture to students and professionals remains a very important task. However, it is still a challenging matter for teachers and learners on different levels and contexts. We also lack an updated overview on how such a challenge has been addressed. This paper presents an overview of software architecture education experiences and initiatives. For this, we systematically examined the most relevant studies addressing software architecture education. After analyzing a total of 50 studies, we discuss how software architecture has been taught, the topic mostly taught, the learning objectives, and the learning methods. Based on our findings, we also present open issues that still remain to be further investigated, aiming to mature software architecture education.*

1. Introduction

The software architecture of a system comprises its main software elements, the relation among such elements, and their properties [Bass et al. 2021]. Different responsibilities within the system's context are assigned to such elements and can drastically affect qualities, such as performance, maintainability, and security, which the system must exhibit to achieve its goals. In this sense, designing a software architecture capable of meeting system requirements is a crucial activity during the early stages of the software development process. Just as software architecture is relevant to software development, so is teaching it to students of computer science-related courses and professionals working on software development. The topic of software architecture has been taught since its emergence in 1992.

Several initiatives and experiences of teaching software architecture have been published, pointing to what can be considered a consensus: Teaching software architecture is a challenging task [Mannisto et al. 2008, Lago and Vliet 2005, Rupakheti and Chenoweth 2015, Galster and Angelov 2016, Cervantes et al. 2016, Deursen et al. 2017, Angelov and Beer 2017, Lago et al. 2019]. Several are the reasons for that, such as students of computing-related degree programs often face a large gap between low-level courses (e.g., programming and data structures) and high-level courses, in which they have to design effective systems [Garlan et al. 1992]. Without appropriate directions for teaching software architecture, the already challenging task to define a suitable architecture becomes a barrier to the proper education of future software engineers [Garlan et al. 1992]. Moreover, students have difficulties with problem-solving when the problem can be solved in many ways (i.e., with no single best solution) [Lago and Vliet 2005, Galster and Angelov 2016], which is the case for software architecture design. In turn, the architectural design process is difficult to be learned and performed with confidence since many aspects have to be considered when making architectural decisions, and there are many of them to be made during the software development [Cervantes et al. 2016]. In general, the desired skills of architects are mostly developed or gained through experience over many years of developing and designing software architectures [Rupakheti and Chenoweth 2015, Lago et al. 2019, Cervantes et al. 2016]. It means that instructors have to choose those topics that students will face when they go into the industry and teach them in a way that will ease the path throughout their career. More reasons make teaching software architecture too difficult, as discussed in depth in [Galster and Angelov 2016].

Despite several experiences and initiatives already published, to the best of our knowledge, there is only one study that analyzed how software architecture education has been addressed [Rodrigues and Werner 2009]. This study examined 37 studies that reported on software architecture teaching initiatives and, more specifically, it discussed the maturity of such initiatives, the employment of large and complex systems as part of the content addressed, and the educational approaches and resources used. However, this study was published more than ten years. Considering the relevance of investigating software architecture education and the continuing evolution of both the state of practice and state of the art, an updated review becomes necessary to address other research questions and objectives.

The main goal of this work is to present an overview of software architecture education based on the literature. For this, we examined 50 main studies published on the matter since 1992 and analyzed different aspects, including the types of experience within software architecture education, how the subject has been addressed, which topics have been considered relevant for the learning process, which categories of learning objectives have received more attention, and the educational approaches that have been employed. As a main result, we found many different teaching experiences, which have addressed several perspectives of the learning and teaching process, and various subjects at different cognitive levels; however, little attention has been given to teaching recent or trending topics of software architectures, like microservices and cloud-based architectures. Another important finding is that software architecture is still challenging and difficult to teach and learn; therefore, more attention must be paid to maturing and consolidating the field of software architecture education.

The remainder of this paper is organized as follows. Section 2 presents the method we followed to search, select, and analyze the studies. Section 3 presents the result and findings, whereas Section 4 discusses the results and presents the threats to the validity. Finally, we outline our conclusion in Section 5.

2. Research Method

To provide an overview of software architecture education, we followed the guidelines proposed in [Petersen et al. 2015] for planning, conducting, and reporting systematic mapping studies (SMS). In this section, we outline the most important sections of the SMS protocol, which is fully available online[1].

During planning phase, we established the following research questions:

- **RQ1.** How has software architecture been taught?
- **RQ2.** What topics have been taught in the software architecture area?
- **RQ3.** Which learning objectives have been considered in software architecture teaching?
- **RQ4.** Which learning methods have been adopted to teach software architecture?

Based on such questions, we developed the following search string, after rounds of calibration: *((“software architecture”) AND (“education” OR “educational” OR “course” OR “training” OR “teaching”))*. This string was adapted to each database engine and applied in 2021 to the following databases: ACM Digital Library[2], Engineering Village[3], IEEE Xplore Digital Library[4], and Scopus[5]. Our search was limited to studies published since 1992 and, when possible, we restricted the search to the title, abstract, and keywords of the studies. The number of studies returned by each search engine is detailed in the SMS protocol provided in the external material. Moreover, we considered one inclusion criterion (IC) and five exclusion criteria (EC) to support the selection process:

- IC1: The study reports an experience with software architecture education.

- EC1: The study was published before 1992.
- EC2: The study is not presented in English.
- EC3: The full text of the study is not accessible or available.
- EC4: The study is reported in a book or gray literature.
- EC5: The study is a duplicate of another study included.

The execution phase process is shown in Figure 1. We obtained 4,741 studies from the database search and, after removing the duplicated studies, we started the first selection phase with 2,871 primary studies to be analyzed. In that step, all 2,871 studies had their titles and abstracts read by the reviewers. Sometimes, the introduction section was also analyzed, enabling a better application of selection criteria. After finishing the first selection, 80 studies were thoroughly analyzed during the second selection. During that step, the 80 studies were fully read to confirm whether the selection criteria were correctly applied or not. As a result, we excluded 32 more studies that were not filtered through exclusion criteria during the first selection. For the remaining 48 studies, we extracted all the pieces of information that were registered in our extraction form, including

[1] github.com/brauneroliveira/SAE-SMS/blob/master/Protocol.pdf
[2] dl.acm.org
[3] engineeringvillage.com
[4] ieeexplore.ieee.org
[5] scopus.com

the references flagged as potential candidates for snowballing [Wohlin 2014]. After finishing this step, we performed the backward snowballing procedure, which allowed us to identify other two primary studies relevant to our research. In total, we included 50 primary studies as relevant for our SMS, as listed in Table 1.

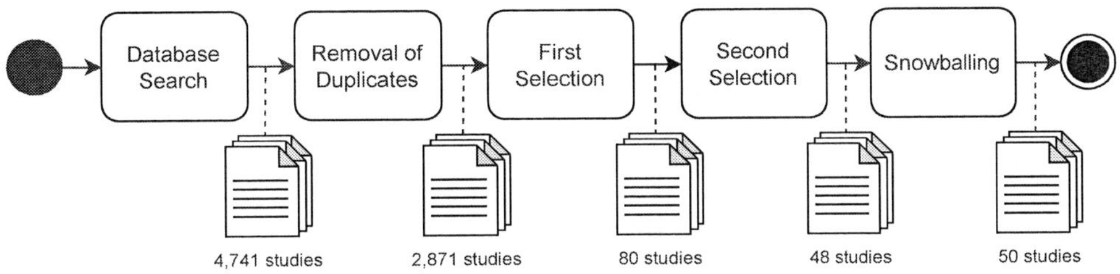

Figure 1. Review process overview

Table 1. Studies included for analysis phase.

ID	Reference
S1	Garlan, D., Shaw, M., Okasaki, C., Scott, C., and Swonger, R. (1992). **Experience with a course on architectures for software systems**. In 6th SEI Conference on Software Engineering Education, pages 23–43.
S2	Royce, W., Boehm, B. , and Druffel, C. (1994). **Employing UNAS technology for software architecture at the University of Southern California**. In 11th Annual Washington Ada Symposium and SIGAda Summer Meeting (WAdaS/SIGAda), page 113
S3	Butler, S. (1999). **A client/server case study for software engineering students**. In 12th Conference on Software Engineering Education and Training (CSEE&T), pages 156–165.
S4	Fairbanks, G. (2003). **Why can't they create architecture models like "developer x"? an experience report**. In 25th International Conference on Software Engineering (ICSE), pages 548–552.
S5	Karam, O., Qian, K., and Diaz-Herrera, J. (2004). **A model for SWE course "software architecture and design"**. In 34th Frontiers in Education (FIE), pages 4–8.
S6	Vickers, B. (2004). **Architecting a software architect**. IEEE Aerospace Conference, pages 4155–4161.
S7	Lago, P. and Vliet, H. (2005). **Teaching a course on software architecture**. In 18th Conference on Software Engineering Education and Training (CSEE&T), pages 35–42.
S8	Wang, A. and Stalhane, T. (2005). **Using post mortem analysis to evaluate software architecture student projects**. 18th Conference on Software Engineering Education and Training (CSEE&T), pages 43–50.
S9	Jarzabek, S. and Eng, P. (2005). **Teaching an advanced design, team-oriented software project course**. 18th Conference on Software Engineering Education and Training (CSEE&T), pages 223–232.
S10	Wang, A. and Sørensen, C. (2006). **Writing as a tool for learning software engineering**. Software Engineering Education Conference, Proceedings, 2006(7491):35–42.
S11	Golden, E. and Bass, L. (2007). **Creating Meaningful Assessments for Professional Development Education in Software Architecture**. In 20th Conference on Software Engineering Education & Training (CSEE&T), pages 283–290.
S12	McGregor, J. D., Bachman, F., Bass, L., Bianco, P., and Klein, M. (2007). **Using an architecture reasoning tool to teach software architecture**. 20th Conference on Software Engineering Education & Training (CSEE&T), pages 275–282.
S13	Svahnberg, M. and Martensson, F. (2007). **Six years of evaluating software architectures in student projects**. Journal of Systems and Software (JSS), 80(11):1893–1901.
S14	Wang, A. I., Arisholm, E., and Jaccheri, L. (2007). **Educational approach to an experiment in a software architecture course**. In 20th Conference on Software Engineering Education & Training (CSEE&T), pages 291–298.
S15	Andrade, R. M. and Arakaki, R. (2007). **Teaching Software Architecture Quality based on run-time metrics**. In International Conference on Engineering Education (ICEE), pages 1–6.
S16	Chenoweth, S., Ardis, M., and Dugas, C. (2007). **Adapting cooperative learning to teach software architecture in multiple role-teams**. ASEE Annual Conference and Exposition, Conference Proceedings.
S17	Gast, H. (2008). **Patterns and traceability in teaching software architecture**. In 6th PPPJ, pages 23–31.
S18	Mannisto, T., Savolainen, J., and Myllarniemi, V. (2008). **Teaching Software Architecture Design**. In 7th Working IEEE/IFIP Conference on Software Architecture (WICSA), pages 117–124.
S19	Boer, R., Farenhorst, R., and Vliet, H. (2009). **A community of learners approach to soft ware architecture education**. In 22nd Conference on Software Engineering Education and Training (CSEE&T), pages 190–197.
S20	Wang, A. I. (2009). **Post-mortem analysis of student game projects in a software architecture course: Successes and challenges in student software architecture game projects**. 1st International IEEE Consumer Electronic Society's Games Innovation Conference, ICE-GiC 09, pages 78–91.
S21	Wu, B., Wang, A. I., Strom, J.-E., and Kvamme, T. B. (2009). **XQUEST used in soft- ware architecture education**. In International Consumer Electronics Society's Games Innovations Conference (ICE-GIC), pages 70–77.
S22	Gu, Q., Lago, P., and van Vliet, H. (2010). **A Template for SOA Design Decision Mak- ing in an Educational Setting**. In 2010 36th EUROMICRO Conference on Software Engineering and Advanced Applications, pages 175–182. IEEE

Continued on next page

Table 1 – *Continued from previous page*

ID	Reference
S23	Giraldo, F. D., Ochoa, S. F., Herrera, M., Neyem, A., Arciniegas, J. L., Clunie, C., Zapata, S., and Lizano, F. (2011). **Applying a distributed CSCL activity for teaching software architecture**. In i-Society, pages 208–214.
S24	Wang, A. I. (2011). **Extensive Evaluation of Using a Game Project in a Software Architecture Course**. ACM Transactions on Computing Education, 11(1):1–28.
S25	Wang, A. I. and Wu, B. (2011). **Using game development to teach software architecture**. International Journal of Computer Games Technology, 2011.
S26	Christensen, H. B. and Corry, A. (2012). **Lectures abandoned: active learning by active seminars**. In 17th Conference on Innovation and Technology in Computer Science Education (ITiCSE), pages 16–21, Haifa, Israel.
S27	Wu, B. and Wang, A. I. (2012). **Comparison of learning software architecture by developing social applications versus games on the android platform**. International Journal of Computer Games Technology.
S28	Urrego, J. S. and Correal, D. (2013). **Archinotes: A tool for assisting software architecture courses**. In 26th CSEET, pages 80–88.
S29	Cleland-Huang, J., Babar, M. A., and Mirakhorli, M. (2014). **An inverted classroom experience: Engaging students in architectural thinking for agile projects**. In 36th International Conference on Software Engineering (ICSE).
S30	Kiwelekar, A. W. and Wankhede, H. S. (2015). **Learning objectives for a course on software architecture**. In ECSA, volume 9278, pages 169–180.
S31	Rupakheti, C. and Chenoweth, S. (2015). **Teaching software architecture to undergraduate students: An experience report**. In 37th International Conference on Software Engineering (ICSE), pages 445–454.
S32	Grbac, T. G., Car, Z., and Vukovic, M. (2015). **Requirements and Architecture Modeling in Software Engineering Courses**. In Proceedings of the 2015 European Conference on Software Architecture Workshops, volume 07-11-Sept, pages 1–8, New York, NY, USA. ACM.
S33	Cervantes, H., Haziyev, S., Hrytsay, O., and Kazman, R. (2016). **Smart Decisions: An Architectural Design Game**. In 38th International Conference on Software Engineering (ICSE), pages 327–335.
S34	Georgas, J. C., Palmer, J. D., and McCormick, M. J. (2016). **Supporting software architecture learning using runtime visualization**. In 29th CSEET, pages 101–110.
S35	Ciancarini, P., Russo, S., and Sabbatino, V. (2016). **A Course on Software Architecture for Defense Applications**. In 4th International Conference in Software Engineering for Defence Applications, pages 321—330.
S36	Angelov, S. and Beer, P. (2017). **Designing and applying an approach to software architecting in agile projects in education**. Journal of Systems and Software, 127:78–90.
S37	Montenegro, C. H. and Astudillo, H. (2014). **A role-playing game to teach ATAM (Ar- chitecture Trade-off Analysis Method) a simulation tool and case study**. In IEEE ANDESCON 2014.
S38	Deursen, A., Aniche, M., Aue, J., Slag, R., de Jong, M., Nederlof, A., and Bouwers, E. (2017). **A Collaborative Approach to Teaching Software Architecture**. In ACM Technical Symposium on Computer Science Education (SIGCSE), pages 69–80.
S39	Tsur, E. E. (2018). **Delivering the fundamentals of software architecture, design and abstraction by developing a ray tracer for 3-dimensional graphical scenes**. Computer Applications in Engineering Education, (November 2017):1–10.
S40	Greising, L., Bartel, A., and Hagel, G. (2018). **Introducing a deployment pipeline for continuous delivery in a software architecture course**. In 3rd European Conference of Software Engineering Education (ECSEE), pages 102–107, Seeon/Bavaria, Germany.
S41	Vidoni, M., Montagna, J. M., and Vecchietti, A. (2018). **Project and team-based strategies for teaching software architecture**. IJEE, 34(5):1701–1708.
S42	Wedemann, G. (2018). **Scrum as a method of teaching software architecture**. In 3rd European Conference of Software Engineering Education (ECSEE), pages 108–112, Seeon/Bavaria, Germany.
S43	Lieh, O. E. and Irawan, Y. (2018). **Teaching Adult Learners on Software Architecture Design Skills**. In FIE. IEEE.
S44	Lieh, O. E. and Irawan, Y. (2018). **Exploring Experiential Learning Model and Risk Management Process for an Undergraduate Software Architecture Course**. In IEEE Frontiers in Education Conference (FIE), pages 1–9.
S45	Lago, P., Cai, J., De Boer, R., Kruchten, P., and Verdecchia, R. (2019). **DecidArch: Playing cards as software architects**. In 52nd Hawaii International Conference on System Sciences (HICCS), pages 7815–7824.
S46	Ouh, E. L. and Irawan, Y. (2019). **Applying case-based learning for a postgraduate software architecture course**. In Conference on Innovation and Technology in Computer Science Education (ITiCSE), pages 457–463.
S47	Backert, M., Blum, T., Kreuter, R., Paulisch, F., and Zimmerer, P. (2020). **Software Curriculum @ Siemens — The Architecture of a Training Program for Architects**. In 2020 IEEE 32nd Conference on Software Engineering Education and Training (CSEET), pages 1–6. IEEE.
S48	Lieh Ouh, E., Kok Siew Gan, B., and Irawan, Y. (2020). **Did our Course Design on Software Architecture meet our Student's Learning Expectations?** In 2020 IEEE Frontiers in Education Conference (FIE), volume 2020-Octob, pages 1–9. IEEE.
S49	Gonçalves, A. C., Vicente Graciano Neto, V., Ferreira, D. J., and Ferreira Silva, U. (2020). **Flipped Classroom Applied to Software Architecture Teaching**. In 2020 IEEE Frontiers in Education Conference (FIE), volume 2020-Octob, pages 1–8. IEEE.
S50	Capilla, R., Zimmermann, O., Carrillo, C., and Astudillo, H. (2020). **Teaching students software architecture decision making**. In ECSA 2020, pages 231–246.

3. Results

The studies included in our SMS cover a period of 28 years, with three studies published before 2003 and most of them (47) after that year, as shown in Figure 2. The higher num-

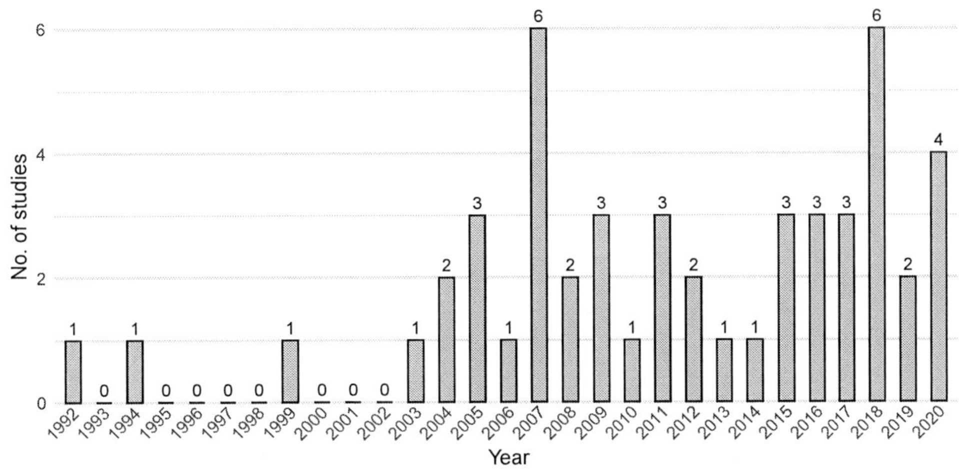

Figure 2. Number of studies by year from 1992 to 2020

ber of studies after 2003 may be related to the popularization phase of software architecture, as discussed in [Shaw and Clements 2006]. The most cited textbook on software architecture (entitled *Software Architecture in Practice* [Bass et al. 2003]) was published in that year as well, and its influence is present in the studies we investigated in this SMS. Regarding the publication venue, most experiences were published in event proceedings (i.e., 44 studies), whereas only six works were published in journals.

We also categorized the studies according to a broad classification of teaching experiences, i.e., course, activity, tool, game, and industry training, as shown in Figure 3. The most frequent category is **course**, which accounts for 36 studies. This category represents experiences in universities that have computing-related courses, such as computer science, computer engineering, and information systems. Studies in this category are still split into single or multiple experiences. **Single experience** encompasses studies that reports only one instance of a course whereas **multiple experience** reports on two or more (the highest number of course instances reported on was 28). The remaining categories account for 14 studies split in four additional categories: activities, tools, games, and industry training. **Activities** refer to single educational instructions that take place in one day for a limited amount of time, and have been split into single and multiple experiences as well (which refers to how many times an activity has been conducted). **Games** propose some sort of non-digital game (e.g., card games) to support or provide means for learning. With the same goal are **tools**, which represent software developed to specifically support activities within experiences. Finally, **industry training** accounts for training experiences that took place in industry or targeting industry professionals. This category is split into single and multiple experiences as well.

The following four subsections present the answer for each RQ previously defined.

3.1. RQ1. How has software architecture been taught?

Aiming to understand the curricular program of software architecture courses reported by the included studies, we investigated whether these courses were planned as a whole independent course, or were included as a sub-topic within a broader course. We found that 61.1% (22 studies) proposed an exclusive course to teach software architecture, while

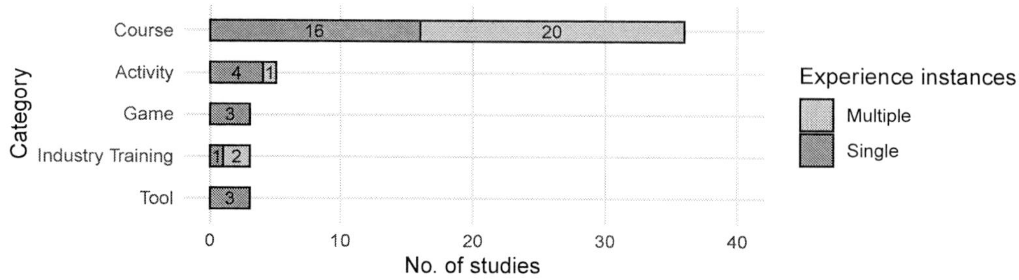

Figure 3. Classification of studies

22.2% (8 studies) included software architecture as a sub-topic of a software engineering or related courses. The remaining studies (16.7%) (6 studies) did not mention it explicitly. Regarding the course duration, we identified that 24% (12 studies) did not mention its duration, whereas 48% (24) had reported their duration ranging from five to 12 weeks. In particular, most courses (52.8% or 19 studies) had a duration of 12 weeks or more. Considering these numbers, we can say the duration of software architecture courses were not very different from other regular courses in computing programs (between three and six months).

Considering only those 36 studies that report an teaching experience during the courses, we also found that 44.4% of courses (16 studies) were proposed specifically as part of the curricula of graduate courses, and 30.6% (11) were defined at undergraduate studies level. Moreover, 11.1% (4 studies) were proposed for teaching software architecture in both undergraduate and graduate levels. Three courses (8.3%) involved industry professionals whereas two courses (5.6%) targeted graduate students and industry professionals. These percentages show some evidence that teaching software architecture for graduated students draw more attention than to others students. Moreover, most studies (2/3 or 24 studies) presented the number of students that enrolled in the courses. More specifically, 25% (9 studies) reported the course was lectured to class sizes smaller than 50 students, 27.8% (10) had between 51 and 100 students, 11.1% (4) had between 101 and 150 students, and 1 study had between 151 and 200 students. These numbers show that software architecture was taught to a good variety of class sizes regardless of the inherent challenges. The number of students attending a course, however, can be explained by external factors, such as those related to university characteristics or students' interests.

Considering the broad classification previously mentioned, for the category activity, five studies report diverse activities designed and applied to achieve particular learning objectives. An example is a 2-hour session in which students work as a team to extract architecturally significant requirements (S29, previously shown in Table 1). Other examples of activities are: S23, in which students of six universities distributed over different countries remotely participate in a computer-aided session to design the software architecture of a system. In S10 the *Writing to Learn* method is used for teaching the theory about software architecture tactics. Students individually wrote down every architectural tactic that they knew for achieving a list of quality attributes. In these studies, all activities had their outcomes assessed in different ways, such as student's feedback (gathered by means of oral evaluation (e.g., S10), questionnaires (e.g., S23) and controlled experiments (e.g., S29 and S49).

In the category tools, we found three software tools in three studies (S12, S28, and S34). These tools were developed specifically to assist software architecture courses. These tools are in fact GUI applications that provide functionality to manage and share architectural knowledge, or to visualize run-time metrics of a system under execution. Just one of the tools (S28) supports multi-user interaction, which is done by means of a mobile application installed in the student's phones to have access to a centralized repository.

Following the trend of adopting games in software engineering, three games were proposed for software architecture education (reported in S33, S37, and S45). Two are card games and one is an RPG (Role-Play Game), a classic and old game style in which players are assigned to a particular role for a given story. Both card games focus on the architectural decision process and can be fully played in sessions around one or two hours. The RPG focuses on ATAM (Architecture Tradeoff Analysis Method) for evaluating software architectures, relying on information from a case and from the ATAM specification for the assignment of roles to participants. This game was played in 1-hour sessions but it can take more time as in a real-world ATAM evaluation.

When it comes to industry experiences, we found three studies (S4, S6, and S47). Two of them (S6 and S47) report on long-term company programs for training professionals in the software architecture discipline. These programs have been improved over a considerable amount of years. The other study (S4) presents a particular training experience involving a development team of a large financial company facing problems with the integration of legacy systems.

We can observe that the RQ1 was able to provide us an overview of how software architecture has been taught along several years. We also observe that teaching has focused on different levels (undergraduate and graduate students, and professionals) with diverse course duration and formats (e.g., diverse activities) and using different means (e.g., games and tools). This panorama shows us that teaching software architecture (including its reporting through scientific studies) has been a concern and a diversity of initiatives have emerged dealing with different and complementary perspectives.

3.2. RQ2. What topics have been taught in the software architecture area?

We identified a broad variety of software architecture topics addressed by the studies included in our SMS. Figure 4 shows all topics and their frequency (one study sometimes considered more than one topic). Most of them address quality attributes, such as performance, portability, and fault tolerance. This finding was expected as the quality attributes refer to a basic requirement for addressing core architectural concepts, such as design and evaluation. The architectural evaluation method **ATAM** was the second most frequent topic in the list. ATAM is a well-known method for evaluating software architectures, and its conduction takes into account a number of core concepts associated with software architecture, such as quality attributes, trade-offs, scenarios, and decisions. So teaching ATAM can provide a learning opportunity for several topics at different cognitive levels.

Following ATAM, we found well-known topics, such as architectural design, styles, patterns, tactics, views, viewpoints, and trade-off analysis. Moreover, quality attribute scenarios and the method ADD (Attribute-Driven Design) were also considered in a relevant number of studies. Other important topics were also found but addressed in a few studies, as shown in Figure 4. Moreover other 30 different topics were addressed in

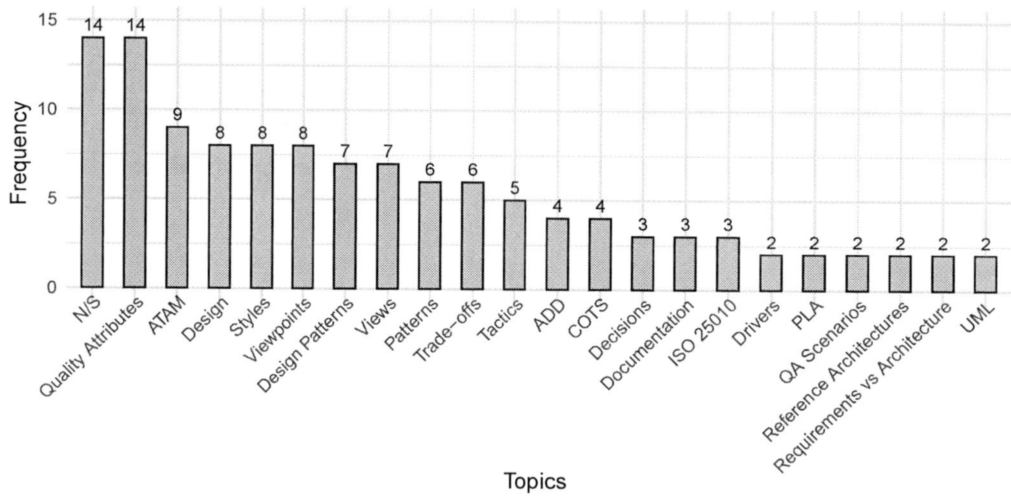

Figure 4. Topics addressed in two or more studies

single studies; they are listed in the external material.

The answer for this RQ shows us that diverse topics in the software architecture area have been taught. However, the two most taught ones are directly related to *quality attributes*, pointing out their relevance in the context of software architecture. We also observe that those topics were directly influenced by textbooks published on software architecture, including [Shaw and Garlan 1996, Bass et al. 2003, Van Vliet 2008, Clements et al. 2010, Rozanski and Woods 2011], as they have been used as reference in many experiences. In particular, an influential textbook is the second edition of "*Software Architecture in Practice*" [Bass et al. 2003].

3.3. RQ3. Which learning objectives have been considered in software architecture teaching?

In our SMS, we also investigated the studies regarding their learning objectives. An important finding is that most studies did not refer to any instrument, such as the original Bloom's Taxonomies [Bloom et al. 1956] or Revised Bloom's Taxonomies [Anderson et al. 2001], to support the definition of learning objectives (which refer to explicit formulations of what teachers intend students to learn [Anderson et al. 2001]). However, most studies (84% or 42 studies) stated explicitly one or more learning objectives, even when not employing the usual definition given by [Bloom et al. 1956] or [Anderson et al. 2001]. Only eight studies did not mention learning objectives (S2, S6, S8, S11, S17, S27, S28, and S50.

Aiming to better understand the studies included in our mapping regarding their learning objectives, we deeply analyzed and interpreted all 50 studies and classified their learning objectives within one (or more when pertinent) of the six cognitive levels (i.e., remember, understand, apply, analyze, evaluate, and create) [Anderson et al. 2001]. More specifically, **remember** refers to the capacity of retrieving relevant knowledge from long-term memory, **understand** refers to constructing meaning from instructional messages (e.g., oral, written, and graphic communication), **apply** refers to carrying out or using a procedure in a given situation, **analyze** refers to breaking material into smaller parts, determining how such parts relate to each other and to an overall structure, **evaluate** refers to making judgments based on criteria and standards, and **create** refers to forming a coherent or functional whole by putting elements together as well as to reorganizing elements to create a new pattern or structure [Anderson et al. 2001]. As result, we found that emphasis was given to four levels: understand, apply, evaluate, and create, while remember and analyze appear in just a few studies, as illustrated in Figure 5.

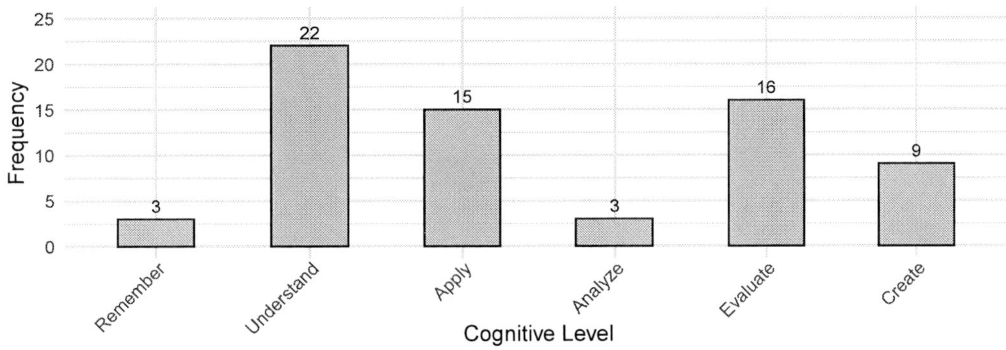

Figure 5. Bloom Cognitive Process Levels addressed in Learning Objectives

Understand appears in several learning objectives (22 studies) related to basic concepts, such as quality attributes, architectural styles, patterns, etc., whereas **apply** (15 studies) is related to the application of methods, such as ATAM, ADD, and trade-off analysis or even abstract concepts, such as styles and patterns. **Evaluate** (16 studies) is mostly present due to the high employment of ATAM for architecture evaluation. We understand, however, that applying ATAM does not imply the capability for evaluating software architectures as it possibly requires way more efforts to be developed for an individual. Lastly and perhaps the most expected level is **create**, which is surprisingly addressed in several (9) but not all studies, and is concerned with the definition (or creation) of an architecture for a specific or open-ended problem.

This RQ reveals that the cognitive process levels were considered in the learning objectives (reported by the studies) but more attention was paid in some of them. Remember is not less important than the other levels. In fact, it is required for solving more complex problems, applying methods or conducting procedures. However, remember as an ultimate goal for a software architecture course would not make much sense. On the other hand, analyze is a core cognitive process for many architectural activities but was not explicitly targeted in learning objectives of most studies.

3.4. RQ4. Which learning methods have been adopted to teach software architecture?

Different learning methods (which include resources and approaches) were adopted by one or more studies, as illustrated in Figure 6. In particular, learning methods refer to methodologies that put the students in a passive or active position towards the learning objective and uses physical, virtual or theoretical resources to support this process. However, it is important to highlight that most studies did not explicitly address learning methods/theories/practices or even the literature related to the education area, as expected in studies that deal with education.

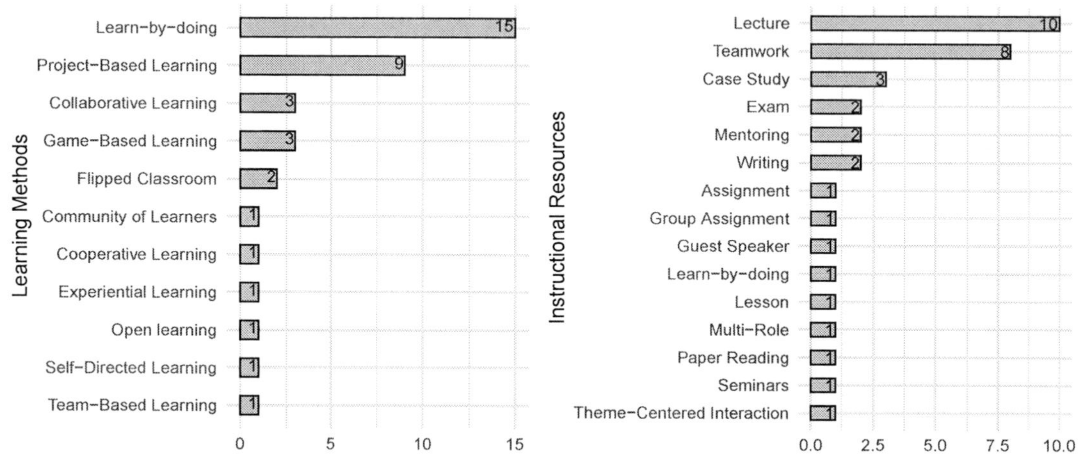

Figure 6. Learning Methods and Resources used by the Studies

We observe that traditional teaching methods that instructors have commonly used to present content to students (e.g., Learn-by-doing and Lecture) have been also adopted to introduce fundamental topics/concepts associated with software architecture. The most frequent approach is **Learn-by-doing** (found in 16 studies), in which learners perform one or a few architectural activities, such as design (reported for example in S7 and S18) or evaluation (e.g., S13 and S20), based on knowledge acquired before or during the actual experience. **Lectures** are also part of many experiences reported (10 studies).

Another interesting approach is **Project-Based Learning** that follows up as an way to mimic the software development in industry. We observe that projects with different sizes were used, from small projects (as those used in S3, S9, and S39) to large projects developed in partnership with software companies (as in S1, S2, and S4). Independently from the projects' size, studies reported advantages of this learning method, such as promoting soft skills by means of teamwork and developing good practices which can be later transferred to industry. In some cases, the projects are supposed to deliver value to real-world stakeholders. In this direction, **teamwork** is an approach that can involve different stakeholders and is frequent in our mapping (found in 8 studies).

There are also several other approaches but to a lesser extent in a few studies. For instance, **case studies** have been employed as a mean to promote learning based in real-world systems and architectures. In general, this approach was used in a later phase of the experiences to promote relevant discussions and show how software architecture concepts are present in real-world projects (as discussed in S3, S30, and S38). Another perspective is to ask learners to conduct case studies, gathering relevant information from real-world software projects, and documenting the findings (as discussed in S38).

Game-Based Learning was found in three studies (S33, S37, and S45) that describe the development and employment of games to support the learning process of specific topics, such as ATAM, Software Architecture Design Decision Making (SADDM) and Attribute-Driven Development (ADD). This approach has only been explored more recently and the games developed have usually followed a card style, requiring face-to-face interaction among players. **Collaborative Learning** also appears in a few studies

(S38, S50, and S23) and refers to practices where all students contribute somehow to achieve a particular goal such as the definition of an architecture or the writing of a book with knowledge acquired through the course. Many other interesting learning methods were explored to teach software architecture, and reported in one or two studies, as illustrated in Figure 6.

This RQ shows us that the studies employed a wide range of learning methods and resources but a great amount of methods were explored in just a few studies. The most recurring methods emphasize the practical nature of software architecture, as discussed in [Galster and Angelov 2016]. However, more experiences exploring other methods can help understand their benefits and drawbacks when they come to the software architecture education.

4. Discussion

This section presents the main findings of our work, some future research perspectives, and threats to validity.

The distribution of studies included in our SMS over the years made us believe that software architecture education&training is still an important topic to be investigated, even though the first study ever reported dates 1992. Considering the time span analyzed (1992-2020), 80% of studies were published after 2006 (i.e., the median year); this may indicate an increasing interest in the topic from the software architecture community, including researchers, events, and journals in the field. We also observe that even after many studies have been conducted and published, the difficulties and challenges of teaching and learning software architecture still remain.

Another finding worth highlighting is that the target audience of courses (or experiences teaching software architecture) was split into nearly two halves, undergraduate and graduate (Master/Ph.D.) students. In just one case, professionals were also part of the target audience. One may believe that teaching software architecture to graduate students would be more suitable as they are more likely to understand and learn the concepts due to prior experience with theory and practice. On the other hand, one may find it suitable to start teaching undergraduate students so they can understand software architecture concepts as early as possible, enabling them to develop capabilities to better deal with real-world software projects.

Regarding the software architecture topics addressed by the studies, an emphasis has been put on fundamental concepts associated with software architecture as well as well-known methods, like ATAM. However, new architectural styles and patterns, such as microservices and serverless, cloud-native architectures, IoT architectures, were not addressed, although they are trending in several domains and industry projects, so proper education regarding them can be very relevant. Other current relevant topics related to continuous architecting in the context of agile development have not been considered; only one study addresses it (S40). in particular, in this study, students conduct a project in which a continuous delivery pipeline is developed. Therefore, we can say that the teaching of software architecture should also encompass new trends, including those relevant to the current real-world project.

The most recurrent learning methods used to teach software architecture were those that we expected to find, following the nature of other engineering-related courses.

Less common and intuitive approaches were found as well, showing us a continuous interest in innovating the learning experiences. Teaching with games, for example, has only been addressed more recently, but its potential can improve the education of new generations of software architects/engineers. Collaborative approaches, which were explored in a few studies, can be attractive due to an increase of remote/hybrid job positions (most of them due to the pandemic). However, many supportive tools and platforms are still required to enable fast and suitable collaboration.

Our investigation was also interested in finding a correlation between the topics taught and the learning methods, but no relevant correlation was found in the studies. Therefore, it would be valuable for future investigation to find if such a correlation exists, aiming at success in the software architecture education experiences. We also intend to investigate whether the learning methods adopted are related to the instructional resources used and whether the learning objectives match the instructional activities employed.

4.1. Threats to Validity

The threats to the validity of our SMS are listed below along with the measures taken to mitigate their impact. We followed the classification proposed in [Wohlin et al. 2012], which is composed of four threat categories:

- **Internal validity**: During the data extraction from primary studies, in some cases, the authors did not clearly provide information with sufficient detail about one or more concepts, which may have led us to misconceptions. In this sense, some pieces of information had to be interpreted during our analysis. To minimize this threat, we assumed as less as possible and report the cases in which the information necessary to answer our research questions were not available or not clear to allow interpretation. In some cases the reviewers participated in consensus meetings to mitigate misinterpretation of some data extracted;
- **External validity**: In this category, another possible threat was the incorrect selection of primary studies according to the inclusion/exclusion criteria. To mitigate this threat, we had three reviewers participating during the selection process, ensuring all studies were reviewed by at least two of them. Consensus was achieved with the help of the third reviewer when necessary. Also, we created a detailed protocol, which was validated prior to the execution phase by members of our research group;
- **Construct validity**: Missing relevant studies was big a concern for this study. In some cases, a relevant study may not be found as a result of not having any of the search string terms in their title, abstract, or keywords. To mitigate this threat, we performed several interactions of a pilot test using the Scopus database and calibrated our search string analyzing carefully the results and confirming that the terms contained in our string were capable of finding a list of core studies we already knew prior to this study. Another construct validity threat might be our judgment concerning the selection of each study; hence, to minimize this threat, the decisions of inclusion or exclusion of studies were discussed by all researchers from this SMS; and
- **Conclusion validity**: Since some data had to be interpreted, there was a potential threat to the reliability of the results. To minimize this threat, we performed several brainstorming sessions to better define all elements of the SMS protocol (e.g., research questions, search string, databases, and selection strategy). Besides, the data extracted was

carefully reviewed by all authors of this work and any conflict was solved in a meeting using consensus.

5. Conclusion

The knowledge and experience in software architecture (which can be to some extent gathered via training courses) are sometimes essential for students who initiate in software companies. Hence, software architecture education is an important subject for curricula of computing-related courses. In this scenario, we provide an overview of the state of the art in the field of software architecture education through a deep analysis of 50 studies published from 1992. Different experiences were found, and we elicited important information, including the topics taught, the cognitive process categories (which are usually aimed by teachers and instructors when defining learning objectives), and the learning methods used. Such information can provide the current panorama of the field as well as the future directions to be followed to mature this field. Despite many years of research in the software architecture area, we can also conclude that education in this area still remains a challenging task.

Acknowledgment

This study was financed in part by CAPES - Brasil (Coordenação de Aperfeiçoamento de Pessoal de Nível Superior) (Finance Code 001 and Grant No.: 88882.328820/2019-01), National Council for Scientific and Technological (CNPq) (Grant No.: 313245/2021-5), and São Paulo Research Foundation (FAPESP) (Grant No.: 2015/24144-7).

References

Anderson, L., Krathwohl, D., and Bloom, B. (2001). *A taxonomy for learning, teaching, and assessing: a revision of Bloom's taxonomy of educational objectives*. Longman.

Angelov, S. and Beer, P. (2017). Designing and applying an approach to software architecting in agile projects in education. *Journal of Systems and Software*, 127:78–90.

Bass, L., Clements, P., and Kazman, R. (2003). *Software Architecture in Practice*. Addison-Wesley, 2nd edition.

Bass, L., Clements, P., and Kazman, R. (2021). *Software Architecture in Practice*. Addison-Wesley Professional, 4th edition.

Bloom, B., Engelhart, M., Furst, E., Hill, W., and Krathwohl, D. (1956). *Taxonomy of Educational Objectives: The Classification of Educational Goals: Handbook I Cognitive Domain*. David McKay Company, Inc.

Cervantes, H., Haziyev, S., Hrytsay, O., and Kazman, R. (2016). Smart Decisions: An Architectural Design Game. In *38th International Conference on Software Engineering (ICSE)*, pages 327–335.

Clements, P., Bachmann, F., Bass, L., Garlan, D., Ivers, J., Little, R., Merson, P., Nord, R., and Stafford, J. (2010). *Documenting Software Architectures: Views and Beyond*. Addison-Wesley Professional.

Deursen, A., Aniche, M., Aué, J., Slag, R., de Jong, M., Nederlof, A., and Bouwers, E. (2017). A Collaborative Approach to Teaching Software Architecture. In *ACM Technical Symposium on Computer Science Education (SIGCSE)*, pages 69–80.

Galster, M. and Angelov, S. (2016). What makes teaching software architecture difficult? In *38th International Conference on Software Engineering (ICSE)*, pages 356–359.

Garlan, D., Shaw, M., Okasaki, C., Scott, C., and Swonger, R. (1992). Experience with a course on architectures for software systems. In *6th SEI Conference on Software Engineering Education*, pages 23–43.

Lago, P., Cai, J., De Boer, R., Kruchten, P., and Verdecchia, R. (2019). DecidArch: Playing cards as software architects. In *52nd Hawaii International Conference on System Sciences (HICCS)*, pages 7815–7824.

Lago, P. and Vliet, H. (2005). Teaching a course on software architecture. In *18th Conference on Software Engineering Education and Training (CSEE&T)*, pages 35–42.

Mannisto, T., Savolainen, J., and Myllarniemi, V. (2008). Teaching Software Architecture Design. In *7th Working IEEE/IFIP Conference on Software Architecture (WICSA)*, pages 117–124.

Petersen, K., Vakkalanka, S., and Kuzniarz, L. (2015). Guidelines for conducting systematic mapping studies in software engineering: An update. *Information and Software Technology*, 64:1–18.

Rodrigues, C. and Werner, C. (2009). Software architecture teaching: A systematic review. In *9th IFIP World Conference on Computers in Education (WCCE)*, pages 1–10.

Rozanski, N. and Woods, E. (2011). *Software Systems Architecture: Working with Stakeholders Using Viewpoints and Perspectives*. Pearson Education.

Rupakheti, C. and Chenoweth, S. (2015). Teaching software architecture to undergraduate students: An experience report. In *37th International Conference on Software Engineering (ICSE)*, pages 445–454.

Shaw, M. and Clements, P. (2006). The Golden Age of Software Architecture: A Comprehensive Survey. Technical Report CMU-ISRI-06-101, Institute for Software Research International.

Shaw, M. and Garlan, D. (1996). *Software Architecture - Perspectives on an Emerging Discipline*. Prentice Hall.

Van Vliet, H. (2008). *Software engineering: principles and practice*, volume 13. John Wiley & Sons Hoboken, NJ.

Wohlin, C. (2014). Guidelines for snowballing in systematic literature studies and a replication in software engineering. In *18th International Conference on Evaluation and Assessment in Software Engineering (EASE)*, pages 1–10.

Wohlin, C., Runeson, P., Höst, M., Ohlsson, M., Regnell, B., and Wesslén, A. (2012). *Experimentation in Software Engineering*. Springer Berlin Heidelberg.

Automatic identification of web API change types in consumer applications

Graciela Vidal[1], Franco Herrera[2], Sandra Casas[3]

[1,2,3]Instituto de Tecnología Aplicada – Universidad Nacional de la Patagonia Austral
Campus Universitario – Piloto Lero Rivera S/Nro. Río Gallegos – Santa Cruz - Argentina

gvidal@uarg.unpa.edu.ar,
fherrera@uarg.unpa.edu.ar, scasas@uarg.unpa.edu.ar

Abstract. *The evolution of the web API affects consuming applications. Its modification and/or adaptation to be compatible with API changes is usually critical, since it is manual, and requires higher costs and efforts. Previous studies record types and/or patterns of changes in web APIs. However, proposals that help developers automatically identify changes in their applications are insufficient. This work proposes an approach that allows to automatically identify a set of types of changes. The strategy is to use a dictionary of consumed APIs and automatic checking for inconsistencies with the current selection of APIs included in the dictionary.*

Resumen *La evolución de las API web afecta a las aplicaciones consumidoras. Su modificación y/o adaptación para que sea compatible con los cambios de las APIs suele ser crítica, ya que es manual, y requiere mayores costes y esfuerzos. Estudios previos registran tipos y/o patrones de cambios en APIs web. Sin embargo, las propuestas que ayuden a los desarrolladores a identificar automáticamente cambios en sus aplicaciones son insuficientes. Este trabajo propone un enfoque que permite identificar automáticamente un conjunto de tipos de cambios. La estrategia consiste en utilizar un diccionario de APIs consumidas y la verificación automática de inconsistencias con la especificación actual de las APIs incluidas en el diccionario.*

1. Introducción

Las APIs (Interfaz de Programación de Aplicaciones) permiten reutilizar componentes de software en el contexto del desarrollo de software y así mejorar la productividad [Robbes y otros, 2019]. Una API puede verse como un contrato entre un proveedor y un consumidor de una funcionalidad dada [Maalej y Robillar, 2013]. Las APIs se han convertido en grandes aliadas del desarrollo de software moderno, tanto de aplicaciones móviles como aplicaciones web.

La nueva generación de APIs, denominadas API de servicios web, ofrecen un enfoque sistemático y extensible, a diferencia de las APIs vinculadas estáticamente o locales [Curbera y otros, 2002][Vinoski, 2008]. En particular las APIs web facilitan el intercambio de datos inter e intra organizacionales disponibles a través de endpoints específicos [Dekel y Herbsleb, 2009]. Los catálogos como API Harmony, PublicAPI o

ProgrammableWeb enumeran miles de APIs web y dan cuenta de la proliferación de este tipo de recursos.

Las APIs web evolucionan y cambian por diversos motivos tales como proporcionar nueva funcionalidad, solucionar problemas de seguridad, aumentar la facilidad de uso de la API a los consumidores, etc. En [Stocker y Zimmermann , 2021] se proporcionan diversas causas que impulsan a los proveedores de APIs web a realizar cambios. La cooperación entre los proveedores y los consumidores de APIs idealmente consistiría en que los proveedores desarrollan APIs estables, proporcionando documentación detallada y útil para que los consumidores de la API la utilicen sin dificultad, y que además las mejoras adicionales de la API no afecten el funcionamiento de las aplicaciones. No obstante, esto no siempre sucede, puesto que ante la evolución de las APIs se suelen presentar incompatibilidades con las aplicaciones consumidoras, produciendo generalmente impactos negativos [R. Koçi y otros, 2019][Espinha y otros, 2014][Dig y Johnson, 2006][Li y otros, 2013].

Se ha denominado co-evolución [Eilertsen y Bagge, 2018] cuando el software del cliente debe modificarse para mantenerse compatible con los cambios de las APIs. En el caso de APIs web, puede ser crítico, en tanto las aplicaciones consumidoras pueden perder la robustez, si la evolución tiene efectos conocidos como "breaking changes" (el código del cliente se "rompe", no compila, o se ejecuta erróneamente) y requiere que se reescriba el código correspondiente [Jezek y Dietrich, 2017][Xavier y otros, 2017]. Los cambios de metadatos o cambios sintácticos y varios niveles de cambios semánticos, cuando suceden, pueden requerir un esfuerzo significativo de reparación e incluso descubrimiento a partir del fallo. Esto se ve agravado en el contexto de APIs, los componentes de software se caracterizan por presentar ciclos de lanzamiento independientes. Según [Brito y otros, 2020] los "breaking changes" tienen impactos importantes en las apps clientes. Otros inconvenientes para los desarrolladores de app consumidoras se presentan, como el hecho de que el mecanismo de informar la obsolescencia (deprecado) de un elemento de la API, no es una práctica habitual en el contexto de APIs web, según los estudios empíricos de [Yasmin y otros, 2020].

Existen estudios que registran tipos y/o patrones de cambios de las APIs web [R. Koçi y otros, 2019] [Sohan y otros, 2015][Espinha y otros, 2015], sin embargo, aún son insuficientes las propuestas que ayuden a los desarrolladores de las aplicaciones consumidoras de APIs web a identificar automáticamente los cambios en relación directa a las aplicaciones. Es notable que la evolución de las APIs locales (estáticas) cuenta con diversas herramientas que asisten con diferentes niveles de automatización al mantenimiento (la identificación, migración, refactorización de los cambios), no obstante, en el ámbito de las APIs web, estas tareas continúan siendo manuales [Lamothe y otros, 2021].

En esta dirección, este trabajo propone un enfoque que permite identificar automáticamente un conjunto de tipos de cambios que afectan a una aplicación consumidora (web o móvil). La estrategia consiste en usar un diccionario de las APIs consumidas (DAC) y un proceso que automáticamente verifica incompatibilidades y discordancias con la OAS (OpenAPI Specification) vigente de las APIs incluidas en el diccionario.

Este trabajo está estructurado de la siguiente manera, en la Sección II se describe la metodología, en la Sección III se brindan conceptos sobre evolución y tipos de cambio en la APIs web, en la Sección IV se presenta la propuesta para identificar cambios en aplicaciones consumidoras, en la Sección V se desarrollan ejemplos de uso, en la Sección VI se presentan los trabajos relacionados, en la Sección VII se exponen las limitaciones de la propuesta, finalmente en la Sección VIII se presentan las conclusiones.

2. Metodología

En este trabajo se aplicó el enfoque denominado Design Science Research (DSR) [Peffers y otros, 2007]. Generalmente se utiliza en investigaciones relacionadas con la ingeniería, la informática y los sistemas de información. DSR propone la producción de artefactos, como instancias, construcciones, modelos o métodos. La Fig. 1 presenta los pasos que se han seguido en este estudio.

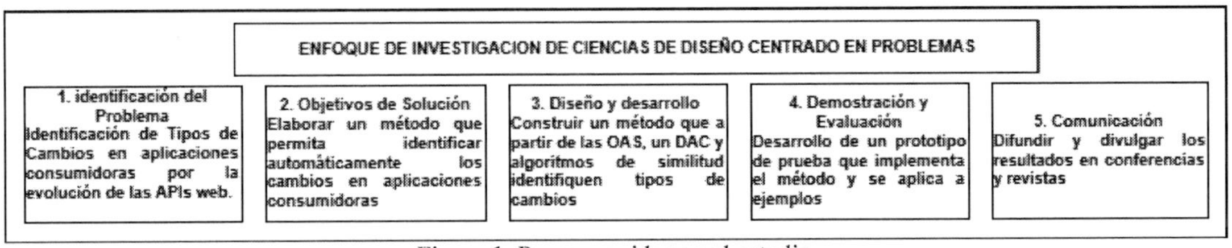

Figura 1. Pasos seguidos en el estudio.

El primer paso (1) fue la identificación del problema para el que se busca una solución. El segundo paso (2) fue establecer los objetivos de una solución inferida del problema identificado que ayudó a determinar los requisitos del marco. El tercer paso (3) fue el diseño y desarrollo del artefacto, este consiste en la definición de un diccionario de APIs web consumidas (DAC), la selección de tipos de cambios que se pretenden identificar y el proceso de verificación automática de cambios. El DAC se implementa en JSON. Los cambios resultan ser un subconjunto que ha sido reportado por estudios de otros autores. La verificación se realiza con la OAS, y es de carácter sintáctica. El cuarto paso (4) se refiere a la evaluación, para lo cual se desarrolló un prototipo de herramienta que da soporte a los artefactos presentados en el paso anterior y mediante algunos ejemplos muestra la factibilidad de la propuesta.

3. Evolución y Tipos de Cambios en APIs web

Durante el ciclo de vida las APIs experimentan iteraciones producto de su evolución, en cada fase del ciclo, los proveedores realizan modificaciones, lo que a veces hace necesario el lanzamiento de nuevas versiones [R. Koçi y otros, 2019]. Esto significa que las aplicaciones consumidoras también deben adaptarse (co-evolución) a estos cambios para continuar funcionando correctamente.

En contextos de APIs vinculadas estáticamente, algunos autores afirman que pueden surgir numerosos cambios, sin embargo, los consumidores pueden elegir no migrar a la nueva versión de la API. Cuando se trata de la evolución de una API web esto no es posible y los desarrolladores deben migrar y adaptarse a los cambios [R. Koçi y otros, 2019] [Espinha y otros, 2015].

Diversos tipos de cambios, producto de la evolución de las APIs web han sido reportados, los cuales están relacionados a diferentes componentes de una API. En la Tabla 1, se mencionan algunos que se han informado en estudios recientes, según el componente de la API al que afectan.

Tabla 1: Tipos de cambios agrupados por componente

Endpoints
▪ Modificación de endpoints - [R. Koçi y otros, 2019] ▪ Cambios en los métodos de solicitud (GET,POST,DELETE) - [R. Koçi y otros, 2019] ▪ Cambios en valores por defecto de parámetros - [Li y otros, 2013] ▪ Cambios en encabezados HTTP - [Sohan y otros, 2015] ▪ Cambio de home de API - [Sohan y otros, 2015]
Operaciones
▪ Remoción de operación /método (GET, POST, DELETE) - [Li y otros, 2013] [Fokaefs y otros, 2011] [Sohan y otros, 2015] ▪ Renombrar método - [Li y otros, 2013] [Sohan y otros, 2015] ▪ Combinación de métodos - [Li y otros, 2013] ▪ Separación de métodos - [Li y otros, 2013] ▪ Método request no soportado - [Li y otros, 2013] ▪ Cambio de post condiciones - [Sohan y otros, 2015]
Parámetros
▪ Cambios en tipo de parámetro - [Li y otros, 2013] [Espinha y otros, 2015] ▪ Modificación de parámetros - [R. Koçi y otros, 2019] ▪ Renombrar parámetros - [Li y otros, 2013] [Sohan y otros, 2015] ▪ Cambio en el formato del parámetro - [Li y otros, 2013] ▪ Cambio en los valores límites de los parámetros - [Li y otros, 2013] ▪ Cambios en los tipos de las entradas - [Fokaefs y otros, 2011] ▪ Remover parámetro - [Li y otros, 2013] [Sohan y otros, 2015] ▪ Agregar atributos en los parámetros - [Fokaefs y otros, 2011]
Campos
▪ Remoción de campos - [Sohan y otros, 2015] [Espinha y otros, 2015] ▪ Cambio en el valor de retorno - [Li y otros, 2013] ▪ Cambio en tags de XML - [Li y otros, 2013] ▪ Renombrar campos - [Sohan y otros, 2015] ▪ Cambios en los tipos de salida - [Fokaefs y otros, 2011]
Seguridad
▪ Cambios en niveles de autoridad - [R. Koçi y otros, 2019] ▪ Restricciones de acceso a la api - [Li y otros, 2013] ▪ Cambio en los protocolos de autorización - [Sohan y otros, 2015] ▪ Cambio de autenticación [Sohan y otros, 2015]
Errores
▪ Cambio en condiciones de error - [Sohan y otros, 2015]
Estructura - Formato
▪ Cambiar de formato de la respuesta (XML por JSON) - [Li y otros, 2013] ▪ Modificar la jerarquía (ubicación) de un componente en la respuesta - [Li y otros, 2013]

La evolución de las APIs web ocasiona diferentes tipos de cambios, los cuales afectarán a los consumidores de diferentes formas. Acciones como identificar el tipo de cambio, examinar el código de las aplicaciones para analizar el impacto que el cambio provoca y finalmente realizar las modificaciones para adaptarse a la nueva versión, son todas tareas que requieren tiempo y esfuerzo extra y por lo tanto son costosas.

4. Identificación de cambios en APIs web en aplicaciones consumidoras

La propuesta consiste en verificar automáticamente si las APIs web consumidas por una determinada aplicación, han experimentado un cambio y ofrecer información que reporte y proporcione detalles del mismo. El eje que fundamenta la estrategia, reside en que cuando una API web evoluciona, los cambios se reflejan en la especificación OAS. Así una nueva versión de la OAS se genera, lo cual está denotado en la misma descripción. Para realizar el proceso de identificación, se utiliza un artefacto que se denomina Diccionario de APIs web Consumidas (DAC) y la/s OAS vigentes (al momento de la verificación). A continuación, se presenta el DAC, los tipos de cambio a verificar y el proceso de verificación.

Diccionario de APIs web consumidoras

El registro de las APIs web consumidas por una aplicación en un diccionario sirve de documentación a las aplicaciones consumidoras y además permite identificar inconsistencias, incompatibilidades y cambios en las APIs. Este artefacto, debe ser creado durante el proceso de desarrollo de aplicaciones, comprende una estructura general para todas las aplicaciones. Cada aplicación dispondrá de su propio diccionario, el cual incluirá todas las APIs consumidas.

La información que describe la aplicación en el DAC, también en formato JSON, se agrupa en tres objetos: info, server y apis. El objeto info describe datos generales tales como title y description, el objeto servers indica el acceso a la página principal del sitio y apis es un vector que contiene las APIs web consumidas, ya que puede utilizar *n* APIs (n>=1). Los elementos definidos para cada API son: name, version, servers, paths (endPoints) y components. Los objetos paths y components definen la información más importante de cada API utilizada, en paths se especifican las operaciones (GET, POST, DELETE, etc.), se incluyen parameters con sus atributos (in, name, type) de cada uno de ellos. En components se definen schemas y security schema, el objeto schemas permite definir datos de entrada y salida como también sus propiedades (required, style, type, etc.) en este caso se definen campos esperados en response. Estos últimos representan los campos que el usuario utiliza de la API, de no contar con estos datos la aplicación web no estaría funcionando correctamente. En el objeto security schema se define el tipo de autenticación que requiere la API, la cual puede tomar los valores APIkey o auth2.

En la Fig. 2 se presenta la estructura del DAC para la aplicación web Kitelife[1]. El objeto info incluye la siguiente información, el nombre de la aplicación que consume la API, una breve descripción del sitio y además el número de versión de la aplicación. En este caso, se define un sitio web que permite buscar el lugar apropiado para hacer

[1] https://clayjuneau.com/Kiteflite/

volar una cometa dependiendo de las condiciones climáticas, se trata de la versión 1.0 de la aplicación.

Fig.2 Estructura del DAC del sitio web Kiteflite

En el objeto servers se especifica la url de acceso a la aplicación. En el objeto apis se detallan los elementos utilizados de cada API consumida. La API utilizada es Weather API y su es versión 1.0. De cada API utilizada se registra la siguiente información: name, version y servers de acceso, los paths y components. En este DAC se define un path, luego se refiere a dos schemas y finalmente los datos de seguridad, precisamente es el tipo de autenticación requerido para acceder a la Weather API versión 1.0.

Tipos de cambios

La Tabla 2 presenta los siete tipos de cambios que este estudio aborda.

Tabla 2. Tipos de cambios y elementos OAS asociados

Tipo de Cambio	Elemento OAS
Modificación de endPoint	Elemento path
Cambio de Tipo de Propiedad	Elemento type del objeto properties
Remoción de Parámetro	Propiedad name del objeto parameter
Cambio de esquema	Propiedad name del objeto Schema
Cambio de Tipo de Dato de Parámetro	Propiedad type del objeto parameter
Cambio de Tipo de Autenticación	Propiedad type del objeto Schema Security
Modificación de Condición de Parámetro	Propiedad required del objeto parameter

Para cada uno, además se indica el elemento de la OAS que se puede analizar para identificar la ocurrencia del evento. Los mismos son un subconjunto de los mencionados en la Sección 3 y afectan a distintos elementos como los parámetros, los endPoints, componentes tales como esquemas (datos de entrada y salida) y esquemas de seguridad (autenticación).

Para verificar cada tipo de cambio se accede a cada objeto y luego a sus propiedades. Si alguna de las propiedades o sus valores definidos en el DAC son modificados o removidos de la OAS dejan de ser compatibles y significa que se produjo un tipo de cambio.

Proceso de verificación de cambios

El objetivo de este proceso es identificar automáticamente si se han producido cambios y proporcionar información sobre tales inconsistencias. En esta instancia la verificación es capaz de identificar los siete tipos de cambios antes descriptos.

El proceso requiere dos entradas, el DAC y la última versión de la especificación OAS, sobre la cual se realizará el análisis, ambos documentos en formato JSON. Luego se debe acceder a cada uno de los elementos definidos en el DAC y se lo compara con su equivalente en la OAS. Cada vez que encuentra una desigualdad, informa el tipo de cambio, el objeto sobre el cual se produce y de ser posible, los nuevos valores. En Listado 1 se describe el algoritmo que realiza el análisis de los parámetros y endPoints.

```
Entrada: dac(app) and OAS(x)
Salida : Cambio : reporte / set?

FOR EACH elemento in dac(app) where apis.api.name = x
|  FOR EACH dac.path
|  |  IF dac.apis.api.paths !found() in x
|  |     Cambio ← Cambio + Modificacion Punto Final
|  |  ELSE
|  |  |  FOR EACH dac.apis.api.paths.parameters
|  |  |  |  IF dac.apis.api.paths.parameters.name !found() in x
|  |  |  |     Cambio← Cambio + Remocion de Parametro (name)
|  |  |  |  ELSE
|  |  |  |  |  IF dac.apis.api.paths.parameters.name.type < > en x
|  |  |  |  |     Cambio← Cambio + Cambio de tipo de dato de parametro (name)
|  |  |  |  |  ELSE
|  |  |  |  |  |  IF dac.apis.api.paths.operationId.parameters.requerid < > en x
|  |  |  |  |  |     Cambio← Cambio + Cambio de condicion de parametro (name)
|  |  |  |  |  |  endIf
|  |  |  |  |  endIf
|  |  |  |  endIf
|  |  |  endForeach
|  |  endIf
|  endForeach
```

Listado 1. Algoritmo que identifica cambios en los endPoints y parámetros.

De manera similar, se han definido dos algoritmos que analizan los schemas y aspectos de seguridad.

5. Ejemplos de Uso

El proceso de verificación de cambios fue implementado en un prototipo desarrollado en Python y Django. El prototipo permite seleccionar el DAC y la OAS de la API web sobre la cual se realiza la verificación.

En la Fig.3 se presenta el prototipo, sobre la imagen a la izquierda, en primer lugar (a) se debe seleccionar el archivo correspondiente al diccionario de la aplicación consumidora, luego (b) se debe seleccionar la API web sobre la cual se realizará el proceso. A la derecha de la imagen se presentan los resultados luego de la ejecución del proceso de verificación. En este caso, aplicado al diccionario denominado artefactoClima3.json y a la OAS de la API Weather versión 1.0. Se encontraron cuatro cambios en la OAS Weather: (a) modificación de condición de parámetro, se trata del parámetro city del endPoints /weather/get, en el cual se modificó la condición required, el nuevo valor es true, (b) remoción de parámetro, el parámetro state perteneciente al endPoints /weather no se encontró disponible, ahora se denomina states, (c) modificación de tipo de dato propiedad, el tipo de dato de la propiedad lon del esquema inline_response_200 fue modificada a string, (d) cambio de tipo de autenticación, se registró cambio en el schema de seguridad, el tipo de autenticación ahora es api_key.

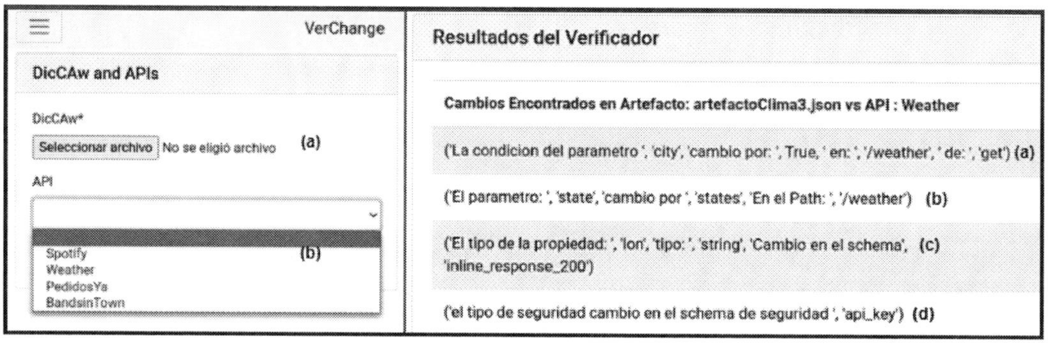

Fig.3 Prototipo de verificación y resultados

A continuación, se describen dos de los tipos de cambio identificados:

Modificación en condición de parámetro: Primero se analiza la coincidencia del nombre de la API y luego del endPoint, en este caso es "/weather". Luego se verificaron los parámetros, primero el atributo *name*, cuyo valor es "city", el cual se encontraba en la especificación, es decir que no existían anomalías hasta ese punto. Luego se analizaron las demás propiedades de este parámetro, en el caso de *required* que en el DAC está definido "false", y en la OAS fue modificado a "true". Entonces el verificador informó el tipo de cambio y el nuevo valor del campo. Con esta información el desarrollador es capaz de tomar decisiones respecto a las actualizaciones necesarias para que la aplicación consumidora continúe siendo compatible con la API utilizada. En Fig.4 se muestran las estructuras analizadas, (a) corresponde a la OAS vigente, (b) es el DAC y en (c) se presentan los resultados obtenidos por el prototipo.

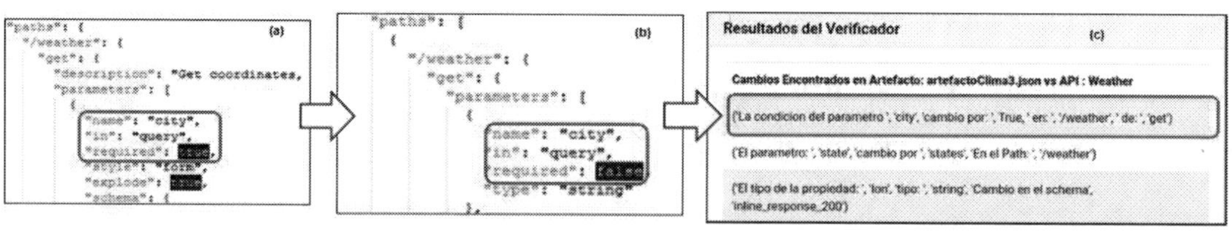

Fig.4 . Identificación del cambio: modificación de condición de parámetro

Remoción de parámetros: nuevamente el proceso se inició verificando el nombre de la API y los endPoints, luego se accedió a los parámetros definidos para el mismo, para cada uno de ellos se buscó su equivalente en la especificación OAS verificando el atributo *name*. Cada parámetro fue verificado sobre la OAS, en este caso el *name* del parámetro definido en el diccionario es "state". El mismo no se encontraba en la especificación, por lo tanto, se informó el tipo de cambio al desarrollador. En la Fig.5 se presentan las especificaciones analizadas y los resultados obtenidos por el verificador.

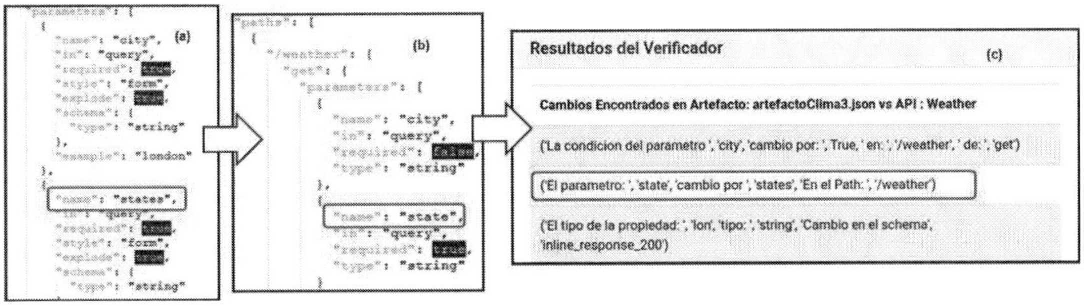

Fig.5. Identificación del cambio: remoción de parámetro

6. Trabajos Relacionados

En [Lamothe y otros, 2021] se presenta una revisión sistemática de la literatura (RSL) referente a la evolución de las APIs, que analiza 369 artículos en el periodo 1994-2020, con el objetivo de examinar la evolución del tema e identificar los desafíos de investigación. El estudio demuestra claramente que una mayor cantidad de trabajos de investigación en APIs locales, y particularmente en relación a las APIs de Java y Android. En consecuencia, existen mayores evidencias y soluciones a problemas de este nicho, se reportan numerosas herramientas, técnicas, recomendaciones con los objetivos de documentación, migración, adaptación, deprecación, etc. La evolución y cambios de APIs locales por su naturaleza estática orientan a soluciones y enfoques que no son aplicables al mismo fenómeno, pero si en el contexto de APIs web. La RSL destaca como uno de los desafíos actuales y futuros, la propuesta de herramientas que ayuden a los desarrolladores que usan APIs web a manejar la evolución, ya que se ha realizado escaso esfuerzo en este tema [Wittern, 2018].

En [Stocker y Zimmermann, 2021], se presenta una encuesta a proveedores de APIs web, cuyo objetivo fue comprender las razones que obligan a los arquitectos de software y desarrolladores de API a cambiar una API y también las consecuencias de dichos cambios. Los autores llegan a las siguientes conclusiones: a) las modificaciones a las API suelen ser causadas principalmente por cambios en los requisitos funcionales, impulsados por el cliente o el proveedor, y menos por problemas no funcionales. b) en cuanto al segundo factor de cambios (no funcionales) se indicó que ocurren problemas de calidad y también dan como resultado cambios en la API. La usabilidad y mantenibilidad, seguidos de rendimiento y escalabilidad, son los atributos de calidad que más cambios impulsan. c) en cuanto a las tácticas de cambio y mitigación que los proveedores aplican al realizar los cambios en las APIs que ofrecen, estas son, actualizar la especificación o el código, actualizar la documentación de la API, ajustan el número de versión de la API, y ajustar los clientes de la API. Luego los autores proponen un catálogo de refactoring candidatos pero para desarrolladores de APIs.

El estudio de [R. Koçi y otros, 2019] está orientado a la identificación y clasificación de tipos de cambios, que se producen en una API e investigan como estos cambios se reflejan en distintos artefactos tales como la documentación, notas de versión, seguimiento de problemas, y los registros de uso de APIs. El análisis de cada paso del cambio, su implementación y el impacto sobre los consumidores permite una amplia visión de la evolución de la API. Para esto, proponen un framework de clasificación de cambios que pueden ocurrir en una API y las causas que los originan. El Framework se limita a la identificación y clasificación de los cambios. Principalmente el trabajo se enfoca en cómo se reflejan los cambios y en qué medida son documentados.

En [Li y otros, 2013] presentan un estudio empírico sobre la evolución de las APIs web, como resultado presentan un conjunto de patrones de cambio. Estos patrones y su frecuencia son presentados a los desarrolladores como información de referencia sobre los cambios que pueden descubrir. Afirman que es posible que los patrones sirvan en un proceso de migración automatizado en un futuro. Por último, presentan un análisis comparativo con APIs locales.

En [Sohan y otros, 2015] se presenta un conjunto de recomendaciones para profesionales e investigadores basadas en un caso de estudio realizado sobre un conjunto de APIs. El mismo consiste en un esquema de codificación de tipos de cambios, para definir patrones de cambio, además identificaron las formas de documentar y comunicar los cambios. Si bien las recomendaciones se ajustan a diversas aplicaciones web que utilizan APIs, no ofrecen automaticidad que asista a los consumidores de APIs en el proceso de identificar y tratar los cambios ocasionados por la evolución.

En [Espinha y otros, 2015] sostienen que las APIs web son necesarias en el desarrollo de software moderno y al mismo tiempo reconocen que su evolución es inevitable. Por lo cual, también es necesaria la actualización del software para que siga siendo compatible con la API web que utiliza. Presentan un estudio sobre la reacción de aplicaciones móviles, ante cambios o fallas en una API web utilizadas. La experiencia sobre 48 aplicaciones y la simulación de mutaciones en API web, proporciona información sobre los enfoques de control de versiones, además realizaron entrevistas a desarrolladores.

En [Fokaefs y otros, 2011] se presenta un trabajo empírico sobre la evolución de servicios web, para esto utilizó las descripciones WSDL. Luego un algoritmo fue diseñado para identificar cambios sobre estos documentos. Finalmente, con los resultados se analizan los cambios que pueden ocurrir entre versiones de diferentes servicios, esto permite discutir los posibles efectos en el mantenimiento de estos sistemas. A diferencia de nuestro trabajo, se enfoca en especificaciones de servicios web.

Analizar los cambios y evolución de software ayuda al desarrollador en la tarea de mantenimiento de sistemas, en [Chaturvedi y otros, 2021] se presenta un trabajo en el cual aplicaron minería de cambios y de evolución a sistemas distribuidos. El mismo se enfoca en descubrir cambios provocados por la evolución de servicios. Para esto utilizan como entradas dos versiones de especificaciones de servicios, posteriormente aplican la minería de cambios. Luego proponen cuatro métricas de evolución del sistema. Ambos son la base de un modelo de análisis de evolución, además crearon una herramienta inteligente denominada gestión automática de cambios de servicios web. Las métricas pueden ser útiles en el mantenimiento de versiones y el desarrollo de futuras versiones. También pueden ayudar al consumidor a analizar funcionalidades. Si bien se trata de un proceso que analiza dos especificaciones como entrada, la diferencia con este trabajo se encuentra en que es aplicada a especificaciones de servicios web y en esta propuesta se utiliza una OAS y un DAC, este último es un documento técnico personalizado y definido por el desarrollador. El mismo, no solamente documenta a la aplicación, sino que también asiste en un paso importante en la identificación automática de los cambios en las APIs web.

Diversos tipos de fallas que afectan a la producción de las aplicaciones que consumen APIs web, son analizadas por [Aué y otros, 2018] El trabajo identifica 11 causas generales de fallos, las cuales se pueden atribuir principalmente a los datos de solicitud no válidos o faltantes. Consideramos que algunos de estos tipos de fallos también podrían estar relacionados a cambios por evolución de las APIs web. Si los cambios de las APIs web se producen de forma brusca y no informada o documentada, solicitudes que eran válidas dejarán de serlo.

El estudio empírico de [Yasmin y otros, 2020] revela que más del 80% de los cambios que producen "breaking changes" no fueron informados en las versiones de OAS anteriores mediante el uso del protocolo "deprecar-remover", aplicado para anunciar la futura obsolescencia de elementos. En consecuencia, los desarrolladores no tienen la oportunidad de adaptar y/o migrar las aplicaciones consumidoras de manera anticipada y evitar los impactos. Por ello, propuestas como la que nuestro trabajo presenta resultan necesarias.

En [Tashtoush y otros, 2019][Wittern y otros, 2017][SungGyeong y otros, 2014] se presentan herramientas que usando alguna especificación (OpenApi/Swagger o Web IDL), verifican la consistencia y coherencia de las peticiones o solicitudes codificadas en las aplicaciones consumidoras. Las herramientas son específicas para aplicaciones basadas en tecnologías Ajax, Jquery y Javascript. Estas herramientas están dirigidas a identificar errores por solicitudes inválidas, ocasionados principalmente por documentación incompleta de las APIs, como los enumerados por [Aué y otros, 2018]. También pueden ser útiles para identificar algunos de los errores de ejecución causados por la evolución de las APIs, como ser los que implican cambios y modificaciones en los endPoints.

Como se abordó en la Sección 3, existen diversos estudios empíricos, que han identificado y caracterizado los tipos de cambios producto de la evolución de las APIS web. Estos trabajos [Stocker y Zimmermann, 2021][R. Koçi y otros, 2019][Li y otros, 2013][Sohan y otros, 2015][Espinha y otros, 2015][Fokaefs y otros, 2011] sirven para catalogar, clasificar y analizar los cambios, pero en ninguno de ellos se presentan propuestas de identificación, asistencia o manejo destinada a los desarrollares de aplicaciones consumidoras de APIs web.

7. Amenazas a la validez y limitaciones

En cuanto a la validez interna, nuestra propuesta requiere de las OAS de las APIs web. Mientras las OAS a utilizar por el verificador estén correctamente elaboradas y actualizadas, el proceso de verificación y el DAC identificarán los cambios definidos. En el caso de OAS incompletas, con errores o desactualizadas, el verificador podría no detectar los cambios y/o informar cambios incorrectos. En cuanto a la validez externa, dado que el proceso de verificación solo requiere de entradas documentos JSON (OAS y DAC) nuestra propuesta es independiente de todo detalle de implementación (lenguajes de programación, frameworks, sistemas operativos, etc.) de las aplicaciones consumidoras. Por otro lado, para aquellas APIs web cuyas especificaciones respondan a otros esquemas (WADL, API Blueprint, RAML), existen diversos procesos automáticos de conversión entre especificaciones, lo cual amplia la aplicación de nuestro enfoque.

Observamos algunas limitaciones en nuestra propuesta. Como se dijo anteriormente es válida para aplicaciones que utilicen APIs web cuya especificación se encuentre disponible en formato OAS. Además, requiere que el desarrollador analice y registre en el DAC, por un lado, los datos de la aplicación consumidora y además los elementos que utiliza de cada una de las APIs web. Esto demandará tiempo y esfuerzo inicialmente, sin embargo, es posible compensarlo en el futuro, en la tarea de descubrimiento de cambios en las APIs una vez que la aplicación está en línea.

8. Conclusiones

Este trabajo presentó un enfoque para identificar un conjunto de cambios que ocurren frecuentemente en APIs web en aplicaciones consumidoras. La propuesta consiste en un Diccionario de Aplicaciones Consumidoras de APIs y un proceso que automáticamente identifica siete tipos de cambios de APIs web. El DAC y la OAS más reciente de una API web seleccionada, representan las entradas del proceso. El mismo analiza ambos archivos y en caso de encontrar diferencias informa el tipo de cambio y los elementos que han sido modificados o ya no están disponibles, como así también los nuevos valores, cuando es posible.

El DAC también sirve para documentar a la aplicación web consumidora de manera personalizada, es definido por el desarrollador e incluye únicamente la información requerida por la aplicación. Además, puede ser utilizado para otros procesos o integrarse a herramientas en el proceso de desarrollo.

El DAC es compatible con el estándar OpenAPI, debido a que su contenido posee una estructura equivalente a OAS, pero incluye únicamente los campos necesarios para describir la aplicación consumidora. Esto significa que el diccionario es comprendido fácilmente por los desarrolladores familiarizados con OAS.

El trabajo continúa con la extensión del diccionario ya sea para incorporar nueva información de la aplicación, como así también para adaptar su estructura a nuevos campos en las nuevas versiones de OpenAPI. No se descarta trabajar en la automatización de la creación del diccionario, lo cual representaría una tarea menos para el desarrollador. La extensión del diccionario posibilitará ampliar las capacidades del verificador, es decir aumentar la cantidad y la naturaleza de los tipos de cambios a identificar.

Los tipos de cambios han sido abordados por estudios previos, sin embargo, escasos están orientados a APIs web, nuestro trabajo se enfoca específicamente sobre aplicaciones web consumidoras de APIs web.

Referencias

Aué, J., Aniche, M., Lobbezoo, M., & van Deursen, A. (2018). "An Exploratory Study on Faults in Web API Integration in a Large-Scale Payment Company". In ICSE-SEIP '18: 40th International Conference on Software Engineering: Software

Engineering in Practice Track (pp. 13-22). Association for Computing Machinery (ACM). https://doi.org/10.1145/3183519.3183537

Brito A., Valente M.T, Xavier L. (2020) "You broke my code: understanding the motivations for breaking changes in APIs," Empirical Software Engineering 25, 1458–1492.

Chaturvedi, A. Tiwari A., Binkley D. and Chaturvedi S.(2021) "Service Evolution Analytics: Change and Evolution Mining of a Distributed System," in *IEEE Transactions on Engineering Management*, vol. 68, no. 1, pp. 137-148. doi: 10.1109/TEM.2020.2987641.

Curbera F., Duftler M., Khalaf R., Nagy W., Mukhi N., and Weerawarana S.. (2002) "Unraveling the web services web: an introduction to SOAP, WSDL, and UDDI," Internet Computing, vol. 6, no. 2, pp. 86–93, 2002.

Dekel U. and Herbsleb J.D. (2009) "Reading the documentation of invoked API functions in program comprehension" ICPC'09, pp. 168–177.

Dig D. and Johnson R.E (2006) "How do APIs evolve? A story of refactoring." In Journal of Software Maintenance, vol. 18, pp. 83-107.

Eilertsen A.M. and Bagge A.H. (2018) "Exploring API / Client Co-Evolution", Gothenburg, Sweden 2nd International Workshop on API Usage and Evolution.

Espinha T. Zaidman A. and Gross H.G (2014) "Web API growing pains: Stories from client developers and their code". IEEE Conference on Software Maintenance, Reengineering, and Reverse Engineering (CSMR-WCRE). IEEE CS, pp. 84–93.

Espinha T., Zaidman A., and Gross H.G. (2015) "Web API Fragility: How Robust is Your Mobile Application?" in Proceedings of the IEEE MOBILESoft, pp. 12–21.

Fokaefs M., Mikhaiel R., Tsantalis N, Stroulia E., Lau A. (2011) "An Empirical Study on Web Service Evolution". IEEE International Conference on Web Services.

Jezek K. and Dietrich J.(2017) "API Evolution and Compatibility: A Data Corpus and Tool Evaluation". Journal of Object Technology , 2:1–23. https://doi.org/10.5381/jot.2017.16.4.a2

Lamothe M., Guéhéneuc Y.G, and Shang W.(2021) " A Systematic Review of API Evolution Literature". ACM Comput. Surv. 54, 8, Article 171 .36 pages. https://doi.org/10.1145/3470133

Li J, Xiong Y., Liu X., and Zhang L. (2013) "How does web service API evolution affect clients?" 20th Conf. on Web Services (ICWS). IEEE, pp. 300–307.

Maalej W. and Robillard M.P. (2013) "Patterns of knowledge in API reference documentation," IEEE Trans. Softw. Eng., vol. 39, no. 9, pp. 1264–1282.

Peffers K, Tuunanen T., Rothenberger A. and Chatterjee S. (2007) "A design science research methodology for information systems research". Journal of Management Information Systems, 24(3). Pp 45–77 https://doi.org/10.2753/MIS0742-1222240302

R. Koçi R., Franch X., Janovic P and Abelló A (2019) "Classification of Changes in API Evolution". IEEE 23rd International Enterprise Distributed Object Computing Conference (EDOC)

Robbes R., Lungu M. and Janes A.(2019) “API fluency” ICSE-NIER '19: Proceedings of the 41st International Conference on Software Engineering: New Ideas and Emerging Results. pp 97–100. https://doi.org/10.1109/ICSE-NIER.2019.00033

Sohan S.M., Anslow C, Maurer F. (2015) “A Case Study of Web API Evolution”. IEEE World Congress on Services. Doi: 10.1109/SERVICES.2015.43.

Stocker M. and Zimmermann O. (2021) “From Code Refactoring to API Refactoring: Agile Service Design and Evolution”.Conférence Symposium and Summer School on Service-Oriented Computing Pages 174-193 - Éditeur Springer, doi 10.1007/978-3-030-87568-8_11.

SungGyeong B., Hyunghun Ch., Inho L., and Sukyoung R. (2014). SAFEWAPI: web API misuse detector for web applications. Proceedings of the 22nd ACM SIGSOFT International Symposium on Foundations of Software Engineering . Pages 507–517. DOI:https://doi.org/10.1145/2635868.2635916

Tashtoush T., AlRashdan M.N., Salameh O. and Alsmirat M. (2019) "Swagger-based jQuery Ajax Validation," IEEE 9th Annual Computing and Communication Workshop and Conference (CCWC) pp. 0069-0072, doi: 10.1109/CCWC.2019.8666542.

Vinoski S.(2008) “Restful web services development checklist,” IEEE Internet Computing, vol. 12, no. 6, pp. 96–95.

Wittern E. (2018).”Web APIs—Challenges, design points, and research opportunities”. In Proceedings of the 2nd International Workshop on API Usage and Evolution. ACM Press, New York, NY, 18–18.

Wittern E., Ying A.T.T, Zheng Y, Dolby J. and Laredo J.A. (2017) "Statically Checking Web API Requests in JavaScript," IEEE/ACM 39th International Conference on Software Engineering (ICSE) pp. 244-254, doi: 10.1109/ICSE.2017.30.

Xavier L., Brito A., Hora A., Valente M.T. (2017) Historical and Impact Analysis of API Breaking Changes: A Large-Scale Study. IEEE 24th International Conference on Software Analysis, Evolution and Reengineering (SANER). Doi 10.1109/SANER.2017.7884616.

Yasmin J., Tian Y. and Yang J. (2020) "A First Look at the Deprecation of RESTful APIs: An Empirical Study," in IEEE International Conference on Software Maintenance and Evolution (ICSME), Adelaide, Australia, pp. 151-161.doi: 10.1109/ICSME46990.2020.00024

Autonomy and Turnover in Distributed Software Development Projects: a Systematic Literature Review

Amanda Chaves[1], Luís Amorim[2], Marcelo Marinho[2], Ivaldir de Farias Júnior[3], Hermano Moura [1]

[1]Centro de Informática (CIn) – Universidade Federal de Pernambuco (UFPE)
50740-560 – Recife – PE – Brazil

[2]Departamento de Computação (DC) – Universidade Federal Rural de Pernambuco (UFRPE)
52071-000 – Recife – PE – Brazil

[3]Departamento de Computação
Universidade de Pernambuco (UPE) – Garanhuns – PE – Brazil

amc5@cin.ufpe.br, luis.fcamorim@ufrpe.br,marcelo.marinho@ufrpe.br,

ivaldir.farias@upe.br, hermano@cin.ufpe.br

Abstract. *Distributed teams have become a tendency among software companies. However, companies that apply Distributed Software Development (DSD) suffer from high developer turnover. Research shows that autonomy factors can mitigate or prevent team turnover. In this research, we investigate the role of autonomy on turnover in distributed teams through a Systematic Literature Review (SLR). Our findings revealed a set of autonomy dimensions that influence turnover in DSD projects. Besides, we identified the main factors related to autonomy linked to turnover in DSD projects. These findings provide software companies and organizations with a better understanding of the importance of autonomy factors to battle the DSD projects turnover problem.*

1. Introduction

Turnover originates different changes on the company's human resources departments and software projects [Khan et al. 2010]. Studies point out that there are different factors negatively or positively related to turnover happening [Sulayman et al. 2014]. Since 1979, literature has created models trying to relate determining factors to turnover, for example, Mobley's model [Goldenson and Herbsleb 1995], which developed a motivation action model in an individual level at user behaviour.

Software companies show high levels of turnover and this constant change and turnover generates some problems such as increasing companies costs, the difficulty of managing a team, the decrease in the workplace harmonia, impact on project success and others [Rainer and Hall 2002, Khan et al. 2010]. For example, Ramasubbu [Ramasubbu 2013], pointed out that 90% of projects suffer from turnover .

A high level of turnover becomes a problem because it indicates that professionals do not stay in the company for a long time, making companies and projects show a low retention level. Furthermore, turnover itself causes significant costs whether they are considered as a pecuniary classification or also a work quality level, and individual work [El Emam and Koru 2008]. In DSD projects, turnover levels are reported to be even higher than in localized projects, which can be related to the specifics of the job related to geographic location, communication, etc [Armstrong et al. 2018].

Models show positive and negative factors to have a turnover occurrence, differing turnover when the professional has already left the project and company, and turnover intentions. It is possible to notice professional intentions in a determined moment where he lived and acted in the project [Khan and Khan 2013]. Some factors are stated in literature because of their turnover impact and turnover intentions [Khan and Khan 2013, Kautz and Nielsen 2000]. Autonomy is an essential factor and a motivator for software engineering in this context. One dissatisfaction among autonomy needs provenience from software engineers, and autonomy degree is that he/she owns might have an impact on performance and motivation [Sulayman et al. 2014]. Therefore, our primary focus in this paper is to present a relationship between autonomy and turnover from Software Engineers that are inserted in Distributed Software Development (DSD) projects.

Thus, to answer the research question, "What is the relationship between autonomy and turnover in distributed software projects?" we elaborated two subquestions:

- RQ1.1 - What are the main dimensions of autonomy that influence turnover in distributed software projects?
- RQ1.2 - What are the main factors related to autonomy linked to turnover in distributed software projects?

This paper is organized as follows: in Section 2, we introduce the background. Section 3 describes the method we apply. Section 4 presents the results, their implications and limitations, respectively. Furthermore, Section 5 presents discussion and limitations. Finally, Section 6 presents conclusion and future research directions.

2. Background

2.1. Autonomy

Autonomy is known as one of the most studied job characteristics, and it plays a central role in motivation's work design [Campion 1988]. In an early stage, autonomy was seen as a synonym of how much freedom and independence in an individual perspective a team member had while executing a project or work task [Hackman and Oldham 1976].

After that, researches [Wall et al. 1992, Bass et al. 2018, Marinho et al. 2021] regarding this theme made explicit that the concept of autonomy in workplaces was mentioned when there were some characteristics such as freedom, independence, decision making, choices of working routine and methods to task execution.

Nevertheless, Morgeson *et al.* [Morgeson and Humphrey 2006] also pointed out three aspects interrelated to autonomy focused on freedom such as working routine, decision making and working methods.

Autonomy is strongly related to Self-Determination theory stated by [Deci and Ryan 2012] which aims to explain the factors that could mediate motivation. In this context, competency, identification with work and autonomy are three psychological necessities innate to a person to feel satisfied in a workplace are expressed by this theory. Furthermore, Ryan and Deci pointed out that the higher the autonomy one feels, the more motivated one is [Deci and Ryan 2012].

According [Noll et al. 2017] the autonomy at work was recognized as a central factor in work design, leading to many positive outcomes. Even so, [Dysvik and Kuvaas 2013] have rightly questioned its predictive role for several outcomes, including turnover intention, as well as the relationship between them.

In software engineering, the Self-Determination factors may be described as barriers to motivation and satisfaction with work. Professional demotivation is considered a predictive factor for turnover, which is considered a specific and different context when working on distributed projects [Cruzes and Dyba 2011].

Autonomy has been identified as an important motivational factor for software engineers who work in distributed models. Those professionals are also more tolerant of motivational changes because they are naturally exposed to hours of antisocial work and travel necessities [Ivarsson and Gorschek 2011].

In a distributed project context, autonomy itself is not referred to as a factor that might motivate a team member. However, when it is not present, an individual's needs for autonomy might contribute to a higher dissatisfaction with work and result in this team member turnover [Wall et al. 1992].

2.2. Turnover

Team members' turnover negatively impacts software development. Even though many authors consider turnover as a natural part of an organization, high levels usually result in negative impacts on processes efficiency [Bass et al. 2018].

Turnover may be classified as external when team members leave the organization or internal when they remain in the company but change their previous work. This process can happen voluntarily when the employee himself decides to abandon the company and their role or involuntarily, which happens when the organization decides to terminate its relationship with the employee [Chatzipetrou et al. 2018].

Furthermore, turnover rates can be calculated by dividing the number of employees who left the organization in a determined time by the total amount of employees during this same period. However, in daily organizational practice, the data needs to be more detailed to identify the reasons that resulted in a turnover. This understanding is shown as one of the main barriers. Such data are highly relevant for strategies creation that might be applied in an efficient way to deal with turnover and its consequences properly [Chatzipetrou et al. 2018].

Articles show that perceived intention job autonomy was negatively related to turnover reporting only for employees with high levels of perceived support. However, these results must be integrated with new ways of working, such as the Distributed Software Development (DSD) [Dysvik and Kuvaas 2013].

DSD has become a common practice worldwide, intensified by financial, structural and global factors [Bass et al. 2018].

Among the several characteristics related to DSD is the organization's potential to attract qualified professionals, even being in a local context with professionals' scarcity.

This incredible capacity to attract and hire specialized professionals positively impacts productivity and services, and products' quality [Dysvik and Kuvaas 2013].

DSD projects might have turnover levels raised because of physical distance, and on Ebert and Jha study [Ebert et al. 2016], turnover is mentioned as one of the five most significant risks for DSD projects. Previous short research related to the relevance of motivational factors to prevent this phenomenon in distributed projects [Deci and Ryan 2012].

2.3. Distributed Software Development

A distributed project is a group of people among different locations that work united in a single project for an extended period. This kind of software project in which the human resources involved are spread by distance, regionally, nationally or globally, is defined as Distributed Software Development (DSD) [Sulayman et al. 2012, Marinho et al. 2018, Marinho et al. 2019].

Furthermore, DSD can be classified on two factors: the distance among work teams which presents itself as Onshore (teams located in the same country) and Offshore (teams located in different countries). Besides, on the other hand, the control relationship the central organization has over the remote teams presents itself as Outsourcing (hiring of third party company) or Insourcing (creation of a company remote unit) [Richardson et al. 2010].

Research indicates that offshore outsourcing service providers could reduce staff member turnover by improving work-life balance and adopting more family-friendly employment policies, such as increased autonomy. Further, outsourcing service providers could reward innovation more effectively and structure contracts to enable software product ownership to improve staff retention [Bass et al. 2018, Marinho et al. 2018].

3. Research Method

In this paper, we conducted a Systematic Literature Review (SLR), which aimed to answer the research question: *What is the relationship between autonomy and turnover in distributed software projects?* We follow kitchenham and Charters' guidelines [Kitchenham and Charters 2007], and it had its execution based on a research protocol that contains our research questions, inclusion and exclusion criteria for gathered studies, search string, chosen digital libraries and a quality evaluation guideline. They are all presented below.

We used the boolean search string shown as following to ensure that we captured a wide variety of papers.

> *("global software engineering" OR "global software development" OR "distributed software engineering" OR "distributed software development" OR GSE OR GSD OR "distributed teams" OR "global team" OR "dispersed team" OR "spread team" OR "virtual team" OR offshore OR outsource OR DSD OR DSE) AND (turnover OR "turnover intention" OR departure OR "rate of replacement" OR "employee retention") AND (autonomy OR "self-government" OR independence OR "self-rule" OR freedom OR "self-sufficiency" OR "job control" OR "schedule control" OR "self-management" OR isolation OR "job autonomy")*

The following criteria guided the selection of papers that helped us address the research questions. We *included*: (i) complete, peer-reviewed, published papers; (ii) papers directly related to the research questions; and (iii) the study is available via the university library services accessible to the authors during the time of the research. We *excluded*: (i) texts not published in English; (ii) technical content, e.g: editorials, tutorials, key-note speech, white papers, thesis, dissertations, technical reports, books; and (iii) Studies not related to Software Engineering.

Our search string returned 1752 studies from 5 engines as noticed in the Table 1. We identified 95 duplicate papers and no replicates. After excluding duplicate results from the dataset, we identified papers for inclusion in the initial selection (phase 1). Of these papers, 85 were passed on to phase 2, in which 25 were eliminated and 60 (`https://bit.ly/3wWUV0Q`) were finally passed on to the data extraction and data synthesis phase (see Table 1).

Engine	Selection	Phase 1	Phase 2
ACM	759	40	33
Scopus	148	27	20
Wiley	175	5	3
Springer	353	3	2
IEEE	317	10	2
Total	**1752**	**85**	**60**

Table 1. Papers by engine.

A spreadsheet was used to record the extracted data. Two researchers performed the data extraction independently to reduce the bias of the data extraction. Before the formal data extraction process, two researchers discussed the definitions of the data, in pairs, items to be extracted to ensure that both researchers had a common understanding. After we completed the data extraction, a discussion was held to resolve conflicts for reaching a consensus on the data extraction results.

We opted for a mixed approach based on quasi schemes(standard) where the research type of facet was selected as described by [Wieringa et al. 2006]. The rigour and relevance model used was the one proposed by [Ivarsson and Gorschek 2011] in order to establish a qualified point of view regarding SLR's found paper's relevance. To measure the maturity of the themes, a scheme proposed by [Ebert et al. 2016] was carried out, where the results found in research facets and contribution facets over time are crossed.

After that, a thorough reading was done to extract as many quotes that somehow answered our questions as possible. All data were categorized in a digital sheet, using Google Sheets tool, which contained the following fields: study's sequence ID, study's quotes ID, related research questions, quote's field itself with each extracted quote and yet the reason why each one of them was chosen. In the end, it was possible to identify 161 quotes that answered the proposed research questions. They were all exported to MaxQDA 2020 software (version 20.2.1) for proper codification.

In order to codify and to attribute themes for some groups of quotes, we followed Cruzes and Dyba [Cruzes and Dyba 2011]. The initial papers' codification was executed by building a list of codes with 388 categorizations. Then, codes were grouped into themes that resulted in 5 main groups: organizational culture, Autonomy and Global Software Development (GSD) relationship, Autonomy and Turnover relationship, Autonomy dimensions in GSD, and Factors related to Autonomy in the event of Turnover.

4. Results

4.1. Overview of primary studies

We executed an overview of all papers found. The first year the theme was found was in 1998, and it reached its apex in 2018 with eight papers found. It was noticed that after 2010, autonomy related to Turnover in GSD projects had a constant recurrence on literature with an average of 4 papers per year as seen in Figure 1.

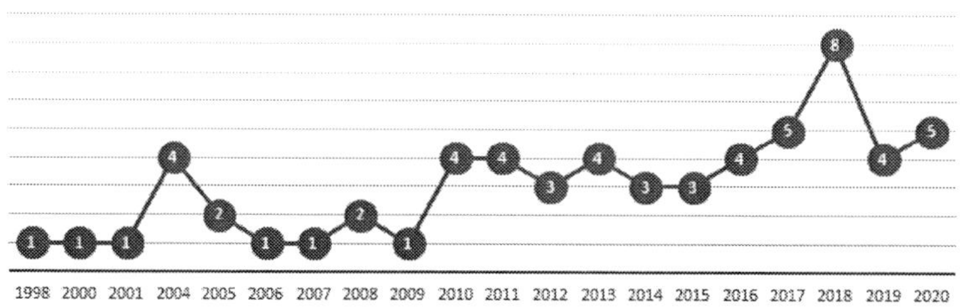

Figure 1. Papers distribution by year.

The researches type facets according to [Wieringa et al. 2006] is presented by year in Figure 2 where most of the analyzed papers were classified as Lessons Learned(32), Theory (12) and Model (8). Also, it was possible to observe that since 2010 there was a theory and Lessons Learned tendency seen. It is also relevant to state the increase of Framework facets types since 2016.

The distribution of contribution type facets of the reviewed studies derived from Petersen *et al.* [Petersen et al. 2008] is presented in Figure 3 by year. Most papers were classified as Evaluation (32) followed by papers of Experience (17) and Solution Proposal (5) in the context of research type facets classification regarding contribution. It was noticeable an increase of Evaluation type tendency over time through found papers contribution analysis.

Based on [Ivarsson and Gorschek 2011] we assessed the rigour and relevance studies. The Rigor consists of combining three concepts: context, study design and discussed validity. They received a score where 0 indicated weakly, 0.5 medium, and 1

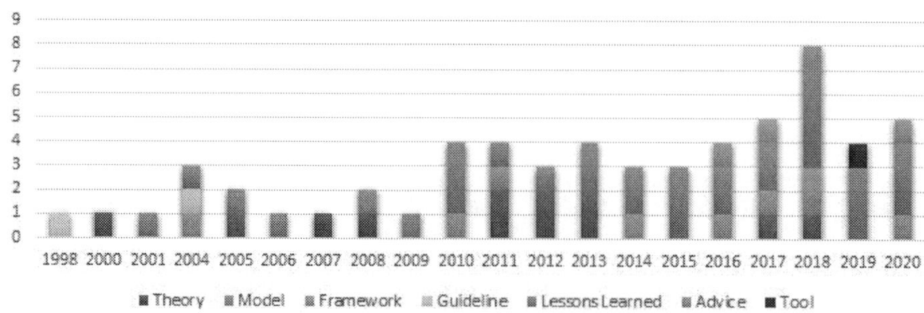

Figure 2. Research type facets over time.

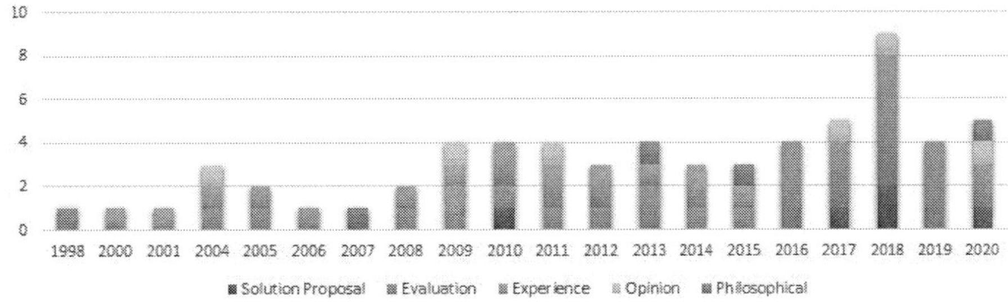

Figure 3
Contribution type facets over time.

strong. The most of the papers were classified as strong on the three concepts mentioned before (25).

Furthermore, we calculated the relevance amount in order to analyze papers relevance which consisted of combining four classifications: Relevance subject, context, scale and method and each one of them were scored with 0 (weak), 0.5 (medium) and 1 (strong). As a result, most papers (38) were classified with a score of 4, which meant strong relevance.

In order to analyze the different contributions' maturity published about autonomy impact on turnover in distributed projects, Figure 4 provides a systematic map to illustrate maturity achieved by the gathered papers. The map shows a focus on collecting lessons learned to guide the knowledge about the theme. Lessons learned (33) represented the most significant part among results and, from them, 19 corresponded to Evaluation papers. This map also shows a kind of maturity in terms of theory based on experiences and evaluation models.

Experience Paper	2	7	0	0	8	0	0
Evaluation Paper	6	3	1	2	19	1	0
Philosophical Paper	0	1	0	0	3	0	0
Solution Proposion	0	1	3	0	1	0	0
Opinion Paper	0	0	0	0	2	0	0
-	Model	Theory	Framework	Guideline	Lessons Learned	Advice	Tool

Figure 4. Systematic Map

4.2. RQ1.1 - What are the main dimensions of autonomy that influence turnover in DSD projects?

Some autonomy dimensions related to concepts that specified and had a relationship with the kind of autonomy given to an employee were identified in the paper extraction phase. There were found eight autonomy dimensions listed on Table 2. Following, we describe the dimensions found.

Table 2. Autonomy Dimensions by references

Dimensions	References	Occurrences
Relatedness	Bass, Beecham, Abdur (2018), Smith, Speight (2006), Lin, Robles,Serebrenik (2017), Gopalakrishnan, Halgin, Borgatti (2013),Moquin,Riemenschneider (2013).	5
Competence	Bass, Beecham, Abdur (2018), Smith, Speight (2006), Meland, Waage, Sein(2005), Moquin, Riemenschneider (2013),Ferratt, Enns, Prasad (2001), Mgaya,Uzoka, Kitindi, Shemi (2009).	6
Context	Mourmant, Niederman, Kalika (2013), Monteiro, Silva, Santos, Farias (2011), Adya, Cotton (2012).	3
Internal	Lundene, Mohagheghi (2018), Monteiro, Silva, Santos, Farias (2011),Uzoka, Mgaya, Shemi, Kitindi (2011),Bao, Xing, Xia, Lo, Li (2017).	4
External	Lundene, Mohagheghi (2018), Monteiro, Silva, Santos, Farias (2011),Uzoka, Mgaya, Shemi, Kitindi (2011),Bao, Xing, Xia, Lo, Li (2017).	4
Individual	Lundene, Mohagheghi (2018), Monteiro, Silva, Santos, Farias (2011),Uzoka, Mgaya, Shemi, Kitindi (2011), Bao, Xing, Xia, Lo, Li (2017).	4
Adaptation	Lundene, Mohagheghi (2018), Mgaya, Uzoka, Kitindi, Shemi (2009), Bao, Xing, Xia, Lo, Li (2017).	3
Variety	Setor, Joseph (2020), Lundene, Mohagheghi (2018), Monteiro, Silva, Santos, Farias (2011)	3

Relatedness and *competence* were connected with the professional need to feel part of the team and identify with the project, and have the opportunity to learn new skills and develop the existent ones. Therefore, autonomy should be balanced between these two dimensions because feelings of stress and demotivation may flourish without competence to execute tasks with higher autonomy. In this sense, it is also stated that professionals who do not feel connected with work might feel isolated when high levels of autonomy are given [Richardson et al. 2010].

The *context* dimension is related to the context in which this autonomy is applicable, whether it is about a product, personal factors, planning or decision making. The context can be summarized in individual, internal and external autonomy [Bass et al. 2018].

Individual autonomy refers to the amount of freedom and discretion an individual has in carrying out assigned tasks. On the other hand, external autonomy is described as the influence applied by managers on other individuals, whether they are involved or not in a team's activities. Internal autonomy refers to how all team members jointly share decision authority. Furthermore, those autonomy dimensions must be balanced to avoid turnover on distributed projects [Bass et al. 2018].

The *adaptation* dimension is related to the work's characteristics that might lead to turnover. Those distributed projects' own characteristics might be related to the team's distribution because the offshore projects show a higher turnover level when compared to onshore ones [Sumner et al. 2005].

Offshore distributed projects have antissocial work hours as a strong characteristic thereby decreasing autonomy related to work routine and also decreasing professional motivation. On the other hand, distributed projects (onshore and offshore) are positively related with work variety and team connection through agile methodologies which is identified as a positive factor for software engineers's motivation [Richardson et al. 2010].

The *variety* is a dimension related to a professional's expertise. So jobs that offer an individual autonomy that might awaken an employee's creativity and provide his learns tend to be a career anchor and are considered a guardian to precursors of turnover intentions [Sumner et al. 2005].

4.3. RQ1.2 - What are the main factors related to autonomy linked to turnover in DSD projects?

We identified the main factors related to autonomy linked to turnover in DSD projects (See Table 3). The literature has widely addressed the importance of considering *employees'*

Table 3. Related Factors by references

Related Factors	References	Occorrences
Employees' wishes	Noll, Razzak, Beecham (2017), Mourmant, Niederman, Kalika (2013), Choi,Tausczik (2017), Hynninen, Piri, Niinimaki (2010).	4
Communication	Lundene, Mohagheghi (2018), Zhou, Gifford, Ratakinda, Westerwick, Engel (2014), Beecham (2014).	3
Contributor's opinion	Lundene, Mohagheghi (2018), Mgaya, Uzoka, Kitindi, Shemi (2009), Bao, Xing, Xia, Lo, Li (2017).	3
Individual factors	Bass, Beecham, Abdur (2018), Noll, Razzak, Beecham (2017), Lundene, Mohagheghi (2018), Robert Jr, Sangseok (2017).	4
Career Satisfaction	Bass, Beecham, Abdur (2018), Smith, Speight (2006), Garrison, Wakefield,Xu, Sang (2010), Uzoka, Mgaya, Shemi, Kitindi (2011).	4
Job opportunities	Uzoka, Mgaya, Shemi, Kitindi (2011), Johri, Teo (2018), Mgaya, Uzoka, Kitindi, Shemi (2009).	3
Work Regime	Bass, Beecham, Abdur (2018), Noll, Razzak, Beecham (2017), Uzoka, Mgaya,Shemi, Kitindi (2011), Foerderer, Kude, Mithas, Heinzl (2016), Johri, Teo(2018).	5
Work Routine	Setor, Joseph (2020), Lundene, Mohagheghi (2018), Monteiro, Silva, Santos, Farias (2011)	3

wishes and aligning them with what the organization can offer. Furthermore, software engineer's opinions about autonomy and its levels in an organizational context need to be investigated, considering the specificities of work [Smith and Speight 2006].

Communication was also pointed as an important factor related to autonomy, mainly in distributed projects. When a company cannot establish an adequate communication flow is common to find inefficient work processes and employees with low levels of commitment to the organization and, thereby, high turnover levels [Noll et al. 2017].

Other factors related to *individuals* are also relevant such as mental overload, conflicts related to roles, social support, organizational noticed support, job demands, engagement and burnout. Individuals factors are directly related to autonomy because they can strongly influence motivation and satisfaction at work and might still contribute to more significant intentions of turnover if they are not balanced [Bellini et al. 2019].

Job opportunities and *career satisfaction* directly influence turnover intentions. Autonomy relates to these factors because it can significantly improve professional satisfaction by allowing the employee to elaborate plan, prioritizations and practices within the work. Autonomy can also improve quality tasks by flourishing feelings of a more specialized work to the ones involved in execution when applied in a motivated team with a high level of satisfaction with their careers [Massoni et al. 2019].

Work regime shows itself as a significant factor related to autonomy because even in a small way, autonomy is commonly perceived as a positive and preventive factor to turnover. However, for that to happen, managers must look for ways to ensure good communication among team members and ensure that team monitoring is not perceived in an authority way because such practice tends to reduce this feeling of individual autonomy [Beecham and Noll 2015].

Furthermore, *work routine* is also an essential factor related to autonomy. A certain level of autonomy is perceived as beneficial to tasks execution because it allows an employee to prioritize the project meant to him and establish practices judged as necessary to its execution. This higher freedom to prioritization gives the employee a feeling of higher control, which becomes a preventive factor for turnover intentions [Remus et al. 2016].

After performing the data extraction and identifying the dimensions of autonomy that influence turnover in DSD and the factors related to autonomy linked to turnover, we analyzed dimensions and factors. Thus, we developed a representative picture of how dimensions can influence factors. We add that the Figure 5 represents the evidence found in the SLR and that future studies are needed to indicate the correlation of this set of variables.

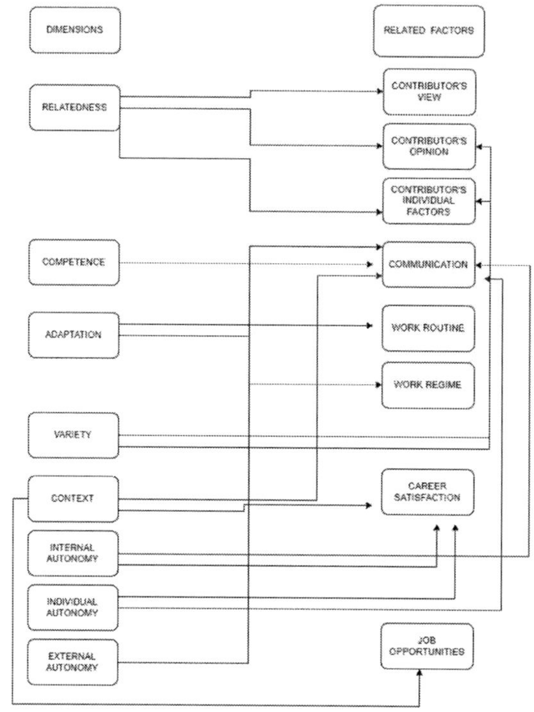

Figure 5. Autonomy Dimensions x Related Factors

5. Discussion

The dimensions of autonomy pointed out that the theme has different divisions, and that they can present themselves differently in the Software Engineer's work routine [Bass et al. 2018, Setor and Joseph 2022]. The factors related to autonomy concern the ways in which autonomy can be modulated by the Software Engineer's perception of his environment and work routine [Smith and Speight 2006, Marinho et al. 2021].

In this sense, some dimensions can be associated with related factors, as they relate to factors to the work environment and their dimensions. For example, the dimension of relatedness [Noll et al. 2017] associates the related factor Contributor's view, opinion and individual factors. In order to feel related to the work, it is important to know the point of view, the opinion and the various individual factors of the employee, analysing this factors for each of them [Smith and Speight 2006, Bellini et al. 2019]. These factors can influence in the motivation factors of the employee as showed in: "A mismatch between an individual's need for autonomy, and the degree of autonomy she or he actually has, may have an impact on motivation levels" [Smith and Speight 2006].

The dimension of competence can also be modulated by the communication factor, since autonomy is considered as a motivating factor when the professional is competent to perform tasks, otherwise his motivation may be reduced, causing stress. Communication is part of this process, as it is important for the employee to be able to communicate with their team and management, even in processes of stress and demotivation.

In distributed projects, communication presents itself as one of the main challenges for management, since many of these employees are on different schedules and activities. As showed in [Lundene and Mohagheghi 2018] "Teams need a shared purpose, the necessary skills, competence and mutual trust among the team members to develop internal autonomy. During the project period the teams gained a complete set of skills to develop, maintain, deploy, monitor and support the applications they have responsibility for. In addition, support was given from legal and communication experts to ensure data protection and clean language applied in the products". Also, according [Beecham 2014] "Individuals can be undermined if head office is heavy handed, and interferes with communication, or if their work is monitored too stringently. For developers working under the spotlight of the customer, autonomy can be problematic" .

The dimension of adaptation, which relates to the characteristics of the project's work, is an example of the distribution of teams. In this sense, the factors of work regime and the individual factors of the employee may be related to that dimension. Individual factors will influence how the employee sees the work routine determined for the team, and the work regime will connect with the way the employee is able to adapt to the management of their workload and the specific characteristics of the same. As shown in [Lundene and Mohagheghi 2018] "Autonomy has some pre-conditions to be realized, among them redundancy of skills (since it affects the team's capability to adapt to changing situations)".

The dimension of variety is closely connected with the creativity of the employee in a work environment, where autonomy can provide a true career anchor. The related factors of opinion and individual employees are linked to the idea that you should know your employee to be able to determine the professional's expertise. In this sense, the task quality factor is also related to the work process and a creative and managerial role through the employee.

The dimensions of the context in which internal and individual autonomy are linked may be connected with factors related to communication and career satisfaction, as punctuated in [Lundene and Mohagheghi 2018]: "Internal autonomy refers to the degree to which all team members jointly share decision authority, while individual autonomy refers to the amount of freedom and discretion an individual has in carrying out assigned tasks and their satisfaction".

External autonomy can also be related to the related factor of communication, as expressed in [Lundene and Mohagheghi 2018]: "Ideally, in high trust organizations, a team should be given a problem to solve, and then the solution should be solely the team's responsibility" . The context dimension can be related to the job opportunity related factor, as [Johri and Teo 2018] study: "The option to work from home was not only beneficial to the employees but also to the firms – giving workers the opportunity to work from home or from cities of their choice resulted in very low turnover". Furthermore, it is vital to know the career orientation of employees because based on such knowledge organizations can reduce high turnover rates by providing job opportunities and incentives that match the career orientation of their employees [Mgaya et al. 2009].

5.1. Limitations

Our study has some limitations that will be discussed on this section. In general, there were used known tools to conduct secondary studies following rigorous methods to analysis and data reports. However, the study was only conducted with a pool of found and related themes. We cannot affirm that we presented a full picture because we did not include all themes found on our SLR.

All numbers and classifcations presented on this paper must be treated carefully because our classification may only provide indications. Furthermore, it remains unknown if the present classification properly reflects the real situation in practice.

In short, information and data collection more well structured based on specialists and cases were not applied in this study but they are made necessary in order to confirm the findings in the present paper. Those limitations, however, motivate more researchers to complete a wider board about this matter in the future. As mentioned earlier, the factors and effects are indicators, needing to consider the organisational aspects of the context in which the company is inserted and the individual factors that are customized for each employee.

6. Conclusion

In this paper we performed a systematic literature review where we searched for the relation between autonomy and turnover in distributed projects as well as its dimensions and attached factors. The analysis of the papers revealed that the theme series addresses both conducting high-quality research, but also fostering to explore the DSD context. Among 16 themes that were defined by using the cluster analysis, it was possible to observe that autonomy dimensions and their related factors are directly related to turnover in distributed projects and they can weather be perceived as preventive or precursors of turnover intentions thereby depending on how they are modulated within the context.

This paper pointed out the relevance of studies that address DSD projects, as they are a growing reality in the middle of Software Engineering. As specificities about this project, the relevance of the study of Turnover in this type of project was raised, since the numbers are high when compared to traditional projects.

Motivation was indicated by several authors as a preventive factor for turnover, with autonomy directly associated with this process. Finally, the main implication of the present research is the need for autonomy modulation in a different way in distributed projects, since they have specific dimensions and related factors that can influence employee motivation, reducing the level of organizational turnover.

We concluded that autonomy in distributed projects needs a good organizational preparation before being implemented or increased because factors like communication, work methodologies and an internal factors analysis need to be analyzed and modulated for a software engineer in order to flourish a higher efficiency to work tasks and professional satisfaction not becoming a possible precursor of turnover by stress and feelings of isolation.

Finally, the main implication of the present research is the need for autonomy modulation in a different way in distributed projects, since they have specific dimensions and related factors that can influence employee motivation, reducing the level of organizational turnover.

References

Armstrong, D. J., Riemenschneider, C. K., and Giddens, L. G. (2018). The advancement and persistence of women in the information technology profession: An extension of ahuja's gendered theory of it career stages. *Information Systems Journal*, 28(6):1082–1124.

Bass, J. M., Sarah, B., Razzak, M. A., and Noll, J. (2018). Employee retention and turnover in global software development: Comparing in-house offshoring and offshore outsourcing. In *2018 IEEE/ACM 13th International Conference on Global Software Engineering (ICGSE)*, pages 77–86. IEEE.

Beecham, S. (2014). Motivating software engineers working in virtual teams across the globe. In *Software project management in a changing world*, pages 247–273. Springer.

Beecham, S. and Noll, J. (2015). What motivates software engineers working in global software development? In *International conference on product-focused software process improvement*, pages 193–209. Springer.

Bellini, C. G. P., Palvia, P., Moreno, V., Jacks, T., and Graeml, A. (2019). Should i stay or should i go? a study of it professionals during a national crisis. *Information Technology & People*.

Campion, M. A. (1988). Interdisciplinary approaches to job design: A constructive replication with extensions. *Journal of applied psychology*, 73(3):467.

Chatzipetrou, P., Šmite, D., and Van Solingen, R. (2018). When and who leaves matters: emerging results from an empirical study of employee turnover. In *Proceedings of the 12th ACM/IEEE International Symposium on Empirical Software Engineering and Measurement*, pages 1–4.

Cruzes, D. S. and Dyba, T. (2011). Recommended steps for thematic synthesis in software engineering. In *2011 international symposium on empirical software engineering and measurement*, pages 275–284. IEEE.

Deci, E. L. and Ryan, R. M. (2012). Self-determination theory.

Dysvik, A. and Kuvaas, B. (2013). Perceived job autonomy and turnover intention: The moderating role of perceived supervisor support. *European Journal of Work and Organizational Psychology*, 22(5):563–573.

Ebert, C., Kuhrmann, M., and Prikladnicki, R. (2016). Global software engineering: Evolution and trends. In *2016 IEEE 11th International Conference on Global Software Engineering (ICGSE)*, pages 144–153. IEEE.

El Emam, K. and Koru, A. G. (2008). A replicated survey of it software project failures. *IEEE software*, 25(5):84–90.

Goldenson, D. R. and Herbsleb, J. D. (1995). After the appraisal: A systematic survey of process improvement, its benefits, and factors that influence success. Technical report, Carnegie Mellon University in Pittsburgh, Pennsylvania.

Hackman, J. R. and Oldham, G. R. (1976). Motivation through the design of work: Test of a theory. *Organizational behavior and human performance*, 16(2):250–279.

Ivarsson, M. and Gorschek, T. (2011). A method for evaluating rigor and industrial relevance of technology evaluations. *Empirical Software Engineering*, 16(3):365–395.

Johri, A. and Teo, H. J. (2018). Achieving equilibrium through coworking: Work-life balance in floss through multiple spaces and media use. In *Proceedings of the 14th international symposium on open collaboration*, pages 1–11.

Kautz, K. and Nielsen, P. A. (2000). Implementing software process improvement: two cases of technology transfer. In *Proceedings of the 33rd Annual Hawaii International Conference on System Sciences*, pages 10–pp. IEEE.

Khan, A. W. and Khan, S. U. (2013). Critical success factors for offshore software outsourcing contract management from vendors' perspective: an exploratory study using a systematic literature review. *IET software*, 7(6):327–338.

Khan, S. U., Niazi, M., and Ahmad, R. (2010). Critical success factors for offshore software development outsourcing vendors: an empirical study. In *International Conference on Product Focused Software Process Improvement*, pages 146–160. Springer.

Kitchenham, B. and Charters, S. (2007). Guidelines for performing systematic literature reviews in software engineering. Technical report, Technical report, EBSE Technical Report EBSE-2007-01.

Lundene, K. and Mohagheghi, P. (2018). How autonomy emerges as agile cross-functional teams mature. In *Proceedings of the 19th International Conference on Agile Software Development: Companion*, pages 1–5.

Marinho, M., Amorim, L., Camara, R., Oliveira, B. R., Sobral, M., and Sampaio, S. (2021). Happier and further by going together: The importance of software team behaviour during the covid-19 pandemic. *Technology in society*, 67:101799.

Marinho, M., Noll, J., and Beecham, S. (2018). Uncertainty management for global software development teams. In *11th International Conference on the Quality of Information and Communications Technology*, pages 238–246, Coimbra, Portugal. IEEE.

Marinho, M., Noll, J., Richardson, I., and Beecham, S. (2019). Plan-driven approaches are alive and kicking in agile global software development. In *International Symposium on Empirical Software Engineering and Measurement (ESEM)*, pages 1–11, Porto de Galinhas, Brazil. IEEE.

Massoni, T., Ginani, N., Silva, W., Barros, Z., and Moura, G. (2019). Relating voluntary turnover with job characteristics, satisfaction and work exhaustion-an initial study with brazilian developers. In *2019 IEEE/ACM 12th International Workshop on Cooperative and Human Aspects of Software Engineering (CHASE)*, pages 85–88. IEEE.

Mgaya, K. V., Uzoka, F.-M. E., Kitindi, E. G., and Shemi, A. P. (2009). Examining career orientations of information systems personnel in an emerging economy context. In *Proceedings of the special interest group on management information system's 47th annual conference on Computer personnel research*, pages 41–56.

Morgeson, F. P. and Humphrey, S. E. (2006). The work design questionnaire (wdq): developing and validating a comprehensive measure for assessing job design and the nature of work. *Journal of applied psychology*, 91(6):1321.

Noll, J., Beecham, S., Razzak, A., Richardson, B., Barcomb, A., and Richardson, I. (2017). Motivation and autonomy in global software development. In *International Workshop on Global Sourcing of Information Technology and Business Processes*, pages 19–38. Springer.

Petersen, K., Feldt, R., Mujtaba, S., and Mattsson, M. (2008). Systematic mapping studies in software engineering. In *12th International Conference on Evaluation and Assessment in Software Engineering (EASE) 12*, pages 1–10.

Rainer, A. and Hall, T. (2002). Key success factors for implementing software process improvement: a maturity-based analysis. *Journal of Systems and Software*, 62(2):71–84.

Ramasubbu, N. (2013). Governing software process improvementsin globally distributed product development. *IEEE Transactions on Software Engineering*, 40(3):235–250.

Remus, U., Wiener, M., Saunders, C., Mähring, M., and Kofler, M. (2016). Control modes versus control styles: Investigating isd project control effects at the individual level.

Richardson, I., Casey, V., Burton, J., and McCaffery, F. (2010). Global software engineering: A software process approach. In *Collaborative software engineering*, pages 35–56. Springer.

Setor, T. K. and Joseph, D. (2022). When agile means staying: A moderated mediated model. *Journal of Computer Information Systems*, 62(1):186–195.

Smith, D. and Speight, H. (2006). Antecedents of turnover intention and actual turnover among information systems personnel in south africa. In *Proceedings of the 2006 ACM SIGMIS CPR conference on computer personnel research: Forty four years of computer personnel research: achievements, challenges & the future*, pages 123–129.

Sulayman, M., Mendes, E., Urquhart, C., Riaz, M., and Tempero, E. (2014). Towards a theoretical framework of spi success factors for small and medium web companies. *Information and Software Technology*, 56(7):807–820.

Sulayman, M., Urquhart, C., Mendes, E., and Seidel, S. (2012). Software process improvement success factors for small and medium web companies: A qualitative study. *Information and Software Technology*, 54(5):479–500.

Sumner, M., Yager, S., and Franke, D. (2005). Career orientation and organizational commitment of it personnel. In *Proceedings of the 2005 ACM SIGMIS CPR conference on Computer personnel research*, pages 75–80.

Wall, T. D., Jackson, P. R., and Davids, K. (1992). Operator work design and robotics system performance: A serendipitous field study. *Journal of applied Psychology*, 77(3):353.

Wieringa, R., Maiden, N., Mead, N., and Rolland, C. (2006). Requirements engineering paper classification and evaluation criteria: a proposal and a discussion. *Requirements engineering*, 11(1):102–107.

Centrarse en las personas para facilitar abordajes de Diseño Participativo

Cynthia L. Corso[1], Cecilia Challiol[2]

[1]CIDS, UTN, FRC and also Facultad de Informática, UNLP
Córdoba, Argentina

[2]LIFIA, Facultad de Informática, UNLP and also CONICET
La Plata, Buenos Aires, Argentina

ccorso@frc.utn.edu.ar, ceciliac@lifia.info.unlp.edu.ar

Abstract. *Facilitating Participatory Design experiences to create software for neurodiverse adults involves many challenges. It is crucial to consider the preferences of people who participate when each activity is planned. In this paper, we propose a conceptual framework to guide facilitators in designing and conducting Participatory Design experiences focused on neurodiverse participants. This framework is based on Design Thinking to innovate in the software creation. A summary of the current state of this topic is presented and a space for discussion is provided to invite designers to reflect.*

Resumen. *Facilitar experiencias de Diseño Participativo para crear software para adultos neurodiversos conlleva muchos desafíos; ya que las preferencias de las personas que participan se deben considerar a la hora de plantear cada actividad. En este trabajo se propone un framework conceptual para guiar a los facilitadores en el diseño y conducción de experiencias de Diseño Participativo centrándose en las personas neurodiversas que participan. Este framework se basa en Design Thinking para innovar en la creación de software. Se presenta un resumen del estado actual de la temática y se plantea un espacio de discusión para invitar a los diseñadores a reflexionar.*

1. Introducción

El Diseño Centrado en las Personas (DCP) se focaliza en las necesidades de las personas para generar, por ejemplo, productos o servicios. DCP tiene como premisa involucrar a las personas destinatarias (del producto/servicio) en todas las etapas del diseño, pero estas no forman parte del equipo que diseña [Sanders 2002]. Existen distintos abordajes para dar solución al DCP; por ejemplo, en los últimos años la disciplina de Design Thinking (DT) [Corso and Challiol 2020] ha sido ampliamente usada en las empresas para generar innovación de productos/servicios; recientemente se ha extendido su uso a otros dominios, por ejemplo, salud, educación. DT [Corso and Challiol 2020] puede ser considerado como: un recurso de la organización, un proceso cognitivo o una teoría general de diseño. El presente trabajo se enfoca en la mirada de DT como un proceso cognitivo que utiliza las prácticas y formas de pensamiento de los diseñadores para innovar en la creación de nuevos productos de software.

En el DCP, incluido DT, es fundamental comprender y más aún empatizar con las necesidades reales de las personas para las que se está diseñando software [Sanders, 2002]; cuando esto no se logra se generan experiencias frustrantes para los usuarios [Kudryashov 2021]. Esto acontece generalmente cuando la brecha entre las vivencias de los diseñadores y las personas para las que están diseñando es muy grande; por ejemplo, diseñar para autistas[1] [Maun et al. 2021]. Para dar solución a esto, ha emergido el Diseño Participativo (DP), en el cual las personas destinatarias del software no solo pasan a ser parte del equipo que diseña sino que además toman un rol esencial en el proceso de diseño [Sanders, 2002]; se convierten en expertos del dominio, por ejemplo, los adultos autistas aportando su mirada en primera persona [Kudryashov 2021].

En [Maun et al. 2021] se destacan las ventajas que tiene el DP para desarrollar software para adultos autistas; remarcando que se necesita considerar al menos seis aspectos críticos: enfoques adecuados, diferencias individuales, ambiente, flexibilidad, comunicación, aspectos sensoriales y desafiar los supuestos. Se vienen explorando distintos aspectos, por ejemplo, cómo indagar sobre preferencias [Thompson et al. 2020] o cómo mejorar un software [Kudryashov 2021]. Sin embargo, todavía no existen guías claras que ayuden a los facilitadores a diseñar y conducir experiencias de DP con personas adultas neurodiversas[2]. Esto motiva el presente trabajo.

Se destaca en [Maun et al. 2021] que DT podría ser muy adecuado para llevar a cabo el DP con autistas, ya que tiene el potencial de innovar en las soluciones que se obtienen; sin embargo los recursos a usar deben considerar las necesidades de los autistas [Kudryashov 2021]. Existen guías generales en relación a DT, por ejemplo, en [Corso and Challiol 2020] se propone un meta-framework para diseñar experiencias o en [Pariz et al. 2020] se aborda la recomendación de recursos; sin embargo, estos trabajos no contemplan los aspectos críticos planteados en [Maun et al. 2021], y enunciados anteriormente, para abordar DT con adultos autistas. Más aún, existe una gran variedad de recursos que se pueden utilizar en DT y DP (los cuales no son exclusivos de estos abordajes, por ejemplo, se pueden usar en las metodologías ágiles); sin embargo estos recursos generalmente no brindan flexibilidad respecto al modo de participación [Maun et al. 2021]. Esto refuerza la motivación del presente trabajo.

El objetivo de este trabajo es proponer un framework conceptual que sirva de guía a los facilitadores para diseñar y conducir experiencias de DP centrándose en las personas neurodiversas que participan; se consideran aspectos de DT para lograr generar soluciones de software innovadoras. Además, se presenta una exploración sobre el estado actual de la temática y se brinda un espacio de discusión que invita a reflexionar.

Este trabajo se estructura de la siguiente manera. En la Sección 2 se presenta un estado del arte en relación a la temática. En la Sección 3 se propone un framework conceptual para generar experiencias de DP centradas en la personas neurodiversas. Un

---

[1] El término a utilizar para nombrar a los autista es controversial [Kenny et al. 2016]. En este trabajo optamos por el concepto de identity-first (identidad primero) que en inglés es "*autistic person*"; traducido al español como *autista* o *persona autista*, este concepto es usado por la comunidad autista de habla hispana [Vance 2020] y también por la mayoría de los adultos autistas en las redes sociales.

[2] Las personas neurodiversas (por ejemplo, los autistas) [Kenny et al. 2016] tienen estilos cognitivos alternativos a los neurotípicos (aquellos que tienen un estilo cognitivo "*normal*").

espacio de discusión es presentado en la Sección 4. En la Sección 5 se mencionan las conclusiones y trabajos futuros.

2. Estado del Arte

La investigación realizada hace foco en las personas autistas las cuales son un subgrupo dentro de las personas neurodiversas; en un futuro se ampliará la exploración a otros subgrupos. Es interesante mencionar que existen varias investigaciones en relación al DP con niños autistas, pero muy pocas con adultos autistas [Kudryashov 2021].

A continuación se describen algunos trabajos de DP con foco tecnológico. En [Maun et al. 2021] se realiza una revisión sistemática, y además se plantean seis aspectos a tener en cuenta cuando se diseña con adultos autistas: usar enfoques y metodologías adecuados, considerar las diferencias individuales de cada persona, flexibilidad respecto al modo de participación, establecer canales de comunicación adecuados, contar con espacios amigables y desafiar los supuestos en torno a los autistas. Si bien en [Maun et al. 2021] se enuncian estos aspectos, no se brinda información de cómo ponerlos en práctica; el framework propuesto en el presente trabajo busca dar las bases iniciales sobre posibles formas de abordar estos aspectos.

Además, existen algunos trabajos que describen experiencias concretas de DP con adultos autistas. En [Politis et al. 2017] y su evolución presentada en [Politis et al. 2019] se propone una plataforma para que los adultos autistas entrenen habilidades de conversación; los mismos participan solo en las fases de testeo y retroalimentación. Si bien en estos trabajos se habla de DP en realidad los autistas no diseñan, sino que testean un producto ya diseñado. Por otro lado, en [Aslam 2018] los adultos autistas generan un kit de herramientas para el diseño de robots sociales; la experiencia se divide en tres estadios: entender las experiencias autistas en relación a los robots, generar un kit de herramientas que facilite el diseño de robots y finalmente cada autista diseña su propio robot. En [Aslam 2018] se utilizan los siguientes recursos: entrevistas semiestructuradas, grupos de discusión, juego de roles y actividades de visualización. Además, se utilizan bloques de construcción a los cuales se les adaptó el tamaño para que fuese más simple y ágil el ensamble. Por último, en [Kudryashov 2021] se generan prototipos de tecnología de Comunicación Aumentativa y Alternativa (CAA), el diseño aborda tres aspectos: entender el problema en relación a los CAA para adultos autistas, visionar posibles modificaciones y bosquejar sus propios diseños. Es importante destacar que el facilitador de esta experiencia es autista, lo cual aporta una mirada en primera persona en relación a los participantes. En [Kudryashov 2021] se utilizan los siguientes recursos: actividades de visualización, lluvia de ideas y bocetos iterativos (brindando la posibilidad que fueran en papel o digital). Otro recurso usado fue la técnica de escenarios brindándoles a los participantes la libertad de comunicar sus experiencias hasta donde se sintiesen cómodos. Además, se utiliza el recurso de mapa ganancia/dolor (gain/pain) donde en vez de usar un personaje ficticio el participante tiene que completarlo en base a su propia visión de las CAA. En relación a los recursos usados en las experiencias descriptas, es de interés mencionar que solo se acondiciona en [Aslam 2018] el tamaño de los bloques de construcción, mientras que en [Kudryashov 2021] se resignifica el uso las técnicas de escenarios y mapa ganancia/dolor considerando a las personas autistas. En [Politis et al. 2017], [Politis et al. 2019], [Aslam 2018] y [Kudryashov 2021] se centran en la experiencia en sí y no brindan ninguna guía de cómo poner en práctica este tipo de abordaje; el framework propuesto en el presente trabajo busca aportar en este sentido, enunciando qué consideraciones deben tenerse en cuenta, por ejemplo, en relación a los recursos.

En [Maun et al. 2021] se destaca que el DP debe ser inclusivo; al buscar bibliografía con foco en esta terminología (y en relación a adultos autistas) se obtienen trabajos orientados a otros ámbitos no tecnológicos (por ejemplo, arquitectura, social entre otros). Acorde a esto, dado que tiene un aporte significativo para el presente trabajo es de interés mencionar lo presentado en [Thompson et al. 2020]; donde se describe una convocatoria buscando autistas para participar de talleres de creación de música. Para la formulación de la encuesta participaron investigadores (autistas y neurotípicos) y luego esta encuesta fue revisada por un grupo de tres autistas; de esta manera logran precisión en el lenguaje y la forma utilizada para plantear cada pregunta. Como parte de la encuesta se consulta a los autistas en relación al rol del facilitador; un dato interesante que recolectaron fue que los autistas tienen muy claro que esperan de esa persona, por ejemplo, que brinde confianza, que sea respetuosa de las diferencias, que valoren sus puntos de vista. En [Thompson et al. 2020] se brinda la posibilidad de responder las encuestas en diferentes modalidades (videollamada, correo electrónico, chats entre otros). Si bien [Thompson et al. 2020] se focaliza solo en la encuesta inicial para una experiencia de DP, se destaca la posibilidad de brindar diferentes modalidades para responderla; esto será considerado en el framework conceptual propuesto a la hora de abordar los distintos recursos dentro de las experiencias de DP.

3. Guía para facilitar experiencias de Diseño Participativo centradas en las personas neurodiversas

En esta sección se propone un framework conceptual para guiar a los facilitadores en el diseño y conducción de experiencias de DP centrándose en las personas neurodiversas, para generar soluciones de software innovadoras. Como se describió en la Sección 2, distintas características se vienen explorando por separado en la bibliografía existente; el framework propuesto tiene por objetivo centralizar distintos aspectos relevantes para ayudar al facilitador en este tipo de abordaje.

Para el planteo del framework se utilizó como base el meta-framework para diseñar experiencias de DT presentado en [Corso and Challiol 2020]; el cual se focaliza en brindar los meta-conceptos que deben considerarse en experiencias en general, y no profundiza en los aspectos críticos (detallados en la Sección 2) que se deben considerar en relación a personas neurodiversas [Maun et al. 2021]. Esto último es incorporado como parte del aporte del presente trabajo. Cabe mencionar que uno de los autores cuenta con experticia[3] para comprender cuál es el rol del facilitador en este tipo de experiencias enriqueciendo así el planteo del framework propuesto, el cual se pude observar en la Figura 1.

---

[3] Uno de los autores del presente trabajo es coach ontológico y facilitador de aprendizaje experiencial. En relación a DT, tiene formación en el ámbito empresarial y ha facilitado varias experiencias en ámbitos áulicos, tanto en modalidad presencial como virtual. Además, es una Persona Altamente Sensible, es decir que tiene un sistema neurosensorial que recibe y procesa en simultáneo más información que la media de las personas, lo cual en algunos momentos puede ser abrumador; esto le permite tener una mirada en primera persona de la neurodiversidad.

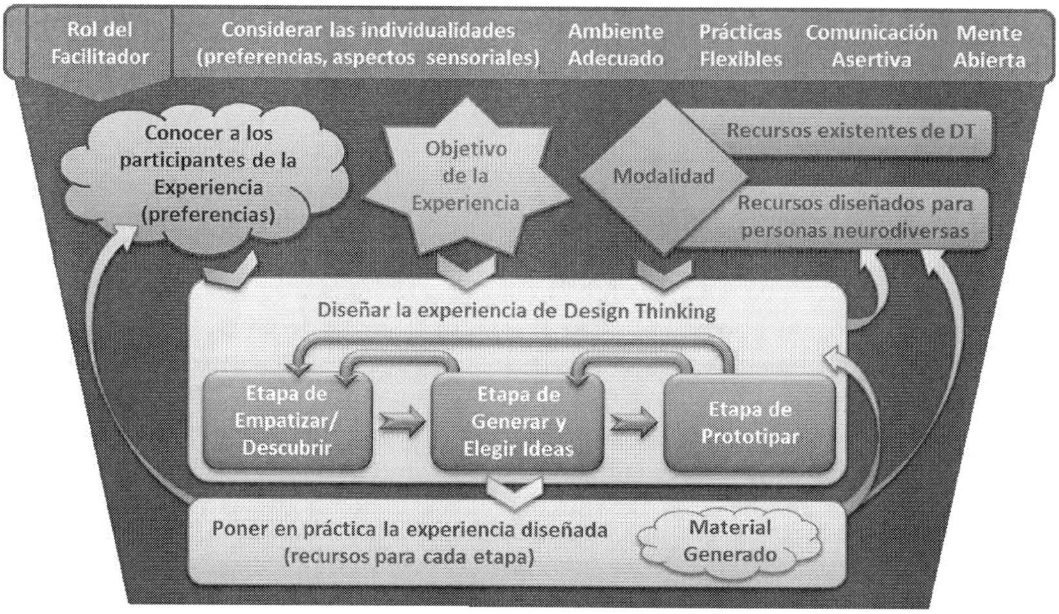

Figura 1. Framework conceptual para guiar a los facilitadores en el diseño y conducción de experiencias de DP centrándose en las personas neurodiversas, para generar soluciones de software innovadoras.

La investigación en relación al framework conceptual propuesto está en una etapa inicial. Para reforzar la viabilidad del mismo a continuación se detalla para cada uno de los conceptos planteados en la Figura 1, una breve descripción del mismo y se cita bibliografía para indicar cómo otros autores abordan ese concepto.

Rol del Facilitador. Es el pilar fundamental del framework propuesto, ya que el éxito de la experiencia se basa en diseñar y poner en práctica experiencias de DP centrándose en las personas neurodiversas que participan. En la Figura 1 se mencionan las habilidades fundamentales con las que debe contar el facilitador (o facilitadores): debe considerar las individualidades de cada persona que participa (tanto preferencias como aspectos sensoriales), generar ambientes adecuados (no solo a nivel físico, sino también el clima que se vivencia durante la experiencia), proponer prácticas flexibles (ajustándose a los cambios que emerjan a partir de la lectura del grupo), tener una comunicación asertiva y una mente abierta (sin prejuicios). Para la formulación de estas habilidades se consideró, por ejemplo, los aspectos críticos que se mencionan en [Maun et al. 2021], los valores/principios descriptos en [Aslam 2018] y las expectativas que los adultos autistas manifestaron en relación al rol del facilitador [Thompson et al. 2020].

Conocer a los participantes de la experiencia. Realizar una indagación adecuada permite recolectar información muy valiosa para identificar, por ejemplo, las preferencias de las personas en relación a la forma de comunicarse (videollamada, correo electrónico, etc.) o las sensibilidades sensoriales que tienen. Esta indagación debe realizarse antes de diseñar la experiencia. También es interesante conocer qué esperan los participantes [Thompson et al. 2020], por ejemplo, en relación al rol del facilitador. En [Thompson et al. 2020] se describen distintos aspectos a considerar en el proceso de formulación del cuestionario inicial para conocer sobre los participantes, notar que en la confección del cuestionario participaron adultos autistas que aportaron precisión en el lenguaje usado y la forma de especificar cada pregunta.

Objetivo de la experiencia. Se puede orientar la experiencia de DT para realizar un único resultado grupal (co-diseñar) o que cada persona diseñe un producto a su medida pudiendo compartir sus avances con el grupo. Por ejemplo, en [Kudryashov 2021] se aborda una aproximación a co-diseñar bosquejos de CAA, aunque no se llega a un único bosquejo; mientras que en [Aslam 2018] cada persona diseña su propio robot. Además, como parte del objetivo se puede plantear que la experiencia sea de carácter exploratoria (por ejemplo, para identificar potenciales puntos de mejoras de un producto [Kudryashov 2021]) o buscar generar un producto concreto [Aslam 2018].

Modalidad. Una modalidad virtual permite aprovechar las ventajas de las comodidades qué cada persona tiene en su propio espacio [Kudryashov 2021]; en el caso de realizarse presencial, se vuelve fundamental acondicionar el espacio físico (niveles de ruido, luminosidad, etc.) para generar una experiencia placentera para todos los participantes [Maun et al. 2021]. Cada modalidad permite utilizar distintos recursos, ya sean existentes de DT [Pariz et al. 2020] como recursos pensados para personas neurodiversas (en la Sección 2 se detallaron algunos recursos acondicionados en [Aslam 2018] y [Kudryashov 2021]). Además, el facilitador siempre puede crear o reformular recursos nuevos acorde al grupo que va a participar de una experiencia concreta.

Diseñar la experiencia de Design Thinking. Basándose en el conocimiento de las personas que van a participar, el objetivo de la experiencia y la modalidad elegida; se seleccionan los recursos a utilizar en cada etapa de la experiencia de DT. Para cada recurso hay que definir, por ejemplo, el tiempo otorgado o las opciones que se brindarán para completarlo [Kudryashov 2021]. Además, cómo se menciona en [Aslam 2018] se podría diseñar el recurso para llevarlo a cabo en una o dos jornadas dependiendo del nivel de agotamiento del grupo. Como se plantea en [Corso and Challiol 2020] las experiencias de DT se pueden diseñar en base a un framework existente de DT o generar uno nuevo (especificando sus etapas). Para ayudar al facilitador a tener un punto de partida, en la Figura 1 se especificaron tres etapas en relación a las experiencias de DT: empatizar/descubrir, generar y seleccionar ideas y prototipar. La elección de estos tres estadios se basa en que estos siempre están presentes en todos los frameworks de DT existentes [Corso and Challiol 2020].

Poner en Práctica la experiencia diseñada. En base al diseño, el facilitador conduce los recursos seleccionados para cada etapa; haciendo lectura del grupo para ir ajustando dinámicamente las actividades (por ejemplo, se podría observar la necesidad de generar nuevos recursos sobre todo para siguientes etapas). Durante la experiencia además se puede enriquecer el conocimiento que se tiene sobre los participantes. Es importante ir recolectando todo el material generado, y que los participantes puedan ir apreciando el progreso [Aslam 2018].

4. Discusión

En esta sección se discuten algunos aspectos interesantes relacionados con la temática abordada. Un primer tema a mencionar es el uso del término DP. Por ejemplo, en [Politis et al. 2017] y [Politis et al. 2019] se utiliza DP pero los autistas sólo participan del testeo de un producto, el cual no fue diseñado por ellos; estos trabajos llevan a la reflexión de qué tan participativos son en realidad, tal vez se clasifican más como un abordaje de DCP [Sanders, 2002].

Es de interés destacar que en algunas experiencias de DT el rol del facilitador pasa inadvertido y con poca relevancia, sin embargo en [Corso and Challiol 2020] se refuerza su importancia. Más aún, en el abordaje de DP con adultos autistas este rol es crítico para el éxito de la experiencia [Maun et al. 2021]; y además existe mucha expectativa por parte de los adultos autistas sobre su desempeño [Thompson et al. 2020]. En [Kudryashov 2021] los participantes se manifiestan asombrados por lo bien que funcionaron las distintas formas de comunicación que tenían con el facilitador, por ejemplo, mediante el chat. Los participantes destacaban que en otros ámbitos esta vía de comunicación no era tan efectiva y no se sentían escuchados. Se espera que el presente trabajo, y el planteo del framework conceptual sirvan como punto de partida para enriquecer el rol del facilitador; e ir generando cada vez más herramientas que lo ayuden a desempeñar mejor su tarea, sobre todo en el DP con personas neurodiversas para la generación de software.

En [Maun et al. 2021] se destaca la necesidad de abordar actividades de diseño acondicionadas para autistas. Sin embargo, como se describió la Sección 2 solo en [Aslam 2018] y [Kudryashov 2021] se mencionan adaptaciones/reformulaciones de uno y dos recursos respectivamente, más allá que ambas experiencias utilizan otros recursos. Tanto en [Aslam 2018] como en [Kudryashov 2021] no queda claro en base a qué se realizaron las adaptaciones ya que no se menciona si hubo un contacto previo con los participantes. Por otro lado, brindar distintas modalidades de participación en paralelo (chat, oral, etc.) para responder/completar cada recurso; lleva al interrogante de cómo co-diseñar cuando luego hay que converger en un único resultado para continuar co-diseñando desde ahí. Por ejemplo, si se tiene en una etapa de ideación respuestas en chats, algunas orales y otras en post-it; cómo todo esto se unifica para clasificarlas y filtrar cuáles ideas terminan siendo elegidas para prototipar. Solo en [Kudryashov 2021] se realiza un principio de co-diseño, los participantes comparten sus bosquejos de CAA y el resto opina sobre los mismos; sin embargo no se avanza a un único bosquejo grupal. En base a esto se puede observar que co-diseñar usando DP con adultos autistas podría requerir de mucha exploración para poder abordarlo adecuadamente.

5. Conclusiones y Trabajos Futuros

Se espera que este trabajo ayude a visibilizar la necesidad de explorar en relación al DP con personas neurodiversas para la generación de software, y el rol fundamental que tiene el facilitador para el éxito de las mismas. El framework conceptual propuesto en este trabajo es un punto de partida para ayudar al facilitador en esta tarea; si bien está en una etapa inicial se ha fundamentado cada concepto con bibliografía, permitiendo apreciar la viabilidad del mismo. Además, el trabajo presentado puede impactar ampliamente en el DP con personas neurodiversas, ya que esto está poco explorado [Maun et al. 2021]. Poder aprender sobre cómo diseñan las personas neurodiversas podría servir en un futuro para conformar grupos de trabajo mixtos; donde se aporta una mirada distinta a la visión neurotípica del mundo.

Como trabajo futuro se espera poder usar el framework propuesto para diseñar y poner en práctica experiencias concretas, esto nos va a permitir aprender más sobre este tipo de abordaje; para enriquecer el framework y contar con más recomendaciones (por ejemplo, cómo acondicionar recursos existentes de DT para usarlos con personas neurodiversas). Además, se realizará una exploración de bibliografía en relación a otros subgrupos neurodivergentes (ya que en este trabajo se abordó la mirada autista); para contar con más conocimiento sobre otras consideraciones que hay que tener en cuenta al momento del DP con personas neurodiversas.

Referencias

Aslam, S. (2018). Participatory Design of a Social Robot Toolkit for Adults with Autism. In *Student Undergraduate Research E-journal!*. TU Delft OPEN.

Corso, C. L. and Challiol, C. (2020) "Meta-framework para diseñar experiencias de Design Thinking", 2020 IEEE Congreso Bienal de Argentina, S. Gramajo, G. Tomaselli and R. Scapinni, Argentina, IEEE Press, p. 1-8.

Kenny, L., Hattersley, C., Molins, B., Buckley, C., Povey, C. and Pellicano, E. (2016). Which terms should be used to describe autism?. In *Autism 20(4)*, pages 442-462. SAGE Publications.

Kudryashov, L. (2021) "Participatory Design of Augmentative and Alternative Communication (AAC) Technology with Autistic Adults", Thesis of Master Science Information, University of Michigan.

Maun, R., Fabri, M. and Trevorrow, P. (2021) "Adapting Participatory Design Activities for Autistic Adults: A Review", International Conference on Human-Computer Interaction, M. M. Soares, E. Rosenzweig and A. Marcus, Washington, Springer Cham, p. 300-314.

Parizi, R., da Silva, M. M., Couto, I., Trindade, K., Prestes, M. P., dos Santos Marczak, S. and Candello, H. (2020) "Design thinking in software requirements: What techniques to use? A Proposal for a Recommendation Tool", XXIII Ibero-American Conference on Software Engineering, C. P. Ayala, L. Murta, D. Soares Cruzes, E. Figueiredo, C. Silva, J. L. de la Vara, B. de França, M. Solari, G. Horta Travassos and I. Machado, Brazil, Curran Associates, p. 320-333.

Politis, Y., Olivia, L., Olivia, T. and Sung, C. (2017). Involving People with Autism in Development of Virtual World for Provision of Skills Training. In *International Journal of E-learning and Distance Education*, Au Press.

Politis, Y., Olivia, L. and Olivia, T. (2019). Empowering autistic adults through their involvement in the development of a virtual world. In *Advances in Autism*, pages 303-317. Emerald Publishing Limited.

Sanders, E. B. N. (2002). From user-centered to participatory design approaches. In *Design and the Social Sciences*, pages 18-25. CRC Press.

Thompson, G., Raine, M., Hayward, S. and Kilpatrick H. (2021). Gathering community perspectives to inform the design of autism-friendly music-making workshops for wellbeing. In *International Journal of Wellbeing*, pages 117-143.

Vance, T. (2020) "Understanding the Autistic Mind 1 (Comprender la Mente Autista 1)", https://neuroclastic.com/guide, Abril.

Detección automática de problemas de accesibilidad a partir de eventos de interacción de usuario

Maximiliano Jonathan Toledo, Julián Grigera[1], Alejandra Garrido[1]

LIFIA, Fac. de Informática, Universidad Nacional de La Plata, Argentina
[1]También CONICET, Argentina

{maximiliano.toledo, juliang, garrido}@lifia.info.unlp.edu.ar

Resumen. *Muchas actividades de nuestra vida cotidiana se encuentran integradas a aplicaciones web, las cuales deben ser accesibles a todos los usuarios. Por esto resulta fundamental incorporar la accesibilidad al proceso de desarrollo. Para facilitar esta integración y la detección de problemas de accesibilidad, en este trabajo se desarrolló una herramienta automática para la detección y reporte de este tipo de problemas denominada ABF (Accessibility BadSmells Finder). La misma busca ayudar a los desarrolladores a proveer sitios web accesibles, gracias a que realiza búsquedas dinámicas de diversos problemas de accesibilidad y que no son detectados por otras herramientas debido a la complejidad de su detección.*

Keywords: Bad Smell, Aplicaciones web, Accesibilidad, Análisis dinámico de eventos.

1. Introducción

La accesibilidad web está enfocada en brindar independencia para permitir autonomía a los usuarios de poder navegar por el contenido presente en la web, más allá de sus discapacidades. A pesar de la gran cantidad de estudios, herramientas y soluciones propuestas, la mayor parte del contenido web que se produce no tiene en cuenta las normas de accesibilidad ni las necesidades de personas con discapacidad [Carvalho2016; Carvaja2020]. Generalmente, las empresas de software tratan de disminuir el tiempo y los recursos afectados a los procesos de desarrollo para competir rápidamente en el mercado, y por ende no invierten en el proceso de accesibilidad de sus productos. Esto igualmente produce que el costo de la **no-accesibilidad** sea alto, lo cual incluye no sólo la pérdida de usuarios y clientes que no encuentran o no pueden acceder a lo que buscan, sino también sanciones que se pueden llegar a recibir por no proveer un producto accesible y eventuales costos de contratación de servicios externos para subsanar los problemas de accesibilidad. Por ende, es necesario que los desarrolladores de pequeñas y medianas empresas puedan contar con mecanismos y herramientas que les permitan generar aplicaciones web accesibles de una manera rápida y a bajo costo.

Con el fin de proveer un mecanismo que la industria pueda adoptar fácilmente para evaluar la accesibilidad de sus sistemas, la W3C ha creado las "Web Content Accessibility Guidelines" [WCAG]. Las mismas constituyen pautas o recomendaciones para lograr que el contenido web sea accesible, que se agrupan con sus criterios de éxito y posibles soluciones cuando los criterios no se cumplen. Las WCAG son consideradas estándares internacionales de accesibilidad Web y constituyen el instrumento más popular utilizado para guiar a los desarrolladores en la creación y evaluación de sitios web accesibles [W3C2005]. Sin embargo, y a pesar de cumplir con las recomendaciones de la W3C, una aplicación puede no ser usable o accesible, debido a que personas con discapacidades podrían aún tener dificultades para navegar e interactuar con el contenido de manera cómoda, fácil y eficaz. Esto se da sobre todo en las aplicaciones con contenido dinámico, por ejemplo, en las llamadas Single Page Applications (SPA) o Rich Internet Applications (RIA), que cambian la página web y el estado de los widgets en la página a medida que el usuario interactúa con ella.

Asociadas a las WCAG se han construido herramientas de detección automática que ayudan a los programadores a identificar violaciones a las pautas [TAW]. Sin embargo, estas herramientas realizan un **análisis estático** a nivel de código y, por lo tanto, la cantidad de problemas que pueden encontrar es limitada. Por ejemplo, la Figura 1 muestra dos sitios web con mensajes de formularios o modales inaccesibles ya que un usuario con discapacidad visual nunca se entera de su presencia. Este problema no puede ser detectado por estas herramientas, dado que se trata de aplicaciones RIA y las herramientas solo chequean y analizan el código HTML estático. La principal característica de estos elementos es que no aparecen desde un principio cuando el usuario ingresa al sitio web, sino que son desplegados luego de alguna acción generada por el mismo usuario. Por esto, una búsqueda estática no es suficiente para detectar este tipo de problemas.

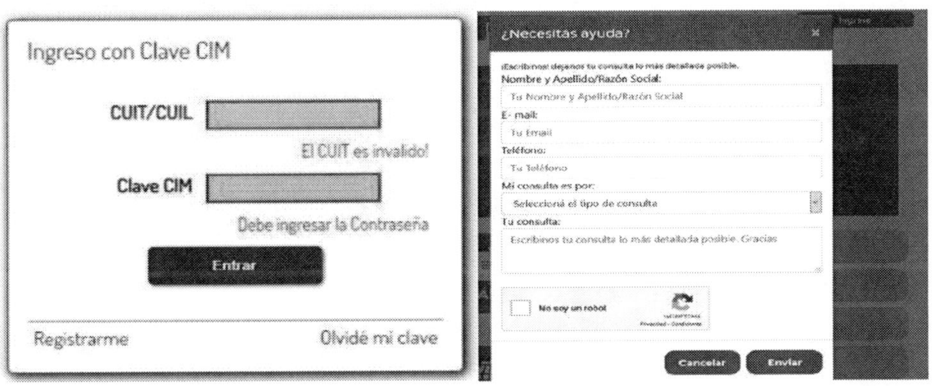

Fig. 1: Formulario de Ingreso con varios mensajes de error desplegados y modal desplegado para completar formulario web.

Para poder detectar estos problemas que aparecen a medida que un usuario interactúa con el sitio, es necesario realizar **búsquedas dinámicas** analizando los patrones de interacción generados por los usuarios. Existen diferentes propuestas en trabajos relacionados para encontrar problemas de accesibilidad que aparecen dinámicamente [Watanabe2016; Antonelli2019]. Sin embargo, solo pueden detectar un número acotado de problemas de accesibilidad, necesitan de la ayuda humana para poder realizar una detección eficaz, generan reportes que solo personas técnicamente preparadas pueden entender, simulan eventos de usuario de forma poco eficiente y generan falsos positivos, entre otras desventajas.

Este trabajo presenta un nuevo enfoque, basado en una herramienta denominada Accessibility BadSmells Finder (ABF)[1], que mediante el uso de varias funcionalidades del lenguaje JavaScript y una extensión web, permite realizar búsquedas dinámicas en aplicaciones web, y así lograr detectar elementos web que generen *accessibility smells* [Toledo2021]. El fin de esta herramienta no es solo detectar estos elementos problemáticos, sino además almacenar su información para luego generar reportes de

[1] Accesible desde http://sedici.unlp.edu.ar/handle/10915/125055

accesibilidad que sean de fácil lectura. Además, a través del desarrollo de algoritmos de detección (*finders*) individuales se logró una herramienta que puede ser extendida sin limitaciones para atacar diferentes tipos de problemas de accesibilidad.

2. Marco teórico y trabajo relacionado

2.1 Evaluación estática de la accesibilidad web

Existen varias herramientas que permiten la evaluación online de accesibilidad de sitios web como Level Access, TAW, AChecker y OAW. Estas herramientas online aplican métodos de **búsqueda estáticos en el código** de la página web, en busca de incumplimientos de las guías de accesibilidad WCAG. No obstante, hay varios problemas de accesibilidad que no pueden ser encontrados de esta manera. Por ejemplo, los botones hechos con elementos HTML `<a>` (para definir links) o `<div>` (para agrupar contenido), impiden a un usuario que utiliza un lector de pantalla poder encontrarlos, lo cual lleva a que realice varios recorridos dentro de la misma sección o página para lograr ubicarlos.

La W3C también ha creado una especificación técnica para el desarrollo de componentes RIA accesibles llamada WAI-ARIA [WAI-ARIA]. La misma permite agregar semántica a elementos dinámicos, especificando su tipo y funcionalidad a través de atributos, pero no se define la manera de asegurar su cumplimiento.

En definitiva, ninguna herramienta en sí misma puede determinar si un sitio cumple o no completamente con las pautas de accesibilidad [Antonelli2019]. Para determinar si un sitio Web es accesible, es necesaria la evaluación humana [W3C2005].

2.2 Refactoring para la mejora de la usabilidad y accesibilidad

Una propuesta para solucionar problemas de usabilidad o accesibilidad que aparecen en las aplicaciones web es el concepto de "Refactoring Web" [Garrido2011; Garrido2014]. La propuesta asociada a este concepto consiste en cambiar aspectos de la navegación o presentación de una aplicación web en producción sin cambiar su comportamiento, con el fin de mejorar su usabilidad o accesibilidad. El mayor inconveniente de esta técnica es que resulta muy difícil para una persona discapacitada reconocer qué refactoring instalar para solucionar los problemas que sufre.

Por otro lado, estos refactorings están catalogados dependiendo del problema o "smell" que solucionan, que en el caso de usabilidad se denominan **usability smells** [Garrido2011;Buono2020]. Grigera et al. han desarrollado una técnica de detección automática de usability smells en aplicaciones web que ya están en producción [Grigera2017]. Esta estrategia está basada en el análisis dinámico de los eventos de interacción del usuario. Sin embargo, se enfoca en las interacciones de usuarios videntes, ya que se basa principalmente en el análisis de eventos de mouse. En base a este trabajo, se ha desarrollado una extensión que permite procesar interacciones que incluyan eventos de accesibilidad [Durgam2020]. Para esta extensión se definió un catálogo de **accessibility smells** para usuarios con dificultades visuales que pueden detectarse automáticamente al observar la interacción a través de teclado y lector de pantalla. En este caso, la principal desventaja es que los reportes de smells deben ser leídos por personas con experiencia técnica y aun así en muchos casos es muy difícil identificar la causa concreta del problema; además existen algunos reportes que no pueden ser solucionados debido a que aún no existen refactorings desarrollados para este fin.

2.3 Detección de problemas de accesibilidad a través de la simulación de eventos

En el trabajo de Antonelli et al. se describe el desafío de las herramientas de evaluación automática de accesibilidad, que no son capaces de identificar componentes RIA en el código [Antonelli2019]. Los enfoques existentes aproximan esta identificación a través de la simulación de la interacción de usuarios [Fernandes2013; Watanabe2016].

El trabajo de Watanabe et al. propone una herramienta que identifica automáticamente a los elementos de tipo menú drop-down en una aplicación web [Watanabe2016]. Una vez que los elementos están identificados son analizados para determinar si están implementados utilizando las recomendaciones de ARIA. Esta herramienta está basada en la simulación de escenarios de interacciones de usuario, Mutation Observers y cambios de visibilidad en la interfaz del browser. Específicamente se simula a los usuarios generando eventos de desplazamiento en los elementos de una página web. Los cambios en el DOM son observados con Mutation Observers para clasificar elementos como menú desplegable o no, a través del análisis del resultado de la ejecución de código HTML, CSS y JavaScript dentro del navegador. Una vez detectados los menús desplegables, se analizan las reglas ARIA aplicadas a estos elementos y se generan los respectivos reportes. Las principales desventajas de este trabajo son la generación de falsos positivos por los simuladores y el gran tiempo requerido para cada simulación. Para evitar esta desventaja nuestro enfoque observa la ejecución de eventos de interacción reales, como describe la próxima sección.

3. Metodología

Nuestro objetivo es la detección automática de los problemas de accesibilidad que ocurren dinámicamente en una aplicación web, y que llamamos "accessibility smells". En especial nos enfocamos en accessibility smells para usuarios con discapacidad visual que utilizan un lector de pantalla. Con este fin hemos desarrollado la herramienta ABF, que genera reportes con el listado de los diferentes accessibility smells detectados por la herramienta junto a la información detallada de los elementos de la página que generaron estos problemas. ABF está constituida por tres componentes principales (ver Figura 2):

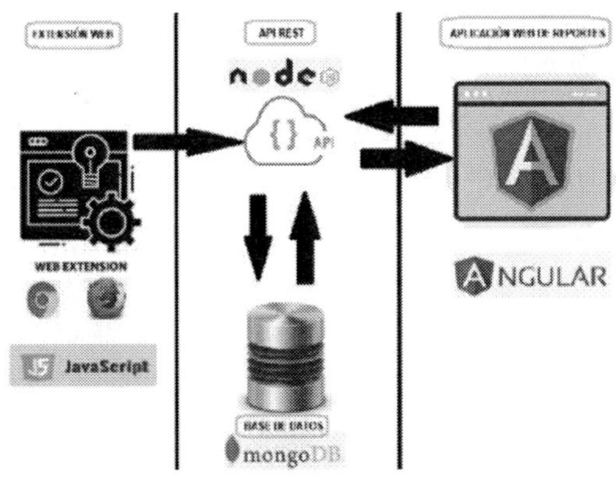

Fig. 2: Arquitectura de ABF

1. **Extensión web**: encargada de detectar elementos web que generen algún tipo de accessibility smell.

2. **API REST**: encargada de proveer la comunicación entre la extensión web, la base de datos y la aplicación de reportes.

3. **Aplicación de reportes**: aplicación web en la cual tanto el propietario del sitio web como los desarrolladores pueden visualizar los accessibility smells de su aplicación.

Dichos componentes integran las siguientes tres etapas dentro del funcionamiento de ABF, respectivamente: *Detección, Almacenamiento y manejo de la información*, y etapa de *Reporte*. La instancia de detección es la más importante de la herramienta, ya que es donde se analiza y se detectan los problemas de accesibilidad en páginas web. Un desarrollador que desee utilizar ABF, debe instalar la extensión web que implementa la detección dentro del mismo browser mientras está navegando en la aplicación web donde desea realizar la evaluación de accesibilidad. De esta forma ABF comenzará a observar los eventos *reales* que disparan los usuarios al acceder al contenido de su aplicación, sin necesidad de utilizar simulación. Cada vez que la extensión web detecte un elemento que genera un accessibility smell, se comunica a través del API REST para almacenar esta información en la base de datos, para luego poder ser consumida por la aplicación de reportes. Accediendo a este reporte cada cierto intervalo de tiempo, el desarrollador podrá obtener el listado de smells ocurridos en ese intervalo.

El componente de detección funciona a través de *finders*. Los finders son algoritmos que analizan el sitio web en busca de elementos que generen un tipo específico de accessibility smell. Varios de estos finders realizan búsquedas dinámicas, es decir que dependen de los eventos de interacción del usuario para poder detectar elementos inaccesibles. En este trabajo nos concentramos en tres tipos específicos de accessibility smells que fueron detectados en búsquedas manuales utilizando el lector de pantalla NVDA. Particularmente se analizaron manualmente más de 20 sitios web conocidos.

La búsqueda de elementos inaccesibles se enfocó en aquellos involucrados en la interacción del usuario, es decir, que mediante NVDA y la interacción utilizando teclado, no es posible acceder a dichos elementos. A continuación, se describirán los tres finders implementados para este trabajo.

3.1 Análisis de accesibilidad en elementos web interactivos con handlers JS asignados

Los **elementos interactivos** son aquellos que pueden reaccionar a eventos que disparan los usuarios y así agregan algún tipo de funcionalidad al sitio. De entre estos, podemos encontrar varios casos de elementos que simulan ser otros mediante el uso de *handlers JavaScript*. Por ejemplo: botones desarrollados con DIV's, elementos link `<a>` sin el atributo HREF con forma de botón y hasta elementos `<span>` que simulan ser links.

Visualmente parecen links y botones, con lo cual un usuario sin discapacidad visual los reconoce. Sin embargo, al utilizar un lector de pantalla como NVDA, estos elementos son ignorados, impidiendo que el usuario con discapacidad acceda contenido o funcionalidad, por ejemplo, impidiéndole el envío de un formulario. Durante el análisis manual preliminar encontramos este problema en elementos HTML de tipo: **div**, **span**, **li** y **a**. Por lo tanto, la búsqueda se centró en este tipo de elementos. No obstante, cabe destacar que no todos los elementos de esos tipos son inaccesibles, ya que algunos desarrolladores consideran la accesibilidad durante el proceso de desarrollo, y mediante la utilización de atributos ARIA y el uso consciente de JavaScript en el código, logran desarrollar elementos interactivos accesibles.

3.1.1 Desarrollo del finder

La sección principal del código del *finder* realiza dos acciones principales:

1. Búsqueda de handlers declarados en el código del elemento HTML. Ejemplo:

```
<div onClick="cancel()"></div>
```

2. Búsqueda de handlers utilizando la función *getEventListeners()* provista por el browser. Estos handlers pueden estar declarados como código JS dentro de tags `<script>` en el mismo documento .html de la página o en archivos .js externos.

Una vez que se detectó si un elemento de la página posee un handler asignado, se almacena junto a diversa información del elemento. Esta información incluye el tipo de elemento (div, span, a ...), su ID, clases, los valores de varios atributos utilizados para brindar accesibilidad como *tabindex*, *aria_label* y *role*(ARIA), e información de los elementos hijos. Es importante notar que si los hijos de un elemento son accesibles gracias a sus atributos, el elemento padre también será accesible. Como validación extra se decidió agregar a cada uno de estos elementos con handlers JS, un *listener* JS, es decir, un objeto oyente de JS para escuchar eventos de foco. Así también podremos corroborar si el usuario logró interactuar con dicho elemento.

La información de los elementos que recibieron el foco es enviada a la API REST, quien es la encargada de almacenarlos en la base de datos, además se almacenan los eventos de foco que cada uno de estos elementos recibió. Luego esta información va a ser consumida por la aplicación de reportes. Para este Finder, se decidió que la lógica de analizar y reportar si un elemento es accesible o no, lo va a realizar la misma aplicación de reportes.

3.2 Análisis de accesibilidad en mensajes dinámicos de formulario web

Los formularios se utilizan para todo tipo de efectos interactivos en la web. Éstos permiten a los usuarios seleccionar y comprar productos, rellenar encuestas y cuestionarios, inscribirse en cursos, buscar información, etc.

Los formularios y otros elementos de interacción pueden ser confusos o difíciles de utilizar para muchas personas, lo cual las induce a cometer errores. Algunos ejemplos de ayuda para prevenir y corregir errores serían:

- Instrucciones descriptivas, mensajes de error y sugerencias de corrección.
- Ayuda contextual para funcionalidades e interacciones más complejas.
- Opción de revisar, corregir o revertir envíos si es necesario.

Esto incluye comentarios en línea o cerca de los campos del formulario y comentarios generales que generalmente se brindan después del envío del formulario. Además de los consejos anteriores, cada mensaje de error debe tener el atributo *role* con valor *alert*, para que puedan percibirlo los usuarios de lectores de pantalla.

3.2.1 Desarrollo del finder

Los mensajes de errores en los formularios son generalmente elementos HTML de texto como `<p>` y `<span>`. La detección de estos mensajes no se puede hacer de forma totalmente estática revisando el código de la aplicación web, ya que estos mensajes se pueden ir generando dinámicamente dentro o fuera del formulario. Por esto, la forma más efectiva de saber si los mensajes son accesibles es generarlos y analizarlos.

El desarrollo e implementación de este finder se basó en el trabajo de Watanabe et al. para identificar drop-down menú widgets utilizando "mutation observers" y "visibility changes" [Watanabe2016]. Es decir, un objeto incorporado a JS que observa un elemento DOM y dispara una función callback cuando hay cambios en él (visibility changes). De esta forma podremos observar dinámicamente cuando aparecen estos mensajes de error mientras el usuario interactúa con el formulario.

En nuestro caso, el primer paso es obtener todos los formularios de la página web actual (elementos <form>). El segundo paso es asignarle a cada elemento `<form>` un listener JavaScript (MutationObserver) que captura los eventos que agregan un elemento al formulario. Luego, cuando un cambio ocurre, filtramos por tipo de elemento: solamente nos quedamos con los elementos **p**, **span** y **label**. En los casos en que estos elementos no poseen atributos rol o aria*, reportamos el elemento y se envía a la API REST para su almacenamiento.

3.3 Análisis de accesibilidad en elementos web flotantes

Los modales son interfaces bastante comunes en la Web. Los desarrolladores y diseñadores pueden darles diferentes nombres: lightbox, modal window, dialog, overlay, etc., pero son básicamente lo mismo. La W3C denomina a estos elementos flotantes como **dialogs** o **modal dialogs**. Por lo general, el resto de la página está atenuado y los usuarios no pueden interactuar con ella hasta que cierren el cuadro de diálogo. En términos de ARIA, este es un diálogo "modal", **modal dialog**.

Los modales al igual que las alertas, interrumpen el flujo de lo que hace un usuario si no puede controlar la apertura de un modal. Para mitigar esta problemática, se pueden agregar controles para la apertura y cierre del modal con botones. Sin embargo, también hay cuadros de diálogo "no modales", non-modal dialogs, que permiten la interacción con el resto de la página y en este caso se ven como "paneles" que flotan en la ventana principal. Estos paneles muestran algún contenido sobre la página web, mientras que el resto de la página continúa siendo 100% funcional y accesible.

Durante nuestra búsqueda utilizando NVDA para detectar problemas de accesibilidad relacionados a elementos flotantes, descubrimos que hay una gran presencia de non-modal dialogs en las diferentes páginas web testeadas. Encontramos sitios webs donde hay hasta más de 5 elementos non-modal dialogs presentes al ingresar a la página.

Los diferentes tipos de non-modal dialogs que podemos encontrar son: *Cookie notifications, Toast messages, Toggletips o Tooltips, Popups activados por el usuario con elementos interactivos*.

WAI-ARIA menciona dos pasos principales para desarrollar estos elementos:

1. **Asignación de roles**: El elemento dialogo, en general de tipo `<div>`, debe contener el rol *dialog*, el cual ayuda a las tecnologías de asistencia a identificar el contenido del diálogo como *agrupado y separado del resto del contenido de la página*.

2. **Asignación de propiedades y relaciones importantes**: Etiquetar a los elementos dentro del diálogo proporcionará información contextual sobre los elementos interactivos dentro del diálogo.

Si un diálogo ya tiene un elemento de título visible, el texto dentro de ese elemento se puede usar para etiquetar el diálogo. Para esto conviene usar el atributo *aria-labelledby* en el elemento *role="dialog"*. Si el diálogo contiene texto descriptivo además de su título, este texto se puede asociar con el diálogo mediante el atributo *aria-describedby*.

3.3.1 Implementación del finder

Durante la investigación para este caso, encontramos que todos los elementos analizados manualmente, están definidos con etiquetas `<div>`. Esto nos provee un punto de partida para detectar este tipo de elemento. Sabiendo que los elementos flotantes que buscamos son `<div>`, debemos encontrar un patrón de diseño que los caracterice y diferencie de los demás *DIVs* de la página. Los modales generalmente poseen estilos CSS particulares que hacen que aparezcan por encima del contenido, diferenciándose del contenido principal. Comúnmente se utilizan las propiedades CSS como **z-index** (mayor a 0 para posicionarse por encima del contenido principal de la página), **Right, Bottom, Left, Top** (para posicionar al elemento en alguna esquina de la pantalla). Siempre están fijos en una misma posición de la pantalla mientras el contenido principal de la página se mueve con la navegación en el contenido), **Position**: fixed y **Display**: flex.

Por lo tanto, nos quedamos con los `<div>` que tengan definidos los estilos CSS mencionados anteriormente, que pueden obtenerse a través del método **getComputedStyle(elem).getPropertyValue()** y así comprobar si cumplen con el patrón de estilos que definimos. En principio, en la búsqueda nos quedamos con los elementos que posean los atributos con los valores *z-index > 1* y *position = 'fixed';* el chequeo de estos valores fue suficiente para detectar con suficiente certeza los elementos que nos interesan. Continuando con la búsqueda de elementos flotantes que se muestran al iniciar la página web, el último paso en la detección, consiste en revisar si los elementos poseen los atributos correspondientes de Rol y ARIA para poder ser accesibles.

Durante esta búsqueda, se lograron capturar y analizar la mayor parte de los elementos flotantes de nuestro interés. Durante la investigación en distintos sitios webs, hemos encontrado que generalmente hay entre 1 y 2 elementos flotantes (*non-modal dialogs*). Incluso, se lograron capturar los casos donde hay *non-modal dialogs* que se muestran dinámicamente al pasar cierto periodo de tiempo dentro de la página web. Cabe destacar que estos elementos no son renderizados por causa de algún evento disparado por parte del usuario, sino que es el mismo sitio web el que automáticamente los muestra.

Para lograr ampliar nuestra detección a elementos flotantes que se despliegan en la página dinámicamente, se utilizó como guía de desarrollo el diseño de la herramienta de detección desarrollada por Watanabe et al. [Watanabe2016], en la cual se realiza una búsqueda previa de los elementos que están ocultos, para luego observar si éstos son mostrados al usuario. En concreto, la solución consiste en observar los elementos que contienen los atributos *display: none* y *visibility: hidden*, como podemos observar en el código de la Figura 3.

```
function obtenerElementosOcultos() {
    let divs = getBodyDiv();
    return [...divs].filter(elem => {
        // Attributos de ocultamiento
        let display = window.getComputedStyle(elem).getPropertyValue('display');
        let visibility = window.getComputedStyle(elem).getPropertyValue('visibility');
        return visibility === 'hidden' || display === 'none';
    });
}
```

Fig. 3: Código de la función JS con la cual se obtienen los elementos ocultos.

Al tener detectados los elementos a los cuales vamos a observar, al igual que en la herramienta de Watanabe et al. [Watanabe2016], se fijan los Mutation Observer a estos elementos ocultos para lograr capturar si en algún momento pasan a ser visibles. Esta detección funciona dinámicamente; por ende, va a detectar aquellos elementos flotantes que cambien de estado oculto a desplegado en cualquier momento.

Cuando se detecta que un elemento estaba oculto y luego pasa a ser visible, se analiza si es un elemento de tipo flotante. Para eso se analizan sus atributos CSS, y si cumple, se busca entre sus atributos la ausencia de roles y atributos *ARIA*. Si no existe ninguno de estos atributos, se reporta el elemento a la *API REST* indicando que contiene el accessibility smell denominado *elemento web flotante inaccesible*.

Esta nueva solución dinámica permitió además detectar otros tipos de modales y elementos flotantes diferentes a los non-modal dialogs que pasan de estar ocultos a mostrarse debido a alguna acción disparadora que realiza el usuario.

3.4 Implementación de API REST y aplicación de reportes

Después de que cada finder finalice con su búsqueda y detección de elementos web inaccesibles, se envía la información de estas detecciones a la API Rest de la herramienta, y ésta se encarga de darle el formato correcto para almacenar la información en la base de datos. Dentro de la API Rest, hay un método que se encarga de realizar toda la lógica necesaria para lograr almacenar toda la información necesaria sobre los eventos de bad smells capturados por la extensión web, el método saveBadSmellEvent(). Dentro de este método se almacena el evento de bad smell en la colección BadSmellEvents. Sobre el evento se guarda las propiedades **BaseURI,** que indica la URL de la página web donde se originó el evento y **Data,** que contiene información sobre atributos del elemento web: contenido del elemento, tipo de elemento, código HTML del elemento, tipo de smell generado por el elemento, fecha y hora en la que se generó el evento.

Además, en este mismo método se registra el evento en otra colección llamada ReportedPages. El propósito de esta es tener almacenados los elementos web que provocaron eventos de accesibilidad en cada página web en donde se ejecutó la herramienta de una manera más organizada. Cada elemento de esta colección lo denominamos ReportedPage, y contiene la siguiente información: BaseURI (URL de la página web donde se ejecutó la web extensión), Reported_elements (contiene una colección de elementos que generaron smells de accesibilidad dentro de la página. De cada elemento almacenamos cierta información útil para lograr identificarlos y llevar un conteo de ocurrencias: tipo de elemento, código HTML del elemento, tipo de bad smell generado, cantidad de veces que se reportó este evento, fecha y hora en la que se generó el evento, fecha y hora en la que se actualizó por última vez).

El paso final es armar el reporte de los bad smells para cada sitio web en los cuales se ejecutó la extensión web, un ejemplo puede verse en la Figura 5 y 9. De esto la encargada es la aplicación web de reportes, la cual se comunica con la API Rest para que esta le brinde la información que se encuentra en la base de datos.

4. Experimentación y evaluación de la propuesta

4.1 Análisis de accesibilidad en elementos web interactivos con handlers JS asignados

Para mostrar el resultado final de la herramienta para la detección de elementos web inaccesibles con handlers JS, se ejecutó la misma en varios sitios web, un ejemplo de los resultados es el siguiente.

Página de principal del portal de APR

URL

www.apronline.gob.ar

Comportamiento de NVDA

En este caso *NVDA* no mencionó ninguno de los dos elementos que están señalados en la Figura 4. Por lo tanto, el usuario no puede utilizar el carrusel de trámites.

Fig. 4: Screenshot de los elementos para controlar el scroll del carrusel.

Como se puede observar en la Figura 5, se reportaron ambos elementos del carrusel. Los cuales son links <a> con handlers JS asignados y sin atributo HREF ni atributos para lograr accesibilidad.

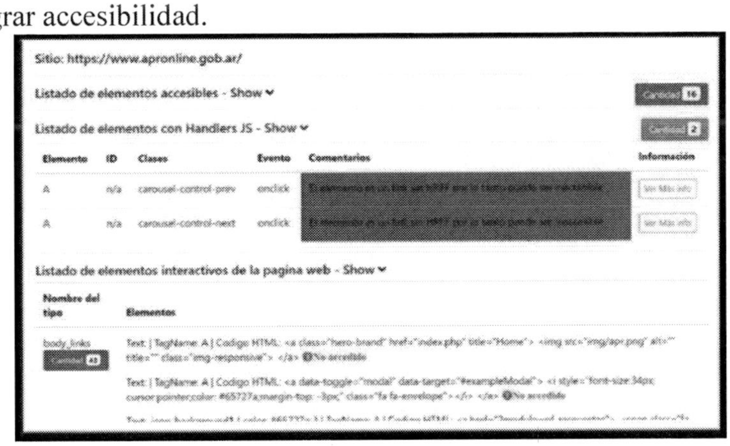

Fig. 5: Reporte generado por ABF para la página principal de APR.

Ampliación de búsqueda para elementos no detectados

Luego de probar la herramienta en varios sitios web, se han logrado detectar la gran mayoría de elementos con handlers JS. Aun así, había algunos elementos que no podían ser detectados, y la causa fue que utilizaban handlers diferentes a los que eran buscados por el finder de búsqueda. Por ejemplo, en un principio el finder buscaba elementos con handlers "onClick", pero esto no detectaba la mayoría ya que existen elementos que manejan el evento "click". Por lo tanto, luego de añadir este evento a la búsqueda del finder, se logró ampliar aún más la cantidad de elementos detectados. Por ejemplo, en el sitio de autogestión de APR, hay elementos de tipo link <a> los cuales antes de incluir eventos "click" en el finder, no podían ser detectados y ahora lo son. Como se puede observar en la Figura 6, se pueden ver los elementos con handlers JS accesibles y los que no lo son.

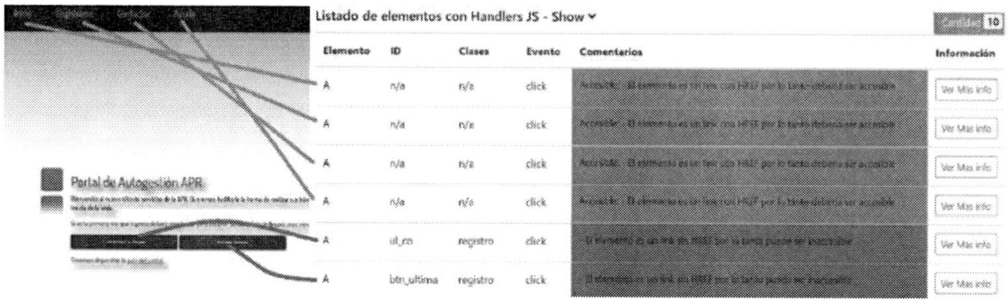

Fig. 6: Diagrama que muestra los elementos con handlers JS de la página de APR reportados y clasificados.

Eventos no detectados

Para seguir ampliando la capacidad de detección de este finder, se necesitó seguir añadiendo más tipos de eventos a la etapa de búsqueda del algoritmo. Para este trabajo nos enfocamos en elementos que reaccionan a eventos **onClick** y **click**, debemos destacar que para elementos de tipo link <a> no solo realizan su acción al recibir el click de mouse sino también al presionar la tecla *enter*. Sin embargo, al igual que los botones, esta es una característica de estos elementos. Para el caso de los <div> y <span> esto no es así, el usuario no los va a poder utilizar si no poseen una handler para recibir eventos de tecla *ENTER* (con handler *onclick* no es suficiente).

Fig. 7: Captura del carrusel de imágenes del sitio web de grupo-urbano.com.ar, junto al código HTML y los handlers asignados.

No obstante, hay casos donde se crean elementos interactivos que reaccionan a otro tipo de eventos, por ejemplo, como se puede ver en la Figura 7, los dos elementos para manipular el carrusel de imágenes están declarados con <div>'s que tienen los siguientes handlers asignados: **mousedown**, **mouseup**, **touchend** y **touchstart**. Sería bueno para trabajos futuros incluir estos eventos a la búsqueda de elementos.

4.2 Análisis de accesibilidad en mensajes dinámicos de formulario web

<u>Página de registro del portal de APR</u>

URL

https://autogestion.apronline.gov.ar/registro

Comportamiento de NVDA

En este caso el lector de pantalla *NVDA* no mencionó ninguno de los errores que se muestran en pantalla. Simplemente hizo un salto al primer input con error.

La herramienta reporta los elementos que representan a un error en el formulario y que no son accesibles. En este ejemplo, los elementos de la Figura 8 que contienen los mensajes de error contienen el atributo for, pero están declarados como *<span>* y no como *<label>*. El atributo *for* solo funciona en elementos *label* y *output*, es decir en este caso no permite que el elemento sea accesible para el lector de pantalla. Estos elementos fueron detectados y reportados por la herramienta como se observa en la Figura 9, por lo tanto, podemos concluir que en este caso la detección funcionó correctamente.

Fig. 8: Formulario web del sitio de APR con mensajes de error desplegados.

Fig. 9: Reporte generado por la aplicación de reportes para la página de registro de APR.

4.3 Análisis de accesibilidad en elementos web flotantes

<u>Página de inicio de APR Online</u>

URL

http://www.apronline.gov.ar/

Comportamiento de NVDA

Continuando con el caso de la página de APR Online encontramos que al ingresar a la página web aparece un modal desplegado. Este modal cubre el contenido de la página con una capa oscura (ver Figura 10). De una manera contraintuitiva, mientras el modal esté desplegado, el usuario puede seguir interactuando con los demás elementos de la página. Más allá de ello, el usuario no es notificado sobre el modal desplegado como debiera suceder.

Fig. 10: Modal al inicio de la página web de APR Online.

Elementos Flotantes web inaccesibles

Mostrar Elementos

Identificador	Tipo Elemento	Último Update	Ocurrencias	Acciones
<div class="chat2" style="cursor: pointer;"> <a href="?modulo=pf_res..	DIV	Apr 28, 2021, 7:43:50 PM	4	Ver Más info
<div class="chat" style="cursor: pointer;"> <a data-toggle="modal" da..	DIV	Apr 28, 2021, 7:43:50 PM	4	Ver Más info
<div class="hide modal fade show" id="events-modal-popup" style="paddi..	DIV	Apr 28, 2021, 7:43:50 PM	3	Ver Más info
<div class="modal-backdrop fade show"></div>	DIV	Apr 28, 2021, 7:43:50 PM	3	Ver Más info

Fig. 11: Resultado final de la detección de elementos flotantes con problemas de accesibilidad.

Analizando el resultado de la herramienta mostrado en la Figura 11, nos detendremos en los últimos dos elementos reportados:

a) class="hide modal fade show" id="events-modal-popup"

b) class="modal-backdrop fade show"

Ambos están relacionados con el modal de la Figura 10; el modal en sí que contiene el contenido es el elemento reportado a), y está correctamente reportado ya que no posee ningún atributo o rol ARIA para ser accesible. El elemento b) también carece de estos atributos, pero no es correcto reportarlo ya que es la sombra del modal. Fue reportado por la herramienta ya que posee las mismas características de un elemento flotante. Este fue el único caso en estos tipos de elemento donde ABF reporta un falso positivo. En futuras versiones se planea ignorar este tipo de elementos durante la detección de elementos flotantes.

5. Conclusiones y trabajo futuro

La accesibilidad web no es algo sencillo de lograr si la misma no está incluida en el proceso de desarrollo. Por otro lado los desarrolladores no suelen tener en cuenta a la accesibilidad durante el desarrollo de una aplicación web, y tampoco poseen capacitación en el tema. En general, recién se comienza a dar importancia a la accesibilidad web luego de que el costo de no incluirla en el desarrollo comienza a aumentar. Para ayudar a los desarrolladores a lograr proveer sitios webs accesibles, actualmente existen varias herramientas online y gratuitas para evaluar un sitio en busca de problemas de accesibilidad. Sin embargo, están limitadas a solo poder encontrar aquellos problemas de accesibilidad que pueden ser detectados a través del análisis estático de código.

En este trabajo se buscó brindar a los desarrolladores y dueños de sitios web una herramienta que facilite la forma en que pueden encontrar diferentes tipos de elementos webs que generen *accessibility smells*. El fin de esta herramienta no es solo la de detectar los elementos problemáticos, sino además almacenar su información para luego generar reportes de accesibilidad que sean de fácil lectura. Una de las principales ventajas de la herramienta ABF es que su código es público, así que puede ser extendido sin limitaciones para lograr detectar más casos de elementos web inaccesibles. Otra ventaja importante es que los *finders* definidos en la extensión web están desarrollados en JavaScript, lo cual debería facilitar la incorporación de nuevos finders de otros *accessibility smell* a detectar. Además, la experimentación ha demostrado que ABF tiene un buen rendimiento [Toledo2021].

Como trabajos futuros se plantean ampliar la búsqueda utilizando nuevos tipos de eventos para el finder *análisis de accesibilidad en elementos web interactivos con handlers JS asignados*. En el caso del finder *análisis de accesibilidad en mensajes dinámicos de formulario web*, hubo algunos casos de mensajes inaccesibles que no fueron detectados debido a que estos elementos son generados fuera del formulario, y la herramienta está desarrollada para detectar solo cambios del DOM dentro del formulario. Como trabajo futuro buscaremos integrar a la herramienta existente, la lógica para poder capturar estos mensajes por fuera del formulario. En el finder *análisis de accesibilidad en elementos web flotantes*, el siguiente desafío consta en continuar mejorando el filtrado de aquellos elementos flotantes que no son deseados en las detecciones, por ende, no es de nuestro interés analizarlos en búsqueda de problemas de accesibilidad.

Además, se desea continuar con la mejora de los finders de la herramienta definidos en este trabajo y continuar con el desarrollo de nuevos finders que ataquen a otras problemáticas de accesibilidad web y diferentes elementos web. También se propone agregar dentro de los reportes, la zona específica en el código de la aplicación web donde se generan los bad smells detectados. Por otro lado también buscaremos incluir la aplicación de *refactorings* de código a los elementos detectados y reportados por la herramienta cuando sea posible, y así lograr aplicar una solución a estos problemas. Asimismo buscaremos avanzar en escalar la herramienta a un ambiente de producción. Esto permitirá que varios usuarios reporten a una misma base de datos, y así poder generar reportes de accesibilidad con datos generados por múltiples usuarios. Además, se va a continuar con la realización de experimentos con usuarios no videntes para testear la funcionalidad de la herramienta y así analizar sus resultados para continuar con la mejora continua de la herramienta.

Referencias

[Antonelli2019] Antonelli, H. L., Sensiate, L., Watanabe, W. M., & de Mattos Fortes, R. P. (2019). Challenges of automatically evaluating Rich Internet Applications accessibility. Proc. of the 37th ACM Int. Conf. Design of Communication, pp. 1-6.

[Buono2020] Buono, P., Caivano, D., Costabile, M., Desolda, G., Lanzilotti, R. (2020). Towards the Detection of UX Smells: The Support of Visualizations, in IEEE Access, vol. 8, pp. 6901-6914.

[Carvaja2020] Carvajal, Carlos Máñez. (2020). Evaluación de accesibilidad web de las universidades chilenas. Formación universitaria, 13(5), pp. 69-76.

[Carvalho2016] Pedroso Carvalho, L. , Pereira Ferreira, L., Pimenta Freire, A. (2016). Accessibility evaluation of rich internet applications interface components for mobile screen readers. In Proc. 31st ACM Symp. on Applied Computing. pp. 181–186.

[Durgam2020] Durgam, F. (2020). Detección de problemas de accesibilidad en la utilización de lectores de pantalla en aplicaciones web. Tesis de Maestría, Fac. de Informática, Univ. Nacional de La Plata.

[Fernandes2013] Fernandes, N., Batista, A. S., Costa, D., Duarte, C., Carriço, L. (2013). Three web accessibility evaluation perspectives for RIA. In Proc. 10th Int. cross-disciplinary conference on web accessibility, pp. 1-9.

[Garrido2011] Garrido, A., Rossi, G., Distante, D. (2011) Refactoring for usability in web applications. IEEE Software 28(3), pp. 60–67.

[Garrido2014] Garrido, A., Rossi, G., Medina-Medina, N., Grigera, J., Firmenich, S. (2014) Improving Accessibility of Web interfaces: refactoring to the rescue. Univ. Access in the Information Society 13, pp. 387-399.

[Grigera2017] Grigera, J.; Garrido, A.; Rivero, J. M.; Rossi, G. (2017) Automatic detection of usability smells in web applications. International Journal of Human-Computer Studies 97, pp. 129-148.

[TAW] Taw. Test de accesibilidad web. https://www.tawdis.net/.

[Toledo2021] Toledo, M. (2021). Detección automática de problemas de accesibilidad a partir de eventos de interacción de usuario. Tesis de Licenciatura, Fac. de Informática, Univ. Nacional de La Plata.

[W3C2005] W3C. 2005 Web Accessibility Initiative (WAI). Accessibility Introduction. https://www.w3.org/WAI/fundamentals/accessibility-intro/

[WAI-ARIA] WAI ARIA, the Accessible Rich Inter net Applications Suite. https://www.w3.org/WAI/standards guidelines/aria/.

[WCAG] WCAG 2.1 2018. Web Content Accessibility Guidelines. https://www.w3.org/TR/WCAG21/.

[Watanabe2016] Watanabe, W. M., & de Mattos Fortes, R. P. (2016, April). Automatic identification of drop-down menu widgets using mutation observers and visibility changes. In Proc. 31st Annual ACM Symp. on Applied Computing (pp. 766-771).

Experimento para evaluar el uso de patrones de negocio para facilitar la comprensión del modelo conceptual de un sistema de gobierno electrónico

Oscar Medina[1], Marcela Genero[2], Marcelo Marciszack[1], Alicia Bratti[1], Ana Strub[1]

[1] Universidad Tecnológica Nacional – Facultad Regional Córdoba, Cruz Roja Argentina y Maestro López s/n, Ciudad Universitaria, Córdoba, Argentina

[2] Universidad de Castilla-La Mancha, Paseo de la Universidad N°4, Ciudad Real, España.

{omedina, marciszack, gbratti, astrub}@frc.utn.edu.ar, marcela.genero@uclm.es

Resumen. *Los patrones son reconocidos como modelos exitosos que favorecen la reusabilidad, y es una de sus características, facilitar la comprensión de un modelo. Este artículo describe un experimento cuyo objetivo es corroborar si el uso de patrones de negocio mejora la comprensión del modelo conceptual de un sistema de gobierno electrónico. El experimento se realizó en el año 2021 con 33 estudiantes del tercer curso de la carrera de Ingeniería en Sistemas de Información. Los resultados obtenidos evidencian que existen diferencias significativas en favor a la efectividad de la comprensión del modelo conceptual al utilizar patrones de negocio. En cambio, no hay diferencias relevantes en la eficiencia al utilizar, o no, patrones.*

1. Introducción

Un patrón es una descripción de una solución común a un problema recurrente que puede ser aplicado a un contexto específico. Los patrones ayudan a aprovechar la experiencia colectiva de software especializado, donde los ingenieros representan la experiencia existente y probada en el desarrollo de sistemas.

Para Alexander [Alexander 1979], un patrón es una *"solución generalizada que puede ser implementada y aplicada en una situación problemática y de ese modo a eliminar uno o más de los problemas inherentes con el fin de satisfacer uno o más objetivos"*. Alexander propuso el término patrón en su libro *"The Timeless Way of Building"* en el año 1979. En 1994 se aplica el concepto de patrones al diseño de software en la obra *"Design Patterns: Elements of Reusable Object-Oriented Software"* [Gamma et al. 1994], acorde al paradigma de la programación orientada a objetos.

Según Eriksson y Penker [Eriksson and Penker 2000], cada patrón se ocupa de un problema específico y recurrente en el diseño o implementación de un sistema de software. Los patrones se pueden utilizar para construir arquitecturas de software con propiedades específicas. Los patrones que se encuentran en un modelo de negocio se denominan patrones de negocio. Dichos autores afirman que los patrones de negocio permiten obtener los recursos del modelo, organizaciones, objetivos, procesos y normas de la empresa.

En el mismo sentido, el modelo conceptual de un sistema de información tiene como finalidad identificar y explicar los conceptos significativos en un dominio de problema, elicitando los atributos y las asociaciones existentes entre ellos [Sommerville 2011]. Los patrones que se aplican al modelado conceptual cumplen la función de reutilizar el conocimiento y experiencia de sistemas anteriores encapsulado en soluciones de análisis y diseño concretas, permitiendo la verificación y validación de los requerimientos funcionales. Los patrones permiten modelar el proceso de negocio como marco situacional en el cual se desarrollará un sistema. Es por ello que el empleo de patrones, al inicio del modelado conceptual, aporta una serie de beneficios significativos en la construcción del sistema, los cuales fueron observados en investigaciones anteriores [Marciszack et al. 2018, Medina et al. 2018, Medina et al. 2021].

El problema que intenta resolver la mencionada propuesta de modelado es la falta de reusabilidad de modelos de negocio que definan el marco para la construcción de un nuevo sistema de un mismo dominio, como por ejemplo el de gobierno electrónico. El uso de patrones de negocio en el modelo conceptual permitiría optimizar la reusabilidad que es además una de las dimensiones de la calidad de software.

Para comprobar dicha afirmación, el presente trabajo expone un experimento que se realizó con el objetivo de evaluar si el uso de patrones mejora o no la facilidad de comprensión del modelo conceptual de un sistema de gobierno electrónico real, comparándolos con el uso de descripción narrativa exclusivamente, o en combinación patrones de negocio más descripción narrativa.

De los resultados obtenidos en las anteriores investigaciones, se destaca un mapeo sistemático de la literatura sobre patrones aplicables al Modelado Conceptual de sistemas de información [Medina et al. 2022b]. En este estudio se pudo identificar los tipos de patrones más relevantes que se aplican en el modelado de sistemas que son los patrones de diseño, negocio, análisis, arquitectura y escenario. Se destacan los patrones de diseño, que son los primeros patrones definidos en Ingeniería de Software; y los patrones de Negocios, debido a que se utilizan para la especificación de procesos en la fase de modelado. Es por ello que se utilizaron patrones de negocio en el experimento.

Se analizó la facilidad de comprensión porque es una de las características de la reusabilidad [Manso 2009], ya que la comprensión es la facultad que posibilita percibir y asimilar un fenómeno, objeto o concepto. Esto nos permite luego reutilizarlo, adaptándolo al contexto si fuera necesario.

El experimento se llevó a cabo con 33 estudiantes del tercer curso de la carrera Ingeniería en Sistemas de Información de la U.T.N. – F.R.C. (Universidad Tecnológica Nacional – Facultad Regional Córdoba) de Argentina en el mes de abril de 2021. Para planificar, ejecutar y reportar este experimento, se siguieron las recomendaciones proporcionadas en [Wohlin et al. 2012, Genero et al. 2014]. Todo el material utilizado en el experimento se encuentra disponible en el sitio web del Centro de Investigación [Medina et al. 2022a].

El resto del artículo está estructurado de la siguiente manera. En la sección 2 se presenta la planificación del experimento. En la sección 3 se describe las características principales de la ejecución del experimento, mientras que en la sección 4 se desarrolla el análisis e interpretación de resultados recopilados en la ejecución, y en la sección 5 se analiza las amenazas a la validez del experimento. Finalmente, en la sección 6 se presenta las conclusiones y los trabajos futuros.

2. Planificación del experimento

La planificación de un experimento, al formular un planteamiento adecuado del problema, ayuda a asegurar que se estén evaluado las variables correctas. A continuación, se detallan los componentes de la planeación de este experimento: la selección del contexto, sujeto y variables del experimento, formulación de hipótesis, diseño experimental, instrumentación y tareas experimentales.

2.1. Selección del contexto

El contexto elegido para este experimento es un entorno académico y trata sobre el modelo conceptual de un sistema real de gobierno electrónico.

Como a la fecha del experimento, en la U.T.N. – F.R.C. se desarrollaban las clases en modalidad virtual por la pandemia del COVID 19, todas las actividades del experimento se realizaron vía internet utilizando las plataformas académicas habituales que son *"Zoom"* para el dictado del taller de formación y la ejecución del experimento, y el sistema *"Moodle"* de aula virtual de la U.T.N. – F.R.C. para la gestión de cuestionarios y materiales utilizados en el experimento.

Los objetos experimentales consistieron en dos patrones de negocio: 1) patrón de objetivos (ver Figura 1), 2) estructura básica del proceso y proceso de interacción; y la descripción narrativa de un sistema de gobierno electrónico.

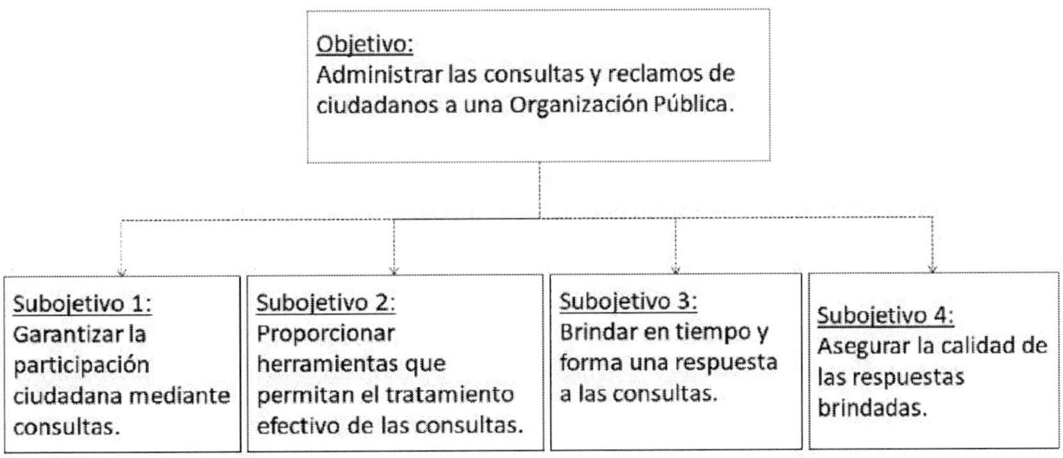

Figura 1. Diagrama del patrón "Gestión de consulta de ciudadanos – Objetivos"

En [Medina et al. 2022a], se puede apreciar con detalle el material del sistema gestión de consulta de ciudadanos que se empleó en el experimento. Sólo se utilizaron estos dos tipos de patrones de negocio porque son los más adecuados, según Eriksson & Penker [Eriksson and Penker 2000], para modelar procesos que soportan a productos de software y lo realizan en el nivel de mayor abstracción del modelo conceptual.

Los patrones utilizados modelan un sistema de gestión de consultas de ciudadanos de un organismo público regional que administra la seguridad previsional de los empleados del estado provincial de Córdoba, Argentina. Los objetos experimentales son parte de los resultados de un proyecto de investigación que fueron transferidos formalmente de la U.T.N. – F.R.C. al organismo público [PDTS 2022]. El patrón de objetivos desagrega el objetivo principal en cuatro subobjetivos con sus correspondientes problemas y soluciones implementadas. El patrón de estructura básica del proceso es un patrón de negocio que permite expresar el concepto principal del proceso considerando el suministro de recursos, el objetivo a alcanzar y la transformación de entradas en salidas. Por último, el patrón proceso de interacción detalla múltiples interacciones que ocurren entre los diferentes procesos de negocio. La descripción narrativa es una síntesis de la documentación funcional del sistema.

Como sujetos se escogieron estudiantes del tercer curso de Ingeniería en Sistemas de Información, como representantes de ingenieros de software principiantes.

2.2. Selección de sujetos

En el experimento participaron 33 estudiantes de la carrera Ingeniería en Sistemas de Información. Los estudiantes cursan la asignatura Gestión de mejora de procesos, asignatura electiva de tercer año que tiene por objetivo adquirir conocimientos que permitan analizar y diseñar procesos de negocio, basados en el concepto de mejora continua, y gestionar los cambios.

Se considera que el conocimiento adquirido sobre modelado conceptual en la carrera es suficiente para que los estudiantes puedan interpretar los patrones de negocio y la descripción narrativa del sistema seleccionado. Además, previo a la ejecución del experimento, se dictó un taller sobre utilización de patrones para comprender procesos de negocio, con el fin de unificar conceptos, y se solicitó a los sujetos responder un pre-cuestionario con calificación numérica [Medina et al. 2022a].

Los 33 sujetos se dividieron en tres grupos de 11 estudiantes cada uno: GP de sólo patrones, GN de sólo descripción narrativa y GPN de patrones más descripción narrativa. Se utilizó la calificación del pre-cuestionario para lograr grupos balanceados con respecto al nivel de conocimiento sobre el modelado conceptual de sistemas de información. Los sujetos participaron voluntariamente y se seleccionaron por conveniencia, es decir todos los sujetos disponibles en dicha asignatura.

Para evitar el temor a la evaluación, que podrían causar amenazas a la validez del experimento, se les comunicó a los sujetos que no serían evaluados por su rendimiento en la resolución de las tareas del experimento. Asimismo, para evitar ausentismo se les dijo a los estudiantes que tareas similares se iban a incluir en los exámenes finales de la asignatura.

Como en esta ocasión se desea validar una tecnología emergente, en cuanto al uso de patrones en el modelado conceptual de sistemas, es válida la justificación de Kitchenham [Kitchenham et al. 2002] y Svahnberg [Svahnberg et al. 2008] de realizar experimentos con estudiantes cumpliendo el rol de ingenieros de software no expertos. Los beneficios adicionales de la selección de estos sujetos son: el nivel de conocimientos homogéneo previo al experimento, la disponibilidad de un número importante de sujetos y la oportunidad de obtener evidencias de una primera validación de la hipótesis en un entorno académico.

2.3. Selección de variables

La variable independiente (también denominada factor principal) es el "Tipo de descripción conceptual", que es una variable nominal que toma tres valores: P (sólo patrones), N (sólo descripción narrativa) y PN (patrones más descripción narrativa).

La variable dependiente es la "Facilidad de comprensión", que se evalúa utilizando las siguientes medidas:

- Efectividad de la Facilidad de comprensión (Efec-Fc): Esta medida está relacionada con la corrección de las respuestas dadas al cuestionario presentado en la Tabla 1 y representa la habilidad de comprender correctamente el proceso que da soporte al sistema seleccionado. Se calcula de la siguiente manera: (Número de respuestas correctas – Número de preguntas respondidas) / Número de preguntas. Cada pregunta respondida puede tener 3 valores de respuesta: 1 si es correcta, 0,5 si es parcialmente correcta y 0 si es incorrecta. Se considera que mientras mayor sea su valor, mayor será la Efectividad de la Facilidad de comprensión.
- Eficiencia de la Facilidad de comprensión (Efic-Fc): Esta variable está relacionada con el tiempo y con la corrección y representa el Número de respuestas correctas por unidad de tiempo. Se calcula de la siguiente manera: (Número de respuestas correctas – Número de preguntas respondidas) / tiempo.

2.4. Formulación de hipótesis

Se formulan las siguientes hipótesis relacionadas con las dos medidas de las dos variables dependientes propuestas, Efec-Fc y Efic-Fc, respectivamente:

- $H_{1,0}$: No existe una diferencia significativa en la Efectividad de los sujetos al realizar tareas de comprensión de modelado conceptual, cuando usan sólo patrones de negocio (P), sólo descripción narrativa (N) o en conjunto, patrones de negocio más descripción narrativa (PN). $H_{1,1}$:$\neg H_{1,0}$.
- $H_{2,0}$: No existe una diferencia significativa en la Eficiencia de los sujetos al realizar tareas de comprensión de modelado conceptual, cuando usan sólo patrones de negocio (P), sólo descripción narrativa (N) o en conjunto, patrones de negocio más descripción narrativa (PN). $H_{2,1}$:$\neg H_{2,0}$.

2.5. Diseño experimental

Se seleccionó un diseño inter-sujetos equilibrado, es decir se asigna un solo tratamiento por sujeto y cada tratamiento se asigna al mismo número de sujetos.

Se intentan mitigar ciertas amenazas inherentes al diseño inter-sujetos. Por ejemplo, para mitigar el efecto de la experiencia, por ello se asignan aleatoriamente los sujetos a cada tratamiento distribuyendo en grupos balanceados de sujetos con el mismo nivel de conocimiento. De esta manera, como se mencionó anteriormente, se conformaron tres grupos: GP, GN y GPN.

2.6. Instrumentación y tareas experimentales

En la instrumentación se prepararon los objetos experimentales que constaban de los patrones de negocio y la descripción narrativa del sistema de gobierno electrónico seleccionado, un sistema de gestión de consultas de ciudadanos de un organismo público regional que administra la seguridad previsional de los empleados del estado provincial de Córdoba, Argentina.

Para la tarea experimental que debían hacer cada uno de los sujetos se diseñó un cuestionario con diez preguntas para evaluar la comprensión del modelo conceptual elegido (ver Tabla 1). Las preguntas seleccionadas se consideraron representativas de la actividad de modelado que realiza inicialmente un ingeniero de software antes de construir una nueva aplicación. La corrección de cada pregunta respondida puede tener tres valores: 1 si es correcta, 0,5 si es parcialmente correcta y 0 si es incorrecta. La máxima puntuación que se puede obtener es de diez puntos, si todas las preguntas son respondidas correctamente.

Tabla 1. Cuestionario del experimento

Id	Preguntas	Fuentes	Respuestas
P1	¿Cuál es el objetivo principal del sistema?	Patrón de objetivos, patrón estructura básica del proceso y descripción narrativa	Administrar las consultas y reclamos de ciudadanos a una Organización Pública
P2	¿Cuál es/son la/s salida/s principal/es del sistema?	Patrón estructura básica del proceso y descripción narrativa	Respuesta a la consulta
P3	¿Cuál es el recurso que aporta el área de Recursos Humanos para la implementación del sistema?	Patrón estructura básica del proceso, patrón proceso de interacción y descripción narrativa	RR.HH. y Capacitación
P4	¿Cuál es el beneficio más importante que garantiza el sistema?	Patrón de objetivos y descripción narrativa	Garantizar la participación ciudadana mediante consultas
P5	¿Cómo se resuelve la limitación habitual de expresar una consulta mediante la escritura de un texto?	Patrón de objetivos y descripción narrativa	Permitir adjuntar imágenes o archivos para completar y respaldar la consulta
P6	¿Se comunica al ciudadano por cada intervención a su consulta antes de cerrarla?	Patrón de objetivos y descripción narrativa	Notificación al ciudadano por diferentes medios simultáneamente: mail, mensaje de texto y sistema
P7	¿Cómo se consigue la identificación correcta del motivo de la consulta?	Patrón de objetivos y Narrativa	Ayuda interactiva para identificar el motivo de la consulta
P8	¿Cuál es el principal beneficio de la publicación del sistema en Internet?	Patrón de objetivos y descripción narrativa	Acceso al sistema de consultas de ciudadanos en línea 7 x 24
P9	¿Cómo se evalúa la calidad, profesionalidad y atención adecuada del personal de la Institución?	Patrón de objetivos y descripción narrativa	Calificación del ciudadano por la respuesta recibida
P10	¿Con qué funcionalidad se comprueba si el trámite resultó ágil y en tiempo para el ciudadano?	Patrón de objetivos y descripción narrativa	Elaboración de indicadores que permitan medir los tiempos de respuesta en el proceso

También se diseñó un cuestionario post-experimento que deben responder los sujetos una vez completado el cuestionario del experimento, con el objetivo de obtener la percepción de los sujetos sobre la ejecución del experimento, que podría ser útil para interpretar y explicar los resultados obtenidos en el cuestionario principal. Este cuestionario consta de seis preguntas con respuesta de tipo Likert de 5 puntos y una pregunta con respuesta de tipo Likert de 3 puntos como se muestra en la Tabla 2.

Tabla 2. Cuestionario post-experimento

Id	Preguntas	Valoración de las respuestas
PP1	Dificultad de las preguntas	(1–5)
PP2	¿El taller de formación fue suficiente para realizar la tarea?	(1–5)
PP3	¿Las preguntas que respondí estaban claras para mí?	(1–5)
PP4	No tuve dificultad para interpretar los patrones	(1–5)
PP5	No tuve dificultad para interpretar la descripción narrativa	(1–5)
PP6	Los diagramas de patrones fueron útiles	(1–5)
PP7	Tuve tiempo suficiente para responder las preguntas	(1–3)
1 = muy fácil; 2 = fácil; 3 = media; 4 = difícil; 5 = muy difícil (PP1)		
1 = muy de acuerdo; 2 = de acuerdo; 3 = neutral; 4 = en desacuerdo; 5 = muy en desacuerdo (PP2, PP3, PP4, PP5, PP6)		
1 = tuve más tiempo del necesario; 2 = tiempo suficiente; 3 = no me alcanzó el tiempo (PP7)		

Vale aclarar que las preguntas PP4 y PP6 sólo se hicieron a los grupos GP y GPN, y la pregunta PP5 sólo se hizo a los grupos GN y GPN.

3. Ejecución del experimento

Dos semanas antes de la ejecución del experimento, con el fin de revisar el material experimental y el tiempo necesario para realizar el experimento, se llevó a cabo una prueba piloto con tres docentes investigadores de la U.T.N. – F.R.C.

El experimento se ejecutó en una sesión de *"Zoom"* y los sujetos fueron supervisados por la coordinadora de la asignatura Gestión de mejora de procesos y por el autor del diseño del experimento. Se realizaron dos actividades en diferentes días.

El primer día, 8 de abril de 2021, se dictó un taller de formación de utilización de patrones para comprender procesos de negocio. La duración del taller fue de una hora y se brindó un ejemplo con una tarea similar a la del experimento. Al finalizar el taller, los sujetos completaron un breve pre-cuestionario para evaluar sus conocimientos y conformar de esta manera grupos homogéneos para el experimento. Para completar este último contaron con quince minutos adicionales. En síntesis, la actividad tuvo una hora quince minutos de duración en total.

Se obtuvo la nota final de la asignatura Análisis de sistemas, de segundo año, de cada estudiante que completó el pre-cuestionario. Se confeccionó la tabla de orden de mérito, promediando la mencionada nota final con la calificación del pre-cuestionario, asignando a cada sujeto un grupo del cuestionario del experimento. Es decir, el primer sujeto se asignó al grupo GP, el segundo al grupo GN, el tercero al grupo GPN, el cuarto al grupo GP y así sucesivamente, para obtener grupos balanceados.

El segundo día, 22 de abril de 2021, se ejecutó el experimento propiamente dicho. Ingresaron los sujetos la sesión de *"Zoom"* y se explicó el procedimiento de la actividad. A partir de ese momento no se permitió la comunicación entre los sujetos y se les comunicó que cualquier duda debe resolverse con el autor del experimento, que para ellos cumple el rol de docente de esa actividad áulica.

Los sujetos se dividieron en tres grupos balanceados, de 11 estudiantes cada uno, teniendo en cuenta los resultados del pre-cuestionario. A continuación, los sujetos accedieron al material para realizar la actividad del experimento que se encontraba en el sistema *"Moodle"* de aula virtual de la U.T.N. – F.R.C. El material de los sujetos del grupo GP se compuso de sólo patrones, el material del grupo GN fue sólo descripción narrativa y el material del grupo GPN consistió en patrones más descripción narrativa.

A partir de que los sujetos accedieron al material se les pidió que completaran el cuestionario presentado en la Tabla 1. Además, se midió el tiempo en forma automática por el sistema de aula virtual, desde que se dio acceso al material hasta que cada sujeto envió el cuestionario, para así obtener los valores de las dos variables dependientes: Efec-Fc y Efic-Fc. Se iniciaron las tareas de lectura y comprensión del modelo conceptual presentado, del rellenado del cuestionario detallado en la Tabla 1 y la medición de tiempos.

Una vez completada esta tarea, se dio acceso a los sujetos el cuestionario post-experimento correspondiente al grupo al que pertenecían. Para la realización de todas estas tareas se dispuso de un máximo de dos horas. Los estudiantes que en ese plazo no enviaron el cuestionario del experimento, se les registró el cuestionario con las preguntas que hayan completado y se le dio acceso al cuestionario post-experimento. Para completar este último contaron con quince minutos adicionales. En síntesis, la actividad tuvo dos horas quince minutos de duración en total.

Para evitar posibles sesgos no se develó el carácter experimental de la actividad, aunque se les dijo a los sujetos que esta actividad de formación es una experiencia piloto sobre una metodología emergente de modelado conceptual de sistemas de información. Además, se les comunicó que el resultado de las tareas era confidencial, que no iban a ser evaluados por su rendimiento en el cuestionario de la actividad, y que tareas similares se incluirían en la evaluación de la asignatura. También se les informó que iba a estar disponible, bajo petición a los autores, el informe donde se documenten los resultados de esta actividad.

Después de la ejecución del experimento, se recolectaron todos los datos en una tabla diseñada para tal fin, en el que se le otorga a cada respuesta un punto si es correcta, 0,5 punto si es parcialmente correcta y cero si es incorrecta (ver Tabla 1). Se buscaron valores atípicos y se observó si todos los sujetos respondieron todas las preguntas en el tiempo asignado.

4. Análisis e interpretación de resultados

En primer lugar, se realizó un estudio de los estadísticos descriptivos correspondientes a las medidas de las variables dependientes (Efec-Fc y Efic-Fc) para describir y resumir los valores de éstas: media, mediana y desviación estándar (ver sección 4.1).

Con el fin de decidir si utilizar test paramétricos o no-paramétricos, para probar las hipótesis, se analizó si los datos tenían una distribución normal o no, utilizando el test de Kolmogorov y también se analizó la homogeneidad de las varianzas con la prueba F de igualdad de varianzas (ver sección 4.2).

Finalmente se realizó el test no paramétrico Kruskal-Wallis para probar las hipótesis (ver secciones 4.3 y 4.4).

A continuación, se presentan los resultados obtenidos en el análisis de datos que se efectuó utilizando el paquete estadístico *"InfoStat"* [Di Rienzo et al. 2022].

4.1. Análisis de los estadísticos descriptivos

La Tabla 3 muestra los estadísticos descriptivos correspondientes a las dos medidas de las variables dependientes (Efec-Fc y Efic-Fc). En esta tabla se presentan las siguientes columnas: N (número de sujetos), $\bar{X}$ (media), Mediana y DS (desviación estándar).

Analizando el contenido de la Tabla 3, se puede observar que las medias son mejores cuando los sujetos usan patrones (P) respecto de los otros tratamientos: cuando se usan patrones de negocio más descripción narrativa en conjunto (PN) o sólo descripción narrativa (N). Aunque las diferencias son menores en las medidas de la variable Efic-Fc respecto las medidas de la variable Efec-Fc, en síntesis, con el uso de patrones se obtienen mejores valores en cuanto Efectividad, y también con diferencias leves en Eficiencia, al realizar tareas de comprensión de modelado conceptual.

Tabla 3. Estadísticos descriptivos de Efec-Fc y Efic-Fc

Tratamiento	N	Efec-Fc			Efic-Fc		
		$\bar{X}$	Mediana	DS	$\bar{X}$	Mediana	DS
P	11	**0,8045**	**0,8500**	**0,1214**	**0,0262**	**0,0253**	**0,0114**
PN	11	0,7409	0,7500	0,1044	0,0206	0,0203	0,0048
N	11	0,6136	0,7500	0,2335	0,0180	0,0182	0,0089

4.2. Prueba de normalidad y análisis de homogeneidad de varianzas

Se realizaron las pruebas de Kolmogorov para determinar la normalidad de las variables dependientes [Medina et al. 2022a]. Al usar Kolmogorov para las variables Efec-Fc y Efic-Fc, al ser el p-valor menor a 0,05 se rechaza la H_0, hipótesis nula, que establece la normalidad de la distribución de ambas. Esto indica que estas variables no tendrían distribución normal.

A continuación, se procedió a analizar la homogeneidad de varianzas con la prueba F para igualdad de varianzas [Medina et al. 2022a]. Se observó para las variables Efec-Fc y Efic-Fc que, al existir algún p-valor menor a 0,05, se rechaza la H_0 que establece la homogeneidad entre varianzas.

Como ambas variables dependientes (Efec-Fc y Efic-Fc) no presentan una aproximación a la distribución normal y no hay homogeneidad de varianzas, se decidió utilizar el test no paramétrico Kruskal-Wallis para probar las hipótesis.

4.3. Pruebas de las hipótesis de la Efectividad de la de la Facilidad de comprensión (Efec-Fc)

Se ejecutó la prueba de tipo no paramétrica Kruskall-Wallis. En el análisis se observó para la variable Efec-Fc que, al ser el p-valor igual a 0,0497 (ver Tabla 4), o sea menor a 0,05, se puede rechazar la $H_{1,0}$ que establece que no existe una diferencia significativa en la Efectividad de los sujetos al realizar tareas de comprensión de modelado conceptual al usar los distintos tipos de tratamientos: cuando se usan sólo patrones de negocio (P), sólo descripción narrativa (N) o patrones de negocio más descripción narrativa en conjunto (PN).

Tabla 4. Resultado del test de Kruskall-Wallis para Efec-Fc

Variable	N	H	p-valor
Efec-Fc	33	5,78	0,0497

Es decir que existen diferencias en la Efectividad al usar los distintos tipos de tratamientos y, de acuerdo con el análisis descriptivo, sería mejor el que presenta la media más alta. En orden descendente: P es más efectivo que PN, y PN es más efectivo que N como se puede observar en la Tabla 3.

4.4. Pruebas de las hipótesis de la Eficiencia de la de la Facilidad de comprensión (Efic-Fc)

Se ejecutó la prueba de tipo no paramétrica Kruskall-Wallis para corroborar la hipótesis $H_{2,0}$ correspondiente a la variable Efic-Fc (ver Tabla 5). Como el p-valor es mayor a 0,05 (0,3862) no se puede rechazar dicha hipótesis nula. Es decir que no existen diferencias en la Eficiencia al realizar tareas de comprensión de modelado conceptual indistintamente si se usan patrones de negocio o descripción narrativa.

Tabla 5. Resultado del test de Kruskall-Wallis para Efic-Fc

Variable	N	H	p-valor
Efic-Fc	33	1,90	0,3862

Es decir que no existen diferencias en la Eficiencia al realizar tareas de comprensión de modelado conceptual indistintamente si se usan patrones de negocio o descripción narrativa.

4.5. Resultados del cuestionario post-experimento

El análisis de las respuestas recogidas en el cuestionario post-experimento revelan que la mayoría de los sujetos consideraron a las preguntas del experimento de dificultad media. Los sujetos estuvieron en su mayoría de acuerdo en la claridad de las preguntas y percibieron que fue suficiente o más del necesario la adecuación del tiempo para realizar la actividad. La mayoría de los sujetos estuvieron de acuerdo y muy de acuerdo con respecto a la adecuación del taller de formación dictado previamente al experimento [Medina et al. 2022a].

En cuanto a la facilidad para interpretar patrones, la mayor cantidad de sujetos opinaron que fue neutral y muy de acuerdo como se aprecia en la Figura 2.

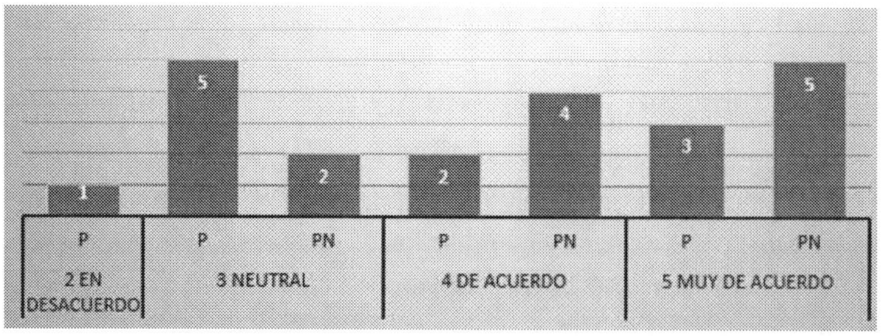

Figura 2. Facilidad para interpretar los patrones

La mayoría de los sujetos estuvo de acuerdo con la facilidad para interpretar la narrativa (ver Figura 3) y muy de acuerdo con la utilidad de los diagramas de patrones para la comprensión del modelo conceptual de un sistema de gobierno electrónico (ver Figura 4).

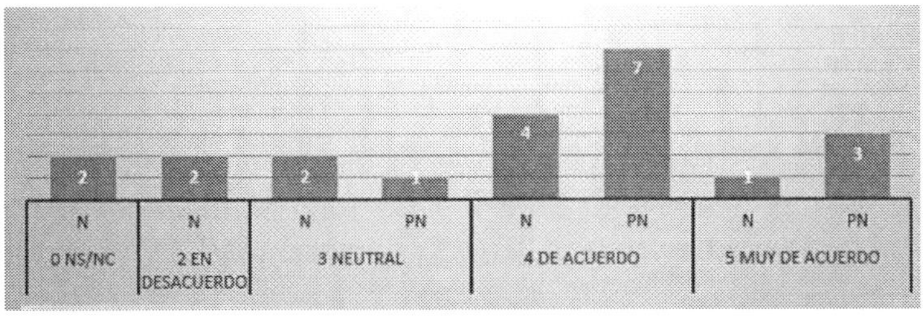

Figura 3. Facilidad para interpretar la descripción narrativa

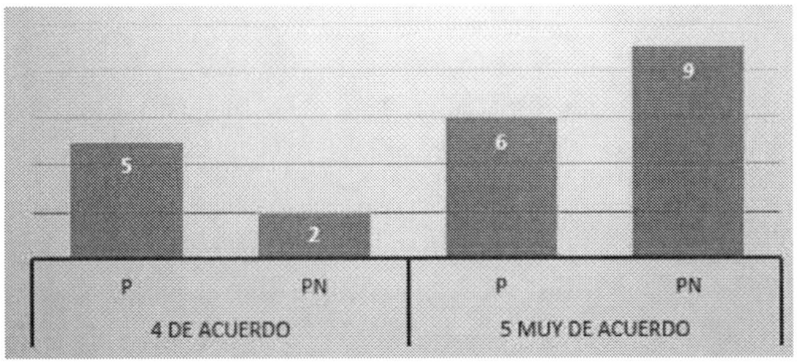

Figura 4. Utilidad de los patrones

Estas percepciones recogidas de los sujetos mostraron mejores resultados en cuanto a la facilidad de comprensión al utilizar patrones.

5. Evaluación de la validez del experimento

Para asegurar la validez de los resultados correspondientes a un experimento controlado, se llevaron a cabo distintas acciones para paliar las posibles amenazas según las recomendaciones propuestas en [Wohlin et al. 2012, Neto y Conte 2013].

Para este experimento se adoptaron acciones agrupadas en cuatro tipos de validez: interna, externa, de constructo y de las conclusiones, que se explican a continuación.

5.1. Validez interna

Representa el grado de confianza con el que pueden extraerse conclusiones en la relación causa efecto, en este caso entre la variable independiente respecto de las dependientes.

Para este experimento se conformaron grupos homogéneos de sujetos en cuanto al conocimiento teórico del modelado conceptual de sistemas y se contempló el temor a la evaluación.

Además, los sujetos manifestaron en el cuestionario post-experimento que el material que el material que recibieron y las tareas estaban bien explicadas, lo que se había corroborado previamente en la prueba piloto.

Por último, para que sea totalmente controlado hubiera sido deseable haberlo de forma presencial. Pero dadas las circunstancias que las clases se dictaban en modalidad virtual, por la pandemia del COVID 19, todas las actividades del experimento se realizaron vía internet utilizando las plataformas académicas habituales. Consideramos que esta situación no afectó a los resultados debido a que se aseguraron todas las condiciones estipuladas para un examen en línea de la asignatura más los recaudos de validez del experimento desarrollados en esta sección.

5.2. Validez externa

Define el grado hasta el que los resultados pueden generalizarse teniendo en cuenta la selección de los sujetos y otros parámetros del experimento.

Se previó la representatividad de los sujetos, estudiantes del tercer curso de Ingeniería en Sistemas de Información, como representantes de ingenieros de software principiantes.

También, la representatividad del objeto de estudio con un sistema de gobierno electrónico real, actualmente en funcionamiento.

En síntesis, los resultados del experimento son válidos en el contexto de ingenieros de software principiantes y sistemas de gobierno electrónico, aunque para poder generalizarlos es necesario realizar réplicas.

5.3. Validez de constructo

Indica hasta dónde las variables del experimento miden con asertividad los constructos teóricos de las hipótesis.

La instrumentación de este experimento se realizó con una característica homogénea de los objetos, ya que los objetos del experimento, tanto los patrones como la descripción narrativa, poseen la misma información sobre el sistema de gobierno electrónico seleccionado.

Las medidas seleccionadas son medidas utilizadas normalmente para medir efectividad y eficiencia, y los cuestionarios del experimento fueron diseñados utilizando cuestionarios y escalas estándares.

Por el número reducido de datos, los resultados de este experimento controlado pueden ser solo considerados como indicadores, y no son concluyentes, y las medidas seleccionadas son medidas usadas normalmente para medir efectividad y la eficiencia.

5.4. Validez de las conclusiones

Representa el grado de confianza de las conclusiones de un experimento, dado un nivel determinado de significación estadística, en la correcta inferencia de la hipótesis.

El material del experimento fue seleccionado de un proyecto real que fue transferido formalmente de U.T.N. – F.R.C. al organismo público, sólo se usaron objetos de estudio de ese sistema y la fuente de los objetos de estudio es la documentación actual del sistema.

Además, para el análisis e interpretación de resultados, se seleccionaron los test estadísticos apropiados teniendo en cuenta la naturaleza de los datos.

6. Conclusiones

En este artículo se presentó un experimento con el objetivo de evaluar si el uso de patrones de negocio mejora la comprensión del modelo conceptual de un sistema de gobierno electrónico. El experimento se realizó en un entorno académico virtual con estudiantes del tercer curso de la carrera Ingeniería en Sistemas de Información de la U.T.N. – F.R.C. de Argentina en el mes de abril de 2021.

Se analizó la facilidad de comprensión de modelos porque es una de las características de la reusabilidad. Los patrones de negocio que se aplican al modelado conceptual cumplen la función de reutilizar el conocimiento y experiencia de sistemas anteriores. Se puede colegir que un modelo que es fácil de comprender tendrá más facilidad de ser reutilizado, y es necesario evaluar en primera instancia la facilidad de comprensión de un modelo usando patrones.

Es por ello, que se buscó obtener evidencias sobre la influencia que pueden tener sobre la Efectividad y Eficiencia en la comprensión del modelado conceptual, el uso de sólo patrones de negocio, sólo descripción narrativa o ambos simultáneamente.

Los estadísticos descriptivos revelaron que los sujetos que utilizaron patrones obtuvieron mejores valores al realizar tareas de comprensión de modelado conceptual en la Efectividad, por el contrario, no hay diferencias relevantes en la Eficiencia al utilizar, o no, patrones.

Con respecto a los resultados de las pruebas de hipótesis planteadas, se comprobó que existen diferencias significativas en la Efectividad de los sujetos al realizar tareas de comprensión de modelado conceptual, cuando se utilizan patrones de negocio. De acuerdo con el análisis descriptivo, sería mejor el que presenta la media más alta. En orden descendente: el uso de sólo patrones es más efectivo que patrones más descripción narrativa, y el uso de éstos, es más efectivo que sólo descripción narrativa.

En cambio, no existe una diferencia significativa en la Eficiencia de los sujetos al realizar tareas de comprensión de modelado conceptual, empleando indistintamente patrones, descripción narrativa o ambos. Es decir, que no se pudo rechazar la hipótesis nula para esta variable, por lo que no se tuvo evidencia suficiente para rechazar que no existen diferencias de Eficiencia entre los distintos tratamientos.

Las evidencias del experimento indican que el uso de patrones impacta de forma visible en la efectividad de la comprensión, que está relacionada con la correctitud de la descripción del modelo conceptual. Pero no lo hace en igual medida con respecto a la eficiencia, que implica la correctitud más la relación con el tiempo en que se realiza la tarea de comprensión. Se corroboran estas conclusiones con los resultados del cuestionario post-experimento donde los sujetos, en su mayoría, estuvieron de acuerdo en la facilidad de interpretación de los patrones y de la utilidad de los diagramas de patrones para la comprensión del modelo conceptual de un sistema de gobierno electrónico.

Por todo lo expresado, los resultados obtenidos llevan a recomendar, con cierta precaución, que es conveniente el uso de patrones de negocio en el modelo conceptual de un sistema de gobierno electrónico para facilitar su comprensión y, en consecuencia, su potencial de ser reutilizado. Estos resultados son válidos en el contexto de ingenieros de software principiantes y sistemas de gobierno electrónico. Resultados que podrían tener impacto tanto a nivel industrial como académico, promoviendo el uso de patrones de negocio en la actividad de modelado de los sistemas en ambos ámbitos. Aunque se considera, con la debida cautela, que para poder hacer recomendaciones firmes sería necesario corroborar la validez de los resultados obtenidos a través de la realización de réplicas. Réplicas que se planifican hacer en un futuro cercano.

Agradecimientos

La investigación presentada en este artículo se desarrolló en el contexto de lo siguientes proyectos: ADAGIO (Consejería de Educación, Cultura y Deportes de la JCCM, España, SBPLY/21/180501/000061), AETHER-UCLM (MICINN, España, PID2020-112540RB-C42) y UTN (CIDS, Argentina, SITCBCO0008152TC).

Referencias

Alexander, C. (1979) "The Timeless Way of Building", Ed. Oxford University Press.

Di Rienzo, J. A., Casanoves, F., Balzarini, M. G., González, L., Tablada, M., Robledo, C. W. "InfoStat: Software Estadístico" versión 2020. Centro de Transferencia InfoStat, FCA, Universidad Nacional de Córdoba. Accedido el 31/01/2022 desde http://www.infostat.com.ar.

Eriksson, H.-E. & Penker, M. (2000) "Business Modeling with UML: Business Patterns at Work", Ed. OMG Press.

Gamma, E., Helm, R., Johnson, R., Vissides, J. (1994) "Design Patterns. Elements of Reusable Object-Oriented Software", Ed. Addison-Wesley.

Genero, M., Cruz-Lemus J.A. y Piattini, M.G. (2014) "Métodos de Investigación en Ingeniería del software", Ed. Ra-ma.

Kitchenham, B., Pfleeger, S., Pickard, L., Jones, P.W., Hoaglin, D., Emam, K., Rosenberg, J. (2002) "Preliminary Guidelines for Empirical Research in Software Engineering", IEEE Transactions on Software Engineering 28(8), págs. 721-734.

Manso, M.E. (2009) "Estudio Empírico para la Validación de Indicadores de la Reusabilidad de Diagramas de Clases UML", Tesis doctoral, Universidad de Valladolid.

Marciszack, M.M., Moreno, J.C., Sánchez, C.E., Medina, O.C., Delgado, A.F., Castro, C.S. (2018) "Patrones en la Construcción del Modelo Conceptual para Sistemas de Información", Ed. edUTecNe, U.T.N.

Medina, O.C, Marciszack, M.M., Groppo, M.A. (2018) "Proposal for the Patterns Definition based on Good Practices for the Electronic Government Systems Development", CISTI 2018 – 13th Iberian Conference on Information Systems and Technologies.

Medina, O.C., Pérez Cota, M., Meloni, B.E., Marciszack, M.M. (2021) "Business Patterns Catalogue and selection proposal for the Conceptual Model of a software product", International Journal of Universal Computer Science (J.UCS) 27(2), págs. 135-151, Editorial J.UCS Consortium.

Medina, O.C., Genero, M., Marciszack, M.M., Bratti, A., Strub, A. (2022). Apéndice con material complementario del presente artículo. Accedido el 31/05/2022 desde http://www.cids.frc.utn.edu.ar/UsoPatrones.

Medina, O.C., Pérez Cota, M., Damiano, L.E., Della Mea, K., Marciszack, M.M. (2022) "Systematic Mapping of Literature on Applicable Patterns in Conceptual Modelling of Information Systems", New Perspectives in Software Engineering, págs. 41-54, Editorial Springer.

Neto, A.A. y Conte, T. (2013) "A conceptual model to address threats to validity in controlled experiments", 17th International Conference on Evaluation and Assessment in Software Engineering (EASE).

PDTS, Banco Nacional de Proyectos de Desarrollo Tecnológico y Social (2022). PDTS-0380 Implementación de patrones en la validación de modelos conceptuales. Accedido el 31/05/2022 desde https://bancopdts.mincyt.gob.ar/proyectos/bancoPdts.zul.

Sommerville, I. (2011) "Ingeniería de Software", 9a Edición en español, Ed. Pearson.

Svahnberg, M., Aurum, A., Claes Wohlin, C. (2008) "Using Students as Subjects - An Empirical Evaluation", 2nd. International Symposium on Empirical Software Engineering and Measurement (ESEM).

Wohlin, C., Runeson, P., Höst, M., Ohlsson, M., Regnell, B. (2012) "Experimentation in Software Engineering", Ed. Springer.

Extending the Sustainability-Quality Model for supporting the design of Persuasive Software Systems

Marcela Quispe-Cruz[1], **Nelly Condori-Fernandez**[2], [3]

[1]Universidad Nacional de San Agustín (UNSA)
Arequipa – Perú

[2]CITIC, Computer Science Department – Universidade da Coruña
Galicia, Spain.

[3]Computer Science department – Vrije Universiteit Amsterdam
The Netherlands.

mquispecr@unsa.edu.pe, n.condori-fernandez@vu.nl

Abstract. *This research aims at providing a guiding support for the selection of relevant features and quality requirements for designing persuasive software systems. To do this, a mapping between the Persuasive System Design (PSD) model and a generic Sustainability-Quality (SQ) model was carried out. As a result of this mapping, we extended the SQ model, by adding certain types of relationships with specific features of the PSD model. A Graph database tool, named Neo4j, was used for facilitating the visualization of the identified relationships. And we also used the query language Cypher in order to retrieve data from the graph Finally, we used an existing persuasive software system for illustrating the usefulness of the extended SQ model represented as graphs.*

1. Introduction

Persuasive technology can be defined as "design, research, and analysis of interactive computing products created to change people's attitudes [1] or behaviors [2]" [Fogg 2003]. As technology can be used as a promoter of sustainable behaviour, many studies have investigated the possibilities to persuade people within the context of environmental sustainability (e.g., increase consumers' awareness of energy consumption [Froehlich 2009]). However, most of these studies have shortcomings that limit their long-term effectiveness. Although behavioral models (e.g., Transtheoretical Model of behavior change [Prochaska and DiClemente 2005], the Goal-setting Theory [Locke and Latham 1991], the Fogg Behavior Model [Fogg 2009]) are very useful for conceptualizing the impact of persuasive technology, most of them cannot be applied directly to the design or assessment of persuasive systems [Harjumaa and Oinas-Kukkonen 2007, Condori-Fernández et al. 2018]. For example, through a user experience assessment of existing persuasive software applications, Condori-Fernandez et al. [Condori-Fernández et al. 2018] found that some relevant non-functional requirements had not been addressed, and consequently users experienced negatively in using such kind of systems.

[1]Attitude represents how a person thinks or feels about someone or something.
[2]Behavior represents an individual's reaction to a particular action, person or environment

As the identification and management of non-functional requirements (NFR) in software projects are challenging [Ameller et al. 2019], various assessment models have been proposed for software product quality (e.g., ISO/IEC 25010 quality model). In the last years, software sustainability has gained more attention from researchers to address sustainability requirements along the software life-cycle (e.g., [Condori-Fernandez and Lago 2018], [Calero et al. 2013], [Venters et al. 2014]). Lago et al. [Lago et al. 2015] defined software sustainability based on a four-dimensional model that adds the technical dimension to the social, environmental and economic dimensions that already appear in the Brundtland report [Brundtland et al. 1987]. Condori-Fernandez and Lago [Condori Fernandez and Lago 2018, Lago and Condori-Fernandez 2022] proposed a Sustainability-Quality (SQ) model, an instrument of the Sustainability Assessment Framework, for supporting the identification of quality requirements that contribute to the four-dimensional model of software-intensive systems [3]. The multidimensional approach of Becker et al. [Becker and et al 2016] adds the individual dimension to the four sustainability dimensions [Lago et al. 2015]. However, Calero et al. [Calero et al. 2013] define sustainability only in terms of energy consumption, resource optimization and perdurability, and they do not consider the individual, social, and economic dimensions.

In this paper, we aim to extend the SQ model [Condori-Fernandez and Lago 2018] in order to provide a guiding support for (i) the NFR identification and (ii) the selection of relevant features from the PSD Model [Oinas-Kukkonen and Harjumaa 2009] for designing persuasive systems. To do this, we first use the PSD Model as a means to extend the SQ model with the inclusion of new type of relationships. It is achieved through a mapping carried out between some elements of the PSD model and the SQ model. Second, given that designers of persuasive systems may achieve more success if adequate methodological support was available, we changed the tabular visualization of the SQL model (static) to a graph-based visualization (dynamic). Therefore, we consider that such kind of visualization can be helpful not only for identifying relevant quality requirements usually ignored in practice, but also for supporting the selection of persuasive software system features.

The following sections provide a detailed account of our paper. Section 2 describes the SQ model and PSD model on which our work is based. Section 3 presents the procedure and results of the mapping carried out between both models. In Section 4, we present the corresponding queries to support the NFR discovery and Feature selection. Section 5 illustrates the application of the most important queries in a specific example. In section 6, we conclude the paper and discuss further work.

2. Background

In this work, we consider the PSD model [Oinas-Kukkonen and Harjumaa 2009], as the theoretical framework for our research, and the SQ model [Condori-Fernandez and Lago 2018].

2.1. The PSD model

The PSD model is a recent conceptualization for designing, developing and evaluating persuasive systems. It consists of the premises behind any persuasive system, the persua-

[3]Systems in which software interacts with other software, systems, devices, sensors and people.

sion context and the persuasive software system features. All persuasive software systems are based on the following premises [Oinas-Kukkonen and Harjumaa 2009]:

- **P1: Useful.** The system really serves the needs of the user.
- **P2: User-friendly.** The system should be easy to use or dealt with.
- **P3: Unobtrusiveness.** The system should avoid being disturbing while the user is performing tasks.
- **P4: Open.** Designers should make the ideas and the goals of persuasion transparent.
- **P5: Cognitive Consistency.** People like their views about the world to be organized and consistent. Inconsistency disturbs people, and they easily want to reorganize their thinking and restore consistency, perhaps even feel obliged to do so.
- **P6: Incremental.** This means that persuasion goes stepwise, and all steps contribute to the goals to be realized.
- **P7: Information Technology (IT) is never neutral.** IT always influences attitudes and behavior.
- **P8: Direct and indirect routes.** Persuasion strategies can be divided into direct and indirect routes, and persuasion will depend on the ability and motivation of people to process information.

The analysis of the *persuasion context* consists of looking into (1) the intent, (2) the event and (3) the strategy. A central feature of analyzing the intent is to consider the change type, in particular whether the persuasion aims at attitude and/or behavior change. The event comprises the use situation, user's characteristics, technological platform and environment. The strategy includes the message itself and the route to be used to achieve a goal.

The PSD model describes 28 *persuasive software system features* grouped in four categories: (i) The **primary activity support category** focuses on supporting the activities that lead to achievement of the persuasive software system goals. (ii) **Dialogue support** refers to techniques/mechanisms to motivate users to use the persuasive software system goals. (iii) The **credibility category** relates to how to design a system so that it is more credible and thereby more persuasive. iv) The **social influence category** describes how to design the system so that it motivates users by leveraging different aspects of social influence. More details of the features can be found in Appendix B.

2.2. The SQ model

It is defined in terms of four *sustainability dimensions*: (i) *Technical dimension* addresses the long-term use of software-intensive systems and their appropriate evolution in an execution environment that continuously changes. (ii) *Economic dimension* focuses on preserving capital and (economic) value. (iii) *Social dimension* focuses on supporting current and future generations to have the same or greater access to social resources by pursuing generational equity. For software-intensive systems, this dimension encompasses the direct support of social communities in any domain, as well as the support of activities or processes that indirectly create benefits for social communities. (iv) *Environmental dimension* aims at improving human welfare while protecting natural resources. For software-intensive systems, this dimension aims at addressing ecologic concerns, including energy efficiency and ecologic awareness creation.

Each dimension is characterized by a set of *Quality attributes*, which can be interdependent. Such dependency can be of two types: (i) it is *inter-dimensional* if it relates a pair of quality attributes defined simultaneously in two different dimensions (e.g. security defined in the *technical* dimension can influence security in the *social* dimension); and (ii) it is *intra-dimensional* if a dependency exists between two different quality requirements defined within the same dimension (e.g. in the *technical* dimension, security may depend on reliability).

Since our SQ model provides support to both identify design concerns, and assess the qualities of the software architecture, a set of metrics are used for measuring the quality requirements, which should be measurable. Instances of metrics can be also defined for *sustainability-related requirements*.

The list of attributes of the SQ model, and corresponding contributions to the four dimensions, can be found at [Condori Fernandez and Lago 2018]. In the following section, we explain how the SQ model has been extended, by means of a mapping with certain elements of the PSD model (i.e., premises and features).

3. Mapping the PSD model to the SQ model

3.1. Procedure

The mapping was carried out iteratively by the first two authors of the paper, which consisted of three iterations. And a first validation of the mapping was carried out in the fourth iteration.

First iteration: The PSD model was analyzed regarding the premises and features that should be considered for designing persuasive systems. Researcher 1 focused on the analysis of the categories and corresponding features of the PSD model. Researcher 2 focused on the analysis of the premises of the PSD model.

During this first iteration, both researchers used independently an Excel template-for marking with an "X" whenever they identified some attributes of the SQ model as relevant.

Second iteration: Two online meetings were organized between both researchers for discussing regarding (i)the QAs identified in the first iteration and (ii) and the relationships that can be identified between the selected QAs of the SQ model and the elements of the PSD model (premises and features). The outcomes of the first iteration were interchanged and reviewed before the meetings. As a result of these meetings, researchers agreed on some type of relationships such as *"Helps to"* that represents a positive contribution and *"Hurts to"* that represents a negative contribution. Both type of relations were adopted from the Non-Functional Requirements framework [Chung et al. 2000]. Therefore, the SQ model is extended by means of the mapping carried out along these two first iterations. The outcome of this mapping can be found in Appendix A.

Third iteration: In this iteration, a visualization of the outcome produced in the previous iterations is implemented, by using a Graph database tool named Neo4j [4] version 4.0. To build the graph database we place the selected characteristics and QAs of the SQ model as well as the features of the PSD model in nodes and the corresponding

[4] https://neo4j.com/

relationships between them as transitions of the graph. To visualize a graph, we use Cypher that is the Neo4j's graph query language.

Fourth iteration: A third participant was involved, a professional in software engineering, for the review of the mapping (only relationships between QAs and Features of the PSD model). This review was in two stages. The first stage was in offline mode, where the reviewer received the corresponding instructions and an excel file that contains (i) definitions of QAs of the SQ model as well as definitions of features of the PSD model; and (ii) the relations to the PSD features with their corresponding explanations. For each identified relationship, the following question was formulated: *Do you agree with the identified relationship? If not, please explain your own rationale.*

In the second stage, an online meeting was held with the participation of our external reviewer and the two researchers that defined the first version of mapping. As a result of this review, two type of changes were implemented regarding:

- Type of relationship: With the purpose of highlighting a greater contribution from some quality attributes to some features of the PSD model, or vice versa, a new relationship *"Strong helps to"* was added. For example, an *"Strong helps to"* was identified for the relationship between the context completeness attribute and two Primary Task Support features: tailoring, and personalization.
- Features: Due to the relevance of some few features (e.g., simulation, reduction) some few relationships were also added to certain QAs. For example, researchers had only considered that unobtrusiveness HELPS to the tunneling feature, when this QA could also helps to the reduction feature.

Figure 1 shows the resulting scheme in the graph database.

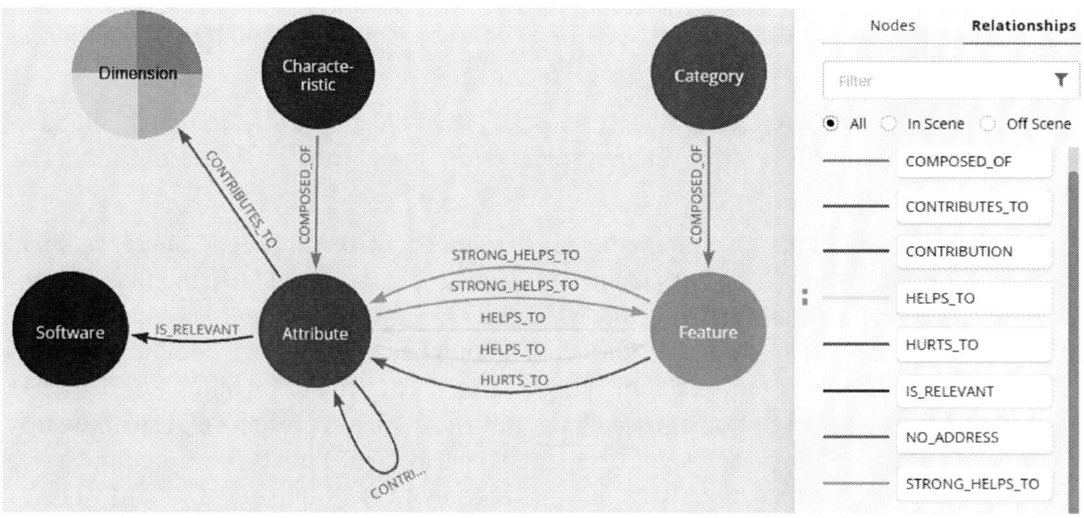

Figure 1. Scheme with types of nodes and relationships in the graph database.

The graph database consists of:

- Four kinds of coloured edges: The edges HELPS_TO (orange), STRONG_HELPS_TO (brown) and HURTS_TO (red) represent that the source node (QA or Feature) helps, strongly helps or hurts the target node (QA or Feature), respectively.

COMPOSED_OF (green) represents a composition relationship.

- Four kinds of coloured nodes: *Characteristic*-node (purple) represents a quality characteristic of the SQ model, *Attribute*-node (fucsia) represents a QA of the SQ model, *Category*-node (olive) represents a features category of the PSD model, *Feature*-node (lime) represents a feature of the PSD model.

3.2. Results

Next, we discuss the type of relations with the PSD model at two levels: Premises and Features.

3.2.1. Premises

Thanks to the mapping with the premises of the PSD model, we were able to identify two new QAs that were not present in the SQ model: Unobtrusiveness (P3) and Transparency (P4). Other premises such as P1 (useful) could be directly related to usefulness of the SQ model; whereas user-friendly (P2) was related to usability (operability). The premise Incremental (P6) was related to maintainability since the system should be easy to modify for adding new suggestions or recommendations.

There were also some premises like Cognitive consistency (P5) and Direct and indirect routes (P8) that could not be related to any specific QA. We consider that both premises could be addressed by more than one QA. For example, attributes regarding context coverage, satisfaction, and effectiveness could enable that software systems can implement their persuasion strategies into direct and indirect routes (P8). It is also important to note that a persuasive system that causes any user disturbance would affect to efficiency (more time to perform tasks) and timeliness (being not opportune). For this reason, Unobtrusiveness (P3) was also related to both QAs.

3.2.2. Features

The mapping with the features of the PSD model allowed us to extend the SQ model, by using some the identified type of relations between QAs and features of the four categories: primary task support, dialog support, system credibility support and social support. Figure 2 summarizes the corresponding features (Fx) and premises (Px) mapped to the quality characteristics that contribute to each sustainability dimension.

An example of graph that shows different type of relationships like COMPOSED_OF (i.e., Satisfaction composed of Trust) HELPS_TO, and HURTS_TO (i.e., relationships between Trust and Features of the *System Credibility Support* category) is shown in Figure 3. In the graph, we considered some features of the *Primary task support* and *System Credibility Support* categories that might *help to* the system in providing information that is truthful. Thus, a system, which incorporates the features like expertise, real-world feeling, leverages roles of authority, and third-party endorsements, makes easy verify the accuracy of site content, and consequently achieves that the stakeholders become confident.

Looking at the same graph (Figure 3), we also see the relationship HELPS_TO from the node labelled "Self-monitoring" (feature) to the node "Trust" (QA). This is be-

QUALITY CHARACTERISTICS	TECH	ENV	ECON	SOC	PREMISES (Px) AND FEATURES (Fx)
Compatibility					F01 to F07
Context coverage					F02 to F05, F07 to F11, F14
Effectiveness					F01, F06, F08 to F21
Efficiency					P3, F01
Freedom from risk					F15 to F28
Functional suitability					F02, F04 to F11, F14, F16, F18 to F20, F22 to F28
Maintainability					P6
Performance efficiency					
Portability					
Reliability					F05, F08 to F14, F21
Satisfaction					P1, F05, F15, F16, F18 to F21
Security					F15
Usability					P2, F02 to F05, F13
Accessibility					F03, F04
Robustness					
Survivability					
Data Privacy					F05
Timeliness					P3, F02, F07
Reguation compliance					
Scalability					
Tailorability					F03
Unobtrusiveness					P3, F2
Transparency					P4, F08-F11

Figure 2. SQ model characteristics related to Features (F) or Premises (P) of the PSD model (Tabular view)

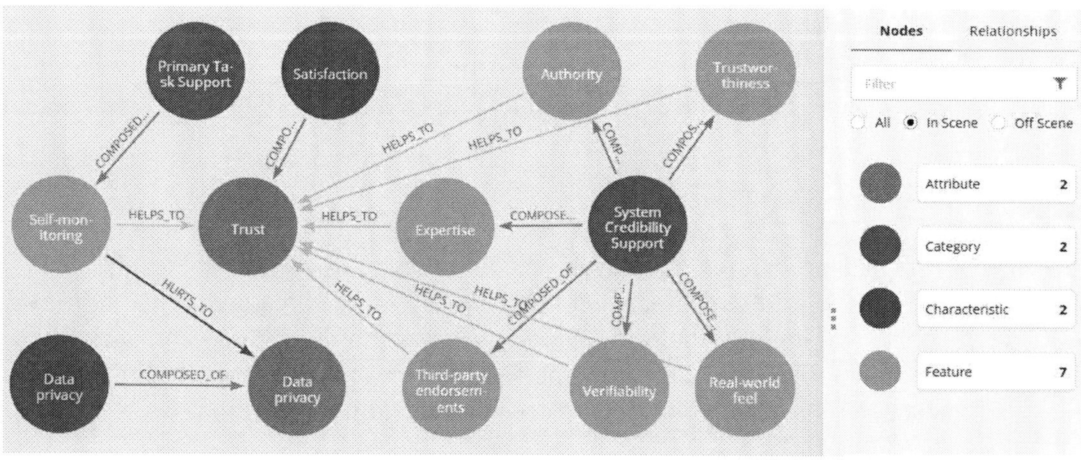

Figure 3. An illustration of relationships: HELPS_TO, HURTS_TO and COMPOSED_OF between the PSD model and the SQ model (Satisfaction in terms of Trust, and Data privacy)

cause having such feature implemented (user can track his/her own performance through the system), it might help to address the quality attribute "Trust" due to stakeholders are confident in that product. However, we can also observe that the "Self-monitoring" feature could also affect negatively to data privacy (HURTS_TO). This is because a system tracking the performance or status might cause some privacy concerns due to the collection of personally identifiable information.

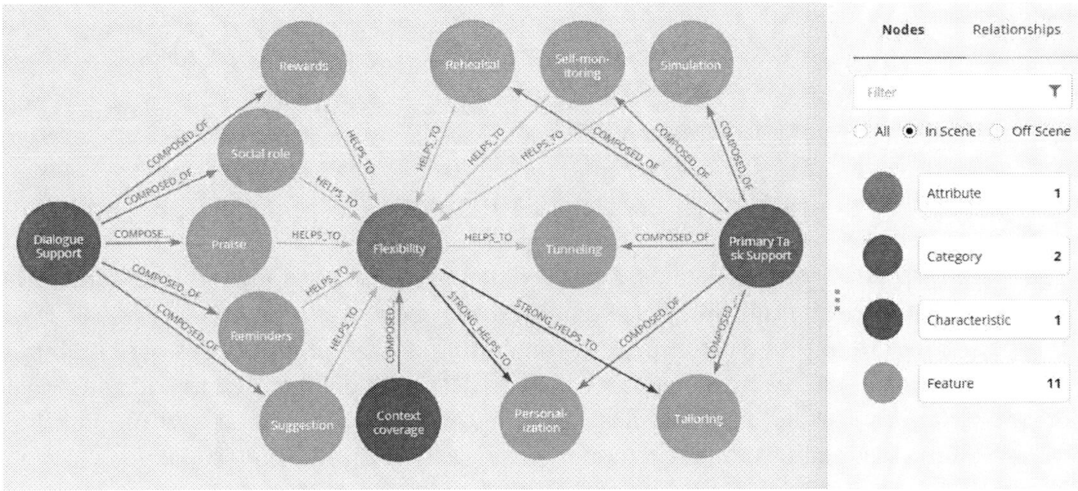

Figure 4. An illustration of relationships: HELPS_TO and COMPOSED_OF between the PSD model and the SQ model (Context coverage in terms of Flexibility)

In Figure 4, we illustrate the relationships for the quality attribute: Flexibility. In this case, we want to remark the arrows direction. For example, five features of the category *Dialogue Support* ("Suggestions", "Praise", "Rewards", "Social role" and "Reminders") contribute (helps to) to address the quality attribute: Flexibility. The implementation of the Praise, Rewards, Reminders, and Suggestions features can help users keep moving towards their goal or target behavior in contexts beyond those initially specified in the requirements. The social role feature might help in communication between users and specialists for example, consequently help the system to be used in contexts beyond those initially specified in the requirements as well.

We can also have contributions in the other direction, (QA→FE), such as Flexibility might help to the Tunneling, Personalization and Tailoring features. This means that if a system can be used in contexts beyond those initially specified in the requirements then the system should be able of: (i) offering personalized content or services; (ii) providing information that should be tailored to the potential needs, interests, personality, usage context, or other factors relevant to a user group; and (iii) guiding the user through a process or experience providing opportunities to persuade it.

4. Retrieval of Features and Quality Attributes using Cypher

The importance of the extended SQ model in a graph database lies in the fact that relationships between features, quality attributes and dimensions of sustainability can be consulted. We take advantage of neo4j's Cypher language to facilitate the designer's query. To better illustrate the retrieval from the graph database using Cypher, we first present the syntax of the language [Neo4j 2022].

Cypher's syntax The Cypher query language depicts patterns of nodes and relationships and filters those patterns based on labels and properties. For instance, nodes are represented with parentheses around the attributes and information regarding the entity. Relationships are depicted with an arrow (either directed or undirected) with the relationship type in brackets.

```
//node
(variable:Label {propertyKey: 'propertyValue'})
//relationship
-[variable:RELATIONSHIP_TYPE]->
//Cypher pattern
(node1:LabelA)-[rel1:RELATIONSHIP_TYPE]->(node2:LabelB)
```

Keywords: Cypher contains a variety of keywords for specifying patterns, filtering patterns, and returning results. Among those most common are: (i) MATCH is used before describing the search pattern for finding nodes, relationships, or combinations of nodes and relationships together. (ii) WHERE in Cypher is used to add additional constraints to patterns and filter out any unwanted patterns. (iii) RETURN formats and organizes how the results should be outputted. Just as with other query languages, you can return the results with specific properties, lists, ordering, and more.

Table 1 illustrates some queries in the graph database (Q1, Q2 and Q3) with a brief description of them. According to the syntax shown above, the query Q1 will search for the pattern of the node (*Characteristic* label) connected by the relationship (*COMPOSED_OF* type and outgoing direction away from the first node) to another node (*Attribute* label and property called name with value of input variable *$attrib*) and this is connected by the relationship (*CONTRIBUTES_TO* type and outgoing direction away from the second node) to the node *Dimension* label). In Q2 and Q3 we have queries of two types of relationships between nodes (of types *HELPS_TO* and *STRONG_HELPS_TO*).

Table 1. Queries

ID	Query in graph database	Description	Input	Output
Q1	MATCH p=(:Characteristic)-[:COMPOSED_OF]->(:Attribute{name:$attrib})-[:CONTRIBUTES_TO]->(:Dimension) RETURN p;	Knowing a quality attribute, the query helps in retrieving the corresponding sustainability dimensions.	Quality attribute	Sustainability dimensions and quality characteristic
Q2	MATCH p=(:Attribute {name:$attrib})- [:HELPS_TO | :STRONG_HELPS_TO]-(:Feature)<- [:COMPOSED_OF]-(:Category) RETURN p;	Knowing a quality attribute, the query helps in retrieving the corresponding feature and category.	Quality attribute	Features, categories
Q3	MATCH p=(:Feature{name:$fea})-[:HELPS_TO | :STRONG_HELPS_TO]-(:Attribute)-[:CONTRIBUTES_TO]->(:Dimension) RETURN p;	Knowing a feature, the query supports retrieving quality attributes helped by it and sustainability dimensions related.	Feature	Quality attributes and sustainability dimensions

5. Use Case: Illustration of Queries in the Graph model

In this section, we firstly describe the case from the well-being domain. Then, the use of the queries, defined in the previous section, is illustrated in two steps, which allow us to: (i) discover the relevant NFR and (ii) identify the features that were not present in the existing software application.

5.1. Case description:

There exists some software applications which aim to prevent and reduce RSIs in office workplaces, where the user has to typically be seated for a long time in front of a screen, typing on the keyboard and using a mouse as main peripheral devices. For illustrating the usefulness of our operationalized model, we have selected the Workrave application.

Workrave is probably one of the most complete applications of its class. It considers micro-pauses, rest breaks, and guidance for exercise routines. This software is based on timers and keyboard/mouse activity, which determine when the actions must be displayed on screen. The user interface offers to configure a good number of parameters and provides a monitor on micro-breaks, rest breaks and working hour limit. The remarkable feature is the Training support, using an animated virtual human to demonstrate the exercises in addition to a textual description (see Figure 5), which could have some positive effects on attaining coaching goals.

5.2. Features selection and NFR discovery

To illustrate the usage of the queries, we will consider only Flexibility and Timelines as relevant NFRs that were not addressed in Workrave:

- **Flexibility.** Workrave can be used in two specified contexts (writing and reading mode). However flexibility is desirable since users might want to use it in another different contexts to the specified. For example during a videoconference (listening).
- **Timeliness.** As Workrave is not aware on the context of usage, the main functionality (i.e., Take-a-break notification) might occur at a non-favourable time.

By considering both NFRs and using the extended SQ model, we were able to identify some new potential features that should be considered in further Workrave versions. In this paper, we illustrate some of the identified features as potential improvements for two functionalities of Workrave.

As shown in Figure 5, one of these functionalities is to provide statistics about user activity. For example, this functionality in the current version is limited to display measures of the keyboard/mouse usage (e.g., how long the mouse has been in use, the total and net distances the mouse has been moved). This means that the statistics of the actual user activity could not become accurate whether a user would be doing anything other than typing. Using query Q2 shown in the Table 1, which receives as input the quality attribute Flexibility, we get as output features (like personalization, tailoring and tunneling) with which they help each other (HELP_TO and STRONG_HELP in both directions). In our case, if workrave was flexible regarding its context of usage, the implementation of the *tailoring feature* would be favoured and consequently the reporting of such type of statistics would be improved as well. Another relation observed in the query Q2, it is that *self-monitoring feature* helps to flexibility. As designers, we think that this feature could effectively help to address the flexibility requirement since Workrave would be able to provide other means to track user status through self-monitoring. This information might enable the system to be used in contexts beyond those initially specified in the requirements. As shown Figure 5, the second functionality of Workrave is regarding "Guided exercises". The fact that this functionality could be done at an opportune moment (timeliness), it would favor the use of Workrave to guide users more appropriately *(tunneling)*, which could provide better opportunities to persuade them along the way. As categories are also output of query Q2 (See Table 1), we can also retrieve the corresponding categories to which the features belong (i.e., Primary task support).

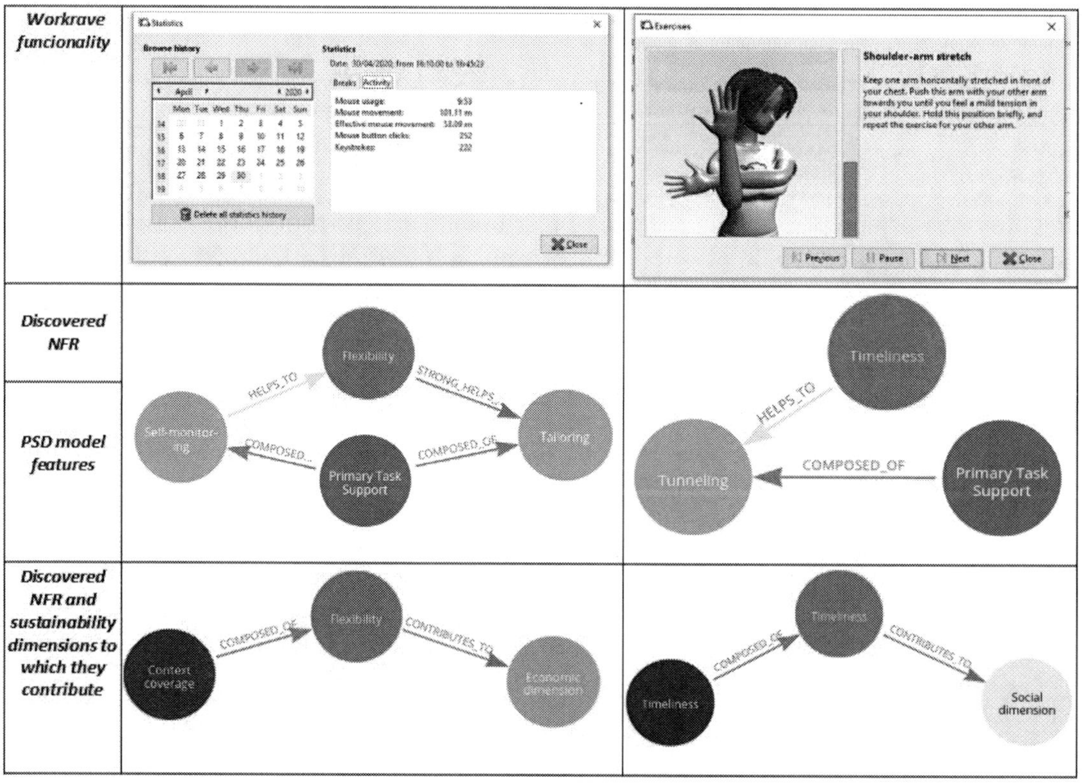

Figure 5. Mapping between NFRs and features for Workrave's functionalities: User activity statistics (left) and Guided exercises (right)

Using Flexibility and Timeliness as inputs, we can also use the query Q1 (see Table 1) to determine which sustainability dimensions can be addressed (output). This is also illustrated in Figure 5, where we obtain the Economic dimension, since there is a relation from flexibility (CONTRIBUTES_TO-type relationship). The quality characteristic Context coverage, is another output from query Q1, since there is a relation (COMPOSED_OF-type relationship) with flexibility. In similar way, we can retrieve the social dimension, by having Timeliness as input for the query Q1.

6. Conclusions and Future Work

The present research aims to operationalize a generic Sustainability-Quality (SQ) model for both assessing and designing persuasive systems through a mapping with the PSD model. As a result of this mapping, the operationalization consisted of identifying: (i) the QAs that might be addressed by the corresponding features or premises of the PSD model; and also those QAs that might help to the implementation of the PSD features, (ii) explicit relationships between QAs and features of the PSD model like *Strong Helps to*, *Helps to* and *Hurts to*. Moreover, the presentation of our operationalized SQ model has been visually represented by using graphs. We consider that this type of visualization might be more efficient because we can take advantage of the graph query language (Cypher).

This mapping (with the PSD model) has also helped us to uncover two new QAs (unobtrusiveness and transparency) that were identified as relevant for designing persuasive systems, which were included in the sustainability-quality model.

This mapping is the first attempt that tries to bridge the gap between both the software engineering and the persuasive technology communities. Our extended SQ model can be a helpful instrument not only for software engineers, who could discover NFR and select specific features for developing persuasive systems in a easier way, but also for researchers from the Persuasive Technology area, who could be interested in the design and evaluation of persuasive techniques/strategies. Besides that, the extended SQ model can be also used as a tool to identify qualities and features that might contribute to one or more dimensions of software sustainability. We also used an existing RSI application (Workrave) for illustrating how the extended SQ model helps in discovering missing quality requirements and potential features that were not present in the software app. Although in this research, we focus on the specific characteristics of persuasive systems, the SQ model can be used for any other type of software-intensive systems.

As future work, we are going to evaluate the implementation of the SQ model(with Neo4jgraph technology), by involving developers or software designers. Their feedback will be very useful not only for reviewing our list of predefined queries, which were formulated for retrieving quality requirements and features, but also for evaluating how usable is our graph-based approach.

Acknowledgment

This work has received support by the projects PDC2021-121239-C31, and KUSISQA 014-2019-FONDECYTBM-INC.INV. The research of Dr. Condori-Fernandez has been carried out as part of CITIC, Research Center accredited by Galician University System, funded by "Consellería de Cultura, Educación e Universidade" from Xunta de Galicia.

References

Ameller, D., Franch, X., Gómez, C., Martínez-Fernández, S., Araujo, J., Biffl, S., Cabot, J., Cortellessa, V., Méndez, D., Moreira, A., Muccini, H., Vallecillo, A., Wimmer, M., Amaral, V., Bühm, W., Bruneliere, H., Burgueño, L., Goulão, M., Teufl, S., and Berardinelli, L. (2019). Dealing with non-functional requirements in model-driven development: A survey. *IEEE Transactions on Software Engineering*, pages 1–1.

Becker, C. and et al (2016). Requirements: The key to sustainability. *IEEE Software*, 33(1):56–65.

Brundtland, G., Khalid, M., Agnelli, S., Al-Athel, S., Chidzero, B., Fadika, L., Hauff, V., Lang, I., Shijun, M., Morino de Botero, M., Singh, M., and Okita, S. (1987). Our common future (brundtland report). Technical report, World Commission on Environment and Development.

Calero, C., Moraga, M. Á., and Bertoa, M. F. (2013). Towards a software product sustainability model. *CoRR*, abs/1309.1640.

Chung, L., Nixon, B., Yu, E., and Mylopoulos, J. (2000). *Non-functional requirements in software engineering*. SPRINGER, LLC, New York, NY, USA.

Condori-Fernández, N., Bolos, A. C., and Lago, P. (2018). Discovering requirements of behaviour change software systems from negative user experience. In *Proceedings of the 40th International Conference on Software Engineering: Companion Proceeedings, ICSE 2018, Gothenburg, Sweden, May 27 - June 03, 2018*, pages 222–223.

Condori-Fernandez, N. and Lago, P. (2018). Characterizing the contribution of quality requirements to software sustainability. *Journal of systems and software*, 137:289–305.

Condori Fernandez, N. and Lago, P. (2018). *A Sustainability-quality Model: (version 1.0)*. VU Technical Report.

Fogg, B. (2003). *Persuasive Technology: Using Computers to Change What We Think and Do*. Morgan Kaufmann Publishers Inc., San Francisco, CA, USA.

Fogg, B. (2009). A behavior model for persuasive design. *Proceedings of the 4th International Conference on Persuasive Technology - Persuasive '09*, page 1.

Froehlich, J. (2009). Promoting energy efficient behaviors in the home through feedback: The role of humancomputer interaction. In *HCIC 2009 Winter Workshop*, volume 9, pages 1–11.

Harjumaa, M. and Oinas-Kukkonen, H. (2007). An analysis of the persuasiveness of smoking cessation web sites. In *The Second International Symposium on Medical Information and Communication Technology*.

Lago, P. and Condori-Fernandez, N. (2022). *The Sustainability Assessment Framework (SAF) Toolkit: Instruments to help Sustainability-driven Software Architecture Design Decision Making*. S2 Group, Vrije Universiteit Amsterdam.

Lago, P., Koçak, S. A., Crnkovic, I., and Penzenstadler, B. (2015). Framing sustainability as a property of software quality. *Communications of the ACM*, 58(10):70–78.

Locke, E. and Latham, G. (1991). A theory of goal setting & task performance. *The Academy of Management Review*, 16:480–483.

Neo4j (2022). Cypher introduction.

Oinas-Kukkonen, H. (2013). A foundation for the study of behavior change support systems. *Personal Ubiquitous Comput.*, 17(6):1223–1235.

Oinas-Kukkonen, H. and Harjumaa, M. (2009). Persuasive systems design: Key issues, process model, and system features. *Communications of the Association for Information Systems*, 24:485–500.

Prochaska, J. O. and DiClemente, C. C. (2005). The transtheoretical approach. *Administration and Policy in Mental Health and Mental Health Services Research*, pages 147—171.

Venters, C., Jay, C., Lau, L., Griffiths, M. K., Holmes, V., Ward, R., Austin, J., Dibsdale, C. E., and Xu, J. (2014). Software sustainability: The modern tower of babel. In *RE4SuSy: Third International Workshop on Requirements Engineering for Sustainable Systems*.

7. Appendix A: Mapping between PSD model and the SQ model

	System credibility			Explanation
Quality attributes	*Strong Helps*	*Helps*	*Hurts*	
Effectiveness		X		A system that incorporates features such as trustworthy, incorporing expertise, surface credibility, incorporing real-world feeling, leverages roles of authority, third-party endorsements and facilitates verifiability of the accuracy of site content achieves (HELPS) that the system be effective.
Economic risk mitigation			X	Social support (all features) might have a negative effect (HURTS) on the user's financial status in medium or long term due to the excessive usage of the (persuasive) software system.
Environmental risk mitigation			X	Social support (all features) might have a negative effect on the environment in medium or long term due to the excessive usage of the (persuasive) software system. For instance, when groups of motivated users became addicts of the system, energy consumption would increase, which can cause a negative effect on the environment.
Health and safety risk mitigation		X		As all features contribute to design more credible systems and thus more persuasive, we think that the likelihood of happening a health and safety risk would be low
Functional appropriateness		X		The functions facilitate (HELP) the accomplishment of specified tasks and objectives related to features that the system should have: Expertise, Real-world feel, Authority, Third-party endorsements.
Functional correctness		X		The correct functions facilitate (HELP) the accomplishment of specified tasks and objectives such as features that the system should have: Expertise, Real-world feel, Authority, Third-party endorsements.
Functional completeness		X		Functional completeness facilitates (HELPS) the accomplishment of specified tasks and objectives such as features that the system should have: Expertise, Real-world feel, Authority, Third-party endorsements.
Maturity		X		If the system facilitates verifiability of the accuracy of site content then the system becomes more reliable
Trust		X		A system that incorporates features such as trustworthy, incorporing expertise, real-world feeling, leverages roles of authority, third-party endorsements and facilitates verifiability of the accuracy of site content achieves (HELPS) that the stakeholders are confident that a product or system will behave as intended, that is, it is seen as trustworthy.
Accountability		X		If actions of an entity can be traced uniquely to the entity, this contributes (HELPS) for the system be viewed as trustworthiness
Authenticity		X		If the identity of a subject or resource can be proved to be the one claimed, this contributes (HELPS) for the system be viewed as trustworthiness
Confidentiality		X		If system ensures that data are accessible only to those authorized to have access, then this contributes (HELPS) for the system be viewed as trustworthiness
Integrity		X		If the system prevents unauthorized access, or modification of, computer programs or data, this contributes (HELPS) to the system be viewed as trustworthiness.
Transparency		X		The transparency of the purpose of the system HELPS make the system more credible (System Credibility Support - all features) and thereby more persuasive.

Figure 6. Relationships between quality attributes (SQ model) and features of system credibility support(category of the PSD model)

8. Appendix B: Features of the PSD model

Categories	Description	Features	Description
Primary Task support	The primary activity support category focuses on supporting the activities that lead to achievement of the BCSS goals.	F01: Reduction	A system that reduces complex behavior into simple tasks helps users perform the target behavior, and it may increase the benefit/cost ratio of a behavior.
		F02: Tunneling	Using the system to guide users through a process or experience provides opportunities to persuade along the way.
		F03: Tailoring	Information provided by the system will be more persuasive if it is tailored to the potential needs, interests, personality, usage context, or other factors relevant to a user group.
		F04: Personalization	A system that offers personalized content or services has a greater capability for persuasion.
		F05: Self-monitoring	A system that keeps track of one's own performance or status supports the user in achieving goals.
		F06: Simulation	Systems that provide simulations can persuade by enabling users to observe immediately the link between cause and effect.
		F07: Rehearsal	A system providing means with which to rehearse a behavior can enable people to change their attitudes or behavior in the real world.
Dialogue Support	Dialogue support refers to techniques/mechanisms to motivate users to use BCSS.	F08: Praise	By offering praise, a system can make users more open to persuasion.
		F09: Rewards	Systems that reward target behaviors may have great persuasive powers.
		F10: Reminders	If a system reminds users of their target behavior, the users will more likely achieve their goals.
		F11: Suggestion	Systems offering fitting suggestions will have greater persuasive powers.
		F12: Similarity	People are more readily persuaded through systems that remind them of themselves in some meaningful way.
		F13: Liking	A system that is visually attractive for its users is likely to be more persuasive.
		F14: Social role	If a system adopts a social role, users will more likely use it for persuasive purposes.
System Credibility Support	The credibility category relates to how to design a system so that it is more credible and thereby more persuasive.	F15: Trustworthiness	A system that is viewed as trustworthy will have increased powers of persuasion.
		F16: Expertise	A system that is viewed as incorporating expertise will have increased powers of persuasion.
		F17: Surface credibility	People make initial assessments of the system credibility based on a firsthand inspection.
		F18: Real-world feel	A system that highlights people or organization behind its content or services will have more credibility.
		F19: Authority	A system that leverages roles of authority will have enhanced powers of persuasion.
		F20: Third-party endorsements	Third-party endorsements, especially from well-known and respected sources, boost perceptions on system credibility.
		F21: Verifiability	Credibility perceptions will be enhanced if a system makes it easy to verify the accuracy of site content via outside sources.
Social support	The social influence category describes how to design the system so that it motivates users by leveraging different aspects of social influence	F22: Social learning	A person will be more motivated to perform a target behavior if (s) he can use a system to observe others performing the behavior.
		F23: Social comparison	System users will have a greater motivation to perform the target behavior if they can compare their performance with the performance of others.
		F24: Normative influence	A system can leverage normative influence or peer pressure to increase the likelihood that a person will adopt a target behavior.
		F25: Social facilitation	System users are more likely to perform target behavior if they discern via the system that others are performing the behavior along with them.
		F26: Cooperation	A system can motivate users to adopt a target attitude or behavior by leveraging human beings' natural drive to co-operate.
		F27: Competition	A system can motivate users to adopt a target attitude or behavior by leveraging human beings' natural drive to compete.
		F28: Recognition	By offering public recognition for an individual or group, a system can increase the likelihood that a person/group will adopt a target behavior.

Figure 7. Features of the PSD model [Oinas-Kukkonen and Harjumaa 2009] [Oinas-Kukkonen 2013]

Investigating the Perception of Success in Software Projects Among Developers from a Brazilian Software Company

Claudio Nascimento[1], **Rafael de Mello**[2]

[1]Centro Federal Tecnológico Celso Suckow da Fonseca, Rio de Janeiro, Brazil

[2]Universidade Federal do Rio de Janeiro, Rio de Janeiro, Brazil

claudio.nascimento@aluno.cefet-rj.br, rafaelmello@ic.ufrj.br

Abstract. *Understanding and properly applying agile practices in software development projects is a common challenge for developers. Consequently, the expected benefits of these practices may not be perceived, hampering developers from reaching critical success factors of software projects. This work aims to investigate the perception of success in software projects in the context of a Brazilian software company whose development process is based on Scrum. Besides, the development teams from this company follow several technical and non-technical agile practices. For this purpose, we conducted an opinion survey with 17 developers distributed among four development teams of this company. The survey findings revealed prevailing gaps in the teams' perception of critical success factors in their projects despite following a common subset of agile practices addressing them. Among others, the gaps include a lack of perceiving realistic schedules, clear requirements, and good quality management. Aiming at improving this scenario in the company, we plan to conduct a collaborative action research with one of the development teams investigated.*

1. Introduction

The agile concepts and methods have been widely disseminated and inserted into the software development practice since the Agile Manifesto [Fowler et al. 2001]. Currently, it is difficult to identify teams applying development processes without any agile inspiration. Consequently, it is common to observe development teams and companies following agile methods. In this way, there are several factors to be considered when choosing a particular method, such as the project scope and the capacity for adaptation of the team members [Dybå and Dingsøyr 2008]. Such factors typically lead development teams to conclude that some agile practices deserve more attention than others. Consequently, it is common to observe development teams or even entire companies depicting and employing customized approaches [Leal and Santos 2015, de Mello et al. 2021]. Not rarely, these approaches include the combination of ceremonies and practices derived from different agile methods [Leal and Santos 2015], such as lean development [Poppendieck and Cusumano 2012], Scrum [Schwaber and Beedle 2002], and Kanban [Ahmad et al. 2013].

Development teams should pursue success in their projects, which may be considerably influenced by the development process employed [Chow and Cao 2008]. The concern on tailoring the software development process is often motivated by a collective and somehow unconscious search for success. Reaching success in software projects goes beyond meeting deadlines and budgets, being directly connected to the organizational climate and the developers' motivation [Dutra et al. 2020]. Therefore, it is important to evaluate the perception of success from a holistic perspective, which includes different critical success factors [Chow and Cao 2008]. In this sense, particular agile practices [de Mello et al. 2014] would contribute for reaching different success factors in software projects [Pimenta and Santos 2016]. For this purpose, it is expected to assure that the agile practices to be followed should be feasible for the project team and properly applied by its members, who should carefully reflect on the benefits and potential drawbacks of these practices in their development contexts [Leal and Santos 2015].

Despite the common concern of developers in tailoring the development process, it is also common to observe a lack of proper following the preconized agile practices. For instance, a development team would argue by following daily meetings despite not following key recommendations such as restricting the discussions about activities and obstacles reported during the meeting time [Schwaber and Beedle 2002]. Besides, several project team members may not be ready to employ different agile practices requiring intense communication and knowledge sharing [Kamei et al. 2017]. Consequently, the effect of these practices on the success of software projects may be minimized or even nullified.

This paper report an investigation on the perception of success in software projects by developers from a Brazilian software company in which developers were fully working remotely due to the COVID-19 pandemics. The company has several development teams specialized in evolving specific modules from an information system for health services. We conducted an opinion survey with 17 developers from this company, distributed among four teams. Both teams reported following several relevant agile practices in common, including daily meetings, product backlog, and whole team. Despite this, the survey results indicate that reaching some critical success factors in software projects tends to be challenging for the developers. In general, we found a trend among developers in not perceiving the feasibility of the projects' schedules and the effectiveness of change management activities. Besides, several developers have negative perceptions about the effectiveness of quality management and risk management activities, among other issues. The survey findings contrast with the expected benefits of the agile practices followed by the teams [Pimenta and Santos 2016].

The replication of the survey protocol introduced in this paper may be employed as a first research step for diagnosing how developers from other companies perceive the success of their projects. Based on the survey findings, alternative research strategies may be applied to overcome the challenging success factors. We opted to plan the conduction of a collaborative action research [Thiollent 1996] with one of these teams aiming to identify, prioritize, and apply interventions for improving the perception of success among its members. The plan of the action research is also introduced in this paper.

Section 2 presents related work on critical success factors in software projects and agile practices. Section 3 describes the settings of the opinion survey conducted with the company's developers. Section 4 presents the survey results. In Section 4.4, we discuss the main threats to validity. Section 5 discusses the main findings of our study. Section 6 introduce the action research to be conducted. Finally, Section 7 concludes the paper and indicates future work.

2. Related Work

Chow and Cao [Chow and Cao 2008] conducted an empirical study on the relationship of critical success factors in software projects following agile practices. Based on the analysis of 408 respondents and 109 projects, the authors identified six critical success factors and corresponding attributes resulting from a proper management process of agile projects. The factors include *delivering strategy*, *agile software engineering techniques*, *team capability*, *project management process*, *team environment*, and *customer involvement*.

Nasir et al. [Nasir and Sahibuddin 2011] analysed the content of 43 research papers aiming at characterizing critical success factors for software projects. The authors found 26 critical success factors, considerably varying in frequency. Most of these factors address non-technical issues such as budget, schedule, and leadership, just to name a few. However, the lack of clear and stable requirements also appeared among the most frequent factors.

One common challenge for development teams addresses the selection of an agile method that best fits their characteristics and needs [Dybå and Dingsøyr 2008]. Regardless of the agile method followed, it is notable that agile principles and practices have been incorporated into the routine of development teams in the last decade [Leal and Santos 2015], which could be considered one great disruption in the field. In this sense, Abrantes and Travassos [Abrantes and Travassos 2013], conducted an extensive systematic literature review for characterizing the principles and practices of agile development. Based on the findings of this review, they carried out an opinion survey with the authors of the relevant papers identified in the review. The survey findings revealed that 16 characteristics of agility and 15 agile practices were perceived as relevant by most researchers. The first column of Table 1 shows an excerpt of these agile practices.

The protocol of the survey conducted by Abrantes and Travassos [Abrantes and Travassos 2013] was then replicated by de Mello et al. [de Mello et al. 2014] over a larger and diverse sample of software professionals. These professionals were identified, stratified, and recruited by following a systematic sampling plan for identifying representative samples [de Mello et al. 2015]. After the analysis of the 272 responses from this replication, the authors found that the perception of software professionals about the relevance of agile practices tends to be predominantly similar to those observed among researchers. Besides, the survey findings allowed expanding the original set of agile practices investigated.

Based on previous research, Pimenta and Santos [Pimenta and Santos 2016] proposed an association between 16 critical success factors in software projects and the relevant agile practices mapped by de Mello et al. [de Mello et al. 2014]. This work may be used by development teams may identify opportunities for introducing/evolving certain agile practices that would enhance the perception of success in their projects. Table 1 show an excerpt of these associations.

It is important to note that following some agile practice in isolation cannot assure reaching some critical success factor satisfactorily. Possible issues on applying certain agile practices may mitigate or even nullify the contributions of these practices to the success of software projects. Besides, other issues related to each agile practice may also

Table 1. Excerpt of the associations between agile critical success factors and agile practices proposed in [Pimenta and Santos 2016]

Agile Practice	Critical Success Factor
product backlog	clear requirements
	clear goals/ objectives
	effective communication/ feedback
	adequate planning
	good risk management
whole team	clear requirements
	realistic schedules
	good leadership
daily meetings	effective communication/ feedback
	updated progress report
	good leadership
small releases	clear requirements
	client-user involvement
	technology familiarity
	committed/ motivated team
project visibility	effective communication/feedback
	updated progress report
	good leadership
continuous integration	good quality management

affect the perception of expected benefits. For instance, a certain development team may build a software system through continuous integration, contributing to good quality management. However, the development team may perceive their configuration management as unsuccessful due to the also continuous introduction of technical debt elements, such as code smells [Zazworka et al. 2014, Iammarino et al. 2019] in the new releases. The incidence of these code smells may be mitigated and combated through the agile practices of pair programming [Hannay et al. 2009] and refactoring [Zazworka et al. 2014].

3. Survey Design

The opinion survey reported in this paper is inserted in the context of a broader investigation aiming at *characterizing the main obstacles perceived by developers for the success of software projects*. In this survey, we want to answer the following research questions:

How are critical success factors of software projects perceived by software developers from teams following agile development approaches?

For this research, we considered the set of relevant agile practices identified by Abrantes and Travassos [Abrantes and Travassos 2013] and de Mello et al.

[de Mello et al. 2014]. The critical success factors considered in this study are those compiled by Pimenta and Santos [Pimenta and Santos 2016]. For answering the research question, we conducted an opinion survey [Linaker et al. 2015] with developers from a Brazilian software company where the first author work. The characteristics of this company and the challenges perceived in the daily work motivated this study with their developers.

3.1. Population and Sample

The survey population is composed of software development professionals working in development teams following agile practices. The sample recruited was established from the developers working for different teams from a Brazilian software company. At the time of the survey execution, the company had around 150 employees, including trainees, effective positions, and temporary ones. The company has two operational headquarters located in the two biggest Brazilian cities (Rio de Janeiro and São Paulo), attending to customers from different parts of the country. Due to the COVID-19 pandemics, all developers were working remotely during the execution of the study.

The company established the adoption of Scrum in 2019 to all development activities. For this purpose, the company hired external consultants to train all developers on the Scrum process and ceremonies. We recruited developers working in four teams from this company to participate. The four teams are responsible for conducting evolutive maintenance projects addressing different modules of the same information system. The system support health companies, such as health insurance operators. The customers frequently requires system evolution addressing new business needs and regulation in the field. These improvements typically result in one-month to three-month projects.

Before performing the recruitment, we mapped the agile practices followed by each team. Besides working in the same software system, we found that all teams surveyed tend to follow similar subsets of relevant agile practices. All teams work with *daily meetings*, *product backlog*, *whole team*, *on-site costumer*, and *pair programming*. Besides, three of the four teams also follow the agile practices of *small releases*, *project visibility*, *continuous integration*, and *simple design*. Therefore, based on the associations presented in Table 1, one could expect that reaching some critical success factors would be less challenging for these teams.

3.2. Instrumentation

The survey questionnaire is composed of 26 items distributed among three blocks. The first block (Table 2) has questions for characterizing the experience of developers in software engineering, based on the schema proposed in [de Mello and Coelho 2021].

The items composing the second block include 16 statements designed for gathering the developers' level of agreement on reaching the critical success factors in their software projects (see Table 3. This level of agreement was gathered through applying the same Likert scale [Joshi et al. 2015] to each item: *totally disagree*, *partially disagree*, *partially agree* and *totally agree*.

The third block of the survey questionnaire is composed of the following two open questions. Through these questions, we aim to gather complementary considerations of the developers about broader points addressing their beliefs about success in software

Table 2. Questionnaire items for characterizing the professional experience of the survey participants.

Questionnaire Item	Answer Type
Higher Academic Degree	Nominal
Years of experience in software development	Number
Years of experience in software development in the current company	Number
Years of experience in software development in the current team	Number
Number of software development projects participated	Number
Number of software development projects participated in the current company	Number
Number of software development projects participated in the current team	Number

projects and the practices that contribute to the success of the projects in their teams. Based on these answers, it will be possible to perform a deeper analysis of the results obtained in the second block.

- *What do you understand by a successful software project?*
- *Which practices followed by the team collaborate to the agility of the development process?*

4. Execution and Results

We conducted the opinion survey in April 2021. Except for the first author, the other 32 developers composing the four selected teams were able to participate in the survey. The developers had five days to answer the survey questionnaire, individually sent by e-mail. After the recruitment, the survey questionnaire were answered by 17 developers: six from the *Billing* module, four from the *Contracts* module, four from the *Operations* module, and three from the *Accounts* module. Most of the 17 survey respondents (88%) declared having at least a Bachelor's degree. Table 4 shows the average working experience (mean/median) of these developers in different contexts.

On average, one may see that the developers have high levels of experience in software development, including at their current working company. These results indicate that the survey participants tend to be experienced and sufficiently immersed in the organizational culture of their working company. Besides, it indicates that most of the developers had participated in the activities for implementing Scrum in the company. Indeed, we identified that the company hired only four of the 17 developers more recently. The mean and median values found for the experience in the team suggest some concern and preference for preserving the team composition. The general characteristics of the developers' experience suggest their opinions will be relevant and well-grounded considering the survey context.

Table 3. Statements composing the second block of the survey questionnaire and the corresponding critical success factor.

Statement	Critical Factor
The project goal remains clear and concise throughout development	clear goals/objectives
The deadlines given for development are realistic	realistic schedule
The project requirements are properly defined from the beginning	clear requirements
The involvement of users and customers in the project is effective	client/user involvement
The stakeholders' communication generates good feedback	effective communication/feedback
Project members are able to apply the tools and the process followed by the company	familiarity with technology/dev. method
The delivering plans are properly defined	adequate planning
It is employed effective ways to share the level of progress of the activities	updated progress report
General details about the development activities are clear and available	effective control/monitoring
Team leadership is well performed	good leadership
The identification of risks in the project and how to deal with them is carried out effectively	risk management
Available work support resources are suited to the complexity of the project	project complexity
The changes performed over development items are properly managed	effective change and config. management
The team is committed to all activities	committed/ motivated team
There is good quality management, following practices that demonstrate and verify the quality of the artifacts created	quality management
Expectations addressing third-party activities are met	good third-party performance

Table 4. Professional experience of the survey participants.

Metric	SW Industry Exp.	Company Exp.	Team Exp.
Years	14.25/13.50	6.90/6.00	4.44/2.00
#Projects	22.00/11.00	7.00/4.00	6.20/4.00

4.1. Perception of Critical Success Factors in Software Projects

From the 272 answers given by the 17 developers to the 16 statements positively addressing the perception of critical success factors in software projects, we found 32,72% answers indicating some level of disagreement with these statements. This overall number *per se* may be interpreted as worrisome once developers are giving opinions about the projects and teams they work on. Besides, we identified that developers perceive the reaching of some critical success factors considerably less than the other factors. Table 5 presents the eight critical success factors worst evaluated by the survey participants. One may see that more than half of the developers somehow disagree that the schedules are realistic and the change management activities are effective.

Table 5. The eight critical success factors worse evaluated by the survey developers (CD-Completely Disagre, PD- Partially Disagree, PA- Partially Agree, CA- Completely Agree).

Factor	CD	PD	PA	CA
realistic schedule	-	9	6	2
effective change/configuration management	1	8	6	2
clear requirements	2	6	9	-
good risk management	3	5	6	3
good quality management	1	7	8	1
adequate planning	1	6	7	3
updated progress report	2	5	9	1
effective control/monitoring	2	5	9	1

Regarding the eight critical success factors better evaluated (Table 6), it is important to point out that *Effective Communication and Feedback*, and *Commited and Motivated Team* were the only factors in which the frequency of total agreement is higher than the incidence of partial agreement. Besides, there is a trend among the developers agreeing (82% or higher) about the effectiveness of *user involvement*, *communication with stakeholders*, *leadership*, and *third-party work*.

Table 6. The eight critical success factors better evaluated by the survey developers (CD-Completely Disagre, PD- Partially Disagree, PA- Partially Agree, CA- Completely Agree).

Factor	CD	PD	PA	CA
commited/motivated team	1	-	6	10
good third-party performance	-	2	13	2
client/user involvement	-	2	10	5
good leadership	1	2	7	7
effective communication/ feedback	-	3	5	9
project complexity	-	4	10	3
familiarity with technolog/dev. method	1	4	6	6
clear goals/objectives	-	6	6	5

4.2. Understanding Successful Software Projects

We also asked what the developers understand about a successful software project. After coding the answers, we found eleven distinct characteristics of successful software projects being evoked (see Table 7). Seven of these characteristics address critical success factors already categorized. From the other four characteristics raised by the developers, one addresses possible consequences of successful projects (customer satisfaction) rather than factors.

On the other hand, *qualified and sufficient team*, *following code standards*, and *realistic budget* may be considered additional critical success factors. One may see that seven of the eleven characteristics coded were spontaneously evoked at least by one-third of the developers, which may be considered a high frequency for open questions. These findings suggest a cohesion in the values and beliefs shared among the development teams investigated, reflecting their experience and the influence of the particular community in which they are inserted.

Table 7. Characteristics of successful software projects evoked by developers.

Characteristics	**Frequency**
clear requirements	9
customer satisfaction*	8
realistic schedule	7
clear goals/objectives	7
updated progress report	6
user/client involvement	6
qualified and sufficient team	6
familiarity with technology/dev. method	5
following code standards*	4
realistic budget*	3
adequate planning	3

4.3. Contributors for the Agility of Software Development

We also asked developers to spontaneously indicate which practices they understand are contributors to the agility of software development. The distribution of the coded answers is presented in Table 8. One can see that nine practices evoked by developers address agile practices already mapped in our research[de Mello et al. 2014]. Of these, six are agile practices largely applied among the development teams (*small releases*, *project visibility*, *whole team*, *daily meetings*, *product backlog*, and *pair programming*). The other two agile practices (*coding standards,collective code ownership*, and *software review*) are followed only by two teams. These findings suggest that developers are aware of the relevance of the practices they follow. However, coding standards seems to be a key concern, being also identified as a critical success factor.

4.4. Threats to Validity

Regarding the construct validity, we strongly grounded our survey questionnaire on results from previous work [de Mello et al. 2014, Pimenta and Santos 2016]. In this sense, we carefully verified whether the statements composed for the second block clearly address the 16 critical success factors mapped in [Pimenta and Santos 2016]. The second block of the survey questionnaire is composed of 16 statements. Long lists of survey items may be exhaustive, negatively influence on the quality of the developers' answers. We mitigate this threat by adopting a standardized model combining short statements with an intuitive four-scale Likert scale.

Table 8. Practices for software development agility evoked by software developers.

Practices	Frequency
daily meetings	7
collective code ownership	6
pair programming	6
coding standardization	5
project visibility	5
whole team	4
small releases	4
software review	4
product backlog	2

The first author of the paper work in the company investigated and also conducted the survey with his colleagues. This scenario is positive to allow performing a deeper analysis of the study findings and we will continue to explore it in the next research steps. However, it may also influence in the answers of the survey participants. In this way, we recruited developers from teams that the first author does not work with to participate. Besides, we applied in the third block open questions that would help to identify possible inconsistencies in the developers answers to the closed questions. We conducted a opinion survey in the particular context of a Brazilian Software Company. Therefore, the generalization of the findings reported in this study may be considerably limited. the general findings points to the contributions of replicating this survey in other companies with similar settings.

5. Discussion

The study involved developers distributed between four development teams from the same company. These teams share a common subset of agile practices identified as relevant in previous investigation [de Mello et al. 2014]. As presented in Section 4.1, most of the survey participants are experienced with software development. Besides, a great part of this experience comes from working in their current company. At a first glance, these overall characteristics may be considered benefic for reaching success in software projects. However, our study revealed that 40% to 53% of the survey participants have difficulty realizing that their projects achieve half of the critical success factors investigated. Despite this unfavourable numbers, we identified that all these factors may be enhanced by agile practices already followed by three or all the four teams involved in the survey sample (see Table 9.

In some cases, contrasting results are more clearly evident. For instance, several developers disagree that the progress reports of the projects are continually updated. However, all teams declared performing daily meetings and three teams declared applying practices for promoting the projects' visibility. Besides, several developers highlighted both agile practices in the open questions. This finding suggest the need of investigating in-depth how these practices have been applied and adapted for the context of remote work. The study findings reveal the need for the teams to find ways to improve how they share their progress during development activities, which may be also harmed by the environmental changing caused by the remote work.

Another example of notable contrasting results address the lack of perception of clear requirements, the only success factor spontaneously evoked by most of developers. It is expected that the combined practices of small releases and product backlog would help the teams to manage the system requirements during the evaluations performed in the source code. One possible reason for this behaviour would address the facility for accessing the customers. Although it is considered an agile practice, teams with this resource should be careful to avoid excessively rely on the informal communication. In this way, we identified that with the managers that the developers are used to frequently keep in touch with the costumers to clarify the system requirements.

The lack of clear requirements harms not only the definition of reliable product backlog and reliable plans, but also establishing realistic schedules despite of the availability of whole teams composed of experienced developers. Without clear requirements, it is hard to estimate the development efforts and consequently feasible deadlines for each development task.

Table 5 also shows that technical agile practices associated with quality management and configuration management are fairly disseminated. These practices include development activities applied for identifying and combating the incidence of technical debt in the source code (*software review*, *refactoring*) and preventing the incidence of defects (*software review*, *TDD*). Here, it is important to note that code review and refactoring activities are important tasks inserted into the context of *pair programming*, which all teams claim to follow. Therefore, this finding point to concrete opportunities for the teams improving the pair programming practice.

Table 9. Mapping of the followed and non-followed agile practices addressing the worse evaluated critcial succes factors.

Critical Success Factors	More Followed Practices	Less Followed Practices
realistic schedule	whole team	-
clear requirements	whole team, product backlog, small releases	-
updated progress report	daily meetings, project visibility	-
good risk management	product backlog	-
good quality management	continuous integration, pair programming	refactoring, TDD, sw review
adequate planning	product backlog	-
effective control/monitoring	daily meetings	-
effective change/config. management	small releases, on site costumer	refactoring

Among the positive results, it is notable the positive effects of the company investing in whole teams predominantly composed of experience developers familiar with the development technologies and methods employed. The internal and external communication (customers/third-party) tend to be positively perceived by the developers. The teams are committed and have experienced leaders available. The adoption of coding standards contributes to the third-party performance.the survey findings also suggest that the overall experience of the developers and the low frequency of rotation among teams may contribute to their positive perception of communication with customers and third-party services providers. In this sense, the availability of the customers on-site is a positive contributor, which was successfully adapted to the remote work.

6. Planning the Action Research

As previously discussed, the survey results indicated gaps and some opportunities for improving the development practice of the teams investigated. This section presents the plan of a collaborative action research [Thiollent 1996] aiming at improving the perception of success in the team the first author works as a developer. The expectation is to run at least one complete action research cycle during a mid-term project. Despite the dynamic nature of action research, it is important to reflect on the main activities to be performed during the first cycle steps.

6.1. Problem Definition

We plan to conduct an open meeting with the participants to start the action research. In this meeting, we will first present the main results of the survey, with a focus on four critical success factors among those worst evaluated by 17 developers. They are *realistic schedule*, *clear requirements*, *good quality management*, and *effective change/configuration management*. We selected this subset once we previously identified with the manager that developers would have more autonomy for applying interventions addressing these factors. After this introduction, the first author will conduct a brainstorming with the team members to map the challenges observed by the developers to apply the agile practices already applied by the team addressing these factors. At the end of the meeting, the team members will be invited to reflect until the next meeting on feasible alternatives to overcome the raised challenges.

6.2. Action Planning

For this step, the first author will moderate a focus group session [Kontio et al. 2004] with the team members to identify and discuss possible interventions to overcome each challenge reported in the problem definition. Therefore, we plan to address a single challenge by focus group section. After the focus group, the validated interventions will be prioritized by the team (vote counting).

6.3. Action

We will identify a feasible subset of the higher prioritized interventions to be applied during the cycle, considering the additional effort and the resources required. The intervention and eventual guidelines/resources will be presented to all team members in a meeting. Then the developers will be oriented to apply the interventions from the beginning of a development project until its end.

6.4. Evaluation and Learning

The first author will work on the projects but he also will be continuously available to follow and orient the team members about the proposed interventions. Besides, he will observe the team dynamics for identifying possible gaps and new challenges. After the end of the project, we will invite the developers to answer an opinion survey on the perceived benefits and challenges of the interventions applied. Depending on the nature of the difficulties observed, we may change the data collection procedure to individual interviews. After that, we intend to conduct a briefing with the whole team to get feedback about the action research experience and gather opportunities for improving the following cycles, if needed.

7. Conclusion and Future Work

Reaching success in software projects is more than achieving budgets and schedules. It is part of a human need, enabled by the unconscious need to feel part of a group that can collaborate and overcome challenges together. As a human feeling, success is a complex thing composed of different and complementary facets.

We may say that the values raised by the agile manifesto two decades ago led the software engineering community to rethink (or remember) the values surrounding success from a holistic perspective. Different studies evidence that several agile practices may significantly contribute to this success when properly applied. However, as part of a complex socio-technical construct, these practices cannot be observed in isolation nor limited to specific methods. Developers should have in mind that agile practices are important resources for a higher purpose: promoting a holistic and collective perception of success among stakeholders.

The study reported in this paper exemplifies how even experienced software teams from companies promoting agile practices may have difficulties in being successful in their projects. The survey protocol reported in this paper may be employed in other software companies as a first step in diagnosing their bottlenecks for reaching success in their projects. This diagnosis should be preceded by an in-depth analysis of the context of each company and the composing teams. In the next step, we will run the action research introduced in this paper. Future work also includes replicating this survey in other companies.

8. Acknowledgements

The authors thank to the study participants for their valuable contributions.

References

Abrantes, J. F. and Travassos, G. H. (2013). Towards pertinent characteristics of agility and agile practices for software processes. *CLEI Electronic Journal*, 16(1):6–6.

Ahmad, M. O., Markkula, J., and Oivo, M. (2013). Kanban in software development: A systematic literature review. In *2013 39th Euromicro conference on software engineering and advanced applications*, pages 9–16. IEEE.

Chow, T. and Cao, D.-B. (2008). A survey study of critical success factors in agile software projects. *Journal of systems and software*, 81(6):961–971.

de Mello, R. and Coelho, M. (2021). Characterizing the experience of subjects in software engineering studies. *Proceedings of the XXIV Iberoamerican Conference on Software Engineering (CIbSE)*, pages 42–55.

de Mello, R., da Costa, J. A., de Oliveira, B., Ribeiro, M., Fonseca, B., Gheyi, R., Garcia, A., and Tiengo, W. (2021). Decoding confusing code: Social representations among developers. In *2021 IEEE/ACM 13th International Workshop on Cooperative and Human Aspects of Software Engineering (CHASE)*, pages 11–20. IEEE.

de Mello, R., da Silva, P., and Travassos, G. (2014). Agilidade em processos de software: Evidências sobre características de agilidade e práticas Ágeis. In *Anais do XIII Simpósio Brasileiro de Qualidade de Software*, pages 151–165, Porto Alegre, RS, Brasil. SBC.

de Mello, R. M., Da Silva, P. C., and Travassos, G. H. (2015). Investigating probabilistic sampling approaches for large-scale surveys in software engineering. *Journal of Software Engineering Research and Development*, 3(1):1–26.

Dutra, E., Lima, P., and Santos, G. (2020). An instrument to assess the organizational climate of agile teams-a preliminary study. In *19th Brazilian Symposium on Software Quality*, pages 1–10.

Dybå, T. and Dingsøyr, T. (2008). Empirical studies of agile software development: A systematic review. *Information and software technology*, 50(9-10):833–859.

Fowler, M., Highsmith, J., et al. (2001). The agile manifesto. *Software development*, 9(8):28–35.

Hannay, J. E., Dybå, T., Arisholm, E., and Sjøberg, D. I. (2009). The effectiveness of pair programming: A meta-analysis. *Information and software technology*, 51(7):1110–1122.

Iammarino, M., Zampetti, F., Aversano, L., and Di Penta, M. (2019). Self-admitted technical debt removal and refactoring actions: Co-occurrence or more? In *2019 IEEE International Conference on Software Maintenance and Evolution (ICSME)*, pages 186–190. IEEE.

Joshi, A., Kale, S., Chandel, S., and Pal, D. K. (2015). Likert scale: Explored and explained. *British journal of applied science & technology*, 7(4):396.

Kamei, F., Pinto, G., Cartaxo, B., and Vasconcelos, A. (2017). On the benefits/limitations of agile software development: an interview study with brazilian companies. In *Proceedings of the 21st International Conference on Evaluation and Assessment in Software engineering*, pages 154–159.

Kontio, J., Lehtola, L., and Bragge, J. (2004). Using the focus group method in software engineering: obtaining practitioner and user experiences. In *Proceedings. 2004 International Symposium on Empirical Software Engineering, 2004. ISESE'04.*, pages 271–280. IEEE.

Leal, T. and Santos, G. (2015). Um survey sobre métodos ágeis e o pós-agilismo. In *Congresso Ibero-Americano de Engenharia de Software-CIBSE.*

Linaker, J., Sulaman, S. M., Höst, M., and de Mello, R. M. (2015). Guidelines for conducting surveys in software engineering v. 1.1. *Lund University.*

Nasir, M. H. N. and Sahibuddin, S. (2011). Critical success factors for software projects: A comparative study. *Scientific research and essays*, 6(10):2174–2186.

Pimenta, D. and Santos, G. (2016). Análise de práticas ágeis no apoio a fatores críticos de sucesso em projetos de software. *RelaTe-DIA*, 9(1).

Poppendieck, M. and Cusumano, M. A. (2012). Lean software development: A tutorial. *IEEE software*, 29(5):26–32.

Schwaber, K. and Beedle, M. (2002). *Agile software development with Scrum*, volume 1. Prentice Hall Upper Saddle River.

Thiollent, M. (1996). *Metodologia da pesquisa–ação (7ª edição)*. São Paulo-SP.

Zazworka, N., Vetro, A., Izurieta, C., Wong, S., Cai, Y., Seaman, C., and Shull, F. (2014). Comparing four approaches for technical debt identification. *Software Quality Journal*, 22(3):403–426.

MethApp4Mob: A Methodological Approach for Mobile Applications Development

Iris Galeano, Mauricio Merín, Magalí González, Luca Cernuzzi

[1]Department of Electronics and Computer Science Engineering
Catholic University "Nuestra Señora de la Asunción" (UC)
Teniente Cantaluppi y G. Molinas – Asunción – Paraguay

iris.ariana07@gmail.com, mimt80@gmail.com, {mgonzalez,lcernuzz}@uc.edu.py

Abstract. *The aspects of mobile technology have introduced challenges for developers, raising the need to improve the software development methodologies traditionally used. As a result of the analysis of the state of the art, an agile methodological approach for its development is presented, consisting of 8 phases: negotiation, planning, design, implementation and alpha testing, beta testing and feedback analysis, application publication, release and maintenance, promotion, and a series of steps, good practices, principles and tools, to offer mechanisms to accompany and streamline the development process. Some validations were carried out including a exploratory study, seeking to propose a robust methodology but at the same time easy to apply in a company.*

1. Introduction

The fast growth of mobile technology and the peculiarities of this type of applications, introduce challenges on how to approach the complete life cycle development of mobile applications in order to achieve the best acceptance from users. Indeed, the development of mobile applications is usually oriented to horizontal or vertical markets rather than specific projects for a single client, which introduces the need to think about the markets of potential users with their own distribution channel with specific rules that must be fulfilled. At the same time, the scope and complexity of mobile applications are often smaller than large systems running on other technology platforms. Furthermore, the current technological market offers a great diversity of mobile devices, giving rise to diverse challenges for those who develop applications for such devices, as they have particular characteristics that should be considered: they have limited space for visualization; need to adapt the user interface to each type of device; technological park in constant evolution; among others [Wasserman 2010]. This introduces for development companies the need to focus not only on the technical aspects of modeling and development, but also to other complementary aspects of management and time-to-market, application acceptance challenges for different target of end-users, promotion plan for the rapid adoption of the application, etc.

The specialized literature presents several proposals for the field of mobile software production [Scharff and Verma 2010][Usman et al. 2014] [El-Kassas et al. 2014] [Heredia et al. 2014] [Ettifouri et al. 2017] [Khan et al. 2019]. However, most of such proposals lack a global vision of software that covers all the particularities of the life cycle of a mobile application [Wasserman 2010] [D. et al. 2012]. Normally the methodological proposals focus on technical stages covered by software engineering (requirements, design, development and testing). However, in several projects the results obtained are not the desired ones [Lee 2014].

Hence, to be successful in the industry, a good development approach must also encompass other relevant phases that are more related to the management aspects, including a project vision to monitor agreements and modifications to the final application, negotiation and planning; to the quality assurance, with emphasis in validations with target users; to the market, covering launch and promotion initiatives, among others.

This study is the result of collaboration between researchers and industry professionals to formulate a methodological proposal that covers both the technical aspects and the complementary aspects of the life cycle of mobile applications. A practical approach is proposed to be used in real mobile projects. The proposal is based on different good practices, mainly from agile methods, and it offers general guidelines to work teamsthat can undertake the development project with support tools in each phasepointing to good levels of product quality. A key aspect of the approach is its simplicity, with a low learning curve that promotes the quick understanding of team members and accelerates their incorporation into the company. Finally, an initial validation in academic environment together with other preliminary validations carried out by developers in the industrial sector provide some insights on the strengths and limitations of the proposal.

The rest of the paper is organized as follows. Section 2 presents related work. Section 3 presents the methodological approach for the development of mobile applications. Section 4 describes different validation experiences including a exploratory study and other partial validations that were carried out by developers in the industrial sector. Finally, section 5 presents the conclusions of this work and some outlines for future work.

2. Related Work

The mobile application development is a hot topic with many publications, as showw the systematic mapping study (SMS) carry out by Galeano *et al.* [Galeano et al. 2016]. The study covers the period between 2007 (launch of the first iphone) and 2015 including 28 articles (out of 601 retrieved) from different sources: IEEE, ACM, Springer, ScienceDirect, Wiley, SAGE and Thomson Reuters.

According to the SMS, most proposals for mobile software development focus on ***Model-Driven Development*** , ***Multiplatform*** approaches , and ***Agile Development with Iterative Development*** , showing no preferential inclination for any existing proposal. Subsequent studies between 2016 and 2020 have yielded similar results [Ettifouri et al. 2017] [Rieger 2017] [Khan et al. 2019].

Considering the perspective of the general approach, Model-Driven Development and Multiplatform proposals allow generating applications capable of running on multiple platforms, without having to develop the same application from scratch for each considered platform, objective sought by many software companies that try to reach the largest number of users. On the other hand, agile methodologies are characterized by better capture of changing requirements and risk management; their main objective is to reduce development time.

On the other hand, Agile methods such as Scrum [Schwaber and Beedle 2001],

Extreme Programming [Beck and Andres 2004] or Kanban [Anderson 2010], are widely adopted for the development of mobile applications [Shen et al. 2012], [O'Hagan et al. 2014]. However, despite their popularity, agile methodologies do not consider some aspects of the life cycle of mobile applications as those tasks related to the publication and promotion of the application after its implementation.

Moreover, the review conducted by Hosbond *et al.*[Hosbond and Nielsen 2005] mentions that the traditional systems development focuses on project-level development tasks with very little focus on company-level or inter-organizational development tasks. However, the development of mobile applications is strongly focused on the business perspective, which extends the reach to higher organizational levels.

Considering more technical perspective, in terms of tools, Joorabchi[Joorabchi et al. 2013] points out that current testing tools do not offer the same level of support for different platforms while lacking important features for testing on mobile devices such as mobility, location services, sensors, gesture control, among others, so testing becomes a significant challenge throughout the application development project. On the other hand, better tools are needed to monitor and analyze certain metrics of applications in development such as memory management, battery usage, network performance, among others. The ***Natives*** applications are the most named in the analyzed studies, followed by the ***Hybrids*** applications and finally the ***Web*** applications. In those applications where the user experience and the use of device-specific features are necessary, the best alternative is the native applications.

In addition, an appreciable aspect is the analysis of the usefulness of the methodologies proposed in the industrial field. In this regard, Picco *et al.*[Picco et al. 2014] suggest a fundamental question to the software engineering community. They focus on an in-depth analysis of the processes that are currently being adopted by large companies such as Google, Apple, which may not be totally consistent with traditional practices that are still taught in universities. The theory dictated must be accompanied by elements demanded by real world as a means to offer real solutions to the problems within the development of mobile applications.

One of the aspects that surprises is the low presence of studies referring to other objectives such as the integration of marketing practices with the rest of the phases, which is a key element currently for the success of an application. Another unexploited objective refers to the productivity of the development team, the lack of support for communication and collaboration among team members, as well as a better organization of activities during the development process.

3. MethApp4Mob: A Methodological Approach for Mobile Applications Development

In addition to the review of the literature we considered the experience of the authors and practitioners of the industry in mobile application development projects. The first author is a semi-senior mobile and web application developer. From industry we collaborate with two senior developers from the same company. One of them has extensive experience in enterprise application development using emerging open source web technologies. The other is a senior developer of mobile and web applications. The company is primarily dedicated to enterprise web and mobile development using open source technology. For the development they mainly use hybrids of agile methodologies. The experience of the company's collaborators enriched the vision of both the technical aspects of development and the project management and interaction with the client. Thus, a methodology based on an incremental iterative model with agile features is designed for tailored native mobile applications development considering its lifecycle. We opted for a focus on the custom mobile applications development because more and more companies contact software enterprises to develop their own mobile application. Likewise, most developers opt for the native applications development due to the user experience, especially in those contexts where accessing the features of the device is essential.

As we seen, the agile methodologies are in agreement with several of the elements present in the ecosystem proposed in this work, which have proven to be appropriate for certain aspects of the mobile application development process. Specifically, the foundations of the Scrum framework have been taken to define the proposed methodology. Scrum seeks early software delivery to the client (between 2 weeks and 2 months) with value to increase the client's satisfaction. Unlike other projects, resistance to change is not encouraged, but this is presented as a strength to take advantage of to increase the customer's competitive advantage and satisfaction. There is a high level of interaction between the team members and the client, which is fundamental considering that the methodology is oriented to the tailored software development, where the client must be an important actor during the execution of the project. On the other hand, it is intended to obtain a constant rhythm of development, where the deliveries are iterative and incremental, providing new features in each iteration or sprint, working in self-organized teams. The choice of Scrum offers two main advantages: on the one hand, it is a method that is easy to learn and put into practice, which is essential for less experienced work teams; and on the other hand, the constant delivery of functional versions provides greater control to the production process because it allows to identify failures in time for immediate correction in future deliveries.

Our experience developing mobile applications allowed also to identify other essential aspects. In the initial negotiations with the client, it is important to analyze and estimate other costs in addition to the development of the application: need for servers, testing infrastructure, payments for the publication channel, among others. Thus, it is paramount to define the scope of application development and services after its publication taking into account that a mobile application can evolve over time. The meetings with the client must be as productive as possible, therefore the exchange of information and the validations that are made must be agile and in a language of quick understanding for the client. An aspect that may be perceived as tedious is the documentation of the specifications and the designs that were agreed and especially the control of changes; however, it is essential to assure the sustainability of the project. This facilitates the incorporation of new people to the work team as well as granting traceability to the requirements. In addition, other exclusive phases for the mobile ecosystem were incorporated, such as: the Mobile Application Publication and Promotion. Depending on the channel chosen to distribute the application, the publication of the mobile application also follows its own process, may incur monetary expenses, time to consider for its release and specific tasks related to the metadata of the application. Likewise, it is well known in the industry that the promotion of an application plays an important role for its quick adoption, that is why we considered to include it in the life cycle, encompassing aspects that the development

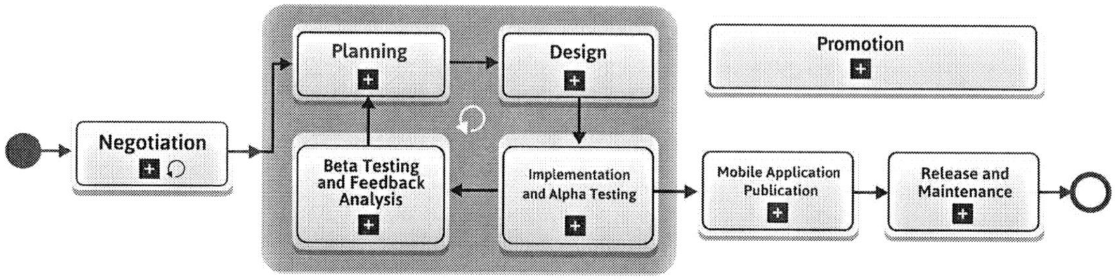

Figure 1. General outline of the phases that make up the methodology.

team can influence.

Finally, the methodological approach includes eight phases: Negotiation, Planning, Design, Implementation and Alpha Testing, Beta Testing and Feedback Analysis, Mobile Application Publication, Release and Maintenance and, lastly, Promotion, as indicated in the Figure 1.

It is important to emphasize that although in Figure 1 the Mobile Application Publication and the Release and Maintenance phases are not within the iterative cycle, its applicability will depend on the client decisions. If the client decides that the deliveries are published and made available to the users, these phases would also be part of an iterative process, otherwise, they would be the last stages once the project is finalized, with its respective connection to the Negotiation phase in case that there were new aspects to incorporate after the publication of the application.

For space limitation, a summary of the main elements that make up each phase of the proposed methodology is presented in Table 1. It includes the output elements of the eight phases along with the main activities and recommendations to obtain the best results according to the needs of the project. In addition, to define a delineation of the tasks to be carried out in each phase, tools are also suggested in each case. In order to access the complete definition of all the aspects that are involved in the described phases, interested readers may access the reference[1].

Table 1. Summary of the main elements and recommendations of the phases of the methodology.

Phase	Output elements	Principles/ Recommendations/ Best practices	Recommended tools
Negotiation	Formal budget	* Constant communication with the customer * Keep the project file updated in the Vision Document (especially when the budget was accepted)	* User stories, Formal Budget, Vision Document templates * Suggested prototyping tools * Effort estimation scheme based on two levels
Planning	Planned tasks	* Take into account the time available for the execution of the project in each incremental planning * Best Scrum practices * Requirements changes control	* XPlanner, Planigle, Assembla, among others * Starfish technique for retrospective meetings * Requirements changes control template (included in the Vision document)

Continued on next page

[1]MethApp4Mob. https://drive.google.com/open?id=0B5GfF1ckQYOmM1hiLTVTOEhuSnM

Table 1 – *Continued from previous page*

Phase	Output elements	Principles/ Recommendations/ Best practices	Recommended tools
Design	* Architecture specification * User interface design * Web services definition * Onboarding design	* Visual representation of the application architecture * MVC design patterns * Heuristics for designing a mobile application interface * Analysis of trends in user interface design according to the chosen platform * Analysis of the most common design errors * Web services with JSON format using a taxonomy for requests/responses between the application and the server * Analysis of Onboarding incorporation for retention	* Rich UML deployment diagram using tools like Gliffy, Microsoft Visio, Dia among others * Prototyping template (included in Vision document) * Spreadsheet proposed by the methodology for the web services definition * Swagger, API Blueprint, Postman as tools for implementing web services * Elasticode, Useronboard, UX Archive and EmptyStat as suggested tools for onboarding design
Implementation and alpha testing	Alpha and beta versions of the application	* Rich project structure for Android applications * Define a naming convention for the development process * Define the criteria to consider "Finished" a task * Consider aspects of the mobile environment for testing * Define the mobile testing infrastructure for tests	* Android Studio * Android project structure proposed by the methodology * Xcode * Visual Studio * Some suggested tools for functional tests are: MITE, MonkeyTal, seeTest Mobile, MobileCloud, among others
Beta testing and feedback analysis	Users feedback	* Choice of distribution channel for beta testing * In-app feedback * Add crash reports within the application * Add questionnaires such as Questionnaire for User Interaction Satisfaction * Categorization and prioritization of users feedback	* Tools like Apptentive and Doorbell.io allow you to implement in-app feedback * Appsee, Apteligent, Buddybuild, Fabric, Fireb, Instabug, among others as some suggested tools for handling crash reports
Mobile Application Publication	Published application	* Consider costs publishing applications in stores * Follow developer policies imposed by app stores	* Google Play and App Store for distribution * Other channels such as websites or emails
Release and Maintenance	Maintenance implementation	* Maintain crash reports for critical error detection * Usage analytics tools * Tracking users feedback left in application stores * Present user surveys within the application at the appropriate time * Add Net Promoter Score * Define with the client the maintenance activities after the launch of the application	* Google Analytics, Mixpanel, Flurry or Localytics are some of the usage analytics available
Promotion	Marketing plan	* Plan on time the marketing activities that make the application known to the users * Consider the App Store Optimization (ASO) suggestions * Provide a landing page for the mobile application	* Some suggested tools for the ASO are: appcodes, appnique, apptweak, ApRankCorner, among others

4. MethApp4Mob Validation

Various validations were carried out under different conditions in which complementary aspects of the methodological proposal were evaluated. For the execution of the validations, it was defined a validation protocol whose activities are summarized in Figure 2. It should be noted that some of the elements that make up the context of a validation did not apply in certain validations, therefore they were not specified.

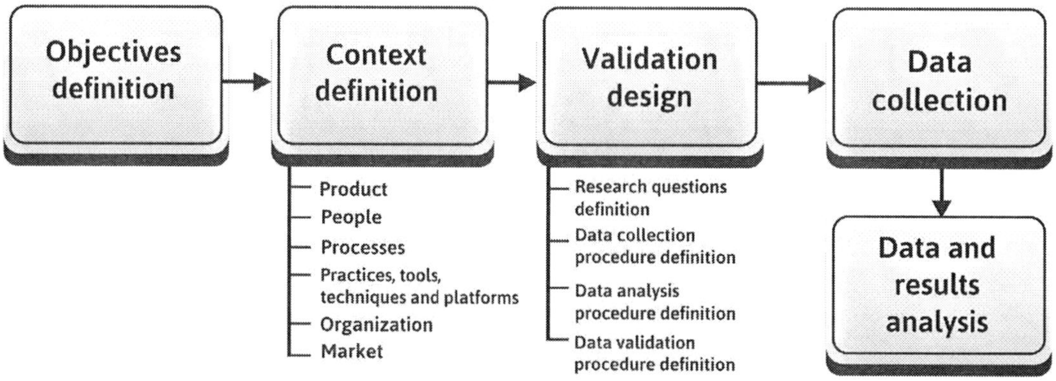

Figure 2. Activities executed in each validation summary.

In order to categorize the different executors of the validations carried out, the years' work experience in the computer science area were used as criteria: Junior, less than 2 years' experience; Semi Senior, between 2 - 6 years' experience; and, Senior, more than 6 years' experience.

Two preliminary validations were executed. The first consisted of a validation of the first 3 phases of the methodology (Negotiation, Planning and Design). The second validation consisted of an evaluation of the user stories usability in the context of the proposed methodology, that is the interest was to evaluate their usefulness according to the characteristics of the defined methodology.

Based on the results, certain adjustments were applied in order to improve some of the proposed activities in the methodological approach, always trying to make a practical proposal and easy to apply but being robust. After that, the developed exploratory study was designed and executed. For reason of space, in this paper we will present the exploratory study developed and its main results.

4.1. Exploratory study

The aim was to apply the proposed methodology to a project in the industrial field to develop a mobile application so that it serves as a guide to approach the project throughout the application development life cycle, and thus determine the impact that the methodology has about the project in order to validate its applicability. Our intent is to explore initial answers to questions such as the following: what benefits offers the methodology for the different actors?; what difficulties has the methodology imposed on the different actors at each stage of the project?; what aspects were not considered during the development of the project; how much time has been invested to understand the methodology?

The product consisted in a native mobile application for Android devices available in the Play Store under the name of ***UCApp***, intended for the students of the UC university. The main functionalities offered by the application were the visualization of the student's academic situation, registration and online payments for exams and career fees. Following the proposed methodology, the application was built iteratively and incrementally. The mobile application communicated with remote servers that simulated the academic, administrative and payment gateway systems which were implemented from scratch for this project. The data communication was made through calls to web services hosted

Table 2. Roles and profiles of the developers in the execution of the exploratory study.

Developer	Role	Profile
Developer E	Developer, Tester , Project configuration manager, Technical writer, System user	* Junior developer * No knowledge about agile methodologies * No experience developing software applications
Developer F	Project manager, System analyst, Designer, Quality assurance, Tester, Technical writer, System user	* Semi-senior developer * No knowledge about agile methodologies * Experience developing web services * Basic knowledge and experience in PHP
Developer G	Designer, Developer, Tester	* Junior developer * No knowledge about agile methodologies * No experience or knowledge developing software applications

on these servers and implemented with PHP. ***UCApp*** had three versions since its launch: Version 1.0, 20/October; Version 1.1, 10/November; and, Version 1.2, 24/November.

The exploratory study was executed by three developers (students of the final years of the Computer Engineering degree) whose roles and profiles are presented in the Table 2. The application was tested in two sessions by a group composed of 12 early-stage students from the same career. Although these students do not possess technical knowledge they were a potential public of interest for the application. The application development process was accompanied by the three researchers mentioned in the previous sections.The three developers participated in three training sessions given by one of the researcher on Android programming (front-end), PHP (back-end) and web hosting administration. The training intention was to provide developers with the necessary tools to face the various activities suggested by the methodology It is important to highlight that although the developers did not have knowledge about several of the programming languages and technologies used, they had enough theoretical knowledge about programming, database engine and other aspects of software engineering that shortened the languages and technologies learning curve. The implementation was carried out over 13 weeks during which the developers performed four iterations of the project whose activities and artifacts generated are described in Table 3.

The practices were carried out with an agile approach such as daily meetings, incremental deliveries, communication with the client and, above all, maintaining a simple, dynamic development framework that is adaptable to changes. The methodology contemplates the use of diverse tools, techniques and platforms throughout the different phases of the mobile application development process. Figure 3 presents the tools, practices, techniques and platforms used in the project specified by phase.

The data collection was carried out using questionnaires and focus group, allowing qualitative and quantitative data to be collected. The main source of data collection were the members of the development team. In order to increase the precision and strengthen the validity of this exploratory study, it was decided to apply two triangulation techniques as part of the data validation procedure: observer triangulation and methodological triangulation. The execution of the focus group was carried out by more than one observer.

Table 3. Executed activities and artifacts generated in the exploratory study.

Iteration	Activity	Artifacts generated
1º	* Functional and non-functional requirements specification through User Stories * Deployment diagram and application prototypes design * Effort estimation using six-dimensional technique	Vision Document
2º	* User stories selection and their decomposition in tasks (academic functionalities) * Web services and MVC architecture specification * Back-end and front-end prototype programming * Mobile Application Releasing in Play Store * Beta testing method and channel for obtaining user feedback definition	Prototype documentation and UCApp 1.0 in the Play Store
3º	* Similar to the previous iteration only that it included the administrative features and the payment gateway * User feedback organization and analysis * Add improvements based on users feedback	Prototype documentation and UCApp 1.1 in the Play Store
4º	* User feedback organization, analysis and implementation * Onboarding implementation * User manual preparation * Acceptance testing definition	Prototype documentation and UCApp 1.2 in the Play Store

In case of the questionnaires, *After-Scenario Questionnaire (ASQ)* was used. The ASQ method has been chosen to measure the degree of users satisfaction with the methodology proposed and executed [Lewis 1991]. Figure 4 presents the questions that make up the ASQ. Three surveys were completed that included the ASQ scenarios regarding the activities carried out in each phase and the use of certain tools and templates recommended in each phase. Different statistical graphs of the scores obtained from the ASQ were elaborated in order to evaluate the results from different perspectives. The different averages calculated are described below:

- The average ASQ score per developer per scenario
- The average ASQ score per developer in each phase
- The average ASQ score per scenario in each phase
- The average ASQ score per phase

The surveys sent to the developers could be found in the following references:

- *Negotiation Phase:* `https://goo.gl/H8pSUq`
- *Planning, Design, Implementation and Alpha Testing phases:* `https://goo.gl/gdEsG9`
- *Beta Testing and Feedback Analysis, Mobile Application Publication, Release and Maintenance phases:* `https://goo.gl/gdMj7K`

Although different statistical graphs were elaborated, due to a limited space, only the graphs that summarize the calculated average ASQ scores will be presented in the following section. At the end of each ASQ survey, a series of exploratory questions were included in order to identify those inconveniences during the phases or elements that were not considered in the proposal if they existed. A question was presented in the format Yes/No waiting for the justification as appropriate. To access the forms used and the full version of the answers obtained, consult the repository of the methodology[1].

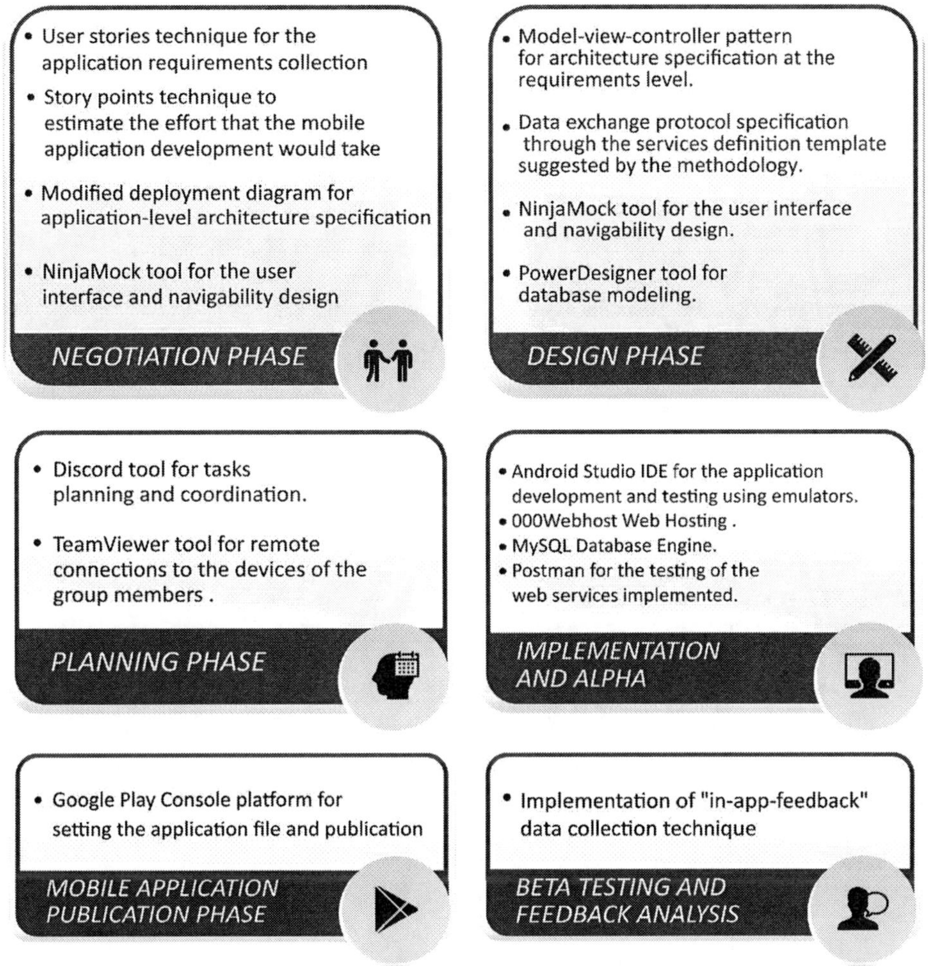

Figure 3. Tools, practices, techniques and platforms used in the project.

After the 4$^{\underline{or}}$ iteration, the three developers and the three researchers carried out a 40 minutes focus group. This, let us identify details that might otherwise be overlooked during data collection and prevent the answers to the questionnaires from being left to the interpretation of the researchers. The researchers asked developers a series of questions related to the User Stories as a requirements gathering technique, the three-level planning, the usefulness of design diagrams, the use of JSON as a communication protocol, the main challenges during alpha and beta testing, experience with the tools used and the learning curve of the methodology.

4.1.1. Data analysis and results

The developers answered the questions based on their experience applying the methodology for the mobile application development. The analysis and data interpretation were carried out by one of the researchers and subsequently verified by two other researchers. The figure 5 describes the summary scores obtained for each developer in the different phases evaluated. It is interesting to note that the developer with the greatest expertise

	After-Scenario Questionnarie (ASQ)	Strongly agree	1	2	3	4	5	6	7	Strongly disagree	NA
1	Overall, I am satisfied with the ease of completing the tasks in this scenario		O	O	O	O	O	O	O		O
2	Overall, I am satisfied with the amount of time it took to complete the tasks in this scenario		O	O	O	O	O	O	O		O
3	Overall, I am satisfied with the support information (online help, messages, documentation) when completing the tasks.		O	O	O	O	O	O	O		O

Figure 4. After-Scenario Questionnaire questions.

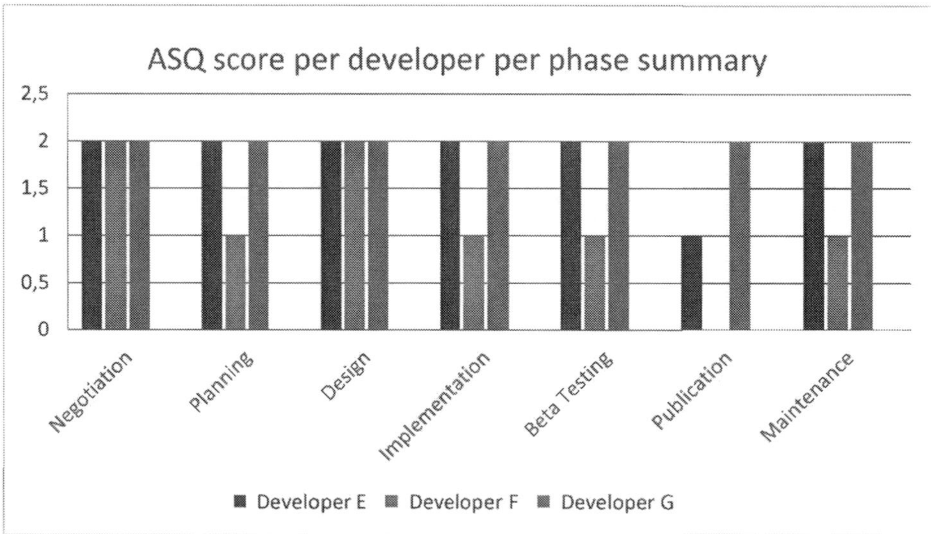

Figure 5. Average ASQ score per developer per phase summary.

(i.e., developer F) was the one who gave the best ASQ scores in most of the evaluated phases.

The usability results of the various activities, tools and techniques proposed in the Negotiation phase, such as the User Stories and the Vision document, were generally quite positive achieving an average score of 2. However, developer E and G commented that elements such as aesthetic requirement and certain fields that should be shown to the end user were not captured by the stories. In this regard it should be noted that both aspects are reflected in the prototypes presented to the client, hence the importance of accompanying the User Stories with the user interface prototypes. Likewise, during the focus group they mentioned that user stories receive significant value as a means of documenting requirements when the work team must work on maintaining the application after the project has finished. Another interesting comment of developer F indicated that it is difficult to identify all the acceptance criteria in the early stages. Also, the developer F mentioned a difficulty in the estimation using story points since they did not have knowledge of the concepts used.

The Planning phase received an average ASQ score of 1,67 (rounded to 2 in the integer scale of ASQ), which is also quite positive. No inconvenience was detected during the execution of the tasks. Despite, the use of a task control tool, suggested by MethApp4Mob, could be a great support to facilitate the project progress and the information exchange anywhere and any time, it is worth noting that the developers did not use it during the project.

The Design phase averaged an ASQ score of 2. The great utility provided by the deployment diagram was rescued for a better understanding of the project context and the prototypes designed for the Implementation phase. The proposed template for the web services definition allowed the independence between the front-end and the back-end team in the Implementation phase where this documentation was sufficient for each team to work on their own. However, developer F expressed the difficulty about the MVC architecture use without having prior knowledge.

The Implementation and Alpha Testing phase resulted in an average ASQ score of 1,67 (rounded to 2). The suggested structure for the Android projects was easy to understand even though the developers lacked prior knowledge of Android. During the focus group it was mentioned that a combination of testing approaches is necessary to cover a greater number of aspects to be controlled. The interaction tests with the interfaces were executed in real devices, since the emulators did not facilitate the user experience. However, the emulators were used instead of those devices that during the validation sessions had problems.

The Beta Testing and Feedback Analysis phase also obtained also very positive ratings with an average ASQ score of 1,67 (rounded to 2). The in-app feedback implementation was quite useful for validation with end users. This technique also facilitated the tasks of feedback organization since all the valuations were centralized in the database During the focus group, the developers indicated the importance of product validation with interested users as a way to constantly improve the quality of the final product.

With an average ASQ score of 1,5 (rounded to 2), the Mobile Application Publication phase was the best evaluated throughout the entire exploratory study. The developer F did not evaluate this phase. The documentation provided by the application store portal, in this case the Google Play Console, facilitated the task to the Applications Store Administrator role who having contact for the first time with this type of platforms.

Finally, the Release and Maintenance phase also averaged an ASQ score of 1,67 (rounded to 2). The developer E expressed the difficulty of evaluating the users' assessments to incorporate them during maintenance tasks, either due to errors in the writing or opinions too generic. In the focus group also a developer mentioned the importance of delimiting the application scope because in many cases the users requests were beyond the project scope. However, at the same time the importance of this process was valued because it allows us to know what real users of the niche market expected from the product.

4.1.2. Threats to validity

Before carrying out the exploratory study, the three developers and the researcher who mainly accompanied the developers, had not worked together. The selection of the developers team was totally arbitrary and it is fundamental to emphasize that no developer had previously knowledge about MethApp4Mob. The group of students who was responsible for testing the application is outside the researchers team. Also, the project specifications definition was made by two researchers and subsequently validated by the third researcher with the aim of ensuring that all the variables that directly affect the methodology evaluation were considered during the project definition process. In addition, several triangulation techniques were used to guarantee reliability or robustness in the validation and to reduce the uncertainty of using only one method during the work.

From the life cycle perspective, the exploratory study does not covered the Promotion phase. However, its exclusion did not affect the project development and at the end the mobile application was available for download in the Play Store.

Considering the artifacts prescribed or recommended by MethApp4Mob, the Vision document generated in the Negotiation phase included the main elements of its structure such as the requirements specification through User Stories, the application prototypes and the effort estimation through story points. Other elements such as positioning and glossary were not included. In addition, beside the methodology does not propose presenting the Gantt diagram to the client, the developers presented such a diagram which introduced some controversial feelings. Also, the methodology recommends many tools for the tasks coordination and tracking but in this case the group was composed of only three developers who were working together the most of the time, therefore the planning was more verbal.

Developers required training sessions of certain technologies and programming languages. We are aware that the training have consequences on the learning curve of the methodology and the better predisposition to evaluate it positively.

The exploratory study was born from a real need to allow academic and administrative processes to students within the UC university. The verification and testing were validated with a group of potential users from the university. Evidently, for the validation of non-functional requirements, such as usability or user experience, it is necessary for further experiences to involve a significant number of end users and adopt specific validation approaches. Moreover, a clear limitation is that the ASQ questionnaires were applied on a small group of participants (three developers). However, considering the complexity of the project, the number of developers involved in the development process was considered reasonable, respecting the established times for the presentation of the deliverables.

Finally, it is worth noting that for more exhaustive and systematic evaluations of MethApp4Mob it is necessary to carry out case studies with other types of projects oriented to mobile applications.

5. Conclusion

The need to implement solutions that support the production line of mobile software, from the creation of the idea to its delivery and maintenance, has led to MethApp4Mob, a methodological proposal development that seeks to accelerate the mobile applications production processes and reduce operating costs linked to projects of this type of scope. MethApp4Mob covers not only the traditional technical phases of the software development but also other relevant dimensions for an industrial project as negotiation, budget preparation, feedback analysis, application publication, promotion, among others.

Two important aspects of the software production process were analyzed: those elements independent of the tools that have to do with the idea; and, those elements that depend on the tools and technologies used. We recognize the resistance of developers to the adoption of a work methodology that organizes, plans and guides the activities execution in a controlled manner throughout a software development project, for this reason, techniques and tools were recommended in each of the phases. A great effort has been made to try to maintain the balance between proposing a simple and practical approach, which reduce the learning curve of the technical staff and points to good levels of product quality, without losing formality and the need of documenting the work done during the process.

Three preliminary validations were carried out and this study focuses mainly on the exploratory study. The global results of the average ASQ scores range from 1,5 to 2 in each phase of MethApp4Mobile. It is encouraging for an approach that could be applicable to an industrial context to simplify their tasks, streamline their communications and improve the work management. However, like any methodology, we are aware that based on its adoption in industrial contexts it will undergo modifications and adaptations.

Some future works related to MethApp4Mobile are: extension of the methodology to other mobile applications types such as web or hybrid applications as well as specific domains like mobile gaming; interoperability mechanisms could be developed that improve the information exchange conditions between the tools suggested in the phases; and, obviously, to further validate the proposed methodology, we require other systematic and rigorous evaluations applying MethApp4Mobile in different industrial projects.

References

Anderson, D. J. (2010). *Kanban: Successful Evolutionary Change for Your Technology Business.* Blue Hole Press.

Beck, K. and Andres, C. (2004). *Extreme Programming Explained: Embrace Change.* Addison-Wesley, 2 edition.

D., F., S., K., and C., W. (2012). A mobile software quality model. *In: Proceedind of the 12th international conference on quality software. IEEE*, pages 154–157.

El-Kassas, W. S., Abdullah, B. A., Yousef, A. H., and Wahba, A. M. (2014). Taxonomy of cross-platform mobile applications development approaches. ELSEVIER.

Ettifouri, E. H., Rhouati, A., Berrich, J., and Bouchentouf, T. (2017). Toward a merged approach for cross-platform applications (web, mobile and desktop). *ICSDE '17: Proceedings of the 2017 International Conference on Smart Digital Environment*, page 207–213.

Galeano, I., González, M., Merín, M., and Casariego, J. (2016). Mobile application development approaches: A systematic mapping study. *2016 35th International Conference of the Chilean Computer Science Society (SCCC)*, pages 1–12.

Heredia, A., Esteban-Santiago, R., Garcia-Guzman, J., and de Amescua, A. (2014). Agile practices adapted to mass-market application development. *Journal of Software: Evolution and Process*, 26(9):818–828.

Hosbond, J. H. and Nielsen, P. A. (2005). *Designing Ubiquitous Information Environments: Socio-Technical Issues and Challenges*, chapter Mobile Systems Development: A Literature Review, pages 215–232. Springer US.

Joorabchi, M. E., Mesbah, A., and Kruchten", P. (2013). "real challenges in mobile app development". pages 15–24, Baltimore, MD. 2013 ACM / IEEE International Symposium on Empirical Software Engineering and Measurement, IEEE.

Khan, M., Azam, F., Anwar, M. W., Samea, F., and Ahmed, M. A. (2019). A model driven approach for state management in mobile applications. *ICSCA '19: Proceedings of the 2019 8th International Conference on Software and Computer Applications*, page 315–319.

Lee, C. (2014). Gartner Says Traditional Development Practices Will Fail for Mobile Apps. Technical report, Gartner.

Lewis, J. R. (1991). Psychometric evaluation of an after-scenario questionnarie for computer usability studies: The asq. *SIGCHI Bulletin*, 23(1):78–81.

O'Hagan, A. O., Coleman, G., and O'Connor, R. V. (2014). *Systems, Software and Services Process Improvement*, chapter Software Development Processes for Games: A Systematic Literature Review, pages 182–193. Springer, New York, Philadelphia.

Picco, G. P., Julienz, C., Murphy, A. L., Musolesi, M., and Roman, G.-C. (2014). Software engineering for mobility: reflecting on the past, peering into the future. *Proceeding FOSE 2014 Proceedings of the on Future of Software Engineering*, pages 13–28.

Rieger, C. (2017). Business apps with maml: A model-driven approach to process-oriented mobile app development. *SAC '17: Proceedings of the Symposium on Applied Computing*, page 1599–1606.

Scharff, C. and Verma, R. (2010). Scrum to support mobile application development projects in a just-in-time learning context. *Proceeding CHASE '10 Proceedings of the 2010 ICSE Workshop on Cooperative and Human Aspects of Software Engineering*, pages 25–31.

Schwaber, K. and Beedle, M. (2001). *Agile Software Development with Scrum*. Prentice Hall, PTR Upper Saddle River, NJ, USA, 1 edition.

Shen, M., Yang, W., Rong, G., and Shao, D. (2012). Applying agile methods to embedded software development: A systematic review.

Usman, M., Iqbal, M. Z., and Khan, M. U. (2014). A model-driven approach to generate mobile applications for multiple platforms. volume 1, pages 111–118, Jeju. 2014 21st Asia-Pacific Software Engineering Conference, IEEE.

Wasserman, A. I. (2010). Software engineering issues for mobile application development. *Proceeding FoSER '10 Proceedings of the FSE/SDP workshop on Future of software engineering research*, pages 397–400.

On the Need to Use Smart Contracts in Enterprise Application Integration

Fernando Parahyba[1], Eldair F. Dornelles[1], Fabricia Roos-Frantz[1], Rafael Z. Frantz[1], Carlos Molina-Jiménez[2], Antonia M. Reina Quintero[3], José Bocanegra[4], Sandro Sawicki[1]

[1]Unijuí University, Brazil

[2]Department of Computer Science and Technology, University of Cambridge, UK

[3]Department of Language and Systems, University of Seville, Spain

[4]Department of Systems and Computing Engineering, Universidad de los Andes, Colombia

{fernando.parahyba,eldair.dornelles}@sou.unijui.edu.br

{frfrantz,rzfrantz,sawicki}@unijui.edu.br

carlos.molina@cl.cam.ac.uk, reinaqu@us.es

j.bocanegra@uniandes.edu.co

Abstract. *Integration processes involve Business Constraints and Service Level Agreements that, with current technology, are not monitored or enforced automatically at run–time. This approach leaves the participants with no means of supervising the development of their interactions or of collecting indisputable evidence to ease the resolution of disputes that can potentially emerge. In this paper, to address the issue, we suggest the inclusion of smart contracts in integration processes to supervise and mediate, at run–time, the agreements to which the participants commit. We discuss the requirements that smart contracts for integration processes need to meet and the challenges involved in writing, executing, deploying, and verifying them.*
Keywords: Smart Contract. Blockchain. Trusted Third Parties. Integration Process. Integration Solution. Service Level Agreement. Business Process. Enterprise Application Integration.

1. Introduction

We conceive the Internet as a repository of applications that are independently run by their owners and offer different computational services and data, for example, business events. It is often convenient for a company to aggregate, i.e., integrate two or more externally provided applications, say for an agreed-upon period, to implement a service rather than implement it from scratch.

The result of an integration is an integration process composed of several independently owned applications, normally conceived without foreseeing possible integration. Therefore, the integration exercise is challenging and the subject of study of Enterprise Applications Integration (EAI) – a branch of Software Engineering that provides methodologies and software tools aimed at helping software engineers in this endeavour [Zimmermann et al. 2016].

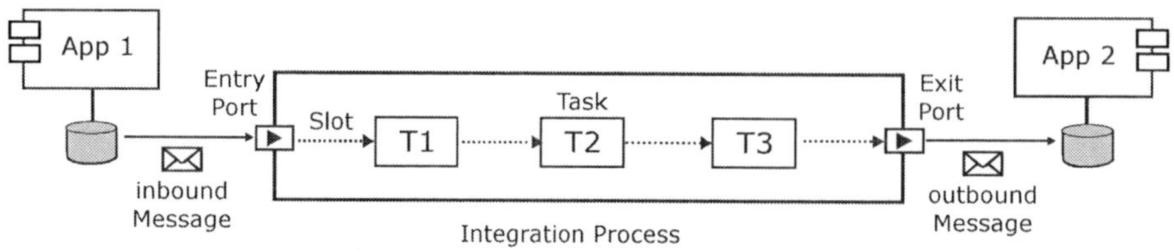

Figure 1. A purchase order integration process.

The challenge is to design an integration process that orchestrates the participating applications to keep them synchronised to provide new functionalities built from their aggregation. The quality of the integration process depends on the quality of the service delivered by the participating applications. Therefore, the owners of the participating applications need to commit to providing data (or services) with certain Quality of Service (QoS) that is specified at: Business Level and Technical Level. At Business Level, QoS is usually specified as Business Constraints (BC), which include commercial rules that must be observed, e.g., "The integration process is prohibited from sending data to the application if the value is less than US$1,000". At Technical Level, QoS is generally specified as a Service Level Agreement (SLA), which defines performance requirements, e.g., "The application is obligated to respond in less than 30 seconds".

An integration process consists of four basic concepts: Messages, Tasks, Slots and Ports. A Message is a container of data that flows through an integration process. Therefore, Messages are abstractions for data. A Message consists of two parts, namely: header and body. The header holds meta-data that identifies the data carried in the body. An integration process includes a set of atomic Tasks that manipulate the body of the Messages, such as: router; spliter; translater and merger. A Slot is a buffer that links one Task to another. Finally, a Port is an abstraction of a communication channel.

Figure 1 shows an example of a typical integration process. Let us assume that the owners of *App 1* and *App 2* have agreed that *App 1* is allowed to send purchase order data to *App 2*, but under certain restrictions: only at certain times of the day and above certain value. *App 1* sends the inbound Message which arrives at the Entry Port and travels through the Task workflow through the Slots. The outbound Message is delivered to the Exit Port and arrives at *App 2*.

The EAI field has been intensively studied and enriched with several integration platforms and tools that simplify the software engineer's work. However, unfortunately, they operate under assumptions that have become unrealistic. For example, some tools assume that a single company owns the applications, e.g., *App 1* and *App 2* and the integration process (see Figure 1). Other tools relax this assumption but consider that the owners of the applications and the integration process trust each other about the QoS delivered by the applications to the integration process and resource consumption of the latter.

With current practice, the integration process and the applications typically belong to companies that are reluctant to trust each other unguardedly. Therefore, these integration processes demand agreements to regulate the interaction to ensure that the participants behave as expected. To be of practical interest, these agreements need to be digitally automated in a manner that potential violations are *detected* and, if possible, *prevented* [Antonopoulos and Wood 2018].

Smart contracts are an emerging technology that can be used to automate the supervision of agreements. Intuitively, a smart contract is an executable piece of code deployed to mediate and regulate contractual interactions. They can be used to automate contracts that include both BC and SLA agreed between two parties. Some progress has been achieved in this direction. For example, some authors have studied Business Level [Khan et al. 2021, Weber et al. 2016, Molina-Jimenez et al. 2018] while others have focused on Service Level Agreements [Kochovski et al. 2020, Uriarte et al. 2018, Tan et al. 2021].

We are unaware of scientific proposals or integration platforms that use smart contracts to specify and mediate agreements between the integration process and the applications. In this paper, to address the gap, we propose enhancing integration platforms with smart contracts that mediate and regulate agreements automatically. The challenge here is to devise languages to encode the original text of the agreement and mechanisms for executing the resulting code (the smart contract).

Ideally, the programmer of smart contracts is provided with a Domain–Specific Language (DSL) with constructs that ease the encoding of the original text. Several DSLs have been proposed for different fields [Varela-Vaca and Quintero 2021]: financial, internet of things, games, data provenance, public sector and business processes. Unfortunately, no DSLs for smart contracts in integration process are available.

In this paper, we argue that a DSL for writing smart contracts should automate the execution of the clauses included in EAI agreements. The smart contract will be responsible for notifying the participants of violations when they take place and for collecting control data. The latter can help to solve legal disputes. Currently, there is no consensus about the legal status of smart contracts [Law Commission 2020, Filippi and Wright 2018]. This discussion falls outside the scope of our work. We only focus on discussing the requirements that smart contracts for integration processes need to meet and the challenges involved in writing, executing, deploying, and verifying them. Our proposal does not consider the automation of penalty payment, as this requires a solution to several technical and legal issues.

The remainder of this paper is organised as follows: Section 2 shows related work. Section 3 defines the basic concepts for Smart Contracts. In Section 4 we discuss the implementation, execution, deployment, and verification of smart contracts for EAI. Section 5 concludes this paper.

2. Related Work

Research on smart contracts to enforce Business Constraints (BC) and Service Level Agreements (SLAs) was pioneered by Minsky in the mid 80s [Minsky and Lockman 1985] and followed by Marshall [Marshall 1993]. Though some of the smart contract tools exhibit some decentralised features [Minsky 2010], those systems took mainly centralised approaches. Within this category falls the contract enforcers discussed in [Molina-Jimenez et al. 2012], [Governatori et al. 2006] and [Perrin and Godart 2004].

Smart contracts are used to monitor Service Level Agreements [Kochovski et al. 2020] to ensure that a service is delivered with the expected Quality of Service (QoS).

[Uriarte et al. 2018] proposes a framework for managing dynamic SLAs in a distributed manner; they rely on a rich and dynamic SLA formalism expressed in smart contracts. [Scheid et al. 2019] proposed an approach which was evaluated by simulating the management of a QoS between a Service Provider and a customer; they successfully automated using a decentralised solution.

[Tan et al. 2021] propose a novel Service Level Agreement model that integrates blockchains and smart contracts where trust issues among cloud service providers, cloud service consumers, and third parties can be supervised through blockchain technologies. The proposed method strengthens data security and enables cloud service providers to provide better services.

In Business Constraints, [Weber et al. 2016] uses smart contracts and blockchain to mediate and execute the steps of a business process. The main contribution is to provide an auditable trail of all stages of the process. Neither party can unfairly accuse the other of breaches of the business process.

[Molina-Jimenez et al. 2018] discuss the advantages and disadvantages of deploying smart contracts on blockchains and alternatively on trusted third parties. They argue that hybrid platforms that integrate on and off–blockchain platforms are more adequate in several applications. They show how a smart contract can be split and executed partially on an off—blockchain contract compliance checker and partially on the Rinkeby Ethereum network. They argue that the hybrid approach avoids the difficulties that afflict blockchains, namely, scalability, performance, transaction costs, and others.

[Khan et al. 2021] discuss the challenges to be faced in the implementation of smart contracts in different areas, including business process and legal issues in the application of automated penalties. In addition, they claim that uniform application of the same rules may not be possible in different countries and that governments attempts at digital standardisation have not been successful.

In our work, we aim to implement smart contracts for integration processes. We are interested in using smart contracts to monitor automatically the observance of clauses included in agreements signed between the participants of an integration process. Due to time and space limitations, leave out of this discussion the automation of penalties. We want to provide a mechanism that either prevents the occurrence of agreements breaches or notifies the parties of their occurrence and provides evidence to help the parties sort out disputes. Existing work fails to address both aspects of BC and SLAs; smart contracts are used for monitoring either of them but not both like in our work.

3. Basic Smart Contract Concepts

Conceptually, smart contracts are similar to conventional agreements. They may include two or more participating parties and clauses. However, smart contracts are executed automatically by means of self-executing computer codes. Therefore, their correctness requirements are higher. Firstly, there should not be logical errors in their original clauses written in natural language. For example, all events that may occur must be foreseen [Mattila 2016], and clauses should not conflict with each other. Secondly, the code that implements the clauses should be written correctly. The term smart contract is attributed to Nick Szabo. He first mentioned smart contracts in [Szabo 1997] and defined them as a computerised transaction protocol that executes the terms of an agreement.

Smart contracts can be modelled as a Finite State Machine or as an Event Condition Action; both models can capture the "if this then that" construct, which means that if a condition is met, an autoresponder is triggered by the program [Molina-Jimenez et al. 2018]. For complete operability, smart contracts need intelligible and unambiguous logic, complete and accurate information. They leave no room for interpretation; they are programs that are always executed exactly as previously programmed. Smart contracts can be modelled at different levels, such as: technological, legal, business, among others. We argue that they should be modelled at the business level, where they expose meaningful concepts to business people, rather than modelling them at lower levels, where they expose meaningful implementation details to software engineers. We believe that, at this level, smart contracts should include constructs to model the following concepts:

- **Contract:** An agreement between two or more parties who do not trust each other unguardedly. A contract can be modelled as an Event Condition Action (ECA) system where events trigger the execution of actions when certain conditions are satisfied.
- **Action:** An action is an operation, for example, send, deliver, pay, delete, among others. Parties execute actions as the contract dictates and only when certain conditions hold. The execution of an action included in a clause produces an event that is expected to enable or disable an action to be executed in another clause.
- **Party:** An entity (typically an enterprise or a human) that agrees with another to sign an agreement with clauses that stipulate terms and conditions.
- **Clause:** A statement that stipulates one or more Rights, Obligations and Prohibitions that the parties are expected to observe.
  - A **Right:** An action (operation) that a party can perform if it wishes to and a condition holds. The party is free to execute the action (for example, send a purchase order) but can choose not to without negative consequences for the party. The execution of a right is illegal if the party tries to execute it when the conditions are not satisfied.
  - An **Obligation:** An action (for example, pay a bill) that a party is expected to execute to comply with the smart contract, when a condition holds. A failure to execute the action that fulfils and obligation results in penalties to be paid by the irresponsible party.
  - A **Prohibition:** An action that a party is not expected to execute when certain conditions hold unless it wishes to take the risk of being penalised.
- **Condition:** A binary statement that can be evaluated to either true or false. For example, the cost of the item included in the purchase order is less than N dollars. In smart contracts, the evaluation of a condition typically enables or disables the execution of an action related to a right, obligation or prohibition. For example, a participant has the right to send (this is the action) a purchase order only if the price of the item is less than N.
- **Event:** An occurrence of something that changes the state of a system. For example, a purchase order has been placed. The occurrence is notified to the interested parties through a Message that is recorded and alters the state of the system, that is, changes the current conditions. In smart contracts, the occurrence of events impacts the evaluation of the conditions.

3.1. Smart Contract Execution

In smart contracts, operations are encoded in executable code that is executed automatically. There are two possible approaches to check if the execution of a given operation (for example, request data from an application) is contract compliant:

- **Smart contract enforcement:** a technique to ensure that a smart contract is never breached. Enforcement is preventive, therefore, it is intrusive rather than non–intrusive like contract monitoring.
- **Smart Contract monitoring:** a technique used to passively observe the execution of a smart contract. Monitoring does not interfere with the development of the smart contract; it only observes and keeps records for potential post–mortem examination, for example, when a dispute is raised.

The two approaches have advantages and disadvantages. We will discuss them within the context of EAI in subsequent sections.

3.2. On TTP and on–blockchain Smart Contract Deployment

Smart contracts deployed on Trusted Third Parties (TTPs) are relatively easy to develop because, with this approach, the TTP operates as a centralised authority responsible for mediating the interaction of the signatories; therefore, it saves the designer from all the issues (for example, consensus, immutability, etc.) that emerge in the absence of a central authority.

Implementing decentralised smart contracts (with no TTP) is far more challenging yet possible. The task significantly simplifies if the designer takes advantage of the facilities offered by emerging blockchain platforms underpinned by Decentralised Ledgers (DLs). Ethereum (one of the leading blockchains) offers immutability, decentralisation, consensus, ubiquity, reliability, security, auditability and other fundamental services that ease the implementation of decentralised contracts.

Blockchains are known to suffer from several limitations like lack of scalability. To address these issues, some authors have suggested a hybrid approach [Molina-Jimenez et al. 2018] where the contract is partially deployed on a TTP (off–blockchain) and partially on a blockchain (on–blockchain).

3.3. Smart Contract Verification

Smart contracts that account only for smooth executions are relatively simple to implement and run. However, they are far too unrealistic to be useful in practical applications. The latter demand smart contracts that include contingency clauses that account exceptional situation that emerge from intentional and accidental diversions from the ideal execution path. These contracts tend to be complex and consequently prone to include logical errors introduced at design time in their original clauses and programming errors introduced at implementation time.

To reduce the risk of implementing unsound smart contracts, we propose formal validation at design time by means of **model checking**. Model checking is aimed at uncovering typical errors that impact contractual clauses, such as contradictions, omissions, and replications [Molina-Jimenez et al. 2012]. To reduce the risk of implementation errors, we suggest systematic testing of the actual executable code. Several authors has studied contract correctness. For example, [Molina-Jimenez and Shrivastava 2013] discusses the implementation of a contract validator tool referred to as **contraval** that accepts abstract models written in epromela (enhanced Promela) and presents them to the Spin model checker [SPIN 2022] to check **safety** and **liveness** properties of claims expressed as basic assertions and Linear Temporal Logic (LTL) [Abdelsadiq et al. 2010]. An example of a typical **liveness** property that can be expressed in LTL is *"always a cancellation operation will be eventually followed by a refund operation"*; likewise *"the auctioneer will never withdraw his item before being sold"*, is an example of a **safety** property.

4. Smart Contracts in Enterprise Application Integration

Enterprise application integration aims at accomplishing an exogenous orchestration of software applications to support companies' business processes. Application integration is normally conducted with the help of integration platforms which are specialised software that helps to design, implement, and execute integration processes. In an integration process, data flows are enveloped in the Message format. A Message has a header and a body. The header usually contains the origin and destination of the Message and an identifier. The body contains the data that is usually structured in XML. An integration process communicates with applications through communication channels that are typically abstracted as a Port. Ports are generally configured in two modes: **unidirectional** or **bidirectional**.

- **Unidirectional** the Messages flow only in one direction, that is, the communication channel either sends or receives data. In unidirectional mode, Ports can be **Entry** or **Exit**, and can have *active* or *passive* behaviour. If the **Entry** Port is *passive*, the application injects data into the integration (operation *"push"*). If the **Entry** Port is *active*, the integration process reads the data that is available in the application (operation *"read"*). If the **Exit** Port is *passive*, the application reads the data that is waiting in a queue at this **Exit** Port (operation *"poll"*). If the **Exit** Port is *active*, the integration process writes the data to the application (operation *"write"*). Fig. 2(a) shows the unidirectional mode and operations discussed.
- **Bidirectional** communication flows in two directions, therefore, there are a sending and a receiving channels. **Bidirectional** Ports can be classified into **Solicitor** (*active*) and **Responder** (*passive*), in both there are two operations, *"request"*, in which one of the parties executes a request, and *"response"*, which is executed by a party when it needs to respond. On the **Solicitor** Port, the integration process performs the *"request"* operation and the application performs the *"response"* operation. On the **Responder** Port, the application performs the *"request"* operation and the integration process performs the *"response"* operation. Fig. 2(b) shows the bidirectional mode and operations discussed.

An integration process belongs to a company, and it is used to support business processes that involve third-party applications. Integration processes involve agreements to be fulfilled by both parties. The challenge is to supervise these agreements to mitigate possible breaches of agreements.

An agreement in EAI involves only two parties. Firstly, the integration process represents the company that owns it. Secondly, there are the applications that will be integrated. We believe that a well written agreement should include clauses that stipulate the

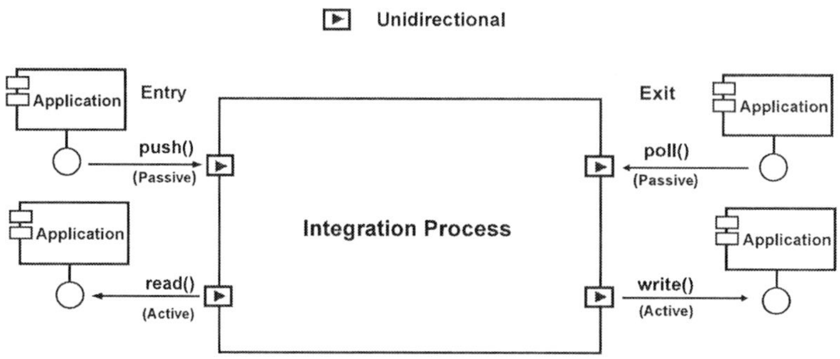

(a) Unidirectional.

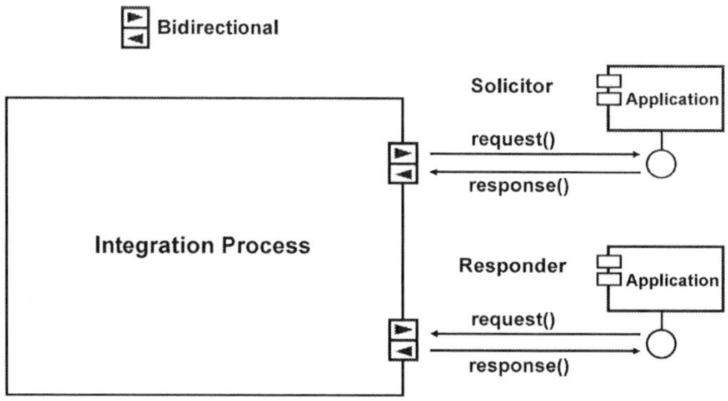

(b) Bidirectional.

Figure 2. Ports and types operations.

behaviour of the participants at two different levels: Business Level and Technical Level. Intuitively, the clauses at Business Level constrain the state of the business process in terms of Business Constraints (BC): they dictate what operations executed by the participants are valid or invalid. For example, what Messages the parties are expected to send to each other and what their contents should be; i.e., the agreement between the integration process and the application may express that the integration process is only allowed to execute write operations if value of the order is greater than US$1,000.

On the other hand, clauses at the Technical Level stipulate the behaviour of the technical infrastructure of the participants, that is, the state of their local systems. In other words, these clauses deal with the Quality of Service (QoS) that the participants' systems are expected to deliver and are expressed typically in terms of Service Level Agreements (SLAs). For example, the integration process may issue a request against an application that is required to respond within 30 seconds. Likewise, the contract might dictate that the integration process is not allowed to issue more than 500 requests per second.

Other researchers have studied the encoding of agreements as smart contracts. However, they either focus on agreements rich in BC or SLAs. That is, they fail to account for both types of clauses [Weber et al. 2016,Kasinathan and Cuellar 2018,Tan et al. 2021]. Consequently, existing work falls short to meet the needs of the smart contracts used in integration processes which include a combination of SLA and BC.

These contracts can be modelled based on the Event Condition Action paradigm. In our model, clauses stipulate Rights, Obligations and Prohibitions. Conditions are

Boolean statements that evaluate either to true or false and enable or disable operations. The events that trigger the clauses are Messages. The workflow tasks have already processed each Message that arrives at a Port, and the data present in the Message body is recorded as a log. This data will be taken by a tool (that has yet to be created to work collaboratively with the integration processes) to be examined by the smart contract that will verify compliance and allow or disallow the execution of operations. When the smart contract is deployed for monitoring, it only notifies of contract breaches and store evidences. Alternatively, when the smart contract is deployed to enforce an agreement, it prevents contract breaches.

4.1. Contract Execution for Enterprise Application Integration

Smart contracts in EAI can be deployed to enforce or monitor agreements signed by the participants. In this section, we discuss the advantages and disadvantages of the two approaches.

4.1.1. Enforcement Execution

With this approach, the smart contract is deployed to act intrusively to prevent the occurrence of contract breaches. We have elaborated on this point in Section 3.1. Therefore, this section will focus only on the particularities that EAI introduces.

The smart contract arbitrates between the integration process and the application so that it will check the clauses and conditions of the agreement. In EAI, enforcement can be implemented through communication channel adaptors. When a Message has already passed through the workflow, it waits in a slot until the communication channel adaptor can perform the operation against the Message. The smart contract is activated when the operation takes place, to verify if it is *contract compliant*, if it is, the execution is enabled. If it is not, the operation is disabled. The Message content that needs to be evaluated to declare the operation *contract compliant* or *non–contract compliant* is made available through the log.

For example, imagine that in an agreement, the integration process has the right to place a request against the application, as long as it is during business hours (from 8:00 am to 6:00 pm). If the operation is requested within business hours, the contract allows the communication channel adaptor to perform the operation on the Message. If it is not, the requested operation is denied to prevent a contract violation.

To use this strategy, the software engineer responsible for the integration project would need to know the implementation details of the adaptors. A technical difficulty is that adaptors vary from one integration platform to another and there are many of them. Another difficulty is that some adaptors are not available as open–source code; therefore, their manipulation is problematic. To avoid these difficulties, we rule out enforcement in favour of monitoring.

4.1.2. Monitoring Execution

With this approach, the smart contract is deployed to passively observe and collect records of operations (legal or illegal) executed by the participants against each other. We have elaborated on this point in Section 3.1. Therefore, this section will focus only on the particularities that EAI introduces.

A smart contract deployed for monitoring in EAI is just a passive observer of the operations that the application and the integration process execute against each other. When a clause is breached, the smart contract notifies the parties that a breach has occurred.

For example, imagine that an integration process has the right to make 1000 requests per day against an application. If this number is exceeded, the owner of the integration process is obliged to pay a fine to the application owners for each extra request. The smart contract detects the breach and log the corresponding records for post–mortem examination.

The main advantage of using monitoring in EAI is that the designer does not need to modify the adaptors that carry out the communication between the integration process and the applications. The information that the contract needs for monitoring can be retrieved from the logs of the operations of each Message. The designer needs only to configure the logs to record all the needed information, for example, the content of the Messages. Log configuration is simpler than adaptor manipulation, consequently, monitoring contracts are easier to deploy in EAI that enforcing contracts. Therefore, we advise the use of monitoring contracts (rather than enforcing) when the consequences of contract breaches are not severe.

4.2. Contract Deployment for Enterprise Application Integration

Smart contracts can be deployed following two approaches: on-blockchain and off-blockchain which is also known as on–TTP deployment. In this section, we discuss the advantages and disadvantages of each approach.

4.2.1. On-blockchain deployment

There are several advantages in deploying smart contracts on public blockchains. Firstly, the blockchain provides a ready to use execution environment. Incidentally, smart contracts written in Solidity language can be deployed on the Ethereum blockchain to take advantage of the Ethereum Virtual Machine available to verify the conditions included in contract clauses to enable or disable the execution of the corresponding operations.

Another advantage is the security provided by the decentralised ledger of the blockchain. The blockchain also provides data immutability and auditability. However, there are some difficulties inherent to the context of EAI. For example, it is well-known that some EAI integration processes involve a large number of Messages that are mapped into events. In these situations, on–blockchain deployment can be costly and therefore impractical because the cost of processing Messages in blockchains is high. Another concern is that in some EAI applications, the arrival rate of Messages is high, of the order of 10.000 msg/s [Parahyba et al. 2021, Frantz et al. 2022]. With arrival rates of these orders, the blockchain is likely to cause unacceptable delays.

Another issue is the language for encoding the smart contracts. Solidity (one of the main contract languages in the Ethereum blockchain) is an alternative. However, being a general purpose contract language, it is also a hurdle for software engineers unfamiliar with smart contract programming. We believe that a domain–specific language for EAI, with constructs for expressing concepts that frequently appear in EAI contracts, is a better approach. Such a language should allow the representation of agreements in EAI at a Platform Independent Model (PIM) level [Wöhrer and Zdun 2020].

A smart contract modelled at the PIM level can be translated automatically by means of model transformations into blockchain specific languages like Solidity. Regarding blockchain transaction costs, it is worth mentioning that an alternative to avoid it is to deploy the smart contract on a private blockchain. This is an suitable alternative to consider if the blockchain offers a sound execution environment for the smart contract and the cost of running the private blockchain is affordable.

4.2.2. On-TTP deployment

As explained in Section 3.2, smart contracts can be deployed on Trusted Third Parties that have the facilities for hosting contracts and provide the security guarantees needed. With this approach, one avoids all the problems that afflict blockchains [Mattila 2016]. However, generally, TTPs are unlikely to provide run-time mechanisms to execute the smart contract. Therefore, such approach would require the implementation of the run-time mechanisms.

An integration process that needs to execute many Messages per second may not be effective if deployed on-blockchain: the waiting time can be too high. A TTP can execute many Messages without long delays. Another factor is that a high volume of data can generate unaffordable costs on a blockchain platform. The use of a TTP can prevent this from happening; however, all the costs required to build or rent a TTP must be analysed by the software engineer. Although, the main issue is that the TTP acts as a central authority that mediates the interaction between the parties and therefore represents a potential risk to privacy. [Molina-Jimenez et al. 2018].

4.3. Formal Verification and Typical Errors in Enterprise Application Integration

A practical approach to reduce the risk of deploying unsound smart contracts is to use model checking techniques to uncover design errors at design time and testing of the actual executable code before production deployment.

Contraval is a tool that has been successfully used to model, check, and test smart contracts deployed on trusted third parties [Abdelsadiq et al. 2010, Abdelsadiq et al. 2011]. We believe that smart contracts for EAI can be validated with *contraval*, possibly, after tuning it and enriching it with new constructs to take into consideration the particularities of EAI. Regarding agreements used in EAI, we have examined several examples and have noticed that their clauses are likely to suffer from the following errors.

- **Message losses:** The arrival rate of Messages in an integration process might be extremely high (of the order of 10.000 msg/s). Such rates can cause resource saturation that results in message loss. However, some integration processes can tolerate the loss of some Messages provided that it is anticipated at design time. Incidentally, the smart contract that is responsible for supervising should be able to ignore missing Messages and continue its work.

- **Conflicting clauses:** The inclusion of clauses that conflict with each other is a typical error in EAI. For example, a clause allows the placement of requests on weekends, and another prohibits them on Saturdays.
- **Incomplete conditions:** A clause can include one or more conditions that constraint the execution of the operations included in the clause. At run time, these conditions are verified to determine if the execution of the operations is contract compliant or not. Conditions might be specified incorrectly. For example, imagine that the integration process has a right to perform a request only during business hours (from 8 am to 6 pm, Monday to Friday). A condition error will occur if only the hours are specified and the days of the week are missing.
- **Missing content:** A particularity of EAI is that to performance of conditions requires examining the actual content of the Messages. For example, a typical error is that a request to read the log returns the wrong content or no content at all, say because the integration process can not obtain this content, the smart contract must have specified how to handle if a condition fed with empty content.

The approach that we intend to follow in the validation of smart contracts for EAI will be based on the extension of the mentioned work. We will evaluate the capacity of *contraval* [Molina-Jimenez 2022] to handle the new challenge. Hopefully, the addition of some new features will suffice. However, we will need to use a more universal tool such as a *Petri Net* based tool, for example, "Maria: The Modular Reachability Analyzer" [Mäkellä 2005]. If this happens, we will take inspiration from [Kasinathan and Cuellar 2018]. Our intention is to select a *Petri Net* tool, use it for validating our use cases, explain how it can be used, including its strengths and weaknesses and produce recommendations to enhance it with features to make it more convenient and intuitive for modelling smart contracts. The actual implementation of the recommendations would be ideal but is something we would consider in the future.

This is an intellectually challenging and innovative task. It demands a deep understanding of i) model checking and testing, and ii) the particularities of model checking and testing smart contracts. This is currently an emerging research field. For example, there is little experience in modelling contract clauses with strict time constraints and contingency execution paths; there is no maturity or tool support either in expressing **safety** and **liveness** properties aimed specifically at uncovering typical bugs that impact smart contracts: What could possibly or likely go wrong in the implementation of smart contracts? What parts of the smart contract can and should be thoroughly scrutinised?

We clarify that *contraval* is a promising tool, but we are not excluding other formalisms and tools for formal validation. Incidentally, we have *Petri Net* in mind also because of two following reasons: i) we are interested in engineering solutions rather than in long-term research in smart contract validation. Thus, we are interested in a mature formalism that has been proven to solve industry problems (as opposed to illustrative academic examples), that is expressive enough to capture smart contract concepts, simple enough to master and, more importantly; ii) *Petri Nets* are supported by good and user–friendly tools that help the user interpret results; these requirements seem to be satisfied by *Petri Net* [Model Checking Contest Committee 2019, CPN Tools 2022];

5. Conclusion and Future Works

In the field of Enterprise Application Integration, companies use the services and data provided by applications owned by other companies. However, relationships are not always between companies that trust each other. Therefore companies that participate in an integration process usually sign legal agreements to stipulate Service Level Agreement and Business Constraints to be observed during their interactions.

Traditional agreements are not digitally automated, therefore, the parties have no mechanisms (software tools) to prevent breaches of contracts. Furthermore, neither they are notified when agreements are breached. To address the problem, in this paper we have proposed the use of smart contracts in EAI to automated the execution of the legal agreements used in the integration process.

For future work, we suggest developing a mathematical formalism that can assist in writing and verifying smart contracts for EAI. In addition, we suggest the use of domain-specific languages for writing smart contracts for EAI. These languages should be high level and with constructs that help the programmer to express, intuitively, concepts that frequently appear in EAI, such as: Operation, Port, Message, among others.

We suggest the use of platform–independent DSLs. The benefit of this approach is that the translation to different contract languages such as Solidity, can be automated relatively simple. We also suggest the use of tools that can help verify smart contracts for EAI with consideration of their particularities. Unfortunately, such tools are not available. Therefore, we suggest the adaptation of existing ones (for example, *contraval*, *Petri Net* and others model–checkers) to tune or tailor them to capture typical errors that afflict smart contracts used in EAI.

Acknowledgements

This work was supported by the Research Support Foundation of the State of Rio Grande do Sul in Brazil (FAPERGS), under grant 19/2551-0001782-0; the Coordination for the Brazilian Improvement of Higher Education Personnel (CAPES); and, the Brazilian National Council for Scientific and Technological (CNPq) under grant number 309315/2020-4. Furthermore, the work of Antonia M. Reina has been funded by projects AETHER-US (PID2020-112540RB-C44/AEI/10.13039/501100011033), COPERNICA (P20_01224) and METAMORFOSIS (US-1381375). Carlos Molina has been partially funded by UKRI CAMB (G115169) project[1].

References

Abdelsadiq, A., Molina-Jimenez, C., and Shrivastava, S. (2010). On model checker based testing of electronic contracting systems. In *12th IEEE International Conference on Commerce and Enterprise Computing (CEC'10)*, pages 88–95.

Abdelsadiq, A., Molina-Jimenez, C., and Shrivastava, S. (2011). A high–level model–checking tool for verifying service agreements. In *6th IEEE International Symposium on Service–Oriented System Engineering (SOSE'2011)*, pages 297–304.

[1]For the purpose of open access, the author has applied a Creative Commons Attribution (CC BY) licence to any Author Accepted Manuscript version arising from this submission.

Antonopoulos, A. M. and Wood, G. (2018). *Mastering Ethereum*. O'Reilly Media, Inc.

CPN Tools (2022). Colored Petri nets and CPN tools. `http://cpntools.org/2018/01/16/publications/`. Visited on 04 Jan 2022.

Filippi, P. D. and Wright, A. (2018). *Blockchain and the Law: The Rule of Code*. Hardvard University Press.

Frantz, R. Z., Sawicki, S., Roos-Frantz, F., Basso, F. P., Zucoloto, B., and Pillat, R. M. (2022). On the analysis of makespan and performance of the task-based execution model for enterprise application integration platforms: An empirical study. *Software: Practice and Experience*, pages 1–19.

Governatori, G., Milosevic, Z., and Sadiq, S. (2006). Compliance checking between business processes and business contracts. In *10th IEEE International Enterprise Distributed Object Computing Conference (EDOC'06)*, pages 221–232.

Kasinathan, P. and Cuellar, J. (2018). Securing the integrity of workflows in IoT. In *International Conference on Embedded Wireless Systems and Networks (EWSN'18)*, pages 252–257.

Khan, S. N., Loukil, F., Ghedira-Guegan, C., Benkhelifa, E., and Bani-Hani, A. (2021). Blockchain smart contracts: Applications, challenges, and future trends. *Peer-to-peer Networking and Applications*, 14(5):2901–2925.

Kochovski, P., Stankovski, V., Gec, S., Faticanti, F., Savi, M., Siracusa, D., and Kum, S. (2020). Smart contracts for service-level agreements in edge-to-cloud computing. *Journal of Grid Computing*, 18(4):673–690.

Law Commission (2020). Smart contracts call for evidence. `https://www.lawcom.gov.uk/project/smart-contracts/`. Visited on 19 Dec 2020.

Mäkellä, M. (2005). Maria: The modular reachability analyzer. `http://www.tcs.hut.fi/Software/maria/index.en.html`.

Marshall, L. F. (1993). Representing management policy using contract objects. In *IEEE First International Workshop on Systems Management*, pages 27–30.

Mattila, J. (2016). The blockchain phenomenon – the disruptive potential of distributed consensus architectures. *Berkeley Roundtable of the International Economy*, 1(38):1–26.

Minsky, N. (2010). A model for the governance of federated healthcare information systems. In *IEEE International Symposium on Policies for Distributed Systems and Networks (Policy'10)*, pages 111–119.

Minsky, N. H. and Lockman, A. D. (1985). Ensuring integrity by adding obligations to privileges. In *8th International Conference on Software Engineering*, pages 92–102.

Model Checking Contest Committee (2019). Model checking contest 2019: 9th edition, prague, czech republic, april 7, 2019. `https://mcc.lip6.fr`. Visited on 10 Jan 2019.

Molina-Jimenez, C. (Visited in Jan 2022). Contraval. `https://github.com/carlos-molina/contraval`.

Molina-Jimenez, C., Sfyrakis, I., Solaiman, E., Ng, I., Wong, M. W., Chun, A., and Crowcroft, J. (2018). Implementation of smart contracts using hybrid architectures with on and off–blockchain components. In *8th IEEE International Symposium on Cloud and Service Computing (SC2) 2018*, pages 83–90.

Molina-Jimenez, C. and Shrivastava, S. (2013). Establishing conformance between contracts and choreographies. In *IEEE Conference on Business Informatics (CBI'13)*, pages 69–78.

Molina-Jimenez, C., Shrivastava, S., and Strano, M. (2012). A model for checking contractual compliance of business interactions. *IEEE Transaction on Service Computing*, 5(2):276–289.

Parahyba, F., Frantz, R. Z., and Roos-Frantz, F. (2021). On the estimation of makespan in runtime systems of enterprise application integration platforms: a mathematical modelling approach. *International Journal of Computer Applications in Technology*, 67(1):17–28.

Perrin, O. and Godart, C. (2004). An approach to implement contracts as trusted intermediaries. In *1st IEEE International Workshop on Electronic Contracting (WEC'04)*, pages 71–78.

Scheid, E. J., Rodrigues, B. B., Granville, L. Z., and Stiller, B. (2019). Enabling dynamic sla compensation using blockchain-based smart contracts. In *IFIP/IEEE Symposium on Integrated Network and Service Management (IM'19)*, pages 53–61. IEEE.

SPIN (2022). On-the-fly, ltl model checking with spin. `http://spinroot.com`. Visited in Jan 2022.

Szabo, N. (1997). Formalizing and securing relationships on public networks. *First monday*, 2(9).

Tan, W., Zhu, H., Tan, J., Zhao, Y., Xu, L. D., and Guo, K. (2021). A novel service level agreement model using blockchain and smart contract for cloud manufacturing in industry 4.0. *Enterprise Information Systems*, 0(0):1–26.

Uriarte, R. B., Nicola, R. D., and Kritikos, K. (2018). Towards distributed sla management with smart contracts and blockchain. In *IEEE International Conference on Cloud Computing Technology and Science (CloudCom)*, pages 266–271.

Varela-Vaca, Á. J. and Quintero, A. M. R. (2021). Smart contract languages: A multivocal mapping study. *ACM Computing Surveys (CSUR)*, 54(1):1–38.

Weber, I., Xu, X., Riveret, R., Governatori, G., Ponomarev, A., and Mendling, J. (2016). Untrusted business process monitoring and execution using blockchain. In *International Conference on Business Process Management (BPM'16)*, pages 329–347. Springer.

Wöhrer, M. and Zdun, U. (2020). From domain-specific language to code: Smart contracts and the application of design patterns. *IEEE Software*, 37(5):37–42.

Zimmermann, O., Pautasso, C., Hohpe, G., and Woolf, B. (2016). A decade of enterprise integration patterns: A conversation with the authors. *IEEE Software*, 33(1):13–19.

Outsourcing with distributed teams in large-scale agile environments

Rafael Camara[1], **Marcelo Marinho**[2], **Suzana Sampaio**[2], **Ivaldir Honório**[1], **Hermano Moura**[1]

[1]Centro de Informática – Universidade Federal de Pernambuco (UFPE)
Caixa Postal 15.064 – 91.501-970 – Recife – PE – Brazil

[2]Departamento de Computação
Universidade Rural de Pernambuco (UFRPE) – Recife, PE – Brazil

`(rcf8,ihfj,hermano)@cin.ufpe.br, (marcelo.marinho,suzana.sampaio)@ufrpe.br`

Abstract. *Outsourcing projects continue to grow through a more distributed and connected environment among teams from all over the globe. Due to it, many customer-vendor relationships are being formed in multi-site settings around a large-scale agile project. Companies are constantly looking for suppliers to assist and develop their complex products, although large-scale agile projects with many teams require some attention to the outsourcing project. Based on it, this study aims to conduct a systematic literature review regarding how outsourced distributed teams from large-scale agile projects are handling their operation. From 23 studies, it was possible to synthesize six distinct themes and 15 patterns of outsourcing distributed teams working in large-scale contexts.*

1. Introduction

The search for lower production costs, access to global talents, and a 24-hour development cycle led modern software engineering (SE) to look for distributed teams over the globe. Such a trend has been shaping the software development approach of many companies. However, by the time the projects grow and the complexity arises, organizations are constantly outsourcing the development of their solutions to achieve similar benefits of Distributed Software Development (DSD) and also acquire scalability [Batra 2009].

Organizations with distributed outsourced teams are usually involved in large-scale projects which require the tailoring and scaling of agile methods to handle the dynamic environment [Krancher 2020]. However, standard agile methods do not fit well in large-scale outsourced projects [Matthiesen and Bjørn 2017]. Since late changes can generate more costs for the client and fixed-bid contracts can be a problem for a vendor that wants to be open to changes, many companies are looking forward to facing the challenges of outsourcing distributed teams with large-scale projects by tailoring the agile methods and the outsource nature [Bass 2016].

Considering this scenario, this study raises a practical question: "How do large-scale agile projects with outsourced distributed teams handle their operation?". To answer such a question, we conducted a Systematic Literature Review (SLR) [Kitchenham and Charters 2007] that extracted studies from 2001 to 2021 that described the outsourcing operation of client and vendors teams in large-scale contexts. A total of

23 studies were selected. From those studies, six themes and 15 patterns regarding the operation activities of those teams have emerged.

This study contributes both practitioners and researchers to a better understanding of how distributed outsourced teams work and handle the challenges of large-scale environments using agile methodologies. By focusing on enriching the body of knowledge, the patterns are presented in a guidance structure with *Problem*, *Context* where the problem exists, *Solution* that describe actions that solved the problem, and *Consequences* that gather results and trade-offs of the patterns.

The remainder of this study is organized as follows: In Section 2, we introduce the background to the present problem. Section 3 describes the research method and research question. Sections 4 and 5 present the results and implications, respectively. Finally, Section 6 provides some concluding remarks and areas of future research directions.

2. Background

2.1. Distributed software development

Distributed Software Development (DSD) is the name given to designate software projects that are developed by teams spread beyond the company's boundaries and in different locations [Marinho et al. 2019]. Such boundaries could be national that describes DSD or international that refers to Global Software Development (GSD) [Marinho et al. 2018].

Despite the nature of the distribution, companies that seek to distribute their development are looking for shared benefits, such as expenses cuts, access to global and high skilled talents, round-the-clock development, and low labor costs [Marinho et al. 2019]. However, those benefits do not come for free; together with them, most organizations need to deal with challenges related to inadequate communication, cultural differences, team coordination, time-zone differences, and control of the development process [Marinho et al. 2018].

2.2. Large-Scale Agile Projects

Large companies constantly looking to distribute their development are often handling large-scale projects. Sometimes, those large-scale projects are complex and belong to critical sectors. A large-scale project also requires development methodologies to scale and fit the environment settings.

Large-scale is also a metric that requires some definition. This study follows the taxonomy presented by Dingsoyr *et al.* [Dingsøyr et al. 2014] which defines the scale of agile software development projects based on the number of teams involved. Small-scale projects are supposed to have only one team. Large-scale projects can have 2 to 9 teams, and the coordination will require scaling approaches. Finally, projects with more than ten teams can be called very large-scale projects; for those projects, a scaling framework is also recommended.

2.3. Outsourcing in large-scale settings

Outsourcing can be described as the relationship between a client and vendor through a contract that aims to deliver a service or a product [Gupta 2022]. Companies outsourcing their software development are constantly handling distributed teams and large-scale projects. Similar to the benefits of DSD, organizations that outsource their development are looking for skilled labor for a low cost and without the full responsibility of coordinating the outsourcing teams. However, those benefits bring some problems. First, clients outsourcing their development cannot always correctly monitor the progress of the vendor team, which can lead to quality control problems [Gupta 2022]. Second, clients need to share their code repositories and documents with the vendor, which can expose them to the risk of losing intellectual property [Gupta 2022].

To handle some of the problems that outsourcing may generate, clients establish rules regarding onshore and offshore software development, concentrating all the complex and vital activities such as design architecture, domain expertise in onshore teams [Bass 2016, Matthiesen and Bjørn 2017], while focusing only on software implementation in offshore teams [Hossain et al. 2009, Noordeloos et al. 2012]. Based on those points, this study focused on describing patterns regarding the operation of outsourcing distributed teams from large-scale projects.

3. Research Method

A Systematic Literature Review [Kitchenham and Charters 2007] was conducted in this study to evaluate most of the relevant literature regarding outsourcing approaches in large-scale distributed environments. Our goal was not to uncover all recorded approaches regarding outsourcing since this study is part of more extensive work regarding agile tailoring practices in large-scale distributed settings. However, we aim to collect sufficient information about the outsourcing theme in those challenging contexts.

We applied automatic search in five large bibliographic databases to identify a set of relevant studiess that the research goals should match. The search string aimed to gather the keywords of each research theme by combining the keywords of "distributed software development", "scaling agile", "large-scale", and "outsourcing". Based on this structure, the search string can be accessed in the research protocol (See in `https://bit.ly/3tV65TD`). We used this string to search the metadata relating to journals and conference proceedings in IEEEXplore, ACM Digital Library, SpringerLink, Scopus, and Wiley bibliographic databases.

3.1. Document selection

The search produced 1520 references from 2001 to 2021 (IEEE = 31; ACM = 836; Springer= 191; Wiley = 58; Scopus = 404). The references were limited from 2001 onwards since the Agile Manifesto was published this year. The selection process had three phases: (i) an initial selection of research results that could reasonably satisfy the selection criteria (outlined next) based on a reading of the studies' titles and abstracts; followed by (ii) a selection against these criteria from the initially selected list of studies based on a reading of their introductions and conclusions; (iii) and finally, the studies were fully read and the ones related to outsourcing with distributed teams in large-scale settings were selected.

3.1.1. Inclusion/Exclusion criteria

The following criteria guided the selection of studies. We *included*: (IC1) complete, peer-reviewed, published studies; (IC2) studies directly related to the research question; (IC3) the study is available via the university library services accessible to the authors during the time of the research; (IC4) keywords of the research string appear on abstract and/or author keywords; (IC5) studies directly related to outsourcing in large-scale distributed settings. We *excluded*: (EC1) texts not published in English; (EC2) technical content, e.g: editorials, tutorials, keynote speech, white studies, thesis, dissertations, technical reports, books; and (EC3) short studies (<=4 pages); (EC4) studies not related to outsourcing in large-scale setting; (EC5) studies related to education matters.

Each study was checked to ensure there was no duplication or replication. For example, if a given study was published in two different journals with a different order of primary authors, only one study would be included; this would usually be the most comprehensive or recent study. By doing this, it was possible to identify 90 duplicated studies and two replication. After excluding the duplicated ones, the selection phase was executed, and we identified 247 studies for phase 1. During phase 1, the introduction and conclusion of each study were read, and 91 studies were selected for the full read. In phase 2, the total read removed ten studies, and the final set consisted of 81. Of those 81 studies, the last phase focused on selecting the ones related to outsourcing with distributed teams on a large scale. Finally, 23 studies [Kommeren and Parviainen 2007, Cho 2007, Hole and Moe 2008, Paasivaara et al. 2008a, Paasivaara et al. 2008b, Hossain et al. 2009, Paasivaara et al. 2009, Batra 2009, Paasivaara and Lassenius 2010, Kussmaul 2010, Batra et al. 2011, Hossain et al. 2011, Noordeloos et al. 2012, Dorairaj et al. 2012, Daneva et al. 2013, Paasivaara et al. 2014, Koch et al. 2014, Lehtinen et al. 2015, Bass 2016, Matthiesen and Bjørn 2017, Vithana et al. 2018, Gupta et al. 2019] passed to the data extraction phase. The 23 studies were selected from IEEE (1), Wiley (1), ACM (4), Scopus (8) and Springer(9).

3.2. Study Evaluation

We based the studies evaluation process on the method of rigor and relevance evaluation assessment proposed by [Ivarsson and Gorschek 2011]. The rigor aspects are evaluated on a scale of 0 ("weak"), 0.5 ("medium"), and 1 ("high"), and it has three dimensions which are (i) context, (ii) study design, and (iii) threats to validity. The maximum value of rigor is 3.

On the other side, the industry relevance is concerned with the impact a study can have on industry and academia, considering relevant research topics and real industry settings. The relevance aspect has a binary score, 1 for present and 0 for not present. The aspects are (i) the subjects of the study that are described as the people involved in the case, e.g industry professionals; (ii) the context in which the study was conducted, e.g industrial settings; (iii) the scale of the applications used in the study, e.g realistic industrial applications; and (iv) the research method used. The maximum value of relevance is 4.

3.3. Data Extraction

Each selected study was fully read to extract information regarding practices of outsourcing distributed teams that work in large-scale environments. This step can be described as the process of gathering all relevant data from the studies to answer a research question [Wohlin et al. 2012]. In order to synthesize the data and ease the management, we decided to conduct some recommended steps by [Cruzes and Dyba 2011]. We also categorized the studies based on contribution facets, as suggested by Petersen et al. [Petersen et al. 2008] and the research facets from Wieringa et al. [Wieringa et al. 2006]. The open-coding activity was executed in the MAXQDA Software [1].

4. Results

In this section, we present an overview of the studies from the SLR. Also, the tailored outsourcing practices are discussed and presented in the following subsections.

4.1. Overview of the Outsourcing Studies

From the 23 studies related to outsourcing, the majority of them, 21 studies, used a qualitative approach, while 3 used a quantitative approach. Based from Wieringa *et al.* [Wieringa et al. 2006] facets, most of the studies were categorized as evaluation studies (15 papers), followed by experience studies (5 papers), solution studies (2 papers) and finally philosophical studies (1 paper) (See figure 1).

The distribution of contribution type facets derived from Petersen *et al.* [Petersen et al. 2008], were classified as lessons learned (18 papers), followed by model contributions (2 papers), framework studies (2 papers), and finally advice studies (1 paper) (See figure 2).

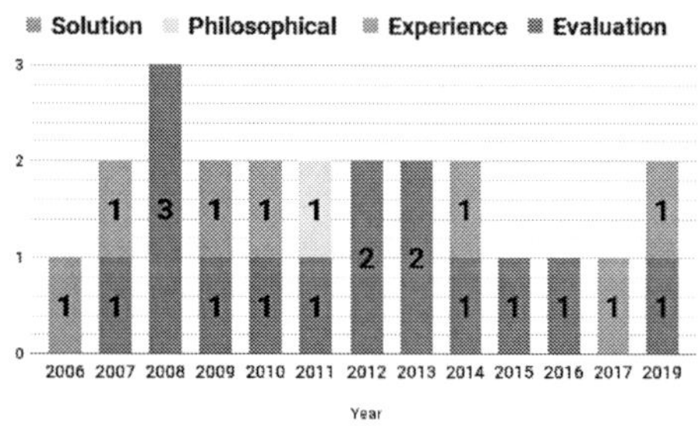

Figure 1. Research type facets over time.

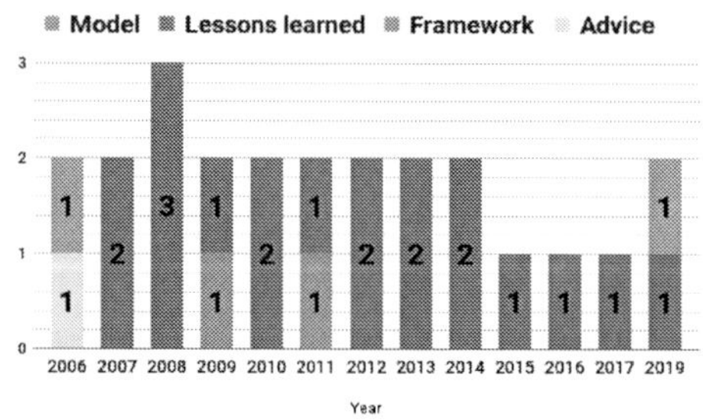

Figure 2. Contribution type facets over time.

Regarding the research methods, most of the studies used the case study methodology (12 papers), although only 2006 has no case studies regarding the theme. Multiple-case studies were the second most used method (5 papers), followed by experience reports (3 papers). Finally, the least used methodologies were ethnography, theory and grounded theory (2 papers each), and literature review with only one study.

In Figure 3, we can see the coefficient of rigor and relevance of each study. Only 2 out of 23 studies had the highest score on rigor and relevance, 3 and 4, respectively. None of the studies reached a score of 0 on rigor, but one study had a 0 on relevance, which can be considered disappointing from the industrial perspective. Finally, the rest of the studies had a rigor aspect value between 1 to 2,5.

Furthermore, the outsourcing theme has a high industry relevance score due to real industrial scenarios that those studies take place (Figure 4). However, since some do not give proper attention to aspects such as threats to validity and study design, the industrial scenario leads them to lower scores.

[1]www.maxqda.com

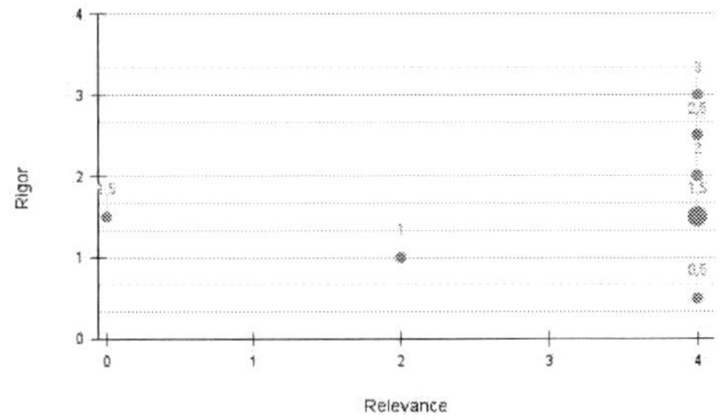

Figure 3. rigor and Relevance of outsourcing studies.

Figure 4. Average Rigor and Relevance over time.

4.2. How do large-scale agile projects with outsourced distributed teams handle their operation?

This section describes the six themes regarding how outsourcing distributed teams were working on large-scale distributed projects. The themes emerged through the steps of thematic synthesizes [Cruzes and Dyba 2011]. From six themes, we have a total of 15 patterns. Each theme and its patterns will be described in the following subsections. For better comprehension, the 15 patterns are described based on the structure suggested by Välimäki and Kääriäinen [Välimäki and Kääriäinen 2008].

4.2.1. Contracts in outsourcing large-scale distributed projects

Contracts in Outsourcing Environment (2): **Problem**: agile values and principles have put the challenge when companies are dealing with third parties. First, the agile value "customer collaborations vs contract negotiation" cannot be followed by the book since standard outsourcing practices work based on contract negotiations [Batra 2009]. Second, welcoming changes can be trouble for fixed-bid contracts or vendors with pre-defined resources [Batra 2009]. **Context**: a client that works with agile methodologies can expect the vendor to be open to customer interaction over contract negotiation. However, it can lead to severe problems regarding development and delivery if the vendor works with pre-defined plans, resources, and fixed-price contracts. **Solution**: Contracts cannot be avoided due to the agreements that protect both client and vendor [Batra et al. 2011]. Further, contracts without fixed prices can also be a way out, although the client must be aware that all changes and new work hours will be counted. **Consequences**: The fixed-price contract can stifle an agile process of a large client, although it can also protect the same client from spending a a lot of money.

Supplier Determine Price After Sprint (1): **Problem**: a study aims to solve the problem regarding price-fixed contracts and also accept late changes [Kussmaul 2010]. However, vendors and clients need to work with closed-range budgets to accomplish such a goal. **Context**: Both customer and supplier agree to work with dynamic contracts during the interactions [Kussmaul 2010]. **Solution**: to minimize the risks, after each sprint, the supplier is responsible for determining the final price based on the actual effort made, and the scope of work completed [Kussmaul 2010]. **Consequences**: the teams become more responsive to uncertainty and change requests during the planning. Also, as a result, both parts could minimize costs since a price range was calculated to accommodate changes in the contracts. Finally, determining the price later avoided conflicts regarding the fixed-price contracts.

4.2.2. Agile ceremonies and artifacts

Planning meetings with onshore and offshore teams (4): **Problem**: synchronizing meeting hours with distributed offshore and onshore teams can be a challenging task in large-scale projects. The planning meetings need to accommodate typical hours of teams with different time zones. **Context**: Planning meetings involving both teams are held in different phases to involve everybody that is spread in global settings. In some cases, the companies can send the offshore team to the onshore site [Paasivaara et al. 2008a, Paasivaara et al. 2008b, Paasivaara et al. 2009]. **Solution**: a phased meeting model which has a distributed meeting, followed by two local meetings in offshore and onshore teams. The distributed meetings can be held during the typical hours of both sites through teleconferences tools, where the Product Owner is responsible for presenting the prioritized backlog items [Paasivaara et al. 2008a, Paasivaara and Lassenius 2010]. After that, the onshore team continues the planning meeting, and the offshore team continues the work done by the onshore team discussing on the draft plan received. **Consequences**: in a distributed environment, the phased planning meeting provided enough visibility for both teams regarding the work that needs to be done and also an open forum for discussion [Paasivaara and Lassenius 2010]. However, separating the meetings regularly in a distributed environment demands a large effort [Paasivaara et al. 2009, Paasivaara and Lassenius 2010].

The Main Supplier as the owner of agile ceremonies (1): **Problem**: the development of a product by two unaffiliated IT suppliers working in the same baseline [Vallon. et al. 2013]. **Context**: one leading supplier (MS) that holds the contract and provides most of the staff, while the additional supplier (AS) is a subcontractor with developers or testers without scrum roles defined [Vallon. et al. 2013]. The MS does not involve the AS in regular scrum events or the scrum board and burndown charts. Consequently, the absence of AS involvement leads to several issues regarding communication and coordination. **Solution**: establish long-lived single-site Scrum teams, enabling electronic tool support, and using BDD to make implicit requirements knowledge explicit and transparent to all parties [Vallon. et al. 2013]. **Consequences**: the refusal to use electronic tools and to seek a healthy relationship with unaffiliated suppliers can lead to several problems. However, if both suppliers are treated in the same way without specific restrictions due to different contracts, their relationship can improve into both seek project success.

4.2.3. Common outsourcing organization designs

Domain expertise stays onshore (8): **Problem**: during the outsourcing of a project, the domain expertise regularly belongs to the client, which is the owner of the business. Also, most of the time, the hired outsourced supplier cannot translate business needs to function requirements since the domain business does not belong to them. **Context**: The necessity to keep domain expertise and requirements elicitation in the onshore site

[Hossain et al. 2011, Bass 2016, Matthiesen and Bjørn 2017, Gupta et al. 2019]. **Solution**: If an offshore team has difficulty keeping up with tasks that need domain expertise, the managers can involve them in less cross-site coordination tasks [Hole and Moe 2008]. In this way, the onshore team focuses on requirements analysis, architecture decisions, and new features while the offshore team works with features implementation and system configuration [Kussmaul 2010]. Finally, the team with domain expertise should actively involve offshore developers and testers to participate in requirements decisions and gradually pass the domain knowledge to them [Noordeloos et al. 2012]. **Consequences**: This approach can cause issues regarding the relationship with the offshore teams, which can feel left out of the project just for not mastering the business. From another perspective, gradually involving the offshore teams can bring benefits, since the seeking for engagement can improve the relation of both teams and also put everybody in the same ruler of business knowledge [Hole and Moe 2008, Kussmaul 2010].

Technical Expertise stays offshore (3): **Problem**: most of the companies that are looking for an offshore team from an outsourcing approach are looking to access high-skilled talents, cheap labor, and a 24/7 development cycle through other regions. However, most of this expertise is used mainly for technical purposes focused only on software development, which can cause issues in the teams' relationships. **Context**: Offshore team with the unique responsibility of implementing the features previously specified by the onshore team [Noordeloos et al. 2012, Bass 2016]. **Solution**: carrying out development activities with adequate onshore support and integration practices between teams [Hossain et al. 2009]. **Consequences**: hire an offshore team to focus specifically on the technical aspects of the project can bring positive impacts as long as they get proper support during all the development phases [Hossain et al. 2009]. However, the lack of support for those team members spread around the globe can create the "us and them" feeling [Noordeloos et al. 2012].

Vendor Responsibilities (2): **Problem**: in an outsourced project, the vendor needs to be aware of its responsibilities, which involve participating in all phases of a development process. Further, the vendor also needs to be aware of the type and size of the project to evaluate how better the development process can be conducted. **Context**: In big projects with many teams, the vendor needs to be close to the customer from the beginning to capture, analyze and transform business requirements into technical stories [Daneva et al. 2013]. However, whether the project is small, the vendor needs to reflect on how the operation activities are worthy of keeping [Dorairaj et al. 2012]. **Solution**: the vendor can be close enough to the customer to capture the requirements in a user story manner with acceptance criteria, followed by other steps such as architecture design, code, and test [Daneva et al. 2013]. In small duration projects, all development activities can be held on the customer site itself [Dorairaj et al. 2012]. **Consequences**: when vendors are genuinely involved in the process of serving the customer by understanding their needs and, based on it building stories that reflect the system specifications, the project has many chances to succeed [Daneva et al. 2013].

Offshore Team relationship (4): **Problem**: working with teams in distributed software development settings can lead to many problems related to communication, coordination, and control of the development process [Marinho et al. 2018]. The vendor can deal with the same issues in outsourced projects while handling both onshore and offshore teams. The difficulty of communication between sites can create the "us and them" feelings, which hinders the development process and diminishes trust in the offshore team [Paasivaara et al. 2014]. Such feelings can be also caused when new developers are hired in one location and developers from other locations do not try to get to know the new ones [Cho 2007]. **Context**: the appearance of a "yes-sir" culture in the offshore team where the members do not try to understand the sprint goal may cause the implementation of failed increments [Koch et al. 2014]. **Solution**: adoption of scrum can increase the feeling of belonging in the offshore team, bringing the team closer to the onshore site as well as the client site with constant interaction with them [Noordeloos et al. 2012]. **Consequences**: due to the agile process of reducing the gap among the offshore team members, the team can increase their knowledge of the client's domain which makes their work more interesting. As another consequence, bringing interactions closer to the offshore team with the client can give them a chance to improve personal skills and also their motivation [Noordeloos et al. 2012].

Outsourcing Organization Models (2): **Problem**: in the process of outsourcing the product development, the customer should choose the suitable model that fits his activities. The model can be a multi-site project in which each site is responsible for a module of the project or a closer approach in which the vendor interacts more closely with the client site to understand the complexities of the project better. **Context**: Depending on the required project communication, different models can fit in the relation of customer and vendor [Batra 2009]. The company decides to work with multi-site projects allocating particular team groups with the required competence to develop specific components of the solution [Kommeren and Parviainen 2007]. **Solution**: customer-supplier should align how agile methods can be adopted in their environments [Kommeren and Parviainen 2007, Batra 2009]. **Consequences**: in a multi-site project approach, the hiring of different team groups for specific components can minimize the problems of concentrating the development in a unique supplier [Kommeren and Parviainen 2007], although it also can lead to an overhead of coordination and communication. On the other side, the regular interaction between customer and vendor through client representatives in both sites can make the development process more expensive when compared to a more direct agile model of interaction [Batra 2009].

4.2.4. Third party suppliers

Third parties suppliers involvement (1): **Problem**: many customers look for hiring third parties and additional suppliers to handle some activities of the development process that can cause overhead to them [Lehtinen et al. 2015]. However, third parties suppliers require much expertise in the customer domain to make those things work right, which sometimes does not happen. **Context**: the customer hires third parties suppliers for a specific activity such as data mass testing, requirement elicitation or design tasks [Lehtinen et al. 2015]. **Solution**: as a consequence of the lack of domain by the POs, the client needed to hire third parties to handle some of their activities to keep the project on the road [Lehtinen et al. 2015]. However, bringing those third-party suppliers may not solve the problem correctly since they might not have the domain expertise. Due to it, the best approach for the clients is to look for specialists suppliers or train their POs in the domain. **Consequences**: as a result of third parties eliciting requirements without a proper domain, the stories can be inaccurate and lead the POs to have difficulty in communicating and prioritizing requirements that they do not understand.

Same backlog for different suppliers (1): **Problem**: when a vendor is dealing with an additional supplier (AS) through subcontracts, it is necessary to pay enough attention to the AS activities. Keeping the same backlog without sharing the whole story can cause problems in the relationship of both suppliers. **Context**: More than one supplier, with the main one and all using the same backlog, although only the main with complete control [Vallon. et al. 2013]. **Solution**: due to the lack of a PO and SM to handle those activities involving the backlog and planning, some developers from the AS site can become unofficial SM, and PO [Vallon. et al. 2013]. Despite the subcontracts, the best way to follow is to engage both suppliers in the development process with their functions clearly defined. **Consequences**: the use of the same backlog for both suppliers cannot cause adverse impacts for itself, although the lack of vital roles in the team can lead to exclusion of the AS from agile ceremonies.

4.2.5. Outsourcing roles and functions

Ambassador and Coordinator Role (6): **Problem**: despite the regular composition of a distributed agile team, an outsourcing project requires some additional roles. Those roles are coordinators, and ambassadors [Paasivaara et al. 2008a, Batra 2009]. **Context**: The ambassador is a client employee responsible for staying in the outsourcing vendor site, interacting with the team members daily, driving the future of the project, and providing business context to the offshore team [Paasivaara et al. 2008a, Paasivaara et al. 2008b, Daneva et al. 2013, Batra 2009, Batra et al. 2011]. The coordinator is a vendor employee responsible for staying with the outsourcing client, interacting with the client team daily, and also being a focal point to the client regarding the vendor's activities [Batra 2009]. **Solution**: the ambassador and coordinator roles can be seen as both ends of a bridge that supports the communication channel between the customer and the outsourcing vendor [Batra 2009, Dorairaj et al. 2012]. The role has some different ways to be implemented; in most cases, hiring a specialist to form the bridge with people that has higher soft skills in communication aspects [Paasivaara et al. 2008a, Paasivaara et al. 2008b, Batra 2009, Batra et al. 2011, Daneva et al. 2013].**Consequences**: establish two different roles can provide better communication among the teams involved in the project.

Outsourcing Team Composition (2): **Problem**: an outsourcing team may have some tailored roles to accommodate the nature of a distributed large-scale context. **Context**: the definition of main roles for an outsourced team with business analysts, tech lead, domain owner, delivery team head, and test scenario team lead which work collaboratively making the requirements decision during iterations [Batra 2009, Daneva et al. 2013]. **Solution**: the ambassador and coordinator roles work as a bridge for customer and vendor communication. The client's design team can help to understand the requirements, while the integration team works closely with the architecture to handle components integration [Batra 2009]. The business analysts must know the business process to be able to translate it into user stories; The teach leads must serve as a technical reference for the team; Domain owners must master the business domain of the client and share it with the others; Delivery Team Heads are responsible to ensure that the development increments will be delivered following all functional and non-functional requirements; Finally, Test Scenario Team Leads are responsible for managing the technology dependencies and constraints related to the project. **Consequences**: tailoring the roles to fit an outsourced environment better is not only a suggestion but sometimes a necessity to achieve project success. Such adaptations were made to the regular roles, and the insertion of new ones can improve the dynamics of the team [Batra 2009, Daneva et al. 2013].

4.2.6. Outsourcing environments characteristics

Regulation problems between Offshore and Onshore team (1): **Problem**: the development of software from a regulated area can bring some additional challenges. Some regulated areas, such as health, aviation or financial, do not allow offshore teams to work on solutions of the onshore site [Noordeloos et al. 2012]. **Context**: The onshore client team is responsible for the design and requirements decision, while the offshore team is mainly responsible for the development and test of the product. In some cases, the financial area is regulated by law or regulatory requirements. **Solution**: the onshore vendor team needs to work more closely on the technical tasks that require access to regulated areas [Noordeloos et al. 2012]. **Consequences**: Due to the regulated environment, some limitations cause delays and bottlenecks in the solution delivery [Noordeloos et al. 2012].

Careful Supplier Selection (2): **Problem**: The unreliable vendor selection can cost the client the whole project [Kommeren and Parviainen 2007]. **Context**: when a company is looking to hire an outsourced vendor to assist or even develop its product, it requires trust in the supplier [Kommeren and Parviainen 2007]. **Solution**: to include the supplier selection as an integral part of the product road-mapping process. The client must evaluate the vendors' capabilities by looking for past experiences or even making an audition [Kommeren and Parviainen 2007]. Build a relationship with the vendor, evolving it into an alliance [Kussmaul 2010].**Consequences**: both approaches to selecting a vendor carefully and also building a healthy relationship with them bring good benefits. However, auditing or conducting a proof-of-concept can become expensive for clients and vendors.

5. Discussion

Our study has shown 15 different patterns spread across six themes regarding the work of distributed outsourcing teams in large-scale contexts. Those patterns reinforce the way of work in outsourcing large-scale distributed environments and how both customer and vendor manage their day-to-day to accomplish project success. Further, it was possible to realize that managing customer-vendor relationships in large-scale projects requires much tailoring in agile methodologies. As presented in the studies of Batra and Daneva [Batra 2009, Daneva et al. 2013], following the agile principles and values by the book may harm the development process of outsourcing distributed teams. However, if these issues are overcome, it can lead to customer-vendor relationship well-being.

It was possible to observe some relationships among patterns from different themes, which can be combined to solve mutual problems. Patterns from theme *Contracts in outsourcing large-scale distributed projects* (See section 4.2.1) and *Common Outsourcing Organization Designs* (See Section 4.2.3) related to fixed-contracts, late changes and vendor responsibilities can be merged to solve the same issues at once. Since late changes, fixed contracts and dynamic prices are not commonly feasible for vendors and customers. It is possible to engage those patterns into the vendor responsibilities pattern. According to Daneva *et al.*, [Daneva et al. 2013] the client PO must be aware of communicating any changes to the vendor early, and also, the vendor assumes that the client master the business value of the solution. Further, the vendor was responsible for allowing only two types of changes: (I) changes from a business perspective related to regulation issues; (ii) changes from a technical perspective that occurs when tech leaders from the vendor find stories too expensive for the architecture. Finally, the approach defined by the vendor of developing "delivery stories" also facilitates the process of avoiding late changes and fixed contracts by refining the user stories that came from the client [Daneva et al. 2013].

The patterns of *Careful Supplier Selection (2)* and *Technical Expertise stays offshore (3)* can be related to some of the success factors studied by Khan *et al.* [Khan et al. 2011]. The most common success factors for vendor selection, according to Khan *et al.* are appropriate infrastructure, cost-saving, and skilled human resources. Keeping the technical expertise offshore is the pattern that most look for cost-saving and access to talented individuals for a cheaper price [Hossain et al. 2009]. However, since the COVID-19 pandemic, remote work has taken hold, and looking for offshore teams became a matter of survival for many companies [NicCanna et al. 2021]. Based on this, to achieve the success factors getting technical expertise from offshore places, the pattern regarding the careful selection of a supplier must be considered. As we saw, clients must audit and evaluate the capabilities of their potential vendors [Kommeren and Parviainen 2007], and according to Khan's study, a large-scale client must also track the record of the successful projects of a vendor, ask for SPI Certifications, and also check the turnover rate. Finally, an efficient outsourcing relationship requires enough knowledge of the client management and culture [Khan et al. 2011], which can avoid problems such as the one presented by Noordeloos *et al.* [Noordeloos et al. 2012].

5.1. Limitations

Limitations are inevitable in any research study. However, in this study, several actions were taken to minimize the impacts that could harm the validity of the SLR. In this section, we discuss three types of threats to validity and how we manage it [Wohlin et al. 2012].

Construct Validity: it was ensured through a peer-review process during the SLR in which both the first and second authors were responsible to evaluate each of the studies to build the patterns. Also, whether any authors disagreed with a study, they would discuss it to reach a consensus. In addition, the third author was involved in an independent pattern assessment. *External Validity:* the SLR was conducted through a rigid research protocol validated and developed by the authors. Further, the studies were extracted from five of the most renowned bibliographic databases, as mentioned in section 3. Also, using a search string in those databases ensures a certain degree of generalism regarding the theme studied. *Internal Validity:* the selected studies were evaluated by the first and second authors, when one of them disagreed with a choice, all of them discussed reaching agreement. All authors were also involved in the analysis of the results and redundancy.

6. Conclusion

Outsourcing in distributed large-scale software development can be considered a way out for many companies that aim to access high-skilled suppliers to develop their complex solutions. However, the nature of those environments requires attention. In this study, we carried out a Systematic Literature Review to better understand how outsourced distributed teams from large-scale contexts handle their operation. Through 23 selected studies from 2006 to 2019, six themes and 15 patterns regarding the operation have emerged. The patterns provide information on how customer and vendor can better coordinate their operation while developing a solution with onshore and offshore teams.

The results and findings of this study will enable researchers and practitioners to better understand the outsourcing nature by providing some solutions to common problems of those types of projects. We hope to evaluate those patterns in a case study of an actual industry project with outsourced teams as future work. Further, we aim to survey outsourced teams from large-scale companies to evaluate better the presence of those patterns and the emergence of new ones. By doing this, we expect to offer solutions to some of the problems encountered in the patterns.

References

Bass, J. M. (2016). Large-scale offshore agile tailoring: Exploring product and service organisations. In *Proceedings of the Scientific Workshop Proceedings of XP2016*, XP '16 Workshops, New York, NY, USA. Association for Computing Machinery.

Batra, D. (2009). Modified agile practices for outsourced software projects. *Commun. ACM*, 52(9):143–148.

Batra, D., VanderMeer, D., and Dutta, K. (2011). Extending agile principles to larger, dynamic software projects: A theoretical assessment. *J. Database Manage.*, 22(4):73–92.

Cho, J. (2007). Distributed scrum for large-scale and mission-critical projects. In *Reaching New Heights. 13th Americas Conference on Information Systems, AMCIS 2007, Colorado, USA, August 9-12, 2007*, page 235. Association for Information Systems.

Cruzes, D. S. and Dyba, T. (2011). Recommended steps for thematic synthesis in software engineering. In *2011 International Symposium on Empirical Software Engineering and Measurement*, pages 275–284.

Daneva, M., van der Veen, E., Amrit, C., Ghaisas, S., Sikkel, K., Kumar, R., Ajmeri, N., Ramteerthkar, U., and Wieringa, R. (2013). Agile requirements prioritization in large-scale outsourced system projects: An empirical study. *Journal of Systems and Software*, 86(5):1333–1353.

Dingsøyr, T., Fægri, T. E., and Itkonen, J. (2014). What is large in large-scale? a taxonomy of scale for agile software development. In *PROFES*.

Dorairaj, S., Noble, J., and Malik, P. (2012). Understanding team dynamics in distributed agile software development. In *Agile Processes in Software Engineering and Extreme Programming*, pages 47–61, Berlin, Heidelberg. Springer.

Gupta, R. K., Venkatachalapathy, M., and Jeberla, F. K. (2019). Challenges in adopting continuous delivery and devops in a globally distributed product team: A case study of a healthcare organization. In *2019 ACM/IEEE 14th International Conference on Global Software Engineering (ICGSE)*, pages 30–34.

Gupta, R. S. (2022). Knowledge management and quality control in software outsourcing projects. In *Research Anthology on Agile Software, Software Development, and Testing*, pages 1484–1510. IGI Global.

Hole, S. and Moe, N. B. (2008). A case study of coordination in distributed agile software development. In *Software Process Improvement*, pages 189–200, Berlin, Heidelberg. Springer.

Hossain, E., Ali Babar, M., and Verner, J. (2009). Towards a framework for using agile approaches in global software development. In *Product-Focused Software Process Improvement*, pages 126–140, Berlin, Heidelberg. Springer Berlin Heidelberg.

Hossain, E., Bannerman, P. L., and Jeffery, R. (2011). Towards an understanding of tailoring scrum in global software development: A multi-case study. In *Proceedings of the 2011 International Conference on Software and Systems Process*, ICSSP '11, page 110–119, New York, NY, USA. Association for Computing Machinery.

Ivarsson, M. and Gorschek, T. (2011). A method for evaluating rigor and industrial relevance of technology evaluations. *Empirical Software Engineering*, 16:365–395.

Khan, S. U., Niazi, M., and Ahmad, R. (2011). Factors influencing clients in the selection of offshore software outsourcing vendors: An exploratory study using a systematic literature review. *Journal of Systems and Software*, 84(4):686–699.

Kitchenham, B. and Charters, S. (2007). Guidelines for performing systematic literature reviews in software engineering. Technical report, Technical report, EBSE Technical Report EBSE-2007-01.

Koch, C., Jørgensen, C., Olsen, M., and Tambo, T. (2014). We all know how, don't we? on the role of scrum in it-offshoring. In *Creating Value for All Through IT*, pages 96–112, Berlin, Heidelberg. Springer Berlin Heidelberg.

Kommeren, R. and Parviainen, P. (2007). Philips experiences in global distributed software development. *Empirical Softw. Engg.*, 12(6):647–660.

Krancher, O. (2020). Agile software development practices and success in outsourced projects: The moderating role of requirements risk. In *Agile Processes in Software Engineering and Extreme Programming*, pages 56–72, Cham. Springer Publishing.

Kussmaul, C. (2010). Onshore and offshore outsourcing with agility: Lessons learned. In *Agility Across Time and Space: Implementing Agile Methods in Global Software Projects*, pages 91–106, Berlin, Heidelberg. Springer Berlin Heidelberg.

Lehtinen, T. O., Virtanen, R., Heikkilä, V. T., and Itkonen, J. (2015). Why the development outcome does not meet the product owners' expectations? In *Agile Processes in Software Engineering and Extreme Programming*, pages 93–104, Cham. Springer.

Marinho, M., Noll, J., and Beecham, S. (2018). Uncertainty management for global software development teams. In *11th International Conference on the Quality of Information and Communications Technology*, pages 238–246, Coimbra, Portugal. IEEE.

Marinho, M., Noll, J., Richardson, I., and Beecham, S. (2019). Plan-driven approaches are alive and kicking in agile global software development. In *International Symposium on Empirical Software Engineering and Measurement (ESEM)*, pages 1–11, Porto de Galinhas, Brazil. IEEE.

Matthiesen, S. and Bjørn, P. (2017). When distribution of tasks and skills are fundamentally problematic: A failure story from global software outsourcing. *Proc. ACM Hum.-Comput. Interact.*, 1(CSCW).

NicCanna, C., Razzak, M. A., Noll, J., and Beecham, S. (2021). Globally distributed development during covid-19. In *2021 IEEE/ACM 8th International Workshop on Software Engineering Research and Industrial Practice (SER IP)*, pages 18–25.

Noordeloos, R., Manteli, C., and Vliet, H. V. (2012). From rup to scrum in global software development: A case study. In *2012 IEEE Seventh International Conference on Global Software Engineering*, pages 31–40.

Paasivaara, M., Durasiewicz, S., and Lassenius, C. (2008a). Distributed agile development: Using scrum in a large project. In *2008 IEEE International Conference on Global Software Engineering*, pages 87–95.

Paasivaara, M., Durasiewicz, S., and Lassenius, C. (2008b). Using scrum in a globally distributed project: a case study. *Softw. Process. Improv. Pract.*, 13:527–544.

Paasivaara, M., Durasiewicz, S., and Lassenius, C. (2009). Using scrum in distributed agile development: A multiple case study. In *2009 Fourth IEEE International Conference on Global Software Engineering*, pages 195–204.

Paasivaara, M. and Lassenius, C. (2010). Using scrum practices in gsd projects. In *Agility Across Time and Space: Implementing Agile Methods in Global Software Projects*, pages 259–278, Berlin, Heidelberg. Springer Berlin Heidelberg.

Paasivaara, M., Väättänen, O., Hallikainen, M., and Lassenius, C. (2014). Supporting a large-scale lean and agile transformation by defining common values. In *Agile Methods. Large-Scale Development, Refactoring, Testing, and Estimation*, pages 73–82, Cham. Springer International Publishing.

Petersen, K., Feldt, R., Mujtaba, S., and Mattsson, M. (2008). Systematic mapping studies in software engineering. In *Proceedings of the 12th International Conference on Evaluation and Assessment in Software Engineering*, EASE'08, page 68–77, Swindon, GBR. BCS Learning & Development Ltd.

Välimäki, A. and Kääriäinen, J. (2008). Patterns for distributed scrum — a case study. In *Enterprise Interoperability III*, pages 85–97, London. Springer London.

Vallon., R., Bayrhammer., K., Strobl., S., Bernhart., M., and Grechenig., T. (2013). Identifying critical areas for improvement in agile multi-site co-development. In *Proceedings of the 8th International Conference on Evaluation of Novel Approaches to Software Engineering - ENASE,*, pages 165–172. INSTICC, SciTePress.

Vithana, V. N., Asirvatham, D., and Johar, M. (2018). An empirical study on using agile methods in global software development. In *2018 18th International Conference on Advances in ICT for Emerging Regions (ICTer)*, pages 150–156.

Wieringa, R., Maiden, N., Mead, N., and Rolland, C. (2006). Requirements engineering paper classification and evaluation criteria: A proposal and a discussion. *Requir. Eng.*, 11:102–107.

Wohlin, C., Runeson, P., Höst, M., Ohlsson, M., Regnell, B., and Wesslén, A. (2012). *Experimentation in Software Engineering*, pages 123–151. Springer.

Perceptions of knowledge management in Brazilian software development companies

Juliana Oliveira dos Santos, Guilherme Augusto dos Reis Martins, Érica Ferreira de Souza, Katia Romero Felizardo, Giovani Volnei Meinerz

[1] Department of Computer, Federal University of Technology – Paraná (UTFPR), Cornélio Procópio/Paraná, Brazil

julianas.2018@alunos.utfpr.edu.br, guimar@alunos.utfpr.edu.br
ericasouza@utfpr.edu.br, katiascannavino@utfpr.edu.br
giovanimeinerz@utfpr.edu.br

Abstract. *The software development companies conduct activities that generate a considerable amount of knowledge. Knowledge Management (KM) allows working with the generated knowledge helping in organizational learning. However, professionals in software companies still face several challenges to articulate and leverage knowledge in the organization. We aim at providing evidence about how KM has been adopted in practical environments of software development. We designed a survey instrument that was distributed to Brazilian software development professionals. The survey results improved the current understanding of KM and how it manifests itself in practical software development environments.*

1. Introduction

Software companies develop projects that generate a considerable amount of knowledge that can be valuable for further projects. Knowledge Management (KM) principles can help organizations to store, distribute and use the generated knowledge [Dalkir 2017]. Such principles have received attention in academia and industry since they support the organizational learning process. KM emerges as a means to manage organizational knowledge and, consequently, to ensure quality in software development [Souza et al. 2021].

Software Engineering is a highly complex area that involves people and a large volume of information. According to Rus and Lindvall (2002) [Rus and Lindvall 2002], knowledge in software engineering is diverse and its proportions are immense and growing. In this context, problems are constantly being solved and new problems arise. So, in this environment, knowledge needs to be updated all the time, since technologies in the domain of Software Engineering are constantly evolving [Vasanthapriyan et al. 2015].

Although KM provides several benefits to software companies, these organizations still grapple with some problems such as difficulty in systematizing information generated throughout the software processes, difficulty in reusing knowledge, loss of organization's intellectual capital, and employees ordinarily reluctant to share their knowledge [Souza et al. 2015]. A possible explanation for this might be that the knowledge generated in organizations is not processed, i.e., the knowledge is not articulated [Souza et al. 2015].

Implementing KM practices, in general, is not an easy task [Menolli et al. 2015]. However, some research has emerged in recent years considering proposals on how to implement new KM solutions in the organization [Napoleão et al. 2021, Souza et al. 2021].

Moreover, knowing how organizations apply KM in the software development domain, such as practices, challenges, and tools, makes it easier to understand how to support such organizations improve the adoption of KM approaches [Napoleão et al. 2021].

In order to provide evidence about how KM has been adopted in practical environments of software development, we designed a survey distributed to professionals working with software development in Brazilian companies. This study provides perceptions of software engineering professionals about tools, KM practices, communication channels, knowledge reuse, and KM hindrance. We investigated these perceptions considering three KM activities: creation, sharing, and application of knowledge. The survey received 80 replies from professionals involved in software companies from different sizes and segments, and demographically distributed throughout Brazil.

The main contribution of this study is to provide a basis with empirical observations on the practice of KM in software development companies from a practitioner's perspective. Furthermore, survey results could help direct future research and support professionals when deciding on the best strategies to apply KM.

The remainder of this study is structured as follows. Section 2 reviews the literature. Section 3 introduces the procedures used to conduct the research. Section 4 presents the results. Section 5 highlights some points of our research. Related works are presented in Section 6. Lastly, conclusions and future directions are described in Section 7.

2. Background

KM formally manages the increase of knowledge in organizations in order to facilitate its access and reuse [Herrera and Martin-B 2015]. Nonaka and Takeuchi (1995) [Nonaka and Takeuchi 1995] define the knowledge generated in an organization as tacit-explicit. Tacit knowledge, as known as personal know-how, is based on people's experience. In turn, explicit knowledge represents the knowledge that can be recorded and, consequently, it becomes easy to disseminate. Generating value from knowledge conversion (tacit to explicit) is to promote conditions for the creation of organizational knowledge [Nonaka and Takeuchi 1995].

KM involves a set of organizational activities that are systematically performed. Effective KM requires executing activities such as identifying, generating, acquiring, diffusing, and capturing knowledge. KM cycles (or models) are responsible for presenting how the different KM activities are organized and promoting their execution within the organization [Dalkir 2017]. KM cycles aim at identifying and disseminating knowledge and knowledge sources within the organization [Dalkir 2017]. Based on different basic KM cycles, Dalkir (2017) proposes an integrated KM cycle represented by the interaction between three activities, described following three activities:

- **Knowledge capture and/or creation:** Knowledge capture refers to the identification of existing knowledge from the environment. In this activity, tacit knowledge is captured or elicited, and explicit knowledge is organized or coded.
- **Knowledge sharing and dissemination:** Once knowledge has been captured, it needs to be shared throughout the organization. Some practices used to share knowledge within the organization are team meetings, written instructions, ad-hoc information, verbally disseminated information, intranet posts.

- **Knowledge acquisition and application:** The knowledge that has been captured and shared is put to use. KM can succeed if the knowledge is used. Consequently, it is crucial to understand which knowledge is used to which set of people and how best to make it available. The use of KM systems, for instance, can be designed to optimize knowledge application in an organization.

The transition between the three KM activities is illustrated in Figure 1. In the integrated KM cycle, the transition from knowledge capture to knowledge sharing, knowledge content is assessed. Knowledge is then contextualized in order to be understood and used. This process then feeds back into the first activity in order to update the knowledge content became an iterative and incremental cycle [Dalkir 2017].

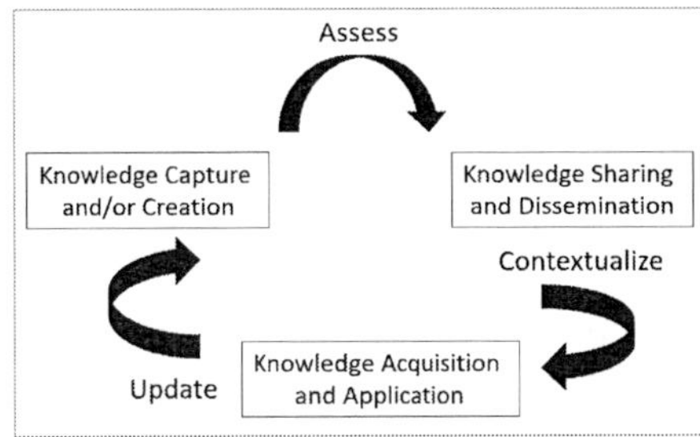

Figure 1. An integrated KM Cycle. Adapted from [Dalkir 2017]

In this study, the integrated KM cycle was used to create the survey questions. We created specific questions to understand how knowledge creation, sharing, and application activities occur in practice in software development companies.

2.1. KM and Software Engineering

Vasanthapriyan et al. (2015) describe that effective management of information in software development processes became a need for organizations to survive in the competitive scenario. In order to get strengths in the development process business, organizations need to execute the software development efficiently and for that, they can introduce KM principles. Introducing KM in software engineering concepts helps the organization to improve the decision-making process, innovation, and organizational performance.

Integrating KM practices with software engineering has brought much discussion about how to manage knowledge in the organization. In a software development environment, for instance, professional company experiences (know-how) can be collected and stored in a knowledge base to be easily reused, and, therefore, accessed by several organization members. In addition, recent research showed that the challenge faced by software organizations is concentrated on how to capture and share this knowledge [Napoleão et al. 2021]. On the other hand, a KM diagnostic[1] conducted in software companies to evaluate KM activities showed that, in practice, the use/application of knowledge is the main point of attention for the investigated software organizations.

3. Survey methodology

We surveyed to collect opinions from professionals working with software development in Brazilian companies. We followed the six phases proposed by [Kitchenham and Pfleeger 2008] to conduct our survey (Figure 2).

– Phase 1: Setting the objectives – Our objective is to provide an empirical basis on the state of KM practice in software development organizations. The base created will

[1]A KM diagnostic analyzes an organization's current state on KM [Bukowitz and Williams 2000].

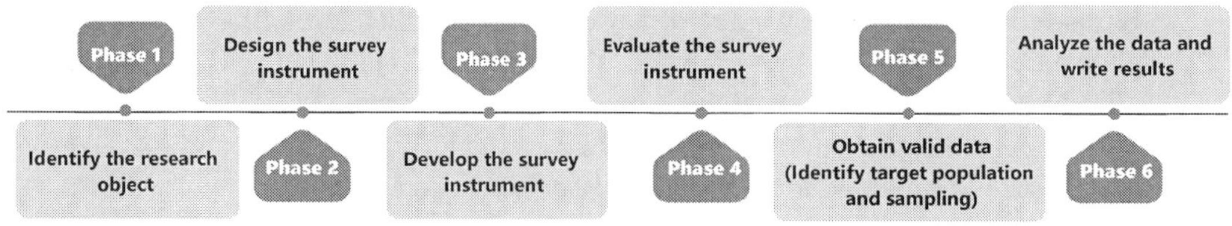

Figure 2. Research phases of this study

present the main KM problems faced by software development organizations and KM practices most used by professionals to create, share, and apply knowledge.

– Phase 2: Designing the survey – Our survey is a cross-sectional study [Kitchenham and Pfleeger 2008]. Software development professionals were asked about KM challenges and practices used to create, share and apply knowledge in their companies.

– Phase 3: Developing the survey instrument – The survey comprises a questionnaire with five sections: 1) Professional Profile; 2) Company Profile; 3) Knowledge creation; 4) Knowledge sharing, and 5) Knowledge application. An online version of the survey is available on *https://doi.org/10.5281/zenodo.6578796.*

The questions of sections 3, 4, and 5 were based on systematic literature reviews and surveys about KM in software engineering, such as [Dingsøyr and Conradi 2002], [Bjørnson and Dingsøyr 2008], [Menolli et al. 2015], [Vasanthapriyan et al. 2015], [Pinto et al. 2018], as well as in classic KM references, such as [Dalkir 2017].

For some questions, participants could choose more than one option as an answer. Therefore the number of answers to the question is greater than the number of respondents. For other questions, some answers' possible choices vary in a scale based on the Likert Scale, which is a metric used in questionnaires such as attitude surveys. At the end of the sections referring to KM activities, an open question was created for participants to provide any comments about challenges on the KM activity. Moreover, in some questions, elements mentioned only once were grouped into the "Others" category.

– Phase 4: Evaluating the survey instrument – We conducted a pre-testing by applying the survey to a smaller sample (6 participants) to identify any problems with the questionnaire. The questionnaire was also evaluated by one experienced researcher in KM and software engineering. The goal of this validation was to mitigate potential threats to validity and correct eventual mistakes.

– Phase 5: Obtaining valid data – Definition of population: In order to identify our population (software development professionals in Brazilian companies), we invited potential respondents to answer the survey in the following ways: (i) a direct request by e-mail was sent to professionals known by the authors. These professionals participated only in the survey pre-testing, and (ii) a request was sent to LinkedIn[2] groups. *Linkedin* is a social network focused on professional relationships. The survey was available for answers during March and June 2021. In the end, 80 participants answered our survey.

– Phase 6: Analyzing the data – The answers were stored directly after the partic-

[2]https://www.linkedin.com

ipants had submitted them. We check the responses in terms of consistency and completeness. After, we define how to analyze each type of response (numerical data, textual data, or ordinal scale). For the open questions, we grouped the answers into categories. The coding technique was used to label the qualitative data and identify different categories.

4. Study Results

Profile Professional. In section 1, we requested that only professionals involved with software development activities respond to the survey. Out of 80 survey participants, 29 (36.25%) work as system analysts, 12 (15%) are information technology (IT) managers, 8 (10%) support analysts, 7 (8.75%) are software engineers, and 24 (30%) are other professions related to IT. Participants have an average of 8.33 years of experience in their positions, with a standard deviation of 13.4.

Regarding KM knowledge level, 28 (35%) participants mentioned to have a basic level of knowledge, 30 (37.5%) answered to possess an intermediate knowledge, 11 (13.75%) mentioned to possess a piece of advanced knowledge in KM, and 11 (13.75%) of the participants reported not know KM.

Profile Companies. Based on the company's names mentioned by the participants who answered the survey, at least 54 companies were identified. Concerning the number of employees in companies, 31 companies have more than 100 employees (38.75%), nine companies between 51 and 100 employees (12.5%), ten companies between 10 and 12 employees (12.5%), and four companies have less than ten employees (5%). Regarding the demographic distribution of companies, 51.25% are in the state of São Paulo, 33.75% in Paraná, 6.25% in Minas Gerais, 3.75% in Bahia, 2.5% in Rio de Janeiro, 1.25% in Distrito Federal, and 1.25% in the Rio Grande do Sul.

The main products developed by the companies are software on demand (23.75%), commercial automation (12.5%), enterprise resource planning (8.75%), software components (7.5%), among others. The principal software development methodologies used by companies are Scrum (45.3%), Incremental Model (14%), Cascade Model (10%), Extreme Programming (XP) (9.3%) and Spiral Model (5.3%).

KM Activities Outcomes. The last survey sections are related to the three main KM activities: i) knowledge creation, ii) knowledge sharing, and iii) knowledge application. In the following, we describe the primary outcomes for these activities:

i) Knowledge Creation

The knowledge creation survey section made it possible to identify how actions related to knowledge creation occur in practice. First, recognize which were the main techniques used to capture tacit knowledge within the companies. Figure 3 presents the main techniques mentioned by the participants.

The technique most cited by participants was short and informal meeting (67 answers – 83.75%). 45.3% of companies use Scrum practices in their development (Section 4). In [Napoleão et al. 2021], synthesis research on KM and Agile Software Development (ASD) was conducted. According to Napoleão et al. (2021), Scrum activities that occur to capture and/or create knowledge are Sprint Planning, Daily Scrum, Development Work,

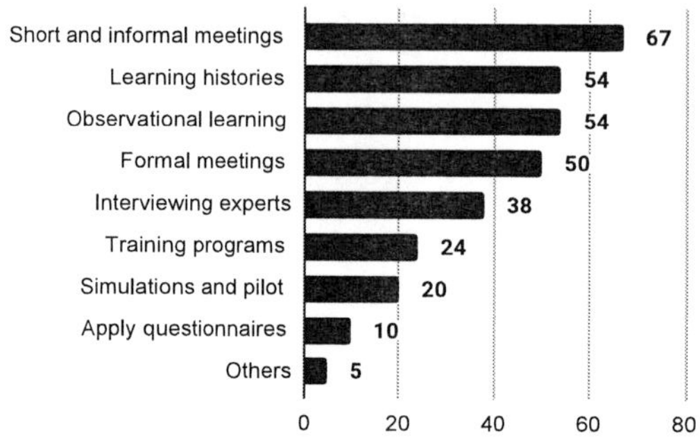

Figure 3. Capture tacit knowledge

Product Backlog, Sprint Backlog, and Increment. Almost all Scrum activities allow to capture or create knowledge. Short and informal meetings support these activities. This behavior aligns with the survey responses.

The techniques "Learning histories" and "Observation learning" were also frequently mentioned, with 54 answers (67.5%). Learning histories are a beneficial means of capturing tacit knowledge. This technique represents a retrospective history of significant events that occurred in the organization's recent past and described by the people who took part in them. Likewise, the observational learning technique is the process of learning by watching the behaviors of others, for example, in the presentations of a sample problem, scenario, or case study [Dalkir 2017].

In knowledge creation, it is crucial to codify this knowledge to the organization. When codifying knowledge into a tangible and explicit form, companies allow that knowledge can be communicated much more widely, with less cost and, build an organizational memory [Dalkir 2017]. As reported by the survey participants, techniques most used to codify knowledge are Unified Modeling Language (UML) (45 answers – 56.25%), Source code and comments (44 answers – 55%), Flowchart (40 answers – 50%) and Manuals (38 answers – 47.5%). Figure 4 presents the techniques mentioned by the participants to codify knowledge.

Finally, in the last survey part, an open question was asked to collect participants' opinions about the companies' main challenges related to knowledge capture. We grouped the main challenges mentioned into categories as shown in Figure 5.

As stated by participants, the main challenges of companies concerning knowledge capture are organizational culture (23 answers – 28.75%) and communication (21 answers – 26.25%). Organizational culture is directly related to the way the company thinks and acts, influencing the behavior of employees [Dalkir 2017], and the communication directly benefits software projects, since skills and experiences cannot be fully mastered in isolation. When there are problems with organizational culture or communication, low productivity is generated [Ouriques et al. 2019].

ii) Knowledge Sharing

In the integrated KM cycle (Figure 1), after knowledge is captured, it must be shared. In this survey section, we ask participants the most used resources to share knowledge in the company. The most resource used is short and informal meetings (55 answers

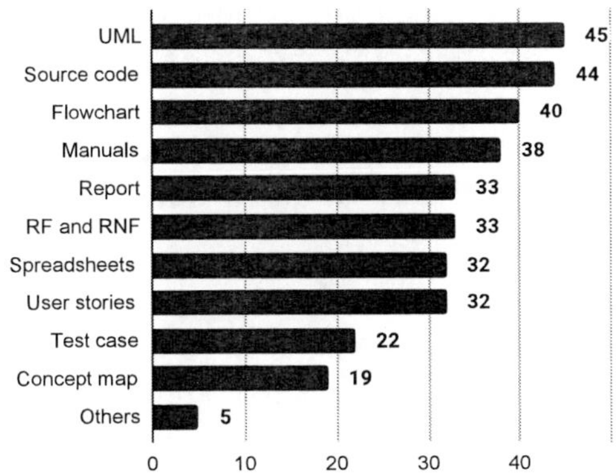

Figure 4. Coding explicit knowledge

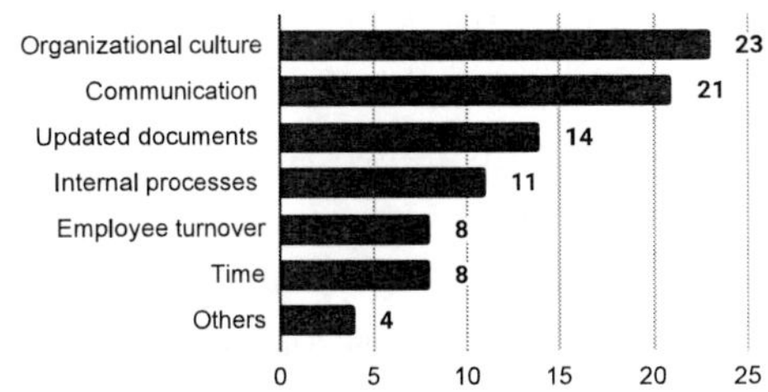

Figure 5. Main knowledge capture challenges

– 68.75%). In addition, internal training programs (46 answers – 57.5%) and formal meetings (42 answers - 52.2%) also was mentioned by participants as resources to share knowledge. Figure 6 presents the resources cited by the participants.

In Napoleão et al. (2021), the most common KM activity adopted in the context of software development organizations is knowledge sharing, mainly when the organization uses ASD. It makes sense since ASD prioritizes the exchange of information and communication among teams. Agile values promote a focus on the people involved in a project and how they interact and communicate. As previously shown, 45.3% of companies use Scrum practices. One of the characteristics of Scrum is the short meetings that take place during the Sprint. This behavior is in agreement with our findings.

When knowledge sharing occurs through the resources mentioned above, we asked participants what knowledge types the company usually shares, as detailed in Figure 7. "Best practices" (68 answers - 85%) was the knowledge most mentioned by professionals. Best practices are those practices that have been shown to produce superior results and judged as exemplary, good, or successfully demonstrated [North and Kumta 2018].

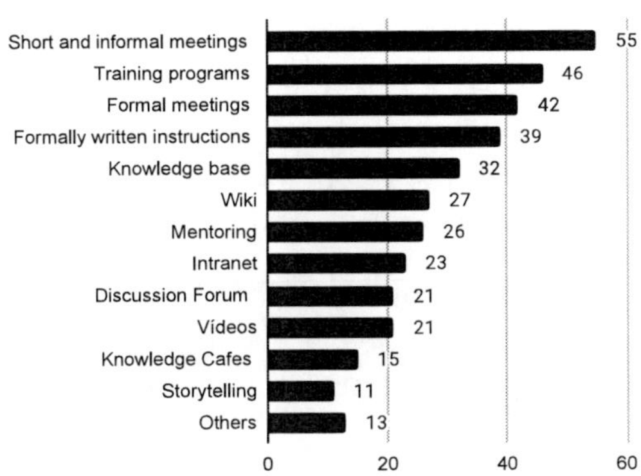

Figure 6. Resources most used to share knowledge

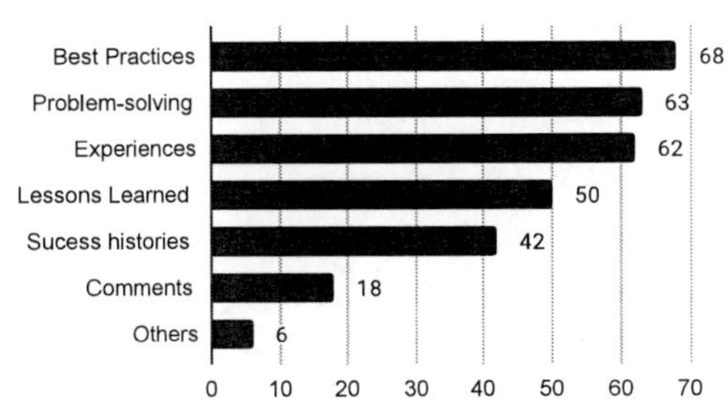

Figure 7. Knowledge types shared

Considering the most valuable communication channel for sharing knowledge, 55 participants (68.75%) responded that virtual meetings are helpful. Contrarily, 25 participants (32.5%) prefer person communication. Most of those who prefer to communicate through a virtual channel mentioned that virtual meetings (e.g., email, forum, wiki, social networks) could keep a history easier to be stored and because of its practicality. On the other hand, those who prefer personal meetings justified that interaction is the main reason for preferring this communication channel.

Figure 8 displayed the results linked to the perception of participants on the frequency that knowledge is shared in the company. We asked about the frequency that they receive motivation to share knowledge, how often they usually share their knowledge, how well they consider that people know each other's knowledge and skills, and how much it is possible to trust in the knowledge shared. The responses are based on the Likert Scale method, which ranges between 1 and 5, where 1 means "Never" and 5 "Always".

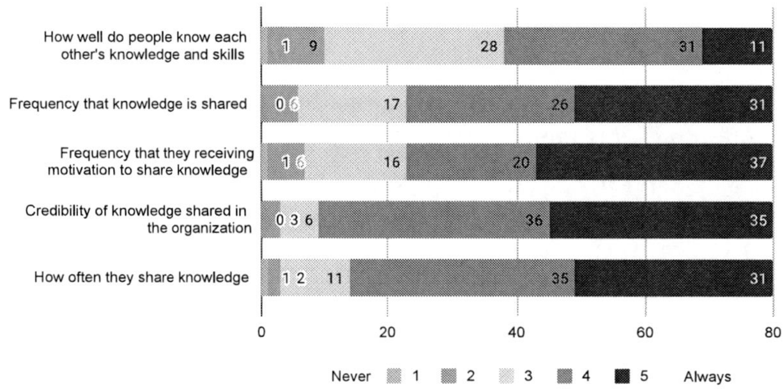

Figure 8. Respondents' perception about the knowledge sharing in the company

In summary, most of the questions presented in this survey section had positive responses (4 and 5 scales). Reflecting on the questions: "How well do people know each other's knowledge and skills" and "Frequency that knowledge is shared" (the first two questions in Figure 8), the concentration of answers is on scales 3 and 4, which means a positive, but with a trend closer to a neutral opinion about them. The question with more positive answers is "Credibility of knowledge shared in the organization" with 36 answers (45%) scale of 4 (very often) and 35 answers (43.75%) scale 5 (always), out 80, totaling 71 (88.75%) answers. This result on the credibility of shared knowledge becomes a good indicator for companies since one of the main hindrances to knowledge sharing is the credibility of the content, and the source [Dalkir 2017].

Several challenges can hinder knowledge sharing within organizations. For this reason, we created a question in the last survey part for participants to express their opinion about the main challenges to sharing knowledge in the company. Figure 9 presents the main challenges mentioned by them.

In participants' opinion, increased workload (86.25%) is the main challenge to work with knowledge sharing in the company. According to [Souza et al. 2015], shortage of time is a potential risk to incorporate the principles of KM and knowledge sharing can imply increasing the employee workload. In the category "Others" (8%), some challenges mentioned were lack of confidence, initiative, awareness, and a clearly-defined process.

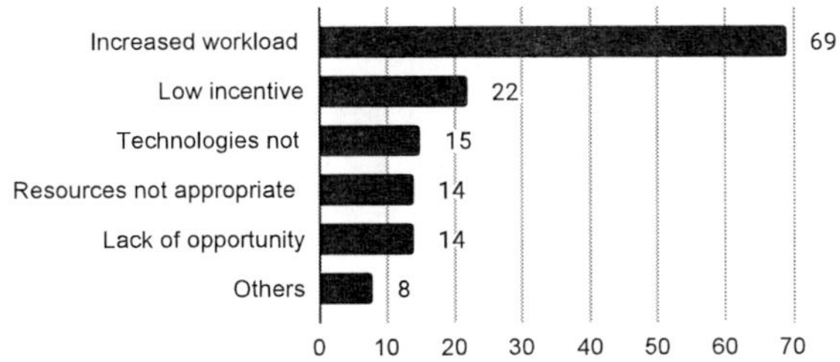

Figure 9. Challenges to sharing knowledge in companies

iii) Knowledge Application

Knowledge application refers to the actual use of knowledge that has been captured or created [Dalkir 2017]. This activity closes the integrated cycle of KM, as proposed by [Dalkir 2017]. The application of knowledge is directly related to the reuse of knowledge. In this survey part, our goal was to understand how participants seek knowledge to solve problems, how knowledge is reused, and the main challenges for applying knowledge in the participants' practical view.

When trying to solve a work problem at the company, participants answered that they usually seek knowledge on the Internet (63 answers – 78.7%) (Figure 10). Currently, individuals and organizations can take advantage of the remarkable possibilities and easy access to information that the Internet provides. In software development, several sites allow seeking knowledge developers, e.g., discussion forums. According to Silva et al. (2020) [Silva et al. 2020], forums have become essential repositories of knowledge to be reused.

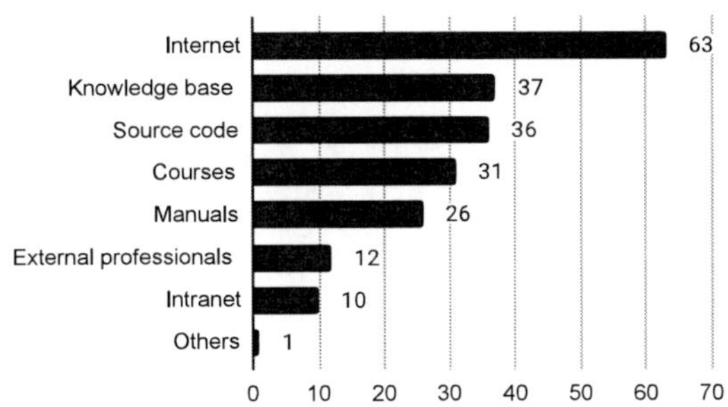

Figure 10. Means to seek knowledge in the company

When knowledge reuse occurs, we ask participants which types of knowledge (tacit and explicit) best contribute to their learning in the company. 42 participants (52.2%) prefer to use tacit knowledge, and 38 (47.5%) mentioned preferring to use the knowledge already explicit. Regarding tacit knowledge, experience from past stories (71 answers – 88.7%) and ideas (77.5%) are the most practiced ways of reusing knowledge in companies. Figure 11 presents the ways to reuse tacit knowledge most mentioned by the participants.

Concerning explicit knowledge, Figure 12 presents the ways most used by participants to reuse knowledge in the company. Functions (methods, classes) (57 answers –

71.2%) is the most reused form of knowledge by participants. In addition, the reuse of system components (subsystems, modules) (43 answers – 53.7%), the entire application system (41 answers – 51.2%), and ready-made libraries (41 answers – 51.2%) were also highlighted. Code reuse, such as functions, components, libraries, test scripts, is a form of knowledge reuse in software development that is essential to minimize costs and reduce development time in new projects [Haefliger et al. 2008].

In knowledge creation, the UML was the most mentioned form for encoding explicit knowledge (Figure 4), and not the most mentioned option for reusing explicit knowledge (Figure 12). Maybe, this happens because professionals who use UML diagrams most often are software architects, followed by software analysts and project managers, corresponding to a very small group in the profile of participants in this study (see Section 4, Profile Professional). In this perception, we can interpret that the UML is not mentioned because it is used more for consultation by the professionals who participated in this research.

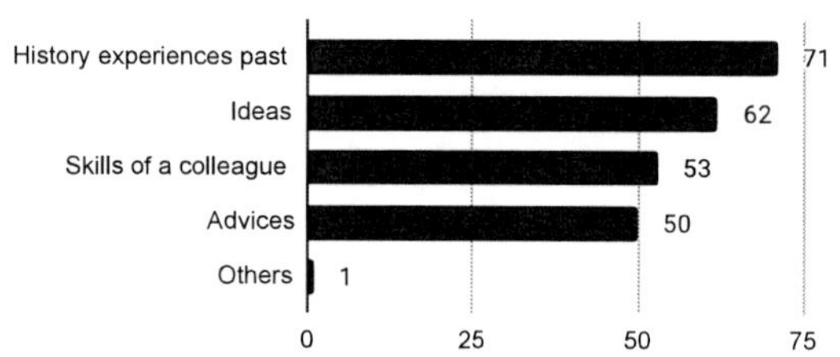

Figure 11. Tacit knowledge reused

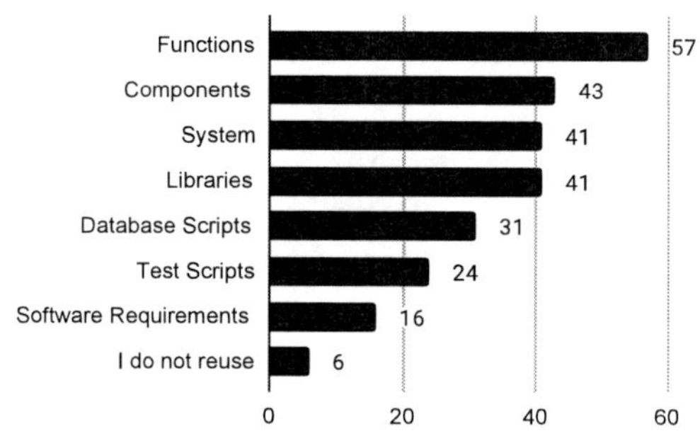

Figure 12. Explicit knowledge reused

It is essential to have tooling support or practices to optimize the process to apply knowledge. In light of this, we seek to know what are the main tools used for KM. Most participants (31 answers – 38.7%) answered that they do not know tools that support KM. Those who mentioned tools affirmed that they do not use specific tools to KM but tools that can support several KM activities, including using/applying knowledge. Some of the most cited tools were: Confluence (12 answers – 15%), Version Control System (VCS) (8 answers – 10%), Microsoft SharePoint (7 answers – 8.7%), and Internal Enterprise System (7 answers – 8.7%). Figure 13 presents the main tools mentioned by participants. Tools mentioned once were added in the "Others" category (33 answers – 41.25%), including Microsoft Teams, ServiceNow, Microsoft Azure, Slack, Degreed, GitHub, Redmine.

Finally, in the last part of the survey, an open question was comprised for participants to externalize their opinion on the main challenges to applying the knowledge. Participants responded that organizing and making knowledge accessible (21 answers – 26.2%) is the biggest challenge for the company concerning the application and/or use of knowledge. Figure 14 presents the company's main challenges regarding the use of knowledge in the opinion of the survey participants.

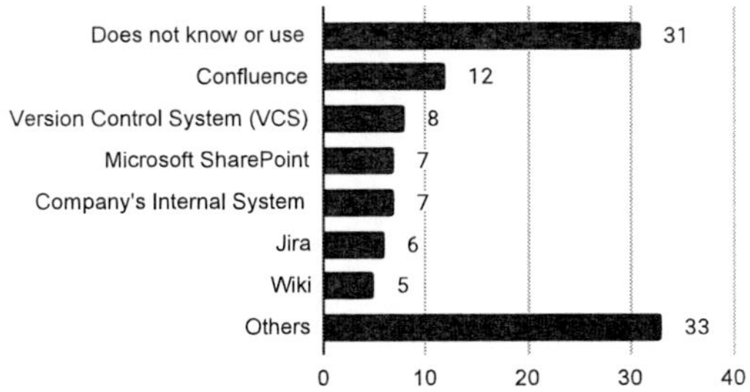

Figure 13. Tools used in the company to support KM

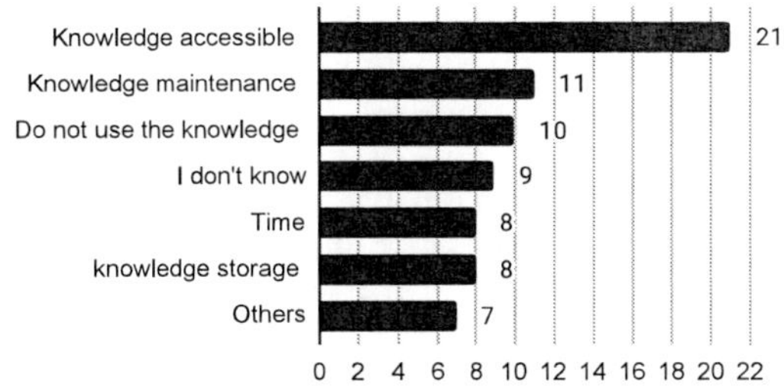

Figure 14. Main challenges in relation to the use of knowledge

5. Discussion

The software has become indispensable in our daily routines and critical and complex application domains, making knowledge increasingly important. KM can provide several benefits for software development companies, but it can also bring several challenges. Our results offer insights into current practices and problems KM as discussed following.

The first KM activity analyzed in our survey was knowledge capture, which refers to the development of new knowledge and know-how innovations that did not have a previous existence within the company [Dalkir 2017]. When analyzing the knowledge capture, the technique most used by participants was short and informal meetings (67 answers – 83.7%). This behavior directly reflects the application of Scrum in the companies in which the participants work. 45.3% adopt Scrum as their development methodology. Scrum activities are based on short and informal meetings, and agile values promote a focus on communication [Ruiz et al. 2018, Napoleão et al. 2021]. Although communication is one of the main principles of agile development, this was identified as one of the main challenges by capturing knowledge in the companies (21 answers – 26.25%). According to Field (2013)[Field 2013], knowledge continuity management is related to communication, i.e., the more critical a job is to the company, the more important is it to be part of a continuity management system. However, the more complex and tacit the professional's knowledge, the more difficult it will be to capture and pass on.

Since the captured knowledge becomes essential to codify before storing it, the techniques most used to codify knowledge are UML and source code. According to Chaudron et al. (2012) [Chaudron et al. 2012], UML modeling contributes to sharing and understanding of the system and more effective communication. As well as the UML, source code can also contribute to the creation and sharing of knowledge. In code review, for example, discussions about coding issues are communicated back and forth between the community or the team members. As a result, developers have the opportunities to reflect, take corrective actions and build concrete experiences.

Regarding knowledge sharing, most participants (55 answers – 68.75%) prefer short and informal meetings which are a trend of the agile development teams. In addition, virtual meetings (55 answers – 68.75%) have also been preferred by most participants, as they believe they are a more practical means. Currently, given the current situation of the COVID-19[3] pandemic and the resulting stay-at-home orders have led to considerable

[3] *https://covid.saude.gov.br/*

changes in the way people work. One of these changes involves increased use of video conferencing as a means of communicating or holding work meetings. While it has been a great challenge for some professionals, it has become the best option, as can be seen from the survey results.

Also, concerning knowledge sharing, most participants demonstrated that they trust in the knowledge shared in the organization (71 answers – 86.25%). However, even though they trust in the knowledge, their biggest challenge is the increased workload to share it (69 answers – 86.25%). The Software Engineering domain is vast, and embedding KM is a real hindrance as it needs commendable efforts from the involved.

The last KM activity analyzed was knowledge application. In order to solve a problem (e.g., implementing a code), most participants (63 answers – 78.7%) are looking for solutions on the Internet, which can make it possible to access and reuse knowledge easily. Knowledge reuse, mainly, is associated with the use of knowledge available in the company. 42 (52.5%) participants believed learning is more accessible when using tacit knowledge to learn within the companies from reuse. The tacit form more commonly reused is the experience from past stories (71 answers – 88.7%). Otherwise, 38 (47.5%) participants prefer to reuse explicit knowledge. In this case, most of them prefer to reuse functions (methods, classes) (57 answers – 71.2%). Source code reuse is crucial for innovation since it can substantially improve the quality of new software products and reduce costs [Haefliger et al. 2008].

Investing in KM is also making use of new technologies or tools. However, according to Menolli et al. (2015), employees have a natural resistance to new technologies, which makes KM implantation more difficult. Our survey results showed that many participants do not know or do not use specific tools for KM (31 answers – 38.7%).

The survey results gave a better understanding of the current state of KM. The results achieved give insights into the current practices and problems of KM in Brazilian software development companies. Concerning professionals, the results of this survey allowed the construction of an empirical base capable of supporting project decisions. From the results, the practitioners can evaluate their own KM situation against companies participating in the research. On the other hand, for research in KM, the results can guide future research, such as solutions to the problems/challenges presented.

5.1. Threats to the Validity

There are some main limitations to our study. Firstly, even not knowing, it is common for professionals to carry out KM activities in their daily lives, mainly those who mentioned using agile practices. Even so, 28 (35%) participants mentioned having a basic level of knowledge regarding KM. Still not possible to state that the responses of these 28 participants can be a bias for this research. Therefore, a pilot study was performed and a survey validated by a KM researcher, so any problem could be identified and corrected before the survey was opened.

Secondly, the data sample was 80. We consider this sample to be representative. We defend that the data collected provided a solid basis for our analysis. However, this study only reflects the situation in Brazil, and we cannot confirm that the findings are valid for companies from other countries.

6. Related Works

Although the first reports of KM in Software Engineering appeared around the year 2000, it is still a relatively new field to be investigated and there are still many challenges about how to apply KM in a software development organization [Bjørnson and Dingsøyr 2008, Souza et al. 2021]. The following are presented some studies that conducted surveys to understand the application of KM in software development companies.

In Maciel et al. (2018) [Maciel et al. 2018], a survey was conducted in software companies in order to identify the perception of professionals in software testing on the use of KM initiatives. The survey was applied to 39 companies. Regarding the main results, testing planning activity and test case reuse have received more attention from companies. According to Maciel et al. (2018), strategic planning and test cases reuse have the potential to reduce software development costs and time significantly.

Ruiz et al. (2018) [Ruiz et al. 2018] surveyed with professionals working with agile tests to understand how knowledge is shared in Brazilian companies that incorporated agile methodology. The survey was answered by 150 professionals. The main results observed were that the knowledge is shared into the team (89.3%), informal communication is most used (52%), tools are used to share knowledge, the future decisions are based on past problems (88%), and the success stories are stored by team (70.9%). Based on the survey results, agile practices support companies to make use of KM principles.

In Menolli et al. (2015), the main tools and technologies to KM used by software-development companies in Brazil are identified. A survey was conducted in Thirteen Brazilian software development companies with high levels of process software maturity. The results show that some of the tools used by the companies do not apply the concepts described in the theories as they do not help promote organizational learning. Furthermore, the tools are not often used, mainly because they are not organized efficiently.

More recently, Mathew and Rodrigues (2019) [Mathew and Rodrigues 2019] presented a study on the KM implementation in Indian software organizations. Critical success factors, process capability, and effectiveness of KM were analyzed by a survey. 423 knowledge workers from 66 large software companies participated in the survey. The results indicated that the overall implementation of KM in Indian software firms was in the right direction with above-average considering the score values of the factors used for analysis in the study.

7. Conclusions

This study sought to understand the three KM activities: creation, sharing, and application of knowledge in Brazilian software development organizations. A survey instrument was distributed and 80 software development professionals participated in this research. This study showed some potential results to be investigated in the future: several no KM specific tools and technologies are used to support the KM activities; ASD practices strongly support KM activities; best practices are the knowledge types the company usually shares; experiences from past stories and source code are fundamental to be reused; and organizational culture, increased workload, and how to make knowledge accessible are the main challenges mentioned by survey participants.

Although our goal in the survey is broader in the sense of knowing the means of creating, sharing, and applying knowledge, it is still essential to deepen this research in order to understand how certain factors could influence the research responses, for example, the companies and/or project characteristics, knowledge level of KM by participants. A deep investigation with other mechanisms to perception about KM in software companies also is part of future work. Moreover, we intend to conduct the same survey for a longer time to collect more data to improve its representativeness. We also intend to replicate the survey in an international context, and conduct interviews to compare the results. Finally, from the survey results analysis, especially the highlighted problems, we also intend to investigate possible solutions to support software organizations in relation to KM.

Acknowledgement

The author Juliana Oliveira dos Santos acknowledges Institutional Scholarship Program in Scientific Initiation (PIBIC-UTFPR) for the financial support. Dr. Érica Ferreira de Souza is supported by a research grant from the Brazilian funding agency CNPq (432247/2018-1). We also would like to thank the professionals that agreed to answer the survey.

References

Bjørnson, F. O. and Dingsøyr, T. (2008). Knowledge management in software engineering: A systematic review of studied concepts, findings and research methods used. *Information and Software Technology*, 50:1055–1068.

Bukowitz, W. and Williams, R. L. (2000). *The knowledge management fieldbook*. Financial Times Prentice Hall, Great Britain.

Chaudron, M., Heijstek, W., and Nugroho, A. (2012). How effective is uml modeling? *Softw Syst Model*, 11:571–580.

Dalkir, K. (2017). *Knowledge Management in Theory and Practice*. Elsevier, USA, 3 edition.

Dingsøyr, T. and Conradi, R. (2002). A survey of case studies of the use of knowledge management in software engineering. *International Journal of Software Engineering and Knowledge Engineering*, 12:391–414.

Field, A. (2013). When employees leave the company, how can you make sure their expertise doesn't? Harvard Business Publishing.

Haefliger, S., von Krogh, G., and Spaeth, S. (2008). Code reuse in open source software. *Management Science*, 54:180–193.

Herrera, R. J. G. and Martin-B, M. J. (2015). A novel process-based KMS success framework empowered by ontology learning technology. *Engineering Applications of Artificial Intelligence*, 45:295–312.

Kitchenham, B. A. and Pfleeger, S. L. (2008). Personal opinion surveys. In *Guide to Advanced Empirical Software Engineering*, pages 63–92. Springer London.

Maciel, C. P. C., Souza, E. F., Vijaykumar, N. L., Falbo, R. A., Meinerz, G. V., and Felizardo, K. R. (2018). An empirical study on the knowledge management practice in software testing. In *XXI Ibero-American Conference on Software Engineering (CIBSE) - Experimental Software Engineering (ESELAW) Track*.

Mathew, A. O. and Rodrigues, L. L. R. (2019). Holistic evaluation of knowledge management practices in large indian software organisations. *International Journal of Web Engineering and Technology (IJWET)*, 14.

Menolli, A., Cunha, M. A., Reinehr, S., and Malucelli, A. (2015). "old" theories, "new" technologies: Understanding knowledge sharing and learning in brazilian software development companies. *Information and Software Technology*, 58:289–303.

Napoleão, B. M., Souza, E. F., Ruiz, G. A., Felizardo, K. R., Meinerz, G. V., and Vijaykumar, N. L. (2021). Synthesizing researches on knowledge management and agile software development using the meta-ethnography method. *Journal of Systems and Software*, 178:110973.

Nonaka, I. and Takeuchi, H. (1995). *The knowledge creation company: how Japanese companies create the dynamics of innovation*. Oxford University Press, New York.

North, K. and Kumta, G. (2018). *Knowledge Management: Value Creation Through Organizational Learning*. Springer, 2 edition.

Ouriques, R. A. B., Wnuk, K., Gorschek, T., and Svensson, R. B. (2019). Knowledge management strategies and processes in agile software development: a systematic literature review. *International journal of software engineering and knowledge engineering*, 29(03):345–380.

Pinto, D., Oliveira, M., Bortolozzi, F., Matta, N., and Tenório, N. (2018). Investigating knowledge management in the software industry: The proof of concept's findings of a questionnaire addressed to small and medium-sized companies. In *Int. Joint Conference on Knowledge Discovery, Knowledge Engineering and Knowledge Management*.

Ruiz, G. A., Silva, P. R., Souza, E. F., Vijaykumar, N. L., Felizardo, K. R., and Meinerz, G. V. (2018). Knowledge management in agile testing teams: a survey. In *XXI Ibero-American Conference on Software Engineering (CIBSE) - Experimental Software Engineering (ESELAW) Track*.

Rus, I. and Lindvall, M. (2002). Knowledge management in software engineering. *IEEE Software*, 19(3):26–38.

Silva, P. R., Santos, V., Souza, E. F., Meinerz, G. V., Felizardo, K. R., and Vijaykumar, N. L. (2020). Extraction of useful information from unstructured data in software engineering: A systematic mapping. In *Ibero-American Conference on Software Engineering (CIBSE) - Experimental Software Engineering (ESELAW) Track*, pages 406–419.

Souza, E. F., Falbo, R. A., and Vijaykumar, N. L. (2015). Knowledge management initiatives in software testing: A mapping study. *Information and Software Technology*, 57:378–391.

Souza, E. F., Falbo, R. A., Vijaykumar, N. L., Felizardo, K. R., Meinerz, G. V., Specimille, M. S., and Coelho, A. G. N. (2021). Development of an ontology-based approach for knowledge management in software testing an experience report. *Journal of Software Engineering Research and Development*, 9(1):12–21.

Vasanthapriyan, S., Tian, J., and Xiang, J. (2015). A survey on knowledge management in software engineering. In *International Conference on Software Quality, Reliability and Security Companion (QRS-C)*, pages 237–244, Vancouver, BC, Canada.

Pivoting in software startups. Motivations, process and evaluation

Karina Lanata[1], Pablo Benítez[1], Gerardo Maturro[1]

[1]Facultad de Ingeniería - Universidad ORT Uruguay
Cuareim 1451, Montevideo, Uruguay

kl146400@fi365.ort.edu.uy, pb179924@fi365.ort.edu.uy, matturro@fi365.ort.edu.uy

Abstract: *Various studies affirm that software startups fail in the first months or years, generally because they did not validate their business hypothesis, and they refuse to implement changes called pivots. In this paper we present the results of a field study whose purpose was to identify how pivots are decided, implemented, and evaluated in software startups. From interviews with founders of ten software startups, it is found that the most common factors that generate the need to pivot are: "negative reaction from customers", "positive reaction from an unforeseen customer segment" and "focus on the target market", and the most used types of pivots are "Technology", "Value capture" and "Customer segment".*

Resumen: *Diversos estudios afirman que las startups de software fracasan en los primeros meses o años, generalmente porque no validaron su hipótesis de negocio, y reusan implementar cambios denominados pivotes. En este trabajo presentamos los resultados del estudio de campo cuyo propósito fue identificar cómo se deciden, implementan y evalúan los "pivot" en las startups de software. A partir de entrevistas a fundadores de diez startups de software, se encuentra que los factores más comunes que generan la necesidad de pivotar son: "reacción negativa de los clientes", "reacción positiva de un segmento de clientes no previsto" y "enfoque en el mercado objetivo", y los pivotes más utilizados son "Tecnología", "Captura de valor" y "Segmento de clientes".*

1. Introducción

Giardino y colegas (2016) definen emprendimiento de software como una empresa con escasez de recursos, altamente reactiva, formada por pequeños equipos con poca experiencia y que opera en un entorno de incertidumbre. Según Blank y Dorf (2020) estas organizaciones buscan un modelo de negocio que sea escalable, repetible y rentable. Unterkalmsteiner y colegas (2016) añaden que es una empresa enfocada en la creación y desarrollo de un producto o servicio innovador e intensivo en software, como base para la creación de valor de negocio.

Por su parte, en la metodología Lean Startup desarrollada por Ries (2011), se utiliza el término pivote como un desvío de curso diseñado específicamente para probar y validar una nueva hipótesis sobre un producto, modelo de negocio y el motor de crecimiento.

Bajwa (2017) considera al pivote como una actividad imprescindible para los emprendimientos de software, pero sin embargo encuentra que las comunidades de investigadores y profesionales aún carecen de una guía sensata y evidencias sobre cómo un emprendimiento de software debe tomar decisiones de pivoteo para eventualmente obtener el éxito. Así mismo, agrega que en los últimos años pocos estudios se han llevado a cabo para comprender los pivotes.

Pocos estudios en la literatura abordan los factores que indican la necesidad de realizar pivotes en los emprendimientos de software, cuáles son los más utilizados, cómo realmente se implementan y evalúan.

Este artículo aborda esta brecha de conocimiento proporcionando al ecosistema emprendedor evidencias empíricas para ayudar al proceso de toma de decisiones relacionadas a los pivotes, aumentando la posibilidad de lograr los objetivos de estos emprendimientos. Según indica Ries (2011), la mayoría de los emprendimientos de software fracasan, en parte por utilizar metodologías tradicionales y por perseverar durante mucho tiempo con la idea original. Debido a la incertidumbre con la que operan, es necesario que los fundadores se encuentren abiertos a realizar cambios, ya que prácticamente todos los emprendimientos de software que sobreviven lo deben hacer.

El propósito de este artículo es reportar los resultados de la investigación realizada a partir de las entrevistas efectuadas a socios fundadores de startups uruguayas. El foco de la investigación fue conocer cuáles son las circunstancias técnicas y de negocio que ponen de manifiesto la necesidad de realizar un pivote, listar los tipos de pivotes más empleados, conocer cómo se planifica e implementa un pivote y conocer de qué manera se evalúa el resultado del pivote ejecutado.

El resto de este artículo se organiza de la siguiente manera. En la sección 2 se presenta una breve revisión de la literatura general relacionada a pivoting. La sección 3 explica el diseño metodológico utilizado para este estudio, donde se presentan las preguntas de investigación, la selección de los emprendimientos de software a estudiar y los informantes claves, así como los procedimientos de recolección, preparación, y análisis de datos. En la sección 4 se exponen los principales resultados obtenidos, mientras que en la sección 5 se discuten estos resultados. En la sección 6 se abordan las amenazas a la validez del presente estudio y en la sección 7 se presentan las conclusiones y los trabajos futuros.

2. Antecedentes

2.1. Tipos de pivotes

Según Ries (2011), existen diez tipos distintos de pivote que se pueden realizar en un emprendimiento de software. Estos se pueden observar en la Tabla 1.

Tabla 1. Tipos de pivotes según Ries

Tipo de pivote	Descripción
Acercamiento	Convierte una característica de un producto en el producto en sí

Alejamiento	El producto entero se convierte en una característica de un nuevo producto más grande.
Segmento de cliente	Se cambia el segmento de clientes al que se apuntaba inicialmente.
Necesidad del cliente	Se cambia el problema a resolver que tienen los clientes.
Plataforma	Se refiere a que la aplicación se convierte en su plataforma de soporte o viceversa.
Arquitectura del negocio	En este pivote un emprendimiento de software cambia la arquitectura del negocio, pasando de un alto margen y bajo volumen a bajo margen y alto volumen, o viceversa
Captura del valor	Para capturar el valor que crea una empresa se cambian los métodos de monetización o modelos de ingresos.
Motor de crecimiento	En este tipo de pivote, la empresa cambia su estrategia de crecimiento para buscar un crecimiento más rápido o rentable.
Canal	Se produce cuando se cambia la forma de llegar a los clientes a un modo más eficaz.
Tecnología	Brinda la misma solución utilizando una tecnología completamente diferente.

Por otro lado, Bajwa (2017) propone la existencia de pivotes que no se corresponden con los diez tipos descritos por Ries. Por esta razón introduce cinco nuevos tipos de pivote adicionales que se detallan en la Tabla 2.

Tabla 2. Tipos de pivotes según Bajwa

Tipo de pivote	Descripción
Acercamiento de mercado	Propone enfocarse en un sector del mercado específico, en vez de enfocarse en todo el mercado.
Alejamiento de mercado	Es el proceso inverso al anterior, pasa de centrarse solo en un mercado específico a ingresar en otros sectores.
Completo	Este pivote se produce cuando hay un cambio significativo en el producto, mercado y dimensión financiera, pero el equipo emprendedor sigue siendo el mismo.
Proyecto secundario	Una idea de negocio diferente, paralela y no relacionada con el proyecto principal que se convierte en el nuevo proyecto.
Equipo	Se basa en agregar un nuevo cofundador con experiencia en negocios de software o cambiar el equipo de desarrollo y contratar a nuevos profesionales que conozcan del negocio y la tecnología.

2.2. Trabajos relacionados

Bajwa (2020) propone que hay una falta de evidencia empírica con respecto a por qué y cómo los emprendimientos de software pivotean. También plantea que hay varios casos de éxito de empresas que pivotaron durante su pasaje emprendedor. El estudio intenta explicar los pivotes, los diferentes tipos y los factores que disparan un pivote. Identifica que los principales tipos de pivoteo que los emprendimientos de software hicieron son: "necesidad del cliente", "segmento de cliente", "zoom-in de producto" y "tecnología".

Bohn y Kundisch (2018) trabajaron con emprendimientos que realizaron pivotes de tecnología. Un pivote tecnológico es aquel en el que se llega a una misma solución usando tecnología completamente diferente [Ries 2011]. En su estudio, que incluyó a catorce emprendimientos de software, diseñaron un modelo que identifica tres prerrequisitos, cinco antecedentes y nueve categorías de consecuencias de ejecutar un pivote tecnológico. El estudio provee evidencia empírica que relaciona la tecnología, el desarrollo del modelo de negocios y la innovación en startups de software.

Bajwa y colegas (2017) se plantean en este trabajo identificar los tipos de pivotes que los emprendimientos de software realizan. Además, buscan destacar aquellos factores que hacen fracasar a los emprendimientos de software y por lo tanto dan lugar a un pivote. Para el estudio utilizaron datos secundarios de estudios sobre pivotes que fueron llevados a cabo en cuarenta y nueve emprendimientos de software. En el trabajo identifica que el 23% del total de los pivotes estudiados no se relacionan con los pivotes descritos por Ries (2011), sino que corresponden con los descubiertos por Bajwa en el estudio.

Terho y colegas (2015) trabajaron con tres empresas finlandesas con el objetivo de averiguar cómo estos emprendimientos de software están desarrollando su negocio y si realmente ejecutan pivotes. En el estudio encontraron que algunos de los pivotes causaron cambios más drásticos, siendo la facturación la principal métrica de evaluación de los pivotes ejecutados. También observaron que en algunos casos sucedía un efecto dominó, es decir que un pivoteo causaba otro, y así sucesivamente.

3. Diseño metodológico

El diseño metodológico se basó en la definición de las preguntas de investigación, la selección de los informantes claves, el armado del instrumento de recolección de datos, para su posterior aplicación en entrevistas semiestructuradas. Luego se prepararon los datos y se codificaron las respuestas obtenidas, para finalmente realizar un análisis e interpretación de los resultados obtenidos.

3.1 Preguntas de investigación

Las preguntas de investigación planteadas para este estudio son las siguientes:

- RQ1: ¿Cuáles son las circunstancias técnicas y de negocio, que indican a los emprendedores que es necesario pivotear?
- RQ2: ¿Qué tipo de pivote es el que se ejecuta con más frecuencia?
- RQ3: ¿De qué manera se planifica y ejecuta un pivote?
- RQ4: ¿De qué manera los emprendedores evalúan el éxito o fracaso de un pivote?

3.2 Informantes claves

Se contactaron catorce emprendimientos incubados en los últimos años en la incubadora Ingenio (https://ingenio.org.uy/) y en el Centro de Innovación y Emprendimientos (CIE - https://cie.ort.edu.uy/); esta última es la incubadora universitaria de la Universidad ORT Uruguay.

Si bien todos los emprendedores contactados accedieron a participar de este estudio, para esta investigación era relevante que sus emprendimientos hubieran realizado pivotes y que se encontraran en funcionamiento actualmente. Por esta razón finalmente se efectuaron diez entrevistas. Para dichas entrevistas se utilizó un enfoque cualitativo, según lo sugerido por Hernández-Sampieri [Hernández-Sampieri 2014].

3.3 Recolección de datos

Para recolectar los datos brindados por los fundadores de los emprendimientos de software se utilizó un cuestionario con preguntas abiertas y cerradas, a modo de guion para el desarrollo de las entrevistas. La mayoría de las preguntas fueron abiertas, por lo que, si bien son más dificultosas de codificar, clasificar y preparar para el posterior análisis, se prefirió incluir este tipo de preguntas para recibir respuestas amplias, donde los entrevistados pudieran profundizar una opinión o los motivos consultados.

El proceso de recolección de datos comenzó con la comunicación y coordinación con los emprendedores de los emprendimientos de software. En la entrevista se les solicitó la autorización para grabar el audio para facilitar la posterior extracción de respuestas obtenidas, se utilizó un cuestionario con veintiún preguntas para responder las cuatro preguntas de investigación, y se empleó una diapositiva con las preguntas a modo de apoyo fundamentalmente para las preguntas con opciones. Por último, se procesaron los audios para realizar la transcripción completa de las entrevistas.

El guion para las entrevistas y las transcripciones de las respuestas pueden obtenerse del primer autor o en el siguiente enlace: link.

4. Resultados obtenidos

En esta sección se muestran datos demográficos relevantes de los emprendimientos participantes de este estudio y se presentan las respuestas a las preguntas de investigación planteadas.

4.1 Sobre los emprendimientos de software participantes y sus fundadores

Se realizaron entrevistas a fundadores de diez emprendimientos de software, con diferente grado de desarrollo, según se muestra en la Tabla 3.

Tabla 3. Grado de desarrollo de los emprendimientos

Grado de desarrollo	Cantidad
Egresadas	7
En incubación	3

En la etapa de incubación los emprendimientos se centran en ingresar al mercado, y cuando alcanzan un estatus de autosuficiencia, pasan al estado de egresados, ya sin dependencia de la incubadora. Los emprendedores al estar incubados tienen acceso a una asistencia especializada para la elaboración de los materiales requeridos, para presentarse frente a inversores o agencias que promueven la innovación y el desarrollo. De esta forma pueden lograr acceder a fondos y subsidios que impulsen sus emprendimientos.

De los diez emprendimientos considerados en este estudio, la Tabla 4 muestra las cantidades de emprendimientos en función de la formación de grado de al menos uno de los fundadores.

Tabla 4. Formación de grado de fundadores de los emprendimientos

Formación de grado	Cantidad
Ingeniería y desarrollo de software	9
Administración y Negocios	3
Otras disciplinas	1

Se puede observar que la amplia mayoría de los emprendimientos estudiados cuenta con al menos un fundador con formación tecnológica con perfil de Sistemas, mientras que en tres casos presentan al menos un fundador con titulación de Administrador de Empresas o Economista.

Existe el caso particular de un emprendimiento estudiado que cuenta con uno de los fundadores con formación en Gestión Agropecuaria y el otro fundador es Doctor en Ciencias Veterinarias, por lo que se consideraron ambos como formación en "Otras disciplinas".

4.2 Sobre las circunstancias técnicas y de negocio para pivotear (RQ1)

En relación con las circunstancias técnicas y de negocio que indican la necesidad de pivotear, se tuvieron como referencia los factores expuestos por Bajwa (2017), ya que según la literatura revisada este era el único estudio que los presentaba.

En la Tabla 5 se lista el ranking de los principales factores mencionados por los emprendedores, donde se observa que la mitad de los emprendimientos entrevistados indicó una "reacción negativa de los clientes" como factor determinante para la ejecución de pivotes.

Tabla 5. Principales factores determinantes para la realización de cambios tecnológicos

Factores	Cantidad
Reacción negativa de los clientes	5
Reacción positiva de un segmento de clientes no previsto	4
Enfocar el mercado objetivo	4
Modelo de negocio con imperfecciones	3
Imposibilidad de sobrevivir a la competencia	3
La influencia de un inversor, mentor o socio	3

Los usuarios valoran una funcionalidad	3

En relación con los factores que les indicaron a los emprendedores que debían hacer cambios tecnológicos, en la Tabla 6 se resumen las respuestas de los entrevistados, en base a los factores que desencadenan pivotes detectados por Bohn y Kundisch (2018). En dicha tabla se indica para cada factor cuántos son los emprendimientos que afirman haber tenido estos motivos.

Tabla 6. Principales factores determinantes para la realización de cambios tecnológicos

Factores	Cantidad
Nuevas oportunidades	6
Mantenibilidad	4
Reducir costos del negocio	4
Otro	4
Viabilidad de la arquitectura a futuro	3

En el caso de los factores que llevaron a ejecutar pivotes tecnológicos, se descubrieron tres nuevos motivos que no se encontraban en el estudio de Bohn y Kundisch (2018), estos son: "mejorar la usabilidad del sistema", "seguridad" y "adaptarse a las normativas existentes". El primero de ellos mencionado por dos emprendimientos.

4.3 Sobre los tipos de pivotes (RQ2)

De las respuestas obtenidas por los emprendedores, se observa que los pivotes que más se ejecutaron son los pivotes de: "tecnología", "captura del valor" y "equipo", todos ellos realizados por ocho de los diez emprendimientos entrevistados (Tablas 7 y 8). El siguiente pivote más utilizado es el pivote de "segmento de cliente", el cual fue aplicado por cinco emprendimientos, siendo ejecutado en 6 ocasiones.

Tabla 7. Tipos de pivotes ejecutados (Ries)

Tipos de pivotes	Cantidad
Captura de valor	8
Tecnología	8
Segmento del cliente	6
Necesidad del cliente	4
Alejamiento de producto	3
Canal	3
Motor de crecimiento	1

Los pivotes de "tecnología", "captura del valor" y "segmento de cliente" corresponden a los diez pivotes presentados en Lean Startup, mientras que el pivote de equipo pertenece a los cinco pivotes descubiertos por Bajwa en su tesis doctoral.

Con el propósito de conocer la cantidad total de pivotes ejecutados por los diez emprendimientos entrevistados, se realizó un conteo el cual se muestra en la Tabla 9. Se puede advertir que en total se ejecutaron cuarenta y tres pivotes.

Tabla 8. Tipos de pivotes ejecutados (Bajwa)

Tipos de pivotes	Cantidad
Equipo	8
Acercamiento del mercado	1
Proyecto secundario	1

Tabla 9. Cantidad de pivotes ejecutados en total

Tipos de pivotes	Cantidad
Ries	33
Bajwa	10

4.4 Sobre la planificación e implementación de los pivotes (RQ3)

En relación con la forma en que planifican e implementan los pivotes, en la Tabla 10 se lista el ranking de los métodos más usados por los entrevistados para ejecutar los pivotes.

Tabla 10. Métodos más utilizados para ejecutar los pivotes

Métodos de ejecución	Cantidad
Basarse en el feedback del cliente	4
Mantener solamente el nuevo producto	2
Cobrar por uso del servicio	2
Involucrar en el proceso de cambio a los clientes	2

Se consultó a los emprendedores sobre las dificultades encontradas en la implementación del primer pivote y las respuestas más repetidas fueron las que se pueden observar en la Tabla 11.

Tabla 11. Dificultades enfrentadas al ejecutar el primer pivote

Dificultades encontradas en el primer pivote	Cantidad
Comunicación del cambio	3
Falta de conocimiento tecnológico	3
Financiación	2

Se constata que la mayoría de los emprendimientos tuvieron la necesidad de aprender habilidades comerciales, siendo mencionado por ocho de los diez emprendimientos. Le siguen las habilidades financieras con tres menciones y marketing y ventas con la misma cantidad de ocurrencias, tal cual se observa en la Tabla 12.

Tabla 12. Habilidades aprendidas por los emprendedores

Habilidades	Cantidad
Habilidades comerciales	8
Habilidades financieras	3
Marketing y ventas	3

4.5 Sobre la evaluación de los pivotes (RQ4)

Con respecto a la manera en que los emprendedores evalúan los pivotes ejecutados, se muestra en la Tabla 13 los criterios de evaluación más utilizados.

Tabla 13. Criterios de evaluación

Criterios de evaluación	Cantidad
Facturación	6
Uso del producto	5
Cantidad de usuarios	3

Con el fin de aprender a partir de las experiencias y evaluaciones de los emprendedores, se les consultó acerca de las acciones que volverían a hacer y las que no al pivotear. Las respuestas más repetidas se pueden visualizar en la Tabla 14, donde se obtuvo que volverían a tener en cuenta la opinión de los clientes, ya que es clave para conocer lo que realmente quieren y necesitan.

Tabla 14. Acciones que los emprendedores volverían a hacer al pivotear

Volverían a hacer	Cantidad
Obtener *feedback* del cliente	4
Probar el producto con clientes	3
Pivotear activamente	2
Medir	2

Por otra parte, se les preguntó a los emprendedores acerca de las acciones que no volverían a realizar ya que no les resultaron útiles al momento de ejecutar los pivotes. En la Tabla 15 se muestran los resultados más significativos.

Tabla 15. Acciones que los emprendedores no volverían a hacer al pivotear

No volverían a hacer	Cantidad
Cerrarse a una idea o preconcepto	2
Demorar la ejecución del pivote	1
Hacer inicialmente un desarrollo completo del producto	1
Tomar decisiones basadas en la percepción	1

5. Discusión

5.1 Circunstancias técnicas y de negocio para pivotear

A partir de las entrevistas realizadas, se puede observar que los síntomas más comunes que generan en el equipo fundador el plantearse la eventual necesidad de accionar un cambio en algún aspecto fundamental del emprendimiento son:

- **Reacción negativa de los clientes**: la adopción y retención de los clientes no sucede a la velocidad esperada y los clientes brindan retroalimentación negativa o no dan reacción alguna.
- **Reacción positiva de un segmento de clientes no previsto**: entre los diferentes segmentos de clientes, un segmento en específico muestra más interés en el producto.
- **Enfocar el mercado objetivo**: el mercado objetivo inicial muestra ser muy pequeño para que el emprendimiento pueda sobrevivir y crecer.

Cabe destacar que estos valores obtenidos reafirman el estudio de Bajwa (2017), siendo la mayoría de los factores de origen externo y el más predominante de ellos la reacción negativa de los clientes. Asimismo, se detectó un nuevo factor que no se encuentra en otros estudios relacionados, al cual se denominó de la siguiente manera:

- **Cultural**: el país o región en donde se brinda el servicio tiende a tener una cultura instaurada de eludir los procesos formales de negocio.

Este factor provocó que tuvieran que implementar posteriormente un pivote de segmento de cliente. Otro factor que impulsó a otros emprendimientos a realizar este mismo tipo de pivote fue contar con un modelo de negocio con imperfecciones, pasando de clientes finales generales a clientes empresariales.

Se constató que el motivo predominante que implica la necesidad de realizar pivotes tecnológicos es la búsqueda de nuevas oportunidades de negocio, estas surgen continuamente a lo largo del desarrollo del emprendimiento.

En el caso de los factores que llevaron a ejecutar pivotes tecnológicos, se descubrieron tres nuevos motivos que no se encontraban en el estudio de Bohn y Kundisch (2018), estos son:

- **Mejorar la usabilidad del sistema**: elevar la calidad en la experiencia que tiene un usuario cuando interactúa con un producto o sistema, siguiendo ciertos estándares para que se brinde un servicio más amigable y fácil de utilizar.
- **Seguridad**: la seguridad de los sistemas informáticos comprende un conjunto de medidas y uso de herramientas para prevenir, resguardar, proteger y poder reaccionar ante cualquier intento que atente contra el sistema y sus datos.
- **Adaptarse a las normativas existentes**: refiere a ajustarse a las normas vigentes que regulan determinada actividad.

A causa del impacto que tuvo la pandemia de COVID-19 en el mundo, algunos emprendimientos tuvieron la necesidad de reinventarse para sobrevivir, lo que los llevó a realizar pivotes de alejamiento de producto, proyecto secundario, captura del valor y tecnológicos.

Los investigadores entienden que los fundadores deben desde un comienzo validar la idea con los clientes, ya que la retroalimentación que estos brindan al emprendimiento es clave para evitar los preconceptos y percepciones que tienen los emprendedores. En definitiva, se vio que todos los disparadores de pivotes están de alguna medida relacionado a los clientes, por lo que es fundamental conocer su opinión.

5.2 Tipos de pivotes

Según lo contestado por los entrevistados los pivotes que se ejecutan con mayor frecuencia, dentro de los tipos de pivotes propuestos por Lean Startup son "tecnología", "captura del valor" y "segmento de cliente". Estos valores obtenidos coinciden con el estudio realizado por Bajwa (2017). Es interesante notar que uno de los emprendimientos ejecutó el pivote de "segmento de cliente" en dos oportunidades.

Por otra parte, se identificó que los emprendimientos también ejecutaron pivotes descubiertos por Bajwa, siendo el más aplicado por amplia diferencia el pivote de "equipo", el cual fue efectuado en ocho ocasiones al igual que "tecnología" y "captura del valor", siendo estos los más ejecutados.

Se puede observar que en total se ejecutaron cuarenta y tres pivotes y que todos los emprendimientos entrevistados realizaron más de un pivote. En promedio se ejecutaron cuatro pivotes por emprendimiento, siendo en promedio tres de ellos de los mencionados por Ries (2011) y uno de los propuestos por Bajwa. Estos valores corresponden con el estudio de Bajwa (2017), encontrando en ambos estudios que el 23% del total de pivotes ejecutados son los descubiertos por el autor.

Además, se nota que en algunos casos se presentó el "efecto dominó" mencionado por Terho y colegas (2015), donde se identificó repetidamente que al ejecutar el pivote de "segmento de cliente" desencadenó la ejecución del pivote de "captura del valor" y al realizar el pivote de "equipo" provocó uno de "tecnología".

Dentro de los tipos de pivotes implementados, se advierte que los pivotes que les resultaron más difíciles son "equipo" y "tecnología". Según informan el de "equipo" les resultó complicado el hecho de conseguir personal, tomar ciertas decisiones, alinearlos y delegar responsabilidades. Por otra parte, si bien muchos tienen perfil técnico, les resultó desafiante el pivote de "tecnología" principalmente por el tamaño del mismo y por la utilización de tecnologías desconocidas por ellos. Al mismo tiempo, otros indicaron el pivote de "tecnología" como sencillo de realizar, ya que al contar con formación en el área se sienten cómodos al hacer estos cambios.

En cuanto al pivote más aplicado de Bajwa, se encontró que en algunos casos existieron cambios en el equipo fundador y en otros cambios en el equipo de desarrollo. Por un lado, unos añadieron cofundadores con el fin de agregar nuevas habilidades al equipo, mientras que otros tuvieron desvinculaciones por objetivos personales que no se alineaban con el emprendimiento. Un caso tuvo cambios en el equipo de desarrollo de forma total, en tanto que otro de manera parcial. Solo un emprendimiento no presentó ningún cambio en el equipo.

Se puede decir que los pivotes se disparan principalmente por dos factores externos que son: "enfocar el mercado objetivo" y "reacción positiva de un segmento de clientes no previsto"; y además por un factor interno: "modelo de negocio con imperfecciones". Se coincide con Bajwa (2017) en cuánto a que los pivotes son disparados principalmente por factores externos.

5.3 Planificación e implementación de los pivotes

En base a las respuestas obtenidas de los emprendedores, se observa que generalmente no siguieron el método propuesto por Ries y no se constatan reuniones regulares para considerar pivotear. Se puede argumentar que quizás esto se deba a que los emprendimientos aún no tienen la estructura organizativa que Ries plantea, ya que el o los fundadores se desempeñan en el rol de producto y negocio al mismo tiempo.

Al ser consultados sobre la utilización de guías de buenas prácticas, se descubrió que la mayoría no hacen uso de estas. Los emprendedores realizan los pivotes a prueba y error, mediante un aprendizaje directo de lo que sucedía y en función de esto deciden cambiar o perseverar. Varios de los emprendedores que no usaron guías de buenas prácticas, mencionaron que no sabían si existían guías para hacer pivotes, y que nunca les presentaron algo similar mientras que incubaron, por lo que se apoyaban en la intuición.

La amplia mayoría de los emprendedores se basa firmemente en el *feedback* de los clientes, el cual consideran fundamental para conocer realmente sus necesidades y pivotear apoyados en sus opiniones. En menor medida algunos emprendimientos consideran importante el *feedback* de referentes y del público en general.

Las dificultades que se enfrentaron al implementar los pivotes fueron principalmente: la comunicación del cambio, la falta de conocimiento tecnológico y la financiación. En referencia a la "comunicación del cambio", los emprendimientos indicaron que lo resolvieron involucrando a los clientes en el proceso y transmitiéndoles con tiempo suficiente el impacto de los cambios que se realizarían. La "falta de conocimiento tecnológico" lo solucionaron estudiando la tecnología particular, ya que al ser técnicos del área tienen las herramientas para hacerlo. En cuanto a la "falta de financiación" fue resuelta por los emprendedores acudiendo a agencias que promueven la innovación y el desarrollo e inversores privados. En algún caso mencionaron que fue un obstáculo no contar con un manual de pivoteo y reconocer que se habían equivocado.

En el proceso de la ejecución de los pivotes tuvieron la necesidad de aprender nuevas habilidades, las cuales en su amplia mayoría fueron habilidades comerciales, financieras y de marketing y ventas. Todos los emprendimientos de software necesitaron aprender al menos una de estas habilidades y solo en dos casos mencionaron habilidades tecnológicas, esto se puede atribuir a que la mayor parte de los emprendimientos entrevistados tienen fundadores con perfil de Sistemas.

5.4 Evaluación de los pivotes

En base a las respuestas de los emprendedores se puede ver que los criterios de evaluación más usados son: la "facturación" y el "uso del producto", seguido por la "cantidad de usuarios activos". La forma que aplican para medir el impacto de los pivotes ejecutados es comparar la métrica obtenida con su valor anterior, pero no utilizan ningún marco de trabajo o metodología para medir el éxito o fracaso de los pivotes. La métrica predominante es la facturación, la cual coincide con los resultados similares del estudio de Terho y colegas (2015). Solo un emprendimiento sostuvo que no midieron el impacto del pivote porque no tenían con qué comparar.

Se infiere a que esto se podría deber en parte al desconocimiento de los emprendedores acerca de los marcos de referencia existentes para la medición, como así también a la falta de recursos, sobre todo el tiempo y foco, para establecer un proceso de medición con el fin de evaluar los pivotes.

Se descubre que es sumamente importante la opinión de los clientes en el proceso de pivoteo, a modo de conocer lo que estos realmente quieren y necesitan. Dicha retroalimentación la obtienen mayoritariamente mediante reuniones presenciales o remotas y encuestas de satisfacción por mail. Algunas otras acciones que volverían a hacer los emprendedores al ejecutar un nuevo pivote serían probar el producto con clientes, medir el pivote y pivotear activamente.

En cuanto a las acciones que no repetirían al hacer un nuevo pivote se repite la idea de no cerrarse a una idea o preconcepto, lo cual se relaciona con la famosa frase de Blank "*get out of the building*", es decir abrirse a nuevas ideas, aprender y escuchar. Otros indican que no volverían a hacer inicialmente un desarrollo completo del producto, para no malgastar recursos y tiempo en algo que aún no se encuentra validado.

Para conocer el resultado final de los pivotes de forma global, se les consultó a los emprendedores si se imaginaron estar donde se encuentran ahora con el emprendimiento. Se recibieron respuestas muy variadas en similar cantidad. Dentro de los que consideran estar mejor de lo pensado, se encontró que recibieron inversión y respaldo por parte de personas ajenas al emprendimiento y realizaron el pivote de captura del valor. Por otra parte, los emprendimientos que se encuentran peor de lo esperado se vieron afectados negativamente por la pandemia de COVID-19 y aspiraban a que al menos uno de los fundadores estuviese trabajando a tiempo completo en estos momentos.

6. Amenazas a la validez

Según Hernández-Sampieri y colegas [Hernández-Sampieri et al. 2014], en una investigación de tipo cualitativo los habituales criterios de amenazas a la validez deben sustituirse por una serie de criterios más específicos para este tipo de investigaciones.

El criterio de **dependencia** se define como el grado en que diferentes investigadores que recolectan datos similares en el campo y efectúan los mismos análisis, generen resultados equivalentes. A modo de cumplir con el criterio de dependencia interna, el análisis de los datos recolectados se hizo en forma independiente por los autores con el fin de discutir las diferencias que pudieran surgir y arribar a resultados unificados. El criterio de dependencia externa no se pudo verificar pues no hay otros investigadores que hayan recolectado datos de los mismos entrevistados y en circunstancias similares, es decir en un mismo ambiente y período.

Por otra parte, el criterio de **credibilidad**, también llamado "máxima validez", hace referencia a si los investigadores han captado el significado completo y profundo de las experiencias de los participantes, particularmente de aquellas vinculadas con el planteamiento del problema. Dado que todas las entrevistas a los emprendedores han sido grabadas y se dispone de los audios, fue posible volver a escuchar, con el fin de no omitir nada importante, lo declarado por los entrevistados tantas veces sea necesario. Así mismo, se cuenta con las transcripciones completas de cada entrevista de forma literal, lo que facilitó la lectura de las respuestas de los entrevistados.

En cuanto al criterio de **transferencia** (aplicabilidad de los resultados), no se refiere a generalizar los resultados a una población más amplia, ya que ésta no es una finalidad de un estudio cualitativo, sino que parte de ellos o su esencia puedan aplicarse en otros contextos. En relación con este criterio, solo se entrevistaron emprendedores incubados en el CIE e Ingenio, por lo que los resultados de la investigación, en principio, no pueden aplicarse a otro tipo de emprendimientos, incubados en otras incubadoras u otros países.

El criterio de **autenticidad**, indica que tanto los participantes como los investigadores se expresen tal y como son, y las descripciones sean equilibradas y justas. Los investigadores dan fe de que se expresaron los pensamientos y opiniones reales y la información expuesta es fidedigna. En cuanto a los entrevistados, se confía y se asume que los datos vertidos son ciertos, pero no existe forma de comprobarlo.

Finalmente, el criterio de la **representatividad de voces** sugiere incluir a la mayor parte posible de los grupos de interés. Para este estudio, los autores se aseguraron de que los emprendimientos participantes sean específicamente de software.

7. Conclusiones y trabajos a futuro

En términos generales, el presente trabajo de investigación permitió identificar los principales motivos de pivoteo, las acciones que suelen tomar para implementarlos y elaborar una propuesta de modelo de proceso de pivoteo, así como la evaluación de la ejecución de los pivotes realizados.

Los factores más comunes que generan a los emprendimientos la necesidad de llevar a cabo pivotes son: "la reacción negativa de los clientes", "la reacción positiva de un segmento de clientes no previsto" y "enfocar el mercado objetivo". Por otra parte, el principal motivo para realizar pivotes tecnológicos es la búsqueda de "nuevas oportunidades" de negocio.

Los tipos de pivotes más empleados son "tecnología", "captura del valor", "equipo" y "segmento de cliente". Se aprecia que todos los emprendimientos ejecutaron pivotes y que en promedio cada uno de ellos realizó cuatro pivotes, siendo el primero efectuado antes de los dos primeros años.

Se encuentra que los emprendedores no siguen un método formal para pivotear, ni realizan reuniones regulares para ello, ya que la mayoría ejecuta los pivotes a prueba y error, mediante un aprendizaje directo de lo que sucede para decidir cambiar o perseverar. La mayor parte de los emprendimientos necesitó aprender habilidades comerciales, financieras y de marketing y ventas.

Los principales criterios de evaluación utilizados para medir el impacto de los pivotes son "facturación", "uso del producto" y "cantidad de usuarios", pero no emplean ningún marco de trabajo para medir el éxito o fracaso.

Se comprueba que realizar los pivotes no es una tarea sencilla, pero si existieran más emprendimientos que se animaran a realizar pivotes, podrían sobrevivir y crecer, reduciendo los altos niveles de fracaso en los primeros años de actividad. Además, se encontró que el *feedback* del cliente es fundamental para adaptar el producto o servicio a las necesidades del mercado, lo que les permite no perder demasiado tiempo y dinero.

Otro aspecto que se entiende relevante a la hora de pivotear es estar abierto a nuevas ideas y dejar de lado los preconceptos. Esto puede ser incómodo al principio, ya que implica reconocer que estaban equivocados inicialmente, pero es necesario para poder innovar y generar un mejor producto o servicio.

Como trabajos a futuro se plantea replicar el estudio, ampliando la muestra para incluir otros tipos de emprendimientos o incubadoras, y analizar si se puede hacer una generalización de los resultados. Así como realizar un estudio de caso para los emprendimientos de software participantes que presentan alguna particularidad, como el hecho de haber realizado más variedad de pivotes o haber realizado un mismo pivote más de una vez. Se proyecta utilizar el cuestionario cerrado como base para una encuesta y poder expandir el estudio a más emprendimientos de software y verificar si se dan resultados similares, al incluir los nuevos factores encontrados en este estudio.

Referencias

Bajwa, S. (2017) "Pivoting in Software Startups". PhD thesis, Free University of Bozen-Bolzano.

Bajwa, S. *et al.* (2017) "Start-Ups Must Be Ready to Pivot", *IEEE Software.*, Vol. 34, No. 3, pp. 18–22.

Bajwa, S., Wang, X., Nguyen Duc, A. and Abrahamsson, P. (2017) "'Failures' to be celebrated: an analysis of major pivots of software startups", Empirical Software Engineering, Vol. 22, No. 5, pp. 2373–2408.

Blank, S. and Dorf, B. (2020) "*The Startup Owner's Manual: The Step-By-Step Guide for Building a Great Company*", John Wiley & Sons.

Bohn, N. and Kundisch, D. (2018) "Much more than 'same solution using a different technology': antecedents and consequences of technology pivots in software startups", Multikonferenz Wirtschaftsinformatik, Lüneburg.

Giardino, C., N. Paternoster, Unterkalmsteiner, M, Gorschek, T. and Abrahamsson.P. (2016) "Software Development in Startup Companies: The Greenfield Startup Model", Information and Software Technology, Vol. 42, No. 6, pp. 585–604.

Grinnell. R. and Unrau, Y. A. Eds. (2004) "*Social Work Research and Evaluation: Quantitative and Qualitative Approaches",* 7th edition, New York: Oxford University Press.

Hernández Sampieri, R. Fernandez Collado, C. and Baptista Lucio, M. del P. (2014) "Metodología de la Investigación", 6th edition, México.

Ries, E. (2011) "The Lean Startup: How Today's Entrepreneurs Use Continuous Innovation to Create Radically Successful Businesses". Crown Publishing, New York

Terho, H., Suonsyrjä, S., Karisalo, A. and Mikkonen, T. (2015) "Ways to Cross the 'Rubicon: Pivoting in Software Startups", *Product-Focused Software Process Improvement*, pp. 555–568.

Unterkalmsteiner, M. *et al.* (2016) "Software Startups - A Research Agenda", e-Informatica Software Engineering Journal, Vol. 10, No. 1, pp. 89–123.autore

Refactoring Assertion Roulette and Duplicate Assert test smells: a controlled experiment

Railana Santana[1], Luana Martins[1], Tássio Virgínio[2], Larissa Soares[1,3], Heitor Costa[4], Ivan Machado[1]

[1] Federal University of Bahia (UFBA) – Salvador, BA – Brazil
[2]Federal Institute of Tocantins (IFTO) – Paraíso do Tocantins, TO – Brazil
[3]State University of Feira de Santana (UEFS) – Feira de Santana, BA – Brazil
[4]Federal University of Lavras (UFLA) – Lavras, MG – Brazil

railana.santana@ufba.br, martins.luana@ufba.br, lrsoares@uefs.br, tassio.virginio@ifto.edu.br, heitor@ufla.br, ivan.machado@ufba.br

Abstract. *Test smells can reduce the developers' ability to interact with the test code. Refactoring test code offers a safe strategy to handle test smells. However, the manual refactoring activity is not a trivial process, and it is often tedious and error-prone. This study aims to evaluate* `RAIDE`*, a tool for automatic identification and refactoring of test smells. We present an empirical assessment of* `RAIDE`*, in which we analyzed its capability at refactoring Assertion Roulette and Duplicate Assert test smells and compared the results against both manual refactoring and a state-of-the-art approach. The results show that* `RAIDE` *provides a faster and more intuitive approach for handling test smells than using an automated tool for smells detection combined with manual refactoring.*

1. Introduction

Writing automated tests requires more than just understanding the business rules implemented in the source code, as the test engineer should be skilled enough to build well-structured test cases. In addition, the complexity of the system under test aligned with the lack of knowledge and experience may lead test engineers to use bad practices to either design or implement the test code [Garousi and Küçük 2018].

Bad design practices in the test code are commonly referred to as test smells [Van Deursen et al. 2001]. Test smells have recently gained importance given their effects on the performance of software testing activities, especially from a maintenance perspective [Virgínio et al. 2020b, Aljedaani et al. 2021]. For instance, *Empty Test* is a test smell that occurs when a test method does not contain any executable instructions. Since the method does not have a body, the test always passes. When developers introduce behavior-breaking changes, an empty test does not notify alternated outcomes [Van Deursen et al. 2001, Peruma et al. 2019].

While good testing practices and guidelines can prevent test smells, test engineers do not always follow them. In particular, whether a software project already comprises a large set of tests, it may not be cost-effective to create novel tests from scratch. An alternative is to employ test-specific refactoring strategies to improve the test code quality without changing its behavior [Van Deursen et al. 2001]. Due to the lack of test suites aimed to test themselves, there is a need for automated tools to refactor the test code and keep its behavior.

The literature has introduced a small set of automated tools to refactor test code [Aljedaani et al. 2021]. For example, `RTj` [Martinez et al. 2020] is a command-line tool that supports detecting and refactoring Rotten Green Tests, i.e., a test that passes during execution but has assertions rarely executed. `DARTS` [Lambiase et al. 2020] is an IntelliJ plugin that supports detecting and refactoring three test smells (General Fixture, Eager Test, and Lack of Cohesion of Test Methods). These tools address a small number of test smells when using the JUnit framework to develop test cases. [Aljedaani et al. 2021] point out that the existing tools do not provide details concerning the accuracy of their refactoring capabilities or usability. To expand the set of refactoring strategies for test smells, we previously presented a systematic approach to detect and refactor two test smells: *Assertion Roulette* (AR) and *Duplicate Assert* (DA). In addition, we implemented `RAIDE`, automated tool support for test smell refactoring [Santana et al. 2020]. `RAIDE` is an open-source tool with a user-friendly interface that can detect and refactor test smells with just a few clicks.

In this paper, we present an empirical study to evaluate `RAIDE`. We aimed to answer the Research Question: ***How does `RAIDE` support users to detect test smells and refactor the test code?*** As the related tools do not support refactoring strategies for the AR and DA test smells, we compared `RAIDE` with manual refactoring. We asked twenty test engineers to refactor test code from two projects. While using `RAIDE`, the test engineers had access to an interface integrated into the Eclipse IDE. They could detect and refactor the test smells. Otherwise, for the manual refactoring, the test engineers used the `tsDetect` to detect the test smells. This is a state-of-the-art test smell detection tool [Peruma et al. 2019], Given that `tsDetect` does not allow automated refactoring, the participants had to use their strategies to refactor the test smells.

In summary, we contributed with a controlled experiment to compare `RAIDE` with one state-of-the-art approach and discuss the usefulness of an IDE-integrated tool that automatically detects and refactors test smells. Controlled experiment findings can support the community of researchers and developers in building and maintaining intuitive tools to detect and refactor test code automatically. Besides, we collected the participants' perceptions of the tools, e.g., the `RAIDE` and `tsDetect` limitations, a feedback key to the continuity and evolution of these tools.

The remainder of this paper is structured as follows. Section 2 introduces the concept of test smells and the `RAIDE` and `tsDetect` tools. Section 3 details the experiment design and the main results. Section 4 discusses the evaluation results. Section 5 presents the threats to the validity. Section 6 presents related work. Section 7 concludes the paper.

2. Background

Test smells result from bad design choices implemented in the test code [Greiler et al. 2013b]. Smells in test code can affect its quality, mainly understandability and maintainability. Consequently, test smells can reduce the effectiveness of test cases to detect faults and the developers' ability to interact with the test code [Yusifoğlu et al. 2015].

Although there are several test smells, some of them are more prevalent. [Palomba et al. 2016] empirically evaluated the diffusion of test smells in automatically generated JUnit test classes in 110 open-source software projects. The results showed that

83% of those classes are affected by at least one test smell. The most frequent test smells were the *AR* (54%) and *Test Code Duplication* (33%). In our study, we considered *DA*, once it is a representative type of *Test Code Duplication* test smell.

In addition, [Peruma 2018] conducted a large-scale empirical study on the test smells occurrence, distribution, and impact in the maintenance of open-source Android applications. They also observed that the *AR* test smell occurred in more than 50% of the test classes. In a multivocal literature review, [Garousi and Küçük 2018] reported the most extensive catalog of test smells and a summary of guidelines, techniques, and tools to handle test smells. The authors pointed out that test smells related to code duplication and code complexity (test redundancy and long test, respectively) have been the most discussed ones in the literature.

The recurring number of studies reporting on the occurrence of the *AR* test smell [Peruma 2018, Palomba et al. 2016] and the repercussion on test smells related to code duplication [Garousi and Küçük 2018] led us to investigate those two test smells and then propose `RAIDE`. We next introduce these test smells.

2.1. Assertion Roulette (AR)

In JUnit, *assertions* have an optional first argument of the String type to explain what each *assertion* is testing. AR occurs when a test method has several undocumented *assertions*, making understanding difficult during maintenance and challenging to detect the *assertion* if the method fails. Listing 1 presents a code excerpt with multiple *assertions* without a return message (lines 93 to 95). The example presents a method from the `TestAbstractPartial.java`[1] test class of the **Joda-Time** project.

```
90 public void testGetValues() throws Throwable {
91     MockPartial mock = new MockPartial();
92     int[] vals = mock.getValues();
93     assertEquals(2, vals.length);
94     assertEquals(1970, vals[0]);
95     assertEquals(1, vals[1]);
96 }
```

Listing 1. Test code with the Assertion Roulette test smell

Possible Effect: Multiple *assertion* statements in a test method without a descriptive message can affect test readability, comprehensibility, and maintainability. Multiple *assertions* make it difficult to detect which assertion gave an error in a test failure.

Detection: To check if a test method has *assertions* without explanation/message (parameter in the *assertion* method).

Refactoring: To include *assertion* explanations in each *assertion*. Listing 2 shows the Listing 1 code refactored with the appropriate explanations for each assert (text highlighted in yellow).

2.2. Duplicate Assert (DA)

DA occurs when a test method tests the same condition multiple times in the same test method [Peruma et al. 2019]. Listing 3 shows a code excerpt with two *assertions* with

[1]Available at `https://bit.ly/35Q56KV`

```java
public void testGetValues() throws Throwable {
    MockPartial mock = new MockPartial();
    int[] vals = mock.getValues();
    assertEquals("Vals size 2", 2, vals.length);
    assertEquals("Year Equal 1970", 1970, vals[0]);
    assertEquals("Month 1", 1, vals[1]);
}
```

Listing 2. Test code after refactoring the Assertion Roulette test smell

the same parameters (lines 361 and 363). The example presents one method from the `TestPeriodFormatterBuilder.java`[2] test class of the **Joda-Time** project.

```java
356 public void testPluralAffixParseOrder() {
357     PeriodFormatter f = builder.appendDays()
358         .appendSuffix("day", "days").toFormatter();
359     String twoDays = Period.days(2).toString(f);
360     Period period = f.parsePeriod(twoDays);
361     assertEquals(Period.days(2), period);
362     period = f.parsePeriod(twoDays.toUpperCase(Locale.ENGLISH));
363     assertEquals(Period.days(2), period);
364 }
```

Listing 3. Test code with the Duplicate Assert test smell

Possible Effect: That test smell hinders test readability and maintenance, as there are repeated assertions (with the same parameters) without explaining the purpose/objective of the test method. In general, DA creates a scenario that violates the responsibility of each method to fulfill a single objective.

Detection: To check if the test method contains two or more *assertion* statements with the same parameters.

Refactoring: To create one test method for testing the same condition with different values. Listing 4 shows a code excerpt from Listing 3 refactored (text highlighted in yellow), which extracts the duplication for a new method (`testPluralAffixParseOrderExtracted`).

```java
public void testPluralAffixParseOrder() {
    PeriodFormatter f = builder.appendDays().
        appendSuffix("day", "days").toFormatter();
    String twoDays = Period.days(2).toString(f);
    Period period = f.parsePeriod(twoDays);
    assertEquals(Period.days(2), period);
}

/* Extracted Method */
public void testPluralAffixParseOrderExtracted() {
    PeriodFormatter f = builder.appendDays().
        appendSuffix("day","days").toFormatter();
    String twoDays = Period.days(2).toString(f);
    Period period = f.parsePeriod(twoDays.toUpperCase(Locale.ENGLISH));
    assertEquals(Period.days(2), period);
}
```

Listing 4. Test code after refactoring the Duplicate Assert test smell

[2] Available at `https://bit.ly/3oriGL1`

2.3. `tsDetect`

`tsDetect` has been reported in a recently published literature review as a comprehensive tool for detecting test smells in Java projects [Aljedaani et al. 2021]. The tool covers 19 test smells with a precision score ranging from 85% to 100% and a recall score from 90% to 100% in open-source Android apps [Peruma et al. 2019]. Given those precision and recall scores, researchers built `tsDetect`-based tools [Virgínio et al. 2020a, Kim et al. 2021]. `tsDetect` tool indicates the existence of test smells in a test class based on a three-step detection process (Figure 1): 1) *Test File Detector* - reads the project test files; 2) *Test File Mapping* - links the test files to the production files under test; and 3) *Test Smell Detector* - detects smells in test code.

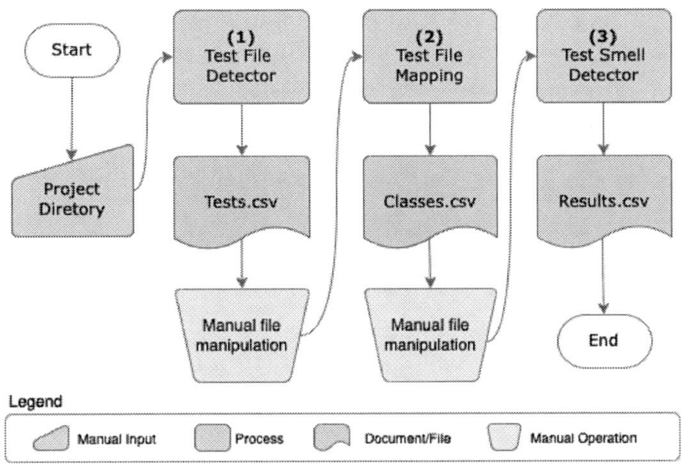

Figure 1. Process for running the `tsDetect` tool

In step (1), *Test File Detector* generates the `Tests.csv` file, which contains the path of the test classes from one software project. That file is input to *Test File Mapping*. Next, step (2) establishes the relationship between the test and production classes. It creates the `Classes.csv` file, which contains the project name, the path of each test class, and the production classes. That file is input to *Test Smell Detector*. Step (3) is responsible for analyzing test smells for the project based on the `Classes.csv` file. The output is the `Results.csv` file, which indicates the presence (true) or absence (false) of test smells in the test classes.

2.4. `RAIDE`

`RAIDE` is an AST (Abstract Syntax Tree)-based tool developed as an Eclipse open-source plugin to detect and refactor test smells [Santana et al. 2020]. We reused rule-based components from `tsDetect` and performed improvements to detect test smells. Whereas `tsDetect` works as a command-line tool that indicates the presence of test smells, `RAIDE` has a user-friendly Graphical User Interface (GUI), which identifies and indicates the exact location (code lines) of the AR and DA test smells. Besides, it includes one feature for automated refactoring of those test smells.

For the test code refactoring activity to succeed, the detection must be precise and explicit, pointing to the source code line where the test smell is located. However, not all tools report the exact location of test smells. For instance, the `tsDetect` only informs whether a class is affected by a test smell. Thus, the users need to analyze the entire test class to identify the test smells and refactor them. Conversely, `RAIDE` exhibits the test smells exact location for users and provides a user-friendly GUI.

`RAIDE` uses graphical components from `JDeodorant`[3], an Eclipse plugin, to detect and refactor code smells in java code and reuses the components `tsDetect` tool: i) AST of the project, responsible for detecting test classes and code structure; and ii) AR test smell detection rules. In addition, we improved the detection rules to meet the scenario with an empty string ("") or space string (" ") in the explanation parameter and inform the line affected by the test smell. The way `tsDetect` implements the DA test smell detection does not allow code reuse for accurately detecting each test smell in `RAIDE`. Therefore, we built modules from scratch in `RAIDE` to detect and refactor the DA test smell and to refactor the AR test smell. Some limitations of `RAIDE` include: i) the implementation of detection rules is based on JUnit 4, other JUnit versions may require adaptations in such rules; and ii) the tool's execution detects the *Assertion Roulette* or *Duplicate Assert*, not both at the same time.

Figure 2 shows the `RAIDE` tool process to identify and refactor test smells. The user should provide as input: the **test package** of the project under analysis, and the test smell the plugin should detect and refactor. In step (1), the **test classes detection** identifies all JUnit classes in the **test package**. In step (2), the **test smells detection** detects a specific type of test smell and presents the **test smell detection results** in an Eclipse view. In step (3), **manual test smells selection** requires the user intervention to select which test smell instances(s) he would like to refactor. Then, in step (4), `Test smells refactoring` shows the user how to refactor the code, and the user can take the decision of accepting the **refactored test code**.

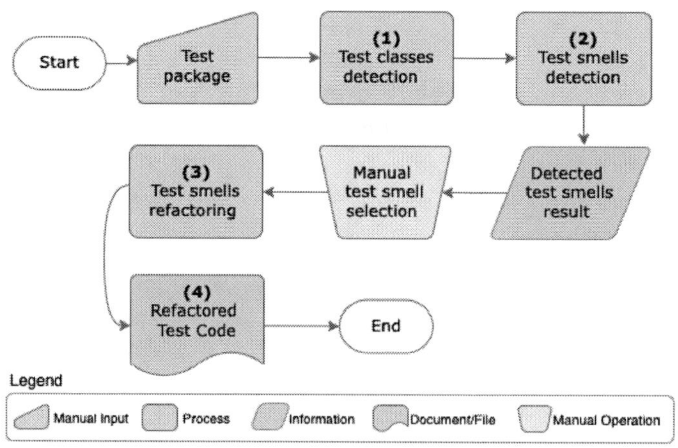

Figure 2. Process for running the RAIDE tool

Figure 3 shows a screenshot of the Eclipse IDE with the `RAIDE` plugin running on the Joda-Time[4] project. `RAIDE` refactored line 131 of method `testGetFieldTypes()` after detecting the AR test smell. `RAIDE` included the explain parameter "Add Assertion Explanation here" to correct that test smell. The user

[3]Available at `https://github.com/tsantalis/JDeodorant`
[4]Available at `https://github.com/JodaOrg/joda-time`

must replace the default string with an explanatory message about the assertion to remove the AR test smell from the code. In Figure 3, it is also possible to see that RAIDE also detected the AR test smell on line 132. After double-clicking on the detected test smell, the tool redirects the user to the highlighted line.

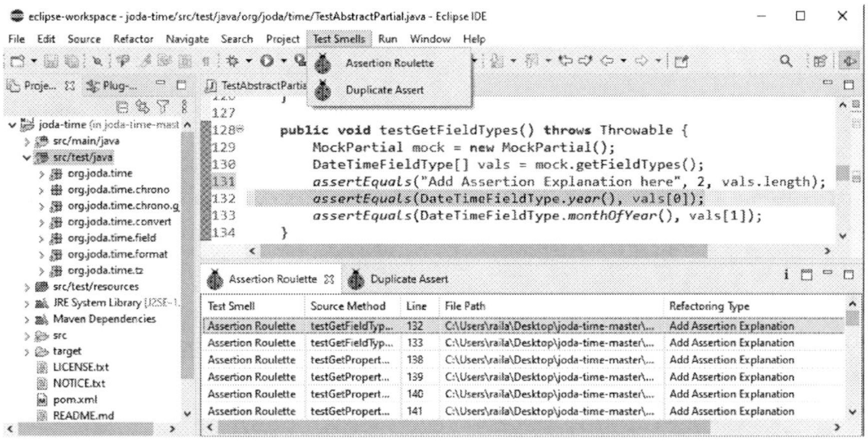

Figure 3. Screenshot of the RAIDE plugin under execution

3. Empirical Assessment

In this study, we carried out a controlled experiment to evaluate how the automated process proposed by RAIDE assists the test engineers to (i) detect test smells and (ii) refactor test code. To answer the main research question (RQ), we split it into two sub-RQs: **RQ_1)** How does RAIDE facilitate the AR and DA test smells detection compared to tsDetect? **RQ_2)** How does RAIDE facilitate the smelly test code refactoring with the AR and DA test smells compared to manual refactoring? For RQ_1, we compared RAIDE and tsDetect concerning how both detect test smells and show the results. For RQ_2, we compared refactorings with RAIDE to manual refactorings. Thus, we measured the participants' time taken to identify the test smells in the test code with the support of RAIDE and tsDetect. After, we measured the refactorings time performed manually and with RAIDE.

Experiment Overview. Before joining the experiment session, the participants filled out an online form with questions regarding their experience in software programming and testing, Java language, JUnit framework, Eclipse, and test smells. Next, we presented the concepts about test smells (AR and DA, particularly) and detection and refactoring processes. We also informed the objective of the experiment. Figure 4 shows an overview of the experiment steps. The participants performed two tasks, one for RAIDE and the other for tsDetect. Each task encompassed the analysis of a different software project. Before running the experiment, the participants received training on using and executing the tool shortly after. We used the same project in the training sessions of both tools (*Project 1* - Figure 4). After training, the participants performed the actual experiment tasks, as follows: (i) they used RAIDE and tsDetect to detect two test smells (AR and DA) and informed the location (code lines) of the test smells, and (ii) they refactored the code to remove the two test smells. Tasks 1 and 2 are similar, but the participants used different tools (either *Tool 1* or *Tool 2*) and projects (either *Project 2* or *Project 3*) (Figure

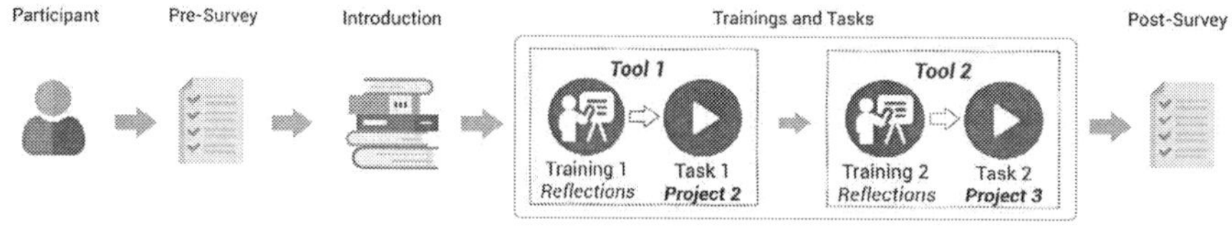

Figure 4. Experiment Flow

4). In the end, the participants answered an online post-survey[5], comprising questions about the experiment execution and their perception of each tool.

Pilot Study. We performed a pilot study with five participants, two graduate students, two practitioners, and another acting in both roles. We found that they took 47 seconds, on average, using `RAIDE` and 15 minutes, on average, using `tsDetect` to detect the test smells. The pilot study was critical in reviewing the concepts and standardizing the training, especially the commands needed to use `tsDetect`. It also was helpful to assess whether the participants could understand the tasks and tools. Data gathered in this pilot study was not considered in the final analysis.

Participants. We recruited twenty participants, where ten participants (50%) were from the academy, five participants (25%) were from industry, and five participants (25%) acted in both roles. All participants held at least a B.Sc. degree, seven participants (35%) were M.Sc. students, and seven participants (35%) were Ph.D. students. They come from sixteen different Brazilian institutions, eight different universities (U1 to U8), and eight different software development companies (C1 to C8). Some of them also belong to more than one institution (P1, P7, P12, P15, P17, P18, and P20). In addition, they have different roles: Agile Coach (AC), Developer (D), Database Admin (DA), Lecturer (L), Researcher (R), and Requirements Analyst (RA). Most participants (80%) had already heard about test smells. Six participants (30%) had specific knowledge about test smell in either industry or academia. Table 1 shows detailed information. Although the participant's profile was collected, we did not investigate the relationship between their experience and performance in carrying out the tasks.

Experiment Material and Tasks. We selected three open-source projects for this experiment: *Reflections* project for training and *Joda-Time* and *Commons-collections* projects for executing tasks 1 and 2 (*Project 2* and *Project 3* - Figure 4, but not necessarily in that order). We chose the projects considering the limitations of `RAIDE` and `tsDetect`, which support Maven projects and tests with JUnit (version 4). Due to the size of the projects, we decided to consider only two test classes for the experiment. Therefore, the *Reflections*, *Joda-Time*, and *Commons-collections* projects would have a similar complexity level, number of methods, and number of test smells. Regarding the test smells in the projects, one method has the AR test smell (4 *assertions* without explanation), and another one has two pairs of the DA test smell (4 *assertions* in the same method).

Design and Procedure. In our experiment, we used a crossover design [Vegas et al. 2015] to avoid the learning effect, as the participants performed two tasks in a row. The projects and the tools are the independent variables, and time is the dependent

[5]Available at `https://zenodo.org/record/5978022#.Yf55hOrMKUk`

Table 1. Participants' profile and experience (in years)

ID	Group	Education	Profile	Institution	Programming	JAVA	Eclipse	Testing	JUnit	Test Smells
P01	1	Ph.D. student	R/L	U1/U2	10+	10+	10+	10+	1⊢ 5	✓
P02	2	M.Sc. student	R	U1	10+	0-1	0-1	5⊢ 10	0-1	✳
P03	3	Ph.D. student	R	U1	0-1	0	1⊢5	1 ⊢5	1⊢ 5	✓
P04	4	B.Sc.	RA	C1	1⊢5	1⊢5	1⊢5	1⊢5	0-1	✗
P05	1	B.Sc.	D	C2	5⊢10	1⊢5	0-1	0-1	0-1	✓
P06	2	M.Sc. student	R/L	U1	5⊢10	1⊢5	1⊢5	1⊢5	1⊢5	✓
P07	3	Ph.D. student	R/L	U1/U3	1⊢5	1⊢5	1⊢5	5⊢10	0-1	★
P08	4	B.Sc.	L	U4	5⊢10	1⊢5	1⊢5	0-1	0	✗
P09	1	B.Sc.	D	C1	1⊢5	1⊢5	0	0-1	0-1	✓
P10	2	B.Sc.	D	C3	1⊢5	0-1	0-1	0-1	0	✗
P11	3	M.Sc. student	R/DA	U5	1⊢5	1⊢5	1⊢5	0	0	✳
P12	4	Ph.D. student	R/L	U1/U6	5⊢10	1⊢5	1⊢5	0-1	0-1	★
P13	1	Ph.D. student	R	U7	10+	1⊢5	1⊢5	0	0	★
P14	2	Ph.D. student	R	U1	1⊢5	1⊢5	0-1	0-1	0	☆
P15	3	M.Sc. student	R/D	U1/C4	1⊢5	1⊢5	0-1	0	0	✓
P16	4	B.Sc.	D	C5	5⊢10	1⊢5	1⊢5	1⊢5	1⊢5	✓
P17	1	M.Sc. student	R/AC	U5/C6	5⊢10	5⊢10	5⊢10	0-1	0-1	✓
P18	2	M.Sc. student	R/D	U1/C7	5⊢10	1⊢5	1⊢5	0	0	★
P19	3	Ph.D. student	R	U8	10+	10+	10+	10+	10+	✓
P20	4	M.Sc. student	R/D	U1/C8	1⊢5	1⊢5	1⊢5	0	0	✗

Labels: (✗) Never heard about them; (✓) Already heard anything about itthem, but had never worked with them; (☆) Knew a little bit about them; (★) Heard about test smells and had already worked with them; and (✳) Researcher investigating the topic of test smells.

variable of the experiment. During the experiment with each participant, we captured the audio and the computer screen to count later the time spent by them to detect and refactor the test smells in each task of the experiment. When a participant inaccurately identified or refactored the test smell, the researcher reported that the task had not been completed yet, and the time continued counting until the task be completed correctly.

Data Analysis. We performed the Shapiro-Wilk test, with a significance level of 5%, to verify the data distribution for the data analysis. As a result, the data distribution is not normal. Then, we selected the Mann-Whitney paired test [Mann and Whitney 1947], with a significance level of 5%, to answer RQ_1 and RQ_2 (sub-RQs). We defined the null hypothesis to investigate the RQ_1: *The detection time of AR and DA test smells with `RAIDE` is similar to detection with `tsDetect`.* Regarding the RQ_2, we defined the null hypothesis: *The refactoring time of AR and DA test smells with `RAIDE` is similar to manual refactoring.*

4. Results and Discussion

This section presents and discusses the results gathered from the empirical assessment.

4.1. Detection of Test Smells (RQ1)

We collected and analyzed the time spent by the participants to complete the task of detecting and locating the AR and DA test smells with `RAIDE` and `tsDetect` to answer RQ_1. The participants completed that task in 63.95 seconds (s) on average with a standard deviation (*sd*) of 28.12s using `RAIDE` and 679.20s on average with *sd* = 248.71s using `tsDetect`. Thus, those values suggest that detecting and locating the AR and DA test smells with `tsDetect` is slower than with `RAIDE`.

The difference between RAIDE and tsDetect is the first one to be an IDE-integrated tool, in which participants select the test smell they want to analyze and report the lines with the smells highlighted by the tool. In tsDetect, the participants need to run three different tools, open a .csv file to check which classes have test smells, and manually inspect the source code. Therefore, the participants spend most of the time using the Test File Detector and Test File Mapping tools and performing adjustments in the .csv files. Although the tools are similar in execution time, they present a wide difference in their efficiency regarding how fast they place the user in front of the test smells.

We also analyzed whether there is a statistically significant difference in identifying the AR and DA test smells. Since our data did not have a normal distribution (*p-value* = 7.748e-05), we performed the non-parametric Mann-Whitney test. The test indicated a significant difference (*p-value* = 9.537e-07) between the average time spent using tsDetect and RAIDE. Thus, we refuted the null hypothesis ($H_0 1$) and answered RQ_1. We also observed that data resulting from the time measures with tsDetect is more dispersed than the time using RAIDE. Figure 5 shows boxplots on a logarithmic scale comparing data gathered from RAIDE and tsDetect. There is no overlap between the boxes of RAIDE and tsDetect, which means a difference between them. In addition, the longest reported time for detecting the AR and AD test smells with RAIDE was much shorter than the shortest time to detect them with tsDetect. The participants using RAIDE achieved similar results in terms of efficiency. However, we can not say the same when they used tsDetect, which indicates that RAIDE standardizes how participants detect the AR and AD test smells, regardless of their experience.

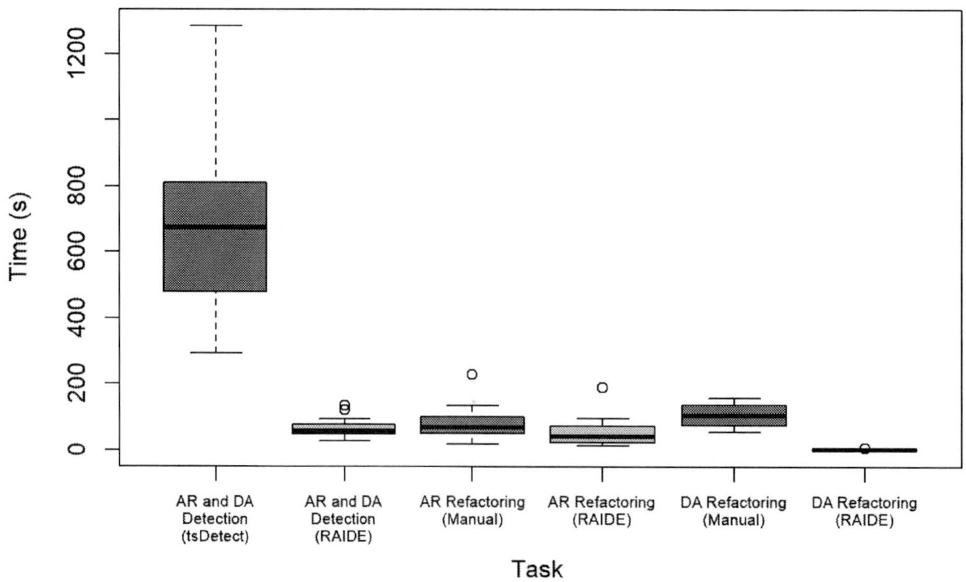

Figure 5. Comparison of the test smell detection and refactoring times between RAIDE and tsDetect

Our findings show that all participants encountered the AR and DA test smells faster with RAIDE than using tsDetect. The mean difference between the time of each task was more than 615s, considering all the steps needed to run tsDetect. Moreover, the participants pointed out many advantages that RAIDE would have over tsDetect related to identifying the AR and DA test smells. For example, according to P02, RAIDE stood out because *"The learning process is easier and faster, it has fewer steps to take. It integrates into a development tool with a graphical interface, facilitating its use. It also identifies the lines that each test smell occurs and suggests refactorings."*

Summary: The AR and DA test smells could be identified ten times faster with RAIDE than with the state-of-the-art tool. RAIDE offers a better user experience, e.g., it enables detecting test smells with just one click and highlights their location in the source code.

4.2. Test Code Refactoring (RQ2)

We collected and analyzed the time spent by the participants to refactor test code with the AR and DA test smells using RAIDE and tsDetect.

AR Refactoring. The participants could refactor the test code with RAIDE on an average of 49.9s (*sd* = 41.35s), while the manual refactoring took 78.30s (*sd* = 46.39s). As the refactoring of RAIDE is by line, we need to count the time spent by the user to select each test smell of the method correctly and refactor them individually. For the statistical analysis, we performed the Shapiro-Wilk normality test. We found that the refactoring time of the AR test smell does not have a normal distribution (*p-value* = 6.607e-05). Therefore, we also used the Mann-Whitney test. Although the refactoring with RAIDE has shown similar dispersion to manual refactoring, the results indicated a significant difference between automated refactoring and manual refactoring (*p-value* = 0.022). It leads us to understand that RAIDE has a shorter detection time, which refutes the null hypothesis ($H_0 2$). Figure 5 shows boxplots with such comparisons, the median line of the box of RAIDE is outside the box of manual refactoring, which confirms a difference between them.

DA Refactoring. Likewise the former, this analysis also considered the Shapiro-Wilk normality test (*p-value* = 7.69e-06) beforehand. Data normality test indicated no normal distribution, then used the non-parametric Mann-Whitney test. Our results showed a significant statistical difference between the refactoring of DA (*p-value* = 4.764e-05), confirming a significant difference between the refactoring with RAIDE and manual refactoring. Therefore, we refute the null hypothesis ($H_0 2$). The average time was 107.2s (*sd* = 35.86) and 2.55s (*sd* = 1.57s) for manual refactoring and using RAIDE, respectively. Figure 5 shows that the median line of the box of RAIDE is outside the box of manual refactoring, which confirms a difference between them.

In addition, from a more qualitative standpoint, we also considered the participants' comments on the refactoring with and without RAIDE. P01, P13, and P16 indicated that they would use RAIDE in their projects due to detecting and refactoring the AR and DA test smells. According to P17, RAIDE can increase productivity in the identification and refactoring process, and such resources try to decrease the chance of human error. According to P19, RAIDE is convenient because it visually shows the AR and DA test smells, and their removal is automated, which allows the user to understand the steps taken.

Summary: The difference between RAIDE and the manual process for refactoring the AR and DA test smells is significant. RAIDE was more than forty-two times faster than the manual process for refactoring the DA test smell. Also, there is a consensus regarding the participants' opinion about RAIDE. There is an indication that RAIDE makes it easier to refactor the AR and DA test smells.

4.3. Discussion

After analyzing the gathered data, we could infer that detecting the AR and DA test smells with tsDetect was the most time-consuming task. That result is related to the fragmentation of the tsDetect, which has three intermediary steps until it presents the results. We also highlight the tool's low usability and the laborious process to detect the location of the test smells in the test code.

The participants' feedback includes essential data we should consider. For example, P01 and P02 reported that although tsDetect treats more test smells than RAIDE, detecting test smells in the former is more cumbersome. They stated that it is necessary to manipulate several files, and the command-line interaction might make it difficult for the identification process. P03 and P06 highlighted that the test smells detection process with tsDetect takes longer than with the RAIDE. P04 claimed that the process performed by tsDetect is counterintuitive, i.e., users would need to repeat the steps more often to learn the process (the order of entry and exit of the files). P06 also mentioned that the results of tsDetect are not very expressive because it only reports the existence or not of test smells, which can lead to misinterpretation, especially when dealing with long test classes.

Furthermore, the tasks performed with RAIDE took an average of 1.94 minutes, against an average of 14.42 minutes to perform the tasks with tsDetect. In addition, we limited the number of classes and tested the smells of the projects used to experiment. Therefore, gathered data indicate that manual test code refactoring would take longer in real-world environments, even without RAIDE. Indeed, it is necessary to carry out further studies in this direction to either confirm or refute this statement.

5. Threats to Validity

Internal Validity. It refers to the effects of the treatments on the variables due to uncontrolled factors in the environment [Wohlin et al. 2012]. We used system training to introduce the tools and participants' tasks to mitigate this threat. We used randomization to assign the order of participants to the tasks to mitigate the learning effect. However, in realizing the assigned tasks, some participants presented difficulties in manually accomplishing the refactoring task (i.e., using the tsDetect). In this case, we guided them to find a solution that may positively influence those participants' performance using tsDetect.

External Validity. It concerns whether the results can be generalized outside the experimental settings [Wohlin et al. 2012]. To mitigate this threat, we counted on experts with different backgrounds. Although there was not a big difference in the number of practitioners and academics, we introduced the detection and refactoring concepts with the tools using a training system. Although the participants had no experience in the context of the experiment, they were skilled enough to perform the tasks.

Construct Validity. It represents the cause and effect concepts to measure in the experiment through dependent and independent variables [Wohlin et al. 2012]. In this study, we did not compare RAIDE with a tool that presents the same features. tsDetect tool detects several test smells but does not assist in refactoring them. Conversely, RAIDE detects two test smells and support their refactoring. In the end, we could compare the effects of both manual and automated refactoring. Also, we conducted a pilot study that helped us improve the experiment design and materials.

Conclusion Validity. It refers to the extension of the conclusions about the relationship between the treatments and the outcomes [Wohlin et al. 2012]. The main threat to conclusion validity is the small size of the sample. Although we carried out the controlled experiment with 20 participants, we selected most of them with some prior knowledge about test smell.

6. Related Work

[Greiler et al. 2013a] introduced the TestHound tool, which performs a test code static analysis to detect the smells: Dead Field, General Fixture, Lack of Cohesion of Test Method, Obscure In-Line Setup, Test Maverick, and Vague Header Setup. The tool suggests refactoring candidates for removing test smells. The authors conducted a study with users and showed that the tool helps developers understand and adjust the test code.

[Baker et al. 2006] proposed TRex, an Eclipse plugin that detects refactoring opportunities to Standardized Tree and Tabular Combined Notation (TTCN-3) test suites. TRex calculates metrics to measure the overall quality of a TTCN-3 test suite and applies a pattern-based analysis to suggest candidate test refactorings. Its accuracy in detecting/refactoring test smells in TTCN-3 test suites, and evaluation with practitioners are unknown.

[Martinez et al. 2020] released RTj, a command-line tool that performs static and dynamic analysis to detect rotten green test smells. RTj also suggests to developers candidate test refactorings. The authors pointed out that RTj detects some false positives due to using conditionals or multiple test contexts. However, there are no details concerning the accuracy of its refactoring capabilities nor experiments validating its usability.

[Lambiase et al. 2020] released DARTS (Detection And Refactoring of Test Smells), a plugin for IntelliJ that utilizes information retrieval to detect three smells (General Fixture, Eager Test, and Lack of Cohesion of Test Methods). They built the tool on top of TASTE [Palomba et al. 2018], a textual-based detector with an overall f-measure of 67%, 76%, and 72% for the three test smells mentioned above, respectively. The tool also offers refactoring support. As for the refactoring support available in the tool, DARTS exploits the IntelliJ APIs to ensure that the refactored code is compilable and error-free.

Compared with the related tools, RAIDE expands the support to detect and refactor other test smells [Santana et al. 2020]. During plugin development researchers with experience in test smells validated the automated refactorings applied by RAIDE.

7. Conclusion

Software test code refactoring is highly dependent on automated support, so it might be cost-effective. Current literature encompasses a few tools supporting automated test code refactoring. However, there is little evidence of automated support to handle test smells refactoring. In prior work, we introduced `RAIDE`, an Eclipse IDE plugin to automate the test smells detection and refactoring from the JUnit test code. That tool can handle Assertion Roulette and Duplicate Assert test smells in the current version. In this paper, we presented an empirical assessment of the `RAIDE`. We carried out a controlled experiment with twenty participants to evaluate the tool. The results indicate that `RAIDE` can detect test smells faster than a comparable state-of-the-art approach. Also, `RAIDE` was able to refactor a test method in a tiny fraction of time. In particular, the results were very favorable compared to the state-of-the-art approach. Future work directions include extending the `RAIDE` to consider other test smells and refactoring techniques. Furthermore, there is a need to conduct further empirical studies to validate whether the tool is valuable and effective in real-world practice.

Acknowledgments

This study was financed in part by the Coordenação de Aperfeiçoamento de Pessoal de Nível Superior - Brasil (CAPES) - Finance Code 001; and FAPESB grants JCB0060/2016 and BOL0188/2020.

References

Aljedaani, W., Peruma, A., Aljohani, A., Alotaibi, M., Mkaouer, M. W., Ouni, A., Newman, C. D., Ghallab, A., and Ludi, S. (2021). Test smell detection tools: A systematic mapping study. In *Evaluation and Assessment in Software Engineering*, page 170–180, New York, NY, USA. ACM.

Baker, P., Evans, D., Grabowski, J., Neukirchen, H., and Zeiss, B. (2006). Trex-the refactoring and metrics tool for ttcn-3 test specifications. In *Testing: Academic & Industrial Conference-Practice And Research Techniques*, pages 90–94, UK. IEEE.

Garousi, V. and Küçük, B. (2018). Smells in software test code: A survey of knowledge in industry and academia. *Journal of systems and software*, 138:52–81.

Greiler, M., van Deursen, A., and Storey, M.-A. (2013a). Automated detection of test fixture strategies and smells. In *60th International Conference on Software Testing, Verification and Validation*, pages 322–331, Luxembourg. IEEE.

Greiler, M., Zaidman, A., Deursen, A. v., and Storey, M.-A. (2013b). Strategies for avoiding text fixture smells during software evolution. In *Proc. of the 10th Working Conference on Mining Software Repositories*, pages 387–396, San Francisco, CA, USA. IEEE Press.

Kim, D. J., Chen, T.-H. P., and Yang, J. (2021). The secret life of test smells-an empirical study on test smell evolution and maintenance. *Empirical Software Engineering*, 26(5):1–47.

Lambiase, S., Cupito, A., Pecorelli, F., De Lucia, A., and Palomba, F. (2020). Just-in-time test smell detection and refactoring: The darts project. In *Proc. of the 28th International Conference on Program Comprehension*, page 441–445, New York, NY, USA. ACM.

Mann, H. B. and Whitney, D. R. (1947). On a test of whether one of two random variables is stochastically larger than the other. In *The annals of mathematical statistics*, volume 18, pages 50–60, Michigan. JSTOR.

Martinez, M., Etien, A., Ducasse, S., and Fuhrman, C. (2020). Rtj: A java framework for detecting and refactoring rotten green test cases. In *Proc. of the 42nd International Conference on Software Engineering: Companion Proceedings*, page 69–72, New York, NY, USA. ACM.

Palomba, F., Di Nucci, D., Panichella, A., Oliveto, R., and De Lucia, A. (2016). On the diffusion of test smells in automatically generated test code: An empirical study. In *Proc. of the 9th international workshop on search-based software testing*, pages 5–14, Austin, TX, USA. ACM, IEEE.

Palomba, F., Zaidman, A., and De Lucia, A. (2018). Automatic test smell detection using information retrieval techniques. In *2018 IEEE International Conference on Software Maintenance and Evolution (ICSME)*, pages 311–322, Madrid, Spain. IEEE.

Peruma, A., Almalki, K., Newman, C. D., Mkaouer, M. W., Ouni, A., and Palomba, F. (2019). On the distribution of test smells in open source android applications: An exploratory study. In *Proc. of the 29th Annual International Conference on Computer Science and Software Engineering*, page 193–202, USA. IBM Corp.

Peruma, A. S. A. (2018). *What the Smell? An Empirical Investigation on the Distribution and Severity of Test Smells in Open Source Android Applications.* Ph.d. thesis, Rochester Institute of Technology, Rochester, New York.

Santana, R., Martins, L., Rocha, L., Virgínio, T., Cruz, A., Costa, H., and Machado, I. (2020). RAIDE: a tool for assertion roulette and duplicate assert identification and refactoring. In *Proc. of the XXXIV Brazilian Symposium on Software Engineering - Tools Track*, pages 374–379, NY, USA. ACM.

Van Deursen, A., Moonen, L., Van Den Bergh, A., and Kok, G. (2001). Refactoring test code. In *Proc. of the 2nd international conference on extreme programming and flexible processes in software engineering (XP2001)*, pages 92–95, NLD. CWI (Centre for Mathematics and Computer Science).

Vegas, S., Apa, C., and Juristo, N. (2015). Crossover designs in software engineering experiments: Benefits and perils. *IEEE Transactions on Software Engineering*, 42(2):120–135.

Virgínio, T., Martins, L., Rocha, L., Santana, R., Cruz, A., Costa, H., and Machado, I. (2020a). Jnose: Java test smell detector. In *Proc. of the 34th Brazilian Symposium on Software Engineering*, SBES '20, page 564–569, New York, NY, USA. Association for Computing Machinery.

Virgínio, T., Martins, L. A., Soares, L. R., Santana, R., Costa, H., and Machado, I. (2020b). An empirical study of automatically-generated tests from the perspective of test smells. In *Proc. of the 34th Brazilian Symposium on Software Engineering*, page 92–96, New York, NY, USA. ACM.

Wohlin, C., Runeson, P., Höst, M., Ohlsson, M. C., and Regnell, B. (2012). *Experimentation in Software Engineering*. Springer.

Yusifoğlu, V. G., Amannejad, Y., and Can, A. B. (2015). Software test-code engineering: A systematic mapping. *Information and Software Technology*, 58:123–147.

Syntactic and Semantic Similarities and Discrepancies between Terms of Glossaries for Software Testing

Guido Tebes[1], Philip Lew[2], Luis Olsina[1]

[1]GIDIS_Web, Facultad de Ingeniería, UNLPam, General Pico, LP, Argentina

[2]XBOSoft, Woodbridge, VA, USA

{guido_tebes,olsinal}@ing.unlpam.edu.ar, philiplew@gmail.com

Abstract. *For software testing, this work performs a comparison and analysis of syntactic and semantic similarities and discrepancies between 3 glossaries. To conduct the study, 8 terminological categories were conceived, which were used to categorize each glossary term, considering the intended semantics. Also, to count the occurrence frequency of a term in the glossaries, a tool was built that also takes into account the matching of synonyms. Then, the analysis of similarities and discrepancies, as well as absent terms for a subset of them, is performed using metrics and expert interpretations. This study identifies several disagreements in standard terminologies that should merit further attention and efforts to promote harmonization amongst the authors/ publishers of these glossaries with the overarching end goal of assisting their readers in learning and understanding the domain of software testing.*

1. Introduction

Today, the software has penetrated every aspect of life. Marc Andreessen's famous quote "Why software is eating the world"[1] has become more than true. Also, many other similar quotes were declared; Mobile is eating the world, Apps are eating the world, Data is eating the world, etc., but the common theme is that we have become more dependent on software. Even traditional hardware-based companies like stereo speakers and garage door openers have been forced to become software companies as software integrates into their hardware devices and platforms.

But what about the quality of the software that has become so important to us? As new development methodologies and business models drive faster software delivery, what happens to the quality? Normally, when you drive a car faster, you have a higher probability of an accident. Hence, even though the software industry has become more mature in the last five decades, the artifacts produced still require more attention with regard to quality. The huge number of produced artifacts can range, for example, from software applications and technology infrastructures to supporting and training documentation. Software glossaries fall within the latter category of artifacts.

A glossary includes agreed entries, i.e., terms and their definitions –and occasionally synonyms, acronyms, and relevant notes- considering significant sources in a given domain. Glossaries certainly serve as a reference to establish a common ground

---

[1] https://www.ciodive.com/news/software-industry-marc-andreessen/605301/

for terms and definitions not only in learning and understanding but in communicating with others.

Thus, an entire profession and field have been focused on improving software engineering processes and any professional in the field of software engineering will have come across and used many glossaries, either in their formal training or in their daily work. In particular, most professionals in the field of software testing are familiar to some degree with glossaries such as ISTQB (International Software Testing Qualifications Board, (ISTQB, 2021)), TMMi (TMMi, 2018) and ISO 29119-1 (ISO/IEC/IEEE 29119-1, 2013).

Certifications in the software testing field and formal training are often based on some of these glossaries, and in light of this, it is important that these glossaries be of high quality. But what is quality when it comes to evaluating a glossary?

As a starting point, and without giving a complete answer to the previous question, the authors of this work carried out a syntactic and semantic analysis of the similarities and discrepancies of the terms in the three cited glossaries. Through a systematic categorization of terms along with an analysis of them, we have identified inconsistencies in these glossaries that we hope will benefit the profession in eliminating confusion and misunderstanding amongst their readers/users while also providing the authors of these glossaries a foundation for improvement.

Ultimately, we believe our categorization, measurements, metrics, and analysis techniques, can be utilized not only for the current three glossaries that we have analyzed but also for examining the quality of other glossaries from other professions in general.

The rest of the paper is organized as follows. Section 2 outlines some features and numbers of the three standard glossaries analyzed. Section 3 discusses the rationale for dividing testing domain terminologies into conceptual blocks or categories. Section 4 shows the qualitative and quantitative comparison and analysis of syntactic and semantic similarities and discrepancies between the three standard glossaries, highlighting the inconsistent use of the word "testing". Section 5 provides a summary of related work and discussion. Finally, Section 6 contains the conclusions and future work.

2. Overview of the Three Included Software Testing Glossaries

We chose these three glossaries because they are all focused on software testing. Even though their usage context, intended purpose and audience varies, they provide a common foundation and intersection of terms all related to software testing. This gives us common characteristics that can be extracted and analyzed as part of our exploratory study.

The ISO 29119-1 glossary (ISO/IEC/IEEE 29119-1, 2013) is part of a series of standards to be used by an organization when performing software testing as a reference for the other parts of the standard. All terms are thus included to assist those reading and interpreting the five parts of the standard by introducing concepts and vocabulary as a basis for understanding. TMMi (Test Maturity Model integration) is a reference model to support organizations to "improve their software and system testing and achieve higher and sustainable levels of product quality for the systems they are developing and maintaining. With TMMi, these organizations can assess and improve their test processes and, if required, become formally certified" (TMMi, 2018). Hence, the TMMi glossary is intended to support organizations in their test process improvement efforts. ISTQB (International Software Testing Qualifications Board) is a training and certification organization. Thus, its glossary (ISTQB, 2021) is intended to help those taking training and certification syllabus in understanding software testing and specifically to obtain certifications.

As mentioned, each of the glossaries has a different purpose and context, hence different size, scope, and audience related to the other materials in context. For example, ISTQB is intended to assist individuals whereas both ISO 29119-1 and TMMi are intended to assist larger organizational entities. While individuals studying for certifications may have different needs than organizations looking for definitions as a means for collaborative discussion, many of the terms intersect and have different usages as well as synonyms.

There have been other works that analyze glossaries, their structure, and characteristics, but from what we found, other research focuses on one glossary (Arnicane et al., 2016) rather than a comparison of like or similar glossaries, as we discuss later on.

As can be seen in Table 1, we did an initial analysis simply to understand the size and scale of each of the glossaries. The first metric, Total Number of Unique Terms per Glossary in the second row depicts that the ISTQB glossary is overwhelmingly larger than the other two. You might expect this since this glossary is intended to be all-encompassing in the field of software testing for individuals desiring professional certifications. The other two glossaries, intended to be used by organizations in the industry either in the act of software testing or attempting to improve their test processes, are lighter by several orders of magnitude. The third row shows the number of synonyms in each of the glossaries, and the last row shows the total of unique terms plus synonyms to denote the total scale.

We will examine these metrics and many others in subsequent sections.

Table 1. Basic numbers for the three software testing glossaries

Metric name/acronym	ISO 29119-1	TMMi	ISTQB
Glossary Standard version/year	1st Ed./2013	v1.2/2018	v3.5/2021
Total Number of Unique Terms per Glossary (#UTxG)	88	279	588
Number of Synonyms per Glossary (#Sy= #TwithSxG - #UTxG)	17	4	160
Total Number of Terms with Synonyms per Glossary (#TwithSxG)	105	283	748

3. Terminological Categories for Terms in Software Testing

Despite the many attempts to standardize testing terms structured in glossaries by different official and *de facto* initiatives, such as ISO, TMMi, and ISTQB, as well as attempts to document testing terms, properties, and relationships structured in ontologies by different researchers as recently analyzed in Tebes et al., (2020), there is often a lack of a broad consensus in the software testing literature and among practitioners on the explicit definition of the terms and their usage. Regarding software testing glossaries, Arnicane et al., (2016) found quality issues in the ISTQB glossary related to consistency, completeness, and correctness. Instead of this study focusing only on a glossary, the present work attempts to obtain evidence for syntactic and semantic similarities and discrepancies between the three aforementioned glossaries for a subset of categorized terms.

To perform the study, eight terminological categories were conceived, which were used to categorize each glossary term, considering the semantics intended by the authors of the standards. The inclusion of terms in categories was carried out at first independently by the authors of the present work, and then we met many times to verify consistency. As a result of this verification via video streaming, some issues were raised and categorization discrepancies in the placement of terms according to the given semantics were agreed upon and resolved.

Table 2 shows the eight terminological categories we designed for domain terms in software testing glossaries. The terms included in categories 1 (C1) to 6 (C6) are specific to the testing domain. Additionally, C7 encompasses terms somewhat related to testing, while C8 includes terms beyond the testing domain that pertains to broader fields such as software engineering or quality.

Table 2. Names of the eight terminological categories for terms in software testing glossaries

Category ID	Terminological Category name
C1	Test Project-, Strategy-, Organizational Test-related Terms
C2	Testing Work Process-, Activity-related Terms
C3	Test Goal-, Requirements-, Entity-related Terms
C4	Test Work Product-related Terms (e.g. Artifact, Report, Result, Specification)
C5	Testing Method-, Technique-, Procedure-, Rule-related Terms
C6	Testing Agent-, Role-, Tool-related Terms
C7	Other Terms somewhat related to Test (e.g., Anomaly, Defect, etc.)
C8	Terms beyond the Test Domain related to Quality or Software Engineering

The main rationale for designing categories C1 to C6 is as follows. After analyzing both the results of the conducted Systematic Literature Review of primary studies on conceptualized software testing ontologies (Tebes et al., 2020) and the state-of-the-art testing-related standards, we decided to develop a software testing top-domain ontology named TestTDO (Tebes et al., 2021). In the process of defining the ontology scope using competency questions, we found it helpful to devise conceptual blocks for them. From these blocks, we now design the categories C1 to C6 shown in Table 2. The key terms used in the label of each category name are terms or properties in TestTDO, so the reader can refer to their definitions in Tebes et al., (2021) or, for a quick reference, in http://arxiv.org/abs/2104.09232.

Let's briefly analyze C2 and C5. Category 2 is labeled "Testing Work Process-, Activity-related Terms". It is intended to include glossary terms with the semantics of the testing process, activity or task. In other words, the terms testing process, activity, or task encompass the meaning of 'what to do' rather than 'how to do' a testing activity. Instead, Category 5 is devoted to including testing method terms, which have the semantics of 'how to do' a testing activity/task description. C5 is labeled "Testing Method-, Technique-, Procedure-, Rule-related Terms" in Table 2. For example, the term Testing Method is defined in Tebes et al., (2021) as "a specific and particular way to perform the specified steps for a task included in a Testing Activity". The explicit semantic distinction between glossary terms that represent 'what to do' and 'how to do' has a clear benefit for understanding. For instance, for the same Design Testing activity (what to do), different Testing Design Methods (how to do) can be assigned (Tebes et al., 2021). About a decade ago, Henderson-Sellers et al., (2014) noted that a highly visible and challenging definition that is urgently needed to ensure that ISO standards are consistent with other industry usage is that of 'method' versus 'process'.

When searching terminological categories for software testing glossary terms, we found two works in the literature. One of them is the test classification of the ISTQB glossary represented in a recent draft document. It has the following categories: Testing, Software Engineering, Requirements, Quality, and General. Note that the Testing category is the only one specific to the testing domain; although the Requirements category includes some terms specific to testing as well. Thus, in order to categorize glossary terms, we have designed six categories as stated above, in which terms for Test Requirements fall in C3. Therefore, for the rest of the ISTQB categories, we have conceived C7 and C8. It is worth noting that the scope of a glossary is generally a bit broader than the domain of software testing. According to the authors of ISTQB: "Some related non-testing terms are also included if they play a major role in testing, such as terms used in software quality assurance and software lifecycle models".

The other somewhat related work for categorization carried out by Kuļešovs et al., (2013) aims at structuring testing ideas into eight classes. For example, the class called "How to test (approach, method, technique)?" corresponds mainly to C5 and, to a lesser extent to C1, in which the testing approach and strategy-related terms are placed. However, an explicit class for C2 (Testing Work Process-, Activity-related Terms) is missing in Kuļešovs et al., (2013).

As a result of our classification, the reader can find the ISO glossary terms categorized in Appendix II of the document at http://bit.ly/ComplementaryResults. The TMMi glossary terms and the ISTQB glossary terms are classified in Appendixes III and IV, respectively.

Table 3 shows the numbers of classified terms and percentages for categories 2 and 5 of the three analyzed glossaries. The numbers for all categories and proportions are in Appendix V of the aforementioned linked document.

Table 3. Numbers and percentages for Categories 2 and 5 of the three software testing glossaries. Recall that the values for #UTxG (Total Number of Unique Terms per Glossary) are in Table 1

Metric name/acronym	ISO 29119-1	TMMi	ISTQB
Number of Unique Terms per Glossary for Category2 (#UTxGC2)	45	43	103
Percentage of Unique Terms per Glossary for Category2 [%UTxGC2 = (#UTxGC2 / #UTxG) * 100]	51.14%	15.41%	17.52%
Number of Unique Terms per Glossary for Category5 (#UTxGC5)	2	27	46
Percentage of Unique Terms per Glossary for Category5 [%UTxGC5 = (#UTxGC5 / #UTxG) * 100]	2.27%	9.68%	7.82%

The next section deals with the qualitative and quantitative comparison and analysis of syntactic and semantic similarities and discrepancies between the analyzed standard glossaries only for C2 and C5.

The underlying hypothesis in this work is that considering both the syntactic and semantic aspects of the terms according to the authors of the glossaries, many of those that fell into C2 should be in C5, and vice versa. In other words, there are syntactic and/or semantic inconsistencies between terms of glossaries found in C2 (what to do) and C5 (how to do), which could hinder understandability.

To carry out this exploratory study, we calculated the Total Sum of Unique Terms considering the summed values shown in Table 1. This result is in the first row of Table 4. Then, the sum of unique terms for the categories C2 and C5 is 266, which represents 27.85% of the total of unique terms (955). It is important to remark that C8, which includes 334 terms beyond the testing domain represents 34.97%.

Table 4. Summed values of the three software testing glossaries just for Categories 2 and 5. Recall that the #UTxG (Total Number of Unique Terms per Glossary) values are in tables 1 and 3

Metric name/acronym	Value
Total Sum of Unique Terms [TUT = (#UTxISO + #UTxTMMi + #UTxISTQB)]	955
Total Sum of Unique Terms for Category2 [TUTC2 = (#UTC2xISO + #UTC2xTMMi + #UTC2xISTQB)]	191
Total Sum of Unique Terms for Category5 [TUTC5 = (#UTC5xISO + #UTC5xTMMi + #UTC5xISTQB)]	75
Total Sum of Unique Terms for Categories2&5 [TUTC2&5 = (TUTC2+ TUTC5)]	266
Percentage of Unique Terms for Categories2&5 [%TUTC2&5 = (TUTC2&5 / TUT) * 100]	27.85%

4. Analysis of Glossary Terms considering Syntactic and Semantic Similarities and Discrepancies

This Section illustrates our analysis results of syntactic and semantic similarities and discrepancies amongst the three glossaries as shown in subsection 4.2. It is important to remark that we have developed a tool to support the syntactic frequency calculation between the three glossaries. The followed procedure by the tool to calculate syntactic matching between glossary terms is documented in subsection 4.1. Finally, subsection 4.3 documents other issues detected in the glossaries such as absences and inconsistencies, among others.

4.1. Procedure to Syntactically Match Terms Between Glossaries

When we started to collect all terms and their corresponding synonyms in each software testing glossary we observed several situations. For example, the ISO glossary has the Organizational Test Strategy term, the TMMi glossary has the Test Strategy term and the ISTQB glossary also has the Test Strategy as a main term in addition to the term Organizational Test Strategy as a synonym of Test Strategy. In analyzing this situation, we have concluded that the term Test Strategy (or Organizational Test Strategy as a synonym) has a syntactic frequency of 3. This result means that the term Test Strategy is present in the three analyzed glossaries. We have concluded this result since we consider that if we have a term with one or more synonyms, we take into account the name of the term or any of its synonyms to calculate the syntactic comparison with another term (or synonym) from another glossary. In other words, in the previous example, the ISTQB glossary terms named Test Strategy or Organizational Test Strategy are used interchangeably in the frequency calculation but count as a single term.

Another situation we had was the following. The ISTQB glossary has the main term "white-box testing" with the following synonyms: clear-box testing, code-based testing, glass-box testing, logic-coverage testing, logic-driven testing, **structural testing**, and structure-based testing. In addition, the ISO glossary has the main term "structure-based testing" with the following synonyms: **structural testing**, glass-box testing, and white box testing. Finally, the TMMi glossary has only the term "white-box testing" without synonyms.

In conclusion, the term "white-box testing" has a syntactic frequency of 3. One way to obtain this result is that "white-box testing" has as a synonym the term "structural testing" in the ISTQB glossary, and the ISO glossary has the term "structural testing" as a synonym of the "structure-based testing" term. Therefore, we have a syntactic matching between the terms of these two glossaries. In addition, the TMMi glossary has the term "white-box testing" which syntactically matches with the term "white-box testing" of the ISTQB glossary and, therefore, the TMMi glossary "white-box testing" term syntactically matches with the term structure-based testing of the ISO glossary or any of its synonyms (structural testing, glass-box testing, and white box testing) by transitivity between glossary terms and synonyms. Note that we can obtain the same result (i.e., a frequency of 3) in different ways, for example considering the "structure-based testing" synonym in ISTQB and the main term "structure-based testing" in ISO. Additionally, at this point, it is important to remark that we consider removing the hyphens in the terms for the syntactic analysis. Note that ISO has the term "white box testing" and the other glossaries have the term "white-box testing".

Therefore, considering the above examples, we have used the following rule when we calculated the syntactic frequency between glossary terms: *Let's suppose that we have the term T1 in the glossary G1, and T2 is a synonym of T1. Also, we have the term T2 in the glossary G2, and T3 is a synonym of T2. Then, if we have the term T3 in the glossary G3, the term T1 syntactically matches with the term T3 by transitivity of terms and synonyms between glossaries. Therefore, T1 (or T2 or T3) has a syntactical frequency of 3.*

We have developed a tool that follows this rule to automatically calculate the syntactic matching between glossary terms and their synonyms.

4.2. Analysis of Syntactic and Semantic Similarities and Discrepancies

Once obtained the results of the syntactic frequency for each glossary term by using the procedure described in subsection 4.1, we calculated the numbers and percentages shown in Table 5. Note that we used a set of metrics, as described below.

The first metric shown in Table 5 is the Number of Terms with Frequency 3 in Categories2&5 (#TFq3C2&5). Note that frequency 3 implies a syntactic similarity of the same term, considering the synonyms, in the three glossaries, e.g., we found the same term "static testing" in the three glossaries. Also, we found 15 terms more with a frequency of 3, so the #TFq3C2&5 is 16 in total.

Table 5. Metrics and their values for the terms' syntactic frequencies of the three software testing glossaries. Recall that TUTC2&5 (Total Sum of Unique Terms for Categories2&5) = 266 according to Table 4

Metric name/acronym	Value
Number of Terms with Frequency 3 in Categories2&5 (#TFq3C2&5)	16
Percentage of Terms with Full Syntactic Similarity in Categories2&5 [%TFSySC2&5 = ((#TFq3C2&5*3) / TUTC2&5) * 100]	18.05%
Number of Terms with Frequency 2 in Categories2&5 (#TFq2C2&5)	48
Percentage of Terms with Partial Syntactic Similarity in Categories2&5 [%TPSySC2&5 = ((#TFq2C2&5*2) / TUTC2&5) * 100]	36.09%
Number of Terms with Frequency 1 in Categories2&5 (#TFq1C2&5)	122
Percentage of Terms without Syntactic Similarity in Categories2&5 [%TwSySC2&5 = (#TFq1C2&5 / TUTC2&5) * 100]	45.86%
Percentage of Terms with Full Syntactic Similarity for All categories C1-C8 (%TFSySforAll)	13.51%
Percentage of Terms with Partial Syntactic Similarity for All categories C1-C8 (%TPSySforAll)	32.67%
Percentage of Terms without Syntactic Similarity for All categories C1-C8 (%TwSySforAll)	53.82%

Then, we calculated the Percentage of Terms with Full Syntactic Similarity in Categories2&5 (%TFSySC2&5) and it resulted in 18.05%. At this point, it is important to remark that the metric %TFSySC2&5 uses the value obtained in #TFq3C2&5 multiplied by 3 since we have 3 terms for each term with frequency 3. Also, the total amount of terms in the calculated percentage is 266 corresponding with TUTC2&5 since we consider only C2 and C5 in this work.

Additionally, we have calculated the same metrics but considering all categories (C1-C8) and we obtained that the Percentage of Terms with Full Syntactic Similarity for All categories C1-C8 (%TFSySforAll) is 13.51% ≅ ((43*3)/955)*100 (note that 955 corresponds with TUT in Table 4).

Analogously to what we did for terms with syntactic frequency 3, we did the same for terms with syntactic frequency 2 and 1. For frequency 2, the Number of Terms with Frequency 2 in Categories2&5 (#TFq2C2&5) is 48. This implies that a term in a certain glossary syntactically matches with another term of only one of the other 2 remaining glossaries. For example, the term "acceptance testing" is in ISTQB and TMMi glossaries, and the term "accessibility testing" is in ISTQB and ISO glossaries. Hence, the Percentage of Terms with Partial Syntactic Similarity in C2 and C5 (%TPSySC2&5) is 36.09% (((48*2)/266)*100). Additionally, the Percentage of Terms with Partial Syntactic Similarity for All categories C1-C8 (%TPSySforAll) is 32.67% (((156*2)/955)*100).

The reader can see the other obtained values for frequency 1 in Table 5. Note that a term with frequency 1 implies that the term name is only in one of the glossaries.

If we compare the obtained results shown in Table 5, we can conclude that the three glossaries have few terms included in C2 and C5 with full syntactic similarity (18.05%) and in general (for all categories) as well (13.51%). Moreover, most glossaries terms in C2 and C5 have a frequency of 1 (45.86%) and, considering all categories, also most terms have a frequency of 1 (53.82% ≅ (514/955)*100).

Table 6. Metrics and their values for syntactic frequencies and semantic similarities/discrepancies of glossaries' terms are taken from the data processed and recorded in Appendix VI at http://bit.ly/ComplementaryResults. Recall that TUTC2&5 (Total Sum of Unique Terms for Categories2&5) = 266 according to Table 4

Metric name/acronym	Value
Number of Terms with Full Semantic Similarity for Frequency 3 in Categories2&5 (#TFSSFq3C2&5)	11
Number of Terms with Partial Semantic Similarity for Frequency 3 in Categories2&5 (#TPSSFq3C2&5)	5
Number of Terms with Full Semantic Similarity for Frequency 2 in Categories2&5 (#TFSSFq2C2&5)	47
Number of Terms without Semantic Similarity for Frequency 2 in Categories2&5 (#TwSSFq2C2&5)	1
Percentage of Total Terms with Full Syntactic and Semantic Similarity in Categories2&5 [%TTFSSSC2&5 = (#TFSSFq3C2&5 * 3/ TUTC2&5) * 100]	12.41%
Percentage of Total Terms with Partial Semantic Similarity in Categories2&5 [%TTPSSC2&5 = ((#TPSSFq3C2&5 * 2 + #TFSSFq2C2&5 * 2)/ TUTC2&5) * 100]	39.10%
Percentage of Total Terms without any Semantic Similarity for Categories2&5 [%TTwSSC2&5 = ((#TPSSFq3C2&5 + #TwSSFq2C2&5 * 2 + #TFq1C2&5) / TUTC2&5) * 100]	48.49%

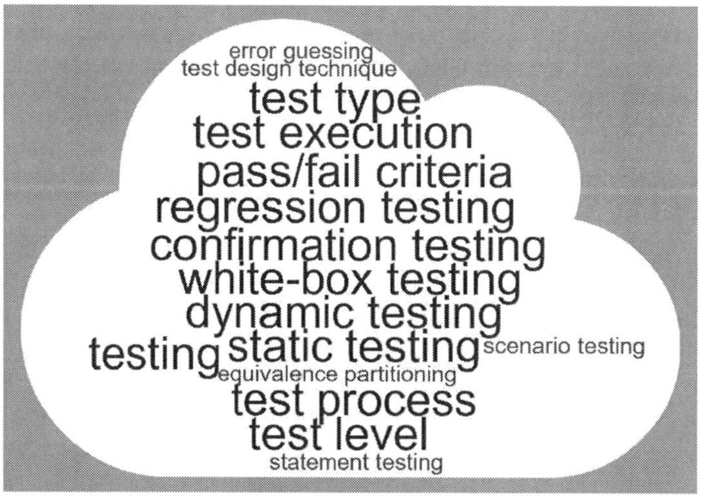

Figure 1. Word cloud for glossary terms with a full syntactic similarity that includes 16 terms with a syntactic frequency of 3 in Categories 2 and 5. Among them, the largest terms (11 blue terms) have full semantic similarity, while the smallest terms (5 red terms) have partial semantic similarity

On the other hand, in Table 6, we illustrate the results of metrics related to semantic similarities. Regarding the semantic similarities and discrepancies of the 16 terms with a syntactic frequency of 3, only 11 terms have full semantic similarity, i.e., the 3 syntactically same terms in the three glossaries have the same intended semantics as well. The remainder 5 terms have a partial semantic similarity, i.e., they have a semantic similarity of only 2 terms out of 3.

We show in Figure 1 a word cloud that illustrates the names of the abovementioned 16 terms with a syntactic frequency of 3. Note that the biggest size terms (blue highlighted) have a full semantic similarity while the smaller ones (red highlighted) have a partial semantic similarity. For example, the term "white-box testing" has a full semantic/syntactic similarity, and the term "test design technique" has a full syntactic similarity but partial semantic similarity.

In order to explain what a "semantic matching" between two terms from 2 glossaries with the same syntax means in this work, we will use Table 7.

As shown in Table 7, the term "white-box testing" (or structure-based testing) is a kind of "dynamic testing" in ISO. Also, the term "dynamic testing" is a kind of "testing", which in turn is a set of activities. Then, we conclude that testing, dynamic testing, and structure-based testing fall in C2 since they are terms related to processes and activities according to their definitions. Something similar happens for the term "white-box testing" in the other 2 glossaries.

Therefore, the term "white-box testing" falls in the same category for the three glossaries. In addition, if we analyze the 3 definitions in-depth, we can conclude that the three glossaries mention the structure of the test object (i.e., the test item, system or component) and therefore the intended semantics of the term is the same for the three glossaries according to our judgment.

Table 7. Definitions of the "white-box testing" and "test design technique" terms in the three analyzed glossaries, as well as some related terms with their definitions

Term	Definition	Glossary	Category
structure-based testing	**Dynamic testing** in which the tests are derived from an examination of the **structure** of the **test item**. *Recall that "structure-based testing" is a synonym of "white-box testing" in ISO 29119-1.*	ISO 29119-1	C2
white-box testing	**Testing** based on an analysis of the **internal structure** of the **component or system**.	ISTQB	C2
white-box testing	**Testing** based on an analysis of the **internal structure** of the **component or system**.	TMMi	C2
dynamic testing	**Testing** that requires the execution of the test item.	ISO 29119-1	C2
testing	**Set of activities** conducted to facilitate discovery and/or evaluation of properties of one or more test items	ISO 29119-1	C2
testing	**The process** consisting of all lifecycle activities, both static and dynamic…	ISTQB	C2
testing	**The process** consisting of all lifecycle activities, both static and dynamic…	TMMi	C2
test design technique	**activities**, concepts, **processes**, and patterns used to construct a test model that…	ISO 29119-1	C2
test technique	A **procedure** used to define test conditions, design test cases, and specify test data. *Recall that "test technique" is a synonym of "test design technique" in ISTQB.*	ISTQB	C5
test design technique	**Procedure** used to derive and/or select test cases.	TMMi	C5

On the other hand, if we do the same analysis for the term "test design technique", we conclude that the intended semantics for the term in the TMMi and ISTQB glossaries is technique/procedure and, therefore, falls in C5, unlike ISO glossary that has process/activity semantics (C2).

In the literature is recognized that "white-box testing" and "black-box testing" are 2 common terms broadly used in the software testing community. We were surprised by the fact that the term "black-box testing" does not have a syntactic frequency of 3. We investigated this situation and we realize that the term "black-box testing" with the semantics of process/activity (C2) appears only in the ISO and TMMi glossaries, but in the ISTQB it only has the term "black-box test technique" with the semantics of method/technique (C5).

4.3. Other Detected Issues

When we look at the results of the Percentage of Terms without Syntactic Similarity in Categories2&5 (%TwSySC2&5 = 45.86%) and Percentage of Terms without Syntactic Similarity for All categories C1-C8 (%TwSyS-forAll = 53.82%) in Table 5, we can note that most glossaries' terms do not have a syntactic similarity with other glossary terms.

This issue implies, on the one hand, a large absence of terms in the glossaries. A cause of this is the different proportions of glossaries' terms. As shown in Figure 2 (a), ISTQB contributes to TUTC2&5 (Total Sum of Unique Terms for Categories2&5 in Table 4) with more than half of all the glossaries' terms. Likewise, as shown in Figure 2 (b), the same happens for the glossaries' terms considering all categories (C1-C8).

On the other hand, another cause of this problem is that we found some terms with the same semantic but with different syntax, and therefore these terms have a syntactic frequency of 1. Just to mention a few examples, the terms "test completion" in ISTQB and "test completion process" in ISO; "maintenance testing" (ISTQB) and "maintainability testing" (ISO); "test monitoring" (ISTQB) and "test monitoring and control process" (ISO); among others.

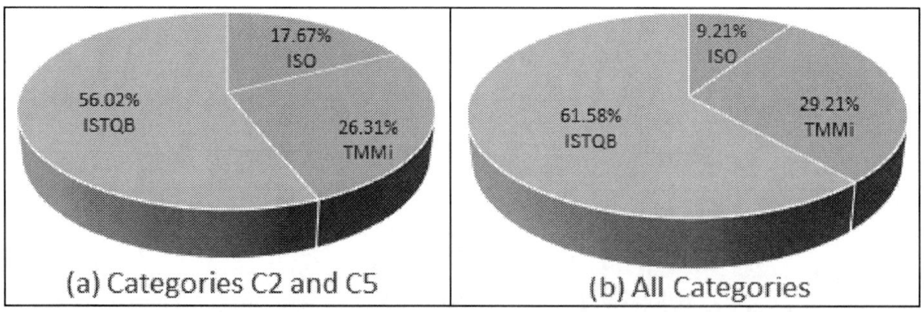

Figure 2. The ratio of glossaries' terms for C2 and C5 (a); and for all categories C1-C8 (b)

Another detected issue is related to the inconsistent use of the term "testing". The three glossaries consider that the term "testing" has the semantics of process/activity (i.e., related to C2). Table 8 shows in the %TTeTC2xG (Percentage of Total Terms that end with the word "Testing" in Category2 per Glossary) metric that most of the terms ending with the "testing" word in their names (or synonymous) fall in

C2 in these glossaries. Recall that we classified the terms by analyzing their given semantics and not the term name.

However, only ISO uses the "testing" word consistently (%TTeTC2xG = 100%). ISO includes 28 terms that end with the word "testing" in the term name and, considering that the "testing" term definition has the semantics of activity/process, these 28 terms fall in the category C2 accordingly. The same does not happen in the other two glossaries, since the metric %TTeTC2xG gives 62.07% in TMMi and 75% in ISTQB. This could lead to interpretation problems and ambiguities in these glossaries.

Although ISO uses the "testing" word consistently in C2, we noted in the definition of the term "test design technique" that it has the given process/activity semantics when it should have the method/technique semantics (i.e., related to C5 as TMMi and ISTQB did). Besides, ISO has the terms "statement testing" and "scenario testing", and we categorized them in C2 since their definitions mention that are a kind of "test design technique" and therefore, considering that in ISO semantically a "test design technique" falls in C2, then these 2 terms fall in C2 as well.

However, if the given semantics of "test design technique" were more coherent, some terms such as "statement testing" and "scenario testing" would fall in C5 and ISO will not be 100% consistent with using the word "testing" in the terms' names.

Table 8. Metrics and their values related to terms' names that end with the word "testing" in Categories 2 and 5

Metric name/acronym	Values per Glossary		
	ISO 29119-1	TMMi	ISTQB
Total Number of Terms that end with the word "Testing" in Categories2&5 per Glossary (#TeTC2&5xG = #TeTC2xG + #TeTC5xG)	28	29	84
Total Number of Terms that end with the word "Testing" in Category2 per Glossary (#TeTC2xG)	28	18	63
Percentage of Total Terms that end with the word "Testing" in Category2 per Glossary [%TTeTC2xG = (#TeTC2xG / #TeTC2&5xG) * 100]	100%	62.07%	75%
Total Number of Terms that end with the word "Testing" in Category5 per Glossary (#TeTC5xG)	0	11	21
Percentage of Total Terms that end with the word "Testing" in Category5 per Glossary [%TTeTC5xG = (#TeTC5xG / #TeTC2&5xG) * 100]	0%	37.93%	25%

5. Related Work and Discussion

To the best of our knowledge, no directly related work in the literature considers a comparative analysis of syntactic and semantic similarities and discrepancies for a set of software testing glossaries.

In order to look at related work in digital libraries, we primarily searched Scopus with a variety of keywords and operators, even including glossaries outside the software testing domain. The result was less than 10 papers, which two authors of this work analyzed in depth. Among them, the most relevant research was carried out by Arnicane et al., (2016). Contrary to our research, they analyzed only inconsistencies in one software testing glossary, without conducting a comparative analysis.

In Arnicane et al., (2016) the authors detected many syntactic and semantic issues in the ISTQB glossary. For example, they detected that the terms “test process” and “testing” have the same semantics in ISTQB, that is, one of them can be supposed as a redundant term in the glossary and they should be synonymous. We noted that the same situation happens in the other 2 glossaries.

Focusing on the results evidenced in Section 4 and taking into account the underlying hypothesis stated in Section 3, we would like to outline at least one simple suggestion that can promote harmonization, homogeneity, and ultimately quality improvement.

Regarding the syntactic aspect of naming terms in C2 (what to do) and C5 (how to do), we recommend a clear distinction between them, for example, adding the word “technique” to some terms in C5. Thus, “regression testing” has the meaning of process/activity in all three glossaries due to the definition of the word “testing” (recall Table 7), and the intended semantics given to it by the authors of the glossaries. So, this is reasonable, but, “statement testing” has the method/technique/procedure semantic in ISTQB and TMMi, so we suggest syntactically disambiguating it by using the term “statement testing technique”. Instead, in ISO there is also a semantic inconsistency, as noted at the end of subsection 4.3.

6. Concluding Remarks and Future Work

This paper has presented the results of analyzing the syntactic and semantic similarities and discrepancies between terms of three analyzed glossaries for software testing documented in ISO 29119-1 (ISO/IEC/IEEE 29119-1, 2013), TMMi (TMMi, 2018) and ISTQB (ISTQB, 2021). We have supported this analysis by using a set of metrics in addition to a set of categories which helped us to semantically categorize all glossaries' terms.

It is important to point out that the analysis carried out in this paper focused only on categories 2 and 5, namely: software testing terms for work processes/activities and method/techniques/procedure, respectively. In conclusion, as shown in Table 6, we found few syntactic/semantic matching between the terms of the three analyzed glossaries. Also, among other issues, we noticed an inconsistent use of the word “testing”, as we have documented in subsection 4.3.

Recalling the hypothesis mentioned in Section 3, which states that many terms with the semantics of process/activity (category 2 –what to do) should have the semantics of method/technique (category 5 –how to do it) and vice versa, we can confirm that hypothesis based on the obtained results.

Therefore, we recommend to the authors of the glossaries make a clear distinction between terms with the semantics of process/activity (e.g., those terms that finish with the word “testing”) and terms with the semantics of method/technique/procedure, which should finish with the words “testing technique” or “testing design technique”. We argue that by making this distinction explicit, the glossaries can foster terminological homogeneity and improve understandability when learning concepts.

In future work, we will include category 1 (C1, Test Project-, Strategy-, Organizational Test-related Terms) in the analysis of the glossaries' terms. We already observed that exist some terms that end with the word "testing" in the term name that fall in C1. This issue could cause misunderstanding in the glossary reader since the term "testing" has the semantics of process/activity, and in C1 the reader would expect to find terms with the semantics of strategy/approach/project/organization.

Additionally, in future work, we will put more emphasis on the sub-characteristics and attributes of information quality that can be considered for evaluation and comparison, such as semantic correctness, completeness of coverage, and non-redundancy of coverage, syntactic and semantic consistency, among others.

Acknowledgments. This line of research is supported partially by the Engineering School at UNLPam, Argentina, in the project coded 09/F079, and named "Family of Strategies for Functional and Non-Functional Software Testing considering Different Test Goal Purposes".

References

Arnicane, V., Arnicans, G., & Borzovs, J. (2016). Building of Concept System to Improve Systematic Collection of Terminology. *Frontiers in Artificial Intelligence and Applications*, volume *291*, 313–326. https://doi.org/10.3233/978-1-61499-714-6-313.

Henderson-Sellers, B., Gonzalez-Perez, C., McBride, T., Low, G. (2014). An ontology for ISO software engineering standards: 1) Creating the infrastructure. *Computer Standards & Interfaces*, *36*(3), 563–576. https://doi.org/10.1016/j.csi.2013.11.001.

ISTQB. (2021). International Software Testing Qualifications Board. *ISTQB®: Standard Glossary of Terms used in Software Testing*, version 3.5. https://www.istqb.org/

ISO/IEC/IEEE 29119-1. (2013). *Software and systems engineering – Software Testing – Part 1: Concepts and definitions.*

Kuļešovs, I., Arnicane, V., Arnicans, G., & Borzovs, J. (2013). Inventory of Testing Ideas and Structuring of Testing Terms. *Baltic Journal of Modern Computing*, *1*(3–4), 210–227.

Tebes, G., Olsina, L., Peppino, D., & Becker, P. (2021). Specifying and Analyzing a Software Testing Ontology at the Top-Domain Ontological Level. *Journal of Computer Science & Technology (JCS&T)*, *21*(2), 126–145. https://doi.org/10.24215/16666038.21.e12

Tebes, G., Peppino, D., Becker, P., Matturro, G., Solari, M., & Olsina, L. (2020). Analyzing and documenting the systematic review results of software testing ontologies. *Information and Software Technology*, volume *123*, 1–23. https://doi.org/10.1016/j.infsof.2020.106298

TMMi. (2018). TMMi Foundation. *Test Maturity Model Integration (TMMi®) - Guidelines for Test Process Improvement*, Release 1.2.

Tool support to aligning requirements and testing through behaviour-driven requirements patterns

Pollyana de Queiroz Ribeiro[1], Ernesto F. Veiga[2], Mariana C. Martins[2], Auri M. R. Vincenzi[3], Taciana N. Kudo[2], Renato F. Bulcão-Neto[2]

[1]Universidade Estadual de Goiás, Santa Helena de Goiás, Brazil

[2]Instituto de Informática, Universidade Federal de Goiás, Goiânia, Brazil

[3]Departamento de Computação, UFSCAR, São Carlos, Brazil

`pollyana.queiroz@ueg.br, auri@ufscar.br, {taciana,rbulcao}@ufg.br`

Abstract. *The software industry still struggles with adverse effects of a weak alignment between requirements and testing. The Software Pattern Metamodel (SoPaMM) aligns requirements and test patterns under the influence of agile practices. However, these patterns will be more beneficial for professionals if development activities are supported by a software tool. This paper presents the behaviour-DRivEn Application Model generator (DREAM) tool, automatically generating requirements and test specifications from SoPaMM-based patterns. We show how DREAM supports requirements elicitation and specification, test case elaboration, and software documentation using a patterns catalogue for electronic health record systems.*

1. Introduction

Requirements reuse is a feasible approach to lessen the negative impacts on software projects whenever Requirements Engineering (RE) activities are inadequately executed [Irshad et al. 2018]. Reusing the knowledge acquired in previous projects allows making the RE activities more prescriptive and systematic while facilitating the reuse of existing requirements artifacts and improve teams' productivity [Barros-Justo et al. 2018].

Among the requirements reuse approaches existing, we have investigated the theory and practice of software requirements patterns (SRP). An SRP is an abstraction that combines behaviours and services common to several systems and that can be reused in similar software [Withall 2007]. The use of SRP in software projects positively affects RE activities, e.g., saving time and improving the quality of requirements regarding completeness, uniformity, consistency, and clarity [Da Silva and Benitti 2013].

Recent work [Kudo et al. 2019a] shows that those benefits acquired with SRP are primarily focused on the RE process, despite the intrinsic relationship between RE outcomes and the remaining software development phases. For instance, consider the established association between requirements and system tests and between business cases and acceptance tests. However, despite the knowledge accumulated over the years, the industry still copes with adverse effects resulting from a weak alignment between requirements and testing [Bjarnason and Borg 2017].

In light of this, we elaborated on a metamodeling solution to relate SRP to outcomes produced over the software development life cycle [Kudo et al. 2022]. Our solution called

Software Pattern MetaModel (SoPaMM) associates SRP with software test patterns (STP) that are high-value testing solutions to recurrent behaviours in various scenarios. Besides, we implemented the Terminal Model Editor (TMEd) tool for supporting the development process of pattern catalogues as SoPaMM instance models [Kudo et al. 2020]. Using TMEd, we have built pattern catalogues, e.g., for Brazilian Electronic Health Record (EHR) systems. [Kiatake et al. 2021, Kudo et al. 2020].

However, aligning requirements and testing through SoPaMM, pattern catalogues, and TMEd is not enough for the software industry. TMEd-supported pattern catalogues compile recurrent requirements and test cases for a given application domain. These catalogues are built upon domain experts' knowledge and represented under the SoPaMM grammar, i.e., in such abstract form not suitable for professionals [Kudo et al. 2020]. Thus, there is a need for a tool that automates RE and testing activities, reducing software team members' cognitive load.

This paper presents the behaviour-DRivEn Application Model generator prototype (DREAM). The DREAM's current version focuses on the automatic generation of software artifacts from pattern catalogues built using TMEd. We show how DREAM maps each element of a pattern catalogue to produce specification documents of requirements and test cases and a requirement traceability matrix. Information items applicable to RE and testing [ISO/IEC/IEEE 2018, ISO/IEC/IEEE 2013] and their content influenced the generation of documents by the DREAM tool.

To illustrate the DREAM capabilities, we describe a scenario in which it reads the pattern catalogue we made for EHR systems [Kudo et al. 2020]. The DREAM tool is the first ongoing work capable of generating software specifications from behaviour-driven requirement pattern catalogues to the best of our knowledge. As developed, we believe DREAM can automate RE and testing-related tasks, save development time, and reduce the team's workload.

This paper is organised as follows: Section 2 analyses related work; Section 3 presents theoretical background; Section 4 describes how DREAM supports RE and testing activities; and Section 5 brings final remarks and future work.

2. Related Work

The SERS tool [Benitti and Silva 2013] provides requirement analysts with user and project management facilities, search, selection, and reuse of requirement patterns, requirements recommendation and tracing, and requirements specification documentation and printing. Similarly, PABRE-Proj [Palomares et al. 2013] users can manage projects, import and browse catalogues, reuse requirement patterns, and generate requirements specifications. Also, PABRE-Proj allows the generation of calls for tender documents and usage statistics for patterns. PABRE-Proj is the one that most resembles DREAM because the catalogues' information items also rely on a metamodel.

Besides aiding requirements elicitation and specification through pattern catalogues reuse, the computational support proposed in [Barcelos and Penteado 2017] provides requirement professionals with pattern catalogues specification and management. This functionality is similar to TMEd's, whose pattern catalogues generated are DREAM inputs. In turn, the InstRP Editor [Beckers et al. 2013] assists professionals in selecting and instantiating cloud-based security requirements using a cloud system analysis pattern.

In brief, every tool, including DREAM, reads requirement pattern catalogues, allows patterns reuse aiding elicitation, and generates requirements specifications as instances of the catalogue's content. As the SoPaMM-based catalogues bridge requirement and test patterns, DREAM goes further by also documenting test case specifications traced to requirements.

3. Background

This section presents components required to comprehend the DREAM support in our behaviour-driven requirement pattern approach: the Software Pattern MetaModel (SoPaMM) and the Terminal Model Editor (TMEd) tool.

3.1. The SoPaMM Metamodel

The SoPaMM metamodel describes how requirement patterns and test patterns are specified, related, and classified [Kudo et al. 2022]. The Catalogue is the coarsest grained reuse unit for collecting software pattern-related concepts in SoPaMM. A Software Pattern Bag (SPB) comprises Software Pattern (SP) elements that, in turn, are extensible points to allow different types of SP, such as requirement, test, or other software patterns. Thus, the SPB concept allows organising, in the same catalogue, software patterns for problems at various software development stages. SoPaMM is flexible regarding relationship types between catalogues, SPBs, and SPs by not predefining them (e.g., dependence and usage [Withall 2007]).

We have focused on how to bridge functional requirement patterns (FRP) and acceptance test patterns (ATP). Under the influence of the BDD agile methodology, an FRP is a composition of Features, written as user stories, whose behaviours are described as scenarios using the BDD's Gherkin syntax.

Consider the following excerpt of the FRP for user account creation. Its feature describes the administrator user allowed to register a new user for the system. This feature has two behaviours represented: a successful and an unsuccessful scenario, both linked to the same precondition (the attempt of creating a new user). However, the scenarios' execution steps are distinct regarding the user data's validity. Similarly, one different outcome is represented for each scenario, i.e., the new user registration and the display of an error message.

Finally, the Example concept allows defining and linking multiple data to each scenario. Thus, each scenario has one data instance so that one scenario registers a new user successfully. In contrast, the other scenario does not due to an invalid example of user identification number. This FRP-Feature-Scenario-Example representation is what defines our *behaviour-driven functional requirement pattern* approach.

```
FRP Name: FRP_User_Creation
  FEATURE User creation
    As: an administrator
    I_can: create a new user
    So_that: he/she is registered for the system
    SCENARIO Successful user creation
      Given: I am trying to create a new user
      When: I enter <ITRN>, <name>, <gender>, <date of birth>,
            <father's name>, <mother's name>, <role>
      Then: the system should register a new user with these data
      EXAMPLE
        735.101.320-92 | Carlos Chagas | Male | 01.01.2000 |
```

```
    Jose Chagas | Carla Chagas | Doctor
  SCENARIO Not successful user creation - Invalid ITRN
   Given: I am trying to create a new user
   When: I enter an invalid <ITRN>
   Then: the system should display the <message> error message
   EXAMPLE
    735.101.320-00 | "This is an invalid individual taxpayer
    registration number (ITRN)"
ATP Name: ATP_User_Creation
 TEST CASE Successful user creation
  InputData = EXAMPLE of SCENARIO Successful user creation
  OutputData = EXAMPLE of SCENARIO Successful user creation
 TEST CASE Not successful user creation - Invalid ITRN
  InputData = EXAMPLE of SCENARIO Not successful user creation -
  Invalid ITRN
  OutputData = EXAMPLE of SCENARIO Not successful user creation -
  Invalid ITRN
```

Aligned to the FRP_User_Creation, the ATP_User_Creation is composed of two test cases, each related to a particular test scenario: (un)successful user creation. Each test case contains preconditions (Given), expected results (When), and postconditions (Then), as well as input and output test data from the respective Example of Scenario. Thus, this is how an ATP verifies compliance against a specific FRP in our approach. Further details about the SoPaMM metamodel can be found elsewhere [Kudo et al. 2019b, Kudo et al. 2022].

3.2. *Terminal Model Editor* (TMEd)

SoPaMM borrows the MetaObject Facility's (MOF) four-layered architecture [OMG 2002] in which lower-layer models are instances of immediately upper-layer models. In the M2 layer, SoPaMM has the MOF metametamodel as a reference model. In the M1 layer, SoPaMM instances are pattern catalogues (or terminal models) built on our TMEd tool. These pattern catalogues follow the SoPaMM grammar constructors presented in Section 3.1, such as Catalogue, SPB, FRP, Feature, Scenario, Example, ATP, etc.

As pattern catalogues' development is not a trivial task, domain experts usually build these through tool support. Developed on top of the Eclipse Modeling Framework (EMF), the TMEd's user interface allows the creation and edition of every SoPaMM component (e.g., SPB, FRP, and ATP) and the generation of an XML output file following the SoPaMM grammar. That output file then feeds the DREAM tool to generate real-world software specifications (or application models, as in the M0 layer).

4. The DREAM tool

DREAM is a web tool developed in these technologies: Java and JavaScript languages, Spring framework (backend), Angular with TypeScript (frontend), and PostgreSQL as DBMS. DREAM supports RE and testing activities through pattern catalogues produced by the TMEd tool. These catalogues include FRP and ATP represented following the SoPaMM metamodel grammar presented previously. DREAM helps requirements teams in the elicitation, specification, and documentation activities. Besides, it also aids testing professionals in elaborating and documenting test cases.

Overall, the DREAM's main requirements include, but are not limited to: user account management; basic software project management; TMEd-based pattern catalogue importing;

imported catalogues search; the exhibition of each catalogue element's contents (e.g., SPB and SP); the association of catalogues with a software project; the reuse of individual catalogue elements supporting requirements elicitation and test case elaboration; and the automatic generation of requirement and test case specifications based on international standards, such as ISO/IEC 29148 [ISO/IEC/IEEE 2018] and ISO/IEC 29119-3 [ISO/IEC/IEEE 2013].

4.1. Supporting requirements elicitation and test case elaboration through patterns reuse

DREAM provides a set of functionalities to support requirements elicitation and test case development through reuse and the automatic generation of artifacts, i.e., software requirements specification (SRS), test case specification (TCS), and traceability matrix (TM). The DREAM user can create and manage software projects as well as register new catalogues or reuse ones already registered. Figure 1(i) depicts a DREAM user interface with the following functionalities: (A) project update; (B) project members; (C) project statistics (mainly related to reuse); (D) associate a patterns catalogue to the current project; (E) view patterns reused; (F) reuse patterns catalogues; (G) edition of requirements and test cases specifications; and (H) automatic generation of SRS, TCS, and TM.

During requirements elicitation, a user can reuse a specific pattern (FRP, NFRP, or ATP), a set of patterns, or the complete catalogue. Os ATPs estão vinculados aos FRPs e/ou NFRs em um mesmo catálogo. This is achieved by accessing the "Associate Catalog" option available on the project's main page, as shown in Figure 1(i)D. A list of the catalogues registered into the DREAM database is exhibited so that the user choose one or more patterns.

When clicking on the "Reuse" option, the user is redirected to the screen in Figure 1(ii), which contains detailed information about each element of the pattern catalogue (FRP, NFRP, or ATP). Reuse options include one or more patterns or the entire catalogue. We implemented such reuse options in DREAM to make requirements elicitation faster. The same effect is expected for test case elaboration when the user reuses ATPs linked to FRPs.

4.2. Supporting requirements and test cases specification

DREAM allows users to edit patterns reused according to a project's needs. The fields on the requirements editing screen, shown in Figure 1(iii), are automatically filled in with the reused patterns' content and can even be edited (except for the reserved words As, I can, So that.

Filling the Priority (1 to 5) and Mandatory (yes or no) fields is optional. The remaining fields (Name, As, I can, So that) are automatically filled by the information from the corresponding FRP reused. Their contents can also be edited by the user if necessary. Information about the source catalogue and the original pattern bag (NOT shown in Figure 1(iii)) can not be changed to maintain reuse traceability and generate software pattern usage reports.

Similarly, Figure 1(iv) illustrates the test case editing screen in which the fields Name, Given, When, Then, and Examples are extracted from the corresponding ATP reused. Likewise, the Scenario's name and the FR id come from the FRP-ATP aligned but are not editable.

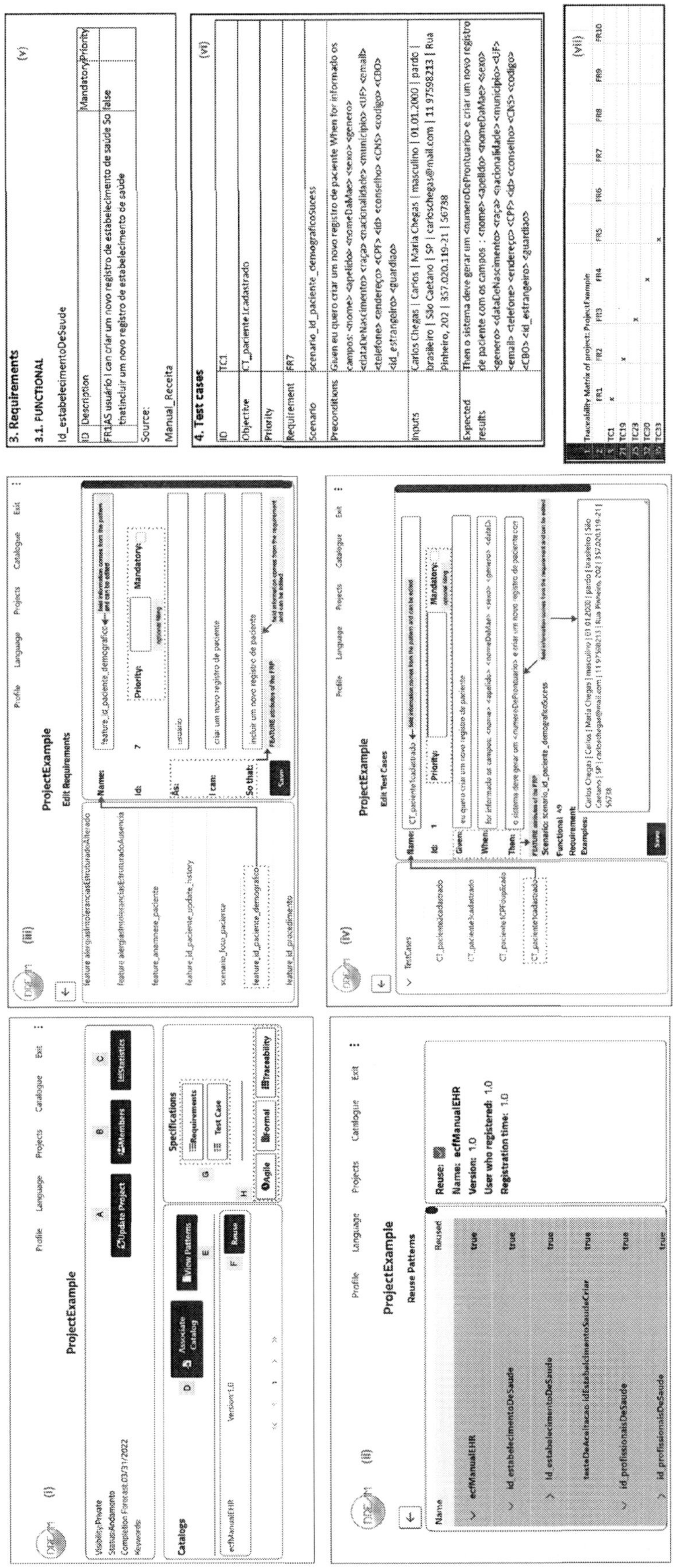

Figure 1. The DREAM user interface: (i) main functionalities for a sample project; (ii) patterns reuse; (iii) requirements edition; (iv) test cases edition; and excerpts of (v) a requirements specification document, (vi) a test case specification document, and (vii) a traceability matrix.

4.3. Automatic documentation of software artifacts

Once a user has reused and edited the definitions of requirements and test cases from pattern catalogues, the DREAM tool also allows the automatic generation of software artifacts. For example, Figure 1(v) illustrates an excerpt of a requirements specification document describing an FR1 functional requirement for the registering of a new health institution. Specified as a user story, FR1 is not mandatory and its source is the electronic prescription section of our catalogue for EHR systems. This document structure, encoded in the .docx format, conforms to the ISO/IEC 29148 standard [ISO/IEC/IEEE 2018].

In turn, Figure 1(vi) depicts an excerpt of a test case specification document describing a TC1 test case for the registering of a new patient. The TC1 contents include preconditions, inputs, and expected results. In addition, observe that TC1 links to an FR7 functional requirement for tracing purposes. This document structure, encoded in .docx, adheres to the ISO/IEC 29119-3 standard [ISO/IEC/IEEE 2013].

Finally, DREAM can generate a traceability matrix document encoded in the .xlsx format. Figure 1(vii) presents the association between FR and TC following the relationships between FRPs and ATPs imported from pattern catalogues.

The generation of agile documentation is a work in progress – see H in Figure 1(i). We have produced a graphical view with individual cards with user stories and acceptance test scenarios to support professionals' tasks. This functionality will be available soon.

5. Final remarks and future work

The DREAM tool is innovative in relating different types of software patterns, i.e., FRP and ATP, to assist requirements and testing activities. None of the similar tools represents and processes the alignment between requirements and testing. In addition, DREAM maintains traceability between reused standards when generating documentation, allowing the management of these requirements throughout a project.

We are aware that, as a CASE tool, DREAM is at an early stage of the investigation. But, on the other hand, we claim we advance state of the art by developing tool support for our reuse approach based on requirement patterns linked to acceptance test patterns.

In future work, we will conduct experimental studies using DREAM in software requirements courses to evaluate to which extent it supports elicitation, specification, documentation, and even validation of requirements through acceptance tests. The goal is to gather the first pieces of evidence about the appropriateness of the DREAM-supported reuse approach. Experimentation results will also be used to identify the need for new features and promote the continuous improvement of the tool. We also plan to experiment with DREAM in professional scenarios later.

References

Barcelos, L. and Penteado, R. (2017). Elaboration of software requirements documents by means of patterns instantiation. *J Softw Eng Res Dev*, 5(3):1–23.

Barros-Justo, J. L., Benitti, F. B. V., and Leal, A. C. (2018). Software patterns and requirements engineering activities in real-world settings:a systematic mapping study. *Comp. Standards & Interfaces*, 58:23–42.

Beckers, K., Heisel, M., Côté, I., Goeke, L., and Güler, S. (2013). Structured pattern-based security requirements elicitation for clouds. In *2013 International Conference on Availability, Reliability and Security*, pages 465–474.

Benitti, F. and Silva, R. (2013). Evaluation of a systematic approach to requirements reuse. *Journal of Universal Computer Science*, 19:254.

Bjarnason, E. and Borg, M. (2017). Aligning requirements and testing: Working together toward the same goal. *IEEE Software*, 34(1):20–23.

Da Silva, R. and Benitti, F. (2013). Evaluation of a systematic approach to requirements reuse. *Journal of Universal Computer Science*, 19(2):254–280.

Irshad, M., Petersen, K., and Poulding, S. (2018). A systematic literature review of software requirements reuse approaches. *Inf. Softw. Technol.*, 93(C):223–245.

ISO/IEC/IEEE (2013). *29119-3:2013 Software and systems engineering - Software testing*. International Organization for Standardization, 5 edition.

ISO/IEC/IEEE (2018). *29148:2018 Systems and software engineering - Life cycle processes - Requirements engineering*. International Organization for Standardization, 2 edition.

Kiatake, L. G. G., Junior, L. A. V., da Silva, M. L., and Sanzovo, O. A. C. (2021). *Manual de Certificação de Sistemas de Registro Eletrônico em Saúde*. Sociedade Brasileira de Informática em Saúde. Versão 5.1. Instituído e regido pela Resolução CFM nº 1821/2007.

Kudo, T. N., Bulcão Neto, R. F., Macedo, A. A., and Vincenzi, A. M. R. (2019a). A revisited systematic literature mapping on the support of requirement patterns for the software development life cycle. *Journal of Software Engineering Research and Development*, 7:9:1–9:11.

Kudo, T. N., Bulcão Neto, R. F., and Vincenzi, A. M. R. (2019b). A conceptual metamodel to bridging requirement patterns to test patterns. In *Proceedings of the XXXIII Brazilian Symposium on Software Engineering*, pages 155–160, New York, NY, USA. ACM.

Kudo, T. N., Bulcão-Neto, R. F., and Vincenzi, A. M. R. (2020). Uma ferramenta para construção de catálogos de padrões de requisitos com comportamento. In *Proceedings of WER20 - Workshop em Engenharia de Requisitos, São José dos Campos, Brazil, Agosto 24-28, 2020*, pages 1–14. Editora PUC-Rio.

Kudo, T. N., Bulcão-Neto, R. F., Graciano Neto, V. V., and Vincenzi, A. M. R. (2022). Aligning requirements and testing through metamodeling and patterns: design and evaluation. *Requirements Eng*, pages 1–19.

OMG (2002). Meta Object Facility (MOF) Specification, version 1.4. *Object Management Group, Inc.*

Palomares, C., Quer, C., and Franch, X. (2013). Pabre-proj: Applying patterns in requirements elicitation. In *2013 21st IEEE International Requirements Engineering Conference (RE)*, pages 332–333.

Withall, S. (2007). *Software Requirement Patterns*. Best practices. Microsoft Press, Redmond, Washington.

Towards an ontology-based recommender system for agile practices adoption

M. Luciana Roldán[1], Verónica A. Bollati[2], Silvio M. Gonnet[1]

[1]Instituto de Desarrollo y Diseño (INGAR) – CONICET / UTN
Avellaneda 3657 – Santa Fe – Argentina

[2]UTN Fac. Reg. Resistencia / CONICET,
Resistencia, Argentina.

{lroldan,sgonnet}@santafe-conicet.gov.ar, vbollati@gmail.com

Abstract. *Choosing the right agile practices to be adopted in a software development process is complex, especially for organizations with little experience and a high turnover of human resources. To select the best practices, it is necessary to consider the characteristics that describe the team, the project, and the context in which they will be applied. In this paper, we propose an ontology-based agile practices recommender. The ontology was built and populated with knowledge obtained from software projects of Argentine organizations. The recommender applies the FP-Growth algorithm to find the most suitable practices for the target profile. In addition, it discovers potential conflicts between the profile and the recommended practices.*

1. Introduction

In the last decades, the software development industry has been increasingly adopting agile methods and practices instead of traditional software development methods as they are more flexible and can bring benefits such as handling requirements changes, productivity gains, and business alignment [Campanelli et al. 2018]. In fact, the well-known survey of Digital.ai [Digital.ai 2021] reports that the two most urgent reasons for adopting Agile are the speed and flexibility required by working environments that continue to be both unpredictable and volatile (64% Enhance ability to manage changing priorities; 64% Accelerate software delivery). These are closely followed by a continued need to focus on alignment across teams to streamline the software delivery process (47% Increase team productivity).

Digital.ai survey also shows that organizations still face a variety of challenges as they introduce agile techniques, practices, and tools. In fact, 30% of respondents identified no fewer than ten different challenges faced while adopting Agile. The key challenges organizations face when adopting Agile have remained largely unchanged for the past several years. Challenges with organizational culture, resistance to change, and lack of skills and experience continue to be problems.

Choosing the right strategy for the adoption of agile practices is key for organizations to take advantage of the benefits of agile and overcome the common problems found in the adoption process and achieve their business goals. Currently, the main difficulty in the agile adoption process lies in selecting the right set of practices for each situation. Numerous research efforts have been reported to address this problem, but there is still no definitive answer [Kurapati et al. 2012; Letelier and Penades 2017; Nishijima and Dos Santos 2013].

The complexity of the agile adoption process is high, especially for organizations with little experience and a high turnover of human resources. Often, companies hire external coaches to provide initial training and kick-start agile development [Stray et al. 2020]. However, consulting costs are high, especially for organizations in countries with economic difficulties, such as Argentina. To select the right practices for an organization, it is important to have experience with agile development projects to know which practices will give the best results, and to consider the characteristics that describe the team, the project and the context in which the practices will be applied. In today's organizations, it is common for two teams in the same organization to have different characteristics in terms of the background of their members, the history of projects developed in the past, and the environment in which they are immersed (such as legal, budgetary, technological), which adds complexity when selecting the optimal set of practices for a particular "profile" (team/project/context).

To overcome those issues, in this work a preliminary agile practices recommender system is proposed. The system is based on an ontology that represents agile knowledge gained from literature, technical websites and forums, and industry experiences. It constitutes a decision support tool for the process of adopting agile practices. The system was developed on top of an Agile Practices Ontology (AgiPrOnt) to provide an organization or team with the N agile practices best suited to adopt in a particular software development project and context. The contributions of this paper are: an ontology of agile practices, a recommender system based in that ontology, and a conflict resolution mechanism.

The rest of the paper is organized as follows. Section 2 presents related works regarding ontology-based recommending techniques and approaches for Agile process adoption. In Section 3, we present the research methodology followed. In Section 4, we present an overview of the Agile Practices Recommender system. Then, the details of construction and population of the AgiPrOnt ontology are given, and we expose the recommendation algorithm and the conflicts detection approach. In Section 5, some aspects of the proposal are evaluated, and the limitations are discussed. Finally, in Section 6 the conclusions are presented.

2. Related works

Recommender systems (RS) have been proposed as a decision-making strategy for users in complex information environments. Recommender systems [Isinkaye et al. 2015] handle the problem of information overload that users normally encounter by providing them with personalized, exclusive content and services. They are also a means of assisting and augmenting the social process of using recommendations of others to make choices when there is not sufficient personal knowledge or experience.

Ontologies play an important role in knowledge representation as well as in knowledge sharing and reuse in recommendation systems. Previous studies have shown that the incorporation of an ontology domain knowledge to a recommender improves the accuracy and quality of recommendations as well as alleviates other drawbacks associated with conventional recommendation techniques such as cold-start and rating sparsity problems. The effectiveness of ontology-based recommender systems depends mainly on the completeness and accuracy of knowledge maintained in the ontology domain knowledge [Tarus et al. 2018]. RS use domain ontologies to establish the relationships between users and their preferences about the recommendation subject. The semantic information of an item includes the attributes, the relationships among the items, and the relationship between meta-information and items. Many RS employ domain ontologies to measure user preferences with content elements. Moreover, using knowledge about items and users helps to produce a recommendation based on knowledge and reasoning about which item meets the needs of the users [Burke 2000].

There has been prolific literature regarding approaches for agile process implementation and tailoring. A probabilistic model to identify problems related to a project and the team is defined in [Perkusich et al. 2013]. The approach is aimed to help Scrum Masters to be aware of the project's problems and have enough information to guide the team and improve the project's chances of success. The model is a Bayesian network that represents a Scrum-based software development project composed by one development team. One of the limitations of this work is that it focuses on the Scrum framework, which makes it useful only for development projects that apply Scrum.

AgileRoadmap [Letelier and Penades 2017] is an approach for implementing ASD in companies. The proposal includes a model and a strategy for agile implementation, which integrates the most popular agile practices, focusing on the practice application and not on the application of a particular method.

In the literature, some authors propose ontologies, taxonomies, or metamodels to describe ASD knowledge. However, most of these works focus on one or two methods or a bunch of practices and do not cover comprehensively the knowledge related to ASD, regarding the variety of agile practices, characteristics of the teams that use them, and the projects and the environments where they are applied [Júnior et al. 2021]. [Minoli 2011] proposes a framework that suggests solutions tailored to the configurations of projects in the context of A-GSD (Global Agile Software Development). The ontology-based solution framework aims to classify, organize, and unify all the existing knowledge on A-GSD, for which it includes an ontology that represents the knowledge in terms of agile and distributed projects features, and a tool that uses the knowledge of this ontology to make available to the community the existing knowledge about A-GSD. [Ortega-Ordoñez et al. 2019] suggested a common and consistent terminology that allows sharing the knowledge generated from implementing agile approaches in the software processes. The proposal focuses on facilitating the assessment of the agility of the software processes, from the identification of the relationships between the elements of the software processes and the agile principles and values. These ontologies lack concepts to characterize the teams, projects, and contexts where agile processes were performed making it difficult to reuse the shared knowledge in the ontology.

[Kiv et al. 2019] proposed an ontology for representing agile methods knowledge, so that the knowledge and experience on agile adoption reported in the literature may be reusable and systematic. This work has similar goals as ours, as it includes concepts to define certain characteristics of the situation of an organization, its goals, and the practices the organizations want to adopt. The approach is based on the knowledge of ASD cases studies and a set of inferences rules. It provides a list of potential problems that could arise when a team adopts a practice, and, for each problem, propose a solution. However, it requires the user to have expert knowledge about practices to adopt, since he/she must decide in advance which practices the team will adopt. In addition, the tool does not provide support to find teams/organizations with similar characteristics to the user organization.

To the best of our knowledge, no proposal integrates a recommending algorithm based on team, project, and context characteristics, with ontologies to suggest a starter pack of practices to a team initiating a new agile project.

3. Methodology

We employ the Design Science Research paradigm, as the research method adopted in this work, which is concerned with extending "human and organizational capabilities by creating new and innovative artifacts" [Peffers et al. 2007]. It comprises five steps, which are organized in an iterative process: (i) Problem identification and Motivation, (ii) Definition of the objectives for a solution, (iii) Design and Development, (iv) Demonstration, (v) Evaluation, and (vi) Communication.

Regarding the *Problem identification and motivation* step, the problem was identified by the second author when working as a consultant in some organizations on the Northeast region of Argentina. Additionally, the "lack of skills and experience" has been identified as a barrier to Agile adoption from multiple studies [Digital.ai 2021; PMIBA 2020]. The problem means that organizations are forced to invest heavily in training programs and hiring coaches to gain insight into which practices to select when facing a new project.

At the *Definition of the objectives for a solution* step, we decided to develop *AgiPront*, an ontology-based recommender system for agile practices adoption. As requirements of the proposed approach, we defined that it must: (R1) allow identifying the team's characteristics, the project characteristics, and the context in which the new project will be inserted, (R2) provide meaningful and comprehensive data on agile practices, as well as an assessment of the impact of their use on past completed projects, and (R3) recommend a set of agile practices appropriate to the characteristics of the team, project, and context of the organization that uses the tool.

4. The Agile Practices Recommender System

In this section, we address the *Design and Development* step prescribed by the followed research methodology, outlining the system architecture first. The main stakeholders of the Agile Recommender Systems are: i) the *Target Agile Profile* (*TAP*), a person, team or organization that requires support to select the set of best practices to adopt for a given project and context; ii) the *Expert*, who is the responsible to feed the ontology with ASD knowledge from several sources like the literature, web forums, self-experience, open projects repositories, etc. Another actor (not shown in Figure 1) is the *Surveyed Agile Profile*, which interacts with the system by providing data on cases studies, and data from completed ASD projects.

In Fig. 1 the central component of the RS is the semantic model, formalized in an ontology, which represents the concepts involved in Agile Software Development. A web questionnaire is used to collect part of the data required to feed the ontology, by inquiring to diverse agile organizations about their characteristics, the practices they employed in their projects, and the contribution of each practice adopted to the success of the project. The Profile Loader component populates the ontology from the knowledge obtained with the questionnaire. A SPARQL endpoint is a service that allows applications to perform SPARQL queries on data stored in RDF format. Through the Agile Knowledge Interface, users can access the ontology and employ it for learning/training purposes. The Recommender Algorithm consists of three parts: a) a profile matching stage, where the characteristics of the Target Agile Profile are identified and used to find other similar profiles in the knowledge base; b) a stage in which a set of the most successful practices used jointly by similar profiles is obtained, , which constitute the practices that are candidates for recommendation; and c) a conflicts detection and ranking stage, where rules are applied to discover potential conflicts among the candidate practices.

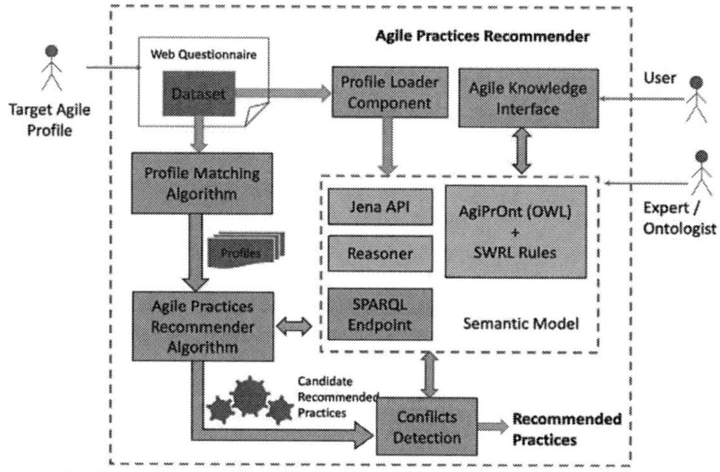

Figure 1. Overview of the Agile Practices Recommender System

4.1. The AgiPrOnt ontology

To develop AgiPrOnt, an ad-hoc methodology was applied that comprises four stages, which are common to most popular ontology development methodologies [Suárez-Figueroa et al., 2012]: i) an Ontology requirements specification stage, which consists of identifying the purpose for constructing the ontology and set its scope; ii) a Conceptualization stage, which consists of organizing the involved concepts in an informally perceived view of the domain and, then, converting it in a semi-formal UML-based specification; iii) a Formalization stage, which comprises the implementation of the ontology using a formal language, as well as populating it with knowledge from different sources; and iv) an Evaluation stage, which allows making a technical judgment of the ontology quality and its usefulness with respect to the requirements specification, competency questions and/or the real world.

The requirements specification stage began with the elicitation of a set of competency questions, which, due to lack of space, are given in [Roldan et al. 2022] (*AgiPrOnt Competency questions* file).

At the conceptualization stage, we decided to build AgiPrOnt as a domain-specific ontology based on the concepts defined by the Software Process Ontology

(SPO) [Oliveira Bringuente et al. 2011]. SPO is a core ontology that is part of SEON (Software Engineering Ontology Network) and provides the general concepts for software processes. SEON [Borges Ruy et al. 2016] provides a network of Software Engineering reference ontologies, and mechanisms to derive and incorporate new integrated subdomain ontologies into the network. The foundational layer of SEON, is the Unified Foundational Ontology (UFO) [Guizzardi 2005], which is developed based on a number of theories from Formal Ontology, Philosophical Logics, Philosophy of Language, Linguistics and Cognitive Psychology. Then, the definition of the concepts and relationships of AgiPrOnt was made by extending the specific concepts and relationships included in SEON network ontology, particularly in UFO and SPO.

From the elicited competency questions, we identified the terms of the ASD domain. Initially, we generated a list of terms without considering the existence of any overlapping, the possible relationships among them, or the properties that characterize each concept. Then, each term was defined as an extension of the general concepts in the upper ontologies.

To organize the concepts in *AgiPrOnt*, four semantic submodels were defined (Fig. 2): the Fundamental Agile Concepts Model (*FACM*), the Agile Practices Model (*APrM*), the Agile Characteristics Model (*AChM*), and the Agile Assessment Model (*AAM*). The *FACM* Model comprises the definitions of fundamental concepts of ASD and a canonical model for representing agile developing processes. *Agile Values* are part of the *Agile Manifesto*, which defines the philosophy of agile [Beck. K. et al., 2001]. From these values, twelve *AgilePrinciples* are derived, which enable mapping the agile practices to the business goals the organizations want to achieve. Agile values and principles are implemented through *Agile Practices*. An agile practice is an activity or a mode of working, which can be applied repeatedly, thus performed regularly (in the case of an activity) or enforced systematically (in the case of a mode of working) [Meyer 2014].

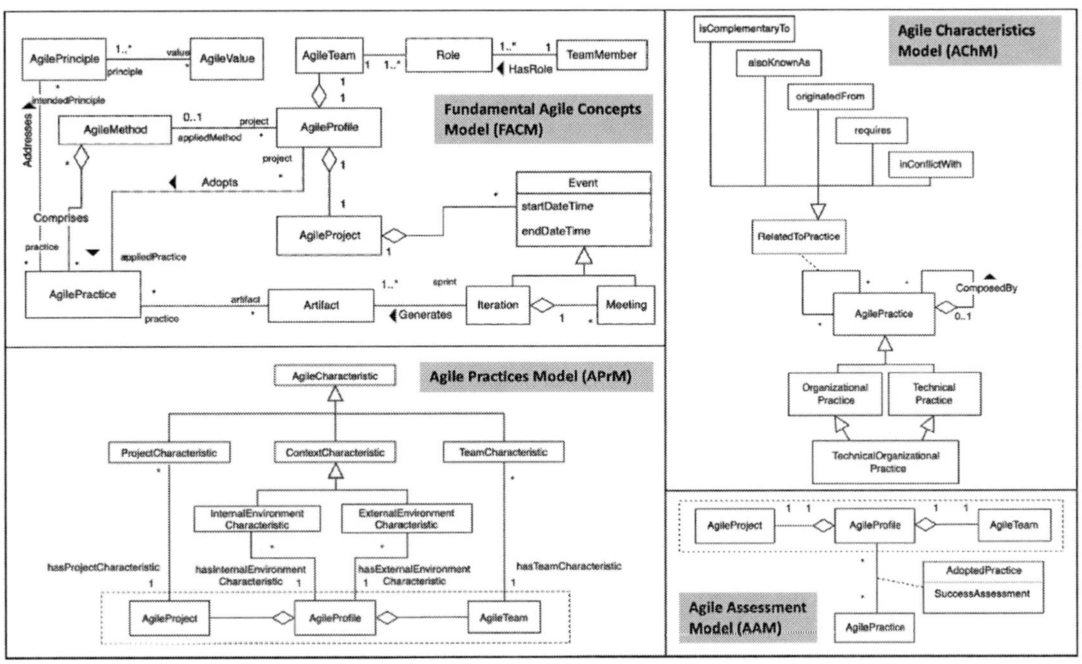

Figure 2. Ontology Conceptual Model

The application of agile practices gives rise to different artifacts or work products (*Artifact*). Some practices can be part of a specific *Agile method*, although it is not required for a practice to be part of a method (*Comprises* relationship).

The concept of *AgileProfile* is key in this proposal, as it acts as the "container" of the concepts *AgileTeam* and *AgileProject*. An agile project is a software development project that follows an extremely iterative and incremental life cycle, where the development team works in a highly collaborative and self-organized manner. An agile project is composed by events. Events are time-boxed, which means that they have a fixed and predefined maximum duration and can be classified as *Iterations* or *Meetings*. An *Agile Team* is defined as a set of persons involved in the development of the project. An organization may have multiple projects in progress, and different teams in charge of their development. Each *Team Member*, who participates in an agile team, has a specific *Role* (a set of functions that are fulfilled within the agile team).

The *APrM* model represents that an *AgilePractice* can be an *OrganizationalPractice*, a *TechnicalPractice*, or both (*TechnicalOrganizationalPractice*). While organizational practices affect the cost, schedule and team sustainability of a project, the technical practices support product quality and effectiveness. The model includes some relationships among practices, which are defined by the Agile Alliance Glossary [Agile Alliance [S.d.]]: *composedBy alsoKnownAs*, and *originatedFrom*. Other relationships included in the model are: *inConflictWith* (to indicate that two practices cannot coexist in the same project), *isComplementaryTo* (to represent that if a practice A is adopted, then, it is highly recommended to adopt also practice B) and *requires* (to represent that if practice A is adopted, practice B must be also adopted for A to work properly).

The *AChM* Model includes the concepts for representing the properties or attributes that characterize to the agile teams, the projects they carry on, and their contexts. The central concept is *AgileCharacteristic*, which is specialized in *TeamCharacteristic* (how the team is composed and how their members interact), *ProjectCharacteristic* (budget, schedule, resources, and technological aspects of the system or software to be developed), and *ContextCharacteristic*. The last one refers to the environment of a Team+Project pair, and it is specialized in *ExternalEnvironmentCharacteristic* (aspects from the outside of the organization) and *InternalEnvironmentCharacteristic* (aspects from the inside of the organization).

The *AAA* model represents the knowledge about the success of the practices adopted by agile profiles. The recorded knowledge from past experiences is useful for new agile teams that face a new agile project in a new context. To explicitly represent this knowledge, the model incorporates a relationship between the *AgileProfile* and *AgilePractice* concepts. This relationship, called *AdoptedPractice*, also maintains information about in what extent a given practice contributed to the overall success of a project (*SuccessAssesment* attribute).

The next step was the formalization of the conceptual model in OWL, in terms of classes, individuals, and properties (Fig. 3), using Protegé[1]. When implementing the *APrM* model in OWL, two possible design decisions were considered on how to define

[1] https://protege.stanford.edu/

the agile practices. The first option was to create an instance of *AgilePractice* class for each existent practice. The alternative option was to create a subclass by each existent agile practice extending the *AgilePractice* concept, and then generate a singleton instance for each subclass. We selected the second option because it allows us to define richer rules in the ontology and work with a reasoner to get meaningful results from the inferences. Over 70 agile practices were collected and consolidated from various sources (literature, websites, and agile community forums), and defined in AgiPrOnt [Agile Alliance [S.d.]; Campanelli et al. 2018; Digital.ai 2021]. As there is no consensus in the literature on the names of agile practices, some relationships of "aliases" were established by means of inference rules. In addition, annotation properties were added to the practices (*definition*, *benefits*, and *pitfalls*).

Like practices, profiles' characteristics were also defined as classes. The complete set of practices and characteristics that were regarded in this proposal are available in the *Datasets* folder in [Roldan et al. 2022]. To represent that an agile profile has certain characteristics, the *AgileCharacteristic* instances are related to an instance of *AgileProfile* through the *hasCharacteristic* object property (either *hasTeamCharacteristic*, *hasProjectCharacteristic*, *hasExternalEnvironmentCharacteristic*, or *hasInternalEnvironmentCharacteristic* object properties). Characteristics have values (*hasValue* object property), which are used to assign a specific meaning to the characteristic for a profile. The values can be of different types (Fig. 3): categorical values (binary, nominal, or ordinal) and numerical values. While nominal values represent discrete units and are used to label variables that have no quantitative value and no order, ordinal values represent discrete and ordered units. On the other hand, numerical values can be continuous, interval, or discrete.

The *AdoptedPractice* relation (Fig. 2) was reified in an OWL class called *AdoptsPracticeRelationship*, in such a way that it is possible to assign it a property value to maintain the assessment value given by a profile to the practice based on the success of the project. The assessment value is represented on a *Likert scale* value.

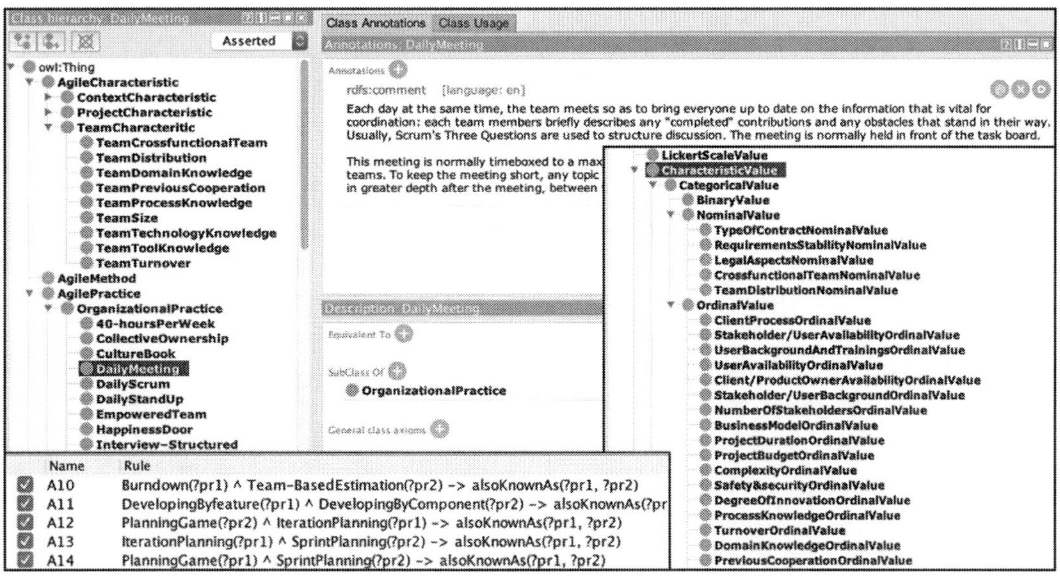

Figure 3. Partial view of the ontology model formalized in OWL

The OWL ontology was enhanced regarding completeness, expressiveness, and logic by adding SWRL (Semantic Web Rules Language) rules. The first set of rules was specified to infer associations between instances, and other ones to express alias relationships (*alsoKnownAs* object property) between practices (Fig. 3).

The next step was to *populate the ontology*. First, an *owl:allDifferents* axiom was added to the ontology to explicitly state that all individuals are different. The sources of knowledge to populate the ontology were diverse. Mainly, several case studies and data were gathered during a previous research project in which one of the authors participate. In that project a framework and a tool were developed to support management and evaluation of ASD projects, with the aim of facilitating the adoption of quality assurance practices [Pinto et al. 2018]. In this project, 47 case studies of participating agile organizations were collected.

A structured web questionnaire helped to systematize the task of characterizing the agile profiles for the different case studies collected. The questionnaire is made up of a set of closed questions, which provide the possible response values for each characteristic of a profile. Additionally, the questionnaire inquiries about the practices that a profile has adopted or implemented during an ASD process and asks the respondent to rate or evaluate the contribution of each practice to the success of the project. One participant from each project answered the questionnaire. In other cases, the questionnaire was answered by a consultant that had been involved with the organization during the project.

The first set of questions aims to characterize the team, the attributes of the developed project (system/software), and the characteristics of the context (internal and external environment) in which the team and project are immersed. The possible answers are categorical, and their values can be, according to the characteristic considered, ordinal, nominal, or binary types. The ordinal and nominal values take integer values between 1 and 5, where each number has an associated meaning. For example, the team characteristic "*Crossfunctional Team*" takes the nominal values "*siloed teams*" (1), "*most members are specialists*" (2), "*50/50*" (3), "*most members have multiple skills*" (4) and "*full crossfunctional*" (5). Each possible value is mapped to instances of *CrossfunctionalTeamNominalValue* (a subclass of *NominalValue*) in the ontology. The project characteristic "*Project budget*" takes ordinal values, such as "*< \$1 million*", "*\$ 1-2 millions*", "*\$ 2-3 millions*", "*\$ 3-4 millions*", and "*\$ 5 millions Ordinal*". "*Management support*" is an internal context characteristic, that takes the binary values "No" or "Yes". The *Datasets* folder in [Roldan et al. 2022] includes the complete definition of the values of the characteristics. Most of the characteristics and their values were taken from [Campanelli et al. 2018], then adapted and categorized to design the questionnaire. The data gathered with the questionnaire were used to create instances (individuals) of the *AgileProfile* class, and the instances of the correspondent *TeamCharacteristic*, *ProjectCharacteristic*, and *ContextCharacteristic* subclasses.

The second set of questions inquiries about what practices the agile team adopted and employed during the development of the project. For each selected practice, the participant is asked: "Did the practice contribute to the overall success of the project?". The answer provided must be a Likert scale value, which is associated with a numerical score: *Strongly Disagree* (1), *Disagree* (2), *Neutral* (3), *Agree* (4), and *Strongly Agree* (5). These values provide a rating or assessment based on the respondent's perception of the contribution of the practice to the overall success of the project. The data collected with the questionnaire are available in the *Datasets* folder in [Roldan et al. 2022] (*Profiles.xls* and *AdoptedPractices.xls* files). They were used to populate the ontology by employing the *Profile Loader* component (developed in Java and the Apache Jena API).

4.2. The recommending algorithm

The proposed recommendation algorithm has two phases: 1) to find the right set of candidate practices for an agile objective profile, 2) to detect conflicts, discard practices and obtain the final recommendation. To find the set of candidate practices to recommend, the algorithm follows the following steps:

Step 0: creation of the *target* agile profile. To instantiate the target profile the User stakeholder answers the first set of questions in the questionnaire. An instance of the class *TargetAgileProfile* is generated (AP_T) and the instances for their characteristics, which are related through an object property to their assigned values.. This profile has particular values for the Team / Project / Context characteristics $\{TC_{1T}, TC_{2T}, ..., TC_{tT}, PC_{1T}, PC_{2T}, ..., PC_{pT}, ..., CC_{1T}, CC_{2T}, ..., CC_{cT}\}$. The user also is asked about the *minimum rating value* (MRV) the algorithm should employ to consider as successful the adoption of a certain practice by a profile.

Step 1. Find the k agile profiles AP_i most similar to the target profile AP_T, calculating the similarity according to the values of their characteristics. The result of this step is a set of the k agile profiles $\{AP_1, AP_2, ..., AP_k\}$ most similar to AP_T. Given that the values of the characteristics are categorical (nominal, ordinal and binary values), the similarity algorithm uses a distance function for categorical/binary data (*SimpleMatchingSimilarity*).

Step 2. For each AP_i in $\{AP_1, AP_2, ..., AP_k\}$, retrieve the practices (P_j) each profile adopted during the development of a project and the corresponding assessment about its degree of success. These data are represented by a matrix of ratings, where the rows (i index) are the similar agile profiles, and columns are the practices (j index). In other words, each row in the matrix is the tuple of ratings ($r_{i,1}, r_{i,2}, ..., r_{i,j}, ..., r_{i,m}$). A rating $r_{i,j}$ is a value on the Likert scale between 1 and 5 given by a profile i to a practice j. If an agile practice P_j has not been adopted by the APi profile, a rating $r_{i,j}$ with a value of 0 is considered.

Step 3. The $r_{i,j}$ values (ratings) are converted from nominal (Likert scale value or zero) to binary (True/False). That is made using a mapping function, which, in case the value of a $r_{i,j}$ rating is between the selected MRV and 5 (the highest Likert scale value), it becomes true, otherwise false. The result is a new "dataset" that for each profile (rows) and each practice (columns) has "*true*" or "*false*", being *false* if the practice was not adopted or the success rating was low, or *true* in case it was adopted with a neutral or positive degree of success for the project.

Step 4. Calculate the frequently co-occurring successful practices used by the similar agile profiles, using the *FP-Growth algorithm. FP-Growth algorithm* (derived from A-Priori) is an efficient algorithm for calculating frequently co-occurring items in a transaction database. FP-Growth algorithm is commonly applied in domains such as market basket analysis, but also has been applied to software engineering problems

[Muhairat et al. 2020]. To apply FP-Growth algorithm in the ASD domain, we consider the following:

- an item = an agile practice
- a transaction = a complete set of agile practices successfully adopted by an organization/team in the development of a project, in a certain context.
- an itemset = any subset of practices that were applied together by the same agile profile. For example, two possible *itemsets* could be (*daily meeting*, *continuous delivery*, *face-to-face communication*, *poker planning*) and (*daily meeting*, *continuous delivery*, *poker planning*).

The input of the FP-Growth algorithm is the result obtained in step 3, which is in the format "items in dummy coded columns". After applying it, the frequently occurring practices are provided. The *itemset of practices* with the maximum length and an acceptable support value contains the candidate practices CP_{kT} for the target agile profile $\{CP_{1T}, ..., CP_{iT}, ..., CP_{mT}\}$. The steps 1 to 4 of the algorithm were implemented in RapidMiner[2] using a plain dataset and not directly the instances in AgiPrOnt, for better performance [Roldan et al. 2022].

The set of candidate practices needs to be validated to avoid recommending practices that conflict with each other or with the target profile. The conflict resolution phase is addressed with the usage of OWL DL and SWRL rules. The technique for conflict detection employed is based on introducing inconsistency in the ontology and the use of disjoint classes [Alcaraz Calero et al. 2010]. Since the models are described in OWL DL which is based on Description Logic, a DL reasoner is used to deal with inconsistencies, that is, two conflicting facts are held in the knowledge base. When an inconsistency is detected by the DL reasoner, it fires a conflict detection alert.

To detect a possible conflict, we add to the ontology a class called *ConflictiveAgileProfile*, an "artificial" concept for the domain. The *ConflictiveAgileProfile* class is defined as *disjoint with* the *TargetAgileProfile* class. An OWL disjoint axiom (*disjointWith*) is defined between the two classes, which determines that these classes cannot have instances in common. Therefore, if a disjoint statement is specified for two different classes, a reasoner can deduce an inconsistency when an individual is stated to be an instance of both classes. For the conflict detection mechanism to work, the *Expert* user has to define a set of SWRL rules (Fig. 4), which express potential conflicts between practices, or between practices and profiles that have certain characteristics.

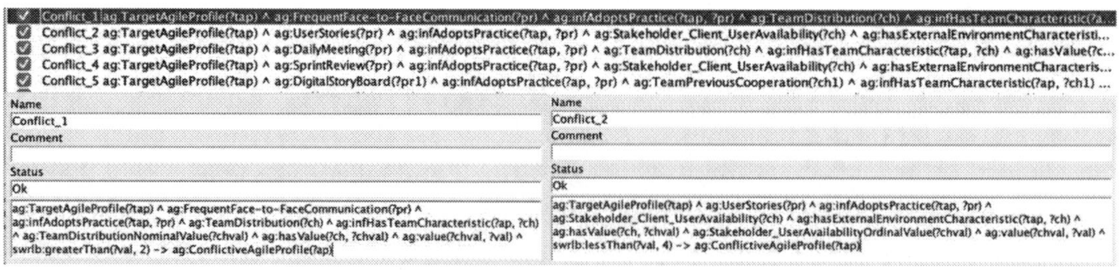

Figure 4. SRWL rules to conflict detection

[2] https://rapidminer.com/

A rule-based reasoner is used to perform inferences on the ontology by applying the SWRL rules. Each conflict rule defined for detecting a conflict between the target profile AP_T and a candidate practice CP_j has an antecedent that is the conjunction of facts that cause a conflict, and a consequent that is the inferred fact *ConflictiveAgileProfile*(AP_T). For each candidate practice CP_{jT} the following steps are performed:

i. An axiom is added to the ontology that sets an *AdoptsPracticeRelation* "relationship" between the target profile AP_T and the singleton instance corresponding to the practice CP_j. In this way, it is "temporarily" stated in the ontology that the AP_T (target agile profile) adopts the practice CP_j.

ii. The reasoner is synchronized, which implies that the rules for detecting conflicts are applied. If the antecedent of a conflict detection rule is true, the *TargetAgileProfile* instance (AP_T) is classified as *ConflictiveAgileProfile*. However, since previously the AP_T had been created as an instance of *TargetAgileProfile*, an inconsistency is reported since the AP_T instance cannot be instance of two disjoint classes. This means that the adoption of the CP_j by the target profile AP_T incurs in a practice-profile conflict, or practice-practice conflict, so the candidate practice CP_j should be dismissed.

iv. The user is informed about the existent conflict, and the practice is eliminated from the recommendation set. When the conflict is between two practices, the user can choose the practice to discard. Then, the axioms added in step *i* are deleted.

Some examples of SWRL rules for conflict detection are below. Due to lack of space, the SRWL rules are detailed in the OWL ontology in [Roldan et al. 2022].

Rule example 1: An agile team that wants to apply the practice "Frequent face-to-face communication" needs all its members to work in the same physical location (city or office), or at most, in the same country (which means that traveling for meetings is feasible). To express that in a rule, the characteristic *TeamDistribution* of the target profile should not have the values greater than 2, being "Same location" or "Same country" categorical/nominal values with values 1 and 2.

Rule example 2: To successfully employ the practice "User Stories", the target profile should have the external context characteristic "Product Owner/Client Availability" with value "Medium-to-High" or "High" (the categorical/nominal values that correspond to 4 and 5). This means that the client (Product Owner) is involved in the project to write the user stories. Besides, there must be support from the management (from the client's organization) to allow employees to participate and commit to the project. In case that is not true, a conflict is detected.

Rule example 3: When team members have little experience working together on agile projects (the value of the *TeamPreviousCooperation* characteristic is "Never"), the Kanban/Scrum board should not be digital.

An optional phase of the algorithm is to recommend additional candidate practices based on the specific characteristics of the target profile. To this end, a series of SPARQL queries is defined. These queries materialize the experts' knowledge about the ASD domain. When a performed SPARQL query for a practice returns a result, this means that the target profile satisfies certain characteristics required by the practice. Due to lack of space, just one example is shown, omitting the PREFIX definition. More SPARQL queries to improve recommendations can be found in [Roldan et al. 2022].

SPARQL Query 1: If the team of the target profile has more than 10 members (time size characteristic has value "10+(too large)"), the "ScrumOfScrums" practice is added to the set of candidate practices. The goal is to divide the team into smaller groups.

```
SELECT ?profile ?value WHERE {?profile rdf:type ag:TargetAgileProfile ;
                    ag:hasTeam ?team .
  ?team   ag:hasTeamCharacteristic ?teamch .
  ?teamch rdf:type ag:TeamSize ;
                   ag:hasValue ?value .
Filter (?value=<http://www.semanticweb.org/utn/AgileOntology#10+(toolarge)>)}
```

SPARQL Query 2: If the team characteristic "Turnover" of the target profile has a value between 3 and 5 (medium, medium-to-high, or high-rate), it is advisable to do short sprints to allow team members to get to know each other quickly. Therefore, the practice "PersonalMaps" is added to the set of candidate practices. This practice can also be recommended when the members of the team of the target profile have little previous cooperation or poor domain/technology knowledge. Therefore, the SPARQL query is defined as a UNION that comprises all the situations.

6. Evaluation

We have started some activities regarding the *Demonstration* and *Evaluation* steps of the research method. The first activity was mainly focused on validating the quality of the AgiPrOnt ontology. We used an automated ontology evaluation tool named OOPS! (OntOlogy Pitfall Scanner) to verify the quality of the ontology, which helps to detect some of the most common pitfalls when developing ontologies. We evaluated the AgiPrOnt ontology (at Tbox level) by submitting it to OOPS!. Some pitfalls were detected by OOPS!, which were considered to improve the ontology. On the other hand, to validate the satisfaction of the ontology requirements, we verified the coverage of the competency questions that were identified in Section 2. To prove that the requirements were satisfied, a set of SPARQL queries were performed to answer the competency questions. Due to lack of space, the queries are provided in [Roldan et al. 2022]. In addition, AgiPrOnt has been informally reviewed by human experts during its development. The reviewers were some of the organizations, which have participated in previous research studies carried out by the authors and answered the questionnaire. Several validation activities were carried out during working technical meetings and workshops. The resulting comments led to a continuous ontology improvement in order to be functionally integrated into the recommender system.

Regarding the evaluation of the recommendation algorithm, we generated 12 test cases for different scenarios, each one representing an agile profile with a particular configuration of Team/Project/Context characteristics, with clear differences between the cases. Six of them were obtained from collaborating organizations that provided actual situations prior to the start of an ASD project. The recommender provided a different set of practices for each case. However, we note that in 3 cases, the set of practices recommended was insufficient and very basic, as the ontology lack of enough data to give a better result. Despite this limitation, the performed tests were useful for adjusting the parameters of FP-growth, such us support, frequency, minimum support and frequency, minimum and maximum items per itemset, in order to obtain the best result.

The validation of the proposed recommender has other limitations. Although several tests and recommendations were conducted, it is not possible to obtain feedback in the short term on user satisfaction regarding the usefulness of the recommendations. Until the projects in which the recommended practices were adopted have not been completed, the degree of success achieved cannot be known. Finally, the knowledge represented in AgiPrOnt is still limited; with only 47 case studies, there are situations that the model cannot answer. To address this limitation, we plan to add more knowledge to the ontology in the future.

6. Conclusion

This research proposes an ontology-based recommender system of agile practices. The ontology enables the representation of agile software development knowledge so that the experiences on agile adoption can be reusable and systematic. The original approach of the Agile Practice Recommender resides in the combination of an ontology, data mining techniques, and semantic rules to detect conflicts in the recommended practices. The representation of expert knowledge using SWRL rules and SPARQL queries is useful to compensate for the deficiencies of datamining techniques applied to a small number of cases. For future work, we are working on integrating the recommender with agile development frameworks like Jira and SonarQube. Such integration would make it possible to recommend the practices at the beginning of a new project and record the ones adopted, some of which can be supported by the framework in use. In addition, the recommender could be fed with the metrics generated by these frameworks, which can help to automatically characterize the agile profiles (regarding team, project, and environment), record experiences, and add new cases to the recommender.

References

Agile Alliance ([S.d.]). Agile Glossary and Terminology. https://www.agilealliance.org/agile101/agile-glossary/, [accessed on Apr 1].

Alcaraz Calero, J. M., Marín Pérez, J. M., Bernal Bernabé, J., et al. (1 nov 2010). Detection of semantic conflicts in ontology and rule-based information systems. *Data and Knowledge Engineering*, v. 69, n. 11, p. 1117–1137.

Borges Ruy, F., Falbo, R. de A., Barcellos, M. P., Costa, S. D. and Guizzardi, G. (2016). SEON: A software engineering ontology network. In *Lecture Notes in Computer Science (LNAI volume 10024)*. Springer Verlag.

Burke, R. (2000). Knowledge-Based Recommender Systems. *ENCYCLOPEDIA OF LIBRARY AND INFORMATION SYSTEMS*, v. 69, p. 2000.

Campanelli, A. S., Camilo, R. D. and Parreiras, F. S. (1 mar 2018). The impact of tailoring criteria on agile practices adoption: A survey with novice agile practitioners in Brazil. *Journal of Systems and Software*, v. 137, p. 366–379.

Digital.ai (2021). 15th Annual State Of Agile Report. https://digital.ai/resource-center/analyst-reports/state-of-agile-report, [accessed on Mar 29].

Guizzardi, G. (2005). Ontological foundations for structural conceptual models. Telematica Instituut / CTIT.

Isinkaye, F. O., Folajimi, Y. O. and Ojokoh, B. A. (2015). Recommendation systems: Principles, methods and evaluation. *Egyptian Informatics Journal*. Elsevier.

Júnior, P. S. S., Barcellos, M. P., Falbo, R. de A. and Almeida, J. P. A. (17 mar 2021). From a Scrum Reference Ontology to the Integration of Applications for Data-Driven Software Development. *Information and Software Technology*, p. 106570.

Kiv, S., Heng, S., Kolp, M. and Wautelet, Y. (21 may 2019). Agile methods knowledge representation for systematic practices adoption. In *Lecture Notes in Business Information Processing*. . Springer Verlag.

Kurapati, N., Manyam, V. S. C. and Petersen, K. (2012). Agile software development practice adoption survey. In *Lecture Notes in Business Information Processing*. . Springer Verlag.

Letelier, P. and Penades, M. C. (2017). AgileRoadmap: An Approach to Implement Agile Practices in Teams. *IEEE Latin America Transactions*, v. 15, n. 7, p. 1295–1300.

Meyer, B. (2014). *Agile!* Springer International Publishing.

Minoli, M. (2011). Marco de Soluciones basado en Ontologías para Desarrollo Global Ágil. Universidad Rey Juan Carlos.

Muhairat, M., ALZu'bi, S., Hawashin, B., Elbes, M. and Al-Ayyoub, M. (jan 2020). An Intelligent Recommender System Based on Association Rule Analysis for Requirement Engineering. *Journal of Universal Computer Science*, v. 26, n. 1, p. 33–49.

Nishijima, R. T. and Dos Santos, P. D. J. G. (27 jul 2013). The challenge of implementing Scrum agile methodoloy in a traditional development environment. *International Journal of Computers & Technology*, v. 5, n. 2, p. 98–108.

Oliveira Bringuente, A., Almeida Falbo, R. and Guizzardi, G. (2011). Using a foundational ontology for reengineering a software process ontology. *Journal of Information and Data Management*, v. 2, n. 3, p. 511–511.

Ortega-Ordoñez, W. A., Pardo-Calvache, C. J. and Pino-Correa, F. J. (1 apr 2019). Ontoagile: An ontology for agile software development processes. *DYNA (Colombia)*, v. 86, n. 209, p. 79–90.

Perkusich, M., De Almeida, H. O. and Perkusich, A. (2013). A model to detect problems on scrum-based software development projects. In *Proceedings of the ACM Symposium on Applied Computing*. . ACM Press.

Pinto, N., Tortosa, N., Cabas Geat, B., Ibanez, L. and Bollati, V. (26 dec 2018). Quality evaluation of agile processes: Measurement of requirements management using AQF v2. In *Proceedings - 2018 QUATIC 2018*. IEEE.

PMIBA, C. Á. (2020). 2° Estudio sobre el Pulso de la Agilidad en Argentina 2020.

Roldan, M. L., Bollati, V. and Gonnet, S. (2022). Agile practices adoption by Argentine software organizations. Mendeley Data, V3, doi: 10.17632/3chkfjxxk5.3

Stray, V., Memon, B. and Paruch, L. (2020). A Systematic Literature Review on Agile Coaching and the Role of the Agile Coach. *LNCS (subseries Lecture Notes in Artificial Intelligence and Lecture Notes in Bioinformatics)*, v. 12562 LNCS, p. 3–19.

Tarus, J. K., Niu, Z. and Mustafa, G. (1 jun 2018). Knowledge-based recommendation: a review of ontology-based recommender systems for e-learning. *Artificial Intelligence Review*, v. 50, n. 1, p. 21–48.

Tratamento de Requisitos de Confiabilidade de Sistemas-de-Sistemas: Um Mapeamento Sistemático da Literatura

Sidny de Almeida Molina, Débora Maria Barroso Paiva, Maria Istela Cagnin

[1]Faculdade de Computação – Universidade Federal de Mato Grosso do Sul (UFMS)
CEP 79070-900 – Campo Grande – MS – Brasil

{sidny.molina,debora.paiva,istela.machado}@ufms.br

Abstract. *Systems-of-Systems (SoS) is a set of software systems from distinct organizations that form alliances of organizations. These systems work together to reach broader business goals, which cannot be achieved by a system alone. Due to SoS characteristics, their requirements change over time, bringing challenges for Requirements Engineering. This paper aims to discover how reliability requirements are addressed during the SoS life cycle. As the main results, there is evidence that this requirement type is being commonly handled at a phase later than the requirement phase, and there is a lack of techniques to address them appropriately.*

Resumo. *Sistemas-de-Sistemas (SoS) é um agrupamento de sistemas de software de diversas organizações que formam alianças de organizações. Esses sistemas trabalham em conjunto para alcançar objetivos de negócio mais complexos, não obtidos por um único sistema de software. Devido às características do SoS, seus requisitos mudam ao longo do tempo, trazendo desafios para a Engenharia de Requisitos. O objetivo deste artigo é descobrir como os requisitos de confiabilidade são tratados durante o ciclo de vida do SoS. Evidenciou-se que esse tipo de requisito está sendo geralmente considerado em fase posterior à fase de requisitos e que há carência de técnicas para tratá-los de maneira apropriada.*

1. Introdução

Sistemas-de-Sistemas (SoS) resultam da necessidade de interoperabilidade entre sistemas de software individuais (constituintes) para oferecem recursos e funcionalidades mais amplas (ou seja, missões) que não poderiam ser entregues pelos sistemas constituintes individualmente [Dersin 2014]. SoS possuem algumas características peculiares que os diferenciam de outros sistemas complexos, como independência operacional e gerencial dos seus constituintes, comportamento emergente e desenvolvimento evolucionário [Maier 1998]. Os sistemas constituintes de um SoS podem pertencer a diferentes organizações que têm seus processos de negócios específicos. Tais processos, quando reunidos para alcançar objetivos estratégicos de alianças de organizações (tais como parcerias, fusões ou aquisições de empresas), fazem surgir processos de negócios grandes, complexos e dinâmicos que são automatizados por SoS e são denominados como Processos-de-Processos de Negócio (PoP - *Processes-of-Business Processes*) [Cagnin and Nakagawa 2021].

O SoS evolui continuamente para responder as mudanças das missões e, assim, obter comportamentos emergentes resultantes da comunicação entre os constituintes para alcançar os objetivos estratégicos de negócio das alianças de organizações. Por consequência, podem haver falhas nos próprios sistemas constituintes, na comunicação entre eles [Ferreira et al. 2021] (por exemplo, atrasos de comunicação, indisponibilidade do serviço e problemas de perda de pacotes de dados [Alexander et al. 2004]) ou durante a reorganização da arquitetura dinâmica do SoS quando os constituintes são adicionados, alterados ou removidos durante a sua execução [Batista 2013], afetando o funcionamento e a confiabilidade do SoS como um todo [Ferreira et al. 2021]. Diante desse cenário, é primordial manter a estabilidade do SoS mesmo quando ocorre algum tipo de falha ou comportamento inesperado. Apesar da importância dos requisitos de confiabilidade para a estabilidade do SoS, eles ainda não são muito explorados na literatura [Bianchi et al. 2015, Cadavid et al. 2020, Ferreira et al. 2021].

Em paralelo, devido às peculiaridades do SoS, diversos aspectos podem dificultar a Engenharia de Requisitos (que envolve a extração, análise, especificação, validação e gerenciamento das mudanças de requisitos [Dick et al. 2017]), por exemplo, múltiplas interações entre diversos sistemas constituintes que têm necessidades de uso diferentes com as suas particularidades; constituintes podem pertencer a diferentes domínios e conter conceitos homônimos com significados divergentes entre os domínios; variação da capacidade do SoS de acordo com situações operacionais específicas do negócio, mesmo dentro de um único domínio de negócio; fatores internos ou externos ao SoS que podem levar a demandas de mudanças rápidas nos constituintes e no próprio SoS [Lewis et al. 2009]. A partir desses desafios, é crucial utilizar técnicas e mecanismos apropriados para realizar o gerenciamento de requisitos durante todo o ciclo de vida do SoS [Ncube and Lim 2018].

Diante da importância dos requisitos de confiabilidade e dos desafios inerentes à Engenharia de Requisitos no contexto de SoS, o principal objetivo deste artigo é descobrir como esse tipo de requisito não funcional têm sido extraído, especificado e validado na literatura. Para isso, foi conduzido um mapeamento sistemático da literatura [Kitchenham and Charters 2007], em que foram selecionados 12 estudos primários. Os principais resultados obtidos indicam que os estudos dão maior enfoque na representação de requisitos de confiabilidade, principalmente de tolerância a falhas e de recuperabilidade. Esses requisitos são extraídos principalmente a partir de falhas que podem ocorrer durante a comunicação entre os sistemas constituintes e, em geral, são especificados por meio de modelos e diagramas em nível de projeto arquitetural.

A escrita deste artigo está organizada em mais quatro seções. A Seção 2 aborda sobre requisitos de confiabilidade no contexto de SoS. A Seção 3 detalha o processo do mapeamento sistemático conduzido no âmbito deste trabalho. A Seção 4 discute os resultados e, por último, a Seção 5 apresenta a conclusão.

2. Requisitos de Confiabilidade de SoS

De acordo com a norma ISO/IEC 25010 [2011], *confiabilidade* é uma característica de qualidade de software e se refere ao grau em que um sistema executa suas funções sob condições específicas por um determinado período de tempo. *Confiabilidade* é composta pelas seguintes subcaracterísticas [ISO/IEC 25010 2011]: (i) *tolerância a falhas*: grau em que um sistema opera conforme planejado, apesar da presença de falhas de hardware ou software. Devido aos comportamentos emergentes de um SoS, resultantes das interações intrínsecas entre seus constituintes, existe a possibilidade de ocorrerem falhas ou erros [Hyun et al. 2020] que são considerados excepcionais em sistemas monolíticos tradicionais [Andrews et al. 2013]. De maneira complementar, dependendo de como os elementos do SoS colaboram, falhas podem ser propagadas e reveladas como outros tipos de falhas em diferentes elementos do sistema [Despotou and Kelly 2009]; (ii) *recuperabilidade*: grau em que, em caso de interrupção ou falha, um sistema pode se recuperar e retornar a um estado pretendido. No contexto de SoS, é a capacidade de recuperar dados do SoS diretamente afetados após uma falha (por exemplo, durante a interoperabilidade entre os constituintes) e restabelecer o SoS a um estado desejado. Porém, nem sempre é claro entender o processo da recuperação dos sistemas constituintes quando um SoS está sendo recuperado como um todo [Andrews et al. 2013]; (iii) *disponibilidade*: grau em que um sistema está operacional e acessível quando for utilizado. No contexto de SoS, como os constituintes podem ser inseridos, alterados ou removidos em tempo de execução, é primordial garantir que os constituintes essenciais para o funcionamento do SoS estejam disponíveis no momento adequado para o cumprimento de uma determinada missão; e (iv) *maturidade*: grau em que um sistema atende às necessidades de confiabilidade sob operação normal. Sob a perspectiva de SoS, é necessário garantir a sua estabilidade durante o seu uso pelos diferentes *stakeholders*. Para isso, é primordial assegurar a reconfiguração do SoS, devido à sua natureza dinâmica [Garro and Tundis 2014], em que os constituintes podem ser atualizados, fazer parte ou deixar de fazer parte de um SoS.

3. Mapeamento Sistemático

Para a execução do Mapeamento Sistemático da Literatura (MSL) foi adotado o processo proposto por Kitchenham and Charters [2007]. As etapas planejamento, condução e apresentação dos resultados estão descritas, respectivamente, nas Seções 3.1, 3.2 e 3.3. A ferramenta Parsifal[1] forneceu apoio para registrar principalmente as duas primeiras etapas. A ferramenta MS Excel também foi utilizada para tabular os dados dos estudos primários e confeccionar os gráficos.

3.1. Planejamento

O principal objetivo do MSL apresentado neste artigo é descobrir como os requisitos de confiabilidade de SoS têm sido extraídos, especificados e validados na literatura. Para isso, foi elaborada a seguinte questão de pesquisa principal **(QP)**: *Como os requisitos de confiabilidade de SoS estão sendo elicitados, especificados e validados?*

Com o intuito de fornecer uma resposta mais detalhada para a QP, foram estabelecidas as seguintes subquestões de pesquisa:

- **Sub-QP1.1:** *Quais tipos de requisitos (subcaracterísticas) de confiabilidade, de acordo com a norma [ISO/IEC 25010 2011], estão sendo tratados pelos estudos primários no contexto de SoS?*
- **Sub-QP1.2:** *Em qual fase do ciclo de vida de SoS os requisitos de confiabilidade estão sendo extraídos e especificados?*

[1]https://parsif.al/

- **Sub-QP1.3:** *Quais mecanismos (ou seja, método, técnica, abordagem, framework e etc) estão sendo utilizados para extrair requisitos de confiabilidade de SoS e quais fontes de informação estão sendo adotadas para isso?*
- **Sub-QP1.4:** *Quais técnicas estão sendo utilizadas para especificar ou representar os requisitos de confiabilidade de SoS?*
- **Sub-QP1.5:** *Quais critérios são utilizados para validar os requisitos de confiabilidade de SoS?*
- **Sub-QP1.6:** *Como os mecanismos de elicitação e técnicas de especificação de requisitos de confiabilidade têm sido avaliados?*

A estratégia de busca envolveu buscas eletrônicas em três bibliotecas digitais (*Scopus*[2], *ACM Digital Library*[3], *IEEE Xplore*[4]) frequentemente adotadas em mapeamentos e revisões sistemáticas da literatura na área de Engenharia de Software. Como a *Scopus* indexa artigos de diferentes bibliotecas digitais, ela foi utilizada pelos autores para realizar a calibragem da string de busca padrão, tomando como base cinco artigos de controle destacados em negrito na Tabela 3. Esses artigos foram identificados pelos autores a partir de um levantamento realizado antes da execução do MSL.

Para a elaboração da string de busca padrão, foram selecionadas três palavras-chaves relacionadas aos tópicos de interesse do MSL (*Systems-of-Systems*, *Reliability* e *Discover*). Para obter uma string de busca mais abrangente, os autores identificaram sinônimos para cada palavra-chave. Esses sinônimos foram encontrados em artigos publicados em conferências e periódicos da área de pesquisa. Após vários refinamentos durante a calibragem da string de busca preliminar, com o apoio dos artigos de controle, obteve-se a string de busca padrão:

*("Systems of Systems" **OR** "SoS" **OR** "System of System" **OR** "Systems of System" **OR** "System of Systems" **OR** "Systems-of-Systems" **OR** "System-of-System" **OR** "Systems-of-System" **OR** "System-of-Systems" **OR** "Systems of Information Systems" **OR** "SoIS" **OR** "Systems of Information System" **OR** "Systems-of-Information Systems" **OR** "Systems-of-Information System") **AND** (reliability **OR** fault **OR** failure **OR** recoverability) **AND** (discover **OR** discovery **OR** elicitation **OR** obtaining **OR** gaining **OR** acquisition **OR** capture **OR** capturing **OR** extracting **OR** specification **OR** representation **OR** modeling)*

Como os motores das bibliotecas digitais selecionadas possuem sintaxe distintas, a string de busca padrão foi adaptada para cada uma delas. Adicionalmente, para apoiar a seleção dos estudos primários foram estabelecidos critérios de inclusão (CI) e de exclusão (CE) exibidos, respectivamente, nas Tabelas 1 e 2. Com base nesses critérios, estudos devem ser incluídos se atendem pelo menos um dos CI e excluídos se atendem ao menos um dos CE.

Com o intuito de facilitar a extração dos dados dos estudos primários para responder as questões de pesquisa, os autores definiram um formulário de extração contendo os seguintes campos: (1) identificador do artigo (id), (2) ano de publicação, (3) tipo de publicação, (4) tipo dos autores (academia, indústria ou ambos), (5) resumo, (6) pontos

[2]https://www.scopus.com/
[3]https://www.acm.org/
[4]https://ieeexplore.ieee.org/

Tabela 1. Critérios de inclusão

Código	Descrição
CI1	O estudo propõe uma solução de extração de requisitos de confiabilidade de Sistemas-de-Sistemas
CI2	O estudo avalia o mecanismo de extração de requisitos de confiabilidade de Sistemas-de-Sistemas
CI3	O estudo avalia requisitos de confiabilidade de Sistemas-de-Sistemas
CI4	O estudo considera fatores/elementos que influenciam a confiabilidade em Sistemas-de-Sistemas

Tabela 2. Critérios de exclusão

Código	Descrição
CE1	O estudo não atende a pelo menos um dos critérios de inclusão
CE2	O estudo não está disponível
CE3	O estudo está escrito em uma linguagem diferente do inglês
CE4	O estudo é similar a outro que reporta os mesmos resultados, no qual o mais recente é base para a análise
CE5	O estudo é um documento não avaliado por pares (por exemplo, prefácio, livro, editorial, resumo, pôster, painel, palestra, mesa redonda, oficina ou demonstração)

fortes, (7) pontos fracos, (8) domínio de aplicação, (9) subcaracterísticas de confiabilidade, (10) fase do ciclo de vida do SoS que ocorre a extração, (11) fase do ciclo de vida do SoS que ocorre a especificação, (12) mecanismos utilizados para a extração, (13) fontes de informação utilizadas para apoiar a extração, (14) técnicas utilizadas para a especificação, (15) elemento(s) da técnica utilizado(s), (16) linguagem/notação adotada pela técnica, (17) desafios/problemas de confiabilidade tratados, (18) solução, (19) técnica utilizada para validar os requisitos, (20) critérios utilizados para validar os requisitos e (21) método de avaliação do estudo.

As principais ameaças à validade deste trabalho estão relacionadas a: (i) *possível perda de estudos relevantes:* para contornar essa ameaça, conduzimos as buscas em bibliotecas digitais variadas e efetuamos diversos refinamentos na string de busca utilizando termos encontrados nos artigos de controle. O termo "requisito" não foi incluído na string para não correr o risco de limitar o escopo da busca. (ii) *parcialidade na seleção dos estudos:* para mitigar essa ameaça nós seguimos rigorosamente o processo de MSL utilizado [Kitchenham and Charters 2007] e todos os autores participaram das duas etapas de seleção; todas as divergências foram discutidas e resolvidas por todos os autores. (iii) *falta de padronização na extração dos dados e de confiabilidade dos resultados:* para tratar essa ameaça um formulário de extração foi criado na ferramenta Parsifal e validado por todos autores. Os dados dos estudos primários foram extraídos pelo primeiro autor e validados e refinados pelos demais. Todo resultado obtido foi discutido entre os autores para melhor síntese das respostas das questões de pesquisa.

3.2. Condução

A etapa de condução do MSL foi sistematizada em cinco passos. No **passo 1**, foram realizadas buscas no período de 27/09/2021 a 17/11/2021 em cada biblioteca digital selecionada (IEEE Xplore, ACM e Scopus), considerando a string de busca correspondente. As buscas retornaram um total de 603 estudos, que foram importados na ferramenta Parsifal. No **passo 2**, 107 estudos duplicados foram identificados e removidos com o apoio da Parsifal, obtendo-se 496 estudos para serem submetidos à primeira seleção **(passo 3)**. Nesse passo, a seleção se deu por meio da leitura do título e resumo dos artigos, eliminando um total de 392 estudos de acordo com os critérios de inclusão (Tabela 1) e exclusão (Tabela 2), obtendo-se um total de 104 artigos. No **passo 4**, foi realizada leitura completa dos 104 artigos obtidos no passo anterior, aplicando os critérios mencionados previamente. Nesse penúltimo passo foram selecionados 12 estudos primários (Tabela 3[5]), cujos dados foram extraídos no **passo 5** com o apoio do formulário de extração, definido na etapa de planejamento.

Tabela 3. Estudos primários selecionados

ID	Ano	Tipo de Publ.	Título
E1	2015	Workshop	A Conceptual Model of System of Systems [Damm and Vincentelli 2015]
E2	2018	Conferência	Irrational System Behavior in a System of Systems [Van Bossuyt et al. 2018]
E3	**2020**	**Conferência**	**Pattern-based Analysis of Interaction Failures in Systems-of-Systems: a Case Study on Platooning [Hyun et al. 2020]**
E4	2008	Conferência	Autonomous verification architectures for complex systems [Prasad and Milks 2008]
E5	**2014**	**Conferência**	**Research on the task process reliability modeling of SoS** [Tianjian and Xin 2014]
E6	2017	Conferência	Systems architecture in failure analysis (Applications of architecture modeling to system failure analysis) [Rambikur et al. 2017]
E7	2016	Conferência	Model Driven Software Security Architecture of Systems-of-Systems [El Hachem et al. 2016]
E8	2014	Periódico	On the Reliability Analysis of Systems and SoS: The RAMSAS Method and Related Extensions [Garro and Tundis 2014]
E9	2009	Conferência	A deviation based systems of systems safety view for modelling architectural frameworks [Despotou and Kelly 2009]
E10	**2021**	**Conferência**	**System-of-Systems Reliability: An Exploratory Study in a Brazilian Public Organization [Imamura et al. 2021]**
E11	**2013**	**Conferência**	**Fault modelling for systems of systems [Andrews et al. 2013]**
E12	**2014**	**Conferência**	**SysML fault modelling in a traffic management system of systems [Ingram et al. 2014]**

Os resultados detalhados da primeira (passo 3) e da segunda seleção (passo 4) são apresentados, respectivamente, nas Tabelas 4 e 5.

3.3. Resultados

Os dados dos estudos primários, extraídos na etapa anterior (Seção 3.2), foram tabulados e analisados para obter uma visão geral dos estudos (Seção 3.3.1) e responder as questões de pesquisa deste MSL (Seções 3.3.2 a 3.3.6).

[5]Os estudos destacados em negrito se referem aos artigos de controle.

Tabela 4. Resultado da primeira seleção dos estudos

Bases	Total	Dupl.	CE1	CE2	CE3	CE4	CE5	CI1	CI2	CI3	CI4	1ª Sel.
Scopus	398	60	-278	0	-2	0	-4	+1	+11	+14	+28	54
IEEE	185	47	-96	0	0	0	-1	+4	+7	+10	+20	41
ACM	20	0	-10	0	0	0	-1	0	0	+2	+7	9
Total	603	107	-384	0	-2	0	-6	+5	+18	+26	+55	104

Tabela 5. Resultado da segunda seleção dos estudos

Bases	CE1	CE2	CE3	CE4	CE5	CI1	CI2	CI3	CI4	2ª Sel.
Scopus	-37	-9	-2	0	-1	+1	+1	+1	+2	5
IEEE	-33	-2	0	0	0	0	+1	+4	+1	6
ACM	-8	0	0	0	0	0	0	0	+1	1
Total	-78	-11	-2	0	-1	+1	+2	+5	+4	12

3.3.1. Visão geral dos estudos primários

A Figura 1 apresenta um panorama geral dos estudos primários. Observa-se que a publicação dos estudos está distribuída, em geral, de maneira equilibrada ao longo dos anos (exceto no período 2010 a 2012) e que a maioria dos autores é da academia. Apenas um estudo foi publicado em periódico da área (*IEEE Systems Journal*) e a maioria deles foi publicado em conferências relevantes, como *System of Systems Engineering* (SoSE), *Asia-Pacific Software Engineering Conference* (APSEC), *International Symposium on Autonomous Decentralized Systems* (ISADS) e *Brazilian Symposium on Information Systems* (SBSI).

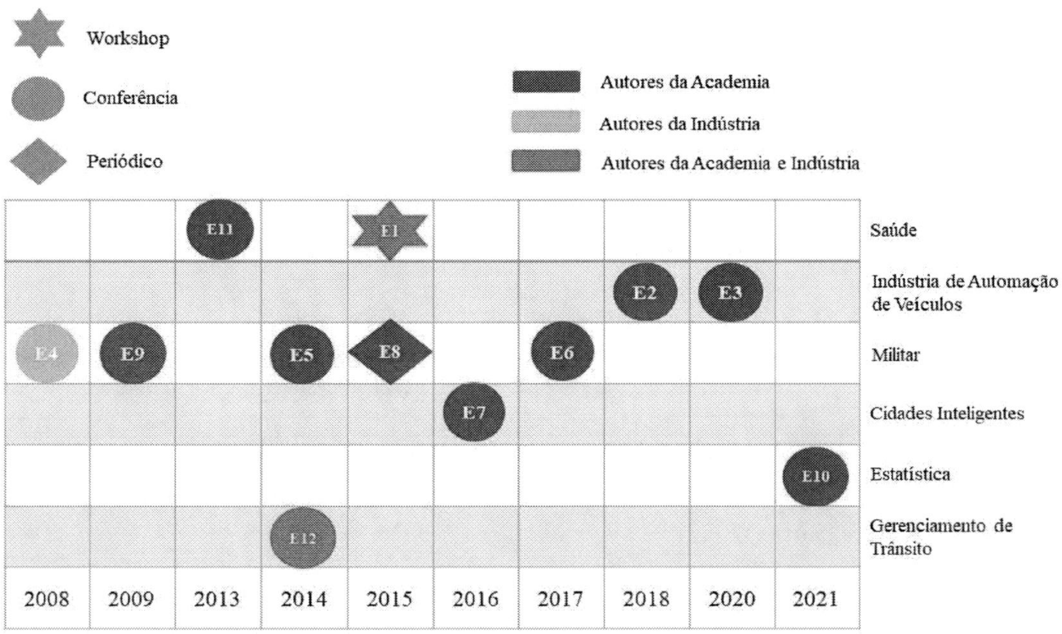

Figura 1. Visão geral dos estudos primários

Considerando o domínio em que os estudos foram aplicados, destaca-se o domínio militar (5 de 12 estudos). Além desses, os domínios Saúde, Indústria de Automação de Veículos, Cidades Inteligentes, Estatística e Gerenciamento de Trânsito também estão presentes porém com menos recorrência.

Em relação ao país de origem dos autores dos estudos primários, se destacam os países da Europa e da América (em particular do Norte e do Sul), que totalizam 7 e 5 autores, respectivamente. O continente asiático possui 2 autores e a Oceania possui um. Assim, observa-se que o tópico de pesquisa deste MSL está sendo investigado em diversas partes do globo terrestre. Além disso, há colaboração de pesquisa entre autores de alguns países, como é o caso de autores da Alemanha e Estados Unidos (E1), França e Austrália (E7), Reino Unido e Holanda (E12), contribuindo para o fortalecimento dos grupos de pesquisa e para o amadurecimento do tópico sobre confiabilidade de SoS.

3.3.2. Requisitos de Confiabilidade Tratados (Sub-QP1.1)

Os estudos se preocupam mais especificamente com requisitos de tolerância a falhas (12 de 12 estudos) e de recuperabilidade (5 de 12), conforme ilustrado na Tabela 6. O primeiro tipo de requisito é bastante relevante no contexto de SoS pois podem ocorrer diversas falhas principalmente devido à sua arquitetura dinâmica, já que seus constituintes podem ser alterados, removidos ou inseridos, a qualquer momento, em tempo de execução. Além disso, podem ocorrer atrasos de comunicação (por exemplo, devido a dados que dependem da uma coleta manual e são enviados em lote para algum sistema, podendo levar algum tempo para serem incorporados ao banco de dados), indisponibilidade do serviço (por exemplo, em razão do excesso de chamadas de serviços) e também alteração em interfaces dos serviços sem notificar previamente os envolvidos [Imamura et al. 2021]. Assim, justifica-se o segundo tipo de requisito mais tratado pelos estudos pois, uma vez que as possíveis falhas são identificadas, é necessário definir procedimentos adequados para contornar os problemas levantados a fim de manter a estabilidade do SoS para cumprir as suas missões e, consequentemente, para atender os objetivos estratégicos de negócio das alianças de organizações. Devido à relação intrínseca entre requisitos de tolerância a falhas e de recuperabilidade, 5 de 12 estudos tratam ambos requisitos.

Tabela 6. Tipos de requisitos de confiabilidade cobertos pelos estudos primários

Tipo	ID
Tolerância a falha	E1, E2, E3, E4, E5, E6, E7, E8, E9, E10, E11 e E12
Recuperabilidade	E7, E8, E10, E11 e E12

3.3.3. Elicitação e especificação de requisitos de confiabilidade durante o ciclo de vida do SoS (Sub-QP1.2)

Poucos estudos tratam da descoberta de requisitos de confiabilidade (5 de 12) e em uma fase posterior à fase de requisitos, ou seja, na fase de projeto arquitetural (4 de 12), conforme indicado na Tabela 7. Apenas um estudo (E10) se preocupa em levantar e especificar esse tipo de requisito na fase de requisitos, porém não discute como isso poderia ser feito durante o desenvolvimento evolucionário do SoS. Esse resultado evidencia que a área de Engenharia de Requisitos de SoS precisa ser mais explorada [Ncube and Lim 2018], visto que os esforços ainda estão bastante concentrados em nível arquitetural [Cadavid et al. 2020].

Tabela 7. Extração e especificação de requisitos de confiabilidade no ciclo de vida do SoS

Fase	**ID (Extração)**	**ID (Especificação)**
Requisito	E10	E10
Projeto Arquitetural	E2, E3, E5 e E9	E1, E2, E3, E4, E5, E7, E8, E11 e E12

Na fase de projeto arquitetural, as capacidades dos constituintes já foram identificadas em fases anteriores do ciclo de vida do SoS, utilizando técnicas apropriadas, como mKAOS [Silva et al. 2015]. Diante disso, o interesse maior dos estudos está em definir *como* as potenciais falhas, que podem surgir durante a interoperabilidade entre os sistemas constituintes ou em algum outro momento da execução do SoS, devem ser tratadas em nível arquitetural para garantir a estabilidade do SoS.

3.3.4. Mecanismos de extração de requisitos de confiabilidade de SoS (Sub-QP1.3)

Conforme já mencionado na Seção 3.3.3, os estudos E2, E3, E5, E9 e E10 tratam da extração de requisitos de confiabilidade de SoS voltados a tolerância a falhas. Para isso, esses estudos utilizam mecanismos distintos (Tabela 8).

Tabela 8. Mecanismos de extração de requisitos de confiabilidade de SoS

Mecanismo	**Fonte de informação**	**ID**
Abordagem para identificar vulnerabilidades do SoS	Interação entre constituintes representada em modelos funcionais	E2
Técnica para extrair sequências de interação impróprias entre constituintes	Dados de interação entre constituintes obtidos a partir de *logs* de execução do SoS	E3
Abordagem para identificar causas de falhas	Diagrama causal	E5
Abordagem DDA (*Dependability Deviation Analysis*)	Elementos do SoS	E9
Grupo focal[6]	Equipe de engenharia do SoS	E10

Em mais detalhes, o estudo E2 identifica comportamentos impróprios a partir da análise dos fluxos que saem de cada constituinte do SoS e são eventos iniciais inesperados em outro constituinte. A análise é feita em modelos funcionais, que representam a comunicação entre os sistemas constituintes. Após a identificação dos comportamentos impróprios, os autores atribuem uma probabilidade de ocorrência a cada um deles. De acordo com os autores, a análise dos fluxos e a atribuição de probabilidade podem ser apoiados por técnicas existentes de análise de falhas de produtos (como FMEA (*Failure Modes and Effects Analysis*) e PRA (*Probabilistic Risk Assessment*)). No estudo E3, os autores propõem uma técnica de análise baseada em padrões para processar os dados de interação entre constituintes e extrair sequências de interação impróprias que levam a falhas e dificultam o cumprimento das missões do SoS. Os dados de interação, gerados por simulador, são obtidos a partir de *logs* de execução de cenários do mundo real que falharam. Já o estudo E5 analisa cada possível falha que pode ocorrer durante o processo de tarefa do SoS, visto que esse processo é composto por outros processos e a falha de cada processo provavelmente afetará todo o processo do SoS. A análise é realizada em um diagrama causal[7], que representa o processo de tarefa do SoS, e é baseada em uma técnica de análise de falhas de produtos (FMEA). No estudo E9, os autores utilizam a abordagem DDA *(Dependability Deviation Analysis)* para identificar as condições de falhas e efeitos atrelados a cada elemento do SoS. Cada elemento do SoS é investigado com o intuito de levantar desvios do comportamento pretendido (por exemplo, omissão de determinado serviço). Se os efeitos do desvio afetarem a operação do SoS, uma condição de falha é identificada. Em seguida, os elementos do SoS, as respectivas condições de falhas identificadas e os efeitos associados são representados em um modelo de falhas (F-Maps), a partir do qual são extraídos os requisitos de tolerância a falhas. Esses requisitos refletem o contexto de como as falhas afetarão toda a operação do SoS, e não o contexto local de uma única condição de falha. Por outro lado, no E10 os autores conduziram um grupo focal com a equipe de engenharia de SoS de uma organização pública na área de estatística (para apoio a tomada de decisões) para levantar situações que poderiam prejudicar a confiabilidade geral do SoS (por exemplo, chamadas excessivas para serviços de dados, atrasos de comunicação entre os sistemas constituintes e alteração nas interfaces dos serviços fornecidos pelos constituintes).

3.3.5. Técnicas para especificação de requisitos de confiabilidade de SoS (Sub-QP1.4)

Conforme apresentado na Tabela 9, os estudos utilizam diferentes técnicas para especificar os requisitos de confiabilidade, sendo que 8 de 12 estudos (E1, E3, E5, E7, E8, E10, E11 e E12) representam esses requisitos por meio de modelos ou diagramas. Desses estudos, quatro deles (E7, E8, E11 e E12) representam os requisitos de confiabilidade em diagramas distintos da notação SysML[8], que é uma linguagem utilizada para documentar a arquitetura de sistemas complexos, como o SoS. Em particular, o estudo E7 estendeu o diagrama de blocos da SysML para criar dois outros modelos (de segurança e de objetivos) e o estudo E12 criou um perfil para a SysML, utilizando estereótipos específicos para representar mais apropriadamente as falhas de um SoS. Por outro lado, dois estudos (E8 e E11) utilizam na íntegra alguns diagramas (de requisitos, de definição de bloco, de bloco interno, de sequência e de atividades) da SysML para especificar os requisitos de confiabilidade do SoS com foco em tolerância a falhas.

Considerando os outros estudos que representam os requisitos de confiabilidade em diagramas ou modelos, o estudo E1 utiliza mapa conceitual para representar um panorama geral das falhas que podem ocorrer durante a execução de um SoS. Em outra perspectiva, o estudo E10 estendeu o modelo de missões da mKAOS [Silva et al. 2015], que é uma linguagem orientada a missões criada para representar informação associada a missões do SoS. O modelo estendido possui novos elementos inspirados em três elementos (evento *timer*, evento *cancel* e *gateway* exclusivo) da notação BPMN (*Business Process Model and Notation*). Já o estudo E3 utiliza um modelo de interação, com notação

[7]Esse diagrama mostra a hierarquia dos processos do SoS e suas respectivas tarefas [Tianjian and Xin 2014].

[8]https://sysml.org/

Tabela 9. Técnicas para especificação de requisitos de confiabilidade de SoS

Técnica	Notação	ID
Mapa conceitual	Mapa Conceitual	E1
Lista de caminhos de falhas	Textual	E2
Modelo de interação	Próprio autor	E3
Ontologia de falhas	Modelo de dados relacional	E4
Planilha	Textual	E5
Diagrama	IDEF3	E5
Modelo de segurança e modelo de objetivos	Extensão do diagrama de blocos da SySML	E7
Diagrama de requisitos	SysML	E8
Modelo de missões com confiabilidade representada	Extensão da mKAOS	E10
Diagramas de definição de bloco, de bloco interno, de sequência e de atividades	SysML	E11
Diagramas de atividades	SysML	E12

própria, para representar interações entre os sistemas constituintes com comportamento inesperado.

Três estudos (E2, E4 e E5) utilizam representação textual para especificar requisitos de confiabilidade de SoS. Em mais detalhes, E2 apresenta um listagem de cada caminho de execução do SoS que leva a falhas, enquanto que E5 utiliza uma planilha para documentar todas as falhas identificadas do SoS. Essa planilha contém, dentre outras informações, cada tarefa do processo com o respectivo modo, efeito e causa da falha, e também como mitigar a falha. A partir dessa panilha, são gerados diagramas na notação IDEF3 (*Integrated DEFinition for Process Description Capture Method*) para representar graficamente as falhas que podem ocorrer durante o fluxo de tarefas do processo. Por outro lado, E4 representa uma ontologia de falhas em um modelo de dados relacional semântico baseado em axiomas, que possibilita gerar ou atualizar um conjunto exaustivo de falhas de SoS.

3.3.6. Validação dos requisitos de confiabilidade do SoS ((Sub-QP1.5) e avaliação dos mecanismos de extração e das técnicas de especificação (Sub-QP1.6)

Ressalta-se que nenhum dos estudos primários, principalmente aqueles que propõem mecanismos para extrair requisitos de confiabilidade de SoS, explicitaram a forma que esses requisitos foram validados. Em relação à avaliação dos mecanismos de extração e das técnicas de especificação de requisitos de confiabilidade, todos os estudos primários correspondentes foram avaliados por meio de estudos de caso em domínios variados conforme mencionado na Seção 3.3.1. A maioria desses estudos de caso abordou desafios principalmente atrelados a tolerância a falhas (E2, E3, E5, E9 e E10) e recuperabilidade (E10).

4. Discussão e Perspectivas de Trabalhos Futuros

Os sistemas constituintes de um SoS comumente são controlados por diferentes organizações ou podem estar geograficamente distribuídos dentro de uma mesma organização [Maier 1998]. Nesse contexto, a Engenharia de Requisitos de SoS deve ser realizada por meio de colaboração de vários *stakeholders* durante o desenvolvimento evolucionário do SoS para que seu ciclo de vida seja perene [Andrews et al. 2013]. Essa forma de desenvolvimento é uma das características inerentes ao SoS em que os sistemas constituintes podem evoluir a qualquer momento, resultando na evolução do próprio SoS; por outro lado, SoS também evolui devido a mudanças em seu ambiente e, por isso, possui arquitetura dinâmica que causa um novo arranjo de seus constituintes [Maier 1998]. Apesar dessa preocupação, os estudos primários deste MSL dão maior enfoque na elicitação e especificação de requisitos de confiabilidade durante a fase de projeto arquitetural e não apresentam métodos e técnicas específicos para tratar esse tipo de requisito durante a fase de requisitos ao longo de todo o ciclo de desenvolvimento e evolução do SoS.

Outra característica peculiar é o dinamismo do SoS, visto que os sistemas constituintes podem, a qualquer momento, ser adicionados, alterados ou removidos durante a sua execução [Maier 1998], tornando vital garantir a confiabilidade do SoS [Batista 2013]. Compreender os comportamentos dos sistemas constituintes e as comunicações entre eles, bem como identificar anomalias e interrupções que impactem as operações durante a execução do SoS é primordial para estabelecer mecanismos que garantam a sua estabilidade [Ncube and Lim 2018]. Nessa direção, quase metade dos estudos primários que se preocupam com extração de requisitos de confiabilidade consideram como fonte de informação a interação entre os sistemas constituintes e, inclusive, sequências de interação que levam a falhas e prejudicam o alcance das missões do SoS. Entretanto, apesar da informação valiosa dos grandes, complexos e dinâmicos processos de negócios das alianças de organizações e dos diversos benefícios em extrair requisitos a partir de modelos de processos de negócio, dentre eles o alinhamento entre os níveis técnico e de negócio [Cruz et al. 2015], visto que confiabilidade deve ser considerada e gerenciada desde o nível de negócio, nenhum estudo primário utiliza esse artefato como fonte de informação. Os mecanismos de extração de requisitos de confiabilidade dos estudos primários também não se preocupam com possíveis falhas que podem ocorrer quando os constituintes evoluem, devido às características inerentes ao SoS (como independência operacional e gerencial, e desenvolvimento evolucionário), e podem deixar de oferecer as capacidades necessárias para o cumprimento das missões do SoS.

Diferentemente do pouco enfoque dado pelos estudos em extração de requisitos de confiabilidade de SoS, a especificação é abordada por quase todos devido à importância de registrar requisitos não funcionais (dentre eles, requisitos de confiabilidade) como parte da documentação do SoS, especialmente na fase de projeto arquitetural. A maioria dos estudos utiliza modelos ou diagramas para documentar os requisitos de confiabilidade, já que esse tipo de artefato é comumente adotado para representar arquitetura de SoS [Guessi et al. 2019]. Porém, nenhum estudo discutiu uma representação ou *template* padrão para especificar de maneira completa e adequada os requisitos de confiabilidade, considerando as particularidades do SoS, destacando-se a independência operacional e gerencial dos sistemas constituintes, bem como o comportamento emergente e o desenvolvimento evolucionário do SoS.

Com base nas respostas das questões de pesquisa (Seção 3.3) e nas discussões supramencionadas, a seguir são sugeridos alguns desdobramentos de pesquisas futuras para a área de Engenharia de Requisitos de Confiabilidade de SoS: (i) definir métodos e técnicas específicos para tratar requisitos de confiabilidade durante todo o desenvolvimento evolucionário do SoS, considerando inclusive outros tipos de requisitos, como maturidade e disponibilidade, e também o gerenciamento adequado das mudanças dos requisitos de confiabilidade dos sistemas constituintes que podem impactar no alcance da estabilidade do SoS como um todo; (ii) definir técnicas para extrair requisitos de confiabilidade a partir de modelos dos grandes, complexos e dinâmicos processos de negócis de alianças de organizações com o intuito de garantir o alinhamento entre os níveis técnico e de negócio a fim de alcançar de maneira mais efetiva as missões do SoS e, consequentemente, os objetivos estratégicos de negócio das alianças de organizações; (iii) estabelecer uma representação adequada, por exemplo, no formato de um *template*, para especificar de maneira completa requisitos de confiabilidade levando em consideração as diferentes características particulares do SoS; (iv) estabelecer técnicas apropriadas para validar os requisitos de confiabilidade, envolvendo os diferentes tipos de *stakeholders* do SoS e os diferentes fatores que afetam a falta de confiabilidade de SoS levantados por Ferreira et al. [2021]; e (v) conduzir estudos de casos e estudos empíricos para avaliar quantitativamente e qualitativamente os métodos e técnicas propostos.

5. Conclusão

Com os resultados obtidos no mapeamento sistemático conduzido no âmbito trabalho, espera-se contribuir para um melhor entendimento sobre como os requisitos de confiabilidade de SoS estão sendo tratados na literatura. Foi constatado que os requisitos de confiabilidade de SoS estão concentrados em tolerância a falhas e recuperabilidade e estão sendo identificados e especificados em fase posterior à fase de requisitos. Por essa razão, as especificações são baseadas principalmente em modelos e diagramas, dentre eles destacando-se os da SysML. A descoberta dos requisitos de confiabilidade é realizada principalmente com base em comportamentes inesperados que podem ocorrer durante a comunicação entre os constituintes. Ademais, este trabalho pode despertar o interesse de especialistas e pesquisadores da área sobre a importância de considerar os grandes, complexos e dinâmicos processos de negócios de alianças de organizações como uma fonte de informação valiosa para extrair os requisitos de confiabilidade do SoS, uma vez que é importante considerar desde o nível de processos de negócio as potenciais falhas (por exemplo, comportamentos não previstos ou interrupções inesperadas) que podem dificultar ou afetar a estabilidade e disponibilidade desses processos. Com essa fonte de informação, é possível manter o alinhamento entre os níveis técnico e de negócio, colaborando para que o SoS ajude as alianças a alcançarem seus objetivos estratégicos de negócio, tornando-as mais eficientes, competitivas e lucrativas. Além disso, é fundamental gerenciar os requisitos de confiabilidade de maneira apropriada durante todo o ciclo do SoS principalmente devido a sua característica evolutiva em que tanto os constituintes quanto o próprio SoS podem evoluir a qualquer momento, culminando em uma nova organização arquitetural do SoS.

Agradecimentos

O presente trabalho foi realizado com apoio da UFMS e da Coordenação de Aperfeiçoamento de Pessoal de Nível Superior (CAPES) - Código de financiamento 001.

Referências

Alexander, R., Hall-May, M., and Kelly, T. (2004). Characterisation of Systems of Systems failures. In *22nd International System Safety Conference*, pages 499–508. IEEE.

Andrews, Z., Fitzgerald, J., Payne, R., and Romanovsky, A. (2013). Fault modelling for systems of systems. In *11th International Symposium on Autonomous Decentralized Systems (ISADS)*, pages 1–8. IEEE.

Batista, T. (2013). Challenges for SoS architecture description. In *1st International Workshop on Software Engineering for Systems-of-Systems*, pages 35–37. ACM.

Bianchi, T., Santos, D. S., and Felizardo, K. R. (2015). Quality attributes of Systems-of-Systems: A systematic literature review. In *3rd International Workshop on Software Engineering for Systems-of-Systems*, pages 23–30. IEEE.

Cadavid, H., Andrikopoulos, V., and Avgeriou, P. (2020). Architecting Systems of Systems: A tertiary study. *Information and Software Technology*, 118:106202.

Cagnin, M. I. and Nakagawa, E. Y. (2021). Towards dynamic Processes-of-Business Processes: A new understanding. *Business Process Management Journal*, 27(5):1545–1568.

Cruz, E., Machado, R., and Santos, M. (2015). Bridging the gap between a set of interrelated business process models and software models. In *17th International Conference on Enterprise Information Systems(ICEIS)*, pages 338–345.

Damm, W. and Vincentelli, A. S. (2015). A conceptual model of System of Systems. In *2nd International Workshop on the Swarm at the Edge of the Cloud*, pages 19–27. ACM.

Dersin, P. (2014). Systems of Systems. IEEE-Reliability Society. Technical Committee on "Systems of Systems", `https://rs.ieee.org/technical-activities/technical-committees/systems-of-systems.html` (Acesso em 28/01/2022).

Despotou, G. and Kelly, T. (2009). A deviation based systems of systems safety view for modelling architectural frameworks. *IET Journals*, 1:13.

Dick, J., Hull, E., and Jackson, K. (2017). *Requirements engineering*. Springer, London.

El Hachem, J., Pang, Z. Y., Chiprianov, V., Babar, A., and Aniorte, P. (2016). Model driven software security architecture of Systems-of-Systems. In *23rd Asia-Pacific Software Engineering Conference (APSEC)*, pages 89–96. IEEE.

Ferreira, F. H., Nakagawa, E. Y., and dos Santos, R. P. (2021). Reliability in software-intensive systems: Challenges, solutions, and future perspectives. In *47th Euromicro Conference on Software Engineering and Advanced Applications (SEAA)*, pages 54–61.

Garro, A. and Tundis, A. (2014). On the reliability analysis of systems and SoS: The RAMSAS method and related extensions. *IEEE Systems Journal*, 9(1):232–241.

Guessi, M., Graciano-Neto, V. V., and Nakagawa, E. Y. (2019). Architectural description of Systems-of-Information Systems. *Minicourse of Brazilian Symposium on Information Systems*, 1:29–52.

Hyun, S., Song, J., Shin, S., Baek, Y.-M., and Bae, D.-H. (2020). Pattern-based analysis of interaction failures in Systems-of-Systems: a case study on platooning. In *27th Asia-Pacific Software Engineering Conference (APSEC)*, pages 326–335. IEEE.

Imamura, M., Ferreira, F. H., Fernandes, J. C., and Santos, R. (2021). System-of-Systems reliability: An exploratory study in a brazilian public organization. In *17th Brazilian Symposium on Information Systems (SBSI)*, pages 1–8. ACM.

Ingram, C., Andrews, Z., Payne, R., and Plat, N. (2014). Sysml fault modelling in a traffic management system of systems. In *9th International Conference on System of Systems Engineering (SOSE)*, pages 124–129. IEEE.

ISO/IEC 25010 (2011). ISO/IEC 25010:2011 - Systems and software engineering — Systems and software Quality Requirements and Evaluation (SQuaRE) — System and software quality models.

Kitchenham, B. and Charters, S. (2007). Guidelines for performing systematic literature reviews in software engineering. Technical Report Technical Report EBSE 2007-001, Keele University and Durham University, Keele, UK.

Lewis, G. A., Morris, E., Place, P., Simanta, S., and Smith, D. B. (2009). Requirements engineering for systems of systems. In *3rd Annual IEEE International Systems Conference (SysCon)*, pages 247–252. IEEE.

Maier, M. (1998). Architecting Principles for Systems-of-Systems. *Systems Engineering*, 1(4):267–284.

Morgan, D. L. and Krueger, R. A. (1998). *The focus group guidebook*. Sage.

Ncube, C. and Lim, S. L. (2018). On Systems of Systems engineering: A requirements engineering perspective and research agenda. In *26th International Requirements Engineering Conference (RE)*, pages 112–123. IEEE.

Prasad, G. and Milks, W. A. (2008). Autonomous verification architectures for complex systems. In *International Multi-Conference on Engineering and Technological Innovation (IMETI)*, volume 2, pages 159–163.

Rambikur, A., Giammarco, K., and O'Halloran, B. (2017). Systems architecture in failure analysis (applications of architecture modeling to system failure analysis). In *12th System of Systems Engineering Conference (SoSE)*, pages 1–6. IEEE.

Silva, E., Batista, T., and Oquendo, F. (2015). A mission-oriented approach for designing System-of-Systems. In *10th System of Systems Engineering Conference (SoSE)*, pages 346–351. IEEE.

Tianjian, W. and Xin, P. (2014). Research on the task process reliability modeling of SoS. In *26th Chinese Control and Decision Conference (CCDC)*, pages 2262–2266. IEEE.

Van Bossuyt, D. L., O'Halloran, B. M., and Arlitt, R. M. (2018). Irrational system behavior in a System of Systems. In *13th Annual Conference on System of Systems Engineering (SoSE)*, pages 343–349. IEEE.

Understanding Refactoring Tasks over Time: A Study Using Refactoring Graphs

Aline Brito, Andre Hora, Marco Tulio Valente

[1] ASERG Group, Department of Computer Science (DCC),
Federal University of Minas Gerais (UFMG) – Belo Horizonte, Brazil

{alinebrito,mtov,andrehora}@dcc.ufmg.br

Abstract. *Refactoring is a fundamental practice in modern software development. Therefore, it is essential that practitioners have a solid understanding of refactoring, both in theory and in practice. In this paper, we rely on a graph-based abstraction—called refactoring graphs—to visualize and analyze refactorings performed by students in a canonical refactoring application: the Video Store System, proposed by Fowler. We asked 46 students to perform the refactorings included in this example under two scenarios: according to a list of explicit guidelines, where most students performed the tasks successfully; and by using flexible ones, in which a part of the students faced problems identifying the appropriate operations. We conclude by presenting discussions and implications.*

1. Introduction

Refactoring is a common and indispensable practice during software evolution. Developers frequently refactor the source code for different proposes [Murphy-Hill et al. 2009, Pantiuchina et al. 2020, Silva et al. 2016]. As a consequence, a large number of studies investigate refactoring practices in the last 30 years [Abid et al. 2020]. Many of those studies focus on refactoring comprehension, for example, assessing motivations, benefits, impact, and challenges of refactoring operations [Pantiuchina et al. 2020, Kim et al. 2014, Sellitto et al. 2022]. There are also approaches and tools to understand source code affected by refactoring [Silva et al. 2020, Tsantalis et al. 2020, Brito and Valente 2021, Grund et al. 2021]. However, typically, prior literature does not rely on abstractions to extract, visualize, and understand complex refactoring tasks performed over time, which is a relevant aspect for researchers and practitioners [Bogart et al. 2020, AlOmar et al. 2021a].

Therefore, in this paper, we explore an abstraction called *refactoring graphs* [Brito et al. 2020, Brito et al. 2021] to visualize, interpret, and evaluate refactoring tasks performed over time. For this purpose, we rely on a canonical refactoring example: a Video Store System, proposed by Fowler [Fowler 1999]. This example is used by Fowler to present and discuss refactoring operations, practices, and benefits. Specifically, we invited 46 students from a Software Engineering undergraduate course to perform refactoring operations in the Video Store System under two distinct scenarios. The first one includes a list of *explicit* and well-defined guidelines, i.e., refactoring tasks with detail instructions about the piece of code that should be refactored and the expected operations. The second scenario comprises *flexible* and open guidelines, in which we asked the students to implement the Template Method design pattern [Gamma et al. 1995].

After that, we detect the refactorings performed by the students in distinct commits (i.e., over time) [Silva et al. 2020]. Next, we generated *refactoring graphs* to describe the refactorings performed by each student. In such graphs, the nodes are methods, and the edges represent refactoring operations. Particularly, our guidelines generate a large refactoring graph with 24 vertices and 26 edges.

To better understand the tasks performed by the students, we first rely on a graph-based metric. Specifically, for *explicit guidelines*, we used a similarity metric called *edit distance* to compare each student's graph with our ground truth [Sanfeliu and Fu 1983]. This strategy allowed us to automate the analysis of the tasks performed by the students and to rapidly conclude whether they matched our proposed ground truth. It also allowed us to rapidly identify and analyze the divergences between the student's solution and the ground truth. In the case of *flexible guidelines*, we performed a visual inspection by navigating in the graph-based structure to verify, for example, refactoring operations, sequence of operations, and affected elements. Our key results are summarized as follows:

1. When following *explicit guidelines*, most students performed refactoring tasks successfully (93.5%). The few mistakes refer to refactorings performed in multiples commits.
2. When following *flexible guidelines*, less students implemented the design pattern successfully (70%). Particularly, a significant part of the students faced difficulties identifying the appropriate refactorings operations.

Our contributions are twofold. First, we show that *refactoring graphs* can be used to understand, evaluate, and visualize large refactoring tasks. In some cases, this analysis can be automated using standard graph metrics, such as *edit distance*. Second, we complement research on refactoring practices, mainly on the educational side, by exploring the student's understanding of refactoring.

Structure: Section 2 includes details about the Video Store System and the representation of refactoring operations as graphs. Section 3 describes the study design, while Section 4 shows the results. Section 5 states threats to validity, and Section 6 presents related work. We conclude by prospecting future studies in Section 8.

2. Background

2.1. Video Store System

In the study described in this paper, the students followed the steps proposed by Fowler to refactor a well-known example designed to illustrate the benefits and the mechanisms of refactoring: a system to calculate and print clients' charges at a Video Store [Fowler 1999].[1] Basically, the system prints the movies rented by a client with prices and the number of rented days. The price depends on the movie's category (i.e., regular, children, and new releases) and the number of rented days. The initial system version contains three classes:

- *Movie*: class that represents a movie with the respective data, i.e., title, price, and category.

[1] In the 2nd edition of his book, Fowler changed the system to JavaScript. However, we decided to use the original system since it is still widely known.

- *Rental*: class that represents a client renting a movie. It includes information about the movie and the number of rented days.
- *Customer*: class to represent the store' clients. It comprises information as the client's name and a list of rented movies. There is also a method, named `statement()`, which prints the statement in text format.

The new code design is a consequence of several refactoring operations to improve existing code and incorporate a new feature. Among these refactorings, most cases aim to decompose the large method `statement()` by extracting and moving distinct pieces of the code. Other refactorings generate the class `Price` and their subclasses in seven main steps, as proposed by the State design pattern. In this case, the goal is to remove a conditional statement that determines the price of each video category. There are also classes to print the statement in different formats (i.e., `HTMLStatement` and `TextStatement`), as proposed by the Template Method pattern.[2]

2.2. Refactoring Graphs

We use refactoring graphs to visualize and understand the operations performed by the students in our experiment [Brito et al. 2020, Brito et al. 2021]. Formally, a refactoring graph G contains a set of disconnected subgraphs $G' = (V', E')$. In these graphs, the vertices represent the full signature of methods. The edges refer to the refactoring type (e.g., extract method), and it includes additional information about the operation (e.g., author name, date, and commit). Figure 1 shows an example: extracting method `amountFor(Rental)` from `statement()`, and moving it with a new name to a class `Rental` creates a sequence with two edges in the subgraph. A second refactoring to extract and move the method `getFrequentRenterPoints()` from `statement()` generates another node in the graph.

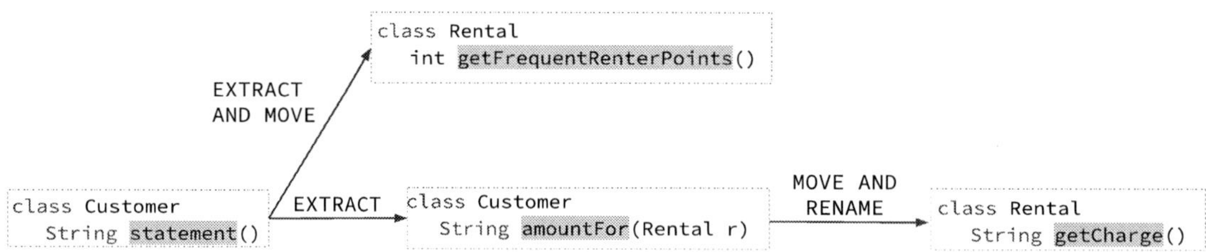

Figure 1. Example of a fragment of ref. subgraph from Video Store System

In this context, following all the steps to refactor the Video Store System creates a large subgraph with 24 vertices and 26 edges, as presented in Figure 2. As we can notice, 14 edges refer to *extract* operations, generating one or more methods, i.e., new vertices in the subgraph. The subgraph also includes two *pull up* methods, six *pull up signatures* (when only the signature is pulled up, preserving the method body in the subclass), and three *push down implementations* (when the signature is kept in the superclass, as an abstract method). There is a single operation called *move and rename* method, which moves a method to a distinct class, changing its name.

[2]The class diagram of the system before and after applying the refactoring tasks is publicly available at: `github.com/alinebrito/refgraph-fowler-study#class-diagram`

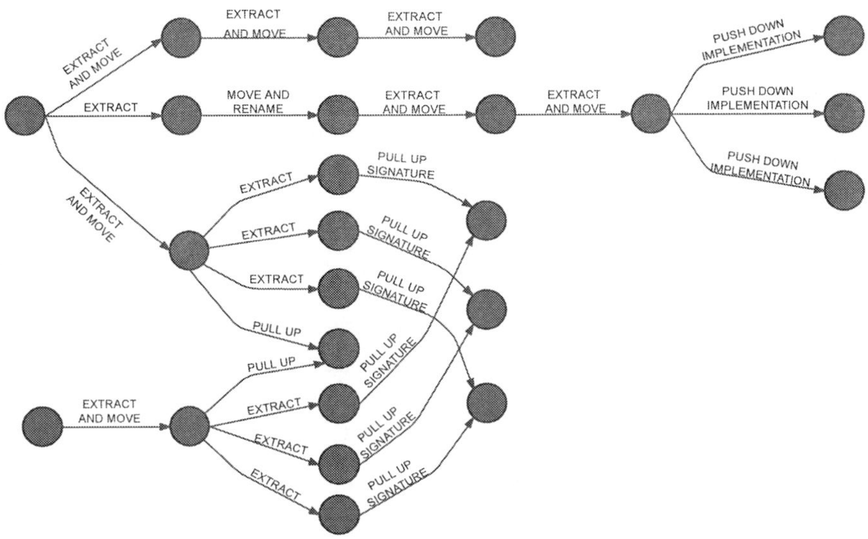

Figure 2. Refactoring subgraph from Video Store System (*ground-truth*)

3. Study Design

3.1. Study Participants

We perform our study with 46 undergraduate students in Computer Science (10 women and 36 men), which we label from $S01$ to $S46$. Specifically, they are students concluding a Software Engineering course. In this course, they have studied topics such as refactoring, testing, design patterns, and clean code. The students could decline participation in the study. Also, we inform the participants that the results could be reported exclusively in an anonymous format. The period to perform the proposed refactoring exercise was one week. The results do not include three students who completed the set of tasks in less than ten minutes.

3.2. Refactoring Tasks & Research Questions

Each student received the three initial classes—`Movie`, `Rental`, and `Customer`—and the instructions to perform the refactorings. We separate the study into two main parts: *explicit* and *flexible* guidelines.

The first part refers to *explicit guidelines*, in which the students received explicit information about the expected refactoring tasks. Specifically, these guidelines indicate the piece of code that should be refactored, the refactoring type, and the signature of the new methods. There are 15 main steps. Three of them introduce new methods or classes, and the other cases involve refactoring operations to make the source code cleaner or to apply changes in the inheritance hierarchy. There is also large refactoring to replace a conditional to polymorphism, which results in a new `Price` hierarchy. Each step finishes with a commit indicating the conclusion of a refactoring task.

After finishing the first part, there are two similar methods in class `Customer`, `statement()` and `htmlStatement()`, which print the statement in ASCII and HTML formats, respectively. Therefore, in the second part of the study, we described to the students the problems of this design structure. For example, it is necessary to duplicate the code to print the statement in other formats, such as CSV, JSON, etc. To mitigate this issue, Fowler proposes the usage of a Template Method. To implement this pattern, it is necessary to extract and move a set of similar methods to new classes. Then, multiple extract operations are needed to make the methods identical. As a final operation, a set of pull up operations should be performed to generate the template code.

Therefore, the second part includes a set of *flexible guidelines*. We invite the students to implement the Template Method pattern to eliminate duplicated code as we previously described. Different from the *explicit guidelines*, we do not indicate operations or details about the piece of code that should be refactored. Each student received only high-level instructions to refactor the methods, in order to create a template method.

We report each guideline results in distinct research questions, which are described in Section 4. Specifically, we present the findings from *explicit guidelines* in RQ1, and the results from *flexible guidelines* in RQ2. We use refactoring graphs as an abstraction to understanding and visualizing the sequence of refactoring operations performed by the students. In RQ1, we rely on a graph similarity metric to detect results that diverge from our ground truth [Sanfeliu and Fu 1983]. In RQ2, we perform a manual inspection of the refactoring subgraphs created from the refactorings performed by the students.

3.3. Detecting Refactoring Operations

We used REFDIFF to identify the refactorings performed by the students [Silva et al. 2020]. As mentioned in a previous section, our study concentrates on six distinct refactoring operations over methods (i.e., *extract*, *extract and move*, *move and rename*, *push down implementation*, *pull up*, and *pull up signature*). REFDIFF is a tool that detects refactorings by analyzing the commits of git-based projects. Therefore, for the 46 projects (i.e., one project per participant), we iterate in the list of commits, comparing each commit with its parent one.

3.4. Execution time

We also computed the time to generate the refactoring graphs. To this purpose, we used a Core i7-8550U workstation with 16 GB of RAM, 5,400 RPM HDD, and Ubuntu 18.04. The process to build our ground truth executed in 18 seconds. As we can observe in Figure 3, regarding the students' projects, the execution times are also low, ranging from 20 to 31 seconds, with a median of 23 seconds. These runtime measures consider the whole process, which includes getting the list of commits, detection of refactoring operations by RefDiff, and generation of refactoring subgraphs. In total, we were able to generate all refactoring subgraphs (of all students) in approximately 18 minutes.

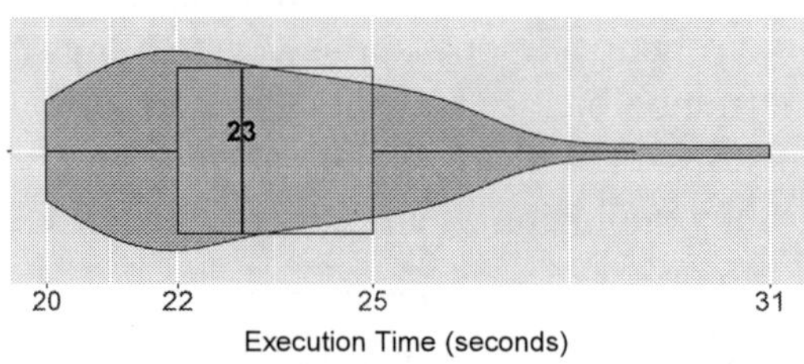

Figure 3. Distribution of the time to generate refactoring graphs per student

4. Results

In this section, we discuss our results. We divide the discussion in two parts: refactorings performed using *explicit guidelines* and refactorings performed using *flexible guidelines*. We rely on refactoring graphs to interpret the refactoring tasks performed by the students.

4.1. (RQ1) How do Students Apply Refactorings When Following Explicit Guidelines?

The instructions from the *explicit guidelines* generate ten edges in the expected refactoring subgraph (top of Figure 2). We compare this subgraph with our ground truth, reporting the number of extra and missing edges. We also assess the similarity by computing the subgraph edit distance. This distance is defined as the minimum number of addition, deletion, and replacement of vertices or edges that makes the student's subgraph identical to the ground-truth graph. As shown in Table 1, only three students made mistakes (6.5%). The other 43 students (93.5%) completed the tasks successfully, i.e., the distance to the ground truth is zero.

Table 1. Subgraphs with mistakes in the explicit guidelines

Student	Edges			Distance
	Total	Extra	Absent	
S02	7	-	3	6
S22	9	-	1	1
S44	12	2	-	2

These three students only made minor errors. For example, in the sixth refactoring task, the students should extract and move the method `Rental.getFrequentRenterPoints()` from `Customer.statement()`. However, $S22$ performed this refactoring in two steps. In the first commit, the student copied the code from `statement()` to `getFrequentRenterPoints()`. In other words, the student created a duplicated code. However, in a second commit, the student removed the duplication, replacing the code with a call to the new method.

There is a similar mistake in $S02$'s subgraph. In the thirteenth refactoring task, the students received instructions to change method `Price.getCharge()` by pushing down the implementation to three subclasses. But, $S02$ also performed this refactoring in two steps, creating a duplicated code. In the first commit, the student copied the code to the subclasses. In a subsequent commit, the student updated the superclass, keeping only the method signature. Since the student did not perform the three *push down implementations* in a single commit, our refactoring mining tool had not detected the refactorings. As a result, the distance between the refactoring graphs is six. In other words, it is necessary to add three edges and three vertices to make the subgraph identical to the ground truth, as shown in Figure 4.

Finally, $S44$ reverted a refactoring task, which generates two extra edges in the subgraph. In this case, the reason is that the student created the new method with only a piece of the expected code. Therefore, $S44$ reverted the operation and after that performed it correctly.

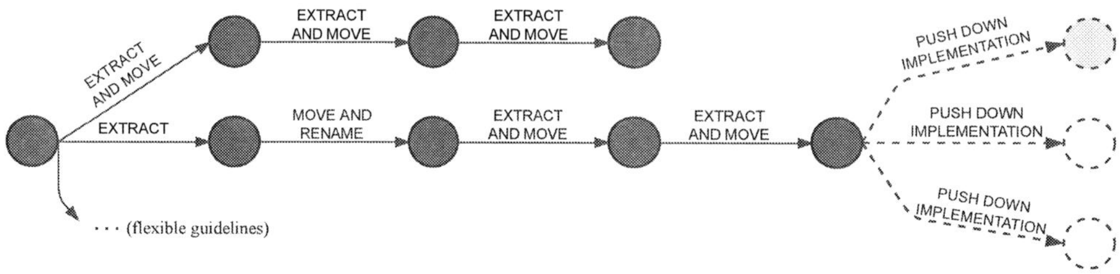

Figure 4. Example of a student's refactoring subgraph. Dashed lines represent missing edges and vertices (*explicit guidelines*, S02).

Summary: When following explicit guidelines on refactoring operations, 93.5% of the students perform the refactoring tasks successfully. The few mistakes refer to refactorings performed in multiple commits. To evaluate the tasks, we used a similarity metric to compare each student's subgraph with the ground truth. We were able to obtain each assessment in a few milliseconds.

4.2. (RQ2) How do Students Apply Refactorings When Following Flexible Guidelines?

The *flexible guidelines* can be finished with three refactoring tasks. These tasks refer to the implementation of the Template Method pattern, which generates 16 edges in the ground truth refactoring subgraph (bottom of Figure 2). For this study part, we performed a qualitative analysis by manually inspecting the 46 subgraphs and the source code to investigate the students' strategies. In the following paragraphs, we describe the results. Overall, 32 students (70%) performed the *flexible guidelines* successfully.

Task 1. In the first task, the students received instructions to create the superclass `Statement`, as well as the respective subclasses (i.e., `TextStatement` and `HtmlStatement`). Next, they were instructed to extract and move method `statement()` to subclass `TextStatement`, which must contain the code to print the statement in ASCII format. Similarly, it is necessary to extract and move method `htmlStatement()` to subclass `HtmlStatement`, which contains the code to print the statement in HTML format. The two moved methods should have the name `value()`. Most students performed these steps correctly, generating two edges in the subgraph (44 students, 96%). In two cases, minor mistakes refer to unfinished refactorings.

Task 2. In the second task, we invited the students to perform all refactoring operations in order to make the two methods identical, i.e., `HtmlStatement.value()` and `TextStatement.value()`. For each method, we expect at least three extract operations, as presented in Figure 5.

The first operation extracts a method to build the statement's header, returning the client's name in a specific format (HTML or ASCII). The second refactoring generates a method to retrieve the movie's title and charge. Finally, the third extracted method returns the statement's footer, which contains information about the price and the client's renter points. In Figure 5, vertices A, B, and C indicate the operations to decompose `HtmlStatement.value()`. Similarly, there are three extract operations to decompose method `TextStatement.value()`.

We detect that 33 students (72%) performed the expected operations, i.e., they

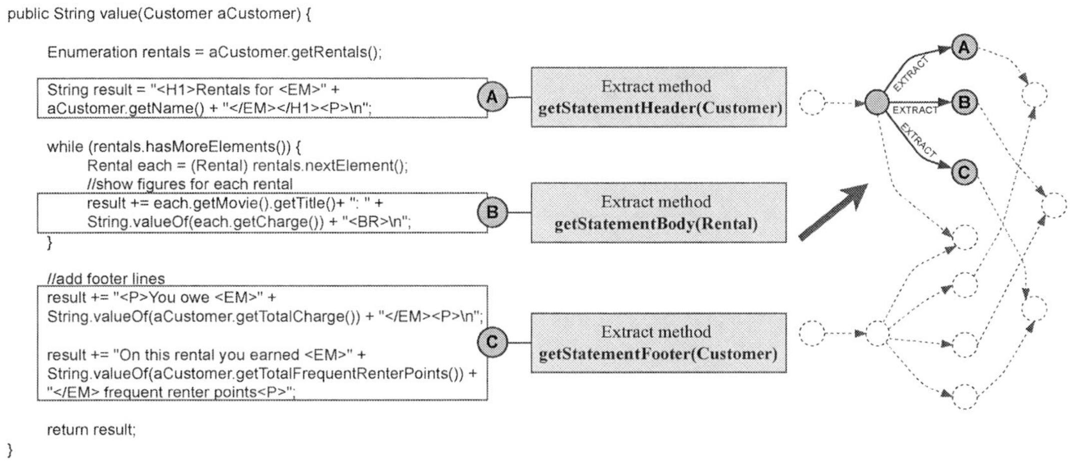

Figure 5. Refactoring operations to decompose method value() in subclass Html-Statement (*flexible guidelines, task 2*)

decomposed the methods by extracting three new ones in each subclass. Interestingly, five students (11%) used a different strategy. They divided the statement footer into two methods. The first method returns the price and the second one returns the client's renter points. As a consequence, these students created eight vertices in the subgraph (i.e, four *extract* operations in each subclass).

Eight students (17%) did not perform extract operations to remove the code duplication. Among these cases, five students (11%) added fields. For example, $S22$ used fields to customize the strings, as presented in Figure 6. The values of the fields are defined in the constructors. For instance, field `_preName` receives the value *"<H1>Rentals for <EM>"* in subclass `HtmlStatement`. The same field receives the value *"Rental Record for"* in the subclass `TextStatement`. Finally, $S17$ only added empty methods, and two students did not make the methods identical.

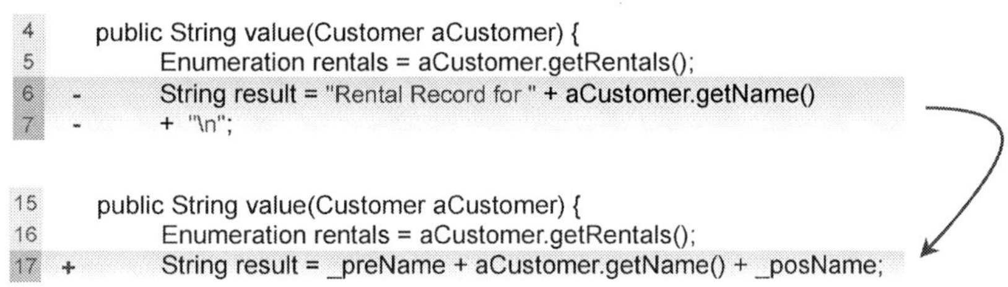

Figure 6. Textual diff produced by GitHub. S22 added two fields (_preName and _posName) in the header line (*explicit guidelines, task 3*)

Task 3. Assuming the students performed the refactoring tasks as expected, we should have in this step two identical methods `value()` in `TextStatement` and `HtmlStatement`. As a final operation, we requested the students to remove this duplicated code. It is expected at least six *pull up signatures* and two *pull up* methods in this last task, which generates eight edges in the subgraph. Among the 46 students, 74% completed this task successfully (34 occurrences).

Summary: When following flexible guidelines for refactoring operations, most students implemented the *Template Method* pattern successfully (70%). Most mistakes refer to students who faced problems identifying the appropriate operations. Refactoring graphs assisted in visualization and understanding the sequence of refactoring tasks performed by the students.

5. Threats to Validity

5.1. Construct Validity

Refactoring tasks. First, the communication among the students is a possible threat in our study. However, the participants received instructions to avoid sharing their source code. To mitigate this threat, we removed outliers from our results. The period to perform the proposed refactoring exercise was one week. For the *explicit guidelines* (RQ1), about 75% of the students complete the tasks up to 198 minutes (i.e., approximately three hours), with a median of 106 minutes. In case of *flexible guidelines* (RQ2), 75% of the students spent about one hour to conclude the three refactoring tasks (i.e., 65 minutes), with a median of 44 minutes. The highest intervals probably refer to students that paused the refactoring tasks for a while, returning on a distinct day. Considering the distribution of the time, we eliminated the projects of three students, who performed the *explicit* or *flexible* guidelines in less than ten minutes since this is not a viable time to conclude the refactoring tasks. Second, the refactoring tasks include examples and discussions, which are spread over eleven chapters of Fowler's book. In other words, it is not trivial to obtain the answers directly from the book. Still, the usage of Fowler's book by students is a possible threat. We relied on two different strategies to alleviate this threat, i.e., creating not only *explicit* but also *flexible* (or open) guidelines. All students followed these guidelines, and we obtained different results. Particularly, when following the flexible guidelines, a significant part of them faced problems performing the refactoring tasks. Third, the Video Store System may represent a nonessential software project nowadays. We decided to keep this system to preserve consistency with Fowler's catalog, which is widely used in Software Engineering courses. In future studies, we plan to use the new book version [Fowler 2018], which relies on JavaScript and adaption of the system to another context.

Detection of refactoring operations. We removed a single refactoring operation and two projects due to compilation errors or false positives. These cases represent a small piece of the sample. Thus, it is not likely to influence our results. In addition, we used REFDIFF to detect the refactorings [Silva et al. 2020]. We adopted this tool due to its support to multiple programming languages. Therefore, it is possible to replicate the study with the refactorings described in the last edition of Fowler's book, which relies on JavaScript [Fowler 2018]. It is also possible to adapt the guidelines to other programming languages, such as *C* [Silva et al. 2020] and *Go* [Brito and Valente 2020].

5.2. Internal Validity

Student's mistakes. We used *refactoring graphs* as a visual instrument to understand and evaluate the refactoring operations performed by the students. Also, we used a similarity metric called *graph edit distance* to compare our ground-truth subgraph with the students' subgraphs. For this purpose, we rely on a well-known Python library that implements this similarity algorithm.[3] However, our results also rely on the manual inspection of the commits of each student. Thus, we reinforce their subjective nature. The refactoring operations performed by the students (and our analysis) are publicly available at: `alinebrito.github.io/refgraph-fowler-study`

5.3. External Validity

Generalization of the results. Our guidelines relied on the Java programming language and on a canonical refactoring example to introduce refactoring concepts, i.e., the Video Store System proposed by Fowler [Fowler 1999]. Thus, as unusual in empirical software studies, the results can not be generalized to other scenarios, such as different refactoring tasks or programming languages.

Sample size and students' experience. The 46 participants might not be a representative sample. However, they have previously studied several topics in the Software Engineering course (e.g., refactoring, testing, design patterns, and clean code).

6. Related Work

Refactoring is a fundamental practice in software development and evolution. For this reason, several studies focused on this research line over the last 30 years [Abid et al. 2020]. Among them, there are several studies aiming to understand refactoring activities [Kim et al. 2012, Kim et al. 2014, Mahmoudi et al. 2019, Pantiuchina et al. 2020, Paixao et al. 2020]. However, there is also a need for abstractions and tools to organize, visualize, and evaluating large and complex refactorings [Bogart et al. 2020, AlOmar et al. 2021a].

Most studies focus on developers' perception of refactoring. Murphy-Hill *et al.* [Murphy-Hill et al. 2009] used four Eclipse IDE datasets to investigate how developers perform refactoring operations. Considering these metadata, the authors discuss the frequency of refactoring operations, the usage of tools, and refactoring occurring in batches (i.e., in a 60-second time window). Among the main findings, the authors point out that 40% of refactorings occur in batches and developers alternate refactorings with other software activities. Silva *et al.* [Silva et al. 2016] investigated the motivations behind refactoring operations by performing a *firehouse* interview with 195 developers. The authors report 44 distinct reasons, such as improving testability or readability and eliminating duplicated pieces of code. The study also discusses the usage of tools for supporting refactoring, reinforcing a previous study about the prevalence of manual refactorings [Murphy-Hill et al. 2009]. A recent study expands this catalog, by adding 26 new motivations [Pantiuchina et al. 2020]. In this case, the author analyzed a set of 551 pull requests and the respective commits. However, the mentioned studies do not explore abstractions to visualize and understand refactoring tasks over time. In this paper, we rely on *refactoring graphs* to extract and interpret large refactoring tasks performed by students. In the wild, *refactoring graphs* have been used to explore refactorings performed over time, showing that a significant part of the operations is not a sole transformation [Brito et al. 2020, Brito et al. 2021].

On the educational side, research on refactoring covers distinct scenarios. Demeyer *et al.* [Demeyer et al. 2005] propose examples for students. López *et al.* [López

[3] networkx.org/documentation/stable/reference/algorithms/similarity.html

et al. 2014] propose activities to teach refactoring. The study suggests a set of tasks, such as reading texts, comprehension of refactoring catalogs, and practical exercises. Other studies discuss approaches and lessons to promote refactoring practices [Stoecklin et al. 2007, Hebig et al. 2020]. There are also tools to improve the student's perception of refactoring [Agrahari and Chimalakonda 2020]. However, the mentioned studies do not consider graph-based concepts to evaluate refactoring activities over time.

Keuning *et al.* [Keuning et al. 2020] performed a study with 133 students from the second year of a Software Engineering course. The experiment uses a tutoring system, which contains a set of refactoring exercises and provides feedback during the refactoring tasks. Specifically, there is an option to check the student progress, and a second functionality to get hints (i.e., to diagnose and provide suggestions). The students' mistakes were extracted from log entries of the system. However, most of them are outside the scope of refactoring. For example, the authors report compiler errors due to language unsupported constructs, runtime errors, and failed tests. Besides, each of the five exercises involved an isolated issue. For example, two tasks are from a website that contains a list of code problems. In our paper, we use a canonical refactoring example (proposed by Fowler [Fowler 1999], with 18 refactoring tasks) and leverage refactoring graphs to assess refactoring operations performed over time.

Abid *et al.* [Abid et al. 2015] conducted a study with 23 students. Each group performed a kind of project scheme in a real system. The first scheme contains a set of software changes, ending with refactoring tasks. In contrast, the second scheme starts with refactoring issues. The authors reported better results in the second one. However, the study does not concentrate exactly on refactoring comprehension. The authors focus on the main differences by performing refactoring operations before and after functional improvements of the system. Besides, the tasks are performed by two or three students. Thus, different students' perceptions of refactoring can influence the results. In our study, each result refers to a single student. In addition, our guidelines are based on a well-known refactoring example.

Karac *et al.* [Karac et al. 2019] investigated the impact of task granularity on Test-Driven Development (TDD). Overall, the study encompasses five main steps. For example, there are steps to implement a feature and the respective tests. The last step involves refactoring operations to improve code quality. The study involves 52 students, most of them are novice programs. The tasks rely on programming exercises, which are essentially algorithmic. A group of students performed decomposed tasks. In contrast, the second group received tasks without decomposition in small steps. Among the main results, the authors argue about the importance of breaking larger work into smaller ones, mainly for novice practitioners. However, the study concentrates on the granularity of issues, and the refactoring operations are just a step of the experiment.

7. Discussion

First, among the most recurring students' mistakes, there are refactoring operations completed in two steps (i.e., two commits). Refactorings performed along multiple commits represent a threat to current studies on refactoring practices. Particularly, the ones based on tools such as RefactoringMiner [Silva et al. 2016, Tsantalis et al. 2018, Tsantalis et al. 2020] and RefDiff [Brito and Valente 2020, Silva and Valente 2017, Silva et al. 2020].

These tools detect refactorings by computing the "diff" between one commit and its parent. For example, if we assume three sequential commits $C1$, $C2$, and $C3$, the tools will miss a refactoring that starts in $C1$, but that is only finished in $C2$, as we observed when manually analyzing the results of both RQs. Since studies on refactoring rely on the default configuration of RefactoringMiner and RefDiff [Bibiano et al. 2019, Sousa et al. 2020, Hora et al. 2018, Paixao et al. 2020, AlOmar et al. 2021b, Brito et al. 2018], they do not consider refactorings performed over multiple commits. Therefore, we also envision research on new heuristics and techniques to detect refactoring in multiples commits, as well as the investigation of their impact on mining software studies.

Second, several well-known graph algorithms can be used with refactoring graphs, such as algorithms to mine graph patterns and metrics [Xifeng Yan and Jiawei Han 2002, Leung 2010, Sanfeliu and Fu 1983]. For example, in the first research question, we used a similarity metric called *graph edit distance* to compare our ground-truth subgraph with the students' subgraphs. Refactoring graphs also allow easy navigation on refactoring operations. We can inspect, for example, entity names, visualize sequences of refactoring tasks, and identify missing and extra operations (i.e., edges and vertices). In this context, researchers can rely on refactoring graphs to perform empirical studies on complex and large refactoring practices over time, which is a hurdle recently pointed in the literature [AlOmar et al. 2021a].

8. Conclusion

In this paper, we explore the usage of *refactoring graphs* to represent, visualize, and assess large refactoring tasks over time. For this purpose, we invited 46 undergraduate students from a Software Engineering course to refactor a well-known example proposed by Fowler, a Video Store System [Fowler 1999]. Each student received two groups of refactoring tasks. The first group included explicit guidelines, i.e., the precise indication of the piece of code to be refactored and the expected operation. In contrast, the second group received flexible instructions. Specifically, in this second case, we invited the students to implement a design pattern without details about the piece of code to be refactored.

The refactoring tasks create a large refactoring subgraph with 24 vertices and 26 edges. The genereration of all refactoring graphs demanded about 18 minutes, i.e, a median of 23 seconds per student. After building such graphs, we assessed the refactoring tasks using graph-based metrics and performing visual inspections. We summarize our findings as follows:

- When following *explicit guidelines*, most students performed refactoring tasks successfully (93.5%). The few mistakes refer to refactorings performed in multiples commits.
- When following *flexible guidelines*, most students implemented the proposed design pattern successfully (70%). However, a significant number of students faced problems identifying the appropriate refactoring operations.

Based on our results, we provided implications for different scenarios. Specifically, we discuss our contributions regarding graph-based abstractions to support comprehension of large and complex refactoring operations. Finally, we argue about a possible thread in studies based on state-of-the-art mining tools [Tsantalis et al. 2018, Tsantalis et al. 2020, Brito and Valente 2020, Silva and Valente 2017, Silva et al. 2020], which do not detect refactoring performed in multiples commits.

Further studies can include other programming languages and ecosystems (e.g., the current version of Fowler's book uses JavaScript [Fowler 2018]) and novel techniques to detect refactorings in multiples commits. Also, future works can perform experiments with practitioners using *refactoring graphs*. For example, in this study, we consider the professors' perspectives to understand refactoring operations performed by students. Other studies can contemplate the student or developer viewpoint, using refactoring graphs as a tool to visualize refactoring tasks. The dataset is publicly available at: alinebrito.github.io/refgraph-fowler-study

Acknowledgments

This research is supported by grants from FAPEMIG, CNPq, and CAPES.

References

Abid, C., Alizadeh, V., Kessentini, M., Ferreira, T., and Dig, D. (2020). 30 years of software refactoring research: A systematic literature review. *ArXiv*, abs/2007.02194.

Abid, S., Abdul Basit, H., and Arshad, N. (2015). Reflections on teaching refactoring: A tale of two projects. In *20th ACM Conference on Innovation and Technology in Computer Science Education (ITiCSE)*, page 225–230.

Agrahari, V. and Chimalakonda, S. (2020). Refactor4green: A game for novice programmers to learn code smells. In *42nd International Conference on Software Engineering: Companion Proceedings (ICSE-Companion)*, pages 324–325.

AlOmar, E., Mkaouer, M., and Ouni, A. (2021a). *Knowledge Management in the Development of Data-Intensive Systems*, chapter Mining and Managing Big Data Refactoring for Design Improvement: Are We There Yet? Auerbach Publications.

AlOmar, E. A., Mkaouer, M. W., and Ouni, A. (2021b). Toward the automatic classification of self-affirmed refactoring. *Journal of Systems and Software (JSS)*, 171:110821.

Bibiano, A. C., Fernandes, E., Oliveira, D., Garcia, A., Kalinowski, M., Fonseca, B., Oliveira, R., Oliveira, A., and Cedrim, D. (2019). A quantitative study on characteristics and effect of batch refactoring on code smells. In *13th International Symposium on Empirical Software Engineering and Measurement (ESEM)*, pages 1–11.

Bogart, A., AlOmar, E. A., Mkaouer, M. W., and Ouni, A. (2020). Increasing the trust in refactoring through visualization. In *42nd International Conference on Software Engineering Workshops (ICSEW)*, pages 334–341.

Brito, A., Hora, A., and Valente, M. T. (2020). Refactoring graphs: Assessing refactoring over time. In *27th International Conference on Software Analysis, Evolution and Reengineering (SANER)*, pages 367–377.

Brito, A., Hora, A., and Valente, M. T. (2021). Characterizing refactoring graphs in Java and JavaScript projects. *Empirical Software Engineering*, 26(6):1–43.

Brito, A., Xavier, L., Hora, A., and Valente, M. T. (2018). APIDiff: Detecting API breaking changes. In *25th International Conference on Software Analysis, Evolution and Reengineering (SANER), Tool Track*, pages 507–511.

Brito, R. and Valente, M. T. (2020). RefDiff4Go: Detecting refactorings in Go. In *14th Brazilian Symposium on Software Components, Architectures, and Reuse (SBCARS)*, pages 101–110.

Brito, R. and Valente, M. T. (2021). RAID - Refactoring aware and intelligent diffs. In *29th International Conference on Program Comprehension (ICPC)*, pages 1–11.

Demeyer, S., Van Rysselberghe, F., Girba, T., Ratzinger, J., Marinescu, R., Mens, T., Du Bois, B., Janssens, D., Ducasse, S., Lanza, M., Rieger, M., Gall, H., and El-Ramly, M. (2005). The LAN-simulation: a refactoring teaching example. In *8th International Workshop on Principles of Software Evolution (IWPSE)*, pages 123–131.

Fowler, M. (1999). *Refactoring: Improving the Design of Existing Code*. Addison-Wesley.

Fowler, M. (2018). *Refactoring: improving the design of existing code*. Addison-Wesley.

Gamma, E., Helm, R., Johnson, R., and Vlissides, J. (1995). *Design Patterns: Elements of Reusable Object-Oriented Software*. Addison-Wesley Longman Publishing Co., Inc., USA.

Grund, F., Chowdhury, S., Bradley, N., Hall, B., and Holmes, R. (2021). CodeShovel: Constructing method-level source code histories. In *43rd International Conference on Software Engineering: Companion Proceedings (ICSE)*, pages 1–13.

Hebig, R., Ho-Quang, T., Jolak, R., Schröder, J., Linero, H., Ågren, M., and Maro, S. H. (2020). How do students experience and judge software comprehension techniques? In *28th International Conference on Program Comprehension (ICPC)*, page 425–435.

Hora, A., Silva, D., Robbes, R., and Valente, M. T. (2018). Assessing the threat of untracked changes in software evolution. In *40th International Conference on Software Engineering (ICSE)*, pages 1102–1113.

Karac, E. I., Turhan, B., and Juristo, N. (2019). A controlled experiment with novice developers on the impact of task description granularity on software quality in test-driven development. *IEEE Transactions on Software Engineering (TSE)*, pages 1–16.

Keuning, H., Heeren, B., and Jeuring, J. (2020). Student refactoring behaviour in a programming tutor. In *20th Koli Calling International Conference on Computing Education Research (Koli Calling)*, pages 1–10.

Kim, M., Zimmermann, T., and Nagappan, N. (2012). A field study of refactoring challenges and benefits. In *20th International Symposium on the Foundations of Software Engineering (FSE)*, pages 50:1–50:11.

Kim, M., Zimmermann, T., and Nagappan, N. (2014). An empirical study of refactoring challenge and benefits at Microsoft. *IEEE Transactions on Software Engineering (TSE)*, 40(7):633–649.

Leung, C. (2010). Technical notes on extending gSpan to directed graphs. Technical report, Singapore Management University.

López, C., Alonso, J. M., Marticorena, R., and Maudes, J. M. (2014). Design of e-activities for the learning of code refactoring tasks. In *2014 16th International Symposium on Computers in Education (SIIE)*, pages 35–40.

Mahmoudi, M., Nadi, S., and Tsantalis, N. (2019). Are refactorings to blame? an empirical study of refactorings in merge conflicts. In *26th International Conference on Software Analysis, Evolution and Reengineering (SANER)*, pages 151–162.

Murphy-Hill, E., Parnin, C., and Black, A. P. (2009). How we refactor, and how we know it. In *31st International Conference on Software Engineering (ICSE)*, pages 287–297.

Paixao, M., Uchôa, A., Bibiano, A. C., Oliveira, D., Garcia, A., Krinke, J., and Arvonio, E. (2020). Behind the intents: An in-depth empirical study on software refactoring in modern code review. In *17th International Conference on Mining Software Repositories (MSR)*, pages 1–12.

Pantiuchina, J., Zampetti, F., Scalabrino, S., Piantadosi, V., Oliveto, R., Bavota, G., and Penta, M. D. (2020). Why developers refactor source code: A mining-based study. *ACM Transactions on Software Engineering and Methodology (TOSEM)*, 37(4):1–32.

Sanfeliu, A. and Fu, K.-S. (1983). A distance measure between attributed relational graphs for pattern recognition. *IEEE Transactions on Systems, Man, and Cybernetics (SMC)*, SMC-13(3):353–362.

Sellitto, G., Iannone, E., Codabux, Z., Lenarduzzi, V., Lucia, A. D., Palomba, F., and Ferrucci1, F. (2022). Toward understanding the impact of refactoring on program comprehension. In *29th International Conference on Software Analysis, Evolution, and Reengineering (SANER)*, pages 1–12.

Silva, D., da Silva, J. P., Santos, G., Terra, R., and Valente, M. T. (2020). RefDiff 2.0: A multi-language refactoring detection tool. *IEEE Transactions on Software Engineering (TSE)*, 1(1):1–17.

Silva, D., Tsantalis, N., and Valente, M. T. (2016). Why we refactor? Confessions of GitHub contributors. In *24th International Symposium on the Foundations of Software Engineering (FSE)*, pages 858–870.

Silva, D. and Valente, M. T. (2017). RefDiff: Detecting refactorings in version histories. In *14th International Conference on Mining Software Repositories (MSR)*, pages 1–11.

Sousa, L., Cedrim, D., Garcia, A., Oizumi, W., Bibiano, A. C., Oliveira, D., Kim, M., and Oliveira, A. (2020). Characterizing and identifying composite refactorings: Concepts, heuristics and patterns. In *17th International Conference on Mining Software Repositories (MSR)*, pages 186–197.

Stoecklin, S., Smith, S., and Serino, C. (2007). Teaching students to build well formed object-oriented methods through refactoring. In *38th Technical Symposium on Computer Science Education (SIGCSE)*, pages 145–149.

Tsantalis, N., Ketkar, A., and Dig, D. (2020). RefactoringMiner 2.0. *IEEE Transactions on Software Engineering (TSE)*.

Tsantalis, N., Mansouri, M., Eshkevari, L. M., Mazinanian, D., and Dig, D. (2018). Accurate and efficient refactoring detection in commit history. In *40th International Conference on Software Engineering (ICSE)*, pages 483–494.

Xifeng Yan and Jiawei Han (2002). gSpan: graph-based substructure pattern mining. In *2nd International Conference on Data Mining (ICDM)*, pages 721–724.

Blockchain Governance using Reference Architectures

Luis Florez[1]

[1]Departamento de Ingeniería de Sistemas y Computación - Universidad de los Andes
Cra 1 Nº 18A - 12, Bogotá, Colombia

le.florez602@uniandes.edu.co

Abstract. *Although Blockchain has grown in importance, great barriers still remain, including high failure rates, governance concerns and issues with quality attributes. These barriers have complex interactions and many trade-offs which suggests the need for design tools such as reference governance models and reference architectures. However, these tools are scarce and research in this area, especially governance, is sparse. The object of this research is thus to propose and then validate a new reference governance model and reference architecture to better design systems with desired attributes. The research will be conducted using the design science methodology and validated through case studies.*

1. Introduction

Blockchain has become one of the top 5 priorities for many organizations [Deloitte Insights 2020] which are already investing considerable amounts of money on the technology. This interest has been driven by the technology's perceived potential to remove intermediaries and make processes between multiple organizations more trustworthy and cheaper. Unlike other systems, blockchain has a decentralized architecture designed to operate in adversarial environments. That is, environments where there are malicious actors [Rauchs et al. 2019]. Of the several types of blockchains that exist, consortium blockchains are some of the most popular for the enterprise because unlike others they provide granular access controls, identity management and configurable security settings. However, the failure rate of blockchain projects is considerably high [Rauchs et al. 2019]. The reasons for such high failure rates are complex and involve multidisciplinary factors including laws, regulations, governance, the market, change management, technology and cultural factors [Deloitte Insights 2020, Rauchs et al. 2019]. Of these barriers there are some that stand out because they appear frequently in the literature as significant barriers [Frizzo-Barker et al. 2019, Helliar et al. 2020] and they are highly related to design. These are barriers related to governance and quality attributes.

Blockchain governance relates to how stakeholders exercise bargaining power, who chooses and how choices are made [Allen and Berg 2020]. At a basic level this power can be divided in two. Endogenous power, which comes from the consensus algorithm used and gives certain users abilities such as adding transactions, upgrading nodes and collecting fees. And, exogenous power, which are other mechanisms not related to the consensus algorithms which include forum discussions, voting and change proposals. Governance can also be subdivided by the state of the project, design, operation, evolution/crisis; by level, infrastructure, application, individual, and institutional [Rauchs et al. 2019]; by dimensions like roles, incentives, membership, communication, decision making, formation and context [van Pelt et al. 2021]; by how explicit vs implicit agreements are; or by level of automation [Rikken et al. 2019]. These considerations show how entangled governance and architecture are. The architecture distributes power between stakeholders and may enable some governance processes to take place. At the same time, many governance conflicts have centered on modifying some aspect of the architecture, such as violating immutability, the property that stored data cannot be altered, to recover stolen or lost funds [Zachariadis et al. 2019], seeking to increase performance at the cost of more centralization [Rikken et al. 2019], or the inclusion of features that might impact security. All of these suggest that a reference model for governance would be helpful to navigate concerns, particularly if it includes architectural considerations.

As noted in some works [Tan et al. 2021, Rikken et al. 2019] there are few studies of blockchain governance. Of these, most focus on the blockchain platform and do not consider the governance of other architecturally important elements such as applications and data [Liu et al. 2021]. In addition, the question of how can a system be designed to enable governance is still open [Liu et al. 2021]. The purpose of this research is thus to seek an answer to this question while still achieving the required quality attributes using the reference architecture and reference governance model that will be developed. Unlike existing reference architectures and governance models they will be developed in unison and they will be technology agnostic.

2. Existing Solutions

2.1. Reference Government

In [Alketbi et al. 2020] they present a reference model for blockchain governance based in part on the architecture and processes of the Hyperledger Fabric blockchain. It describes roles, participants, the architecture and model lifecycle. The governance model has two layers, one for the blockchain platform and one for distributed applications dApps. At the platform layer, there is a committee for governance decisions with key stakeholders or regulators and an entity that issues policies and procedures, promotes standards and resolves disputes. To join the network all members must first accept certain terms and conditions. At the dApp layer each dApp is the responsibility of a single member, this member is responsible for the dApp's development, its technical and legal correctness and negotiating with other members the roles and responsibilities required by the dApp.

In [Dursun and Üstünda2021] they propose a framework based on Policy Based Management (PBM) and Decentralized Identity Management (DIM). The framework allows some governance decisions to be described as policies. Decisions like protocol parameters, fees, rewards, access control and voting threshold. These decisions can be proposed on the blockchain, users can vote on them and if approved they can be automatically enforced on nodes. One of the advantages over other approaches is the transparency of the process and that it can be easier to understand, which promotes participation.

2.2. Reference Architectures

In [Viswanathan et al. 2019] they present the Blockchain Solution Reference Architecture that works on solutions built with the Hyperledger Fabric Blockchain. It's a layered architecture that defines several connectors, including blockchain to blockchain connectors. The architecture also includes the Blockchain Member Onboarding Reference Architecture, with different ways a member can participate on the network: as a major member with their own blockchain nodes and infrastructure; as a minor member with blockchain nodes but that uses the same application provided by other members; and as a minor member without blockchain nodes and who connects through the infrastructure of other members.

[Bodkhe et al. 2020] presents a general reference architecture with three networks: a public network that includes mobile devices, web browsers and command line applications; a cloud network that includes blockchain nodes, gateways, security and monitoring services; and the enterprise network with enterprise systems and databases. To add security to the blockchain network they use a VPN to connect nodes, and an Enterprise User directory for authentication and authorization. For integrating different systems, they use event subscription and an enterprise service bus.

In [Xu et al. 2019] they present a layered architecture for blockchain applications. There are 3 main storage zones: the blockchain, with the ledger, smart contracts and tokens; key management, to store keys; and auxiliary databases to store big or private data. Applications communicate with these storage zones through an API. Though not part of the architecture, they also present a comprehensive list of design patterns for blockchains applications that are broadly useful.

In [Ramachandran and Krishnamachari 2019] they present an architecture for IoT with a payment channel, a marketplace, identity management and ratings. It includes a blockchain and DLT platform layer for storing important transactions, an IoT Blockchain interface, and an IoT layer. In [Gong et al. 2021] they present a reference architecture for crowdsourcing platforms with a business rule editor, business rule engine and smart contracts.

In [Yalcinkaya et al. 2020] they present a reference architecture for ISA95 compliant traditional and smart manufacturing systems for distributed smart manufacturing (SMMS) units. It considers scalability, performance, interoperability, data quality and security requirements. In addition it includes six tiers: a device tier with sensors, robots, actuators; the edge tier with programmable logic controllers, manufacturing execution systems and human machine interfaces; cloud tier, with cloud services like AI; Integration tier with Message Queuing Telemetry Transport (MQTT) protocol; the enterprise tier with the ERP, enterprise applications, certificate authorities, off-chain data stores including IPFS, and the enterprise directory service, LDAP; and the ledger tier with the blockchain and smart contracts.

3. Research Question and Objectives

Research question:

Is governance of blockchain systems improved by the use of reference architectures and reference governance models as measured by the ability to implement governance decisions that impact quality attributes of decentralization and performance?

Objectives:

- Propose a reference governance model for consortium blockchain systems.
- Propose a reference architecture for consortium blockchain systems.

- In real world projects, measure the impact of using the proposed artifacts on governance and the system's quality attributes.
- Validate that the proposed artifacts are considered useful by members of the system's government and architects.

4. Research Methodology

This research will follow the design science methodology whose purpose is to make research contributions by building new artifacts that are both useful to practitioners and based on rigorous research [Hevner et al. 2004]. The artifacts that will be built are a reference governance model and a reference architecture for blockchain solutions. Because blockchain is a nascent technology and production networks are scarce these artifacts will be validated only in two scenarios.

The first scenario will act as a baseline in which no reference architecture or reference governance model will be used. While the second scenario will use the proposed artifacts. In these scenarios governance decisions will be documented, their intent, problems encountered, the result of their implementation, and their effect on decentralization and performance. Decentralization will be measured using the Gini coefficient of the distribution of blocks by block producer [Gochhayat et al. 2020]; and the Nakamoto coefficient [Gochhayat et al. 2020], the minimum number of entities required to compromise the system. Performance will be measured using load tests. In addition, interviews and surveys will be carried out to quantify the perceived usefulness of the artifacts in the governance process.

5. Proposed Solution

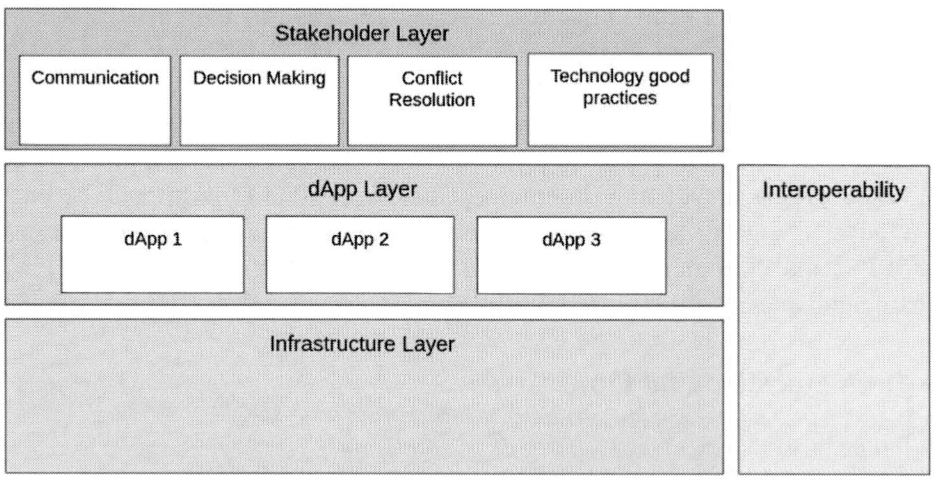

Figure 1. Reference government showing distribution of roles.

Figure 1 shows the main structure of the proposed reference governance model. The infrastructure layer will contain most of the endogenous governance determined by the consensus algorithm, it will also define infrastructure related roles such as admins, infrastructure providers and the like. In the dApp layer there would be one committee for each dApp as they can be developed independently. The interoperability layer contains committees for interoperating with other blockchain networks or external systems. Finally, the stakeholder layer would contain elements of the governance that are mostly outside the network, including communication channels, conflict resolution between members and committees to promote technology standards and good practices.

One of the proposed reference governance model's purposes is to make visible key governance decisions on a blockchain solution. Namely stakeholders, roles, decision process and distribution of power. Unlike other reference governance models, it will explicitly deal with these concerns as well as technological decisions.

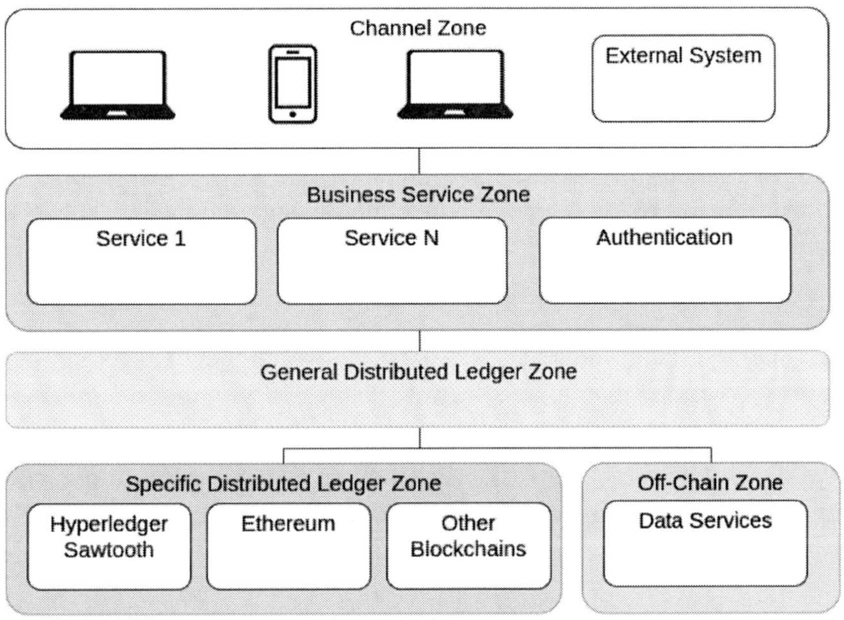

Figure 2. Reference architecture simplified functional view

The proposed reference architecture is divided into three views. A functional view defining services and zones. An integration view with connectors that services can use to communicate between them. And a technology view with deployment diagrams. The proposal has a layered architecture. At the bottom there are two zones, one contains the specific blockchains being used and the other the off-chain storage services. These bottom zones are accessed through a middle zone, the general distributed ledger zone, that hides the zones below. Above these there is the business service zone with domain specific services. Finally, there is the channel zone where clients reside such as web applications, mobile applications and external services. The integration view includes synchronous connectors between zones as well as asynchronous connectors using a message queue. It also details how smart contracts are called.

Unlike other reference architectures, the proposed architecture is designed to be useful in a broad range of domains and not tied to a specific blockchain technology. The reference architecture has been used in several projects at the university's blockchain lab [Blockchain Group Uniandes] with companies, researchers and students prototyping blockchain solutions for diverse domains such as healthcare, additive manufacturing, supply chains and finance. The reference architecture has been used to design these solutions, it's been used as a common language to talk about decisions and to organize development activities. It's also been used in conjunction with model driven engineering tools to deploy these solutions quickly, thus substantially reducing times.

6. Outstanding Issues and Future Work

The proposed governance model requires refinement and the definition of separate views to describe different aspects of the governance model. In particular, work has to be done to better describe roles, responsibilities, power distribution and relationships with the architecture. In addition, validation of the reference governance model has yet to be done. The reference architecture still requires some refining to include services that permit interoperability with other blockchains and it would also benefit from more validation, especially in live networks. Preparing for the validations to come, relations have been established with a bank and a hospital where these validations are planned. Several previous projects have already been made with them, giving more confidence that the validations will go smoothly. The estimated time for the research is 18 additional months, 6 months for the aforementioned refinements on the governance model and architecture, 6 to 8 months for validation and 6 months for writing.

References

Alketbi, A., Nasir, Q., and Talib, M. A. (2020). Novel blockchain reference model for government services: Dubai government case study. *International Journal of System Assurance Engineering and Management*, 11(6):1170–1191.

Allen, D. W. E. and Berg, C. (2020). Blockchain Governance: What we can learn from the economics of corporate governance. *Allen, DWE and Berg, C (Forthcoming)'Blockchain Governance: What can we Learn from the Economics of Corporate Governance*.

Blockchain Group Uniandes. Blockchain Group, ArchiIT Lab, Universidad de los Andes.

Bodkhe, U., Tanwar, S., Parekh, K., Khanpara, P., Tyagi, S., Kumar, N., and Alazab, M. (2020). Blockchain for industry 4.0: A comprehensive review. *IEEE Access*, 8:79764–79800.

Deloitte Insights (2020). Deloitte's 2020 Global Blockchain Survey. Blockchain Gets Down to Business. *Deloitte*.

Dursun, T. and Üstünda, B. B. (2021). A novel framework for policy based on-chain governance of blockchain networks. *Information Processing & Management*, 58(4):102556.

Frizzo-Barker, J., Chow-White, P. A., Adams, P. R., Mentanko, J., Ha, D., and Green, S. (2019). Blockchain as a disruptive technology for business: A systematic review. *International Journal of Information Management*.

Gochhayat, S. P., Shetty, S., Mukkamala, R., Foytik, P., Kamhoua, G. A., and Njilla, L. (2020). Measuring decentrality in blockchain based systems. *IEEE Access*, 8:178372–178390.

Gong, Y., van Engelenburg, S., and Janssen, M. (2021). A Reference Architecture for Blockchain-Based Crowdsourcing Platforms. *Journal of Theoretical and Applied Electronic Commerce Research*, 16(4):937–958.

Helliar, C. V., Crawford, L., Rocca, L., Teodori, C., and Veneziani, M. (2020). Permissionless and permissioned blockchain diffusion. *International Journal of Information Management*, 54:102136.

Hevner, A. R., March, S. T., Park, J., and Ram, S. (2004). Design science in information systems research. *MIS quarterly*, pages 75–105.

Liu, Y., Lu, Q., Zhu, L., Paik, H.-Y., and Staples, M. (2021). A systematic literature review on blockchain governance. *arXiv preprint arXiv:2105.05460.*

Ramachandran, G. S. and Krishnamachari, B. (2019). A reference architecture for blockchain-based peer-to-peer IoT applications. *arXiv preprint arXiv:1905.10643.*

Rauchs, M., Blandin, A., Bear, K., and McKeon, S. B. (2019). 2nd global enterprise blockchain benchmarking study. *Available at SSRN 3461765.*

Rikken, O., Janssen, M., and Kwee, Z. (2019). Governance challenges of blockchain and decentralized autonomous organizations. *Information Polity*, 24(4):397–417.

Tan, E., Mahula, S., and Crompvoets, J. (2021). Blockchain governance in the public sector: A conceptual framework for public management. *Government Information Quarterly*, page 101625.

van Pelt, R., Jansen, S., Baars, D., and Overbeek, S. (2021). Defining blockchain governance: a framework for analysis and comparison. *Information Systems Management*, 38(1):21–41.

Viswanathan, R., Dasgupta, D., and Govindaswamy, S. R. (2019). Blockchain solution reference architecture (BSRA). *IBM Journal of Research and Development*, 63(2/3):1.

Xu, X., Weber, I., and Staples, M. (2019). *Architecture for blockchain applications.* Springer.

Yalcinkaya, E., Maffei, A., and Onori, M. (2020). Blockchain reference system architecture description for the ISA95 compliant traditional and smart manufacturing systems. *Sensors*, 20(22):6456.

Zachariadis, M., Hileman, G., and Scott, S. V. (2019). Governance and control in distributed ledgers: Understanding the challenges facing blockchain technology in financial services. *Information and Organization*, 29(2):105–117.

Definición de patrones a partir de Buenas Prácticas para el desarrollo de sistemas de Gobierno Electrónico

Oscar Medina

Universidad Tecnológica Nacional – Facultad Regional Córdoba, Cruz Roja Argentina y Maestro López s/n, Ciudad Universitaria, Córdoba, Argentina

omedina@frc.utn.edu.ar

Resumen. *La tesis doctoral que se expone tiene por finalidad elaborar un modelo de análisis para definir patrones de Buenas Prácticas de Gobierno Electrónico. Estos patrones se pueden aplicar en el Modelo Conceptual de los sistemas del sector público para facilitar su construcción con mayor nivel de calidad. La reusabilidad de los sistemas es la dimensión de calidad de software que se intenta optimizar con esta propuesta. Se obtuvieron como resultados de la investigación: un conjunto de tipos de patrones que permiten definir Buenas Prácticas de e-Gob, un modelo de análisis para aplicación de dichos patrones, y un método de catalogado y selección de patrones para incorporar un nuevo software público en la fase de modelado.*

1. Introducción

Gobierno Electrónico es la aplicación de las TICs (Tecnologías de la Información y las Comunicaciones) en los procesos de Gobierno. Se considera a las TICs un *"elemento dominante para mejorar factores urbanos como la calidad de vida, la operación urbana y los servicios, y su oferta económica, social y ambiental"* [Estrada et al. 2018]. También llamado e-Gobierno, o e-Gob (el prefijo "e" significa electrónico), abarca a los sistemas de información que dan soporte a los procesos de la Administración Pública.

Asociados a estos procesos se encuentran las Buenas Prácticas de Gobernanza. Se entiende por Buenas Prácticas de Gobernanza *a "todas las iniciativas y experiencias que contribuyen a mejorar la efectividad de las actuaciones gubernamentales y que inciden positivamente en las condiciones de vida de los vecinos, logrando un impacto tangible en las comunidades"* [Varela Rey 2016]. Las Buenas Prácticas de Gobernanza se utilizan como referencia en la construcción del software público [CLAD 2015].

En pos de describir en forma estandarizada mejores prácticas, desde el enfoque de la Ingeniería de Software, los patrones se destacan como herramienta de reusabilidad. Un patrón es una descripción de una solución común a un problema recurrente que puede ser aplicado a un contexto específico. Los patrones ayudan a aprovechar la experiencia colectiva de software especializado, donde los ingenieros representan la experiencia existente y probada en el desarrollo de sistemas.

Las mencionadas Buenas Prácticas de e-Gob pueden ser descritas empleando patrones en la actividad de Modelado Conceptual del software público. La propuesta consiste en caracterizar patrones de Buenas Prácticas de e-Gob que se apliquen en el Modelo Conceptual de los sistemas de las organizaciones públicas, para que facilite su construcción con mayor nivel de calidad. La dimensión que se intenta optimizar es la de reusabilidad de implementaciones exitosas de sistemas de Gobierno Electrónico de Argentina.

En este artículo se desarrollan los principales componentes de la investigación y los resultados obtenidos hasta el momento.

2. Objetivos de la investigación

Basado en el marco conceptual, la investigación se propone dar respuesta a los siguientes interrogantes:

a) ¿Qué son Buenas Prácticas de Gobierno Electrónico?

b) Las Buenas Prácticas de e-Gobierno ¿tienen una metodología de elaboración universalmente instituida? ¿Cuáles son sus principales características?

c) ¿Qué patrones se recomendarían como punto de partida para el desarrollo de sistemas de Gobierno Electrónico?

d) ¿Cómo se pueden catalogar y seleccionar patrones de Buenas Prácticas de Gobierno Electrónico para que puedan aplicarse en el Modelado Conceptual de dichos sistemas?

Para lograrlo, esta tesis doctoral plantea los siguientes objetivos:

2.1. Objetivo general

Definir patrones a partir de Buenas Prácticas que puedan incorporarse en el Modelo Conceptual de sistemas de Gobierno Electrónico de Argentina, en el marco de un modelo iberoamericano de software público.

2.2. Objetivos específicos

- Caracterizar el conjunto de Buenas Prácticas de Gobierno Electrónico más representativas en la actualidad y en un contexto iberoamericano.
- Identificar los tipos de patrones de software existentes que permitan definir Buenas Prácticas de e-Gobierno y describir sus características básicas.
- Describir un método que permita definir patrones de Buenas Prácticas de e-Gobierno.
- Proponer un método de selección y aplicación de patrones de Buenas Prácticas en el Modelo Conceptual de sistemas de Gobierno Electrónico.
- Evaluar la aplicación de estos patrones de Buenas Prácticas en el Modelo Conceptual de sistemas de Gobierno Electrónico.

3. Marco conceptual

Para Alexander [Alexander 1979], patrón es una *"solución generalizada que puede ser implementada y aplicada en una situación problemática y de ese modo a eliminar uno o más de los problemas inherentes con el fin de satisfacer uno o más objetivos"*. Fue este arquitecto quien propuso el término patrón en su libro *"The Timeless Way of Building"* en el año 1979.

Luego, en 1994 Gamma, Helm, Johnson, y Vissides, publican la obra más importante sobre patrones aplicados al diseño de software: *"Design Patterns: Elements of Reusable Object-Oriented Software"* [Gamma et al. 1994], acorde al paradigma de la programación orientada a objetos. A partir de esta publicación se incorporaron patrones a las distintas fases del desarrollo de software creando tipos específicos para cada una de ellas. El empleo de patrones en el inicio de la construcción de un sistema, en las actividades de análisis de requisitos y modelado, aporta una serie de beneficios significativos que fueron observados en los primeros casos de estudio.

Una fase de análisis de requisitos bien realizada es muy importante para permitir el desarrollo de sistemas de alta calidad y su principal resultado es la ERS (Especificación de Requisitos de Software). La ERS supone una especie de contrato entre usuario y diseñadores del software, en el que unos indican sus necesidades, mientras que los otros proponen soluciones para implementar lo que se indica en el documento [Sommerville 2011]. La ERS es el núcleo del Modelo Conceptual de un sistema de información, que tiene como finalidad identificar y explicar los conceptos significativos en un dominio de problema, elicitando los atributos y las asociaciones existentes entre ellos.

Los patrones que se aplican al Modelado Conceptual cumplen la función de reutilizar el conocimiento y experiencia de sistemas anteriores encapsulado en soluciones de análisis y diseño concretas, permitiendo la verificación y validación de los requerimientos funcionales. A partir del Modelado de Negocio es factible una derivación de la arquitectura de software que les da soporte en el marco de la metodología MDD (Model Driven Development), en español Diseño Dirigido por Modelos. El MDD utiliza modelos diagramáticos que se van transformando en las distintas etapas de construcción de un sistema.

Por lo expuesto, el uso de patrones en el Modelado Conceptual de sistemas aportaría una serie de ventajas y sería posible incorporar patrones en esta actividad para formalizar la definición inicial de un nuevo sistema.

Además, las Buenas Prácticas de e-Gob podrían ser descritas empleando patrones en la actividad de Modelado Conceptual del software público y utilizando un modelo de análisis adecuado. El problema que intenta resolver esta investigación es la falta de reusabilidad de soluciones en la construcción de un nuevo sistema del mismo dominio de problema de Gobierno Electrónico. El uso de patrones en el Modelo Conceptual permitiría optimizar la reusabilidad que es además una de las dimensiones de la calidad de software.

Para comprobar dicha afirmación, el presente trabajo debe contemplar un experimento que permita analizar si el uso de patrones mejora la reusabilidad de soluciones en el Modelo Conceptual de un sistema de Gobierno Electrónico, y que esta mejora sea posible de medir en términos de efectividad y eficiencia.

4. Metodología de trabajo

El diseño metodológico de esta tesis tiene un enfoque cualitativo con estudios exploratorios de Buenas Prácticas de Gobierno Electrónico y de patrones dentro del marco teórico de la Ingeniería de Software. Se adopta un enfoque basado en procesos de negocios para el desarrollo de sistemas, en el que los procesos de negocios de la organización se modelan antes del desarrollo del sistema para respaldar la fase de análisis de requisitos.

En primer lugar, se realizó un análisis descriptivo de los patrones de Buenas Prácticas de e-Gob que pueden aplicarse en el Modelo Conceptual de software público de

Argentina. Se confeccionó un mapeo sistemático de la literatura y un trabajo de aproximación descriptiva con la revisión de distintos documentos científicos de bibliotecas digitales virtuales reconocidas a nivel académico. Se realizó una búsqueda exhaustiva de los conceptos esenciales de las Buenas Prácticas de Gobierno Electrónico y de las distintas estructuras y clasificación de patrones.

Se evaluaron las características básicas de las Buenas Prácticas gubernamentales identificadas. Con ellas, se formalizó una heurística de asociación a cada problemática de Gobierno Electrónico. Se definieron conceptos esenciales y aspectos relacionados a la construcción de patrones que se emplean en el desarrollo de software, sobre todo en la etapa de elicitación de requerimientos, en la actividad de creación del Modelo Conceptual. Se seleccionaron los tipos de patrones que permitan definir Buenas Prácticas de e-Gob (ver Figura 1).

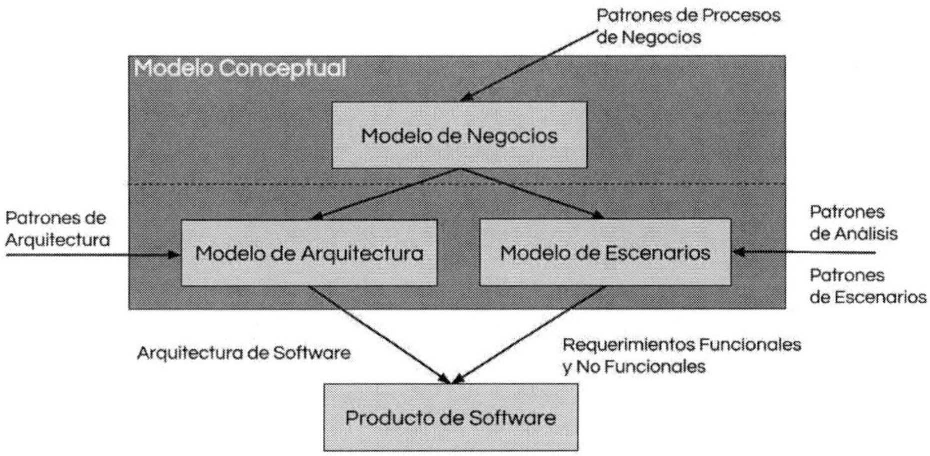

Figura 1. Patrones que permiten definir Buenas Prácticas de e-Gob en el Modelo Conceptual

Se indagó la viabilidad de uso de estos patrones para el modelado de sistemas de Gobierno Electrónico y para verificar si la gestión de patrones contempla, y resuelve, los déficits de reusabilidad identificados en el Modelado Conceptual de software público que no estuvo basado en Buenas Prácticas. Se desarrollaron distintos prototipos de sistemas públicos incorporando los patrones de Buenas Prácticas de e-Gob en la cantidad que sea necesaria para garantizar el resultado de la evaluación. Para la cual, se realizó una triangulación cualitativa al converger dos enfoques de la Ingeniería de Software, patrones y el Modelado Conceptual de sistemas de información.

Se llevó a cabo un experimento para analizar si el uso de patrones de negocio mejora la comprensión del Modelo Conceptual de un sistema de Gobierno Electrónico. El experimento se realizó en el año 2021 con 33 estudiantes del tercer curso de la carrera de Ingeniería en Sistemas de Información de la Universidad Tecnológica Nacional – Facultad Regional Córdoba. Todo el material utilizado en el experimento se encuentra disponible en el sitio web del Centro de Investigación [CIDS 2022].

Se elaboraron trabajos que fueron expuestos a consideración de la comunidad y publicados en revistas científicas y actas de congresos académicos, tanto a nivel nacional como internacional.

5. Resultados obtenidos

Durante el desarrollo de la presente investigación se obtuvieron los siguientes resultados:

- Un conjunto de tipos de patrones que permiten definir Buenas Prácticas de e-Gob,
- Un modelo de análisis para aplicación de patrones de Buenas Prácticas en el Modelo Conceptual de sistemas de Gobierno Electrónico,
- Un método de selección, catalogado e incorporación de estos patrones a un nuevo software público en la actividad de Modelado Conceptual.
- Una evaluación experimental para indagar si el uso de patrones de negocio mejora la comprensión del Modelo Conceptual de un sistema de Gobierno Electrónico.

A continuación, se brindan más detalles de cada uno de estos resultados.

5.1. Patrones que permiten definir Buenas Prácticas de e-Gob

Del análisis del marco conceptual de los temas Buenas Prácticas de Gobierno Electrónico y patrones, se pudo colegir que los tipos de patrones que permiten definir Buenas Prácticas de e-Gob en el Modelado Conceptual del software público son los siguientes: patrones de procesos de negocios, patrones de análisis, patrones de escenario y patrones de arquitectura. Las capas del Modelo Conceptual en las que aplican cada uno de estos tipos de patrones se puede apreciar gráficamente en la Figura 1.

Los patrones de procesos de negocios poseen el mayor nivel de abstracción permitiendo trabajar con el modelado del negocio, posibilitando describir los recursos del modelo, organizaciones, objetivos, procesos y normas de la empresa [Eriksson y Penker 2000]. Los patrones de análisis y patrones de escenarios aplican sobre la capa de requerimientos funcionales y no funcionales del modelado. Los patrones de análisis son grupos de conceptos que representan en conjunto un modelo de negocios relevante dentro de un dominio de aplicación y los patrones de escenarios son *"descripciones narrativas de las interacciones entre los usuarios y los sistemas propuestos"* [Potts 1995]. En cambio, los patrones de arquitectura forman parte de la arquitectura lógica de un sistema, lo que hace necesaria su definición en la fase de construcción, pero es factible y conveniente su inclusión en el Modelo Conceptual. Los patrones de arquitectura son un conjunto predefinido de subsistemas con sus responsabilidades y una serie de recomendaciones para organizar los distintos componentes [Buschmann et al. 1996].

5.2. Modelo de análisis para aplicación de patrones de Buenas Prácticas en el Modelo Conceptual de sistemas de Gobierno Electrónico.

El modelo de análisis que plantea este trabajo posibilita elaborar, clasificar, almacenar y seleccionar patrones de un conjunto acotado de patrones específicos de Gobierno Electrónico denominado catálogo.

En el dominio del Modelado Conceptual nos referimos específicamente a patrones de procesos de negocios, patrones de análisis, patrones de escenarios y patrones de arquitectura. La primera instancia entonces, es definir y catalogar un nuevo patrón a partir de una experiencia exitosa de implementación de un sistema del sector público, por ejemplo, un nuevo patrón de procesos de negocios. De este tipo de patrones, los que adquieren mayor representatividad son los patrones de problema - objetivo ya que explicitan el problema que dio origen a la necesidad del desarrollo del sistema. Al catalogar un patrón de problema – objetivo, se almacena además para el mismo proceso de negocio los otros patrones que complementan la descripción funcional: los patrones de procesos y los patrones de recursos y reglas. En cuanto a otros subtipos de patrones de procesos de negocios se pone a consideración una innovación con un gráfico unificado que permite una ágil visualización de los patrones de modelado de procesos: estructura básica de proceso, proceso de interacción, proceso de suministro en capas y flujo de acción de trabajo [Marciszack et al. 2018]. Además de la información de la *"Plantilla de Patrones de Negocios"* definida por Eriksson y Penker [Eriksson y Penker 2000], se le agregan palabras claves que tiene una valorización o peso de relevancia acorde a la capacidad del patrón para resolver los problemas del proceso de negocio para el cual fue implementado. Este componente es necesario para desarrollar un tesauro estandarizado y específico para el catálogo y que explore con mayor eficiencia las funcionalidades de la minería de texto al analizar la descripción inicial de un problema en la búsqueda.

Por tal motivo, elegir un patrón es otra de las tareas críticas que debe resolver toda actividad de modelado que use patrones. Para esta segunda instancia se pone a consideración un método que es desarrollado en la sección 5.3.

Por último, una vez seleccionado el patrón, o conjunto de patrones, más adecuados se incorpora a cada una de las capas del Modelado Conceptual como línea base del documento de ERS.

5.3. Método de catalogado y selección de patrones para incorporar en el Modelado Conceptual de un software público

Definir un nuevo patrón, y elegir uno preexistente de un conjunto acotado denominado catálogo, son actividades fundamentales que debe resolver todo modelo de análisis que use patrones.

Para validar de forma experimental el modelo de análisis de esta investigación, se elaboró una propuesta para catalogar y seleccionar patrones de procesos de negocios para el Modelado Conceptual de sistemas, y se implementa con un prototipo denominado *"PatCat"*, Pattern Catalogue. Esta aplicación web propia, en su versión inicial, permite la gestión de un catálogo de patrones de procesos de negocios aplicados en casos reales de e-Gob para que facilite su construcción simplificando y brindando mayor claridad en la fase de modelado. Este método, parte del análisis del lenguaje natural en la descripción del problema por parte del diseñador. Para lo cual se utiliza en este prototipo, la búsqueda de palabras claves identificadas en dicha descripción. El primer paso consiste en encontrar un patrón de problema - objetivo del sistema que se está modelando y que tengan asociadas las palabras claves, ya que en este tipo de patrón se describen los problemas que resuelve el proceso. Luego se obtienen los patrones de modelado de procesos en un gráfico unificado, planteado en [Marciszack et al. 2018], que desarrolla el modo en que se relacionan todos los procesos intervinientes y cómo intercambian recursos entre ellos. La especificación del proceso principal de este patrón puede tener otros tipos de patrones asociados, como por ejemplo patrones de análisis y patrones de escenarios, que complementan la especificación funcional de requisitos de software.

5.4. Evaluación experimental sobre el uso de patrones de negocio en el Modelado Conceptual de un sistema de Gobierno Electrónico

Se llevó a cabo un experimento con el objetivo de evaluar si el uso de patrones de negocio mejora la comprensión del modelo conceptual de un sistema de gobierno electrónico. El experimento se realizó en un entorno académico con estudiantes del tercer curso de la carrera Ingeniería en Sistemas de Información de la Universidad Tecnológica Nacional – Facultad Regional Córdoba de Argentina en el mes de abril de 2021.

Se analizó la facilidad de comprensión de modelos porque es una de las características de la reusabilidad. Los patrones de negocio que se aplican al Modelado Conceptual cumplen la función de reutilizar el conocimiento y experiencia de sistemas anteriores. Se puede colegir que un modelo que es fácil de comprender tendrá más facilidad de ser reutilizado, y es necesario evaluar en primera instancia la facilidad de comprensión de un modelo usando patrones.

Es por ello, que se buscó obtener evidencias sobre la influencia que pueden tener sobre la efectividad y eficiencia en la comprensión del modelado conceptual, el uso de sólo patrones de negocio, sólo descripción narrativa o ambos simultáneamente.

6. Conclusiones y trabajos futuros

Del actual desarrollo de la tesis doctoral, se obtuvo en primer lugar, una propuesta de Modelado Conceptual para sistemas de Gobierno Electrónico con un prototipo de catálogo de Buenas Prácticas de patrones e-Gob. También se elaboró un modelo de análisis, asociado al catálogo, y una estrategia que facilita la reusabilidad asegurando la calidad del software desde etapas tempranas mediante el uso de patrones. A su vez, se facilita la utilización de Buenas Prácticas de gobernanza y un desempeño más eficiente de soluciones que contemplan de forma clara y completa, posibles requisitos necesarios para etapas posteriores del ciclo de desarrollo de sistemas de información gubernamentales.

En los casos de estudio, realizados en sistemas de organizaciones públicas locales, se observó que la aplicación de patrones permitió esclarecer la elicitación de requerimientos, plantear problemáticas, encontrar soluciones y similitudes entre los escenarios para simplificar el modelado. Facilita anticipar algunas de las situaciones problema-solución en el circuito del proceso y gestionarlas en el mismo lenguaje del usuario del sistema. La representación de patrones a través de gráficos permite tener una mejor visión del negocio. Posibilita identificar fácilmente el proceso y sus actividades, y validar la reutilización del patrón. Además, conduce a emplear un vocabulario preciso y común entre el responsable de un proceso y su analista, para eliminar ambigüedades y refinar requisitos.

Con respecto a los resultados del experimento, se comprobó que existen diferencias significativas en la efectividad de los sujetos al realizar tareas de comprensión de modelado conceptual, cuando se utilizan patrones de negocio. En cambio, no hay diferencias relevantes en la eficiencia al utilizar, o no, patrones. Los resultados obtenidos indican recomendar, con cierta precaución, que es conveniente el uso de patrones de negocio en el Modelo Conceptual de un sistema de información para facilitar su comprensión.

Desde el punto de vista educativo, se sugiere promover el uso de patrones en la actividad de modelado de los sistemas. Además, las consultoras de software y las universidades tendrán la posibilidad de acceder a los resultados de esta investigación, lo que coadyuvaría a mejores servicios en las diversas organizaciones públicas de la región al contar con patrones y Buenas Prácticas de e-Gobierno contribuyendo también a una mejora en el desarrollo productivo del software local.

Estas recomendaciones son válidas en el contexto de ingenieros de software principiantes y sistemas de Gobierno Electrónico. Para corroborar la validez de los resultados obtenidos, se realizarán réplicas en un futuro cercano. Se prevé la defensa de la presente tesis doctoral en el primer semestre del año 2023.

Agradecimientos

La tesis doctoral presentada en este artículo se desarrolla bajo la dirección del Prof. Dr. Mario Groppo, codirección del Prof. Dr. Marcelo Marciszack y en el contexto del proyecto de U.T.N. – F.R.C. (CIDS, Argentina, SITCBCO0008152TC).

Referencias

Alexander, C. (1979) "The Timeless Way of Building", Ed. Oxford University Press.

Buschmann, F., Sommerlad, P., Stal, M., Meunier, R., Rohnert, H. (1996) "Pattern-Oriented Software Architecture. A System of Patterns", Ed. Wiley.

CIDS, Centro de Investigación, Desarrollo y Transferencia de Sistemas de Infomarción de U.TN. – F.R.C. Experimento para evaluar el uso de patrones de negocio para facilitar la comprensión del modelo conceptual de un sistema de gobierno electrónico. Accedido el 31/05/2022 desde http://www.cids.frc.utn.edu.ar/UsoPatrones.

CLAD, Centro Latinoamericano de Administración para el Desarrollo (2015) "Cartas Iberoamericanas del CLAD", Ed. Secretaría de la Función Pública de la República del Paraguay.

Eriksson, H.-E. y Penker, M. (2000) "Business Modeling with UML: Business Patterns at Work", Ed. OMG Press.

Estrada, E., Maciel, R., Peña Pérez Negrón, A., López Lara, G., Larios, V., Ochoa, A. (2018) "Framework for the Analysis of Smart Cities Models", Trends and Applications in Software Engineering. Proceedings of the 7th International Conference on Software Process Improvement (CIMPS 2018), 261–269, Ed. Springer.

Gamma, E., Helm, R., Johnson, R., Vissides, J. (1994) "Design Patterns. Elements of Reusable Object-Oriented Software", Ed. Addison-Wesley.

Marciszack, M.M., Moreno, J.C., Sánchez, C.E., Medina, O.C., Delgado, A.F., Castro, C.S. (2018) "Patrones en la construcción del Modelo Conceptual para sistemas de información" Ed. edUTecNe, U.T.N.

Potts, C. (1995) "Using Schematic Scenarios to Understand User Needs", 1st Conference on Designing interactive systems: processes, practices, methods, & techniques (DIS'95), 247-256, Ed. ACM.

Sommerville, I. (2011) "Ingeniería de Software", 9a Edición en español, Ed. Pearson.

Varela Rey, A. (2016) "Beneficios del intercambio de buenas prácticas municipales", INNOTEC Gestión, 7, 55-59, Ed. Laboratorio Tecnológico del Uruguay.

Diseño e implementación de un entorno de desarrollo integrado para robótica educativa soportado por una máquina virtual para plataformas de computación física

Ricardo Moran

Universidad Abierta Interamericana, Centro de Altos Estudios en Tecnología Informática, CABA, Argentina

Comisión de Investigaciones Científicas, La Plata, Buenos Aires, Argentina

ricardo.moran@uai.edu.ar

Resumen. *El uso de dispositivos físicos como herramientas de aprendizaje presenta diversos desafíos. Una de las dificultades más grandes a las que se enfrentan los alumnos es la construcción de un modelo mental que permita entender la ejecución de los programas y su relación con el código fuente. El uso de lenguajes visuales no alcanza a resolver este problema y, adicionalmente, puede complicar la eventual transición a lenguajes basados en texto. En este artículo se presenta un entorno de desarrollo integrado para robótica educativa que ofrece una experiencia de programación interactiva basada en un lenguaje híbrido bloques/código.*

1. Introducción

La robótica educativa es una disciplina que tiene como objetivo la utilización de dispositivos robóticos como material pedagógico, poniendo a la enseñanza de la tecnología no como un fin en sí mismo sino como un medio para entender y conocer mejor el mundo que nos rodea (Barrera Lombana, 2015). En este sentido, la robótica educativa presenta numerosos beneficios al proceso de aprendizaje, entre otros podemos mencionar: impacto positivo en la motivación de los estudiantes, reducción del ausentismo escolar (Vega-Moreno et al., 2016), fortalecimiento de las habilidades vinculadas al trabajo en equipo y compañerismo, desarrollo de habilidades que exceden lo meramente intelectual y ayudan en el pasaje del pensamiento concreto al pensamiento abstracto (Zabala et al., 2010).

Asimismo, la robótica educativa fomenta la formación de ciudadanos capaces de interactuar de forma productiva con la tecnología (Factorovich & Sawady O'Connor, 2017), ubicando a los estudiantes en una posición de creador y no de mero consumidor. Considerando además la demanda insatisfecha por profesionales en el área de sistemas (*El Gobierno presentó un plan para formar 111.000 programadores jóvenes y adultos - LA NACION*, s. f.) (*Argentina Programa*, 2020) y el potencial de la robótica educativa para ayudar en la formación de programadores, es comprensible el crecimiento significativo durante los últimos años que ha tenido la inserción de robots en las aulas, tanto en Argentina como en el resto del mundo (Lopes Guedes et al., 2015).

Dada la importancia del tema y los esfuerzos existentes por introducir la robótica en las aulas, resulta fundamental optimizar el uso de los recursos para obtener así el mayor beneficio posible que representa la robótica educativa para la sociedad. Para ello es necesario identificar y resolver los problemas que se observan en las herramientas de programación para robótica educativa disponibles en la actualidad. En este artículo se presenta un proyecto de doctorado cuyo objetivo es aportar soluciones a dichos problemas.

2. Problema

La explosión en popularidad y repentina demanda de soluciones tecnológicas para implementar robótica en las aulas tuvo como consecuencia la proliferación de kits de robótica orientados a usuarios no expertos.

Figura 1. **Kits de robótica: Lego Mindstorms NXT (izquierda) y Arduino (derecha)**

En casi todos los casos, los kits de robótica incluyen algún tipo de software focalizado en el aprendizaje de la programación, de forma que usuarios no expertos (e incluso niños pequeños) puedan no sólo construir un robot sino además programarlo para realizar diferentes tareas. A pesar de que estas herramientas están diseñadas especialmente para ayudar a introducir la robótica y la programación, la mayoría sufre de diversos problemas que reducen su efectividad.

El principal problema que se observa es que la interfaz de programación visual que presentan muchas de estas herramientas es efectiva para el aprendizaje en un estadío inicial, pero puede resultar contraproducente una vez que el estudiante deba incursionar en un lenguaje de programación de propósito general. Al concentrarse exclusivamente en la interfaz visual muchas herramientas introductorias provocan consecuencias negativas:

1. Los estudiantes tienden a considerar los lenguajes visuales (en particular, los lenguajes de bloques) como "programación de juguete" y no cómo "programación real" (Moors et al., 2018).
2. Los estudiantes que pasan de un lenguaje de bloques a aprender un lenguaje de programación basado en texto pueden sufrir un problema denominado "sobrecarga de sintaxis" (Moors et al., 2018).
3. Los estudiantes que aprenden inicialmente con lenguajes basados en bloques pueden potencialmente adquirir malos hábitos de programación que dificultan su capacidad para trabajar satisfactoriamente con lenguajes basados en texto (Meerbaum-Salant et al., 2011).

El segundo problema identificado está vinculado a la necesidad de programar dispositivos que se mueven e interactúan con objetos del mundo real. Normalmente el entorno de programación para robótica educativa se ejecuta en una computadora que, mediante algún mecanismo de comunicación, permite transmitir el programa desarrollado al robot para su posterior ejecución. Al separar el entorno de programación (la computadora del estudiante) del entorno de ejecución (el robot), resulta difícil fomentar un estilo de programación interactivo que reduzca el tiempo entre que el usuario realiza un cambio al programa y se observan los efectos del mismo. Acortar este "feedback loop" tiene efectos positivos sobre el aprendizaje ya que fomenta la experimentación y la prueba a la vez que disminuye los efectos de la frustración ante los errores (Lodi et al., 2019) (Weintrop & Wilensky, 2015).

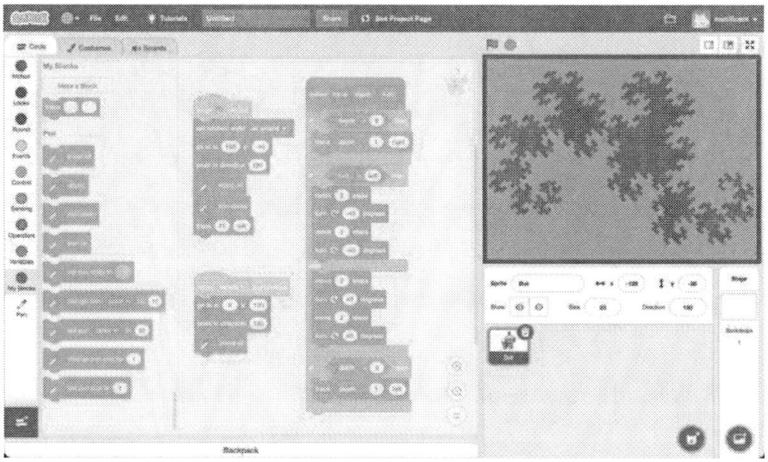

Figura 2. En Scratch tanto el entorno de programación (amarillo) como el espacio de simulación (rojo) forman parte del mismo programa. Esto no es posible en entornos de programación para robótica educativa.

Un tercer problema se refiere a la utilización de abstracciones inadecuadas para el dominio del problema o el nivel de aprendizaje de los alumnos. Un ejemplo claro de este problema es el soporte inadecuado para la concurrencia que tienen algunos entornos. A pesar de que la mayoría de las actividades en robótica educativa requieren la programación de un dispositivo capaz de realizar dos o más tareas en forma simultánea, muchos lenguajes no proveen ningún mecanismo para expresar esta concurrencia de forma sencilla, dejando a los usuarios la responsabilidad de organizar y coordinar el trabajo, muchas veces mediante complicadas máquinas de estado. Si bien el limitado soporte para concurrencia es una de las falencias más visibles en los entornos de programación para robótica educativa, no es el único caso de abstracciones inadecuadas. Otro ejemplo son los detalles del hardware soportado por el entorno, que en algunos lenguajes exponen complicaciones adicionales que podrían evitarse si el entorno los manejara de manera automática (opcionalmente ofreciendo una implementación por defecto que satisfaga los casos más comunes de uso). Se pueden mencionar: la configuración de los pines del GPIO, las interrupciones de hardware (para el control de encoders, por ejemplo), la comunicación con dispositivos I2C, entre otros. Por supuesto, la implementación de dicha funcionalidad es relevante para maximizar la utilidad de la herramienta, pero exponer los detalles de la implementación no necesariamente es pertinente a la educación del alumno. Es importante resaltar que la inserción de robots en las aulas es una excusa para ayudar a cumplir un objetivo mayor, no un fin en sí mismo (Barrera Lombana, 2015), por lo que es crucial evitar distraer al alumno con conceptos innecesarios para que pueda concentrarse en aquellos fundamentales para el aprendizaje (Lopez et al., s. f.).

3. Solución Propuesta

Habiendo identificado entonces los principales problemas que afectan, en mayor o menor medida, a todos los entornos existentes para robótica educativa, la contribución principal del presente trabajo es doble: por un lado, se formularon una serie de principios de diseño y objetivos fundamentales que deberían servir de guía para futuros desarrollos en la materia y, por otro lado, se implementó un entorno de desarrollo integrado (IDE) para robótica educativa que sigue dichos principios y sirve como prueba de concepto de las ideas presentadas.

Los principios de diseño formulados son los siguientes:

1. Autonomía: El entorno debe permitir el desarrollo de programas que se almacenen y ejecuten en el robot de forma independiente, sin requerir una conexión constante con la computadora que se utilizó para la programación.
2. Interactividad: En caso de estar el robot conectado con el entorno, el mismo debe ser capaz de mandar cada cambio realizado al programa de forma automática, permitiendo ver sus efectos inmediatamente y acortar así el "feedback loop".
3. Monitoreo y adquisición de datos: El entorno debe ser capaz de mostrar y almacenar de forma clara y precisa el estado interno del robot y del programa.
4. Modelo híbrido bloques/código: El entorno debe presentar al usuario un lenguaje híbrido basado tanto en bloques como en código, de forma que se fomente una transición gradual hacia el aprendizaje de lenguajes de propósito general.
5. Concurrencia: El lenguaje de programación debe permitir expresar tareas concurrentes sin requerir del usuario la coordinación manual de las diferentes acciones del robot.
6. Depuración: El entorno debe incluir herramientas de depuración que permitan detener la ejecución del programa en cualquier momento, ejecutar las instrucciones paso a paso, y observar cómo el estado del programa cambia ante la ejecución de cada instrucción individual.

Como prueba de concepto, se desarrolló un entorno de programación para robótica educativa denominado Physical Bits (Moran, s. f.). Su implementación es completamente open source, está basado en tecnología web, es compatible con Arduino (una de las plataformas más populares para robótica educativa) y además cuenta con un diseño portable que permitiría soportar otros kits con cambios mínimos al código. Physical Bits fue diseñado bajo los principios formulados previamente, por lo que cuenta con características que lo distinguen de otras herramientas similares.

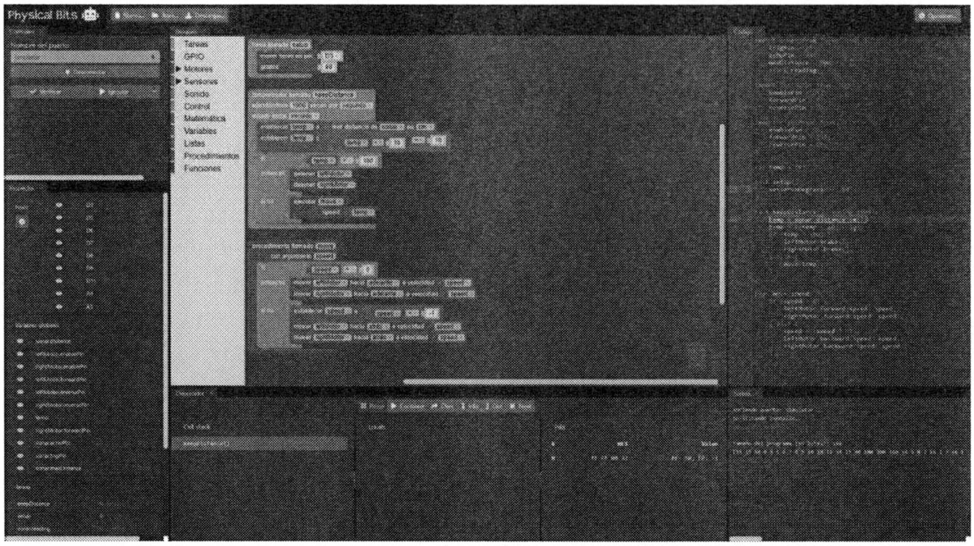

Figura 3. Entorno de desarrollo Physical Bits.

En primer lugar, el entorno soporta un modelo de programación híbrido basado en editores de bloques y de código. Este modelo está diseñado especialmente para facilitar la transición gradual de los alumnos a lenguajes de programación más sofisticados. La interfaz gráfica presenta ambos editores visibles al mismo tiempo y el usuario puede elegir cualquiera de ellos (o ambos) para desarrollar sus programas. Independientemente del editor elegido el entorno se encarga de mantener ambos editores sincronizados generando automáticamente los bloques o el código que sean necesarios.

En segundo lugar, el entorno usa un lenguaje de programación simplificado diseñado específicamente para robótica educativa. La sintaxis de este lenguaje está inspirada en la sintaxis del lenguaje C pero incluye además palabras clave y estructuras diseñadas especialmente para su uso en robótica educativa.

En tercer lugar, el entorno soporta programación interactiva sin sacrificar la autonomía del robot. Es decir que los cambios en el programa tienen un efecto visible inmediato en el comportamiento del robot y la ejecución de los programas se realiza siempre en el robot sin requerir una conexión constante con la computadora. Para ello, se desarrolló un firmware que se instala en el robot y que implementa una máquina virtual encargada de la ejecución de los programas del usuario.

Y finalmente, el entorno incluye herramientas de monitoreo y depuración, algunas de las cuales son prácticamente inexistentes en herramientas similares.

3. Trabajo relacionado

Para entender cómo se compara Physical Bits con otras herramientas similares se llevó a cabo un relevamiento de algunos entornos populares para la programación de robots con fines educativos. En el análisis se seleccionaron un conjunto pequeño de características relacionadas con los principios de diseño formulados previamente. Los resultados de dicho análisis fueron publicados previamente (Moran et al., 2021) pero se presentan a continuación en forma abreviada.

	Interactividad	Monitoreo	Depuración	Autonomía	Interfaz de programación
Physical Bits	✓	✓	✓	✓	Bloques + Código
MicroBlocks	✓	✓	✗	✓	Sólo bloques
Physical Etoys	✓	✓	✓	✗	Bloques + Código
Lego Mindstorms	✗	✓	✗	✓	Sólo bloques
Scratch4Arduino	✓	✓	✗	✗	Sólo bloques
Snap4Arduino	✓	✓	✗	✗	Sólo bloques
XOD	✗	✓	✗	✓	Sólo bloques
Ardublock	✗	✗	✗	✓	Sólo bloques
MakeCode	✗	✗	✗	✓	Bloques + Código
Arduino IDE	✗	✗	✗	✓	Sólo código

Aunque la lista de herramientas relevadas no es exhaustiva, esta selección ofrece una imagen representativa de las estrategias más comunes utilizadas en el desarrollo de entornos de programación para robótica educativa.

La mayoría de los entornos soporta programación visual en forma de bloques pero sólo algunos proveen generación automática del código. A excepción de Physical Bits y Physical Etoys (ambas herramientas desarrolladas por el mismo grupo de investigación), prácticamente ningún entorno provee herramientas de depuración. Y en lo que respecta a la autonomía y la interactividad, la mayoría de las herramientas soportan sólo una de las dos características, a excepción de Physical Bits y microBlocks que soportan ambas al mismo tiempo.

En este sentido, microBlocks (*MicroBlocks*, s. f.) es notable debido a que su implementación sigue un enfoque similar a Physical Bits: usa una máquina virtual para ejecutar programas de forma autónoma en el robot y, al mismo tiempo, brindar una experiencia interactiva y dinámica. Sin embargo, microBlocks no implementa ninguna herramienta de depuración y no es compatible con la programación basada en texto (aunque los autores expresan en su sitio web que es uno de sus objetivos para el futuro). Además, microBlocks soporta una variedad de dispositivos distinta a los que soporta Physical Bits. La máquina virtual de microBlocks está diseñada para microcontroladores de 32 bits, mientras que Physical Bits funciona en microcontroladores de 8 bits. Y microBlocks requiere al menos 12 Kb de RAM y 50 Kb de memoria Flash, mientras que Physical Bits requiere sólo 2 Kb de RAM y 24 Kb de memoria Flash.

Otro entorno interesante es XOD (*XOD*, s. f.). A diferencia de todos los demás entornos de esta lista, XOD es un lenguaje de flujo de datos. Utiliza bloques para representar nodos en un gráfico dirigido, en el que cada nodo puede representar una entrada (normalmente un sensor), algún cálculo, o una salida (normalmente un actuador). Los programas se crean vinculando nodos, que luego se utilizan para generar el programa nativo que el usuario puede cargar en la placa.

MakeCode (*Microsoft MakeCode for Micro*, s. f.) es un entorno web que admite tanto bloques como programación basada en texto utilizando Javascript, y proporciona generación bidireccional tanto del código a partir de los bloques como de los bloques a partir del código. Aunque el entorno MakeCode no proporciona una experiencia de programación interactiva, compensa esta limitación proporcionando un simulador virtual, lo que hace posible ejecutar programas sin un dispositivo físico.

Finalmente, Physical Etoys (Zabala et al., 2010) es una extensión de Etoys desarrollada para interactuar con una amplia gama de dispositivos físicos como LEGO NXT, placas Arduino, joysticks innovadores como Microsoft Kinect o Leap Motion, etc. Permite programar robots usando bloques o un lenguaje de programación basado en texto (Smalltalk). Sin embargo, una vez que un guión (término utilizado por Etoys para referirse a los programas desarrollados por el usuario) ha sido modificado usando el modo textual, no admite volver a los bloques sin perder los cambios realizados. Este problema, sumado a la falta de autonomía, fue el disparador inicial que llevó al desarrollo del entorno Physical Bits.

4. Trabajo Futuro

Habiendo completado el desarrollo del prototipo queda pendiente una validación rigurosa de la propuesta mediante experimentos con usuarios finales. Si bien se han llevado a cabo talleres con alumnos de secundaria (los cuales han permitido mejorar sustancialmente la plataforma), todavía hacen falta más experiencias con usuarios para asegurar la efectividad de la herramienta en un contexto educativo.

Los talleres realizados han servido para resaltar diversos problemas de usabilidad en la interfaz de programación, así como identificar necesarias mejoras en las capacidades del entorno y del lenguaje. Todas estas mejoras fueron incorporadas al software, lo cual ha permitido publicar (hasta el momento) 10 versiones del entorno. Por limitaciones de espacio no se presentará en este artículo un detalle de los cambios realizados en cada versión, pero el lector interesado puede acceder a los mismos en el repositorio de código del proyecto (*Releases · GIRA/PhysicalBits*, s. f.).

Referencias

Argentina Programa: Más de 157 mil inscriptos en 7 días. (2020, noviembre 1). Argentina.gob.ar. https://www.argentina.gob.ar/noticias/argentina-programa-mas-de-157-mil-inscriptos-en-7-dias

Barrera Lombana, N. (2015). USO DE LA ROBÓTICA EDUCATIVA COMO ESTRATEGIA DIDÁCTICA EN EL AULA. *Praxis & Saber*, *6*(11), 215-234.

El Gobierno presentó un plan para formar 111.000 programadores jóvenes y adultos— LA NACION. (s. f.). Recuperado 2 de abril de 2022, de https://www.lanacion.com.ar/tecnologia/el-gobierno-presento-un-plan-para-formar-111000-programadores-jovenes-y-adultos-nid1969143/

Factorovich, P., & Sawady O'Connor, F. (2017). *Actividades para aprender a Program.AR* (I. Miller & T. Alberto, Eds.; Vol. 1). Fundación Sadosky. https://program.ar/descargas/manual-docente-descarga-web-v2017.pdf

Lodi, M., Malchiodi, D., Monga, M., Morpurgo, A., & Spieler, B. (2019). Constructionist Attempts at Supporting the Learning of Computer Programming: A Survey. *Olympiads in Informatics*, *13*, 99-121. https://doi.org/10.15388/ioi.2019.07

Lopes Guedes, A., Lopes Guedes, F., & Guedes Laimer, A. C. (2015). Experiencias de robótica educativa / Experiences with Educational Robot. *Revista Internacional de Tecnología, Ciencia y Sociedad, 4*(2). https://doi.org/10.37467/gka-revtechno.v4.887

Lopez, P. E. M., Bonelli, E. A., & Sawady O'Connor, F. A. (s. f.). *El nombre verdadero de la programación*. 20.

MakeCode for micro:bit. (s. f.). Microsoft MakeCode for Micro:Bit. Recuperado 29 de mayo de 2022, de https://makecode.microbit.org/

Meerbaum-Salant, O., Armoni, M., & Ben-Ari, M. (2011). Habits of programming in scratch. *Proceedings of the 16th Annual Joint Conference on Innovation and Technology in Computer Science Education - ITiCSE '11*, 168. https://doi.org/10.1145/1999747.1999796

MicroBlocks. (s. f.). Recuperado 29 de mayo de 2022, de https://wwww.microblocks.fun/

Moors, L., Luxton-Reilly, A., & Denny, P. (2018). Transitioning from Block-Based to Text-Based Programming Languages. *2018 International Conference on Learning and Teaching in Computing and Engineering (LaTICE)*, 57-64. https://doi.org/10.1109/LaTICE.2018.000-5

Moran, R. (s. f.). *Physical Bits*. Physical Bits - A web-based programming environment for educational robotics that supports live coding and autonomy using a hybrid blocks/text programming language. Recuperado 29 de mayo de 2022, de https://gira.github.io/PhysicalBits/

Moran, R., Teragni, M., & Zabala, G. (2021). Physical Bits: A Live Programming Environment for Educational Robotics. En W. Lepuschitz, M. Merdan, G. Koppensteiner, R. Balogh, & D. Obdržálek (Eds.), *Robotics in Education* (pp. 291-303). Springer International Publishing. https://doi.org/10.1007/978-3-030-67411-3_26

Releases · GIRA/PhysicalBits. (s. f.). GitHub. Recuperado 29 de mayo de 2022, de https://github.com/GIRA/PhysicalBits/releases

Vega-Moreno, D., Cufí Solé, X., Rueda, M. J., & Llinás, D. (2016). *Integración de robótica educativa de bajo coste en el ámbito de la educación secundaria para fomentar el aprendizaje por proyectos*. https://rio.upo.es/xmlui/handle/10433/3504

Weintrop, D., & Wilensky, U. (2015). To block or not to block, that is the question: Students' perceptions of blocks-based programming. *Proceedings of the 14th International Conference on Interaction Design and Children*, 199-208. https://doi.org/10.1145/2771839.2771860

XOD. (s. f.). Recuperado 29 de mayo de 2022, de https://xod.io/

Zabala, G., Morán, R., & Blanco, S. (2010, mayo). *Physical Etoys: Una herramienta libre para el aprendizaje de tecnología con material concreto*. V Congreso de Tecnología en Educación y Educación en Tecnología. http://sedici.unlp.edu.ar/handle/10915/18405

Evaluation and Improvement of Narrative Visualizations

Andrea Lezcano Airaldi[1]

[1]Department of Informatics – Faculty of Exact Sciences
National University of the Northeast (UNNE)

alezcano.exa.unne.edu.ar

Abstract. *In the field of information visualization, storytelling techniques help to communicate facts and enhance comprehension. The use of data storytelling best practices can inform the process of creating narrative visualizations and increase the quality of charts used in software applications by improving aspects such as memorability or engagement, for instance, supporting end users in the decision-making process. The main goal of this doctoral research is to develop a method for assessing and improving the quality of narrative visualizations in software products, like scatter plots, line, bar, or pie charts, among others. This has included a case study and a systematic mapping study.*

1. Introduction

Data visualization has become essential to understand large datasets and communicate findings. As a subfield of visualization research (Post et al., 2003), Information Visualization focuses on the visual representations of abstract data (Keim et al., 2008; Munzner & Maguire, 2014), to enhance understanding and to support and amplify cognition (Card et al., 1999). Visualizations are increasingly used to tell compelling stories in different domains. There are studies that review the use of decision support systems in fields such as agriculture (Gutiérrez et al., 2019) where visualization plays a key role in assisting end-users to interpret the data, or environmental sciences (Grainger et al., 2016), where it is necessary to interact with actors outside of the scientific community and therefore presents the challenge of effective communication to enable users to generate actionable understanding. In more structured contexts, researchers can use these stories to support discussion, decision making and process analysis (Willett et al., 2011).

Storytelling has long been used as an effective way of conveying information and knowledge. Stories aid memory and recall by embedding information into characters, settings, relationships, and events (Henry Riche et al., 2018); hence the importance of integrating data visualization into narrative stories. Many experts in chart design provide guiding principles to create quality visualizations (Bertin, 1983; Nussbaumer Knaflic, 2015; Tufte, 2001). By leveraging the best practices stablished in the literature we can reduce the cognitive workload associated with chart comprehension (Dowding et al., 2018; Gilger, 2006) and prompt positive decision-making (Nussbaumer Knaflic, 2015).

In a software application, the implementation of data storytelling best practices for the design of narrative visualizations can significantly impact comprehension, memorability, and engagement of charts, and assist end users in the decision-making process by addressing issues related to the size and complexity of the data (Dimara et al., 2021). The resulting visualizations should, however, be supported by an evaluation model that allows developers to assess their quality and thus assure effectiveness to a certain degree.

In recent years, evaluation has become a central issue in the field of visualization. There is a diverse set of qualitative and quantitative methods for evaluating different aspects of data-driven stories (Carpendale, 2008). Some of these include controlled experiments, usability tests and case studies (Plaisant, 2004) where participants perform benchmark tasks and researchers collect measures like completion time, error rate and accuracy. These methods, however, only focus on data "facts" and fail to consider other aspects such as decision-making support, or insight generation (Dimara et al., 2018). As Wall et. al. (2019) point out, it would be valuable to have tools that can be deployed rapidly and iteratively during the design process to evaluate visualizations prior to conducting experiments with users.

2. Research Goals

The main purpose of this doctoral research is to "provide a method for evaluating the quality and assisting in the improvement of narrative visualizations". This goal further breaks down into three specific goals, addressing both methodological and technological aspects:

SG1: Identify the best practices for the design of effective narrative visualizations. In general, a visualization is considered effective if it helps people extract accurate information (Card et al., 1999) without further complexity (Haroz & Whitney, 2012).

SG2: Build an evaluation model based on the patterns and best practices found in SG1 to assess the quality of narrative visualizations.

SG3: Develop a software tool to assist in the implementation of the model, and additionally provide improvement recommendations.

The working hypothesis states that: "the development of an evaluation model for narrative visualizations that incorporates best practices and materializes them in a semi-automated support environment, can increase the value of visualizations." In this case, the value is directly linked to decision-making support, which has been identified as the end goal of data visualization (Munzner & Maguire, 2014; Ware, 2020).

The rest of this paper is structured as follows: Section 3 provides a summary of the background and related work, Section 4 describes the methodology and reports the results obtained so far, Section 5 presents the expected contribution of this doctoral research and Section 6 outlines future work.

3. Background and Related Works

This section presents an overview of prior research relevant to our work and contextualizes the aims of the thesis.

3.1. Information Visualization and Storytelling

Over the last two decades there has been a growing interest in visual storytelling and data visualization to communicate findings. Visualization dashboards are commonly used for decision-making but can be insufficient for communication purposes. In a recent study, (Sarikaya et al., 2019) found that people in Business Intelligence often put screenshots of dashboards into slide presentations, suggesting a need for more powerful storytelling features.

Riche et. al. (Riche et al., 2018) define "data-driven stories" as stories that are either based on or contain data, visualized to support one or more intended messages, usually including annotations (labels, pointers, text) or narration. Kosara and Mackinlay (Kosara & MacKinlay, 2013) argue that data-driven storytelling is a natural next step for data analysis and visualization and a pivotal component for effective data exploration.

Many authors have discussed emerging opportunities and challenges in storytelling in the field of visualization. Kosara and Mackinlay (Kosara & MacKinlay, 2013) give an overview of the topic, highlighting the importance of storytelling for data analysis and presentation, as visualizations are increasingly used for decision making. In (Rhyne et al., 2015), the authors take a narrower view of what data storytelling involves, to facilitate discussion around it, and present a comprehensive view of the storytelling process. Ojo and Heravi (Ojo & Heravi, 2017) examined 44 cases of award-winning data stories to identify storytelling practices and characterize the tools and techniques to create them.

Other research discuss the issues regarding visualization and data representation in different fields. In this context, (Gorodov & Gubarev, 2013) describes specific problems in Big Data visualization and defines a set of approaches to avoid them. They provide a useful classification of existing methods for data visualization in application to Big Data. In a similar way, (Gotz & Borland, 2016) reports on the emerging challenges facing the health industry with respect to medical information visualization, as well as some of the major opportunities. The authors suggest that interactive data visualization could become an essential tool for a data-driven healthcare system.

3.2. Evaluation of Visualizations

Given the limitations of formal laboratory methods such as controlled experiments, many researchers seek to go beyond this evaluation approach to determine the effectiveness of a visualization (Wall et al., 2019) and argue that traditional evaluation metrics might not be sufficient in motivating cognitively efficient visualizations (Qu & Hullman, 2016).

Tory and Möller (2005) discuss the use of traditional methods against alternative evaluation techniques in HCI, such as focus groups, field studies and expert reviews, particularly, heuristics evaluations. They argue that such reviews are valuable ways to assess visualizations. North et al. propose an insight-based evaluation (Saraiya et al., 2005) to assess how well a visualization supports people gaining insight from the visual representation.

Lam et al (2012) provide an overview of the different types of evaluation scenarios, categorized into those for understanding data analysis processes and those which evaluate visualizations themselves. They base their categorization on questions and goals, rather than existing methods, encouraging the community to consider the context before choosing an evaluation method.

Regarding evaluation criteria, Bertini, Tatu and Keim (Bertini et al., 2011) presented a systematic analysis of quality metrics to support the exploration of high-dimensional data sets and defined a quality metrics pipeline. More recently, in (Amini et al., 2018) the authors argue that data stories must address different challenges depending on the context and provide a non-exhaustive set of criteria and evaluation methods.

Based on the review outlined above, our evaluation model would be based on the visualization scenario by Lam et al (2012), as we will focus on visualizations as a final product, rather than the process to create them. We intend to develop a software tool to support and automate the evaluation process, providing practical design recommendations based on the guidelines and criteria found in the literature. Our research covers four main types of visualizations, namely: line charts, bar charts, scatter plots, and pie charts, in addition to choropleth maps, area charts, bubble charts and treemaps. We focus on these visualizations as they are the most frequently occurring types, according to (Battle et al., 2018; Lee et al., 2017)

4. Research methodology and obtained results

The development of this doctoral thesis will be conducted following the Design Science (DS) framework (Johannesson & Perjons, 2014), an approach for the creation of artifacts in the form of models, methods and systems to solve problems in a given context. Fig. 1 shows an overview of the high-level activities in the framework. Given that the main goal of this research is the construction of an artifact (the evaluation model discussed in Section 2), the Design Science framework was an appropriate fit for the thesis.

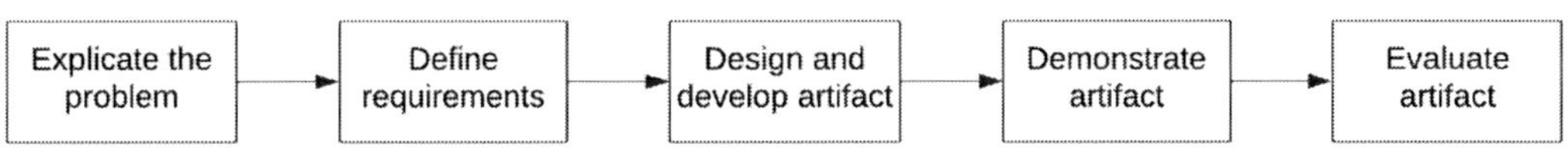

Fig. 1: Overview of the Design Science framework.

To address SG1 we are currently working on the first activity of the framework, that is, to explicate the problem. As a first task, we performed a case study following the guidelines by (Yin, 2017) and (Runeson & Höst, 2009) to gain a deeper understanding of the issue. The goal of the study was to determine the benefits of implementing data visualization best practices in the development of a software product, as well as the impact of not doing so. The system had high volatility in its requirements and short development cycles, prioritizing the delivery of functionality and real-time visualizations. This meant that narrative aspects were set aside and that only some best practices were followed by the development team. The results showed that the use of storytelling techniques in data visualization contributed to an improved decision-making process in terms of increasing information comprehension and memorability by the system stakeholders. In addition, we found that one of the reasons for not applying visualization best practices was the lack of knowledge regarding information visualization and storytelling, rather than the lack of time. In the absence of these skills, developers rely on the default settings of tools, causing stories to lose their potential or become difficult to understand. The full article is published at the Journal of Universal Computer Science and available online (Lezcano Airaldi et al., 2021)

As a second task, we are performing a systematic mapping study (SMS) following the guidelines by (Kitchenham & Charters, 2007), and (Petersen et al., 2015). For this purpose, we formulated the following research questions:

RQ1: *What are the existing definitions of "data storytelling"?* This question seeks to establish what data storytelling is and whether it has a formal and accepted definition for both academics and practitioners.

RQ2: *What are the data storytelling best practices reported in the literature for the design of visualizations and how are they applied?* The goal of this question is to summarize the guidelines and recommendations reported in the literature to create effective narrative visualizations and the diverse ways to apply them.

RQ3: *What are the criteria to evaluate narrative visualizations?* Depending on the goal of a visualization, different criteria is used to assess if that goal has been met (Amini et al., 2018). This question aims at identifying those criteria.

RQ4: *What are the current strategies to evaluate narrative visualizations?* This question identifies the methods by which the criteria defined in the previous question can be evaluated and their characterization: what types of charts they apply to, the metrics they use and the tools to support them.

Due to space limitations, the protocol for the SMS is detailed in Supplementary Materials[1].

The remaining activities in the DS framework will focus on SG2 and SG3. The definition of requirements will be done via a focus group to elicit requirements from stakeholders with different backgrounds and perspectives. For the design and development of the artifact, (Johannesson & Perjons, 2014) suggest drawing upon creative methods such as brainstorming sessions to generate ideas that could later be part of the design, in addition to software engineering techniques to develop it. To demonstrate the artifact, we plan on conducting an action research study to assess its feasibility. Finally, to evaluate the artifact, we will conduct two empirical studies: a controlled experiment that will allow us to achieve high internal validity (Johannesson & Perjons, 2014), and a case study to examine the artifact in a real world context.

5. Expected contribution

The main contribution of this research is an evaluation model implemented via a software tool to assess the quality of narrative visualizations. This model is intended to assist researchers and practitioners from various domains during the design phase of visualizations while also suggesting improvement recommendations based on the best practices and criteria found in the literature.

As an intermediate outcome, the contribution of the SMS is an extensive list of best practices and their corresponding applications that designers and developers can follow during the planning and design of visualizations or use them to compare to the ones they are currently adopting and identify improvement opportunities. Additionally, by understanding the criteria for effective visualizations, they can determine their goals

---

[1] https://bit.ly/cibse_appendix

more clearly (i.e.: to make visualizations more memorable, more comprehensible, or more engaging, for instance) and make informed design choices towards that direction.

6. Future work

We are conducting a systematic mapping study as part of the first activity in the Design Science framework towards SG1. We are currently working on reporting and discussing the results.

Once the review is completed, we will address the subsequent activities discussed in Section 4, detailing the tasks encompassed in each step. This will allow to iteratively build the different layers of the evaluation model proposed. We plan on publishing the resulting articles in journals and conferences relevant to the research field.

References

Amini, F., Brehmer, M., Bolduan, G., Elmer, C., & Wiederkehr, B. (2018). Evaluating Data-Driven Stories and Storytelling Tools *. In *Data-Driven Storytelling* (pp. 249–286). https://doi.org/10.1201/9781315281575-11

Battle, L., Duan, P., Miranda, Z., Mukusheva, D., Chang, R., & Stonebraker, M. (2018). Beagle: Automated Extraction and Interpretation of Visualizations from the Web. *Proceedings of the 2018 CHI Conference on Human Factors in Computing Systems*. https://doi.org/10.1145/3173574

Bertin, J. (1983). *Semiology of graphics*.

Bertini, E., Tatu, A., & Keim, D. (2011). Quality metrics in high-dimensional data visualization: An overview and systematization. In *IEEE Transactions on Visualization and Computer Graphics* (Vol. 17, Issue 12, pp. 2203–2212). https://doi.org/10.1109/TVCG.2011.229

Card, S. K., Mackinlay, J. D., & Shneiderman, B. (1999). *Readings in information visualization : using vision to think*. Morgan Kaufmann Publishers.

Carpendale, S. (2008). Evaluating information visualizations. *Lecture Notes in Computer Science (Including Subseries Lecture Notes in Artificial Intelligence and Lecture Notes in Bioinformatics)*, *4950 LNCS*, 19–45. https://doi.org/10.1007/978-3-540-70956-5_2

Dimara, E., Bezerianos, A., & Dragicevic, P. (2018). Conceptual and Methodological Issues in Evaluating Multidimensional Visualizations for Decision Support. *IEEE Transactions on Visualization and Computer Graphics*, *24*(1), 749–759. https://doi.org/10.1109/TVCG.2017.2745138

Dimara, E., Zhang, H., Tory, M., & Franconeri, S. (2021). The Unmet Data Visualization Needs of Decision Makers within Organizations. *IEEE Transactions on Visualization and Computer Graphics*. https://doi.org/10.1109/TVCG.2021.3074023

Dowding, D., Merrill, J. A., Onorato, N., Barrón, Y., Rosati, R. J., & Russell, D. (2018). The impact of home care nurses' numeracy and graph literacy on comprehension of visual display information: Implications for dashboard design. *Journal of the American Medical Informatics Association*, *25*(2), 175–182. https://doi.org/10.1093/jamia/ocx042

Gilger, M. (2006). Addressing information display weaknesses for situational awareness. *Proceedings - IEEE Military Communications Conference MILCOM*. https://doi.org/10.1109/MILCOM.2006.302129

Gorodov, E. Y. E., & Gubarev, V. V. E. (2013). Analytical review of data visualization methods in application to big data. *Journal of Electrical and Computer Engineering, 2013.* https://doi.org/10.1155/2013/969458

Gotz, D., & Borland, D. (2016). Data-Driven Healthcare: Challenges and Opportunities for Interactive Visualization. *IEEE Computer Graphics and Applications*, *36*(3), 90–96. https://doi.org/10.1109/MCG.2016.59

Grainger, S., Mao, F., & Buytaert, W. (2016). Environmental data visualisation for non-scientific contexts: Literature review and design framework. *Environmental Modelling and Software*, *85*, 299–318. https://doi.org/10.1016/j.envsoft.2016.09.004

Gutiérrez, F., Htun, N. N., Schlenz, F., Kasimati, A., & Verbert, K. (2019). A review of visualisations in agricultural decision support systems: An HCI perspective. *Computers and Electronics in Agriculture*, *163*(May), 104844. https://doi.org/10.1016/j.compag.2019.05.053

Haroz, S., & Whitney, D. (2012). How capacity limits of attention influence information visualization effectiveness. *IEEE Transactions on Visualization and Computer Graphics*, *18*(12), 2402–2410. https://doi.org/10.1109/TVCG.2012.233

Henry Riche, N., Hurter, C., Diakopoulos, N., & Carpendale, S. (2018). Data-Driven Storytelling. In *Data-Driven Storytelling*. https://doi.org/10.1201/9781315281575

Johannesson, P., & Perjons, E. (2014). An introduction to design science. In *An Introduction to Design Science* (Vol. 9783319106328). Springer International Publishing. https://doi.org/10.1007/978-3-319-10632-8

Keim, D., Andrienko, G., Fekete, J. D., Görg, C., Kohlhammer, J., & Melançon, G. (2008). Visual analytics: Definition, process, and challenges. *Lecture Notes in Computer Science (Including Subseries Lecture Notes in Artificial Intelligence and Lecture Notes in Bioinformatics)*, *4950 LNCS*, 154–175. https://doi.org/10.1007/978-3-540-70956-5_7

Kitchenham, B., & Charters, S. M. (2007). Guidelines for performing systematic literature reviews in software engineering. In *Technical report, Ver. 2.3 EBSE Technical Report. EBSE* (Vol. 1).

Kosara, R., & MacKinlay, J. (2013). Storytelling: The next step for visualization. *Computer*, *46*(5), 44–50. https://doi.org/10.1109/MC.2013.36

Lam, H., Bertini, E., Isenberg, P., Plaisant, C., Carpendale Empirical, S., & Lam Enrico Bertini Petra Isenberg Catherine Plaisant Sheelagh Carpendale, H. (2012). Empirical Studies in Information Visualization: Seven Scenarios. *Institute of Electrical and Electronics Engineers*, *18*(9), 1520–1536. https://doi.org/10.1109/TVCG.2011.279ï

Lee, S., Kim, S. H., & Kwon, B. C. (2017). VLAT: Development of a Visualization Literacy Assessment Test. *IEEE Transactions on Visualization and Computer Graphics*, *23*(1), 551–560. https://doi.org/10.1109/TVCG.2016.2598920

Lezcano Airaldi, A., Diaz-Pace, J. A., & Irrazábal, E. (2021). Data-driven Storytelling to Support Decision Making in Crisis Settings: A Case Study. *JUCS - Journal of Universal Computer Science 27(10): 1046-1068*, *27*(10), 1046–1068. https://doi.org/10.3897/JUCS.66714

Munzner, T., & Maguire, E. (Graphic artist). (2014). Visualization analysis & design. In *Cs.Ubc.Ca*. A K Peters/CRC Press.

Nussbaumer Knaflic, C. (2015). *Storytelling with Data: A Data Visualization Guide for Business Professionals*. Wiley. https://www.amazon.com/-/es/Cole-Nussbaumer-Knaflic/dp/1119002257/ref=sr_1_1?crid=4WE4N3JTKA0L&dchild=1&keywords=storytelling+with+data&qid=1616074837&s=books&sprefix=storytelling%2Caps%2C315&sr=1

-1

Ojo, A., & Heravi, B. (2017). Patterns in Award Winning Data Storytelling. *Https://Doi.Org/10.1080/21670811.2017.1403291*, *6*(6), 693–718. https://doi.org/10.1080/21670811.2017.1403291

Petersen, K., Vakkalanka, S., & Kuzniarz, L. (2015). Guidelines for conducting systematic mapping studies in software engineering: An update. *Information and Software Technology*, *64*, 1–18. https://doi.org/10.1016/J.INFSOF.2015.03.007

Plaisant, C. (2004). The challenge of information visualization evaluation. *Proceedings of the Workshop on Advanced Visual Interfaces AVI*, 109–116. https://doi.org/10.1145/989863.989880

Post, F. H., Nielson, G. M., & Bonneau, G.-P. (2003). *Data visualization: the state of the art*. Kluwer Academic.

Qu, Z., & Hullman, J. (n.d.). *Evaluating Visualization Sets: Trade-offs Between Local Effectiveness and Global Consistency*. https://doi.org/10.1145/1235

Rhyne, T.-M., Lee, B., Riche, N. H., Isenberg, P., & Carpendale, S. (2015). *More Than Telling a Story: Transforming Data into Visually Shared Stories*. www.gapminder.org/

Riche, N. H., Hurter, C., Diakopoulos, N., & Carpendale, S. (2018). *Data-driven storytelling*. A K Peters/CRC Press.

Runeson, P., & Höst, M. (2009). Guidelines for conducting and reporting case study research in software engineering. *Empirical Software Engineering*, *14*(2), 131–164. https://doi.org/10.1007/s10664-008-9102-8

Saraiya, P., North, C., & Duca, K. (2005). An insight-based methodology for evaluating bioinformatics visualizations. *IEEE Transactions on Visualization and Computer Graphics*, *11*(4), 443–456. https://doi.org/10.1109/TVCG.2005.53

Sarikaya, A., Correll, M., Bartram, L., Tory, M., & Fisher, D. (2019). What do we talk about when we talk about dashboards? *IEEE Transactions on Visualization and Computer Graphics*, *25*(1), 682–692. https://doi.org/10.1109/TVCG.2018.2864903

Tory, M., & Möller, T. (2005). Evaluating visualizations: Do expert reviews work? *IEEE Computer Graphics and Applications*, *25*(5), 8–11. https://doi.org/10.1109/MCG.2005.102

Tufte, E. R. (2001). *The Visual Display of Quantitative Information* (2nd ed.). Graphics Press. https://www.edwardtufte.com/tufte/books_vdqi

Wall, E., Agnihotri, M., Matzen, L., Divis, K., Haass, M., Endert, A., & Stasko, J. (2019). A heuristic approach to value-driven evaluation of visualizations. *IEEE Transactions on Visualization and Computer Graphics*, *25*(1), 491–500. https://doi.org/10.1109/TVCG.2018.2865146

Ware, C. (2020). *Information visualization : perception for design* (4th ed.). Morgan Kaufmann.

Willett, W., Heer, J., Hellerstein, J. M., & Agrawala, M. (2011). CommentSpace: Structured support for collaborative visual analysis. *Conference on Human Factors in Computing Systems - Proceedings*, 3131–3140. https://doi.org/10.1145/1978942.1979407

Yin, R. K. (2017). Case Study Research and Design. In *Sage Publications* (6th ed.). SAGE Publications, Inc.

Framework socialmente consciente para criação de RPGs para contribuir com o processo de ensino e aprendizagem de Engenharia de Software

Flávia Belintani Blum Haddad[1,2]

[1]Departamento de Informática – Universidade Federal do Paraná (UFPR)
Curitiba – PR – Brasil

[2]Departamento de Computação – Universidade Tecnológica Federal do Paraná (UTFPR)
Cornélio Procópio – PR – Brasil

flaviahaddad@utfpr.edu.br

Abstract. *This paper presents ongoing doctoral research that aims at developing a framework for creating Role-playing games (RPGs) to contribute to the teaching and learning process of Software Engineering (SE). The innovation will be in the design process of the framework, that will implement the Socially Aware Design (SAwD), which enables a social look added to the technical requirements. The research methods include bibliographic research, semi-participatory design workshops, prototyping, and prototype validation with the target audience. It is expected to contribute to the expansion of the production and application of games in the teaching and learning of SE as well as the dissemination of SAwD.*

Resumo. *Este artigo apresenta uma pesquisa de doutorado em andamento que objetiva elaborar um framework para criação de jogos de RPG (Role-playing Game) para contribuir com o processo de ensino e aprendizagem de Engenharia de Software (ES). A inovação estará no processo de design do framework, que irá implementar o Design Socialmente Consciente (DSC), o qual possibilita um olhar social somado aos requisitos técnicos. Os métodos de pesquisa incluem pesquisa bibliográfica, oficinas de design semioparticipativo, prototipação e validação do protótipo com o público alvo. Espera-se contribuir com a ampliação da produção e aplicação de jogos no ensino e aprendizagem de ES bem como a disseminação do DSC.*

1. Introdução

Algumas pesquisas foram desenvolvidas com o objetivo de descobrir os problemas do ensino de Engenharia de Software (ES) e mencionam, principalmente, o excesso de conteúdo teórico, a falta de integração entre as disciplinas, uso de tecnologias desalinhadas com o mercado de trabalho, pouca prática e desinteresse do estudante [Ferreira et al. 2018b]; [Lemos et al. 2019].

Os problemas relacionados ao processo de ensino e aprendizagem de ES refletem a necessidade de mudanças, de tal forma a permitir que os estudantes adquiram conhecimentos e habilidades por meio de práticas, considerando que aulas expositivas da teoria são insuficientes para este fim [Kosa et al. 2016]; [Souza and França 2016]; [Ferreira et al. 2018a]; [Ferreira et al. 2018b].

Os métodos tradicionais de ensino, baseados principalmente em explanações teóricas, dificultam a assimilação do conteúdo, a interdisciplinaridade, a interação e a integração da teoria com a prática. No ensino de ES, o excesso de aulas teóricas é um fator limitante, pois a prática é fundamental para a total compreensão dos conteúdos [Ferreira et al. 2018a]. O desafio em propor mudanças no processo de ensino e aprendizagem de ES é urgente [Ferreira et al. 2018b]. Desta forma, emergem metodologias que propõem uma estratégia de ensino que inserem os estudantes em cenários conectados a realidade do seu cotidiano, ao mesmo tempo em que estudam o conteúdo da disciplina, podendo ser a chave para otimizar o aprendizado [Ferreira et al. 2018a].

Propostas para otimizar ou inovar o processo de ensino e aprendizagem em ES, abordam a aprendizagem baseada em problemas, ambiente integrado automatizado de processos de ES, uso de projetos de software, uso de jogos educacionais, inclusão de atividades lúdicas e gestão interdisciplinar do conteúdo [Ferreira et al. 2018b]; [Lemos et al. 2019].

O uso de jogos educacionais é citado como estratégia de práticas alternativas para o ensino de ES, principalmente por motivar a participação dos estudantes no processo de ensino e aprendizagem [Souza and França 2016]. Os jogos educacionais podem ser considerados uma ferramenta para treinar estudantes ou profissionais de software iniciantes a solucionar problemas causados pela falta de informações práticas [Kosa et al. 2016]. Assim, a utilização de jogos, como objetos de aprendizagem, que possam simular situações problema e a busca por soluções, conciliam o conteúdo e a interdisciplinaridade à prática [Ferreira et al. 2018a].

Os jogos educacionais são utilizados em larga escala na educação como forma auxiliar para obtenção do conhecimento, pois oferecem ao processo de ensino e aprendizagem uma forma de adquirir conhecimento por descoberta e a motivação aos estudantes, que aprendem se divertindo com experiências concretas [Souza and França 2016]. São conhecidos também como jogos sérios, pois o objetivo engloba, além do entretenimento, a abordagem de conteúdos curriculares para aprendizagem [Ahmadi et al. 2016].

Pesquisas recentes realizadas por meio de Mapeamento Sistemático da Literatura (MSL) [Rodríguez et al. 2021], [Ivan et al. 2020] e [Ahmadi et al. 2016], apontam uma quantidade considerável de jogos destinados ao ensino de ES, desenvolvidos ao longo dos últimos 20 anos, sendo que grande parte destes foram desenvolvidos na última década. Observaram que a maioria dos jogos são classificados como digitais, mas também são mencionados jogos de tabuleiros, jogos de cartas, jogos de simulação, *Role-Playing Game* (RPG), Lego e até jogos com papel e lápis.

As áreas cobertas pelos jogos variam entre requisitos, qualidade, processo, testes, gerenciamento de projetos, métodos ágeis e programação. Normalmente, concentram-se em objetivos de ensino específicos, mas falham em fornecer uma abordagem de design de jogos para criar novos jogos para ensinar outras disciplinas de ES [Rodríguez et al. 2021]. Outros problemas apontados por [Lemos et al. 2019] são a indisponibilidade de *links* para acesso e uso dos jogos e poucos trabalhos sobre interdisciplinaridade.

Um ponto relevante é que o aprendizado por meio de jogos não acontece por si só. Deve-se considerar teorias contemporâneas de aprendizagem, como por exemplo aprendizagem situada, construtivismo ou construcionismo, ao projetar jogos educacionais [Ivan et al. 2020] e ampliar o conhecimento do contexto social em que o jogo será inserido [Ferrari et al. 2019]. A construção de narrativas compartilhadas para produção de conhecimento é mencionada por [Baranauskas and Posada 2017] em um estudo sobre a dimensão social do construcionismo, em que define socioconstrucionista como um ambiente de aprendizagem que estimula o usuário a ser ativo, com liberdade para criar objetos concretos ou conceituais que sejam de seu interesse pessoal, sociossituado, o qual favorece a construção conjunta do conhecimento. [Baranauskas and Posada 2017] considera que para a criação de ambientes de aprendizagem baseados em tecnologias que carreguem uma abordagem socioconstrutivista é necessário um processo que inclua o Design Socialmente Consciente (DSC).

O DSC propõe soluções na construção e uso de tecnologias interativas mais humanizadas e sustentáveis que visa descobrir dentro de um grupo social, requisitos nos níveis informal (hábitos, valores e cultura) e formal (procedimentos e regras), que se somem aos requisitos de nível técnico (tecnologias), envolvendo os diferentes tipos de usuários no processo de construção do sistema [Ferrari et al. 2019] para produzir um sistema sustentável, inclusivo e com a devida atenção a possíveis impactos negativos que possa causar [Baranauskas 2014]. É baseado na Semiótica Organizacional [Liu 2000], nas áreas dos Blocos de Construção da Cultura propostos por [Hall 1959], na Teoria de Valores de [Schwartz 2005] e no design participativo [Camargo and Fazani 2014].

A partir desta base, o DSC apresenta a Cebola Semiótica e a Torta de Valores, que guiam sua aplicação na construção de sistemas interativos por meio de oficinas de design semioparticipativo [Pereira et al. 2013]. A Torta de Valores é um esquema que apresenta valores que se manifestam nas camadas informais, formais e técnicas. A Cebola Semiótica é uma representação de como estes níveis interagem uns com os outros e com o design.

O DSC guiará esta pesquisa na criação de jogos que abordem o modelo socioconstrucionista proposto por [Baranauskas and Posada 2017]. O RPG é um tipo de jogo que possui propriedades e atributos para a construção de narrativas compartilhadas, que permite trabalhar características importantes para o desenvolvimento do estudante, tais como: socialização, cooperação, criatividade, interatividade e interdisciplinaridade [Grando and Tarouco 2008].

Neste artigo é apresentada uma pesquisa de doutorado em andamento que visa contribuir com o processo de ensino e aprendizagem de ES. Os objetivos e questões da pesquisa são apresentados na seção 2, na seção 3 o apontamento de alguns trabalhos relacionados, na seção 4 são explicitados os métodos de pesquisa, na seção 5 os resultados preliminares e na seção 6 as consideração finais com o apontamento das contribuições e os próximos passos da pesquisa.

2. Objetivos

O objetivo geral desta pesquisa é contribuir no processo de ensino e aprendizagem de ES possibilitando aos estudantes compreender o conteúdo teórico por meio de práticas lúdicas (jogos) em que eles sejam participantes ativos do processo, considerando o DSC no processo de construção dos jogos.

Para alcançar o objetivo geral são propostos os seguintes objetivos específicos:

1. Relacionar disciplinas e conteúdos de ES para promover a interdisciplinaridade;
2. Elaborar um *framework* socialmente consciente para criação de RPGs (*Role-Playing Games*) em um ambiente de aprendizagem socioconstrucionista aplicado ao ensino de ES;
3. Validar o *framework* por meio da criação e aplicação de RPGs, com a participação de professores e estudantes de cursos de graduação da área de computação.

Com o cumprimento destes objetivos espera-se responder as seguintes questões:

- Q1. Quais são os benefícios do RPG para o ensino de ES contendo elementos de DSC?
- Q2. O quão motivados os professores se sentirão em utilizar o *framework* proposto?
- Q3. Como criar RPGs para ensino de ES considerando elementos sociais, culturais, humanos, legais, conforme preconiza o DSC?

3. Trabalhos Relacionados

Esta seção apresenta alguns trabalhos relacionados ao tema desta pesquisa.

O trabalho de [Grando and Tarouco 2008] apresenta um estudo sobre estratégias dos diversos tipos de jogos educacionais para uma aprendizagem mais efetiva, com ênfase nos jogos de RPG, citando suas características e potencialidades. [Barreto et al. 2008] apresentam um trabalho sobre a utilização de um RPG no ensino de Gerenciamento e Processo de Desenvolvimento de Software, por meio de um jogo chamado SE•RPG (*Software Engineering • Role-playing Game*). Um conjunto de 13 *frameworks* para o desenvolvimento de jogos educacionais é apresentado no resultado de um MSL realizado por [e Rodrigo Cardoso e Juliana Braga e Rafaela Rocha 2018], que são comparados quanto à aplicação no ensino, ciclo de vida, aspectos pedagógicos e jogabilidade.

Em *Tangible and Shared Storytelling: Searching for the Social Dimension of Constructionism*, [Baranauskas and Posada 2017] projetam um ambiente socioconstrucionista, o CPES (Ambiente Programável Colaborativo para Contação de Histórias) e apresentam sua lógica de design e modelo de design de interação. Em *Socially Aware Design of Games: an early workshop for game designers* [Ferrari et al. 2020] realizam oficinas de design semiopartivipativo propostos pelo DSC na concepção de um jogo para apoiar crianças em exercícios fonoaudiológicos.

Os trabalhos citados mostram que os *frameworks* estudados não contemplam o DSC no processo de concepção dos jogos e que é possível aplicar o DSC na construção de jogos para a educação, embora ainda não se encontre trabalhos que o apliquem em RPGs para o ensino de ES.

4. Métodos da pesquisa

O delineamento da pesquisa foi elaborado de acordo com o paradigma *Design Science* proposto por [Engström et al. 2020], que contém a proposta, os métodos para instanciar o problema e criar o design da solução, a forma de validação da solução, qual sua relevância, rigor na execução e contribuições na área representados na Figura 1.

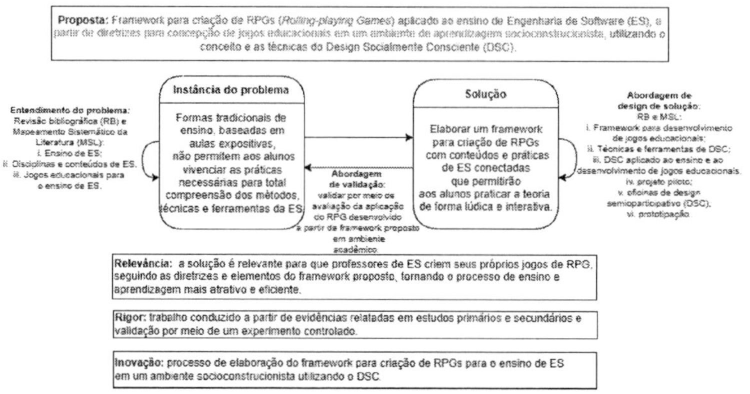

Figura 1. Delineamento da Pesquisa elaborado conforme o paradigma *Design Science*. Fonte: adaptado de [Engström et al. 2020]

Para a instanciação do problema, design da solução e validação são propostas as respectivas atividades apresentadas na Tabela 1.

A execução do projeto piloto possibilitou uma experiência para proposição de uma árvore metodológica, considerando os artefatos do DSC, a ser aplicada na elaboração do *framework*, representada na Figura 2. Esta árvore sugere a realização de quatro oficinas de design semioparticipativo, nas quais serão utilizadas técnicas de *brainstormig* (oficina 1), *brainwriting* (oficinas 2 e 3) e *braindrawing* (oficina 4), com o objetivo de gerar requisitos que abranjam os níveis informal, formal e técnico, conforme preconizado pelo DSC.

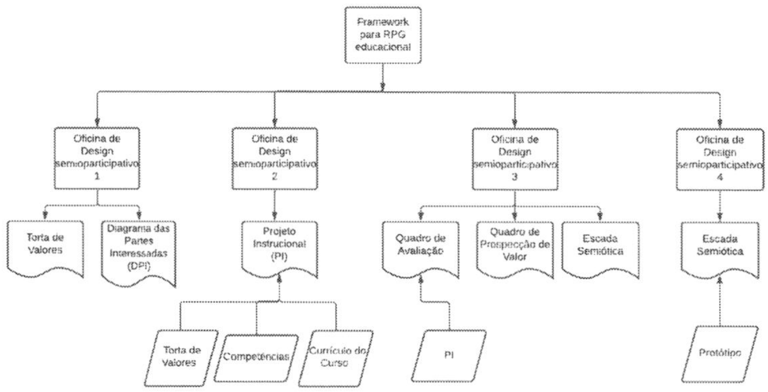

Figura 2. Árvore Metodológica proposta para aplicação do DSC na elaboração do *framework* Fonte: autoria própria.

5. Resultados Preliminares

Esta pesquisa teve início em setembro de 2020 e durante esse período foi possível executar um MSL sobre os pilares e contribuições do DSC para o desenvolvimento de Tecnologias da Informação e Comunicação que apontou como pilares do DSC a sustentabilidade, o design para todos, o envolvimento de diversas partes interessadas no processo de design e a prototipação. Além de uma Revisão Bibiliográfica (RB) para ampliar os conhecimentos sobre o DSC e elaboração de um Mapa Conceitual com disciplinas e conteúdos da ES.

Tabela 1. Atividades da pesquisa. Fonte: Autoria Própria

	Atividade	Descrição
Instanciação do problema	i.RB ii.RB iii.MSL	i.Identificar problemas e soluções relacionados ao ensino de ES. ii.Analisar diretrizes e matrizes curriculares, literatura, planos de ensino e trabalhos científicos sobre ES. iii.Identificar tipos de jogos aplicados ao ensino de ES, áreas e metodologias desenvolvimento.
Design da solução	i.MSL ii.MSL, RB iii.MSL iv.Projeto Piloto v.Oficinas vi.Prototipação	i.Identificar *frameworks* para desenvolvimento de jogos educacionais. ii.Conhecer os pilares, técnicas, ferramentas e artefatos do DSC. iii.Identificar as áreas de atuação do DSC e trabalhos relacionados à educação. iv. Aplicar técnicas e ferramentas de DSC na construção de um jogo educacional. v.Realizar oficinas de design semioparticipativo na elaboração do *framework* para RPG educacional. vi.Criar um RPG baseado no *framework* utilizando prototipação.
Validação	Experimento controlado	Disponibilizar o *framework* para que professores e estudantes de cursos de graduação da área de computação possam criar RPGs e aplicar um instrumento de avaliação (por exemplo, questionários). Selecionar trabalhos correlatos para realizar comparações.

Em 2021 foi conduzido um projeto piloto na construção de um jogo educacional digital para o ensino de Gerenciamento de Projeto de Software Ágil, com a inclusão de artefatos do DSC gerados por meio de oficinas de design semioparticipativo, tais como Diagrama das Partes Interessadas, Quadro de Avaliação e Escada Semiótica. Este projeto piloto trouxe contribuições importantes para melhor compreensão do processo, das técnicas e ferramentas utilizadas pelo DSC gerando uma árvore metodológica (Figura 2). Para a construção do jogo foram realizadas duas oficinas de design, de forma remota devido à pandemia de COVID-19, por meio do Google Meet e da plataforma OpenDesign [da Silva et al. 2018]. O projeto piloto teve duração de 4 meses para o design e 5 meses para codificação. Observou-se que o tempo para desenvolvimento é longo e isto pode desmotivar ao professor, além da necessidade de mão de obra especializada. Na Figura 3 é apresentada a tela inicial do jogo, batizado de Park Man devido ao objetivo do jogo ser a revitalização de um parque. Este jogo será aplicado após exposição teórica do conteúdo da disciplina de Gerenciamento de Projeto de Software, em cursos de graduação, para prática e melhor assimilação do conteúdo.

Figura 3. Tela inicial do jogo

Está sendo finalizado um MSL para identificar trabalhos que implementam o DSC no contexto da educação. Foram retornados 97 trabalhos, selecionados 30 no primeiro filtro e 21 no segundo filtro de seleção de artigos. Dos 21 apenas um relata o uso do DSC na educação, especificamente na educação infantil. A maioria dos trabalhos aplicam o DSC em sistemas de *Internet of Things*. Ainda não foi executado o *snowballing*.

6. Considerações finais

Este artigo apresenta uma pesquisa de doutorado em andamento cujo objetivo é contribuir com o processo de ensino e aprendizagem de ES. A principal contribuição é disponibilizar um *framework* para criação de RPG a ser aplicado no ensino de ES. Este *framework* deverá conduzir os professores à criação colaborativa junto aos estudantes e aplicação dos próprios jogos de forma rápida e eficaz. Com o uso do DSC no processo, pode-se dizer que será um *framework* socialmente consciente. Outra contribuição será a experiência de inserir o DSC no processo de desenvolvimento ampliando e disseminando o seu uso.

Os próximos passos desta pesquisa são a conclusão dos MSLs, cujos resultados servirão de base para a execução desta pesquisa. Outros trabalhos envolvendo a realização de oficinas de design semioparticipativo, a geração dos artefatos de DSC, a elaboração e aplicação do *framework*. Por fim, executar um experimento aplicando o *framework* em cursos de graduação de computação para validá-lo e compará-lo a outros *frameworks*.

Referências

Ahmadi, M., Trescak, T., Bashari Rad, B., and Anisi, Y. (2016). Serious games in software engineering processes, a methodical planning. *Indian Journal of Science and Technology*, 9.

Baranauskas, M. C. C. (2014). Social awareness in hci. *Interactions*, 21(4):66–69.

Baranauskas, M. C. C. and Posada, J. E. G. (2017). Tangible and shared storytelling: Searching for the social dimension of constructionism. In *Proceedings of the 2017 Conference on Interaction Design and Children*, IDC '17, page 193–203, New York, NY, USA. Association for Computing Machinery.

Barreto, F., Benitti, F., and Molleri, J. (2008). Utilização de um rpg no ensino de gerenciamento e processo de desenvolvimento de software.

Camargo, L. S. d. A. and Fazani, A. J. (2014). Explorando o design participativo como prática de desenvolvimento de sistemas de informação. *InCID: Revista de Ciência da Informação e Documentação*, 5(1):138–150.

da Silva, J. V., Pereira, R., Hayashi, E. C. S., and Baranauskas, M. C. C. (2018). Design practices and the sawd tool: Towards the opendesign concept. In Liu, K., Nakata, K., Li, W., and Baranauskas, C., editors, *Digitalisation, Innovation, and Transformation*, pages 208–217, Cham. Springer International Publishing.

e Rodrigo Cardoso e Juliana Braga e Rafaela Rocha, R. O. (2018). Frameworks para desenvolvimento de jogos educacionais: uma revisão e comparação de pesquisas recentes. *Brazilian Symposium on Computers in Education (Simpósio Brasileiro de Informática na Educação - SBIE)*, 29(1):854.

Engström, E., Storey, M.-A., Runeson, P., Höst, M., and Baldassarre, M. (2020). How software engineering research aligns with design science: a review. *Empirical Software Engineering*, 25.

Ferrari, B., da Silva Junior, D. P., Oliveira, C. M., Ortiz, J. S. B., and Pereira, R. (2020). Socially aware design of games: an early workshop for game designers.

Ferrari, B., Junior, D. S., Oliveira, C., Ortiz, J., and Pereira, R. (2019). Design socialmente consciente de jogos: relato de uma oficina prática para o entendimento do problema e prospecção de ideias. In *Anais do I Workshop sobre Interação e Pesquisa de Usuários no Desenvolvimento de Jogos*, pages 11–20, Porto Alegre, RS, Brasil. SBC.

Ferreira, A., Rolim, T., Barbosa, P. L., Silva, J. A., Félix, R., and Silva, P. C. (2018a). Adversidades e intervenções no ensino da engenharia de software: Uma revisão sistemática na literatura. In *Anais da IV Escola Regional de Informática do Piauí*, pages 178–183, Porto Alegre, RS, Brasil. SBC.

Ferreira, T., Viana, D., Fernandes, J., and Santos, R. (2018b). Identifying emerging topics and difficulties in software engineering education in brazil. In *Proceedings of the XXXII Brazilian Symposium on Software Engineering*, SBES '18, page 230–239, New York, NY, USA. Association for Computing Machinery.

Grando, A. and Tarouco, L. M. R. (2008). O uso de jogos educacionais do tipo rpg na educação. *RENOTE*, 6(1).

Hall, E. T. (1959). *The silent language*. Doubleday, Garden City, N. Y.

Ivan, G., Pacheco, C., Méndez, F., and Calvo-Manzano, J. (2020). The effects of game-based learning in the acquisition of "soft skills" on undergraduate software engineering courses: A systematic literature review. *Computer Applications in Engineering Education*, 28:1327–1354.

Kosa, M., Yilmaz, M., O'Connor, R. V., and Clarke, P. M. (2016). Software engineering education and games: A systematic literature review. *Journal of Universal Computer Science*, 22(12):1558–1574. http://www.jucs.org/jucs_22_12/software_engineering_education_and.

Lemos, W., Cunha, J., and Saraiva, J. (2019). Ensino de engenharia de software em um curso de sistemas de informação: Uma análise dos problemas e soluções na perspectiva de professores e alunos. In *Anais do XXVII Workshop sobre Educação em Computação*, pages 305–318, Porto Alegre, RS, Brasil. SBC.

Liu, K. (2000). *Semiotics in Information Systems Engineering*. Cambridge University Press.

Pereira, R., Baranauskas, M. C., and da Silva, S. R. (2013). Social software and educational technology: Informal, formal and technical values. *Educational Technology & Society*, 16:4–14.

Rodríguez, G., González-Caino, P. C., and Resett, S. (2021). Serious games for teaching agile methods: A review of multivocal literature. *Computer Applications in Engineering Education*, 29(6):1931–1949.

Schwartz, S. (2005). *Basic human values: Their content and structure across countries*, pages 21–55.

Souza, M. and França, C. (2016). O que explica o sucesso de jogos no ensino de engenharia de software? uma teoria de motivação. In *Anais do XXIV Workshop sobre Educação em Computação*, pages 260–269, Porto Alegre, RS, Brasil. SBC.

How to Identify Programming Skills from Source Code?

Johnatan Oliveira

[1]Department of Computer Science (DCC)
Federal University of Minas Gerais (UFMG)
Software Engineering Lab (LabSoft)
Belo Horizonte, Brazil
johnatan.si@dcc.ufmg.br

Abstract. *Both open-source and proprietary software systems have become increasingly complex. Despite their growing complexity and increasing size, software systems must satisfy strict release requirements that impose quality, putting significant pressure on developers. Therefore, the success of software projects is dependent on the identification and hiring of qualified developers to build a solid and cohesive team with different programming skills. Our main goal is to develop and evaluate a method able to compute programming skills from source code analysis. Our method uses software metrics such as Changed Files and Changed Lines of Code, to compute the skills. Our results showed that our method is able of identifying programming skills of the developers about mainly libraries used, programming languages, and profile concerning back-end & front-end and unit test.*

Keywords: Skills, Program Skills, Mining Software Repositories

1. Introduction

Both open-source and proprietary software systems have become increasingly complex. Despite their growing complexity and increasing size, software systems must satisfy strict release requirements that impose quality, putting significant pressure on developers. Therefore, software projects' success depends on identifying and hiring qualified developers to build a solid and cohesive team with different programming skills. The current practice in industry and research for assessing programming skills is mainly based on proxy variables of skills, such as education, years of experience, and multiple-choice knowledge tests [Baltes and Diehl 2018]. However, poor hiring decisions may hurt the success of a software system [Marlow and Dabbish 2013]. In particular, software projects have many open positions and not as many qualified candidates [Baltes and Diehl 2018]. In this context, identifying qualified candidates with the right combination of skills is crucial to the success of a software project because these candidates may not actively apply themselves for open job positions.

Several approaches aim at addressing this problem by proposing models [Montandon et al. 2019, Bizer et al. 2011, Constantinou and Kapitsaki 2016, da Silva et al. 2015] and tools [Greene and Fischer 2016, Marlow and Dabbish 2013] to automatically identify the programming skills of developers via source code analysis. These models and tools rely, for instance, on information about who has changed each file to identify developers who might know technology and business logic in these particular parts of a system. With the emergence of social coding platforms, such as

GitHub, a lot of information about developers and projects is available. Such social and programming data about developers have a vast potential to support the effective identification of programming skills and expertise. Greene and Fischer (2016) proposed a tool named CVExplorer to identify developers with programming skills, such as expertise in programming languages.

Although these approaches may potentially identify the programming skills, we still lack approaches able to compute programming skills in 5 perspectives: i) which programming languages each developer knows, ii) main libraries, iii) back-end & front-end profile, iv) if the developer creates unit tests, and v) the developer's experience in mobile devices. Therefore, this project presents a proposal for a Ph.D. thesis in Computer Science to fill this gap. Our contribution targets both researchers and practitioners. Researchers can use our results to design studies related to skills and reflect on the complicated relationship between source code activities and skills. Practitioners can use it to refine the practical evaluation of professional skills for several purposes, from hiring procedures to the evaluation of team formation. Understanding the effectiveness of the different approaches is the first and necessary step for building tools that will genuinely indicate programming skills by analyzing activities in the software repository [Baltes and Diehl 2018].

2. Work Plan

To develop the proposed method, we established a set of tasks to be performed during the Ph.D. course. Figure 1 shows the steps. The tasks may have three possible status: Done, In Progress, and To-Do. Our study is divided in ten steps, as follows: i) As we can observe, the first step of the research was the literature review, from which we could understand the state-of-art of metrics, tools, and models to compute programming skills from the source code (done). We noticed that a few works investigated programming skills from source code in perspectives analyzed in this study. ii) From the previous step, we developed the metrics to compute programming skills (done).

We focus mainly on static metrics, for example, changed files and changed lines of code. iii) From the metrics, we develop a method able to compute programming skills (done). iv) In order to analyze our method, we conducted a clone of repositories from GitHub (done). In steps v and vi, our method made an analysis of changed files and changed lines of code in desktop and mobile app (in progress). We need to improve this method to achieve more accuracy (in progress). vii) From the method developed, we need to conduct an empirical study to evaluate them. For this, we select developers, repositories, programming languages, libraries, and target developers to survey (in progress). viii) From the previous step, we conducted a survey with developers from GitHub in order to identify opportunities to improve the method (in progress). ix) After all previous steps, our aim is to evaluate a tool that supports the method developed (to-do). x) In this last step, we compile all findings to contribute to science and conclude the Ph.D. (to-do).

3. Method Overview

This section presents our method developed to compute programming skills in six perspectives: i) which programming languages are used by developer, ii) main libraries are known by them, iii) profile as develop back-end & front-end, iv) unit test, v) frequency of commits, and vi) experience of the developer in mobile devices (Android).

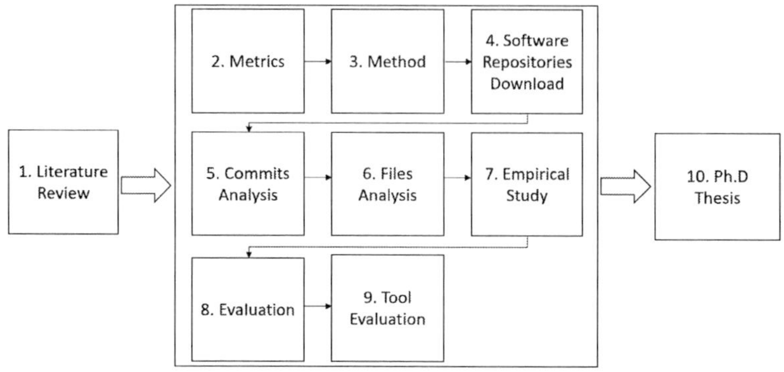

Figure 1. Work plan for quantitative and qualitative studies

3.1. Programming Skills of Library Experts

A library is a collection of objects, functions, and methods [Reif et al. 2016]. Its main benefits are supporting the work performed by developers in such a way that they can implement new features or maintain software systems with more quality [Reif et al. 2016]. Consequently, developers with more knowledge in a library, in particular, can work more actively in open source and proprietary projects [Bailey and Stefaniak 2001, Bailey and Mitchell 2006]. We rely on 3 metrics to identify the library experts. Table 1 shows these metrics and explains them in more details. Each metric is computed in relation to the amount of commits to a specific library. That is, when a commit to a library is identified, the metrics were calculated.

Table 1. Proposed Metrics

Metric	Description
Number of Commits	This metric calculates the activity of each developer through the number of commits using a particular library. Through this metric, it is possible to measure the amount of use of the library in a project that a specific developer works.
Number of Imports	This metric presents the intensity of use of a particular library. For this metric, we count all imports to the library written by a developer. Repeated imports are included.
Lines of Code	To compute this metric, we developed a heuristic to count the amount of LOC related to a specific library, as follows. First, we obtain the ratio of changed LOC by the number of all imports in the file. Then, we multiply the ratio by the number of imports related to the library.

We present the skills of each developer in 5 dimensions: Knowledge Amplitude, Knowledge Intensity, Code Proficiency, Collaboration, and Experience. To rank developers on each of the 5 skills, we created indexes. The indexes range from 1 (beginner) to 5 (senior). Table 2 describes the thresholds used to calculate scores for each skill. This table was designed by empirically analyzing the distribution of data in our study. Thresholds in this table can be adapted to specific contexts.

Knowledge Amplitude– This skill indicates the spread of a developer's knowledge of different libraries. To rank developers in this attribute, we count the number of unique imports written by the developer and related to a specific library.

Knowledge Intensity– This skill shows the intensity of use of a library. We count

Table 2. Thresholds for skill scores

Rank	Knowledge Amplitude	Knowledge Intensity	Code Proficiency	Collaboration	Experience
1	#unique imports between (1 and <=10)	#tota limports between (1 and <=10)	#total LOC between (1 and <=500)	#different file between (0 and <= 5)	#different projects= 0 or 1
2	#unique imports between (11 and <=50)	#tota limports between (11 and <=100)	#total LOC between (501 and <=5,000)	#different files between (6 and <= 10)	#different projects = 2
3	#unique imports between (51 and <=100)	#tota limports between (101 and <=1,000)	#total LOC between (5,001 and <=50,000)	#different files between (11 and <= 20)	#different projects = 3
4	#unique imports between (101 and <=500)	#tota limports between (1,001 and <=10,000)	#total LOC between (50,001 and <=500,000)	#different files between (21 and <= 30)	#different projects = 4
5	#unique imports between (>=501)	#tota limports between (>=10,001)	#total LOC (>=500,001)	#different files >= 31	#different projects >= 5

all imports to the library written by a developer. Repeated imports are included.

Code Proficiency– With this skill, we want to measure how much the developer is productive in a given library. Therefore, we count the total lines of code (LOC) added when this code is related to a library. That is, if the developer adds an import for the library, we assume that this developer is writing code related to the library. We count only non-commented LOC; blank lines and comments are not accounted for this criterion. Table 2 describes the thresholds considered for calculating code proficiency. To compute this metric, we developed a heuristic to count the amount of LOC related to a specific library, as follows. First, it obtains the ratio of changed LOC by the number of all imports in the file. Then, it multiplies the ratio by the number of imports related to the library. The heuristic takes into consideration 3 attributes, the number of library imports, the number of imports in general, and the number of LOC altered by a commit related to the library. The heuristic is then computed as follows:

$$LOC = \frac{\text{\# of LOC Altered by Commit}}{\text{\# of All Imports}} X \text{ \# of Library Imports}$$

Collaboration– This skill measures the developer's ability to collaborate with other peers in the same file. Therefore, we count the number of different source code files that the developer has modified in partnership with other developers.

Experience– This skill denotes the number of additional projects where the developer uses a specific library. Multitasking can produce the developer good dividends if done the right way.

3.2. Programming Skills Profile

Besides compute library experts, we developed 2 other metrics to compute programming skills in 3 dimensions: programming language, back-end & front-end profiles, and unit test. These 2 metrics are, (i) Changed Files and (ii) Changed Lines of Code. Changed Files compute the number of files change made by a specific developer, for example, Mary modified 3 Python, 2 Java, 2 CSS, and 1 HTML files. Therefore, according to the Changed Files, her skill in programming languages is distributed as follows: 37.5% Python, 25% Java, 25% CSS, and 12.5% HTML. In a similar fashion, the metric Changed Lines of Code considers the number of LOC added or removed by a specific developer. For example, to compute the programming skills to Johns in programming languages, we need to count the total number of changed LOC for all files that share the same file extension. John, for instance, has a skill distribution in programming languages as follows: 7 Python, 2 CSS and 1 HTML. Therefore, in percentage we obtain, 70% Python, 20% CSS, and 10% HTML. This data are about programming languages.

Besides compute programming languages, we also analyzed the programmer (a) alignment between back-end front-end profiles and (b) skills in test development. For the former, we classified a set of programming languages as front-end (e.g., CSS), and another set as back-end technologies (e.g., Java). Therefore, we also used the models previously described to calculate back-end front-end profiles. For the latter, to calculate the test skills, we need to identify if a particular folder contains test files. That is, the source code is parsed and we search for directory structures mentioning tests. We manually validated a sample of our script output and verified a precision above 80%. We then consider it good enough for our purpose.

4. Preliminary Results

In this section, we present the dataset used to evaluate our method (section 4.1). Besides, we show the preliminary results in two perspectives: i) library experts (section 4.2) and ii) programming skills profiles (section 4.3).

4.1. Dataset

Our method computed 1,137 curricula from our dataset. To create our dataset, we conduct a process of filtering to select the developers. First, we select 2,000 developers randomly. Second, we made a filter by developers with the top-10 programming languages[1]: JavaScript, Python, Java, Go, C++, Ruby, PHP, TypeScript, C#, and C. Besides, we selected the style sheet language CSS and HTML. Third, from the last filter, we delete developers whose repositories have less than ten projects. Fourth, we select from the previous step developers with at least 100 commits in projects. In the fifth and last step, we select developers with at least a thousand LOC committed and obtained the 1,137 developers able to participate in our analysis.

4.2. Library Experts

In this section, we present a overview of some relevant findings achieved in perspective library experts. Our study shows that a significant amount of expert candidates makes commits, when writing code related to a specific library, performs many imports of particular libraries, and writes LOC in sequence when making an import of the library. The developers were invited (survey) to rank their knowledge using a scale from 1 (one) to 5 (five), where (1) means no knowledge about the library; and (5) means extensive knowledge about the library. If we analyze the data about the precision of the strategy from the sum of levels 3, 4 and 5 of Likert-type scale, we obtain on average 88.49% of accuracy in relation the knowledge of the developers, i.e., identification is correct in more than 88% of the cases. On the other hand, although a score 3 may represent an acceptable knowledge, if we followed a more conservative criterion, only classifying as library experts the developers that informed a higher (≥ 4) knowledge on the libraries, we obtain,

[1]https://madnight.github.io/githut/#/pull_requests/2020/2

on average, 63.31% of precision. This way, we conclude that most of the identified expert candidates identified by the strategy contain high knowledge about the evaluated libraries. In contrast, to a level of knowledge < 3, we achieved only 11.51% of the developers, i.e., possibly the strategy fails by selecting these developers.

4.3. Programming Skills Profiles

This section describes the survey results applied with developers from GitHub. Our dataset had the same setup used in the section 4.1. Figure 2 shows the opinion of the developers about our method. In this figure, we have 3 blocks, one for each evaluated programming skill. The first block of charts represents programming language skills. The second block depicts the back-end & front-end profiles. Finally, the last block shows the test skills. Concerning the Changed Files agreement, we observe in the programming language perspective that 27% of the participants answered "strongly agree" and "agree". On the other hand, we observe that to the Changed LOC, 14% and 22% of the participants answered respectively "strongly agree and "agree". Concerning disagreements, we have 12% and 18% to "strongly disagree" and "disagree" to the Changed Files. While for Changed LOC, we observe 18% and 19%, respectively, to "strongly disagree" and "disagree". This way, we note that the Changed Files models, in general, are better evaluated by developers to capture their programming language skills.

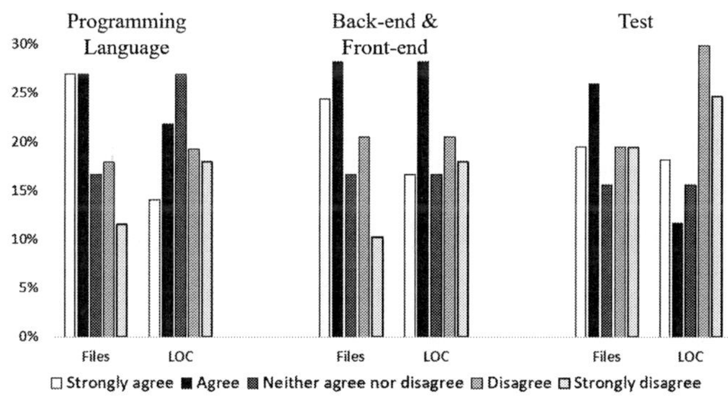

Figure 2. Overview

5. Related Work

The use of data present in GitHub to understand how software developers work and collaborate has become recurrent in software engineering studies [Destefanis et al. 2016]. Some studies seek to understand the behavior of developers concerning interaction with their peers [Ortu et al. 2015]. For example, studies that try to understand who are the developers with peaceful behavior and those with aggressive behavior and if these developers coexist productively in software development projects [Ortu et al. 2016]. Similar studies also try to understand if there is a relationship between bug resolution time and behavior of developers [Ortu et al. 2015]. Also, some studies investigate developers manners [Destefanis et al. 2016] and seek to understand the emotional behavior of software developers [Ortu et al. 2016].

Greene and Fischer (2016) have developed an approach to extracting technical information from GitHub developers. The work of researchers also does not differentiate developers from their level of knowledge of technical skills, since a recruiter has several candidates for the same job position [Greene and Fischer 2016]. In addition, the work only shows the profile of the users in GitHub, and it does not extract other characteristics of their knowledge and skills. Besides, they do not provide actual data about the developer's knowledge production. Singer et al. (2013) investigate the use of profile aggregates in the evaluation of developer skills by developers and recruiters [Singer et al. 2013]. However, these aggregates only gather skills for individual developers, and it is not clear how they support the identification of relevant developers from a large dataset of candidates.

We believe that our method is complementary to the described related work, providing a different approach focusing on the identification of possible experts in specific technologies. To the best of our effort, we did not find a similar strategy. Hence, we cannot compare our proposal to other studies.

6. Conclusion and Future Work

This project presents a proposal for a Ph.D. thesis in Computer Science that focuses on the method to compute programming skills from source code. We believe that mining software repositories to understand how developers use specific technologies provide objective insight into their real expertise. Therefore, our method may be useful to support the assessment of developers' skills, which are often analyzed using curriculum information, interviews, and admission tests. Our method uses data from GitHub to compute programming skills from source code. We rely on a set of metrics and thresholds. Our preliminary results showed that our method is able compute programming skills.

As future work, we intend to conclude the last study steps, publish the study results as papers for the community, complete the study (to-do) and finish this Ph.D.'s is December 2022 or January 2023 with the thesis defense.

References

Bailey, J. and Mitchell, R. B. (2006). Industry perceptions of the competencies needed by computer programmers: technical, business, and soft skills. *Journal of Computer Information Systems*, 47(2):28–33.

Bailey, J. L. and Stefaniak, G. (2001). Industry perceptions of the knowledge, skills, and abilities needed by computer programmers. In *Proceedings of the 2001 ACM SIGCPR conference on Computer personnel research*, pages 93–99. ACM.

Baltes, S. and Diehl, S. (2018). Towards a theory of software development expertise. ESEC/FSE 2018, page 187–200, New York, NY, USA. Association for Computing Machinery.

Bizer, C., Heath, T., and Berners-Lee, T. (2011). Linked data: The story so far. In *Semantic services, interoperability and web applications: emerging concepts*, pages 205–227.

Constantinou, E. and Kapitsaki, G. M. (2016). Identifying developers' expertise in social coding platforms. In *42th Euromicro Conference on Software Engineering and Advanced Applications (SEAA)*.

da Silva, J. R., Clua, E., Murta, L., and Sarma, A. (2015). Niche vs. breadth: Calculating expertise over time through a fine-grained analysis. In *2015 IEEE 22nd International Conference on Software Analysis, Evolution, and Reengineering (SANER)*.

Destefanis, G., Ortu, M., Counsell, S., Swift, S., Marchesi, M., and Tonelli, R. (2016). Software development: do good manners matter? *PeerJ Computer Science*, 2:e73.

Greene, G. J. and Fischer, B. (2016). Cvexplorer: Identifying candidate developers by mining and exploring their open source contributions. In *31st IEEE/ACM International Conference on Automated Software Engineering (ASE)*, pages 804–809.

Marlow, J. and Dabbish, L. (2013). Activity traces and signals in software developer recruitment and hiring. In *Proceedings of the 2013 conference on Computer supported cooperative work*, pages 145–156.

Montandon, J. E., Silva, L. L., and Valente, M. T. (2019). Identifying experts in software libraries and frameworks among GitHub users. In *16th International Conference on Mining Software Repositories (MSR)*, pages 276–287.

Ortu, M., Adams, B., Destefanis, G., Tourani, P., Marchesi, M., and Tonelli, R. (2015). Are bullies more productive?: empirical study of affectiveness vs. issue fixing time. In *Proceedings of the 12th Working Conference on Mining Software Repositories*, pages 303–313. IEEE Press.

Ortu, M., Destefanis, G., Counsell, S., Swift, S., Tonelli, R., and Marchesi, M. (2016). Arsonists or firefighters? affectiveness in agile software development. In *International Conference on Agile Software Development*, pages 144–155. Springer.

Reif, M., Eichberg, M., Hermann, B., Lerch, J., and Mezini, M. (2016). Call graph construction for Java libraries. In *24th Proc. of the ACM Int. Symposium on Foundations of Software Engineering (SIGSOFT)*, pages 474–486.

Singer, L., Figueira Filho, F., Cleary, B., Treude, C., Storey, M.-A., and Schneider, K. (2013). Mutual assessment in the social programmer ecosystem: an empirical investigation of developer profile aggregators. In *Proceedings of the 2013 conference on Computer supported cooperative work*, pages 103–116. ACM.

Metodología Basada en Modelos en Tiempo de Ejecución para la Construcción y Operación de Sistemas Autoconscientes de Internet de las Cosas

Lenin Erazo-Garzón[1]

[1]LIDI – Universidad del Azuay
Cuenca, Ecuador

lerazo@uazuay.edu.ec

Abstract. *Nowadays, one of the technological challenges is the development of software for IoT systems, since they operate in highly changing scenarios, being complex with traditional Software Engineering methodologies to identify all the system requirements in the development stage. An alternative is to increase their autonomy, providing them with self-awareness capabilities with the support of runtime models, to transfer several of the functionalities that are programmed during development to runtime. This doctoral work proposes to develop a methodology based on runtime models for the construction and operation of self-aware IoT systems.*

Resumen. *Hoy en día, uno de los desafíos tecnológicos es el desarrollo de software para sistemas de IoT, ya que operan en escenarios altamente cambiantes, siendo complejo con las metodologías de Ingeniería de Software tradicionales identificar todos los requisitos del sistema en la etapa de desarrollo. Una alternativa es incrementar su autonomía, dotándoles de capacidades de autoconsciencia con el apoyo de los modelos en tiempo de ejecución, a fin de trasladar varias de las funcionalidades que se programan durante el desarrollo al tiempo de ejecución. Este trabajo doctoral propone desarrollar una metodología basada en modelos en tiempo de ejecución para la construcción y operación de sistemas autoconscientes de IoT.*

1. Introducción

El Internet de las Cosas (IoT) es un paradigma tecnológico que se usa para referirse a una infraestructura compuesta por un conjunto de objetos (cosas) inteligentes, ubicuos e interconectados mediante las tecnologías de información para procesar datos del mundo físico y virtual; y, actuar con la mínima intervención humana [Madakam et al. 2015]. El IoT promueve el desarrollo de innovadoras aplicaciones en diversos dominios (p. ej., hogar, ciudad inteligente, industria), agregando una nueva dimensión a la vida de las personas, basada en la interacción permanente con los objetos inteligentes, en cualquier lugar y momento, lo cual impacta favorablemente en el desarrollo de la sociedad.

Los sistemas de IoT operan en entornos altamente cambiantes que deben ser controlados oportunamente para garantizar su correcto y continuo funcionamiento [Miorandi et al. 2012]. Debido a la incertidumbre intrínseca asociada a los cambios, resulta complejo identificar todos los requisitos de un sistema de IoT durante la etapa de desarrollo. Además, las metodologías y herramientas de Ingeniería de Software tradicionales han demostrado ser poco productivas para afrontar el dinamismo y la escalabilidad de los sistemas de IoT, siendo los desarrolladores los que gestionan la evolución del sistema en el tiempo de diseño [Sosa-Reyna et al. 2018]. Esta limitación se agudiza aún más, ya que estos enfoques metodológicos y herramientas se centran en los detalles de implementación (programación a bajo nivel) en lugar del dominio del problema, volviéndose complejo para los desarrolladores por la heterogeneidad de los dispositivos de IoT (sensores, actuadores) que deben ser integrados [Chen et al. 2015].

Un enfoque apropiado es incorporar la autoconsciencia computacional a los sistemas de IoT con el apoyo de los modelos en tiempo de ejecución, a fin de aumentar su capacidad autónoma y resiliente frente a las situaciones imprevistas [Esterle and Grosu 2016]. Un sistema de IoT es considerado autoconsciente, si es capaz de obtener y mantener el conocimiento sobre sí mismo y el entorno (p. ej., estructura, estado, evolución), sin control externo [Kounev et al. 2017]. Dicho conocimiento puede ser capturado directamente de los datos crudos recolectados desde los sensores físicos o virtuales (observación inmediata – perceptual) o extraído de modelos conceptuales internos, construidos a partir de los datos históricos [Lewis et al. 2017].

Los modelos en tiempo de ejecución (models@run.time) constituyen una auto-representación causalmente conectada de un sistema observado. En este sentido, la información recopilada desde el sistema de IoT puede utilizarse para retroalimentar los modelos en tiempo de ejecución. Luego, estos modelos pueden analizarse para conocer el estado y la posible evolución del sistema; y, en caso de ser necesario recomendar acciones correctivas. Por lo tanto, el uso de los models@run.time en los sistemas de IoT contribuye a trasladar varias de las funcionalidades que tradicionalmente se programan durante el desarrollo al tiempo de ejecución, lo cual eleva el nivel de abstracción y automatización del proceso de desarrollo, así como también mejora la gestión de la complejidad, la incertidumbre y el cambio [Bencomo et al. 2019].

La autoconsciencia es un campo emergente dentro de la Ingeniería de Software con importantes desafíos y oportunidades de investigación [Elhabbash et al. 2019]. A su vez, según [Bencomo et al. 2019] uno de los desafíos actuales de los models@run.time es la autoconsciencia computacional. Particularmente, los trabajos de investigación sobre autoconsciencia en IoT son escasos y se orientan principalmente a nivel conceptual [Gurgen et al. 2013; Tammemäe et al. 2017; Esterle et al. 2020].

Este artículo presenta una propuesta de tesis doctoral cuyo propósito es desarrollar una metodología y su infraestructura de soporte basada en modelos en tiempo de ejecución para la construcción y operación de sistemas autoconscientes de IoT. En la actualidad, la solución propuesta se encuentra en la etapa de evaluación experimental y refinamiento, con la finalidad de garantizar un método formal, ordenado, eficaz, eficiente y repetible para el desarrollo de sistemas autoconscientes de IoT.

La estructura de este documento es la siguiente: Sección 2 presenta el estado del arte sobre la autoconsciencia en IoT. Sección 3 plantea los objetivos y preguntas de investigación de la tesis doctoral. Sección 4 explica la metodología de investigación empleada. Secciones 5 y 6 describen la solución propuesta y los resultados preliminares de su evaluación. Finalmente, la Sección 7 presenta las conclusiones y el trabajo futuro.

2. Trabajos Relacionados

Según la revisión sistemática sobre autoconsciencia en Ingeniería de Software elaborada por [Elhabbash et al. 2019], los avances dentro del dominio de IoT son poco significativos. Recién en los últimos años ha crecido el interés de los investigadores sobre la autoconsciencia en IoT, siendo en su mayoría trabajos conceptuales, enfocados en identificar los beneficios, desafíos y recomendaciones en torno a la construcción de sistemas autoconscientes de IoT. En [Tammemäe et al. 2017] se formulan varios estudios de caso para demostrar que incorporar la autoconsciencia a nivel de los nodos edge y fog de una infraestructura de IoT es beneficioso para mejorar el rendimiento de los recursos durante el procesamiento de los datos. A su vez, [Gurgen et al. 2013] describen una arquitectura general para un sistema ciber-físico autoconsciente, basada en el modelo MAPE-K y un middleware orientado a servicios distribuidos, junto con los desafíos y recomendaciones para su implementación en las infraestructuras de una ciudad inteligente. Por su parte, [Götzinger et al. 2020] proponen el framework RoSA, el cual está basado en un modelo jerárquico de agentes que proporciona facilidades para implementar y evaluar aplicaciones autoconscientes para sistemas ciber-físicos.

Con respecto a la autoconsciencia colectiva, [Esterle et al. 2018] presentan un artículo de posición sobre un enfoque de diseño de aplicaciones de IoT, basado en una arquitectura autoconsciente que utiliza modelos de interacción colectiva entre los nodos de IoT para mejorar el rendimiento de la red global. En otro trabajo, [Esterle et al. 2020] amplían la idea de la autoconsciencia de sistemas individuales y proponen una hoja de ruta hacia una autoconsciencia en red, a fin de aumentar la capacidad de los sistemas ciber-físicos para aprender sobre el entorno y las interacciones con otros sistemas. En un ámbito general, [Lewis et al. 2017] presentan un framework conceptual que define los niveles, aspectos y el dominio de un sistema autoconsciencia.

3. Objetivos y Preguntas de Investigación

Este trabajo de investigación doctoral propone como objetivo general: desarrollar una metodología y su infraestructura de soporte basada en modelos en tiempo de ejecución para la construcción y operación de sistemas autoconscientes de IoT. A su vez, el objetivo general se descompone en los siguientes objetivos específicos: i) analizar el estado del arte sobre la autoconsciencia computacional y el uso de los models@run.time en IoT y otros dominios relacionados; ii) definir un proceso metodológico formal, sistémico y repetible que integre las actividades, guías, recursos, artefactos y herramientas necesarias para la construcción y operación de sistemas autoconscientes de IoT; iii) diseñar la arquitectura de la infraestructura que dará soporte al método propuesto; iv) construir los componentes de la infraestructura de soporte, incluyendo metamodelos, lenguajes específicos de domino (DSLs), herramientas de configuración y otras herramientas a nivel de middleware para mantener la relación causal entre los modelos y el sistema de IoT observado, así como para ejecutar las capacidades de autoconsciencia especificadas en los modelos; e, v) instanciar y evaluar la metodología y su infraestructura para conocer la percepción de los desarrolladores sobre su efectividad, eficiencia, facilidad de uso, utilidad e intención de uso futuro.

Para alcanzar los objetivos se definen las siguientes preguntas de investigación: PI-1. ¿Cuáles son los problemas y desafíos sobre el uso de los models@run.time para incorporar la autoconsciencia a los sistemas de IoT? PI-2. ¿Qué actividades, guías, recursos, artefactos y herramientas deben incorporarse en la metodología? PI-3. ¿Cómo organizar las actividades y recursos de la metodología? PI-4. ¿Cómo diseñar la arquitectura de la infraestructura de soporte? PI-5. ¿Cómo construir los artefactos y herramientas de la infraestructura de soporte? PI-6. ¿Cómo evaluar y demostrar que la metodología y su infraestructura es considerada por los desarrolladores como efectiva, eficiente, fácil de usar, útil, y que tienen la intención de utilizarla en el futuro?

4. Metodología de Investigación

La metodología empleada para el desarrollo de la tesis doctoral está basada en el Modelo de Investigación y Transferencia de Tecnología propuesto por [Gorschek et al. 2006]. Este modelo se fundamenta en un proceso que inicia con la formulación del problema y la revisión del estado del arte. Luego se definen las soluciones candidatas, las cuales a través de un ciclo evolutivo son objeto de evaluaciones empíricas y una mejora continua hacia la búsqueda de una solución adecuada y realista. Con respecto a la evaluación empírica de la solución se utilizan cuasi-experimentos basados en el Modelo de Evaluación de Métodos (MEM) [Moody 2001].

5. Solución Propuesta

5.1. Metodología Basada en Modelos en Tiempo de Ejecución

La metodología propuesta integra un conjunto de actividades, guías, recursos y herramientas que indican cómo construir un sistema autoconsciente de IoT. En la Figura 1, se presenta un diagrama de proceso de alto nivel basado en la notación SPEM 2.0, incluyendo las seis actividades principales que conforman la metodología, así como los artefactos de entrada y salida que se utilizan durante el proceso. Las dos primeras actividades requieren de la intervención de los desarrolladores, mientras que las cuatro restantes se ejecutan automáticamente. A continuación, se describen estas actividades:

1. **Diseño de la arquitectura de monitoreo del sistema de IoT**. Tiene como alcance el modelado visual de la arquitectura multi-capa de un sistema de IoT, la cual incluya: i) las entidades de IoT (físicas o digitales) y sus propiedades a ser monitoreadas; ii) las entidades digitales (recursos de hardware / software) que soportan los procesos de recolección, transporte, procesamiento y almacenamiento de datos, a nivel de las capas edge, fog y cloud; y, iii) los flujos de datos entre las entidades digitales, basados en protocolos de comunicación síncronos o asíncronos.
2. **Configuración de las capacidades de autoconsciencia del sistema de IoT**. Construye el modelo de autoconsciencia, el cual incorpora especificaciones sobre: i) el dominio (sujetos y objetos) de autoconsciencia; ii) los aspectos a capturar sobre los objetos de autoconsciencia (p. ej., estado, causalidad, evolución); iii) los procesos pre-reflexivos[1] y reflexivos[2] de autoconsciencia [Lewis et al. 2017], con sus respectivos métodos de recolección, calculo y modelos de análisis que determinan la forma como un sistema de IoT ejecuta sus capacidades de autoconsciencia; iv) las métricas (directas, indirectas e indicadores) para evaluar los aspectos de autoconsciencia; v) los recursos de implementación (fórmulas, funciones o servicios web) que son utilizados por los métodos de autoconsciencia para calcular las métricas; y, vi) las recomendaciones prescriptivas asociadas a los

[1] Proceso capaz de obtener conocimiento subjetivo directamente de los datos crudos recolectados desde los sensores (observación perceptual), permitiendo al sistema de IoT responder a los eventos de manera inmediata.
[2] Proceso capaz de construir modelos conceptuales internos que capturan conocimiento a partir de los datos históricos recopilados por los sensores.

criterios de decisión y umbrales de los indicadores.

3. **Sincronización entre los modelos de arquitectura - autoconsciencia y el sistema de IoT observado (mantiene la relación causal).** A partir de las especificaciones de los modelos y su evolución, esta actividad implementa o reconfigura automáticamente: i) los recursos de software del sistema de IoT (APIs, aplicaciones, servicios, brokers, base de datos) que soportan el monitoreo; y, ii) los recursos de implementación que operacionalizan los métodos de autoconsciencia, a fin de calcular las métricas y evaluar los aspectos de autoconsciencia.

4. **Monitoreo.** Ejecuta los recursos de software creados en la actividad anterior con el propósito de recolectar, transportar, procesar y almacenar los datos crudos obtenidos desde los sensores.

5. **Aprendizaje.** Utiliza los datos generados por la actividad de monitoreo y las especificaciones de los modelos para producir métricas directas e indirectas que valoren los aspectos de autoconsciencia. Las métricas directas son obtenidas mediante los métodos de recolección y representan los datos crudos recolectados directamente desde los sensores u otras fuentes. Mientras que las métricas indirectas se derivan de otras métricas directas e indirectas por medio de la construcción, refinamiento y aplicación de modelos conceptuales (p. ej., modelos de regresión, de aprendizaje automático) especificados en los métodos de cálculo.

6. **Razonamiento.** Utiliza las especificaciones del modelo de autoconsciencia para aplicar modelos de análisis que combinen y comparen los valores obtenidos para ciertas métricas con los criterios de decisión (umbrales), a fin de obtener nuevos indicadores cuantitativos y cualitativos que determinen el estado o la posible evolución futura de un objeto de autoconsciencia; y, en caso de ser necesario recomendar las acciones prescriptivas incluidas en el modelo de autoconsciencia.

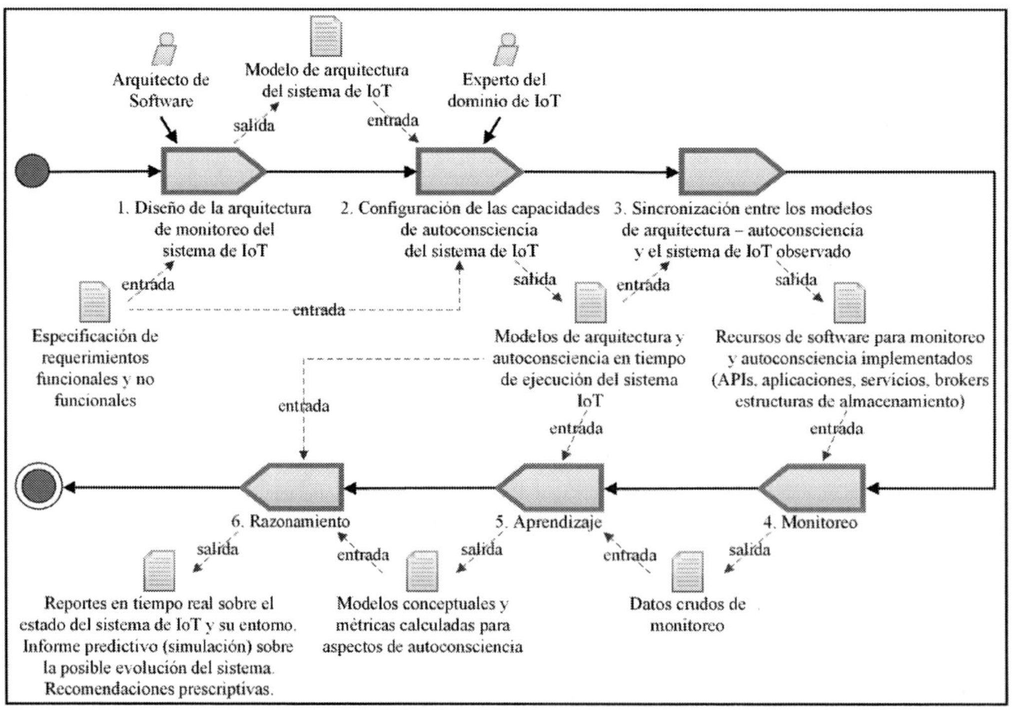

Figura 1. Proceso metodológico de alto nivel basado en models@run.time.

5.2. Infraestructura de Soporte

La Figura 2 presenta la arquitectura de la infraestructura de soporte, cuyos principales componentes se describen brevemente a continuación:

- **Monitor-IoT.** Lenguaje específico de dominio (DSL) para modelar arquitecturas multi-capa que soporten los procesos de monitoreo de un sistema de IoT. Monitor-IoT incluye un diseñador gráfico desarrollado en Obeo Designer y un metamodelo alineado con la arquitectura de referencia para IoT ISO/IEC 30141:2018.
- **Configurador de capacidades de autoconsciencia de sistemas de IoT.** Aplicación web desarrollada en Node.js para mantener y generar el modelo de autoconsciencia en tiempo de ejecución. El configurador utiliza un metamodelo construido a partir del framework conceptual de autoconsciencia de [Lewis et al. 2017] y la ontología de medición de software de [García et al. 2004].
- **Middleware de la infraestructura de soporte.** Integrado por los motores de sincronización y autoconsciencia, los cuales han sido construidos en Node.js. El *motor de sincronización* detecta automáticamente cualquier cambio en los modelos y ejecuta tareas de implementación y reconfiguración de los recursos del sistema de IoT. Mientras que el *motor de autoconsciencia* crea demonios (daemon) que encapsulan y ejecutan los procesos pre-reflexivos y reflexivos en segundo plano, según lo establecido en el modelo de autoconsciencia en tiempo de ejecución.

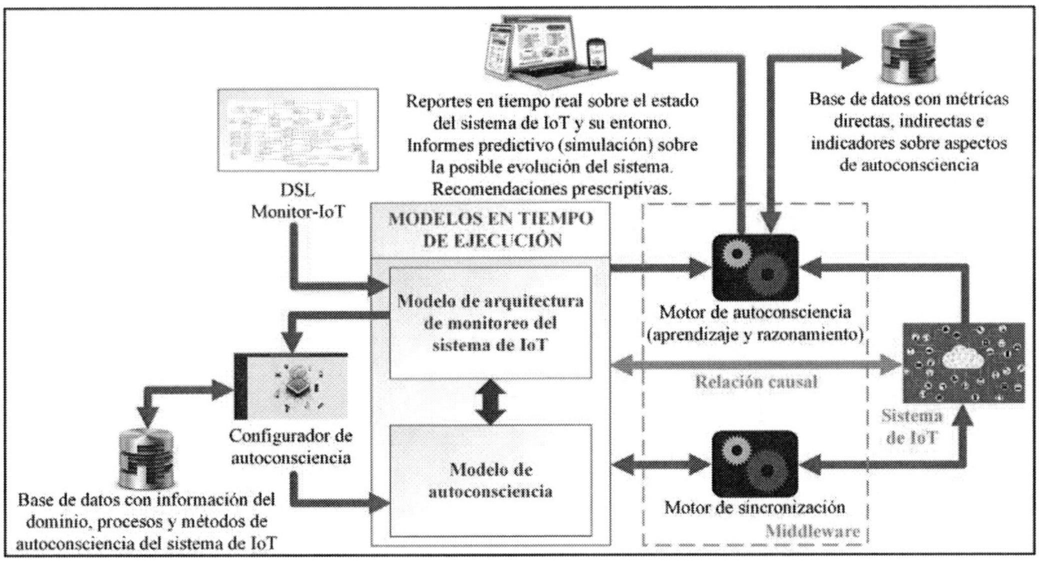

Figura 2. Arquitectura de la infraestructura basada en models@run.time.

6. Resultados Preliminares de la Evaluación de la Solución Propuesta

De acuerdo con el paradigma de Goal-Question Metric (GQM), en la Tabla 1 se define el objetivo de evaluación de la solución propuesta. Al momento, se han evaluado las actividades 1 y 3 de la metodología mediante la aplicación de cuasi-experimentos basados en el MEM. Los experimentos contemplaron el uso de Monitor-IoT para el diseño de la arquitectura de un sistema de gestión de emergencias para adultos mayores que viven solos en su hogar, así como el despliegue del motor de sincronización para la implementación y reconfiguración automática de los recursos de software especificados en el modelo de arquitectura (boletines de los experimentos están disponibles en: http://t.ly/vsPr). En los experimentos se utilizaron formularios de trabajo para recolectar métricas sobre el rendimiento de los participantes y se realizaron encuestas para conocer su percepción sobre las herramientas utilizadas. Para analizar los datos recogidos, se utilizó estadística descriptiva y pruebas de hipótesis. La Tabla 2 presenta un resumen de los resultados obtenidos en los experimentos para las variables de rendimiento (efectividad y eficiencia) y de percepción (facilidad de uso, utilidad e intención de uso). Los valores promedio de efectividad demuestran que los participantes fueron capaces de cumplir en gran medida con las tareas experimentales. A su vez, los tiempos promedio invertidos en el cumplimiento de las tareas experimentales son mínimos en comparación al tiempo que se necesitaría para implementar los recursos de software del escenario experimental con el apoyo de métodos y herramientas de Ingeniería de Software tradicionales. Finalmente, las variables de percepción tienen como común denominador que su promedio es mayor al valor neutro (3) de la escala de Likert, lo que demuestra que los participantes perciben a los componentes evaluados como fáciles de usar, útiles, y que tienen la intención de utilizarlos a futuro.

Tabla 1. Definición de Goal-Question-Metric para la evaluación de la solución

Evaluar:	La metodología y su infraestructura de soporte basada en models@run.time para la construcción y operación de sistemas autoconscientes de IoT.
Con el propósito de:	Analizar y determinar el rendimiento (efectividad y eficiencia) de los usuarios en el uso de la metodología y su infraestructura soporte, así como su percepción con respecto a la facilidad de uso, utilidad e intención de uso futuro de la solución.
Desde el punto de vista del:	Investigador.
En el contexto de:	Un grupo de estudiantes de los últimos semestres de la carrera de Ingeniería de Sistemas de la Universidad del Azuay y Universidad de Cuenca.

Tabla 2. Estadísticos descriptivos de las variables de rendimiento y percepción

Variable	Actividad 1		Actividad 3	
	Media	**Desviación estándar**	**Media**	**Desviación estándar**
Efectividad: Grado de cumplimiento de los objetivos del método.	86,98%	15,69%	94,53%	8,36%
Eficiencia (minutos): Tiempo empleado para aplicar el método.	86,78	16,75	22,09	6,74
Facilidad de uso: Grado en que una persona cree que utilizando un método requerirá menos esfuerzo.	4.43	0.51	4,14	0,71
Utilidad percibida: Grado en que una persona cree que utilizando un método mejorará su desempeño.	4.55	0.49	4,53	0,51
Intención de uso: Medida en que una persona tiene la intención de utilizar un método.	4.56	0.55	4,44	0,76

7. Conclusiones y Trabajo Futuro

La revisión de la literatura evidencia que dotar de autoconsciencia a los sistemas de IoT con el apoyo de los models@run.time representa una brecha de investigación en la actualidad. De ahí que, como parte de los resultados alcanzados en esta tesis doctoral en curso, se propone desde una perspectiva general una metodología e infraestructura de soporte basada en models@run.time para la construcción y operación de sistemas autoconscientes de IoT. Los componentes de la solución metodológica evaluados hasta el momento, han alcanzado indicadores favorables de efectividad, eficiencia y usabilidad. Como trabajo futuro se tiene previsto difundir a través de publicaciones cada una de las actividades y componentes de la metodología y su infraestructura de soporte, junto con los resultados de las evaluaciones que demuestran su utilidad. A su vez, se tiene planificado continuar con las evaluaciones de las restantes actividades de la metodología y con las tareas de mejora continua de la solución.

References

Bencomo, N., Götz, S. and Song, H. (2019). Models@run.time: A Guided Tour of the State of the Art and Research Challenges. *Software & Systems Modeling*, 18(5):3049-3082.

Chen, X. et al. (2015). Runtime Model Based Approach to IoT Application Development. *Frontiers of Computer Science*, 9(4):540-553.

Elhabbash, A., Salama, M., Bahsoon, R. and Tino, P. (2019). Self-Awareness in Software Engineering: A Systematic Literature Review. *ACM Transactions on Autonomous and Adaptive Systems*, 14(2):1-42.

Esterle, L. and Brown, J. (2020). I Think Therefore You Are: Models for Interaction in Collectives of Self-Aware Cyber-Physical Systems. *ACM Transactions on Cyber-Physical Systems*, 4(4):1-25.

Esterle, L. and Grosu, R. (2016). Cyber-physical Systems: Challenge of the 21st Century. *e & i Elektrotechnik und Informationstechnik*, 133(7):299-303.

Esterle, L. and Rinner, B. (2018). An Architecture for Self-Aware IoT Applications. In *2018 IEEE International Conference on Acoustics, Speech and Signal Processing (ICASSP)*, pages 6588-6592.

García, F. et al. (2004). Una Ontología de la Medición del Software. Universidad de Castilla-La Mancha.

Gorschek, T., Garre, P., Larsson, S. and Wohlin, C. (2006). A Model for Technology Transfer in Practice. *IEEE Software*, 23(6):88-95.

Gotzinger, M. et al. (2020). RoSA: A Framework for Modeling Self-Awareness in Cyber-Physical Systems. *IEEE Access*, 8:141373-141394.

Gurgen, L., Gunalp, O., Benazzouz, Y. and Gallissot, M. (2013). Self-Aware Cyber-Physical Systems and Applications in Smart Buildings and Cities. In *2013 Design, Automation & Test in Europe Conference & Exhibition (DATE)*, pages 1149-1154.

Kounev, S. et al. (2017). The Notion of Self-Aware Computing. In *Self-Aware Computing Systems*, pages 3-16. Springer.

Lewis, P. et al. (2017). Towards a Framework for the Levels and Aspects of Self-Aware Computing Systems. In *Self-Aware Computing Systems*, pages 51-85. Springer.

Madakam, S., Ramaswamy, R. and Tripathi, S. (2015). Internet of Things (IoT): A literature review. *Journal of Computer and Communications*, 3(5):164-173.

Miorandi, D., Sicari, S., De Pellegrini, F. and Chlamtac, I. (2012). Internet of Things: Vision, Applications and Research Challenges. *Ad Hoc Networks*, 10(7):1497-1516.

Moody, D. (2001). *A Practical Method for Representing Large Entity Relationship Models*. PhD Thesis. University of Melbourne, Australia.

Sosa-Reyna, C., Tello-Leal, E. and Lara-Alabazares, D. (2018). Methodology for the Model-Driven Development of Service Oriented IoT Applications. *Journal of Systems Architecture*, 90:15-22.

Tammemäe, K. et al. (2017). Self-Aware Fog Computing in Private and Secure Spheres. In *Fog Computing in the Internet of Things*, pages 71-99. Springer.

Modelo para Amparar o Desenvolvimento de Protótipos de Sistemas IoT

Eduarda Maganha de Almeida[1,2]

[1]Departamento de Informática - Universidade Federal do Paraná (UFPR)
Código Postal - 82590-300 -Curitiba - PR - Brasil

[2]Departamento de Computação - Universidade Tecnológica Federal do Paraná (UTFPR)
Código Postal - 86300-000 - Cornélio Procópio - PR - Brasil

eduardamaganha@ufpr.br

Abstract. *The term Internet of Things describes an environment where billions of objects are connected to the Internet and interact autonomously. However, there are challenges in the development of these systems. The different perceptions of those involved and the different use of computing resources can make requirements inconsistent. Thus, the need for a prototyping model that supports the processes of elicitation, analysis and visualization of the requirements of these systems is characterized. This article reports a research that seeks to support the development of prototypes of IoT systems. The model reflects a framework for designing and visually modeling requirements using Socially Conscious Design and Extended Reality.*

Resumo. *O termo Internet das Coisas descreve um ambiente onde bilhões de objetos são conectados à Internet e interagem autonomamente. Entretanto, existem desafios no desenvolvimento destes sistemas. As diferentes percepções dos envolvidos e o uso distintos de recursos computacionais podem tornar os requisitos inconsistentes. Dessa forma, caracteriza-se a necessidade de um modelo de prototipação que ampare nos processos de elicitação, análise e visualização dos requisitos desses sistemas. Este artigo relata uma pesquisa, que busca amparar o desenvolvimento de protótipos de sistemas IoT. O modelo reflete uma estrutura de trabalho, para concepção e modelagem visual dos requisitos, com o uso do Design Socialmente Consciente e Realidade Estendida.*

1. Introdução

O processo de produção passou por mudanças para enfrentar os mercados dinâmicos. As modificações refletem a maneira como as pessoas vivem, trabalham e se relacionam, é caracterizada pelo uso intensivo de tecnologias digitais com o intuito de gerar novos produtos de forma rápida e eficaz [Zabadal and de Castro 2017]. Destacam-se como componentes que envolvem essas modificações, Internet das Coisas (IoT, do inglês *Internet of Things*), Inteligência Artificial, *Big Data*, Realidades virtuais e aumentada, e demais componentes.

Neste escopo, IoT ganhou espaço para além dos ambientes produtivos, como indústrias e escritórios, e passou a se inserir em todos os aspectos da vida das pessoas, seja em instituições de ensino, residências e / ou lazer, por meio de diferentes dispositivos e formas de acesso, tem ampliado seu alcance em todo o mundo [Pereira et al. 2013].

A IoT, envolve funcionalidades inovadoras conectando dispositivos e/ou objetos perfeitamente. Mas há ameaças, suas características e sua grande quantidade de elementos e características de tempo real tendem a aumentar a complexidade de desenvolvimento, pois as diferentes percepções dos envolvidos e o uso distintos de recursos computacionais podem tornar os requisitos inconsistentes [Sommerville et al. 2011] e acarretar ambiguidades no seu desenvolvimento [Weyrich and Ebert 2015]. Além disso, há falta de padrões e modelos que amparar a especificação de requisitos, modelagem, segurança, desempenho, entidades dinâmicas e outras particularidades [Reggio 2018].

Dessa forma, caracteriza-se a necessidade de um modelo de prototipação que ampare no processo de elicitação, análise e visualização dos requisitos em sistemas IoT.

Em busca de soluções de modo que seja possível atender as necessidades das diferentes partes interessadas envolvidas, sem desencadear efeitos nocivos nas pessoas e no meio em que é utilizado, o Design Socialmente Consciente (DSC) [Baranauskas et al. 2009], foi pensado para o processo de design de sistemas computacionais de modo geral, tem potencial de contribuir para o design de sistema, pois informa e provoca reflexões sobre o domínio do problema e o potencial de impacto da soluçãono mundo social [Ferrari et al. 2019].

Assim, a metodologia de DSC, por meio da teoria da semiótica organizacional e da realização de workshops semioparticipatórios - técnicas de design participativo, colaborativo e universal - elicitam requisitos que abrangem o humano, organizacional , valores legais, culturais, econômicos e técnicos, divididos em níveis de projeto informal, formal e técnico [Baranauskas 2014]. Assim, o nível técnico se baseia nas informações que recebe dos níveis formal e informal. O processo de elicitação é iterativo, ou seja, vai do informal ao técnico e do técnico ao informal, enquanto verifica as possíveis necessidades de atualização do modelo[Baranauskas 2014].

Neste contexto, o uso da tecnologia de Realidade Estendida (XR, do inglês *Extended Reality*) é identificada para visualização do protótipo de sistemas IoT em tempo real, pois se une aos ambientes real e virtual, a fim de amparar dispositivos de distintos níveis de realidade na visualização de um cenário [Chuah 2018]. Além disso, o trabalho [Han and Leite 2022] aponta que o uso tecnologia XR pode contribuir para os desafios relacionados à visualização dos requisitos ao longo do ciclo de vida do projeto.

Este artigo relata uma pesquisa de doutorado em andamento, que propõe o uso a tecnologia de Realidade Estendida e a metodologia de Design Socialmente Consciente, para amparar o desenvolvimento de protótipos de sistemas IoT. O artigo está organizado em seções, a seção 2 apresenta os objetivos da pesquisa; a seção 3 relata o embasamento teórico e as soluções existentes; seção 4 descreve a metodologia de pesquisa; a seção 5 destaca os resultados da pesquisa alcançados até o momento; a seção 6, descreve as possíveis contribuições da pesquisa e seu diferencial e; a seção 7 destca os apontamentos paras as próximas atividades da pesquisa.

2. Objetivo

Diante desta contextualização, a fim de atenuar informações ambíguas e conflitantes durante o desenvolvimento de protótipos de sistemas IoT, o objetivo da pesquisa de doutorado é:

- Amparar o desenvolvimento de protótipos de sistemas IoT, usando a tecnologia de Realidade Estendida e a metodologia de Design Socialmente Consciente, por meio de um modelo visual.

Os objetivos específicos são:

1. Gerar os artefatos para identificação dos requisitos específicos de sistemas IoT;
2. Propor um modelo para prototipação de sistemas IoT, para auxiliar na elicitação e visualização dos requisitos;
3. Implementar e validar o modelo visual, por meio de experimentos e estudos de caso;

3. Referencial Teórico

3.1. Modelos para Elicitação de Requisitos de Sistemas IoT

A IoT se tornou um tema relevante, uma vez que viabiliza como as pessoas podem experimentar e usar a tecnologia em um protótipo, no entanto, existem desafios relacionados à identificação dos requisitos específicos de sistemas IoT [Souza Rodrigues et al. 2020].

De acordo com [Silva et al. 2019a], a construção de sistemas IoT requerem um processo definido incluindo atividades desde a elicitação de requisitos até a implantação do sistema de software. Para isso, na literatura foi possível identificar métodos para amparar na elicitação e especificação dos requisitos para um sistema IoT, como o trabalho relatado por [Reggio 2018], apresenta uma versão do IotReq, um método para a elicitação e especificação dos requisitos para um sistema IoT; outros trabalhos, [Zambonelli 2017] e [Larrucea et al. 2017], abordam o tema de requisitos para sistemas IoT, os quais propõem estruturas conceituais para capturar e apresentar os requisitos.

Entrentanto, o autor [Reggio 2018] indica, que não há um conjunto de melhores práticas de engenharia de software para desenvolvimento de sistemas IoT. Ressalta-se ainda, nenhuma proposta associando um modelo visual de prototipação em sistemas IoT foi identificado na literatura.

3.2. Design Socialmente Consciente e IoT

O Design Socialmente Consciente pode afetar diretamente o resultado final de um sistema. Baseia-se na realidade socioeconômica e cultural de um grupo de envolvidos e tem como objetivo obter uma visão de design mais ampla [da Silva et al. 2016]. Propõe práticas participativas, semioparticipativas e inclusivas que envolvem diversas pessoas com diferentes papéis, que serão devidamente identificadas para propor soluções de tecnologia [da Silva et al. 2016].

O estudo [da Silva et al. 2021] destaca o uso do DSC, em fases iniciais do projeto, para resolver o problema de design de requisitos durante um desenvolvimento de software para IoT. Além disso, aponta que as atividades do DSC promovem discussões que impactam sobre os aspectos socioeconômica e suas implicações no cotidiano das pessoas.

Demais estudos, como [Silva et al. 2018] e [Silva et al. 2019b], destacam o uso do DSC para amparar nas atividades de sistemas IoT, como elicitação de requisitos, construção de cenários de interação em tempo real. Reforçam, que o DSC auxilia no entendimento do problema, e geram eficácia no processo de desenvolvimento dos sistemas IoT.

3.3. Realidade Estendida para Desenvolvimento de Sistemas IoT

O conceito de Realidade Estendida é genérico, abrange as tecnologias virtuais, incluindo Realidade Aumentada (RA), Realidade Virtual (RV) e Realidade Mista (RM) em um aspecto que vai desde dispositivos que interagem com o mundo real e virtual simultaneamente àqueles que só trabalham com o mundo virtual [Andrade and Bastos 2019], para fornecer experiências de usuário intuitivas, imersivas e interativas [Han and Leite 2022].

Dado uma busca bibliográfica sobre sistemas IoT com o uso da tecnologia de XR, foi possível identificar um estudo [Andrade and Bastos 2019], que propõe um modelo de comunicação de dados que permite a tradução de dados IoT em objetos, eventos ou cenários de XR. Neste estudo, também são indicados tendências e aplicações sobre IoT e XR, o uso na segurança cibernética, para ajudar as equipes de defesa de segurança a se defenderem contra ataques de softwares maliciosos dos dispositivos.

4. Metodologia de Pesquisa

O Design da Ciência, é um paradigma que apoia a realização de pesquisas aplicadas, a fim de sumarizar, identificar, avaliar e comunicar suas contribuições [Engström et al. 2020]. A metodologia de pesquisa deste trabalho é baseada nos elementos do Design da Ciência [Engström et al. 2020], apresentados na Figura 1.

Figura 1. Visão Geral da Pesquisa conforme o Paradigma Design da Ciência
Fonte: adaptado de [Engström et al. 2020]

A proposta refere-se ao objetivo geral da pesquisa descrito na Seção 2. A instância do problema são as lacunas identificadas na literatura, como as diferentes percepções dos envolvidos, o uso distintos de recursos computacionais e elementos específicos de sistemas IoT, indicam artefatos que devem amparar a solução. O entendimento do problema, descreve atividades que devem serem seguidas para alcançar a proposta, condução de mapeamentos sistemáticos, oficinas semioparticipativas, desenvolvimento de uma estrutura de trabalho, modelos visuais, estudos de viabilidade e experimentos.

A abordagem de design de solução destaca uma estrutura de trabalho com atividades pré-definidas para concepção visual dos requisitos de sistemas IoT, e a implementação e validação, deve acontecer por meio de experimentos, estudos de casos e de viabilidade. Neste cenário é esperado como solução, um modelo para prototipação de sistemas IoT, desenvolvidos a partir de artefatos do DSC, a fim de amparar na elicitação dos requisitos e sua visualização com o uso da tecnologia de Realidade Estendida.

A validação do modelo é dada por meio da execução de experimentos e estudos de caso. Este delineamento da pesquisa também, ressalta o rigor, relevância e inovação da proposta.

Diante deste delineamento, algumas atividades devem acontecer, sendo elas:

a) Mapeamento Sistemático da Literatura (MSL) para verificar como o DSC contribui para o desenvolvimento de tecnologias da informação e comunicação (TIC), seus pilares e artefatos; e MSL para identificar as características específicas de sistemas IoT;
b) Realização de oficinas de design semioparticipativo;
c) Desenvolvimento de um guia de aplicação da metodologia de DSC;
d) Elaborar modelos visuais para auxiliar na elicitação de requisitos para sistemas IoT, com o uso de modelos visuais: UML (do inglês *Unified Modeling Language*, em português Linguagem de Modelagem Unificada) e Histórias em Quadrinhos (HQ);
e) Verificar a aplicabilidade do modelo visual em HQ e UML;
f) Aplicação do teste de aplicabilidade referente ao cenário virtual de IoT com HQ;
g) A partir dos aterfatos gerados na aplicação do modelo em HQ, construir o modelo para prototipar os requisitos e elementos específicos de IoT.
h) Definição da plataforma virtual de visualização do protótipo;
i) Construção do modelo para amparar no desenvolvimento de protótipos de sistemas IoT;
j) Experimentos e estudos de caso para validação do modelo.

5. Resultados Preliminares

Esta pesquisa foi iniciada em agosto de 2020, primeiramente foi realizada a execução de um MSL, para verificar como o DSC contribui para o desenvolvimento de tecnologia da informação e comunicação (TIC), seus pilares e artefatos. Na condução do MSL foram retornados 67 trabalhos, destes 10 passaram pelos filtros de seleção e 2 estudos foram adicionados, por meio da estratégia *backward snowballing*, totalizando 12 trabalhos.

Ao realizar o MSL foi possível observar que o desenvolvimento de produtos e soluções tecnológicas utilizam comumente aspectos do DSC e pilares da sustentabilidade de forma implícita, por outro lado, a utilização de maneira explícita pode possibilitar a inserção dos elementos do DSC em um processo de produção mais ágil e inteligente, atendendo aos pilares de sustentabilidade e inserindo efetivamente os interessados em todo o processo de desenvolvimento, assim como o envolvimento no processo de design dos requisitos e prototipação.

O resultado desse MSL, impulsionou a condução de outro MSL, para identificar as características específicas de sistemas IoT, e como são realizados o processos de design de requisitos e prototipação de sistemas IoT.

Esse MSL, retornou 122 estudos, dos quais 18 atenderam os critérios de seleção e inclusão, além de 4 estudos inseridos por meio da estratégia *backward snowballing*. Como resultado, entende-se que ainda não surgiu nenhum conjunto consolidado, de práticas recomendadas de engenharia de software para a Internet das Coisas [Reggio 2018]. Os resultados apontaram práticas preliminares de métodos utilizados para especificar requisitos de IoT, é válido ressaltar, que não houve relato sobre a atividade de prototipação.

Faz-se necessário, uma geração de ambientes e modelos de Engenharia de Software que ampare o a concepção do design de requisitos de sistemas IoT [Zambonelli 2017].

Os artefatos gerados na execução dos dois MSL, indicam a eficiência do uso de oficinas de DSC para auxiliar no processo de design de requisitos, além de evidências referentes a limitação de técnicas, modelos e abordagem para especificar requisitos de sistemas IoT, decorrência de suas particularidades.

Atualmente estão sendo conduzidas as atividade de execução das oficinas de design semioparticipativas, a fim de desenvolver modelos visuais, com o uso dos modelos UML e HQ, para auxiliar na elicitação de requisitos para sistemas IoT; e o desenvolvimento do guia de aplicação.

A Figura 2 apresenta a sugestão do guia de aplicação, inicialmente devem ser conduzidas oficinas semioparticipativas, envolvendo os interessados do projeto IoT, nesta atividade são geradas as informações e requisitos específicos, que serão visualizados por meio dos modelos UML e/ou HQ. Além disso, a visualização do protótipo de sistemas IoT, pode ocorrer em um ambiente virtual em tempo real com o uso da tecnologia de XR.

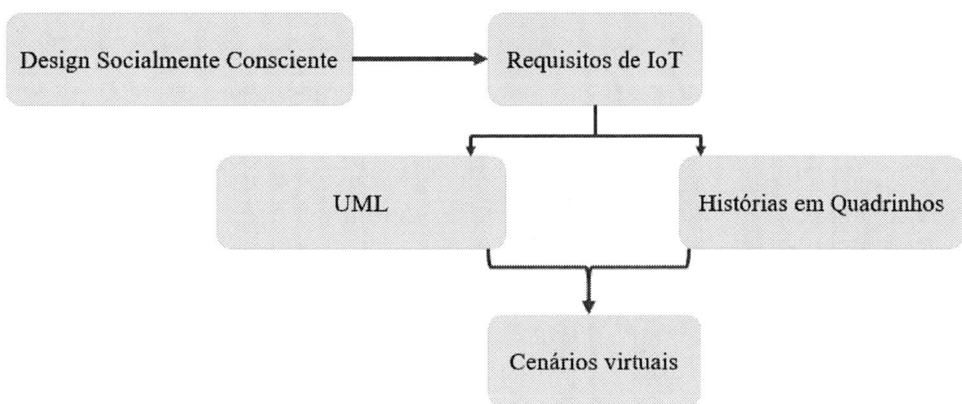

Figura 2. Guia de Aplicação

6. Contribuições

Este trabalho sumarizou uma pesquisa de doutorado em andamento, cujo objetivo é amparar o desenvolvimento de protótipos para sistemas IoT, por meio de um modelo visual.

Diante dos resultados identificados até o momento, a pesquisa aponta diferenciais de implementação como: a construção do modelo visual, é amparada por um guia de aplicação, o qual insere a experiência do DSC como parte do processo de identificação dos requisitos para sistemas IoT, onde a compreensão comum dos envolvidos é uma ação que gera resultados positivos; a prototipação e visualização dos requisitos em cenários virtuais com o uso da Realidade Estendida, pois a mesma pode atrair as partes interessadas com inúmeras oportunidades para criar experiências inovadoras e únicas [Alizadehsalehi and Yitmen 2021].

A proposta do modelo é se tornar uma inovação para o estado da arte atual. Contribuindo para pesquisadores, profissionais de Engenharia de Software, professores, acadêmicos que desejam utilizar um modelo visual para amparar a prototipação de requisitos para sistemas IoT. Além disso, espera-se estabelecer uma integridade na concepção e elicitação dos requisitos de um sistema IoT, colaborando para o desenvolvimento, implementação e implantação do sistema.

7. Trabalhos Futuros

As próximas etapas estão relacionadas aos objetivos específicos deste trabalho, Seção 2 itens 2 e 3, e envolvem as atividades de (b) a (j), disponibilizadas na Seção 3, para a construção de um modelo para amparar o desenvolvimento de protótipos de sistemas IoT.

Referências

Alizadehsalehi, S. and Yitmen, I. (2021). Digital twin-based progress monitoring management model through reality capture to extended reality technologies (drx). *Smart and Sustainable Built Environment.*

Andrade, T. and Bastos, D. (2019). Extended reality in iot scenarios: Concepts, applications and future trends. In *2019 5th Experiment International Conference (exp. at'19)*, pages 107–112. IEEE.

Baranauskas, M. C. C. (2014). Social awareness in hci. *Interactions*, 21(4):66–69.

Baranauskas, M. C. C. et al. (2009). Socially aware computing. In *ICECE 2009 VI International Conference on Engineering and Computer Education*, pages 1–5.

Chuah, S. H.-W. (2018). Why and who will adopt extended reality technology? literature review, synthesis, and future research agenda. *Literature Review, Synthesis, and Future Research Agenda (December 13, 2018).*

da Silva, J. V., Baranauskas, M. C. C., and Pereira, R. (2021). Hands on, heads in: Building iot scenarios for learning software engineering. In *2021 XLVII Latin American Computing Conference (CLEI)*, pages 1–10. IEEE.

da Silva, J. V., Pereira, R., Buchdid, S. B., Duarte, E. F., and Baranauskas, M. C. C. (2016). Sawd - socially aware design: An organizational semiotics-based case tool to support early design activities. In Baranauskas, M. C. C., Liu, K., Sun, L., Neris, V. P. d. A., Bonacin, R., and Nakata, K., editors, *Socially Aware Organisations and Technologies. Impact and Challenges*, pages 59–69, Cham. Springer International Publishing.

Engström, E., Storey, M.-A., Runeson, P., Höst, M., and Baldassarre, M. T. (2020). How software engineering research aligns with design science: a review. *Empirical Software Engineering*, 25(4):2630–2660.

Ferrari, B., Junior, D. S., Oliveira, C. M., Ortiz, J. S., and Pereira, R. (2019). Design socialmente consciente de jogos: relato de uma oficina prática para o entendimento do problema e prospecção de ideias. In *Anais do I Workshop sobre Interação e Pesquisa de Usuários no Desenvolvimento de Jogos*, pages 11–20. SBC.

Han, B. and Leite, F. (2022). Generic extended reality and integrated development for visualization applications in architecture, engineering, and construction. *Automation in Construction*, 140:104329.

Larrucea, X., Combelles, A., Favaro, J., and Taneja, K. (2017). Software engineering for the internet of things. *IEEE Software*, 34(1):24–28.

Pereira, R., Baranauskas, M. C., and da Silva, S. R. (2013). Social software and educational technology: Informal, formal and technical values. *Educational Technology & Society*, 16:4–14.

Reggio, G. (2018). A uml-based proposal for iot system requirements specification. In *Proceedings of the 10th international workshop on modelling in software engineering*, pages 9–16.

Silva, D., Gonçalves, T. G., and da Rocha, A. R. C. (2019a). A requirements engineering process for iot systems. In *Proceedings of the XVIII Brazilian symposium on software quality*, pages 204–209.

Silva, J. V. d., Baranauskas, M. C. C., Moreira, E. A., Muriana, L. M., and Santos, A. C. d. (2019b). Reclaiming human space at iot: Contributions of the socially aware design. In *Proceedings of the 18th Brazilian Symposium on Human Factors in Computing Systems*, pages 1–11.

Silva, J. V. d., Pereira, R., Hayashi, E., and Baranauskas, M. C. C. (2018). Design practices and the sawd tool: Towards the opendesign concept. In *International Conference on Informatics and Semiotics in Organisations*, pages 208–217. Springer.

Sommerville, I. et al. (2011). Engenharia de software.[sl]. *Pearson Education*, 19:60.

Souza Rodrigues, S., Luiz da Silva Genesio, V., Maria Barroso Paiva, D., and Pontin de Mattos Fortes, R. (2020). A case study on how brazilian companies deal with the user experience in iot projects. In *Proceedings of the 38th ACM International Conference on Design of Communication*, pages 1–7.

Weyrich, M. and Ebert, C. (2015). Reference architectures for the internet of things. *IEEE Software*, 33(1):112–116.

Zabadal, B. M. and de Castro, B. F. L. M. (2017). Iot e seus principais desafios. *Revista Interdisciplinar de Tecnologias e Educação*, 3(1).

Zambonelli, F. (2017). Key abstractions for iot-oriented software engineering. *IEEE Software*, 34(1):38–45.

On the Continuous Delivery in IoT Systems

Igor Muzetti Pereira

[1]Federal University of Ouro Preto (UFOP)
Ouro Preto – MG – Brazil

igormuzetti@ufop.edu.br

Abstract. *The development of IoT systems brings the adequacy of software engineering to current paradigms, such as IoT, industry 4.0, smart cities and environments, and wearable devices. IoT systems require the integration of different technologies such as sensors, actuators, edge devices, cloud computing, big data, artificial intelligence, and IT operations. The successful delivery of products depends directly on the continuous cooperation of professionals with different skills. However, we noticed a specific resistance in carrying out continuous and automated software deliveries to hardware devices by professionals. This research investigates the practices and technologies for the continuous software delivery pipeline on hardware devices that make up an IoT system.*

1. Introduction

Companies developing Internet of Things (IoT) systems rely on software components as one of the main assets in their products. As systems become more complex, companies need to adapt to ensure continuous development processes [Luz et al. 2019]. In their development processes, these companies have teams that develop embedded systems that traditionally use plan-oriented methods [Lindgren and Münch 2016]. Moreover, they have software development and operations teams that are familiar with agile methodologies. However, an IoT environment requires ongoing cooperation between hardware and software development and operations teams to ensure quality attributes are met. Although there are studies on using agile methods in hardware teams, these teams do not accept these practices very easily [Mattos et al. 2018].

IoT leads to an era where, instead of just developing software, we need to design software systems that encompass multidisciplinarity and integrate different areas to realize successful products according to their purposes. This means that software is just one facet of IoT, which, along with others, is necessary for IoT solutions [Motta et al. 2018]. Therefore, software engineering is adapting to the construction and maintenance of these complex IoT systems, seeking to reduce development costs and increase the quality of the final product [Beyer et al. 2016].

IoT software systems involve recent technologies that question the traditional way of developing. Software engineering, as a discipline, has undergone constant changes since its conception. Several concepts, methods, tools, and patterns support software development [Bourque et al. 2014]. It is then possible to consider the need to evolve existing development practices to keep the construction of IoT software systems.

Continuous Delivery (CD) can handle this adaptation, such as automating the build, test, and delivery process achieving better time to market, better customer satisfaction, and good product quality [Chen 2015a]. Applying CD in the hardware and firmware development implies various challenges as a resistance of the professionals in using agile practices [Greene 2004, Srinivasan et al. 2009]. This research aims to propose and evaluate a conceptual model capable of assisting in planning continuous delivery pipelines for IoT systems focused on the hardware and firmware development.

The remainder of this document is organized as follows: Section 2 presents the related work necessary to understand this research. In turn, Section 3 presents the details of the different steps used to execute and collect the results obtained so far and how we plan the future steps. Section 4 describes the main and most relevant preliminary and expected results acquired by this research. Finally, Section 5 reports a final remarks and addresses the next steps of this research.

2. Related Work

Usually, the embedded software systems runs continually and does not stop. Its starts when the hardware is started and must run until the hardware has been turned off. Moreover, physical constraints, the need for direct interaction with the hardware, and security and reliability issues can affect the software project [Sommerville 2015].

There was difficulty in getting papers about continuous delivery in the IoT systems. The selected studies approach mainly the use of Extreme Programming (XP) and Scrum on embedded software projects. We consider that the concept of Internet of Things (IoT) systems evolved from the embedded systems and so, we see a correlation between them. Continuous delivery (CD) is an outcome of the agile methods used mainly after continuous integration.

CD is a discipline where teams build valuable software to be released into production at any time [Chen 2015b]. IoT is a computational paradigm that considers objects that communicate and cooperate with software systems to achieve common goals. These objects can be sensors, actuators, radio frequency identification (RFID) tags, gateways, smartphones, wearable devices, etc [Atzori et al. 2010].

Ronkainem and Abrahamsson [Ronkainen and Abrahamsson 2003] explore the possibilities of using agile development techniques in an embedded domain where the hardware sets tight requirements for the software. An empirical study was conducted in the development of low-level telecommunications software. The main challenge identified was a co-design, which means that the development of embedded systems is characterized by the need to develop software and hardware simultaneously. Therefore, this study approaches the software and hardware development of digital signal processors (DSPs) and application-specific integrated circuits (ASICs). The focus of the future of this research is the pipeline development of the hardware and firmware.

Manhart and Schneider [Manhart and Schneider 2004] report a case study of a software development department for buses. This organization is used to traditional software process improvement models like SPICE. However, research shows that the organization has combined the practices of this traditional model with agile elements. According to the authors, this combination fostered an acceptance of agile ideas and helped them break the ice to an extension of the adoption of agile processes. This application of agile practices in the embedded software demonstrated that it is possible to change the culture of the teams. This cultural change is a challenge to this research that focuses on incentive the application of the continuous delivery pipeline in hardware and firmware teams.

Greene [Greene 2004] cited several unique challenges in the embedded software development as many firmware developers are not classically trained software engineers but often have electrical engineering backgrounds and pick up programming as needed to solve reluctant to adopt the latest software tools and methodologies. They strive to develop code as expediently as possible. So, the paper describes the experience of implementing Scrum and XP to build firmware for the Intel Itanium processor family. We expected to find these challenges in IoT systems development teams.

Srinivasan et al. [Srinivasan et al. 2009] describe others challenges about the use of the agile practices in the development of embedded systems as meeting hard real-time requirements, supporting safe experimentation, generating sufficient documentation and, supporting test driven development.

Salo and Abrahamsson [Salo and Abrahamsson 2008] surveyed agile methods in European embedded software development organizations and showed the actual use and usefulness of XP and Scrum. Continuous integration was a fourth practice more used; 44% said that used systematically, mostly, or sometimes. But curiously, TDD was the practice that never applied with 41%. Moreover, all the Scrum practices received a high percentage of never and do not know responses. The paper shows that agile practices are not dominated by the 13 European industrial organizations studied.

The studies [Xie et al. 2012, Shen et al. 2012, Rong et al. 2014, Blašković et al. 2021] conducted a systematic review of the application of agile methods to embedded software development. They identified that XP and Scrum are the methods more used by these projects. But does not exist a depth discussion about the practices as CI are used. The papers too appoint that exists an immature development environment to apply TDD. As CI makes part of the continuous delivery, begin CI a phase important to this, our research could explore it better.

3. Experimental Procedures

This section describes the stages planned for this doctoral research. Figure 1 shows the overview of the four stages. Until this moment, two stages were concluded: the systematic mapping study (SMS) and the exploratory study involving interviews and a questionnaire. The third stage is building a conceptual model of the delivery continuous to hardware and firmware development in the IoT systems projects. Finally, the fourth stage aims to perform a experiment human-oriented.

IoT systems induce an articulation of studies in software engineering to prepare the development and operation of software systems materialized in physical objects and structures interconnected with embedded software and hosted in clouds. At the start of this research, to understand the boundaries between development and operation in the different architectural layers of IoT systems, we performed a systematic literature mapping (SLM) to search for evidence in the scientific literature about DevOps principles applied to IoT systems.

The SLM was divided into two parts and each one was discussed and published in two international conferences. After discussing with the two communities of these conferences, we decided to change DevOps to Continuous Delivery (CD). The main reason was that we realize this traditional practice involved inside the DevOps concept that can

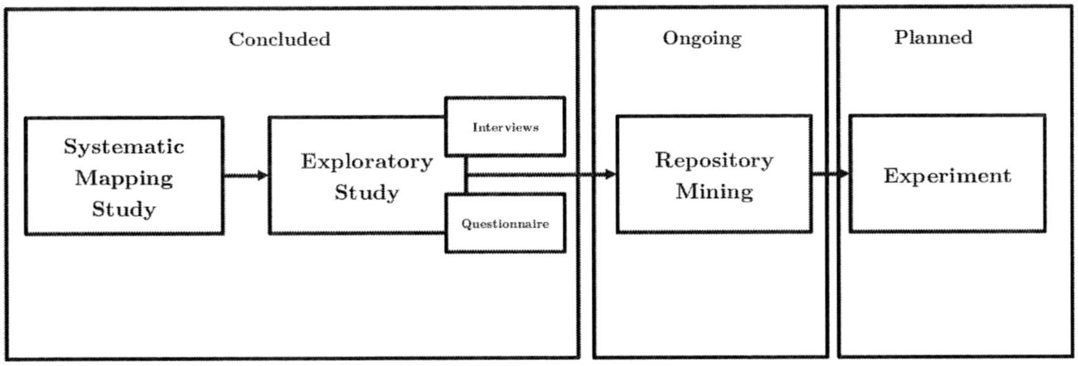

Figure 1. Steps of research experimental procedures

bring more focus on the future of this research. The conduction of this study followed guidelines [Kitchenham and Charters 2007].

We consider the second step as an exploratory study as described by Wohlin et al. [Wohlin et al. 2012]. We use a survey as an empirical strategy to collect information from professionals working with continuous delivery and IoT systems in the industry. In the first phase of this study, we used interviews to collect information and a questionnaire to verify this information in the second phase. To understand IoT system projects seeking continuous delivery, we first interviewed thirty-one experienced professionals. In the second phase, we applied a questionnaire to another group of thirty professionals from these areas to cross-validate our understanding of the collected information.

The third step of this study will focus on quantitatively analyzing a dataset extracted from a platform hosting structured or semi-structured text. We will explore these data in a way continuous and immediate. The data collection and analysis will be simultaneous, and we get a theoretical sampling. This mining is essential to identify evidence of using a continuous delivery pipeline. Most and less popular repositories will study the GitHub platform. We will not consider projects considered "toys" or documentation only. Only IoT software development projects will be valid. We will take into account ethical aspects for this type of study, as discussed in the work of Gold and Krinke [Gold and Krinke 2022]. Finally, we will inspire our process on the lessons learned, and the method proposed in the results by Barros et al. [Barros et al. 2021] and Vidoni [Vidoni 2022], respectively.

An experiment is a study in which an intervention is deliberately introduced to observe its effects on some aspects of reality under controlled conditions. We plan to do a human-oriented experiment to confirm conventional wisdom, i.e., to test people's conceptions and evaluate the conceptual model about continuous delivery pipelines on IoT systems. In the next section, we discuss the obtained and expected results of each experiment.

4. Results

The steps presented in the 1 shows two preliminary results of this research project and two other expected results. SLM enabled our understanding of the challenges and benefits of approaching DevOps in IoT systems and how an automated pipeline is necessary for continuous delivery. The exploratory study addressed the state of practice on this topic from perspectives of the professionals. The conceptual model from repository mining will be based on concepts found in the literature and evidence from open-source IoT system projects. Finally, the human-oriented experiment will allow us to evaluate the proposed conceptual model.

The SMS expanded our previous studies [Pereira et al. 2021a, Pereira et al. 2021d] by adding other recent studies, including the first semester of 2021. There are thirty-three studies now, and we analyzed them more horizontally as a systematic mapping study. A list of the practices and technologies DevOps covered in the studies was presented and discussed. Five categories of benefits and six of the challenges perceived in the studies were analyzed.

A preliminary result about the main differences of DevOps on IoT systems was published in SBES 2021 [Pereira et al. 2021c]. In favor the feedback received from the community, we expanded the research and added two other research questions. Our new focus started with the pursuit of continuous delivery in developing IoT systems. The additional research questions involved understanding what quality practices and the challenges perceived faced for continuous delivery in IoT systems projects by professionals. A follow up paper that describes this research was published in SBQS 2021 [Pereira et al. 2021b].

Participants presented the differences perceived when seeking continuous delivery as benefits for their processes. For instance, when teams use the automated pipelines, adhering to agility even across hardware teams, professionals gain greater possibilities to deliver more often and better meet customer expectations. The participants in this study made some use of quality practices. Of course, they can be applied to other domains. However, we see an effort by hardware and firmware professionals to implement them, either to keep up with what professionals in different areas are already doing or to meet customer requirements. The explored challenges mainly involve bringing professionals specialized in hardware closer to the practices used by development and operations professionals who are already more familiar with the agile way of working. The correct selection of components in the solution in the face of technological advances is a constant pressure that helps in the competitiveness of the market. The support of top management in the transformation is essential to keep business expectations aligned with the teams' technical capacity.

Our research will aim to generate a conceptual model for pipelines of continuous delivery in IoT systems projects. The model will be derived from publicly accessible records of processes and practices in popular open-source IoT software systems. We start our derivation process on continuous delivery practices in IoT systems by collecting and analyzing the publicly available documentation for each project, community mailing lists, websites documenting each project, open-source code repositories, blog posts, web articles, tutorials, and manuals.

With the conceptual model extracted from the repository mining study, a hypothesis is planned to be formalized, and the data collected during the experiment will be used to, if possible, reject the hypothesis. If the hypothesis can be ruled out, conclusions are drawn based on testing the hypothesis under certain risks. We will analyze the density of failures reported by participants when using pipelines for continuous delivery in an IoT system. A possible hypothesis that we are thinking about today would be that: "Contributors of software-to-hardware projects in IoT systems are not very comfortable building a continuous delivery pipeline."

5. Final Remarks

To summarize the doctoral project of the author completed, ongoing, and future activities, this section presents the schedule of activities involved.

Table 1. General Doctoral Schedule

#	Activities	2020/1	2020/2	2021/1	2021/2	2022/1	2022/2	2023/1	2023/2
0	Obtain PPGCC/DECOM/UFOP credits	X	X						
1	Participate in area communities and events	X	X	X	X	X	X	X	X
2	Conduct a literature review	X	X	X					
3	Conduct interviews		X	X					
4	Apply questionnaire			X					
5	Write and submit papers resulting from the studies carried out		X	X	X				
6	Present accepted studies			X	X				
7	Participate in the doctoral qualification exam.					X			
8	Development of a concept model about continuous delivery pipelines in IoT systems				X	X			
9	Evaluation of pipelines composed by the conceptual model.						X	X	
10	Write and submit papers for the second half of the doctorate					X	X	X	
11	Write the thesis							X	X
12	Defend the doctoral thesis								X

In this moment, the author is cursing the 2022/1 semester. This text is part of the Ph.D. project and explains the completed, ongoing and next steps to complete the doctoral research. This paper documents half of this doctorate, and the next steps will be added to these and will be part of a new final document that will become the final thesis.

References

Atzori, L., Iera, A., and Morabito, G. (2010). The internet of things: A survey. *Computer Networks*, 54(15):2787–2805.

Barros, D., Horita, F., Wiese, I., and Silva, K. (2021). *A Mining Software Repository Extended Cookbook: Lessons Learned from a Literature Review*, page 1–10. Association for Computing Machinery, New York, NY, USA.

Beyer, B., Jones, C., Petoff, J., and Murphy, N. R. (2016). *Site reliability engineering: How Google runs production systems*. O'Reilly Media, Inc.

Blaškovic, K., Candrlic, S., and Jakupovic, A. (2021). Systematic review of methodologies for the development of embedded systems. *International Journal of Advanced Computer Science and Applications*, 12(1).

Bourque, P., Fairley, R. E., and Society, I. C. (2014). *Guide to the Software Engineering Body of Knowledge (SWEBOK)*. IEEE Computer Society Press, Washington, DC, USA, 3rd edition.

Chen, L. (2015a). Continuous delivery: Huge benefits, but challenges too. *IEEE Software*, 32(2):50–54.

Chen, L. (2015b). Continuous delivery: Huge benefits, but challenges too. *IEEE Software*, 32(2):50–54.

Gold, N. E. and Krinke, J. (2022). Ethics in the mining of software repositories. *Empirical Software Engineering*, 27(1).

Greene, B. (2004). Agile methods applied to embedded firmware development. In *Agile Development Conference*, pages 71–77.

Kitchenham, B. and Charters, S. M. (2007). Guidelines for performing systematic literature reviews in software engineering.

Lindgren, E. and Münch, J. (2016). Raising the odds of success: the current state of experimentation in product development. *Information and Software Technology*, 77:80–91.

Luz, W. P., Pinto, G., and Bonifácio, R. (2019). Adopting devops in the real world: A theory, a model, and a case study. *Journal of Systems and Software*, 157:110384.

Manhart, P. and Schneider, K. (2004). Breaking the ice for agile development of embedded software: an industry experience report. In *Proceedings. 26th International Conference on Software Engineering*, pages 378–386.

Mattos, D. I., Bosch, J., and Olsson, H. H. (2018). Challenges and strategies for undertaking continuous experimentation to embedded systems: Industry and research perspectives. In *Agile Processes in Software Engineering and Extreme Programming*, pages 277–292, Cham. Springer International Publishing.

Motta, R. C., de Oliveira, K. M., and Travassos, G. H. (2018). On challenges in engineering iot software systems. In *Proceedings of the XXXII Brazilian Symposium on Software Engineering (SBES)*, page 42–51, New York, NY, USA. Association for Computing Machinery.

Pereira, I. M., Carneiro, T., and Figueiredo, E. (2021a). A systematic review on the use of devops in internet of things software systems. In *Proceedings of the 36th Annual ACM Symposium on Applied Computing (ACM/SAC)*, page 1569–1571. Association for Computing Machinery.

Pereira, I. M., de Senna Carneiro, T. G., and Figueiredo, E. (2021b). Investigating continuous delivery on iot systems. In *XX Brazilian Symposium on Software Quality (SBQS)*. Association for Computing Machinery.

Pereira, I. M., de Senna Carneiro, T. G., and Figueiredo, E. (2021c). Main differences of devops on iot systems. In *Brazilian Symposium on Software Engineering (SBES)*, page 315–319. Association for Computing Machinery.

Pereira, I. M., de Senna Carneiro, T. G., and Figueiredo, E. (2021d). Understanding the context of iot software systems in devops. In *3th International Workshop on Software Engineering Research Practices for the Internet of Things (SERP4IoT)*.

Rong, G., Liu, T., Xie, M., Chen, J., Ma, C., and Shao, D. (2014). Processes for embedded systems development: Preliminary results from a systematic review. In *Proceedings of the 2014 International Conference on Software and System Process (ICSSP)*, page 94–98, New York, NY, USA. Association for Computing Machinery.

Ronkainen, J. and Abrahamsson, P. (2003). Software development under stringent hardware constraints: Do agile methods have a chance? In *Extreme Programming and Agile Processes in Software Engineering*, pages 73–79, Berlin, Heidelberg. Springer Berlin Heidelberg.

Salo, O. and Abrahamsson, P. (2008). Agile methods in european embedded software development organisations: A survey on the actual use and usefulness of extreme programming and scrum. *Software, IET*, 2:58 – 64.

Shen, M., Yang, W., Rong, G., and Shao, D. (2012). Applying agile methods to embedded software development: A systematic review. In *2012 Second International Workshop on Software Engineering for Embedded Systems (SEES)*, pages 30–36.

Sommerville, I. (2015). *Software Engineering*. Pearson, 10th edition.

Srinivasan, J., Dobrin, R., and Lundqvist, K. (2009). State of the art in using agile methods for embedded systems development. In *Industrial Experience in Embedded Systems Design (IEESD)*, pages 1195–1200.

Vidoni, M. (2022). A systematic process for mining software repositories: Results from a systematic literature review. *Information and Software Technology*, 144:106791.

Wohlin, C., Runeson, P., Höst, M., Ohlsson, M. C., Regnell, B., and Wesslén, A. (2012). *Experimentation in Software Engineering*, volume Ed. 1ª. Springer Berlin Heidelberg.

Xie, M., Shen, M., Rong, G., and Shao, D. (2012). Empirical studies of embedded software development using agile methods: A systematic review. In *Proceedings of the 2nd International Workshop on Evidential Assessment of Software Technologies (EAST)*, page 21–26, New York, NY, USA. Association for Computing Machinery.

Open-Source Software Projects Curating Model for Empirical Software Engineering Studies

Juan Andrés Carruthers

Departament of Informatics – National University of the Northeast (UNNE)
Corrientes – Argentina

jacarruthers@exa.unne.edu.ar

Abstract. *Software projects are common inputs in Empirical Software Engineering (ESE), and they are often selected without following a specific strategy, leading to biased samples. To avoid this problem, researchers choose to use publicly available datasets instead of picking the projects themselves. However, some datasets are not maintained, containing old versions of projects, or even deprecated ones. This may raise some representativeness issues due to major changes in development practices and technologies over time. The main goal of this research is to develop a procedures model to construct and maintain a software project dataset with their product quality metrics, to support the development of ESE studies.*

1. Introduction

Software Engineering works mainly with the "construction of multi-version software applications" [Parnas 2001]. Thus, many of the activities associated with software application require revisions to improve the functionality or correct errors, especially in agile methodologies [Irrazábal et al. 2001]. Quality in software development can be studied from two angles: the software development process and the source code [Lehman 1996]. In the latter case, empirical methods are necessary to demonstrate the quality of the software [Kitchenham and Pfleeger 1996], using evidence related to the software product in form of metrics and indicators directly linked to quality [Garvin 1984].

The massive use of open source repositories (e.g. Github, SourceForge and Maven) made publicly available vast amounts of software projects data for researchers and software engineers to conduct Empirical Software Engineering (ESE) studies [Vidal et al. 2016], [Vázquez et al. 2019]. However, ESE studies performed with arbitrarily picked samples could lead to unrealistic and potentially inaccurate conclusions due to the proportion of noise in these repositories [Munaiah et al. 2017], contrasting with the ESE notions of replicable and generalizable results. In particular, replicability is essential not only for publications in prestigious journals or conferences of the discipline; but also for software development companies that often want to analyze the evolution of their own projects or use them as a benchmark in software audit reviews.

A common practice to demonstrate the effectiveness of metrics as predictors of software quality characteristics is the construction of datasets [Tempero et al. 2010]. Datasets of software projects work as inputs for researchers and as comparison mechanisms for different types of ESE studies. Examples of popular datasets are:

Qualitas corpus [Tempero et al. 2010], NASA dataset [Shepperd et al. 2013] or Jureczko and Madeyski dataset [Jureczko and Madeyski 2010], which their latest available version has more than seven years. Thus, it is necessary to review the versions of each project and recalculate their metrics.

With that being said, our hypothesis is "have a procedure model to construct, maintain and curate a dataset of software projects with their product quality metrics can provide a sound strategy to conduct ESE studies; improving replicability, experimental consistency, and flexibility for a controlled evolution of a software project dataset over time".

2. Research Goals

The main goal of our research is "develop a procedures model to construct, maintain and curate a dataset of software projects with their product quality metrics, to support the development of ESE studies". This objective is divided into two parts:

- Methodological support. Analyze and design rules to construct and curate a representative sample of open source software projects, and the metadata necessary to motivate ESE studies.
- Technological support. Develop tools to allow automated generation of metadata, to control rules for the curation of software projects, and to help researchers and engineers manage their use for the design and execution of experiments.

3. Related works

In ESE studies the results obtained must be, at some degree, replicable and generalizable. Replicability is important to validate the results of a scientific study and can be tackled by providing the datasets and scripts of the conducted research [Baltes and Ralph 2020].

There were attempts to provide a software project dataset for ESE studies over the years. These datasets include source code repositories [Tempero et al. 2010], information in issue trackers [Rahman and Roy 2018], product quality metrics [Jureczko and Madeyski 2010], [Shepperd et al. 2013], and even evolutionary data such as source code change logs [Palomba et al. 2018]. However, they are often unsuitable for the task due to methodological issues when sampling the software projects, reducing the generalization of their conclusions. The lack of representativeness in a sample can bias the generalization of the findings.

For example, Mockus et al. (2002) stated that free/open-source software contained fewer defects than proprietary systems, basing their conclusions on two open-source projects (Apache and Mozilla). Samples with two subjects cannot provide enough evidence to generalize to the entire population of open-source software.

Jureczko and Madeyski (2010) collected object-oriented product quality metrics and defect information from 48 releases of 15 open source projects and 27 releases of 6 proprietary projects. Shepperd et al. (2013) gathered size and complexity metrics from C and C++ Nasa software. In both cases, the authors provide access to the datasets and they are frequently used in current ESE studies. But, neither of them reported the sampling strategy.

Another popular dataset Qualitas Corpus [Tempero et al. 2010], contains the source code of 100 open-source Java projects and includes the guidelines followed to select the projects, keeping even deprecated ones. Using deprecated projects might guarantee the replicability of experiments but also raises issues about the applicability of the results obtained in current projects.

Few studies take into consideration building samples using a probability sampling technique, and they recur to convenience or purposive sampling techniques. The ideal case would be to randomly select a statistically significant sample of software projects, or maybe apply approaches such as Nagappan et al. (2013), to construct diverse and representative samples.

Finally, we identified scarce efforts to provide a framework or procedure model to maintain the temporal validity of the projects in the datasets. Since constant changes in development practices and technologies over time can produce different outcomes in ESE studies, a dataset of software projects constructed several years ago can rarely be representative of recently developed projects. Lewowski and Madeyski (2020) partially tackled this with their tool to create evolving datasets, but did not precise how to deal with deprecated projects.

4. Methodology

We organized the research strategy following the Design Science Research framework (Johannesson and Perjons, 2014), an approach to create and validate novel artifacts, providing solutions in the form of models, methods, and systems that support people in developing, using, and maintaining IT solutions. Also, it aims at producing and communicating new knowledge relevant for a global practice, thus the results produced are twofold, the artifact created, and the knowledge generated.

The purpose of creating new and generalisable knowledge requires that design science projects make use of rigorous research strategies and methods. Such methods are essential for creating results that can be critically discussed, evaluated, and validated. Finally, the new knowledge should be communicated to both practitioners and researchers.

With that being said, to achieve the main goal we propose the following tasks framed by the mentioned framework:

4.1 Explicate the problem

The goal of the first activity is to formulate the initial problem precisely, justify its importance, and investigate its underlying causes.

A1. Define the knowledge base and establish the state of the art on the datasets of software projects used in ESE studies.

The research methods used will be Systematic Literature Review [Kitchenham 2004] and Systematic Mapping Study [Petersen et al. 2008]. These methods identify, evaluate, and interpret all the information related to the particular research topic, in a systematic and replicable way. The application of systematic reviews in the field of Software Engineering allows giving a scientific value to the review of the literature that is done, defining a search strategy for the articles to be evaluated and finally obtaining a hypothesis for or against the revised literature.

4.2 Define Requirements

This activity goal is to identify and outline the artefact that can address the explicated problem, and elicit requirements on that artefact.

A2. Carry out a literature reviews on the datasets of software projects developed to date, in order to compare them and evaluate the necessary characteristics towards ESE studies.

A3. Perform a survey among research and innovation groups to identify the construction, curation and communication necessities for a dataset of software projects.

Two research methods will be used. First, systematic literature reviews [Kitchenham 2004] and Systematic Mapping Study [Petersen et al. 2008]. Second, surveys [Kitchenham and Pfleeger 2002] will be used to collect information from research groups and innovation teams.

4.3 Design and Develop Artefact

The third activity creates an artefact fulfilling the requirements from the previous activity, including the design of the functionality and structure of the artefact.

A4. Build the methodological support based on the analysis and design of the rules for the construction and curation of a representative sample of open source software projects, as well as the necessary metadata oriented to the ESE studies.

A5. Build the technological support with a source code analysis ecosystem and an extraction tool to obtain reports of software quality metrics from the dataset.

To receive feedback about the developed artifact and refine it we will conduct a focus group. This can be seen as an interview in which a group of respondents participate and discuss a specific topic. The aim is to enable the participants to be more creative and pursue the topic addressed in greater depth than in one-to-one interviews.

4.4 Demonstrate Artefact

The fourth activity of the method framework is to demonstrate the use of the artefact in one case, thereby proving its feasibility.

A6. Create datasets with the technological support and conduct controlled experiments with them in order to evaluate sample representativeness.

We will use Wohlin et al. (2012) guidelines to perform experiments. An experiment is a formal, rigorous and controlled investigation, that its key factors are identified and manipulated, while other factors in the context are kept unchanged.

4.5 Evaluate Artefact

Finally, the fifth activity determines how well the artefact is able to solve the explicated problem and to what extent it fulfils the requirements.

A7. Validate the methodological and technological support through the replication of case studies and action-research experiments.

For resolution and validation, the Research-Action method will be used. Originally, this method [Lewin 1947] sought to link the experimental approach of the social sciences with programs of social action that responded to certain main social problems. This method (with a necessary adaptation) has been widely accepted by the Information Systems community [Avison et al. 1999], [Seaman 1999].

5. Results

As part of this research, we carried out a systematic mapping study following the guidelines proposed by Petersen et al. (2008) to obtain an overview of the current technical development or level of practice of a research area. This study aimed to show research groups followed practices for experimentation with software projects, exposing the problems found that compromise sample representativeness and experiment replication.

For this study, we carried out a manual search in the journal Empirical Software Engineering; and the conferences Empirical Software Engineering and Measurement, and International Conference on Evaluation and Assessment in Software Engineering from 2013 to 2020. The systematic search resulted in 122 empirical studies with software projects. The study was presented at The Journal "Computación y Sistemas".

The results showed that, researchers most common practices are: making their own guidelines to select projects and using existing software project datasets. We did not evidence a unified or automated framework to select software projects, due to the large diversity of aspects considered by the researchers. Also, the main programming language of selected software projects was Java.

On the other hand, we are performing another systematic mapping study, in which we aim to determine and assess the general state of the software projects datasets in ESE studies in terms of their validity, purpose, sampling strategy, information extracted from the projects and the tools employed to extract that information. To that end, we formulated the following research questions:

RQ1: What are the characteristics of the software projects in the dataset for ESE studies?

RQ1.1: What criteria was considered to select the software projects in the dataset for ESE studies?

RQ1.2: What were the main programming languages of the projects selected for the dataset for ESE studies?

RQ2: What data was extracted from the software projects that compose the dataset?

RQ3: What tools were used to obtain the data extracted from the software projects that compose the dataset?

RQ4: Why was the dataset created?

RQ5: Is the dataset updated?

6. Expected Contributions

The expected contribution of this research is two fold. First, provide a procedures model to construct and maintain a dataset of software projects, allowing better replicability and representativeness in ESE studies. The key aspect is that the model can be fed with evolutionary information from projects, and at the same time, is extensible to add quality metrics and other useful artifacts. The model will be implemented as a software solution in order to validate and automatize our approach.

Second, share an open source software project dataset with their quality metrics. The dataset will be created and maintained with the implementation of the aforementioned model.

7. Future Steps

Once the second systematic mapping study is finished, we have two planned studies ahead. In first place, we will perform a replication study of a quasi-experiment originally made with the 20130901 release of the Qualitas Corpus; but instead of that version, we will use the 2021 version of the Qualitas Corpus, updating every non-deprecated project inside the 20130901 release. Our goal is to evaluate the degree of replicability between versions and review if temporal validity plays a role in the representativeness of the sample.

Secondly, we will conduct an academic questionnaire to Software Quality research groups in order to assess the results obtained in the studies mentioned in Section 4.2.

Acknowledgments

This research is supported by CONICET through the Internal Doctoral Grant, with a duration of 60 months.

References

Avison, D., Lau, F., Myers, M. and Nielsen, P. A. (1999). Action Research. Communications of the ACM, 42(1), 94–97.

Baltes, S. and Ralph, P. (2020). Sampling in Software Engineering Research: A Critical Review and Guidelines. https://arxiv.org/abs/2002.07764v5

Garvin, D. A. (1984). What Does "Product Quality" Really Mean? MIT Sloan Management Review, 25–43. https://sloanreview.mit.edu/article/what-does-product-quality-really-mean/

Irrazábal, E., Vásquez, F., Díaz, R. and Garzás, J. (2011). Applying ISO/IEC 12207:2008 with SCRUM and Agile Methods. Communications in Computer and Information Science, 155 CCIS, 169–180. https://doi.org/10.1007/978-3-642-21233-8_15.

Johannesson, P. and Perjons, E. (2014). An introduction to design science (Vol. 10, pp. 978-3). Cham: Springer.

Jureczko, M. and Madeyski, L. (2010). Towards identifying software project clusters with regard to defect prediction. ACM International Conference Proceeding Series, 1. https://doi.org/10.1145/1868328.1868342

Kitchenham, B. (2004). Procedures for Performing Systematic Reviews. Keele University, 33, 1–26. https://www.researchgate.net/publication/228756057

Kitchenham, B. and Pfleeger, S. L. (1996). Software quality: the elusive target. IEEE Software, 13(1), 12–21. https://doi.org/10.1109/52.476281

Lehman, M. M. (1996). Laws of software evolution revisited. Lecture Notes in Computer Science (Including Subseries Lecture Notes in Artificial Intelligence and Lecture Notes in Bioinformatics), 1149, 108–124. https://doi.org/10.1007/BFb0017737

Lewin, K. (1947). Frontiers in Group Dynamics: Concept, Method and Reality in Social Science; Social Equilibria and Social Change. Human Relations, 1(1), 5–41. https://doi.org/10.1177/001872674700100103

Lewowski, T. and Madeyski, L. (2020). Creating Evolving Project Data Sets in Software Engineering. Studies in Computational Intelligence, 851, 1–14. https://doi.org/10.1007/978-3-030-26574-8_1

Mockus, A., Fielding, R. T. and Herbsleb, J. D. (2002). Two case studies of open source software development. ACM Transactions on Software Engineering and Methodology (TOSEM), 11(3), 309–346. https://doi.org/10.1145/567793.567795

Munaiah, N., Kroh, S., Cabrey, C. and Nagappan, M. (2017). Curating GitHub for engineered software projects. Empirical Software Engineering, 22(6), 3219–3253. https://doi.org/10.1007/s10664-017-9512-6

Nagappan, M., Zimmermann, T. and Bird, C. (2013). Diversity in Software Engineering Research. Proceedings of the 2013 9th Joint Meeting on Foundations of Software Engineering - ESEC/FSE 2013. https://doi.org/10.1145/2491411

Palomba, F., Bavota, G., Penta, M. Di, Fasano, F., Oliveto, R., & Lucia, A. De. (2018). On the diffuseness and the impact on maintainability of code smells: a large scale empirical investigation. *Empirical Software Engineering*, *23*(3), 1188–1221. https://doi.org/10.1007/S10664-017-9535-Z/TABLES/11

Parnas, D. L. (2001). Some software engineering principles. In Software fundamentals: collected papers by David L. Parnas (pp. 257–266). https://dl.acm.org/doi/10.5555/376584.376632

Petersen, K., Feldt, R., Mujtaba, S. and Mattsson, M. (2008). Systematic Mapping Studies in Software Engineering. Proceedings of the 12th International Conference on Evaluation and Assessment in Software Engineering, 68–77. www.splc.net

Rahman, M. M. and Roy, C. K. (2018). Improving IR-based bug localization with context-aware query reformulation. *ESEC/FSE 2018 - Proceedings of the 2018 26th ACM Joint Meeting on European Software Engineering Conference and Symposium on the Foundations of Software Engineering*, 621–632. https://doi.org/10.1145/3236024.3236065.

Seaman, C. B. (1999). Qualitative methods in empirical studies of software engineering. IEEE Transactions on Software Engineering, 25(4), 557–572. https://doi.org/10.1109/32.799955

Shepperd, M., Song, Q., Sun, Z. and Mair, C. (2013). Data quality: Some comments on the NASA software defect datasets. IEEE Transactions on Software Engineering, 39(9), 1208–1215. https://doi.org/10.1109/TSE.2013.11

Tempero, E., Anslow, C., Dietrich, J., Han, T., Li, J., Lumpe, M., Melton, H. and Noble, J. (2010). The Qualitas Corpus: A curated collection of Java code for empirical studies. Proceedings - Asia-Pacific Software Engineering Conference, APSEC, 336–345. https://doi.org/10.1109/APSEC.2010.46

Vázquez, H. C., Bergel, A., Vidal, S., Díaz Pace, J. A. and Marcos, C. (2019). Slimming javascript applications: An approach for removing unused functions from javascript libraries. Information and Software Technology, 107, 18–29. https://doi.org/10.1016/J.INFSOF.2018.10.009

Vidal, S. A., Bergel, A., Marcos, C. and Díaz-Pace, J. A. (2016). Understanding and addressing exhibitionism in Java empirical research about method accessibility. Empirical Software Engineering, 21(2), 483–516. https://doi.org/10.1007/s10664-015-9365-9

Vidal, S., Bergel, A., Díaz-Pace, J. A. and Marcos, C. (2016). Over-exposed classes in Java: An empirical study. Computer Languages, Systems & Structures, 46, 1–19. https://doi.org/10.1016/J.CL.2016.04.001

Wohlin, C., Runeson, P., Höst, M., Ohlsson, M. C., Regnell, B., and Wesslén, A. (2012). Experimentation in software engineering. Springer Science & Business Media.